Critical Marxism in Mexico

Historical Materialism Book Series

The Historical Materialism Book Series is a major publishing initiative of the radical left. The capitalist crisis of the twenty-first century has been met by a resurgence of interest in critical Marxist theory. At the same time, the publishing institutions committed to Marxism have contracted markedly since the high point of the 1970s. The Historical Materialism Book Series is dedicated to addressing this situation by making available important works of Marxist theory. The aim of the series is to publish important theoretical contributions as the basis for vigorous intellectual debate and exchange on the left.

The peer-reviewed series publishes original monographs, translated texts, and reprints of classics across the bounds of academic disciplinary agendas and across the divisions of the left. The series is particularly concerned to encourage the internationalization of Marxist debate and aims to translate significant studies from beyond the English-speaking world.

For a full list of titles in the Historical Materialism Book Series available in paperback from Haymarket Books, visit:
www.haymarketbooks.org/category/hm-series

Critical Marxism in Mexico

Adolfo Sánchez Vázquez and Bolívar Echeverría

by
Stefan Gandler

Haymarket Books
Chicago, IL

First published in 2015 by Brill Academic Publishers, The Netherlands
© 2015 Koninklijke Brill NV, Leiden, The Netherlands

Published in paperback in 2016 by
Haymarket Books
P.O. Box 180165
Chicago, IL 60618
773-583-7884
www.haymarketbooks.org

ISBN: 978-1-60846-633-7

Distributed to the trade in the US through Consortium Book Sales and Distribution (www.cbsd.com) and internationally through Ingram Publisher Services International (www.ingramcontent.com).

This book was published with the generous support of Lannan Foundation and Wallace Action Fund.

Special discounts are available for bulk purchases by organizations and institu-tions. Please email info@haymarketbooks.org for more information.

Cover design by Jamie Kerry of Belle Étoile Studios and Ragina Johnson.

This book was published with the generous support of
Lannan Foundation and the Wallace Global Fund.

Printed in the United States.

Library of Congress Cataloging-in-Publication data is available.

*Dedicated
to our unforgettable friend and tireless protagonist
in the struggle against racism and anti-Semitism*

*Elisabeth Link
born on 16 November 1955, died in Frankfurt on 29 January 1997*

∴

CUERPOS XIII

Contents

Prologue to *Critical Marxism in Mexico* xiii
   Michael Löwy
Preface to the English-Language Edition xv
Preface to the Original Edition in German xvii
Preface to the Spanish-Language Edition xix

Introduction: From Eurocentric to Peripheral Marxism 1

PART 1
Historical and Theoretical Context

1 The Life and Work of Adolfo Sánchez Vázquez 15
   Beginning of the Biography 16
   The Spanish Civil War 19
   The First Period in Mexico, Exile 26
   The 'New Theoretical and Practical Posture' 34

2 The Life and Work of Bolívar Echeverría 42
   The Period in West Germany and West Berlin 50
   From the Divided City to the Mexican Capital 64
   Collaboration on the Journal Cuadernos Políticos 67
   Back to Philosophy 77

3 The 'State of Art' 84
   a. On Social Philosophy in Latin America 84
   b. On Adolfo Sánchez Vázquez and Bolívar Echeverría 85

PART 2
Adolfo Sánchez Vázquez: Praxis and Knowledge

4 The Concept of Praxis 93
   a. The Term 'Praxis' in Various European Languages 93
   b. The Terms 'Praxis' and 'Práctica' and the Problem of Their Translation 96
   c. General Introduction to the Concept 98

5   **Everyday Consciousness of Praxis**   101
   a. The Critique of the Everyday Consciousness of Praxis, or, What Is a Theoretical Knowledge of Praxis Good For?   101
   b. Revolutionary Praxis and Everyday Consciousness   108
      Practical Politicism and Practical Apoliticism   112
   c. Artistic Praxis and Everyday Consciousness   113
   d. Concluding the Critique of Everyday Consciousness   113

6   **The Relationship between Philosophy and Praxis in History**   116
   a. Antiquity   117
   b. The Philosophy of Praxis   125

7   **The *Theses on Feuerbach***   127
   a. The Position of the *Theses on Feuerbach* in Marx's Work   127
   b. Interpretation of the *Theses on Feuerbach*   132
      Praxis as the Basis for Knowledge (Thesis I)   134
      Praxis as a Criterion of Truth (Thesis II)   138
      Revolutionary Praxis as the Unity of the Transformation in Human Beings and in Circumstances (Thesis III)   143
      From the Interpretation of the World to its Transformation (Thesis XI)   147
   Epilogue to the *Theses on Feuerbach*   152

8   **Critique of Some Marxist Conceptions of Knowledge**   153
   a. Critique of Certain Conceptions of Marxism in General   154
   b. Critique of Certain Marxist Conceptions of Knowledge   156
      Knowledge as the Direct Result of World-Transformative Praxis   156
      Knowledge as Something Achieved Exclusively in Theory   160

9   **Once Again on the Problem of Knowledge and Praxis**   167
   a. Materialism and Idealism   168
   b. Political and Productive Praxis   176

10   ***The Philosophy of Praxis*: Two Versions**   183

PART 3
Bolívar Echeverría: Use-Value and *Ethos*

11 **Praxis and Use-Value**   195
   a. Theory of Use-Value and Critique of the Abstract Concept of Praxis   195
   b. Differences *vis-à-vis* the Concept of Praxis in Sánchez Vázquez   199
   c. Historical Limitations of the Marxian Concept of Use-Value   206
   d. The Aristotelian Concept of Use-Value as Interpreted by Marx   210
   e. Marx as the Founder of the Critical Concept of Use-Value   215
   f. The Marxian Concept of *Natural Form* and the Theory of *Ethos*   223
   g. The Critique of Political Economy as a Critique of Modernity   226

12 **Concretisation of the Concept of Praxis**   229
   a. Reproduction and Communication   229
   b. Use-Value and Signs   238
   c. Marx's Theory of Tools   242
   d. Concept of Concrete Universalism   249

13 **Modernity and Capitalism**   257
   a. The Critique of Actually-Existing Modernity and the Critique of Actually-Existing Postmodern Thought   257
   b. The Term 'Actually-Existing Modernity'   259
   c. Actually-Existing Modernities as Basis for a Non-Capitalist Modernity   264

14 **The Concept of Historical *Ethos***   268
   a. On the Term *Ethos*   269
      Translation Problems   270
   b. Determination of the Concept of 'Historical *Ethos*'   271
   c. Concept of Modernity   278
   d. The Terms 'Realist', 'Romantic', 'Classic', and 'Baroque *Ethos*'   280
   e. The Concept of the Four *Ethe* of Capitalist Modernity as a Contribution to a Materialist History of Culture   281
   f. The Theoretical Positioning and Explosive Force of the Concept of *Ethos*   282
      Form of Civilisation Versus Mode of Production (for Martin Heidegger)   286

  The Finite of the Dominant Modernity and of All Capitalist
    Modernities (for Karl Marx)   286
  Christianity and Capitalism (for Max Weber)   288
  Excursus: Marx on 'Political Economy and Christianity'   290
  Puritanism and Realism   293

15 The Four *Ethe* of Capitalist Modernity   295
  a. The Realist *Ethos*   295
  b. The Romantic *Ethos*   297
  c. The Classic *Ethos*   299
  d. The Baroque *Ethos*   300
  e. Non-existence of Historical *Ethe* in Pure Form   306
  f. Textual Variations of the Concept of *Ethos*   307

16 *Ethos* and Ideology   311
  a. Limitations of the Concept of *Ethos*   311
  b. Contribution to the Reconstruction of the Concept of Ideology in the Critique of Political Economy   313
    1859 Preface to the Contribution to the Critique of Political Economy   313
    The Text: 'The Fetishism of the Commodity and Its Secret'   315
    The Fetishism of the Commodity   316
    The Historical Dimension of the Fetishism of the Commodity, or Knowledge as a Political-practical Process   320
    On the Relation Between 'Necessity' and 'Interest' in the Formation or Perpetuation of Ideologies   324
    Capital as a Critique of Fetishisms   325
  c. The Concept of *Ethos* as a Toned Down Critique of Ideology   328
  d. An Example of the Limitations of the Concept of *Ethos*   331

17 Utopia: A Non-Capitalist Society of Commodity Producers   335

PART 4
On the Relationship between Praxis and *Ethos*

18 Affirmation or Critique of Praxis?   343

19 The Conceptual Determination of Culture and Nature   350

20   **The Philosophical Critique of Eurocentrism**   355
    a. On the Problem of Focusing on European Authors   355
    b. Critical Concept of Praxis Versus Abstract Universalism, Namely
       Eurocentrism   357

Bibliographical Appendix   361
A Bibliography of Adolfo Sánchez Vázquez   363
B Bibliography of Bolívar Echeverría   409
C Selected Bibliography on Marxist Philosophy in Latin
   America   427
D Sources for the Bibliography   432

References   435
Index of Titles   447
Index of Concepts   451
Index of Names   462

CUERPOS XIV

Prologue to *Critical Marxism in Mexico*

This beautiful book speaks to us about the Latin American – in this case Mexican – contribution to the renewal of critical Marxism. Stefan Gandler succeeds not only in explaining, profoundly and coherently – but not uncritically! – the thought of Adolfo Sánchez Vázquez and Bolívar Echeverría, their biography, the evolution of their ideas, the complete bibliography of their works, their convergences and divergences, but he also demonstrates that breaking with Eurocentrism is an indispensable condition for a true universalisation of critical theory.

In the work of Mariátegui, Latin America was introduced to a first version of critical Marxism, which sought to break with the method of 'copying and pasting' from European experiences. (On this point, I cannot share in the least Gandler's position, according to which Mariátegui simply represents a 'Latin Americanised' way of reading Soviet Marxism.) After his death in 1930, the Soviet vulgate of Stalinised Marxism – with a few, honourable exceptions – predominated for many years in Latin America. It was only after the Cuban Revolution that critical Marxism, in multiple forms, would again develop on the continent. These two Mexican thinkers are some of the most original and innovative manifestations of this process. In spite of belonging to two distinct generations, the two political exiles to Mexico discussed in this book had the Cuban revolutionary experience as a shared departure point for their innovative reflections – and so too, years later, that of the Zapatista Army of National Liberation (EZLN).

Adolfo Sánchez Vázquez not only had the merit of being one of the first Marxists – not only in Latin America, but on an international scale – to criticise Althusserian positivism from the point of view of the philosophy of praxis, but also, as Stefan Gandler emphasises, to successfully develop a critical concept of history within his vision of praxis, doing so without knowing the work of Walter Benjamin; without forgetting his contribution to the political discussion of Marxists, insisting on the centrality of the democratic question for the implementation of a socialist transformation. I share Gandler's admiration for the political and philosophical integrity of the author of *The Philosophy of Praxis*, independent of the critiques one could make of this or that aspect of his work.

I believe that Gandler is also correct when he stresses the novelty and importance of Bolívar Echeverría's work, and his project of radical critique of 'actually-existing modernity' ['modernidad realmente existente'] while questioning his utopia of a 'non-capitalist society of commodity producers'. Echeverría's decisive contribution to overcoming Eurocentrism and reformulating a materialist theory of culture is, without doubt, his concept of four *ethe*. The most interesting and 'productive' of these seems to me to be the concept of the 'baroque *ethos*', which provides us with an extremely valuable key for understanding multiple aspects of Latin American culture; a key which allows us to account not only for the Jesuit Reductions in Paraguay, but also, in the twentieth century, for the phenomenon of 'liberation Christianity' and Christian base communities. (In parentheses: it seems to me that Stefan Gandler is mistaken to consider Samuel Ruiz and the liberation theologians as 'committed' to the 'strong and brutal power' of Karol Wojtyla.)

My principal disagreement with the subtle typology of *ethe* proposed by Echeverría has to do with his definition of the 'romantic *ethos*' as a confusion of mercantile value with use-value which understands capital as a grand venture, thereby naturalising capitalism. Following some of Lukács's intuitions, I believe to the contrary that romanticism, understood not simply as a literary school or artistic style, but rather, in a manner similar to baroque, as an '*ethos*', as the principle for the construction of the world lasting centuries and which is characterised by an attitude of hostility toward capitalism. The 'romantic *ethos*', in its various manifestations from Jean-Jacques Rousseau to the Surrealists, passing through Novalis, Hölderlin, William Morris, José Carlos Mariátegui, and Ernst Bloch – in addition to various social, cultural and religious movements – represents a protest against capitalist civilisation in the name of pre-modern cultural values, and an almost desperate attempt to re-enchant the world.

Stefan Gandler's book is not only an excellent introduction to, but also a sharp reflection on, an important chapter 'outside the West' – in the Latin American periphery of the system – of what has been called 'Western Marxism', but which would be better named, as he does in his title, critical Marxism – that is to say, 'universal/concrete' thought which has as its objective the radicalisation of the Marxist critique of the false existing world.

Michael Löwy

Preface to the English-Language Edition

When I started to live permanently in Mexico, 21 years ago, I never imagined that I would be spending so much time on the philosophical question that I was interested in at that moment: how is it possible that authors of the importance, the intellectual quality and the political relevance of Adolfo Sánchez Vázquez and Bolívar Echeverría are practically unknown in the so-called *First World*? I decided to dedicate some time, not only to criticise that blindness in the *philosophic* institutions from Germany (where I studied at Frankfurt University), and other of these self-glorifying countries, but also – and first of all – to do, in my own philosophical and academic activity, something to counteract that incapacity and self-limitation.

Now, 21 years later, the product of this impulse appears in today's *lingua franca*: perhaps something pertinent has been done against the absurd and – at least – five-hundred-year-old European belief that Europe is the centre of the world, and has the right, and even the obligation, to deny all other philosophical reflections, which are carried out outside of the walls of that brave new European world, constructed inside and outside the aged borders of the *old* continent.

In reality, that project started earlier, in 1989, with my first six-month stay in Mexico City, when I visited the Universidad Nacional Autónoma de México (UNAM), and took some unforgettable classes with Adolfo Sánchez Vázquez and Bolívar Echeverría. From this perspective, I have been involved for exactly half of my lifetime up til now in the teaching, the discussion, the analysis, the defence, the dissemination and the critique of the philosophical thinking of these two authors, both of them Mexican by choice. Even when I did some other things in that time, inside and outside the limits of the philosophical *theme parks*, such as founding a family, writing some other texts, teaching philosophy and social theory or travelling around and sometimes *having fun*, the presence of this book, which you now have in your hands in its English-language edition, was nearly total. Perhaps, I involved my life in this project much more than I ever consciously decided or 'planned'; nevertheless: *je ne regrette rien*.

My hope is that this book will be an impulse for the reading, the teaching, the discussion, the analysis, the high-level philosophical critique, and the translation of Adolfo Sánchez Vázquez's and Bolívar Echeverría's texts. Today, when I write these lines, both have passed away: Bolívar Echeverría on 5 June 2010, only days after his last class at the UNAM and hours after our last telephone call, and Adolfo Sánchez Vázquez one year later, on 8 July 2011, after some years of living in his flat in the south of Mexico City, distanced from public and academic activities for health reasons. At one of my last visits to his home, his daughter Aurora Sánchez Rebolledo advised that he normally didn't receive visits for more than fifteen minutes, because, after more than ninety years, his forces were limited. But when we spoke that day, the conversation soon began to turn around the Spanish Civil War and, for two complete hours, we spoke about and discussed some of the big questions of the 'first battle of World War Two'. It was as if those questions and memories had recovered, for an instant, the exceptionally big forces, which he had possessed throughout his life, and on this day he was as awake as ever before when we said goodbye.

I have no doubt that the overcoming of the absurd, destructive, horrible and absolutely boring way of life (boring in the sense that we repeat unthinkingly, even when it appears to be different, the same senseless stuff), which is today dominant in most parts of our planet, will only be possible if voices from outside of the alleged *First World* are heard and taken seriously. This book tries to make a step towards that generation which is less blind and less deaf towards the necessity, possibility and desirability of a life without exploitation, without repression, without war, without torture and – as Adorno expresses it, as his *negative utopia* – without fear.

...

In order to make comparison with the original German and the Spanish-language edition possible – for example, to corroborate the quotations of texts written in Spanish or German – we have carefully respected the numbering of footnotes, so that those in this edition and the German and Spanish-language editions are identical. The bibliography assembled on Adolfo Sánchez Vázquez and Bolívar Echeverría has been updated to the present day.

In this context heartfelt thanks for all the help received finishing the English version of this book, especially from Julio Echeverría and Aurora Sánchez Rebolledo, as well as from Daniele Cargnelutti, who prepared the index for this edition.

Stefan Gandler
Mexico City, 8 March 2014

Preface to the Original Edition in German

The current work situates within their social and theoretical context two of the most important philosophers of the Universidad Nacional Autónoma de México (UNAM), the oldest university on the American continent and, to this day, the most prestigious department of philosophy in Latin America. We present an introduction to their work, which sets out from a discussion of some select philosophical problems and we seek, ultimately, to present a theoretical confrontation between these two social philosophies. We attempt, on the basis of our discussion of Adolfo Sánchez Vázquez and Bolívar Echeverría, to offer our own contribution to the development of a critical theory of society. The extensive bibliography of both authors is intended to serve as a scientific tool to facilitate and stimulate other studies of these works.

A first version of this work was presented in the summer of 1997 as a doctoral thesis (advisors: Doctor Alfred Schmidt and Doctor Joachim Hirsch) in the Department of Philosophy and History at the Johann Wolfgang Goethe University, in Frankfurt. The version presented here is stylistically altered, with light trimming and enrichment with some new reflections; the bibliographies have likewise been updated. Quotations in the Spanish language are reproduced in their German translation. The German translations, nonexistent as a general rule, were made by the author, and the original quotations – drawn partially from unpublished material – can be found in the appendix.

This investigation would have been unimaginable without the suggestions and criticisms the author received from many parties. Particularly irreplaceable were the suggestions to elaborate the bibliographies and biographies (for which I cordially thank Aurora Sánchez Rebolledo, Raquel Serur and Marco Aurelio García Barrios, in Mexico City, as well as Santiago Álvarez, Ana Lucas and collaborators at the Fundación de Investigaciones Marxistas, in Madrid). Warmest thanks to Adolfo Sánchez Vázquez and Bolívar Echeverría, for their extraordinary and very useful help, and for their great interest in the research. Heartfelt thanks to Alfred Schmidt for supporting without prejudices what is for many German philosophers a 'strange' topic, backing which he offered from the beginning as adviser for this research. My appreciation also goes to my parents, Reinhold and Magrit Gandler, for all of their support, above all for their readiness to help me maintain contact with Europe during my stay in Mexico. Likewise, my cordial thanks to Paul Stein for his important technical help. The Heinrich Böll Foundation and German Academic Exchange Service made possible – with three years of financing from the former and three months' worth from the latter – the completion of this work in its entirety, but more particularly my research period in Mexico City lasting several years.

The discussion of drafts of the different parts of the book were of inestimable importance to its content and, at the same time, an important intellectual stimulus. I give warm thanks for this, and for the patient reading and editing of this work in its various stages, to Virginia Carvajal, Carmen Colinas, Tim Darmstädter, Irina Djassemy, Wilfried Fiebig, Katti Geisenhainer, Charlotte Grell, Gerold Heinke, Cathia Huerta Arellano, Thomas Pascual Camps, Joachim Rauscher, Helen Rottmann, Thomas Sablowski, Mickie R. Schleicher, Gerold Schmidt, Peter Stegemann, Dorothea Stein, Eva Stein, Andrea Weber, Annemarie Wolfer-Melior and, especially, Stephan Bundschuh.

Finally, allow me to offer very special thanks to the residents of the Historical Centre of Mexico City, with whom the author lived for almost three years, and who accepted him in such a spontaneous and friendly way as someone new to the neighborhood, something which he had never experienced before in any other place of residence. Through their daily practice they taught him something which, otherwise, in current social relations, he would only have been able to conceive, in the best of cases, through laborious theoretical studies, namely: that racism is in no way *xenophobia* – meaning 'hatred towards the unknown' – or, put in another way, there is no emptier idea than that of 'being an *alien*' (if you will allow us an Anglicism), an idea which is so widespread today and so vulgarly materialistic.

Stefan Gandler
Mexico, October 1999

Preface to the Spanish-Language Edition

This book closes a cycle which began in 1989, coincidentally the year of the so-called fall of the Berlin wall, which, luckily, the author did not have to witness because he was, for the first time in his life, in the metropolis that is now his own: Mexico City. From this unique city, he saw from a distance those events which provoked a mixture of boredom and repudiation. He has never been a follower of the political current associated with the historical project that had its centre in the Soviet Union, and yet, at the same time, he knew perfectly well that National Socialism – his absolute negative reference point ever since gaining historical consciousness – had only been crushed militarily through the sacrifice of the soldiers of the Red Army. The boredom felt in the face of this much celebrated political and social change, symbolised in the administrative decision to open the borders between the two parts of Berlin precisely on 9 November – exactly fifty-one years after the day in which the Nazis burned the majority of German synagogues in 1938, the *Kristallnacht* – extends to the present day, and nobody now wants to speak of the supposed marvels brought about by the mass introduction of the capitalist mode of reproduction into these countries. The same goes for the sense of repudiation, by this point unquestionable, which this form of social organisation provokes, once again, in more and more human beings. Therefore, and not only for reasons of an individual kind from the author's own life, the appearance of the Spanish-language edition of the present book in Mexico closes a cycle: the first steps taken in conceiving it date back to the real, but at the same time only apparent, triumph of the capitalist mode of production, and its appearance coincides with capitalism's ever more obvious decline.

At the same time, a cycle is closing, because the text returns, to some extent, to the place of its origin. It began with the trip of a young philosophy student to the city which attracted him because of its unique history, full of elements seductive to someone who was tired of German and European hypocrisy, namely its denial that it has been the continent that has caused the most damage to the world over the last five hundred years. This city, from the very first day, offered him a perspective distinct from those offered in Europe: submission or exclusion. The author knows perfectly well that these words will sound strange to the majority of Mexican people, but he cannot avoid them because they are the truth.

In spite of everything, Mexico has the privilege of being one of the few countries of the world which has not had a fascist or crypto-fascist government in the twentieth century. It has, furthermore, a history which, relative to world society over the last two hundred years, stands out for its (relatively) high level of freedom of expression and its bourgeois epoch did not begin by reducing its concept of 'freedom' to economic aspects, as occurred in the majority of countries. This book – and forgive the emotional impulse – could not exist without Morelos, Hidalgo, Juárez and, of course, Zapata. Figures like these, and *last but not least* General Lázaro Cárdenas, are difficult to find in the history of other countries, and in Europe only Robespierre, Danton and the anonymous heroes of the anti-fascist resistance are comparable. Without them and, above all, without the popular movements which they led, the author would not be here – and, without any shadow of a doubt, nor would the two philosophers here studied. Mexico, with all of its very long history, has been the country which made this book possible, and thus a circle is closed: the book, originally written for a German-speaking public and which sought to demonstrate with two examples how absurd, mediocre, and beyond all rationality is the European – and German – pretension of being the intellectual centre of the world, returns to the country of the authors here studied, where the majority of this text was written.

All of this is not said to celebrate anything at all, but is valid from the perspective of someone who has opened his eyes in his own country and could no longer endure the revulsion that it caused him. It is obvious that Mexico is also part of the capitalist world system, with all that this entails, and that it is, moreover, a country situated outside of the arrogantly self-designated First World, hence implying that poverty reaches levels unknown in this day and age in the place where the author himself was raised. However – and to remember this will not cause pleasure in Germany and Austria – the hunger deliberately and systematically brought about in the Jewish ghettos established by the Nazis in the occupied countries has not been left behind in the least and is, rather, beyond any adequate description. And this hunger, the death trains that circulated throughout all of Europe on the same railway tracks on which the author used to so enjoy travelling when he was 18 or 23 years old, and the extermination camps themselves, are not something of the *past* that has now gone away, as we have been told in Austrian and German schools.

It took the author ten years of living in Mexico, ten years of physical, and to a certain degree emotional and intellectual, distance in order to realise that, when he was born right in the heart of militarily extinguished Nazism, barely 18 years and eight months had passed since the military defeat of National Socialism. Eighteen years, which is nothing, absolutely nothing, in historical terms, is what separates us in individual biographical terms from the most destructive social project of any time or place. One could say that only this heightened awareness, which probably only a small number of the generation in question will reach, has justified being away from loved ones there, from the landscapes and the green lakes where one can swim.

The author of this book has 'suffered' not only this radical change in consciousness, but also another one that already existed *in nuce* in the first version of the present text, in German: all the explicit or implicit critique of Eurocentrism – above all the 'philosophical' one – in the pages that follow, fall short of what we now think. Now is not the time to expand on this theme, but it should be noted that the years the author has lived in Mexico, and the trips to Europe during this time, have led him to a much more radical perspective toward Eurocentrism than that which is expressed in this book. Here in these pages, we handle with white gloves something which, in all sincerity, deserves something else. In future texts, hopefully, this limitation will be corrected. As against what is thought even in Mexico itself, we are profoundly convinced that Eurocentrism in its 'philosophical' and general forms – inseparable from the systematic and collective denial and of the limitless brutality and irrationality of recent history and that of the last five hundred years, at least – is one of the principal reasons for the current disaster that humanity is living through at the global level. There is no reason to be hopeful until we have overcome the currently-existing self-limitation in the so-called periphery as regards the right and, above all, the obligation to criticise and analyse the world in its totality, and to denounce as well as directly attack from this 'periphery' the fatal errors of the so-called centre. The critique of Eurocentrism must abandon a position which also characterises this book, one which is merely defensive and which above all demands the right to be heard: the voice of countries without a voice. This defensive attitude is radically limited and, therefore, incorrect. If the world still has any hope of being able to overcome its clearly self-destructive tendency, then this hope can only be based in what emerges from outside the so-called centres, whether in practice or theory.

In gaining consciousness of this, above all in the second, theoretical, aspect, the present book attempts – in spite of its aforementioned limitations – to contribute something. A conclusion immediately arises from this stance: thinkers from the so-called Third World not only have the right to be heard in the 'centres' and by the inhabitants and intellectuals of their own countries – who often prefer to read whatever second- or third-rate European author before having to read an author from their own country or a neighbouring country – but, moreover, have the definitive obligation to criticise, from there, the disasters of contemporary society, disasters which are more difficult to see, and even more difficult to understand, from the centres of global decision-making. It is no longer a matter of demanding nothing more than that one's own specificity has the right to exist, but rather of taking back the universal responsibility belonging to those who live outside the falsely named 'First World' – 'first' for nothing except the number of murders perpetrated throughout the course of history.

Someone who expressed, at a political level, an unforgettable example of this attitude, conscious of his own responsibility from a position in the so-called periphery, was Isidro Fabelo. During the period of the Cárdenas government, in consonance with the President of the Republic, Fabelo raised his voice, completely alone, in the League of Nations to protest in the name of the Mexican people against the annexation of Austria by Nazi Germany in 1938, the *Anschluß*. Meanwhile, the self-described classic democracies, France, Great Britain and the United States, maintained a benevolent silence before Nazi Germany's first international crimes, and the Soviet Union, under Stalin, betrayed the cause of the European Left by means of a secret accord with that country. It had to be a country from the 'periphery', it had to be Mexico, to be the only country to defend international law and reason in the best sense of the word. This was not coincidental: only from the "periphery" was this possible, as is the case today. Only from here will it be possible to stop the train on which we are all travelling and which is heading directly, without any visible stops, toward the abyss.

While the German edition sought to convince German-speaking readers that they are much less of the 'centre' than they think, the Mexican edition seeks, from this new perspective, to demonstrate that reason, if it had a favourite physical place, it would be right here, in the 'navel of the moon'[1] [We do not say this to cause false self-praise now in Mexico, but rather to clear our vision regarding the reflexive and critical obligation that the people of Mexico and their intellectuals also have, an obligation in which self-critique always, of course, enjoys a privileged place.

•••

We want to express our heartfelt thanks for all the help we received finishing the Spanish version of this book, from Marco Aurelio García Barrios, Sofía del Carmen Rodríguez Fernández, Max Rojas, and Robert Zwarg.

In order to make comparison with the original German edition possible – for example, to corroborate the quotations of texts written in German – we have carefully respected the numbering of footnotes, so that those in this edition and the German edition are identical. The bibliography assembled on Adolfo Sánchez Vázquez and Bolívar Echeverría has been updated to the pres-

---

1 Translator's note [henceforth TN] – the literal meaning in Nahuatl of the name Mexico.

ent day. There was no time to do this with the same dedication with which we did it originally for the German edition in 1999, and for which we had, with a few exceptions, all the texts recorded in the bibliography in our hands in order to be completely certain of their corresponding bibliographic dates. However, the electronic databases that now exist in much greater number and with wider thematic coverage from those available in 1999, have helped us to update and extend the bibliographies about Adolfo Sánchez Vázquez and Bolívar Echeverría in a highly reliable manner. The distinction between double quotation marks "..." and single quotation marks '...' represents the distinction between textual quotations and other uses of quotation marks, such as highlighting a word or a free quotation.

Stefan Gandler
Mexico, 23 June 2005

CUERPOS II

Introduction: From Eurocentric to Peripheral Marxism

Written with academic reverence, and drafted to achieve a university degree, this book nevertheless attempts to be rebellious. It seeks to violate a law that has never been written down because each person carries it within him or herself. The text of that secret law is the following:

> PREAMBLE. All reason comes from power. Where there is no power, there is no reason either.
> §1 Beware of thoughts that are not allied with the ruling power in each case.
> §2 Beware of thoughts that are not allied with any power at all.
> §3 Beware of thinkers who are not allied with the ruling power in each case.
> §4 Beware of thinkers who are not allied with any power at all.
> §5 Guard yourself from thinkers who are not allied with any power and who have no ambition to become so.
> §6 But, above all, maintain your distance from thinkers who are not allied with any power and who could not become so even if they so desired.
> §7 Never get involved with thinkers who do not even live in the centres of power.
> §8 The simultaneous contravention of §5 and §7 is punishable by the maximum penalty.
> §9 The simultaneous contravention of §6 and §7 is punishable by double the maximum penalty.

We will look somewhat more closely at the text of the law (source: secret archive of unwritten texts, without date or location). It will surprise the eye trained in logic, of course, that there is an incongruity in §9: how can one give double the maximum penalty? When something can be doubled it necessarily ceases to represent the maximum. A good lawyer would know, without doubt, which side to take, but that does not interest us here. The more important question is, how did it become such a complicated affair? We must start from the fact that it is almost unimaginable to ever reach the application of §9. This is explained by the fact that §6, to which §9 makes reference, would also be difficult to violate in reality. How can there exist a thinker who has not even the slightest possibility of drawing closer to a power, even if it is an oppositional one? (Presumably, therefore, the construction of double the maximum penalty has been devised only for the intimidating purpose of being able to apply the maximum penalty to the lesser crime of violating §8, without breaking the ascending scale imposed in the sequence of numbers).

For this reason, and also admittedly for fear of the unimaginable doubling of the maximum penalty, this book drives its aspired-for rebellion only to the point of violating §8.

What is entailed in the violation of these different rules?

To violate §1 means not selling independent thinking to the slavery of the ruling relations, and, therefore, to investigate those relations in a critical way rather than merely affirming them. A whole series of thinkers (who are not even named in the text of the law) have being doing this up to the present.

To violate §2 means also to avoid chaining independent thought to the competing or dominant power structures in other places. Only a small number of thinkers still do this. Many critics of the capitalist social formation can only imagine their thought as a simultaneous affirmation of a power which predominates elsewhere, namely actually-existing socialism in the Soviet Union and its satellite countries. This type of thinker has generally disappeared from the face of the earth along with the Soviet Union. However, a few thinkers – not always on the Left – still remain, who criticise the ruling relations with reference to another existing power. Perhaps the most important example is the reference to existing religious institutions, and above all to the Catholic Church, which operates practically throughout the entire world. This is, specifically in the countries of the so-called Third World, the point of reference for many authors who are critical of the capitalist mode of production (to a lesser degree among female authors), offering as it does a degree of institutional protection, basic material supplies and infrastructure, and, furthermore – something which must not be underestimated – ideological support in continents as penetrated by Catholicism as, for example, Latin America. A contemporary example is the Bishop Emeritus of San Cristóbal de Las Casas, in the Mexican state of Chiapas, who has settled into the function of mediator, alongside a group of colleagues, against a military solution and in favour of a negotiated settlement of the conflict between the Zapatista Army of National Liberation (EZLN) and Mexico's central government. However, in the final instance, this tendency, as much as it gives expression to an internal critique, is nevertheless committed to a strong, and historically far from rarely brutal power, one that is expressed with special clarity when Karol Wojtyla again imposes a prohibition on one of his intra-religious critics speaking in public, and this is obeyed.

Whoever violates §3 is about to do the same as violators of §1, except that in this case they are taking the detour of consulting other thinkers who, in turn, have violated §1. Now, one could find himself subjected to the same limitations of those who violate §1 but respect §2. Moreover, someone can violate §3 and respect §1. This occurs when a critical author is read and interpreted in an affirmative manner, which is no rare thing. However, as this last case does not arise with any degree of certainty, the anonymous legislators have obviously preferred to play it safe as regards the numbers and to sanction in advance any association with thoughts that fall under the verdict of §1.

Whoever violates §4 enters, with respect to §2, into a similar relationship to that into which one falls with respect to §1 when violating §3, with all the limits already established.

Whoever violates §5 complicates things with regard to §4, because now one is no longer dealing with thinkers who remain outside because they do not have anything to say or because nobody is interested in them, but rather with individuals who in a conscious, and therefore even more reprehensible, act politely declined any pact with power. Again, the limitation whereby the reader of a text might not conceive its critique with the same radicalism applies here; this applies equally for subsequent cases, and from here on we will not repeat it every time.

Whoever violates §6 deserves a great deal of respect, because it is not easy to deal with thinkers who could not align themselves with any power even if they so desired. As was already pointed out, it is difficult to imagine someone who could find himself in such a thankless position. This concerns the existing concept of the thinker, since there is a sufficient number of people *in general* who find themselves in such a position; we could estimate that they constitute the great majority of those living today. But to whom would the idea occur to describe any one of them as a thinker? It is not easy to think clearly with an empty stomach, but nor is it impossible. And even if this is achieved, how to record these ideas if there is no money with which to buy paper, much less to distribute it. What publisher is going to take seriously a manuscript written on old cardboard boxes? Thus it is not likely that someone will arise from these circumstances and be recognised as a 'thinker'. One exception we can imagine would be for some person open to dealing with such thinkers to go to them personally and to begin to talk with them. Here arises, naturally, the problem for whoever tries in any way to infringe §6, which is so difficult to violate: he or she must also master the language of these thinkers, who are of such curious interest. This poses a fresh dilemma. Frequently, such thinkers cannot offer themselves to power precisely because a linguistic barrier prevents it or, put differently, they speak one of the languages classified as unimportant, and which are often not even recognised as 'languages'. The latter is the case in Mexico, for example, with regard to indigenous languages – some 52 in total – which are not designated as such (as 'languages'), but rather, in a pejorative fashion, as scarcely representing 'dialects'.

As an example of someone who, at a minimum, began seriously attempting to rebel against §6 – based firmly on the ideological fossils of our societies, and, therefore, so difficult to violate – it is worth citing the most well known of the aforementioned Zapatistas, Subcomandante Marcos. One can even suspect that his tremendous popularity is precisely a consequence of the fact that it is inconceivable that someone could violate §6. If the secret law remains unpublished to this date, it has always been present in the acts, or as Marx would say: *they do not know it, but they are doing it.*

But as the author of this book prefers to sleep in a bed and not in the mud, to have a roof instead of leaves over his head when it rains, and in general only desires, for now, to be a theoretical 'rebel', he has not been able to violate §6 in this book. It was necessary, certainly, to leap linguistic hurdles and overcome obstacles of a different kind, one being the necessity of changing residence 9,400 kilometres to the West-Southwest, but luckily that was all.

Whoever violates §7 does something unheard of even for violators of §§1 to 5, of which there are not many. For example, Western Marxism, which must be included among the few theoretical currents of Europe to have violated §§1 to 5, has not broken §7.

This must be, therefore, what is specific to this book: it tries to violate §7, which has remained unscathed, almost as fiercely as §6, throughout the entire history of European philosophy. But that is not enough. It is not about analysing a thinker exclusively because they are from the so-called Third World, but rather because the theories of that thinker contribute something of universal importance, which perhaps could not have been thought in the so-called First World.

Today there are, of course, various attempts to violate §7 but (and this is decisive) the majority limit themselves to §7 and do not dare to provoke §8. That is to say, there are attempts in the centre to deal theoretically with thinkers from countries of the periphery but, in general, we are speaking of thinkers who do not fall under the verdict of §5, in the majority not even under §4, and very frequently, not under §3 either. They are, then, for the most part thinkers who while living in countries of the so-called Third World are allied with the ruling power there (for example, in Mexico, the Nobel Prize Laureate for Literature, Octavio Paz) or are committed to another power. Here the two possibilities cited with regard to §2 enter into play, one already extinct and the other very contemporary: support for the Soviet Union (in Mexico, for example, Vicente Lombardo Toledano or other dogmatic Marxists) or the Catholic Church (in Mexico, for example, Enrique Dussel, ex-liberation theologian). On these authors there is a volume of European literature that should not be underestimated.

In this book, we are going to go further: attempting to make a contribution to the philosophical discussion of Marxism and, specifically, to do so with the double objective of avoiding equally dogmatism and Eurocentrism. The effort to break as radically as possible with the unwritten 'philosophical' law that we have described, has led us to concern ourselves theoretically with two non-dogmatic Mexican Marxists: Adolfo Sánchez Vázquez and Bolívar Echeverría.

If the selection of an *extra-European* location falls back specifically to Mexico, it is on the following basis. The focal point of interest for this research, from the beginning, was the Latin-American continent, because the author, over the course of his university studies on Latin America, acquired some knowledge about the continent and learned the Spanish language. Within the continent, Mexico was chosen because this country, given its history (and not only its recent history), possesses an especially rich cultural and intellectual diversity. As a result of the Mexican Revolution of 1910, the country is one of the few on the continent where there was not any attempted military coup in the twentieth century. The policies of the post-revolutionary government, moreover, opened up to innumerable exiles the possibility of living and working there. Mexico City thus became one of the biggest cities in the world for exiles, and the most important one on the continent. The majority of these exiles were Leftists, and among them, at the same time, were many who consciously rejected the alternative of exile in the Soviet Union. Thus emerged through diverse waves of exiles: after the Spanish Civil War, in the epoch of fascism and National Socialism, and in the epoch of military dictatorships in South and Central America, an accumulation (unique at least in Latin America) of critical intellectuals in the biggest city on the planet. Of all of these, Adolfo Sánchez Vázquez and Bolívar Echeverría, both originally from other countries, appeared to us the most interesting and meaningful within non-dogmatic Marxist philosophy.

Non-dogmatic Marxism is, if examined in depth, the theoretical current which breaks most radically with §§1–5 of the unwritten law. The efforts of a movement opposing the enormity of Eurocentrism is the way to most significantly infringe upon §§7 and 8. Eurocentrism, of course, does not only exist on the theoretical terrain, but also on the political; it tends to adhere as well to emancipatory foci of one or another variety and leads, not only in Europe, but also on the other side of the world divided in two, to the most fatal results:

a racism directed against oneself in the daily life of many countries of the so-called Third World, in which, for example, lighter-coloured skin is no less celebrated, revered, and elevated as the ideal of beauty by precisely those who do not possess it, and where there exists in political-social conflict a powerful orientation toward US and European forms of organisation, with their political models and respective theoretical foundations.

During the last four decades, this one-sidely directed relationship appeared to have been modified on the political level with the different national liberation movements of the so-called Third World. It is notable that the European solidarity movement, while captured by a peculiar fixation on those, was unable to leave behind the paternalism, even when the Neo-Zapatistas' rebellion broke with the old guerrilla strategies. But on the theoretical level, in spite of various efforts and with few exceptions, ultimately, practically nothing had changed. While, for example, in Mexico every theoretical 'innovation' in Europe or the United States is followed and commented upon with care – not only are translations prepared, but they are also published and read – in Frankfurt the simple discovery that two philosophers living in Mexico are worth reading arouses exclamations of delight or commotion, both expressions of the same phlegmatic self-satisfaction.[1]

The above-described rebellion against this unwritten law, especially against the Eurocentrism contained within it, is not an end in itself, but rather has a specific motive in existing reality. The weakness of the social forces committed to the emancipation of human beings from oppression and exploitation is not mainly a consequence of these forces being insufficiently 'popular', but rather very often due to the fact that they do not appear to represent any alternative to the existing order. This impression is not always deceptive. There are infinite aspects in which the Left can hardly be distinguished whatsoever from the bourgeois forces whose legacy it has accepted, in the negative sense. But it is precisely these aspects which constitute the weakness of the Left, and not, as is complacently stated, its allegedly excessive distance from the 'voice of the

---

1 The prevailing ignorance, however, does not apply only to theoretical expressions from countries of the so-called Third World, but also (if in a lesser fashion) in the case of neighboring countries. The barrier that exists, for example, in relation to France, would scarcely be imaginable in Mexico, where there exists tremendous interest as to what is happening in the different European countries. The mechanism referred to for systematically blocking discussion of certain themes cannot be defined, of course, only in geographical terms. Also dismissed in Germany are certain themes of the 'theoretical rearguard', and, above all, National Socialism: twenty to thirty years had to pass before central works on the theme, like *Behemoth* by Franz Neumann, or *The Destruction of European Jews* by Raul Hilberg, were translated into the German language.

people'. These bourgeois remnants within the Left not only rob it of all credibility, but moreover eat away at it from within. The emancipation of some *cannot* be achieved at the expense of other people's emancipation. This idea – as old as it is erroneous – which, ultimately, recalls the defence of the ancient slave society, is as present today in the Left as it was at the beginning of its existence. The classical formulation used to get around this evidently absurd position was the 'principal and secondary contradiction', with which the unshakably patriarchal tradition within the Left was justified. In reality, it meant: 'let's fight for us, leave us alone, and then we'll see'. This slogan, of insurmountable narrow-mindedness, continues to prevail. On the Left, the concept of solidarity was always applied, as a general rule, in a severely restricted manner. The principle of competition in bourgeois society was merely collectivised and transformed into another form, between severely defined and narrowly profiled groups. The unity of a national workers' movement, for example, appeared unattainable; little now remains of the international solidarity of the proletariat, the dream of the First International.

It is this bourgeoisification of the Left that has caused its near disappearance. Rather than being destroyed or ignored from the outside, it has undermined itself from the inside out. The most terrible example of this is provided by the Stalinists, who, first in cultural policy and then in all other social spheres, practiced an incredible conservatism. They even attempted to surpass bourgeois methods of brutally increasing productivity, as well as imposing other types of discipline which led to greater repression than existed in moderate bourgeois societies. The lesson in all of this is that the Left, in order to effectively contribute something to the emancipation of human beings, will have to discard thoroughly the remains of the bourgeois logic of oppression and exploitation.

There are many examples that could be mentioned. The most discussed over the last two decades have been the gender-specific forms of oppression and exploitation and the repressive relationship toward external nature (and to a lesser degree toward our own nature). But Eurocentrism (which is one of the distinctive characteristics of the Stalinists) continues merrily on its way: the few critiques that oppose it are, for the most part, either quite tepid or trivial attempts to stand it on its head. Without a doubt, this is one of the decisive causes of the current weakness of the Left at the global level. It is not a question of denouncing it again and again in pamphlets and speeches with the calm certainty that nothing is going to change. Eurocentrism can only be attacked, in any event, through the realisation of things: in political praxis, by way of constructing and establishing international contacts; in theory, by way of organising international discussion.

From the point of view of the current global centre, this is, or should be, an exceedingly painful process. If Eurocentrism were actually surpassed in the formation of leftist theory, it would mean a crisis lasting several decades, at least, for the critical spirits of Europe, for example. The certainty of the superiority of European civilisation, which has been lauded for centuries, would clash in the everyday with this new reality. It would be such a painful process that the author cannot imagine it, even stretching his imagination to the utmost possible degree. If we imagine, for example, a writer or scientist from Germany, who suddenly had to woo the public in the book market, competing for attention and interest not only with German theorists, and some Europeans and citizens of the US, but with those of the rest of the world, would this not be terrible for him or her? What would it mean to expect so-called First World intellectuals not only to know more or less well the literature of the so-called old continent and the United States, but also that of the rest of the planet – which is, after all, a vast expanse? Just imagine this writer or scientist arriving in one of those countries that up until now held Europe up as a privileged location of culture, critique, and brilliant thinking, but which suddenly no longer recognises any great merit in the fact of being from Europe. It could be that he or she would be asked to summarise his or her theory in a few phrases because they had not heard anything about him or her, while in Europe perhaps he is a prestigious man, or she a prestigious woman, something which still today is an absolute guarantee of also being recognised in, for example, Latin America. Would not all of this be humiliating for them?

It would be painful, just as no emancipation can occur without birth pains. Eurocentrism, born historically as the ideology concomitant to the economic and military preponderance of the old continent, has become so apparently natural that the idea does not occur – even to those who would like to see this economy brought down – that Eurocentrism has to be abolished in this very moment *at the latest*. But seeing it more clearly, we must fight it from much further back, like all other ideologies that help to stabilise the existing relations of oppression and exploitation.

A look at the map of the world casts something else into relief also: what would Europe be, in reality, without Eurocentrism, understood simultaneously as an ideological and material force? At best, it would be a peninsula of the Asian continent, and in the geography lessons of other continents it would perhaps be referred to in passing as the 'extreme west of Western Asia' or some similar monstrosity. If the mode of projection of the surface of the globe on the two-dimensional world map had not been chosen with the same skill as the location of the Equator – which almost never appears in the middle, but is instead almost always shifted lower – then Europe would only be seen after looking several times. From the European perspective, a world without Eurocentrism is an impertinence, an incredible underestimation of what *we have*. According to this opinion, the bulk of the European Left is nearly indistinguishable from general bourgeois consciousness.

'Yes, this is all true, but we must admit that those countries have not in reality produced as many theories, and of course, have not produced as many leftist theories; when all is said and done, Marx was not Mexican'. This is the objection that generally emerges at this point. The fact that Marx comes from Trier and not Anenecuilco is inarguable. And nor is the fact that Mexico's economic situation allows fewer human beings to enjoy the leisure of theory than is the case in Germany. But none of this is good reason for the astonishing persistence with which theories produced in countries of the so-called Third World are in Germany either completely ignored or merely noted as some exoticism.[2]

To air out the rancid bourgeois stench that accumulated under the robes during a thousand years means, decisively and without any doubt, to once and for all throw Eurocentric arrogance overboard. This demand is not posed paternalistically in favour of the inhabitants of the Third World, but instead emerges immediately from the needs of Germany and Europe. It is only by breaking radically with these anachronistic traditions that we can make a fresh start in the formation of a leftist theory, and the same can be said of political praxis. To remain stuck in Eurocentrism means clinging to one of the foundational elements of bourgeois ideology, and, as a result, as radical and critical as our praxis and theory might seem in other respects, when all is said and done it will continue reshovelling yesterday's bourgeois snow.

This book hopes to contribute a first step toward overcoming Eurocentric bigotry within the formulation of a non-dogmatic leftist theory (put more precisely: within the non-dogmatic philosophical discussion of Marxism). It will doubtless be unable to settle the enormous deficit which exists in Germany in this respect, but its objective is, at least (to use Marx's phrase once again), to shorten the birth pains of this unavoidable but painful process.

However, overcoming Eurocentrism in our theoretical formulations, or at the very least attempting to avoid it, does not mean that we will now treat the Mexican authors we discuss with the silk gloves of apologism simply because

---

2   Note to the edition in Spanish: this book was written largely in Mexico, but at the same time has Germany as an important reference point, since the author was educated there and because he originally sought to assail this 'philosophical' Eurocentrism in Germany itself (in this respect, see the 'Preface to the Edition in Spanish'). As a result, in the German version the expressions 'here' or 'hierzulande' appear with reference to Germany, expressions which in the Spanish version have been simply replaced by the word 'Germany'.

they have been so long ignored in Germany. In the first place, to do so would be profoundly boring, and in the second place, it would do no service either to them or to the urgently necessary international debates among theorists of emancipation. In this book, then, we will attempt a discussion of the theories of Adolfo Sánchez Vázquez and Bolívar Echeverría, which, as we have said, will also be critical.

To the author of this book, this critique has been branded as Eurocentric on more than one occasion during discussions in Mexico with supporters of the two philosophers here analysed. This reproach, however, results more from the desire to have a protected discursive space without external interference (the inverse of Eurocentrism). In this book, rather, the very opposite is the case, as given that it seeks to provide an introduction to the authors' theories, the critique is left short in comparison with the manner in which the author has formulated it in Mexico, in debates in colloquia, conferences, speeches, and other scientific meetings. It is true that, in both cases, we have entered at some points into aspects of their theories which seem questionable to us, but the framework set in this book limits our critique of Sánchez Vázquez and Bolívar Echeverría to a level considerably lesser than that which has already been put forth in the Mexican context. This is defensible because in the German context this book represents scarcely the beginning of serious debate with these two philosophers, which is to say, we are beginning from zero, which is distinct from the situation in Mexico, where both authors are generally known in the social sciences. If it were the case that a debate had got underway in Germany with regard to Mexican or Latin-American social philosophy, we would certainly intervene in it with specifically critical contributions regarding Adolfo Sánchez Vázquez and Bolívar Echeverría.

In the case of the former, for example, we would need to enter into the question of dogmatic remnants that continue to appear again and again across the whole of his work, remnants which have withstood the first rupture with Soviet orthodoxy by a Marxist philosopher in Latin America, namely that undertaken by Sánchez Vázquez. In the latter case, it would be necessary to study, in greater detail than has been done in this book, whether his efforts to ground a non-ethnocentric, yet at the same time universalist, theory have been successful or if, instead, this theory remained relativist in certain ways, such that he may have deprived himself of the means for a radical critique of society and ideology. Put in more general terms, it is a question of the costs of his effort to overcome an abstract and false – that is, a Eurocentric – universalism.

Sánchez Vázquez's central work, *Filosofía de la praxis* [the first edition of this book was translated into English with the title *The Philosophy of Praxis*], can be seen as the cornerstone of the philosophical discussion of Marxism in

Latin America or, to a certain degree, as the beginning of its non-dogmatic formulation. This work contains some parallels with the Lukács of *History and Class Consciousness*, but is developed independently of the latter's work, as the author insists. For several generations of critical social theorists in Mexico and other Latin-American countries, including Brazil, this book represented the nodal point of their apprenticeship. The fact that it continues to be totally unknown in the German-language debates, in contrast to what has happened in Britain, the United States, and Yugoslavia, speaks volumes about the specific nature of *philosophical* Eurocentrism in the country of Karl Marx. Without it mattering, in the last instance, to our judgement on his theory, knowledge of Sánchez Vázquez's primary work is, to a certain degree, 'obligatory' for a first approach towards contemporary social philosophy in Mexico.

It is mostly due to a 'free decision', that we have chosen to include Bolívar Echeverría as the second author in this book. When the author of this book began studying this philosopher, his theory was in Mexico (if we disregard generally well-informed circles) a kind of secret 'tip'. Since that moment, this has changed radically, what coincided more or less with the publication of his book *Las ilusiones de la modernidad* [*The illusions of modernity*] and a volume that he compiled under the title *Modernidad, mestizaje cultural y ethos barroco* [*Modernity, cultural mestizaje and baroque ethos*], at the beginning of 1995. While there is no direct connection between the two theories, we should note that Adolfo Sánchez Vázquez prepared the terrain in Mexico both institutionally and conceptually for a philosophical discussion of Marxism in its non-dogmatic form, within which Bolívar Echeverría was then able to develop his theory. Despite noteworthy theoretical differences within this 'terrain', Sánchez Vázquez repeatedly offered institutional cover to Echeverría when he needed it.

One decisive difference between the two authors lies in relation to the concept of praxis. Sánchez Vázquez celebrates praxis, distinguishing it from the mechanistic materialism of Soviet Marxism, in the sense of a revaluation of the individual as the subject of history, which cannot be obviated by the inevitable self-drive of history and its 'laws'. For him, praxis in this sense does not include all activity, but rather only that which is already conceptually mediated: that which is reflected. The relationship between theory and action has already been built into the concept of praxis itself, also in the sense that only those objects that have already been touched by the historical praxis of human beings can become the material of human knowledge.

Bolívar Echeverría has a particularly sceptical relationship to praxis. While Sánchez Vázquez, against Marxist orthodoxy, holds in high esteem the possibility of the intervention of the subject, Echeverría doubts that the given situation can be limitlessly changed, and he doubts moreover that it would be desirable to subject it entirely to human praxis. In so doing, he does not feel inspired by ecological debates, which similarly call attention to the fatal consequences of an unrestrained human praxis, but rather doubts all the more that human societies themselves can be simply changed overnight. In so doing, he sets out from the most complex organisational forms of these respective societies, which include substantially more than, for example, the pure and simple circumstance of being capitalist or not. Within the capitalist mode of production, Echeverría also perceives very diverse forms for the everyday organisation of social life, which are powerfully rooted in the respective way of producing and consuming *use-values*, something which he documents through the new concept of 'historical *ethos*'. His references to Marx are more heavily directed toward his economic works, whereas Sánchez Vázquez has in mind more the earlier, 'more philosophical' works, even though both coincide in their rejection of the assumption of a break within Marx's theoretical-conceptual development (between 'early philosophical work/central scientific work').

While for Sánchez Vázquez the brake that slows the revolutionary overcoming of the ruling state of exploitation and oppression lies in the complex intertwining of theory and praxis, which mutually condition one another without either managing to perfect itself without the other doing the same (which is, at first glance, a vicious cycle), this is a false dilemma for Echeverría. According to him, it is a question of discovering political possibilities *within* alienation. To do so, he reduces the radicality of the critique of knowledge and ideology, which allows him simultaneously and with complete calm, without the constant interrogation about what is true or false, to conceptually approach in each case the different forms of capitalist modernities (in plural!). It is precisely here that the explosive force of his critical emphasis on Eurocentrism lies. However, Echeverría's theoretical emphasis, applied to concrete ideological forms and their possible *falsehood*, can find itself in a tight spot and fail; this can be seen in his article on the so-called reunification of Germany.

Here we are again turned back to the much more radical critique of knowledge that Sánchez Vázquez applies, doing so principally on the basis of one of the primary texts of non-dogmatic Marxism: the *Theses on Feuerbach*. Setting out from this, he attempts to determine the complex relationship between idealism and materialism, which cannot be dealt with in terms of simplistic formulas regarding 'basic questions'.

The strength of Echeverría's focus lies in knowing how to analyse how leftist politics has all too frequently overlooked the concrete forms of particular societies, which count on their own very specific forms of production and consumption of use-values, and how this ignorance has prevented them from grasping the real possibilities for a radical transformation.

PART 1

Historical and Theoretical Context

Allow us, at the outset of this book, to enter into the biographical details of the authors under discussion. The need for such a presentation lies in the fact that in Germany they are practically unknown. While it is true that translations of Adolfo Sánchez Vázquez's books into English, Serbo-Croat, Portuguese, and Italian exist, as well as translations of his articles – aside from the mentioned languages – into French, Czech, Romanian, and Russian – in German it has only been possible, up to this moment, to read a very short paper and political theoretical talk published in a student journal,[1] and a single German-speaking author mentions him in one of his texts.[2] It is also true that Bolívar Echeverría occasionally gave minor courses at the Freie Universität Berlin, and that he once spoke at the Johann Wolfgang Goethe University in Frankfurt, but this did little more for the knowledge of his work in Germany than the publication of one of his texts in a political-cultural journal in the same country.[3]

---

1   See the list of translations in the section 'Bibliography of Adolfo Sánchez Vázquez', in this book.
2   Haug 1981, pp. 528ff.
3   See the 'Bibliography of Bolívar Echeverría' in this book.

CHAPTER 1

The Life and Work of Adolfo Sánchez Vázquez

The biography of Sánchez Vázquez will also be of interest to our discussion of 'Praxis and Knowledge' below, because in it we can already find a very definite relationship between (political/social) praxis and theoretical-conceptual efforts and unfoldings. Sánchez Vázquez does not vacillate for a second in presenting his theoretical knowledge as directly dependent upon political transformation and praxis. In an opinion poll carried out by the Cuban journal *Casa de las Américas* on the occasion of the twentieth anniversary of the 1959 Revolution, under the title 'What has the Cuban Revolution meant to you?', he responds as follows, referring to among other things his book *The Philosophy of Praxis*:

> Without my first live and direct encounter with the men and the accomplishments of the Cuban Revolution in 1964, my book *Las ideas estéticas de Marx* [Published in English as: *Art and Society*] would not have been possible, and nor would my effort to make my way through Marxism, in my *Philosophy of Praxis*, casting aside the crutch of the instruction manuals.[4]

But his life also shows the tendency toward the inverse movement (from theory to praxis). Sánchez Vázquez mentions various examples, albeit without the vehemence of the opposite movement: among these, the effects of his early essay 'Ideas estéticas en los *Manuscritos económico-filosóficos* de Marx' ['Aesthetic Ideas in Marx's *Economic-Philosophical Manuscripts*'],[5] on cultural politics during the early stages of post-revolutionary Cuba, as well as the interest displayed by a group of Sandinista leaders – which included the highest leaders of the 'New Nicaragua' – in engaging in a theoretical-political discussion with him.

The following brief and drawing biography does not merely seek to sketch the 'life path' of a thinker that we have chosen by chance, and who is then 'thrown into the world', but rather – on the basis of Sánchez Vázquez as an individual – to provide a glimpse into a generation of antifascist intellectuals

---

4 Sánchez Vázquez 1978c, p. 25.
5 Sánchez Vázquez 1961. A revised English version version is published with the titel "The ideas of Marx on the Source and Nature of the Aesthetic" in: Sánchez Vázquez, 1974, pp. 47–95.

who had put their hope in the Second Spanish Republic and social transformation by democratic and parliamentary means which seemed possible there, and who, after seeing their resistance to the Francoist coup d'état crushed, were forced to suffer the heavy burden of exile.

Beginning of the Biography

To Posterity 11

I came to the cities in a time of disorder,
When hunger ruled.
I came among men in a time of uprising
And I revolted with them.
So the time passed away
Which on earth was given me.

I ate my food between massacres.
The shadow of murder lay upon my sleep.
And when I loved, I loved with indifference
I looked upon nature with impatience.
So the time passed away
Which on earth was given me.

In my time streets led to the quicksand.
Speech betrayed me to the slaughterer.
There was little I could do. But without me
The rulers would have been more secure, this was my hope.
So the time passed away
Which on earth was given me.

Our forces were slight. Our goal
Lay far in the distance
It was clearly visible, though I myself
Was unlikely to reach it.
So the time passed away
which on earth was given me.

BERTOLT BRECHT

Adolfo Sánchez Vázquez was born on 17 September 1915 in Algeciras, a coastal city in the Andalusian province of Cádiz. He is the son of María Remedios Vázquez Rodríguez and Benedicto Sánchez Calderón. His father, lieutenant of a detachment in the Civil Guard, saw his career abruptly cut short at the outset of the Spanish Civil War: detained when Málaga was occupied by Franco's troops, he is condemned to death, a sentence which is commuted to many years in prison. Adolfo was his second child, preceded by his sister Ángela and followed by his brother Gonzalo, who would later be a member of the Communist Party of Spain (PCE).

After some time in El Escorial (a province of Madrid), in 1925 the family moved to the southern city of Málaga.[6] There, he studied middle and high school, and from 1932 to 1934 he studied to be a teacher [*magisterio*]. Life in this powerfully politicised city would leave its mark on his first incursions, in literary and poetic, as well as in political respects. Around 1985, Sánchez Vázquez retrospectively recalled this period: 'This "fierce city", which had given the Republican Courts their first communist deputy, due to the combativeness of its youth and its working class, was at the time called "Malaga: the Red", and was also characterised during the prewar years by its intense cultural life'.[7]

There he was educated in literature and poetry alongside Emilio Prados and the 'thriving poetic group' of Málaga.[8] In 1933 the journal *Octubre*, edited by Rafael Alberti, published a first poetic text by Sánchez Vázquez.[9] That same year, he joined the Revolutionary Student Bloc within the Spanish University Federation (FUE) and then joined the Communist Youth. This 'precocious' political development – as Sánchez Vázquez would later call it – began with the birth of the Second Spanish Republic on 14 April 1931 and emerged through the hopes that the student youth, above all, had placed in it.[10] Some 52 years later, he would write about the Communist Youth of Malaga: an organisation of fewer than a hundred members: 'With its cult of action which bordered on adventurism it could scarcely be distinguished from the (anarchist) Libertarian Youth with which its relations were, conversely, not at all cordial. Its richness in terms of violent praxis corresponded to its poverty on the theoretical terrain, but in those moments that poverty did not concern me'.[11]

It was in these days that his uncle Alfredo Vázquez ('more a romantic rebel than a revolutionary, [who] never wished to be subjected to any party discipline'), who would later be executed by firing squad by the Francoists during

---

6   See Lucas 1987, p. 219.
7   Sánchez Vázquez 1985a, p. 11. The central theme of this edition of *Anthropos* (no. 52) is the life and work of Sánchez Vázquez and it contains, among other things, three autobiographical texts.
8   Caffarena Such 1960, p. 167.
9   'Romance de la ley de fugas': Sánchez Vázquez 1933.
10 Sánchez Vázquez 1985a, p. 11.
11 Sánchez Vázquez 1985a, pp. 10–11.

the first days of the coup, introduced him to his first Marxist- and anarchist-oriented theoretical texts.[12]

In October 1935, Adolfo Sánchez Vázquez moved to Madrid to study at the Central University. Once in the capital, he joined some of the flourishing literary circles: there, for example, he would come to know Pablo Neruda and befriend José Herrera Petere. He frequently wrote for the literary section of *Mundo Obrero*, the PCE daily, and is listed as responsible for two ephemeral periodicals: *Línea*, with a 'political-intellectual' orientation, edited in Madrid, with José Luis Cano, and *Sur*, edited in Malaga: with Enrique Rebolledo. On the eve of the Spanish Civil War, between Madrid and Málaga he wrote the manuscript for his first book, a collection of poems entitled *El Pulso Ardiendo*. The text, rescued by the Spanish editor Manuel Altolaguirre, was brought to Mexico and published there in 1942.[13]

He entred the Faculty of Philosophy and Arts [Facultad de Filosofía y Letras] of the Universidad Central after passing an entrance examination whose failure rate of 80 percent meant that it was known as an 'academic massacre',[14] while the '*spiritus rector*' of the Faculty – José Ortega y Gasset – saw therein the possibility of accomplishing his idea of the university as a 'breeding-ground for "distinguished minorities" '.[15]

Studying there satisfied Adolfo Sánchez Vázquez on an academic level, given the high level of many classes and seminars, especially those given by José F. Montesinos, Juan de la Cruz, and Ortega y Gasset himself, but he was not satisfied on the ideological level.[16] He found nothing even remotely like Marxism, at which he arrived through 'two practices', poetry and politics.[17] He was thus required to perfect himself on this terrain as an autodidact, outside of the university and in conjunction with his political activities. In this, he found help in 'some classic texts [by Marx] in the first and excellent versions of Wenceslao Roces'.[18]

---

12   Sánchez Vázquez 1985a, p. 11.
13   Sánchez Vázquez 1985a, p. 10. The text mentioned is Sánchez Vázquez 1942.
14   Sánchez Vázquez 1985a, p. 11. Sánchez Vázquez would use this designation in Mexico years later against José Gaos, then a confidant of Ortega y Gasset and jointly responsible for these examinations: Ibid.
15   Ibid.
16   Ibid.
17   Sánchez Vázquez 1985a, p. 10.
18   Sánchez Vázquez 1985a, p. 11. The impediments to carrying out studies on this terrain also result, however, from the 'traditional disdain of the Spanish workers' movement and its parties for theory': Ibid.

At that time, the Spanish university was the arena of political battles. The FUE student union, controlled by the Left, was fought by the far-right National-Syndicalist Offensive Juntas, founded in Valladolid in 1931 and which simultaneously trained its members militarily.[19] The far-right Falange here found one of its most important sources: 'The Falange and its student sector, the SEU (Sindicato Español Universitario) were, in the words of one of its prominent leaders, one and the same, since the Falange was born with the "mark of the university youth"'.[20]

The Central University campus would be, shortly thereafter, 'one of the fiercest battlefields',[21] with 'Nationalist' efforts to enter the capital militarily held back there for months, with a large portion of the FUE participating in the struggle on the side of the Republic.[22]

The Spanish Civil War

The Civil War began between 17 and 18 July 1936, with the uprising of the military units under General Franco against the Popular Front government of Azaña, elected on 16 February of the same year, and the spontaneous resistance of large sectors of the population against the coup attempt. This war has been characterised by various authors as the 'first battle of the Second World War', due to its international significance and involvement (the military support provided to the Francoists by fascist Italy and Nazi Germany), as well as the indirect support provided by the 'politics of non-intervention' of the English and French democracies, for example, in not letting arms shipments pass, as well as the support provided to the Republic by the Soviet Union and Mexico – in the case of the former, also through sending troops – and finally, that of the International Brigades.[23] The behaviour of the European

---

19 See Thomas 1961, p. 69.
20 Germani 1970, p. 359. Germani here quotes according to Jato 1953, p. 62.
21 Sánchez Vázquez 1985a, p. 11.
22 See, for example, regarding the death of the acting general secretary of the FUE, Juan López, in the battles in the University City: 'Héroes de la Juventud. Ha muerto el camarada Juan López de la Unión de Estudiantes', in *Ahora. Diario de la Juventud*, Madrid, 2 April 1937, p. 5.
23 Líster 1966, p. 4. 'The Second World War began in Spain', wrote Bowers, at that time ambassador of the United States in Spain (Bowers 1955, p. viii. Cited according to Álvarez 1989, p. 21).

    A connection between the Spanish Civil War and the Second World War can be established, moreover, by the fact that, as a result of the long resistance against the Francoite coup, Franco's Spain was so weakened and unstable after the Spanish Civil War (1939) that, despite the request from the government of the German Reich, it did not enter the

democracies with regard to the Spanish Civil War, as well as the internal struggles in the Republican camp (particularly between socialists, communists, and anarchists) and the fatal role played by the Soviet Union, shed light on the combination of political and social events contributing to making possible that which – as the *rupture of civilisation* – would rewrite history. With the fall of Madrid and the Nationalist triumph on 1 April 1939, the German Luftwaffe (Air Force) considered their task to be over, and exactly five months later, with the attack on Poland, the German advance on the East began.

Sánchez Vázquez was one of the thousands and thousands of Spaniards that spontaneously threw themselves into opposition against this coup d'état, and, before suffering ultimate defeat, prevented the Francoite invasion of significant sections of Spain for almost three years. He did this as a member of the Unified Socialist Youth (JSU), which emerges in April 1936 from the union of the Socialist and Communist youth sections.[24]

At the outset of the War, he was a member, in Málaga – where he had recently returned – of the Regional Committee of the JSU, and was editor of its publication *Octubre*. In mid-January 1937, he participated as a delegate to the National Conference of the JSU, held in Valencia.

Second World War, and as a result the Allies were able to cross the strategically important Strait of Gibraltar unhindered (author's conversation with Santiago Álvarez, political commissar of the V Army Body of the Popular Army during the Civil War. Madrid, 22 March 1991).

24 See Cortada (ed.) 1982, p. 282. Santiago Carrillo Solares, who as president of the Socialist Youth drove the unification, mentions among his motives the following: 'We were convinced [in 1934], after seeing what was happening in other European countries, that fascism was rising everywhere without anyone doing anything to stop it. The Socialist youth and the Socialist Left of the period were convinced that we needed to fight and that in order to win we needed to unite with the Communists', and later: 'there is an event that shocked me ... it was the rebellion of Vienna [in February of 1934] and their failure. ... In 1936, after two years of united action, the unification of the Socialist and Communist youth was established' (See Carrillo 1974, especially the chapters: 'Vingt ans en 1936' and 'La guerre d'Espagne: réflexions et remontres', p. 32 and p. 42).

In the literature, the JSU is granted a curious double-role: J.W. Cortada highlights the function of the JSU in the divisions and internal confrontations of the anti-Francoites, among socialists, communists, and anarchists: 'In the course of the Civil War, the JSU fought in various military units, while offering the Communist Party an armed wing to reduce opposition within the Republican zone' (Cortada [ed.] 1982). Ramón Casterás, on the other hand, in the introduction to his work on the Unified Socialist Youth of Cataluña (JSUC), takes a good look at the history of the JSU (throughout Spain), emphasising that the youth organisations of the Civil War, with absolute independence from their adult parties, practiced a politics of collaboration and unity (Casterás 1977, p. 16).

After the fall of Málaga at the end of January, he moved to Valencia, where Santiago Carrillo, in the name of the Executive Committee of the JSU, put him in charge of editing *Ahora*, the central publication of the JSU. Adolfo Sánchez Vázquez would later write of this position: 'Bearing in mind that we are talking about the central publication of the most important youth organisation in the Republican zone, with more than 200,000 members, and the enormous influence that it exerted through these members on the Popular Army, this was an enormous responsibility given my 21 years of age'.[25]

And on his working situation in the embattled city of Madrid: 'Our [editorial] building was situated between the Republican artillery installations and those of the enemy, and this is why I had to get used to writing leading articles and editorials amid the deafening duels of the cannons'.[26]

Sánchez Vázquez functions from March to September of 1937 as editor of *Ahora*, published every day except Sundays, and which during that period generally consisted of eighteen pages with abundant photographic material from the Republican territories and from the front.[27] In early July of 1937 he

---

25 Sánchez Vázquez 1985a, p. 12. Casterás advances in his aforementioned work the following working thesis: through the political unfolding of the Second Spanish Republic and the significant importance that youth movements gained, we can redefine the role of the youth on Spain's historical stage of that moment as another principal actor (Casterás 1977, p. 15). Understood in his way, the great responsibility that Sánchez Vázquez had to assume at the age of 21 was not an isolated experience, but rather part of a general development. In reality, he himself already expressed this when he suggests in the cited text that the JSU, among other things, achieved great importance through the considerable military role it assumed during the Spanish Civil War.

A coeditor of *Ahora*'s twin publication, *La Hora*, which appeared beginning in the summer of 1937 in Valencia, was evidently Sánchez Vázquez's brother, Gonzalo (See 'Gonzalo Sánchez Vázquez, our beloved director', photo caption accompanying the article: '20 months of a youth daily', in *La Hora, Diario Juvenil*, year 3, no. 526. Valencia, 19 February 1939, p. 1; see moreover p. 17 of this book).

26 Sánchez Vázquez 1985a.

27 See *Ahora. Diario de la Juventud*. Madrid, 1 March to 30 September 1937. Regarding the dates, see A. Sánchez Vázquez, letter to the author, Mexico City, 22 February 1991, p. 1.

Aside from the enormous importance that *Ahora* had in informing, politicising, and mobilising members of the JSU and other Spanish youth, it is also worth mentioning its role in debates with opposing leftist currents. What stands out in this sense is the battle against Trotskyist groups or those characterised as such by others. In this regard, see for example, 'La juventud del POUM continúa su política de chantaje [The POUM youth continue their politics of blackmail]', in *Ahora. Diario de la Juventud*, Madrid, 31 March 1937, p. 5, and 'Marxismo-Leninismo, Lenin y el trotskismo. Cómo pensaba el líder de la Revolución rusa del jefe de las bandas contrarrevolucionarias, Trotsky [Marxism-Leninism,

was invited in this capacity to the Second International Congress of Antifascist Writers in Madrid. At the International Congress for the Defense of Culture, he meets, among others, Juan Marinello,[28] Louis Aragon, Anna Seghers, André Malraux, Ilya Ehrenberg, and Octavio Paz.[29]

On the importance of cultural work in the Republican zone, a Spanish historian would later write the following:

> A symptomatic fact is that during the first year and a half of the War the number of primary schools increased, on top of the 800 created in the fronts of the 'cultural militias', in whose work more than 2,000 educators participated (in October 1937 more than 75,000 soldiers had learned to read and write). A thousand libraries were established in hospitals and barracks, and 150 newspapers were published regularly by military units, in many of which young writers regularly participated.[30]

In September of that same year, after a polemic between the newspaper and an international socialist delegation, Sánchez Vázquez withdrew from his position as editor and requested that the Executive Committee of the JSU transfer him to the front.[31] He joined the 11th Division, which was already legendary for its defense of Madrid and was at that point located on the eastern front under the orders of commander Líster;[32] he thereby, under the command of

---

  Lenin, and Trotskyism. What the leader of the Russian Revolution thought of the boss of the counter-revolutionary gangs, Trotsky]', in the same issue.

28   See Sánchez Vázquez 1978a, p. 113.

29   Sánchez Vázquez 1985a, p. 12. Moreover, Sánchez Vázquez mentions the following literati who he met there: Tristan Tzara, Stephen Spender, César Vallejo, Alejo Carpentier, Félix Pita Rodríguez, Rafael Alberti, José Bergamín, Ramón José Sender, Corpus Barga, Arturo Serrano Plaja, as well as Nicolás Guillén (Sánchez Vázquez 1978a, p. 113).

  Moreover, the following people also participated in this Congress: Pablo Neruda (Chile), Egon Erwin Kisch (Czechoslovakia), Córdoba Iturburo, Sara Tornú, Pablo Rojas Paz (Argentina), J. Braus (Netherlands), Vicente Huidobro, and José Bergamín (Spain) (See Líster 1966, pp. 139–40).

  Santiago Álvarez mentions another hundred participants, including Alexei Tolstoi (USSR), Ernest Hemingway (United States), and Wenceslao Roces (Spain) (Álvarez 1989, pp. 367–8).

30   Tuñón de Lara 1966, p. 213. Tuñón goes on to list those 'young writers' involved: 'Rafael Alberti, Miguel Hernández, Serrano Plaja, Herrera Petere, Emilio Prados, Garfias, Chabás, Altolaguirre, Izcaray, Sánchez Vázquez, Rejano, etc.' On the same topic, see also Álvarez 1989, pp. 143–55.

31   Sánchez Vázquez 1985a.

32   On the history of the 11th Division, see Líster 1966, pp. 79ff, and Álvarez 1986, pp. 121ff.

the political commissar of the division, Santiago Álvarez,[33] assumed the leadership of the press and propaganda commissariat,[34] and published the newspaper of that unit: ¡Pasaremos![35] In mid-August, the 11th Division had already carried out an act that would provoke polemical debates in the historiography of the Spanish Civil War: the dissolution of the 'Council of Aragon', an anarchist-oriented regional government in that region of northern Spain, by order of the multi-party central government.[36]

On 15 December 1937, the 11th Division played a central part in an important military victory: the siege and liberation of the city of Teruel, located 100 kilometres to the northwest of Valencia, seat of the threatened government of the Republic.[37] As an eyewitness, Sánchez Vázquez wrote a very valuable report on this event, which was so important for the 'morale' of the Republic.[38] Four months later, on 27 April 1938, also thanks to Teruel, Enrique Líster and Santiago Álvarez were promoted, respectively, to head and political commissar of the 5th Army Corps, and with them, Adolfo Sánchez Vázquez to press and propaganda commissar and editor-in-chief of the publication Acero.[39] The soldiers called the Commissariat to which Sánchez Vázquez belonged, half in jest

---

33 In conversation with the author, Santiago Álvarez indicates that Sánchez Vázquez had already arrived at this Commissariat some weeks previously (S. Álvarez, conversation with the author, Madrid, 22 March 1991).

34 Sánchez Vázquez, letter to the author, Mexico City, 22 February 1991, p. 2.

35 See Sánchez Vázquez 1985a, p. 12. This newspaper, which almost always consisted of eight pages, generally appeared weekly or biweekly (see Pasaremos, March 1937 to September 1937).

36 In this regard, see, for example, Álvarez 1986, especially chapter XVII: 'The most difficult mission of the civil war: the dissolution of the Regional Council of Aragon', pp. 259–71. The newspaper Pasaremos emphasised this event, for example in the article entitled: 'The people of Aragon can breathe freely. A new life begins for them' (signed by E. Líster, in Pasaremos, Órgano de la 11a. División, year 2, no. 38, Caspe, 22 August 1937, p. 1).

37 See Líster 1966, pp. 171ff.

38 See A. Sánchez Vázquez, 'El Cerco de Teruel', in Pasaremos. Órgano de la 11 División, year 2, no. 67, Teruel Front, 28 December 1937, p. 2. (This is one of three texts that we have found signed by Sánchez Vázquez with his own name in the newspaper he directed. Beginning with this issue, the paper changed its subtitle to Órgano de la 11 División).

39 Sánchez Vázquez 1985a, and his 'Pasaremos a Líster y Rodríguez', in Pasaremos, year 3, no. 80, 27 April 1938, p. 2. See also E. Líster, '¡Bajo nuevos jefes, hacia nuevas victorias! Líster, jefe del 5° Cuerpo, Rodríguez, de la 11ª. División', on p. 1 of the same issue. See also Álvarez 1989, pp. 133 and 135.

and half seriously, the 'Talent Battalion'.⁴⁰ Enrique Líster would later speak of the Commissariat in more eulogistic terms:

> The 'Talent Battalion' was a magnificent combat unit; each of its men, firing with his pen and his word, represented many times more than ten and more than even a hundred combatants firing their rifles. The group of combatants that the soldiers and commanders had affectionately dubbed the 'Talent Battalion' was made up of poets, journalists, artists, sculptors, drivers, and liaisons who brought the materials to the front line of combat.... The men of the 'Talent Battalion' used not only the pen but also the bomb and the rifle when the situation demanded it.⁴¹

Sánchez Vázquez participated in the Civil War as a member of the 5th Army Corps, where he became a battalion political commissar,⁴² until – after serious defeats on the Ebro – the Corps crossed the French border on 9 February 1939.⁴³ For the majority of the survivors, crossing the Pyrenees took them to French concentration camps, in which they were detained by order of the government in Paris, and had to attempt to survive under extremely miserable circumstances.⁴⁴ Sánchez Vázquez, who was supposed to carry out a special mission for the General Staff, remained in Spain. When he attempted to make it to the French border, he nearly fell into the hands of the Francoites. Evading the severe French border checkpoints, he managed to reach Perpignan.⁴⁵ He stayed in the Spanish consulate of that city until the fall of Madrid, and with it

---

40   Sánchez Vázquez 1985a. Santiago Álvarez would later explain, with a smile of satisfaction, what it was that distinguished Sánchez Vázquez above all within that Talent Battalion. 'Many of them knew how to write well, but only Adolfo Sánchez Vázquez could do so without drinking. This was occasionally very important' (S. Álvarez, conversation with the author, Madrid, 22 March 1991, cited liberally according to the authors' notes).

41   E. Líster 1966, p. 66. In his detail-rich eyewitness report, Líster mentions Sánchez Vázquez by name: 'The names of Miguel Hernández, Herrera Petere, Adolfo S. Vázquez, Juan Paredes, José Ramón Alonso, Paco Ganivet, Ramón González, the sculptor Compostela, the poster makers Esperet and Briones, the photographer Faustino Mayo, and other intellectuals from the 5th Regiment, will always be wedded to the history of the struggle ... of the 11th Division and the 5th Army Corps'.

42   Sánchez Vázquez, letter to the author, Mexico City, 22 February 1991, p. 1. On Sánchez Vázquez's role in the Civil War, see Álvarez 1989, for example, pp. 133–5. See also in this regard Sánchez Vázquez 1970, p. 490.

43   Sánchez Vázquez 1985a, p. 12.

44   See, for example, Líster 1966, pp. 140–1 and Sánchez Barbudo 1975.

45   Sánchez Vázquez 1985a.

the definitive seizure of power by the Francoites, who were immediately recognised by the French government. Before the consulate was handed over to the new government, he travelled to Paris with Santiago Álvarez.[46] From the French capital, from which Spanish fugitives were banned, he travelled with Juan Rejano to Roissy-en-Brie, where the Union of French Writers was sheltering some Spanish intellectuals.[47]

Sánchez Vázquez would later summarise his role in the Spanish Civil War in the following terms:

> For me, the Spanish Civil War was a very important life experience, but (naturally) not very favourable for the enrichment of my meager theoretical-philosophical baggage. For a young rank-and-file militant like me, to be a Marxist meant at that time grasping the justness of our fight and the need to act by subordinating everything to a primary objective: winning the War.... Bound up in the struggle, and on the other hand lacking the necessary information and indispensable theoretical-critical equipment and still dazzled by the myth of the 'homeland of the proletariat', it was difficult to see clearly through the veil which... Stalinism had woven at that time.[48]

After three months of waiting, the announcement by Mexican president Lázaro Cárdenas that his country would take in the Spanish refugees promised a new beginning. In late May 1939, Sánchez Vázquez left the Mediterranean port of Sète with the first ship, the *Sinaia*, headed toward Mexico.[49] The author of this book finds the concept of homeland suspicious, but with regard to the author we are discussing, who after abandoning Spain was only twenty years later again able to see his father – consumed by Francoite humiliation and long years of imprisonment[50] – for two days in Biarritz, and who himself could only visit Spain again thirty-six years later,[51] allow us to cite the following

---

46   S. Álvarez, conversation with the author, Madrid, 22 March 1991.
47   Sánchez Vázquez 1985a, p. 13.
48   Sánchez Vázquez 1985a, pp. 12–13.
49   Ibid. General Lázaro Cárdenas del Río, president of Mexico from 1934–40, would be remembered by the Spanish refugees with respect and gratitude long afterward for taking this position. In Mexico City, in a classical exile neighbourhood, the Spanish refugees would erect a monument to this important promoter of the right to exile.
50   Sánchez Vázquez 1985a, p. 15.
51   See the journal *Anthropos*, no. 52. Barcelona, August 1985, p. 31 (photo footer).

autobiographical note: 'It was very moving for me to cross the Strait of Gibraltar after seeing Spanish land for the last time'.[52]

The First Period in Mexico, Exile

The arrival after this crossing and the first years in the country that received him were described later by another Spanish refugee, Antonio Sánchez Barbudo: 'On 13 June 1939 the *Sinaia*, an old ship previously used to transport pilgrims to Mecca, entered the port of Veracruz. With it, the first few hundred Spanish refugees arrived in Mexico from the southeastern coast of France. Many thousand would arrive later'.[53]

Mexico, which during the Spanish Civil War was, aside from the Soviet Union, the only country in the world that supported the Spanish Republic, among other things through its arms shipments, took in the Spanish government in exile after the Francoite victory, provided unlimited work permits for all Spanish refugees, and granted citizenship to those desiring it.[54] In contrast to what happened in the Soviet Union, here the refugees needed not fear a second political persecution, and aside from a shared language, these were the reasons that the majority of those who fought against the Francoites and were able to flee came to Mexico.

When the Spanish exiles arrived in Mexico, the internal relationship between Spanish settlers and their descendents and the indigenous and mestizos was altered. Prior to 1939, 'being Spanish' in Mexico was more or less the same thing as being politically conservative and on the side of the owners of the means of production. The majority of the population, made up of indigenous people and poor mestizos, maintained a powerfully anti-Spanish attitude. 'But', as Antonio Sánchez Barbudo wrote retrospectively in 1973: 'when we arrived, these traditional attitudes were transformed radically. Those who tended to sing the praises of the Motherland attacked us as "reds" and lamented our arrival in Mexico in the press. And in contrast, the leftists and workerists, who were the indigenists and "anti-Iberians", took us in as brothers and comrades in their press and their unions'.[55]

Six of those thousands of refugees, young writers and artists, founded the journal *Romance, Revista Popular Hispanoamericana* around six months after

---

52 Sánchez Vázquez 1985a, p. 13.
53 Sánchez Barbudo 1975, p. 1, column 1.
54 Sánchez Barbudo 1975, p. 1, column 2. After the Francoite triumph, in 1939 Mexico broke off diplomatic relations with the Spanish state, only reestablishing them in 1977 with the democratisation of the old 'motherland'.
55 Sánchez Barbudo 1975, p. 1, column 3.

their arrival, the first issue of which appeared in Mexico City on 1 February 1940. Sánchez Vázquez was among them. The other five founders and editorial board members were the painter Miguel Prieto, who took charge of the journal's graphic design;[56] Lorenzo Varela and Antonio Sánchez Barbudo, who had served as editors of *Hora de España* up to the end of their time in Spain;[57] Juan Rejano, who was simultaneously an editor of *Mundo Obrero*,[58] and José Herrera Petere. As we have said, Sánchez Vázquez came to know the latter two while in Spain Rejano from the period in which he sought refuge with the Union of French Writers in Roissy-en-Brie; with him and with the writer Pedro Garfias he had shared a cabin on the *Sinaia*,[59] on whose first crossing Varela and Sánchez Barbudo also came,[60] and he knew Herrera Petere from the period of the Madrid literary circle and the Commissariat of Press and Propaganda.

Among the 'Collaborators' Council' appeared Pablo Neruda and Juan Marinello, among others.[61] Octavio Paz, who edited the journal of young Mexican writers *Taller*, in which Sánchez Vázquez would also write,[62] published texts in *Romance*.[63] The editorial board presented their intentions as follows:

> Purpose. As neither a group nor a tendency, but clearly supportive of an essential aspect of culture: its popularisation, *Romance* aspires to gather in its pages the most significant expressions – in terms quality of thought and sensibility – of the Hispano-American cultural movement.
>
> We do not claim that the concept: *Hispano-America*, defines the existence of a culture that responds to the tradition of a single race or to the absolute spiritual unity of a group of peoples. And in referring to Hispano-American culture we intend nothing more than to qualify in this way that

---

56   Sánchez Barbudo 1975, p. 2, column 2.
57   Sánchez Barbudo 1975, p. 3, column 1.
58   Sánchez Barbudo 1975, p. 2, column 3.
59   See Sánchez Vázquez 1985a, p. 13.
60   Sánchez Barbudo 1975, p. 2, column 3.
61   See *Romance. Revista Popular Hispanoamericana*, year 1, no. 1, Mexico City, 1 February 1940, p. 2. Other members of the Collaborators' Council included Enrique González Martínez, Martín Luis Guzmán, Enrique Díez Canedo, Pedro Henríquez Ureña, and Rómulo S. Gallegos.
62   Sánchez Vázquez 1970, Vol. II, p. 490.
63   Sánchez Barbudo 1975, p. 3, column 2. See also, for example: Octavio Paz, 'El testimonio de los sentidos' (an article on Rainer Maria Rilke), in *Romance. Revista Popular Hispanoamericana*, year 1, no. 1, Mexico City, 1 February 1940, p. 10.

which has the Spanish language as its means of expression, whatever the racial or national circumstances giving it life may be.[64]

The journal, which sought to be more cultural than political, therefore had as its intention, while maintaining the highest level of artistic and literary quality, to move at the same time far beyond the framework of existing literary and artistic circles, and thereby to be a 'Popular Journal'. This effort was expressed, among other things, by the laborious and amazing design of its large-format pages (which were approximately double-sheets); one artist attended exclusively to the aesthetic quality of the magazine.[65] The journal was published by EDIAPSA,[66] which in that period was run by a Spanish exile in Mexico City, Rafael Giménez Siles, who while in Spain had been editor of 'communist and leftist books',[67] as well as the journal *Cenit* (Madrid).[68]

The first sixteen issues appeared bimonthly between 1 April and 15 September 1940. Issue 17, announced for 1 October, appeared three weeks late and the issues that followed also appeared irregularly; the number of issues sold and distributed across the entire American continent would fall sharply after having at one point reached 50,000,[69] and *Romance* would cease appearing on 31 May 1941 after issue 24.

The break following issue 16 was due to the fact that the editorial board, after having refused to accept a manager with broad powers as proposed by the publisher, found the doors of their workplace closed one morning. From then on until the end, the journal would remain under the direction of Martín Luis Guzmán. A decisive contribution to the new period of the journal came from Juan José Domenchina, a Spanish exile who tended to blame the 'reds' for the defeat of the Second Spanish Republic and who was a fierce adversary of the founding board.[70]

---

64   *Romance. Revista Popular Hispanoamericana*, year 1, no. 1, p. 2.
65   Sánchez Barbudo 1975, p. 1.
66   Edición y Distribución Ibero Americana de Publicaciones, S.A.
67   Sánchez Barbudo 1975 p. 2, column 2. In contrast to Sánchez Vázquez, Sánchez Barbudo writes the name of the editor 'Giménez Siles'.
68   Sánchez Vázquez 1985a, p. 14.
69   Sánchez Barbudo 1975, p. 3, column 1.
70   Sánchez Barbudo 1975, p. 3, column 3. On the possible motives for this rupture between the editorial board and the founders of the journal, Sánchez Barbudo wrote the following: 'Moreover, why did Giménez Siles and the businessmen want so badly to impose Guzmán on us? ... They were looking for and finding new capital to expand the editorial business, and perhaps Guzmán's leadership – which was leftist but not "red" at all, very much a product of the Mexican Revolution – was a condition imposed by the new shareholders.

Adolfo Sánchez Vázquez, who at the age of 25 was the youngest member of the editorial board, was described by Sánchez Barbudo as 'informed, serious, intelligent, and hard-working'.[71] He left the board on 1 July of 1940.[72] But as long as the old editorial board remained, he continued to contribute to *Romance*. He published two articles in this journal under his own name ('La decadencia del héroe'[73] and 'En torno a la picaresca')[74] and a total of twelve reviews of books by various authors, including Juan Marinello, Manuel Ponce, Martín Luis Guzmán, Gil Vicente, Juan Bartolomé Roxas, and Henri Lefebvre, as well as an anthology of young Colombian writers.[75] We should mention, moreover,

---

This probably also responded to some complaints, which held that journal should express a more purely national, Mexican character. They explicitly declared only "economic" reasons, but we suspected that they wanted to use the journal, which had come to be an important propaganda vehicle throughout Latin America, freely toward their shady economic and political ends'. Sánchez Barbudo 1975, p. 4, column 2.

71 Sánchez Barbudo 1975, p. 2, column 3.

72 In issue 11 of the journal, appearing on this date, the editorial board communicated a concise, untitled note to their readers: 'Due to causes beyond our will, José Herrera Petere and Sánchez Vázquez have left the editorial board of *Romance*. In giving this notice to our readers and friends, we note, however, that they will continue to collaborate with *Romance*, and that we continue to consider both writers, founders with us of this journal, to be colleagues' (in *Romance*, year 1, no. 11, Mexico City, 1 July 1940, p. 2).

Regarding the possible background, Sánchez Barbudo wrote in 1973: 'I do not recall the causes for that premature expulsion of Petere and Sánchez Vázquez. Perhaps it had to do with the tension that already existed between ourselves and the company, but it most likely had to do principally with the business owners' desire to save some money, and the fact that they seemed to be the least indispensable of the writers' (Sánchez Barbudo 1975, p. 2, column 3).

73 Sánchez Vázquez, 'La decadencia del héroe', in *Romance*, year 1, no. 4 (Mexico City, 15 March 1940), p. 10.

74 Sánchez Vázquez, 'En torno a la picaresca', in *Romance*, year 1, no. 8 (Mexico City, 15 May 1940), p. 6.

75 We refer to the following books, which Sánchez Vázquez reviews in *Romance* (we indicate in parentheses the exact location in year 1, 1940, of *Romance*):

André Maurois, *Eduardo VII y su época* (no. 1, 1 February, p. 20); Juan Marinello, *Ensayos* (no. 2, 15 February, p. 19); Juvenal Ortiz Soralegui, *Flor Cerrada. Poemas* (no. 5, 1 April, p. 18); Manuel Ponce *Ciclo de vírgenes* (no. 6, 15 April, p. 18); Armond and Maubliac, *Fourier* (no. 6, 15 April, p. 19); Martín Luis Guzmán, *Memorias de Pancho Villa. Tercera parte: panoramas políticos* (no. 7, 1 May, p. 18); Gil Vicente, *Poesías de Gil Vicente* (no. 8, 15 May, p. 18); José Ma. Arguedas, *Pumaccahua* (no. 9, 1 June, p. 19); Juan Bartolomé Roxas, *Tres en uno. Auto sacramental a la usanza antigua, en cinco cuadros y tres jornadas* (no. 12, 15 July, p. 18); Francisco Giner, *La rama viva* (no. 13, 1 August, p. 18); Antonio R. Manzar, *Antología del cuento hispanoamericano* (no. 14, 15 August, p. 18); Henri Lefebvre, *Nietzsche* (no. 16,

that Sánchez Vázquez made many contributions to the journal that were not signed with his name, above all in the film and music sections, which Sánchez Vázquez and Herrera Petere coordinated.[76]

In one of these texts, 'La decadencia del héroe', Adolfo Sánchez Vázquez speaks of the meaning, as he experienced it, of defeat in the Spanish Civil War and exile, of being torn away from Spain and from the struggle against fascism, as well as the role that the discussion of modern literature had in these moments:

> When I left Spain, surrounded by those authentic heroes, I found myself alone once again with my memory. Upon leaving that immense and living ocean that had been my homeland, I felt an anguishing emptiness.... In order to move away from that nightmare that surrounded us in real life, I submerged myself as much as possible in reading. Three years of literary insomnia pushed me passionately toward this. And I began to read Celine, Giono, Jean-Paul Sartre, Kafka, Snoth, Queneau...[77]

That same year, Sánchez Vázquez participated in the journal *España Peregrina*, produced by the *Junta Cultural Española*.[78] In 1941, he moved to Morelia, capital of the state of Michoacán de Ocampo, situated to the west of Mexico City,

---

15 September, p. 18); and a collection of texts by young Colombian writers entitled *Piedra y cielo* (no. 10, 15 June, p. 18).

76   Sánchez Barbudo 1975, p. 3, column 2.

77   Sánchez Vázquez, 'La decadencia del héroe', in *Romance*, year 1, no. 4 (Mexico City, 15 March 1940), p. 10. The quotation continues: 'I came from the absolute and total encounter with the hero of life. Now, in opening my eyes to this new world, I found its death, its transfiguration, or its escape'.

We are not going to enter here into a discussion of his critique of the 'death of the hero' or of the difficulties in his handling of the texts, above all the work of Sartre and Kafka, as well as the fact of simply equating authors as different as Celine and Sartre; nor will we deal with Sánchez Vázquez's later positions with regard to Sartre and Kafka in articles, speeches, and a prologue he wrote.

For this, see, for example, Sánchez Vázquez's following texts on Kafka: 'Un héroe kafkiano: José K' (speech given in August 1963 at the UNAM), Sánchez Vázquez 1963; 'Prólogo' in Franz Kafka's *El proceso* [*The Trial*] (Sánchez Vázquez 1967a), and on Sartre: 'Marxismo y existencialismo' (Sánchez Vázquez 1960); 'Sartre y la música', *El Universal*, Mexico City, 26 September 1977; 'La estética libertaria y comprometida de Sartre (Sánchez Vázquez 1980a), and the speech 'La estética de Sartre', given in November of 1969 (Sánchez Vázquez 1985b, esp. p. 22).

78   Sánchez Vázquez 1985a, p. 14.

'a city of scarcely 60,000 inhabitants but with an intense university and cultural life',[79] to teach undergraduate level philosophy.

There he married Aurora Rebolledo,[80] who he had already known during his youth in Spain,[81] and it was also there that his first son Adolfo was born.[82] In Morelia he once again enjoyed some spare time to perfect his philosophical education and, 'to the degree possible given the scarcity of reliable texts', also to advance on the Marxist terrain.[83] He maintained a lively exchange, for example, with Alfonso Reyes, Xavier Villaurrutia, José Gaos, and Joaquin Xirau, and discussed intensely with Ludwig Renn, a German combatant in Spain, who was then located in Mexico.

In 1943 he was forced to resign from his position as a lecturer in the Colegio de San Nicolás de Hidalgo when, during a conflict within the local University, he took the side of the leftist side there under attack, affiliated with Cárdenas.[84] Soon thereafter, he returned with his family to Mexico City and 'did a little of everything' to make a living: he translated[85] and taught Spanish to employees of the Soviet embassy. During this period he resumed his university studies (interrupted in 1936) in the Faculty of Philosophy and Arts [Facultad de Filosofía y Letras] of the Universidad Nacional Autónoma de Mexico (UNAM), and prepared a master's thesis in Spanish Literature on *El sentido del tiempo en la poesía de Antonio Machado* [*The Sense of time in the poetry of Antonio Machado*].[86] Machado had belonged to the Spanish literary current known as the Generation of 98; during the Spanish Civil War he committed himself to the Republic and its defenders, and was recognised for his role, in this regard, more than any other man of letters. Sánchez Vázquez visited him several times during the Civil War by charge of the 5th Army Corps in order to bring provisions to him and his mother.[87] Due to his work as a translator, which occupied much of his time, as well as his intense political activity among émigrés, he became increasingly distanced from the Faculty and did not complete his thesis.[88]

---

79 Ibid.
80 Ibid.
81 S. Álvarez, conversation with the author. Madrid, 22 March 1991.
82 His children Juan Enrique and María Aurora were born later (Sánchez Vázquez 1985a).
83 Sánchez Vázquez 1985a.
84 Ibid.
85 Over time, Sánchez Vázquez did translations from Russian, French, English, and Italian; in the bibliography we have noted the texts translated by Sánchez Vázquez into Spanish.
86 Sánchez Vázquez 1985a.
87 S. Álvarez, conversation with the author, Madrid, 22 March 1991.
88 Sánchez Vázquez 1985a.

At the beginning of the 1950s, the Cold War and the concomitant increase in US support for Franco, definitively destroyed any hope that his exile would soon end, this having previously remained a hope of his. Yet with this, a sort of calm came to Sánchez Vázquez's life; the struggle for a prompt return was transformed into more long-term political work, theoretical reflection again gaining importance and space, and he returned once more to the University. Thus he would later write of this era:

> The prospect of a long exile did not in any way entail for us an abandonment of our political work, but it did allow – at least in my case – a greater degree of serenity and a greater demand for rationality. I thus felt the need to dedicate more time to reflection, to providing a reasoned foundation for my political activity, above all when deeply-rooted beliefs – in the 'homeland of the proletariat' – began to fall apart. For this reason I decided to improve my understanding of Marxist theory and, as a result, to pay more attention to philosophy than to literature.[89]

In the Faculty of Philosophy and Arts, German idealist philosophy – which had been revitalised by exiled Spanish philosophers, and José Gaos in particular – predominated. Inspired by the latter, a group of young philosophers called the 'Hiperión' attempted to develop a 'filosofía de lo mexicano [philosophy of Mexicanness]'. French existentialism was to serve as a theoretical instrument toward this end. Sánchez Vázquez engaged in a 'fertile dialogue' with this group, which forced him to 'sharpen [the] theoretical tools of Marxism.'[90]

Among those teaching in the Faculty there were few Marxist academics; among the first were the exiled translator Wenceslao Roces in the history department, and in the philosophy department the Mexican Eli de Gortari, with his course on dialectical logic. His teaching assistant was Sánchez Vázquez from 1952 to February of 1955.[91] During this period he published the bulletin of the Union of Spanish Intellectuals in Mexico, for which he served as vice president for several years, a journal that was distributed in Spain and stood in solidarity with persecuted intellectuals there.[92]

In October of 1955 he obtained his Maestría [Master's] Degree[93] in Philosophy with a thesis entitled *Conciencia y realidad en la obra de arte* [*Consciousness*

---

89   Ibid.
90   Sánchez Vázquez 1985a, p. 15.
91   Ibid.
92   Sánchez Vázquez 1985a, p. 14.
93   The *Maestría* [Master's Degree] in Mexico is similar to the Magister Artium in Germany.

and reality in artwork]. Sánchez Vázquez, who by that time already had problems with the predominant Marxist philosophy – Soviet *Diamat* – was in this text still faithful to 'socialist realism'. On this topic, he would later write: 'My thesis, without yet breaking with this framework [of *Diamat*], sought to find more open answers; however, those responses moved definitively within the channels of Diamat which was – and is – the aesthetic of "socialist realism" ... '[94] Some time later, the author would move away from the aesthetic perspective represented there. The publication of this work as a book in 1965 took place without his approval.[95]

In the practical-political sphere conflicts developed which shifted this first anti-dogmatic impulse onto the theoretical terrain. In 1954 a confrontation emerged between the Mexican branch of the Spanish Communist Party and its central committee with regard to the Party's authoritarian internal structures. During this conflict, Sánchez Vázquez represented on various occasions the 'Mexican wing' in Europe: in 1954 at the Fifth Party Congress, held secretly on the outskirts of Prague, and in 1957 at various meetings with the PCE Political Bureau in Paris.[96] Certainly, the events of the Twentieth Congress

---

94   Sánchez Vázquez 1985a p. 15.
95   See Sánchez Vázquez 1985a, p. 19. For the published book, see Sánchez Vázquez 1965a.
96   Sánchez Vázquez 1985a, p. 15. He later recalled this Parisian encounter: 'In those meetings Fernando Claudín and I were the leading voices on either side'. Ibid.

Regarding his adversary of the time, it is worth noting that Sánchez Vázquez had already had more serious encounters with him during his time in the JSU. Claudín was his predecessor as editor of *Ahora* and later editor of its sister newspaper *La Hora*, which appeared from 8 June 1937. This JSU publication was founded in Valencia when the government and JSU headquarters were moved there, while *Ahora* remained in Madrid (see the joint extraordinary issue of *La Hora* and *Ahora* on the anniversary of the beginning of the War: Valencia and Madrid, 18 July 1937, illustrated page 'Fighters for unity', as well as 'For unity, toward victory. Taking stock of three months of unity', in *Ahora. Diario de la Juventud*, no. 107, Madrid, 1 May 1937, p. 10).

Moreover, beginning on 20 September 1936, Claudín (from the Communist Youth) was press director for the Unified Executive Commission of the JSU alongside Serrano Poncela (from the Socialist Youth). See Viñas 1978, p. 64, n. 53.

In 1980, in the second edition of his book *The Philosophy of Praxis*, Sánchez Vázquez spoke in the most laudatory tones about Claudín's theoretical work: 'On the *Communist Manifesto* as a theory of social revolution, and on the concepts of class consciousness and the party therein, as well as on its linkage with the economic, social, and political situation of the period, and in particular on the trial by fire that was the Revolution of '48 for this general text by Marx and Engels, the reader can very beneficially consult Fernando Claudín's excellent work *Marx, Engels y la revolución de 1848*, (Madrid: Siglo XXI, 1975) which on more than one point we have followed closely'. Sánchez Vázquez 1980b, p. 187,

of the Communist Party of the Soviet Union (CPSU) in 1956 (the Secret Report on Stalin's crimes), would shock many PCE members living in Mexico, but not the leadership in Paris that predominated over the 'malcontents' in Latin America. Sánchez Vázquez resigned from his Party posts and returned to the unavoidable need to question on a theoretical level this type of 'Marxism' and its practical implications, which had now become known.[97]

The 'New Theoretical and Practical Posture'

The 1959 Cuban Revolution, which broke with traditional thinking and models, and the 1968 invasion of Czechoslovakia by the Warsaw Pact states were two historical events that changed Adolfo Sánchez Vázquez's theoretical perspective.[98] After these moments, what most mattered to him was to abandon the theoretical framework within which he had up to that point sought innovation. Hence, in this regard, the retrospective assessment: 'After that point, I was at pains to abandon the materialist metaphysics of *Diamat*, to return to the original Marx, and to take the pulse of reality in order to thereby gain access to a Marxism which was understood above all as a philosophy of praxis'.[99]

Both his withdrawal from his activities in the PCE as well as the fact that he obtained, in January 1959, the position of full-time professor at the UNAM, made possible what had become impossible in his country of origin to intensely study Marx 'toward an open and critical mode of thinking guided by these two principles of Marx himself: "doubt everything" and "criticise all that exists" '. This 'all that exists' should also include 'naturally... not only Lenin but Marx himself and, especially, what was theorised or practiced in Marx's name'.[100]

Sánchez Vázquez's first scientific text in which this understanding of Marx's theory features appeared in 1961: the essay 'Ideas estéticas en los "Manuscritos económico-filosóficos" de Marx [Aesthetic ideas in Marx's "Economic-philosophical manuscripts"]',[101] was received with great interest in post-revolutionary Cuba, and led to a first invitation to the island, during which he had the opportunity to meet Che Guevara in person.[102]

---

n. 111. On the footnote from the first edition (1967) that was substituted by this one, see chapter 10 of this book: '*The Philosophy of Praxis*: Two Versions'.

97   Sánchez Vázquez 1985a.
98   Ibid.
99   Sánchez Vázquez 1985a, p. 16.
100 Ibid.
101 Sánchez Vázquez 1961.
102 Sánchez Vázquez 1985a.
     On the history of this text's reception, see p. 63 of this book.

In 1965, his first book appeared in Mexico: *Las ideas estéticas de Marx* [published in English as: *Art and Society. Essays in Marxist Aesthetics*],[103] which bore a dual relationship to the Cuban Revolution: it made use of its first experiences on the terrain of art and cultural policy and, with its re-release in Havana in 1966, 'contributed to a certain degree to driving the open, plural, and anti-dogmatic course of its artistic policy'.[104] He would continue travelling frequently to Cuba to give speeches (and to no other country as frequently), participating for example in the Cultural Congress of Havana in 1968.[105]

In March of 1966, he presented his doctoral thesis in philosophy under the title *Sobre la praxis* [*On Praxis*], from which his 1967 book *Filosofía de la praxis* [published in English as: *The Philosophy of Praxis*] emerged, a text which Sánchez Vázquez classified as 'fundamental',[106] and which would reappear in 1980 considerably reworked and expanded by two chapters.[107] 'In it, the point to which my understanding of Marxism had arrived – above all in its philosophical and theoretical-political aspects – is crystallised'.[108]

In 1985, Sánchez Vázquez would describe two noteworthy aspects of his examination, in which José Gaos, the former collaborator of Ortega y Gasset, participated as his advisor, as well as translator of Marx, Wenceslao Roces, Marxist logician Eli de Gortari, Luis Villoro, and Ricardo Guerra: 'first, its duration (it still holds the UNAM record in this respect), and secondly for the toughness of the judges' replies, which converted the long examination into a veritable pitched battle of . . . ideas'.[109]

His subsequent theoretical development is also influenced by the stimulation of his students, 'in particular, that of those attracted to Marxism'.[110] In this sense, the student movement of the summer of 1968 was a crucial moment, which is still today the country's richest political movement in terms of

---

103   Sánchez Vázquez 1965b.
104   Sánchez Vázquez 1985a.
105   Sánchez Vázquez 1985c, pp. 18f.
106   Sánchez Vázquez 1985a. In 1996 Sánchez Vázquez also considered *The Philosophy of Praxis* to be his main work (Sánchez Vázquez, conversation with the author, Mexico City, September 1996).
107   See Sánchez Vázquez 1967b (the book version of the doctoral thesis entitled *On Praxis*, presented in 1966 to the UNAM), and the second edition, Sánchez Vázquez 1980b. On the difference between the first and second edition of *The Philosophy of Praxis*, see Chapter 10 of this book. See in English: Sánchez Vázquez 1977a.
108   Sánchez Vázquez 1985a. Our explanation in this book of the concept of praxis in Sánchez Vázquez refers fundamentally to his work *The Philosophy of Praxis*.
109   Sánchez Vázquez 1985a.
110   Ibid.

consequences since the Mexican Revolution. In a letter to *Le Monde* this movement was characterised as follows:

> This was a movement, which was very different from May 1968 in France. In Mexico, there were practically no scholastic or academic demands, only political ones: freedom for political prisoners, the dissolution of the 'cuerpo de granaderos' [a militarised police unit deployed for 'internal security'], the dismissal of the mayor of the city, the police chief...
> Is it possible to speak of solid democratic traditions when there is really nothing more than one political party?[111]

Sánchez Vázquez joined the student movement along with the majority of UNAM professors. On 15 August, the highest body of the UNAM – the University Council – agreed to support the student demands[112] and when on 18 September the army seized the University City, the rector Javier Barros Sierra publicly protested by repudiating the occupation.

Sánchez Vázquez, aside from his solidarity with the teaching staff, was connected to this movement through various personal contacts. His assistant, Roberto Escudero, was imprisoned; his former colleague and friend Eli de Gortari was unjustly detained and his son Juan Enrique experienced the 'Night of Tlatelolco'.[113] As evening fell on 2 October 1968 – ten days prior to the beginning of the Olympic Games – the police and the army put an end, through an hour and a half of machine-gun fire, to a student demonstration surrounded by tanks in the Plaza de las Tres Culturas in Tlatelolco, killing – according to investigations carried out by the English newspaper, *The Guardian* – more than 325 people, wounding a far greater number, and detaining some two thousand survivors.[114] This event, to which the then Mexican Ambassador to India, Octavio Paz, responded with his resignation,[115] put an end to the student movement. But its political and theoretical effects cannot be underestimated; Sánchez Vázquez later wrote in this regard:

---

111   M. Mayagoitia, letter to *Le Monde*, 7 October 1968, cited according to Poniatowska 1989, p. 20.
112   See Poniatowska 1989, p. 278.
113   Sánchez Vázquez 1985a.
114   Poniatowska 1989, Part II: pp. 161–273, here: p. 170. According to traditional belief, it was exactly there that the final battle against the Spanish conquistadors occurred in 1521 under the legendary Cuauhtémoc.
115   See, for example, Jean-Claude Buhrer, 'Les yeux ouverts sur le monde' (homage to Paz on the occasion of his winning the Nobel Prize for Literature in 1990), in the 13 October 1990 *Le Monde*, p. 12.

Although it was crushed, the movement of '68 changed the political physiognomy of the country, and from that point onward the Universidad Nacional was never the same again. Marxism with a critical and anti-dogmatic edge became one of the most vigorous currents of thought in the institutions of the UNAM and especially in the humanities. ... [M]y Ética [Ethics] ... was inspired in its elaboration by the objectives, achievements, and sacrifices of that student movement which taught not only political but also moral lessons.[116]

Between the years of 1973 and 1981, Sánchez Vázquez was editor of the *teoría y praxis* [*theory and praxis*] book series of the Mexican publisher Grijalbo. In that post, he made emancipatory European thinkers – for example, Rossana Rossanda, Henri Lefebvre, Karel Kosík, Adam Schaff, Louis Althusser, Jindrich Zelený, and Bertolt Brecht – more widely known in Mexico and Latin America. Furthermore, he published contemporary contributions to local discussions of social theory and philosophy, such as those by Rosa Krauze, Enrique Dussel, María Rosa Palazón, and Leopoldo Zea.[117] The book series, entitled 'tp', was presented as follows:

> tp. We propose to make known, in the Spanish language, texts which elucidate the two dimensions – theoretical and practical – of social praxis.
>
> tp. Rejects all speculation, or theoretical activity closed upon itself, and accepts theory which, linked to praxis, contributes to its enrichment or promotion.
>
> tp. Addresses the reader who, not satisfied with the simple divulgation, with no need for prior specialisation, aspires toward a serious knowledge of the corresponding topics.[118]

In 1974, Sánchez Vázquez served on the organizing committee for the Fifteenth International Philosophy Congress in Varna.[119] Already previously, and also

---

116 Sánchez Vázquez 1985a.
117 A complete list of the book titles that appeared in this series up to 1980 can be found in Sánchez Vázquez 1980b, pp. 465ff. On the last four authors cited, see the anthology *La filosofía actual en América Latina*, Vol. III, on Mexico's 'First National Philosophy Colloquium' (Ardao et al. 1976).
    The fact that Sánchez Vázquez also ordered the translation and publication of a declared theoretical adversary like Louis Althusser shows a liberalism that would benefit some German gentlemen of science. See Althusser 1976.
118 Sánchez Vázquez 1980b, back cover.
119 Sánchez Vázquez 1985c, p. 18.

afterward, he participates in international conferences on philosophy and aesthetics. His first public appearance in the German Federal Republic occured in 1976, at the Seventh International Aesthetics Congress, in Düsseldorf.[120]

With Franco's death in 1975, ETA's previous 1973 assassination of his designated successor Luis Carrero Blanco, and the beginning of the process of democratisation in Spain, the possibility opened up for the first time of a lasting and legal return to his home country. In 1978, Adolfo Sánchez Vázquez gave his first public speech in that country since his flight through the Pyrenees, doing so at the Universidad Autónoma de Madrid on the topic of 'Las revoluciones en la filosofía [The revolutions in philosophy]'.[121]

He decided to remain in Mexico, the country that had in 1939 'made possible his escape from anguish and desperation',[122] where he took the path of science, and on the continent where he had come to be one of the most recognised intellectuals of emancipation. He discovered that a return to Spain could not simply erase his existence as an exile. 'And then the exile discovers, first with astonishment, then with grief, and later with a degree of irony, at the very moment that his exile objectively comes to an end, that the time has not passed with impunity, and that whether he returns or does not return, he would never cease to be an exile'.[123]

In 1976–7, he became president of the Mexican Philosophical Association and, respectively, the vice president and president of the organising committees for the two first National Philosophy Colloquia (Morelia, 1975, and Monterrey, 1977).[124]

Adolfo Sánchez Vázquez kept up with the pulse of the times, and thus the Nicaraguan Revolution represented an important historical event for him. He engaged in a lively theoretical-political exchange with prominent Sandinista leaders and, in 1983, gave speeches in Managua, in the Ministry of Culture and in the Universidad Nacional Autónoma de Nicaragua, on the topic of Marxist

---

120   Ibid. The complete list of these appearances up to 1985 can be found therein.
121   Anonymous 1985, p. 22.
122   Sánchez Vázquez 1942, p. 3. The dedication we here cite, which Sánchez Vázquez added to this book in 1942, says: 'These poems were written in Spain, already vigilantly and dramatically awaiting the collective tragedy of my homeland. Now that they come out into the light, I dedicate them to the people to whom I owe my most valued treasure: an exit from anguish and desperation. Morelia, May 1942'.
123   Sánchez Vázquez, 'Cuando el exilio permanece y dura (a manera de epílogo)', in the collective volume ¡Exilio! Cited here according to the reprint in Sánchez Vázquez 1985c, p. 18.
124   Sánchez Vázquez 1985c, p. 18.

aesthetics (for example, on Brecht and Lukács);[125] as well as giving a speech on the topic of 'Democracy, revolution, and socialism' on the occasion of the tenth anniversary of the fall of the Somoza régime in 1989.[126]

On the centenary of Karl Marx's death, a public commemoration was organised in the Palace of Fine Arts, presided over by Sánchez Vázquez, among others.[127] In 1984, he received a doctorate *honoris causa* from the Universidad Autónoma de Puebla, and on 15 May 1985, by a vote of the University Council of the UNAM, he was named professor emeritus.[128]

The legal successor to that state against whose founding Sánchez Vázquez had fought in his youth, in 1989 honoured him in the person of King Juan Carlos I, conferring upon him Spain's highest cultural award: the Gran Cruz de Alfonso X el Sabio [Great Cross of Alfonso X the Wise].[129] Two universities in his native country conferred upon him *honoris causa* doctorates: the Universidad de Cádiz in 1987, and the Universidad Nacional de Educación a Distancia [National Distance Education University] in 1993.[130] Sánchez Vázquez also achieved increasing institutional recognition in other European countries, for example in the German Federal Republic, where he signed on as a member of the Advisory Council of the Berlin Institute of Critical Theory (INKRIT, by its German acronym).[131]

Sánchez Vázquez was invited as an advisor to the Special Forum for State Reform, called for July 1996 by the Ejército Zapatista de Liberación Nacional [Zapatista Army of National Liberation] (EZLN), and he participated by sending a contribution to the discussion of the question of human rights in Mexico, on the basis of the Zapatista rebellion and its causes. In 1998, the UNAM honoured him with an *honoris causa* doctorate.

Until he was with us, Sánchez Vázquez taught postgraduate seminars in Philosophy at the UNAM and struggled in various settings for a world free of exploitation and oppression, as well as for the theoretical understanding

---

125 Anonymous 1985, p. 22. Thus, for example, his speech 'Brecht and Lukács' conceptions of realism', given at the Ministry of Culture, Managua (29 April 1983).
126 Sánchez Vázquez 1989. On the republications, see the Bibliography in this book.
127 See *Anthropos*, no. 52 (Barcelona, August 1985), p. 48 (photo caption). See also Sánchez Vázquez 1983a (a speech given on the occasion of the centenary of Karl Marx's death, 14 March 1983, at the Palace of Fine Arts in Mexico City).
128 Sánchez Vázquez 1985c, p. 18.
129 'Por decreto del rey Juan Carlos I', in *La Jornada* (Mexico City, 22 July 1989), p. 17.
130 Vargas Lozano 1995, p. 9.
131 See 'Hilferuf für das Historisch-Kritisch Wörterbuch des Marxismus', in *Das Argument. Zeitschrift für Philosophie und Sozialwissenschaft*, year 38, no. 217, issue 5/6 (Hamburg, 1996), pp. 662f, here: p. 662.

necessary to bring it about. Adolfo Sánchez Vázquez concluded his 1985 autobiography as follows:

> Many truths have come to earth; certain ends have not resisted contrast with reality and some hopes have vanished. And, nevertheless, I am today more convinced than ever that socialism – linked with those truths and those ends and hopes – continues to be a necessary, desirable, and possible alternative. I remain likewise convinced that Marxism – those elements of it that must be criticised or abandoned – continues to be the most fertile theory for those of us who are convinced of the need to transform the world in which today there exists not only the exploitation and oppression of men and peoples, but also a mortal risk for the survival of humanity.
>
> And although the path toward the transformation of this world today presents reversals, obstacles, and sufferings which we did not suspect in our younger years, our objective continues to be that other world which, since our youth – as socialism – we have conceived, dreamt, and desired.[132]

> To Posterity III
>
> You who will emerge from the flood
> in which we have gone under
> remember
> when you speak of our failings
> the dark time too
> which you have escaped.
>
> For we went, changing countries oftener than our shoes
> through the wars of the classes, despairing
> when there was injustice only and no rebellion.
>
> And yet we know:
> hatred, even of meanness

---

132   Sánchez Vázquez 1985a, p. 16. [Note to the edition in English: Sánchez Vázquez taught philosophy in the UNAM up to 2003 and participated until 2005 in academic events, such as the homage on the occasion of his ninetieth birthday, arranged at the UNAM that year in October. For some recent reflections on the work and life of Adolfo Sánchez Vázquez, see: Gandler 2011.]

contorts the features.
Anger, even against injustice
makes the voice hoarse. Oh, we
who wanted to prepare the ground
for friendliness,
could not ourselves be friendly.

But you, when the time comes
at last
and man is a helper to man
think of us
with forbearance.
   BERTOLT BRECHT

CHAPTER 2

The Life and Work of Bolívar Echeverría

We will also dedicate a relatively significant space to the biography of the second author under discussion. This is due, among other things, to the experience that the writer of this book had on 10 November 1994 during a speech given by Bolívar Echeverría at the Johann Wolfgang Goethe University in Frankfurt. The presentation, on the topic of 'Die Moderne außerhalb Europas. Der Fall Lateinamerika [Modernity outside Europe: the Case of Latin America]', took place in the context of the 'Theodor W. Adorno' Seminar coordinated by Alfred Schmidt; during the discussion, the massive chasm existing between social philosophy in Mexico and Germany became clear to the author of this book (and co-organiser of the conference); and also that it is not even possible to set out from a similar terminology, much less to speak of a degree of understanding of the facts, above all with regard to contemporary Mexican society and the political and theoretical debates which predominate therein. Therefore, the following chapter will allow us not only to take a look at Bolívar Echeverría as an individual and at the history of the development of his work, but also to situate his formulations within the framework of contemporary social and theoretical-philosophical questions in Mexico and Latin America. To this we must add the fact that Bolívar Echeverría himself considered geographical-cultural factors to be very important in the birth of forms of thinking. This refers as much to theories as to everyday ideas. With regard to the latter, he presented his explanation through his central concept of the 'modern *ethe*'. This concept of '*ethe*' already also includes theoretical postulates which Echeverría did not separate aseptically from everyday forms of imagination – that is, those lacking systematic formulations. As he explained in an interview with the author, he equally emphasised the importance – not to be underestimated – for the manner in which his theory developed, of the location of his activity. This interview sought to determine to what degree there exists some sort of parallel between his theory and that of Herbert Marcuse, since both (each in their respective epoch) sought to tie Heidegger's postulates to those of Marx.

This sketch of his life hopes to avoid converting him into one of those Latin-American intellectuals who, fascinated by one or several European thinkers in specific and seemingly progressive moments of European thought, arrived on the 'Old Continent' as a young adventurer and was molded there both personally and intellectually. Many of these globetrotting academics, however, not only had their head filled with a sense of adventure when they left their own countries, but frequently were forced to do so, either through a direct threat to their body and life or the political impossibility of continuing to elaborate critical theories in their own country. These are distinct from the generation of Spanish exiles in Mexico due to the fact that the majority crossed the Atlantic twice and, in so doing, it was not rare for them to end up landing in a Latin-American country very different from their country of origin. As a result of the 1910 Mexican Revolution, and because of the tradition – atypical for Latin America – of an armed forces which emerged from the soldiers of the Revolution and which, in contrast to the rest of the continent, is not the preferred place for the sons of the ruling class to make their careers (and whose generals, therefore, are not accustomed to having great political ambitions), Mexico has been practically the only major country in the continent which has not experienced a military rebellion since the 1940s. It thus happened that, after the Spanish exile, there arrived in the country a second wave, this time from various South-American countries, with which once again many leftist intellectuals, who would be important in the future, enriched Mexico with their presence. Echeverría was one of them. The majority continues to carry a turbulent mixture of memories of the rejection suffered in Europe and their reduction to 'just another person from the Third World', with the hope that this might at some point come to an end.

Bolívar Echeverría Andrade was born on 31 January 1941 in Riobamba. He was the son of Rosa Andrade Velasco, a housewife, and Bolívar Echeverría Paredes, a farm administrator.[133] His place of birth, situated some fifty kilometres south of the Equator, is the capital of the Ecuadorian province of Chimborazo, which owes its name to Ecuador's highest peak, at whose foot Riobamba sits. The Andean volcano Chimborazo – 6,310 metres in height and covered with glaciers from 4,700 metres above sea level – leaves an indelible impression on visitors to Riobamba. The entire atmosphere of this mountainous city is marked by this dominant presence; the summit is nearly always in the clouds, and when it is visible – so they say – the legend of the mountain

---

133   Bolívar Echeverría: Third interview with the author on 10 July 1996 at the Faculty of Philosophy and Arts of the UNAM in Mexico City. Tape recording (cited hereafter as 'Third interview with Bolívar Echeverría').

Echeverría authorised the cited passages from the interviews in writing in Binghamton, NY, on 26 March 1999. Moreover, we indicate from here on the cassette number, side of the cassette, and the position of the tape from the cited interview. All cassettes are in the author's possession. In the absence of a unified counting method, the tape position is indicated according to the apparatus utilised (Panasonic 608). Here: cassette II, side A, pos. 295.

grows even more.¹³⁴ Despite its meager population, which at the end of the 1980s reached some 71,000 inhabitants,¹³⁵ Riobamba is not lacking in importance for the country's history. It was here that in May 1830 the Republic of Ecuador was declared, which after becoming independent from Spain (in 1822) was, as a province of Quito, a part of the Republic of Gran Colombia. Bolívar was the second of six children, after his sister Elena and before his brothers Eduardo, Marcolo, Julio, and finally, his sister Rosa.¹³⁶

Six years after his birth, the family moved to Quito, the capital of the country, located 130 kilometres north of Riobamba.¹³⁷ There, Bolívar Echeverría,¹³⁸ according to the wishes of his mother, who came from a comfortably-off and very Catholic family, attended the Catholic Lasalle College. Until the age of fourteen, Echeverría remained at this 'upper-class school' and was up to this point 'very Catholic',¹³⁹ practicing his beliefs as an altar boy, among other activities.

In 1955, by decision of his father, he transferred to the Colegio Nacional Mejía,¹⁴⁰ which is state-run and therefore secular, and also located in the capital. At this school, Bolívar Echeverría began to be politicised; he participated in organising student movements and strikes, in which he was an active protestor. At that time, Ecuador had a civilian government led by José María Velasco Ibarra, a 'populist opportunist',¹⁴¹ who was head of state during five non-

---

134   Raquel Serur, interview with the author on 4 July 1996 in San Jerónimo, Federal District (written interview notes). We owe this description to Serur, who will appear later in this biography (see p. 77). She provided some important indications regarding Bolívar Echeverría's life and various clues for researching this biography.
135   'Riobamba', in Anonymous 1987, p. 1108.
136   R. Serur, interview with the author on 4 July 1996.
137   Third interview with Bolívar Echeverría, cassette II, side A, pos. 318.
138   In general, we will speak in this book of Bolívar Echeverría instead of 'Bolívar Echeverría Andrade'. In doing so we follow his self-determined name, for example in all of his publications, as well as the way he tends to be spoken of in Mexico. It is only in 'highly official' affairs that his maternal surname appears. Such affairs include, for example, seminar announcements at the Faculty of Philosophy and Arts of the UNAM or his academic work presented at the same University (see p. 66 and p. 78 of this book).
139   Third interview with Bolívar Echeverría, cassette I, side A, pos. 374–7. 'I studied in an upper-class school, a Lasallean Catholic school for my basic education. I was well-educated and very Catholic. Until the age of fourteen, I believed in God, I received Communion and confessed and everything.
140   Third interview with Bolívar Echeverría, cassette I, side A, pos. 302.
141   Bolívar Echeverría, fourth interview with the author on 28 August 1996 in the Faculty of Philosophy and Arts of the UNAM (referred to hereafter as 'Fourth interview with Bolívar Echeverría').

consecutive periods, governing the 'typical banana republic',[142] occasionally with some democratic forms and occasionally with dictatorial powers (from 1970 to 1972).[143]

Four decades later, our 'Andean' author would recall, when questioned as to the causes for his politicisation during his school years, that the Colegio Nacional Mejía was

> ...a completely secular school...Later a very interesting preparatory school, which was the best in Ecuador with some first-rate teachers, as always happens in our countries, who are very valuable people but completely unemployed. So they were of a very high level, those who needed to teach preparatory school to make a living. I had excellent teachers there, and at the same time, the social composition of that school was very interesting.
>
> All classes converged there. There were those from among the poorest, poorest people, the children of shoe shiners, up to the bourgeoisie. All kinds of people were there. As a result there was an interesting sort of solidarity and struggle there. It was a very powerful social and political environment, since there – of course – there was no alternative to understanding the political and social problematic. Through your friends, you suddenly discover that the mother of a friend of yours is dying of hunger in a hospital... This kid had nothing to eat at all. And at the same time you're friends with another who is a rich landowner. So there is a very violent and very open social conflict. As a result, I believe that this school was a key experience for me.[144]

The decision – a radical one for Echeverría – to send him to the Colegio Nacional Mejía and therefore to take him out of upper-class Catholic school, Lasalle College, is one his father took in order 'to educate him politically'. He was 'a liberal, very well-connected to people on the Left. All of his friends were from the Communist Party... politicians and intellectuals: poets, painters, musicians'.

---

142 Ibid.
143 See Cueva Dávila 1974, 1987. On the most recent political events in Ecuador, see, for example, Cueva Dávila 1990.
144 Third interview with Bolívar Echeverría, cassette I, side A, pos. 377ff.

In contrast to this, his mother was 'very Catholic'.[145] The young Bolívar Echeverría became politically interested and began to participate politically in his fifteenth year, taking as a starting point this force field emerging, on the one hand, between the overprotective Catholic education of his mother, alongside the ecclesiastical institutions, and, on the other hand, the 'violent' experience of social contradictions, of solidarity across classes, and political organising among students at the Colegio Nacional, alongside the secular education it offered. He engaged in these first political activities within the framework of the Socialist Youth, a section of the Ecuadorean Socialist Party.[146] During a student strike, the Ecuadorean police aggressively besieged the school building for several days in an effort to force the strikers to surrender due to hunger and thirst, but they failed.[147]

This period of Bolívar Echeverría's political development in the Colegio Nacional corresponds to the beginning of his interest in philosophical literature and philosophical texts in the strict sense. Upon turning seventeen, he received as a gift from his father the complete essays of Miguel de Unamuno, who Echeverría perceived as a sort of 'Spanish existentialist.'[148] In Spain, Unamuno (Bilbao, 1864–Salamanca, 1936) belonged to the group of writers known as the Generation of 98.[149]

---

145 Third interview with Bolívar Echeverría, cassette 1, side A, pos. 399–411. On another occasion, Bolívar Echeverría mentions that Jorge Enrique Adoum was one of the intellectuals who frequented his father's house (Bolívar Echeverría, first interview with the author on 26 April 1994, in San Ángel, Federal District, cited hereafter as 'First interview with Bolívar Echeverría', side A, pos. 224–6). Adoum is today one of the most well-known writers in Ecuador and also in Latin America as a whole. His best known works include *Entre Marx y una mujer desnuda. Texto con personajes* and *Ciudad sin ángel*.

146 Third interview with Bolívar Echeverría, cassette 1, side A, pos. 352ff. Echeverría underlines in this interview that the Socialist Youth represented only the organisational framework which he needed and, beyond that, he does not attribute additional importance to this membership as a political activist at the school level (Ibid.) Elsewhere, he mentions that during this period his application for membership in the Communist Youth of Ecuador was rejected (First interview with Bolívar Echeverría, side A, pos. 231–3).

147 Third interview with Bolívar Echeverría, cassette 1, side A, pos. 352ff.

148 Third interview with Bolívar Echeverría, cassette 1, side A, pos. 336. For Echeverría, Unamuno's central texts are *Del sentimiento trágico de la vida* and *Vida de Don Quijote y Sancho*.

149 Another important writer from the Generation of '98 was Antonio Machado, who in contrast to the majority of these writers, Unamuno included, took the side of the Republicans after the Francoite coup of 1936. See, in this regard, our biography of Adolfo Sánchez Vázquez, subchapter 'The Spanish Civil War'.

With Unamuno's texts, Echeverría established for the first time 'the connection between politics and theory or philosophy'.[150] With a group of friends, some of whom shared in his political activism, he promoted the reading of existentialist writers, arriving at Jean-Paul Sartre by way of Unamuno. Sartre represented a sort of model of what an intellectual ought to be. Alongside his theoretical contributions, the Quito circle was fascinated by the political commitment of the French author.[151] The circle of friends always attempted to remain at the height of the epoch and to read any translations published of texts related to their interests. Beyond Sartre, they analysed Albert Camus, among others.[152] Aside from Echeverría, other members of this circle included Ulises Estrella, Fernando Tinajero Villamar, Iván Carbajal, and Luis Corral. Agustín Cueva Dávila, who was slightly older, occasionally joined their meetings.[153]

Through the 'model intellectual' Sartre, the circle then came to read Martin Heidegger. Whereas with Sartre what particularly interested them was his political positions and activities, as well as the relation of both to his theory, they admired Heidegger as the 'most philosophical', the 'most profound', the

---

With regard to Unamuno, Sánchez Vázquez mentions that in a first moment, the latter had seen the solution to Spain's problems in a return to pre-modern and pre-bourgeois social forms and therefore, immediately following the coup, he had come to 'endorse and justify Francoism as a crusade in defense of Western Christian civilisation'. Adolfo Sánchez Vázquez, speech given at the ceremony '100 years from the Generation of '98, in Spain, the committed thinker', in *La Jornada* (Mexico City, 3 December 1998). However, shortly before his death, Unamuno, it would seem, shifted from his unconditional adherence to Francoism.

150   Third interview with Bolívar Echeverría, cassette 1, side B, pos. 311–33.
151   'Sartre was very important. For my entire generation, Sartre was incredibly important. He was a sort of model of how the intellectual should be' (Third interview with Bolívar Echeverría, cassette 1, side B, pos. 347f).
152   Third interview with Bolívar Echeverría, cassette 1, side B, pos. 335.
153   Third interview with Bolívar Echeverría, cassette 1, side B, pos. 360. These friends had by 1996 made their name in Ecuador and partially in Latin America; Estrella in the movie industry, Carbajal as a poet, and Corral as the director of the Fundación Quito cultural institution in the capital of Ecuador. Tinajero had already made a name for himself as a novelist. See in this regard: Fernando Tinajero Villamar, *El desencuentro* (Tinajero Villamar 1983), as well as *De la evasión al desencanto* (Tinajero Villamar 1987).

Later, Agustín Cueva Dávila would lecture at the Faculty of Social and Political Sciences at the UNAM and would publish, among other texts 'El marxismo latinoamericano. Historia y problemas actuales' (Cueva Dávila 1986) and *Ideología y sociedad en América Latina* (Cueva Dávila 1988). On these texts by Cueva, see, moreover, note 191 of this section.

'most radical' (in philosophical terms).[154] While Bolívar Echeverría and his friends thus embraced Heidegger on the philosophical terrain, on the political terrain they were followers of the Cuban Revolution, which around this period (in 1959) overthrew the dictator Fulgencio Batista. They read *Sein und Zeit* (*Being and Time*) and listened to Radio Rebelde from Havana on shortwave radio.[155]

In 1996, responding to the question of what the Cuban Revolution had in common with Martin Heidegger, how it is possible to be simultaneously a partisan of the philosopher from Freiburg and of the revolutionaries Ernesto Che Guevara and Fidel Castro, Echeverría explained:

> The truth is that it's not very hard [to explain this] because they link up in their radicality. What connects the two is the radicality of the project.... I saw – a bit like Marx poses it in his early work – that what was important and essential was the overcoming of philosophy. So I saw that it was Heidegger who truly overcame philosophy, philosophical tradition, metaphysics... I saw him as the true revolutionary.
>
> So in that sense what was fascinating about Heidegger was his revolutionary character on the terrain of philosophy. And this connected obviously with what was promised by a revolution in that era, at the end of the '50s and early '60s, which also promised to be a much more radical revolution than the Soviet Revolution, for example. So we in Latin America thought we were in a radical, global revolutionary process which was not merely overcoming capitalism, as with what purportedly existed in the Soviet Union, but rather went beyond modern, European culture and all that ... a revolution that entailed liberation from imperialism, and with this liberation the destruction of capitalism, and with the destruction of capitalism [he laughs a bit here] the global transformation of civilisation as such... this was a truly wild dream that we had. So, Heidegger and the Cuban Revolution are connected in this aspect, the aspect of radicalism.[156]

---

154 Third interview with Bolívar Echeverría, cassette I, side A, pos. 309. Moreover, 'When we began to read Heidegger we saw that, yes, Heidegger's thought was much more radical than that of Sartre. We liked Sartre for his connection to concrete politics, with concrete history, and Heidegger because he was a great philosopher' (Third interview with Bolívar Echeverría, cassette I, side A, pos. 342–6).

155 First interview with Bolívar Echeverría, side A, pos. 217.

156 Third interview with Bolívar Echeverría, cassette I, side A, pos. 039–97. See, in this regard, the biographical parallel with Herbert Marcuse, who is considered in the literature to be 'the first "Heideggerian Marxist"': Schmidt 1977, p. 59.

Heidegger's active participation in National Socialism is unknown among his young leftist supporters in Quito. On the one hand, the philosopher from the Black Forest exists for them only in the sphere of pure thought, and on the other, his thought came to be known in 1950s Ecuador almost exclusively by right-wing Heideggerians, who carefully avoid all mention of such biographical 'details'.[157] Discussion of Heidegger's practical proximity to National Socialism and whether 'there exist relations between the philosophy of National Socialism and the philosophy of being [that is, Heidegger]',[158] a discussion already underway after 1945, was still foreign to these young radicals, fourteen years later and 13,000 kilometres away from the historical location of the unconditional German surrender.[159]

Marcuse was as impressed by the atmosphere of leftist irruption in the 1920s in Europe as he was by his philosophical teacher Martin Heidegger. Some theoretical parallels with Echeverría's work, like the attempt to connect Marx to Heidegger, could also find their origin here.

157 Third interview with Bolívar Echeverría, cassette I, side A.
158 Anders 1947, p. 75. Anders answers this question with 'Of course we believe it' (ibid.) and to corroborate this, he cites certain parallels, among others: 'Both philosophies are *anti-civilisational theories*. And both are *against any kind of universalism* (such as humanity, the international, Catholicism), because both are only concerned with the self, which is to say, one which is enclosed upon itself, excluding other [people] or excluding oneself from a common world' (Anders 1947, p. 76), and he concludes:

'These parallels show that the model of becoming authentic [*Eigentlichwerden*] is very similar in both cases. The national uprising was to a certain degree the national-ritual act through which the amorphous German population (which have been made "inauthentic" by parliamentarism, Judaism, and so on) became animated as a *Volk* (racial people) or a *Reich*. The fact that in the long run, becoming authentic on the private level and private nihilism could no longer be tolerated alongside the purported becoming authentic of the racial people (*Volk*) and collective nihilism, is demonstrated by the very polemical article "Heidegger" in the *Konversationslexikon* of Meyer in 1934. Evidently, Heidegger attempted unsuccessfully to ingratiate himself [with the National Socialists, S.G.], which does not reduce his guilt for the *Gleichschaltung* [voluntarily aligning with National Socialist ideology]. It should not surprise us that already (in French interviews) he shows disdain as a *quantité négligeable* for his famous embrace of the national uprising (inaugural rectoral speech of 1933). For us, of course, it continues to pertain to his existence, and with it ... to his impropriety' (ibid.) See the aforementioned text by Heidegger: 'The Self-Assertion of the German University' (Heidegger 1990).

159 In 1999, a similar position could also be found in various Latin-American countries, Mexico included, among philosophers who consider themselves to be critical. This reference to Heidegger's dark past, which he never saw as worthy of self-criticism, is frequently attacked, even in circles claiming to be leftist, whether with the claim that it was a gratuitous invention or with the 'self-critical' expression that if one had been 'under the same pressure as Heidegger' anyone would have acted similarly. What this 'pressure'

In the force field between these two radicalisms, 'at that time most relevant' – according to Echeverría's understanding of the transition from the sixth to the seventh decade of the twentieth century – he decided to move not to Havana, but to Freiburg. After a year studying philosophy and psychology at the Central University of Ecuador in Quito, Bolívar Echeverría set off for Freiburg in late November 1961, in the company of his friend Luis Corral. Enjoying a slice of fortune, Echeverría had obtained a scholarship from the DAAD (the German Service for Academic Exchange) to study in the German Federal Republic.

The Period in West Germany and West Berlin
Having arrived in Freiburg, the hope of being able to study with Martin Heidegger was quickly shattered, and not only due to his lack of knowledge

---

consisted of is either not specified or it is claimed that Heidegger's life was in danger, which is totally false, but through this gesture of consternated compassion many hope to avoid any critique of Heidegger.

On this topic, the important author, Günther Anders, makes the following telling remarks about his former mentor, Heidegger, who became a Nazi allegedly only out of necessity: 'he hoped to have a firm foundation in the phenomenology of Husserl, who had supported him for years (only to have Heidegger, from the day of the Machtergreifung on, refuse to acknowledge him on the street.)' (Anders 1947, p. 51, the parenthetical phrase appears in Anders as a footnote).

The affirmation that the support – both intellectual and mass – for the Nazis' crimes emerged under pressure, or even through threats to life, is as common as it is false, which is documented and proven in all detail, at least since the appearance of Daniel Jonah Goldhagen's book, repeatedly denigrated by German historians: *Hitler's willing executioners. Ordinary Germans and the Holocaust* (Goldhagen 1996). The generally favoured assertion that complicity with and participation in the Nazi genocide occurred exclusively because people had to save their own skins, which is to say, almost as a legitimate defence, in the end functions to justify current or future atrocities. Moreover, this makes it understandable that even outside of Germany there is a growing 'understanding' for victimisers, while the victims and their descendents are asked not to focus too much on what they have experienced. ('Who doesn't have anything to hide?' is the favourite exculpatory phrase.)

Bolívar Echeverría would later confront the question of Heidegger's behavior and National Socialism. See Bolívar Echeverría, 'Heidegger y el ultranazismo', *La Jornada Semanal* (Mexico City, 10 September 1989, pp. 33–6). An expanded version of this text appears in Echeverría 1995a, pp. 83–96.

of the German language.¹⁶⁰ Heidegger no longer taught anything but an *Oberseminar*, to which only a very select circle had access.¹⁶¹

In the year of Echeverría's arrival in the German Federal Republic, the construction of the Berlin Wall began, and this also influenced his decision to move to West Berlin in December of the same year. 'Rather out of adventurous spirit', he heads to the western part of the old capital of the Reich, to see what was happening there, hoping to be near to the most significant socio-political events of the country he was visiting.¹⁶² Another reason for the joint move of Echeverría and Corral to Berlin is that they have the desire (and the obligation) to learn German, and the Goethe Institute – entrusted with doing so at the time – provided housing for foreign students. Only in the Goethe-Institut of Berlin was there the possibility of living independently while taking courses in German. Our young philosopher from Riobamba and Quito set himself to learning German 'like a wild beast' and devoted seven hours a day to doing so. In the remainder of his time, he attended seminars at the Freie Universität Berlin. At first he understood nothing due to his insufficient grasp of the language, but his attendance was mandatory in light of his scholarship. It was difficult for Echeverría and Corral to deal with this first period in Berlin; alongside the heavy workload demanded of them there were also everyday experiences in West Berlin that entailed great tribulations.

Thus their first night, for example, remains an indelible memory, as the two spent the night together in a small private accommodation. The owner rented them the room belonging to her son, who was a Luftwaffe pilot in the Second World War. The room was packed with 'trophies', and the guests were forbidden to touch anything. Thus, their first night was an encounter with the 'German hero'. For Echeverría this was 'terrifying', and he would later recall the consequences of this and other experiences in Berlin. 'I managed to get over them, but Luis couldn't handle it and returned home'.¹⁶³

---

160 'It was a crazy adventure what we did. The two of us went. Neither of the pair knew any German.... I knew French and English and he didn't know anything, only Spanish' (Third interview with Bolívar Echeverría, cassette 1, side B, pos. 390).

161 First interview with Bolívar Echeverría, side A, pos. 176–83. See: 'Heidegger no longer really taught, I believe he had an *Oberseminar* [the equivalent of a postgraduate seminar] and that he met with a group of first-rate philosophers, very important men. So there was no possibility of attending any class with Heidegger, who was the only one who interested me' (ibid.).

162 First interview with Bolívar Echeverría, side A, pos. 198.

163 Third interview with Bolívar Echeverría, cassette 1, side B, pos. 433 and 435f. The text of this part of the interview says: 'We arrived in Berlin and spent the first night in the same

In Berlin, Echeverría met his future first wife, Ingrid Weikert, who connected him to the intellectual scene of artists and bohemians who meet in the Steinplatz, across from the University of the Arts and extending to the Heydecke bar on the Großgörschenstraße. At the Steinplatz theatre – which he attended nearly every day – he would get to know the foremost European, Japanese, and Latin American cinema of the period. In 1963, Bolívar Echeverría joined a discussion circle around the publication *Der Anschlag*, which was also attended by future exponents of the West-German student movement.[164] In the period prior to Berlin's '68, Echeverría was, as he would later recall, something of a 'specialist on Latin America' and the 'Third World' among this political-social milieu, being tasked, for example, with presenting Frantz Fanon's *The Wretched of the Earth*. These discussions, then, represented an important point of departure for the critical questions and actions that would culminate in 1968, but on the German side they would scarcely be perceived as such or, at least, would be quickly forgotten.[165]

---

bed in a private accommodation or something of the sort belonging to a woman who rented her son's room. But her son was a hero of the Second World War, a German pilot, and the whole room was full of photos and trophies and her son's things, all right there. The guests could not touch anything, they had to get into bed [laughs] and leave without touching anything [laughs] because everything was sacred: the German hero, her son – bahhh. So this was the first night [laughs] in Berlin – the terror.
– *And how did you find that* private accommodation?
In the Goethe there were little cards. But it was fabulous. I managed but Luis [Corral] couldn't and he returned [to Quito]. It was very difficult and besides we were very young' (Third interview with Bolívar Echeverría, cassette I, side B, pos. 26–38. The author's interview questions always appear in italics).

164   First interview with Bolívar Echeverría, side A, pos. 251 and 270.
165   Third interview with Bolívar Echeverría, cassette II, side A, pos. 426. In his autobiographical notes, Rudi Dutschke does not grant these conversations great importance. The only reference to these conversations in these writings says: 'In the spring of 1966 the Viva María group emerged, in which Rudi Dutschke and various other members of SDS, as well as many students from developing and other countries, discussed the problematic of the Third World': Dutschke 1981, p. 196.

There is no mention whatsoever of Bolívar Echeverría. This is even more surprising since Echeverría visited Dutschke several times in his Danish residence in Aarhus – to which he withdrew after the attempt on his life of 11 April 1968 – the final time only a few months prior to his death in 1979 as a delayed effect of the attack. (First interview with Bolívar Echeverría, side A, pos. 350–63). Bolívar Echeverría did not participate in the aforementioned group, since it was founded after his departure from Berlin in 1968, as he himself would later recall. (Fifth interview with Bolívar Echeverría, 11 September 1996,

Echeverría would recall in 1994 that in the 1964 demonstration in Berlin against Congolese Prime Minster Moise Chombé, with which 'everything began', Third-World participants predominated, constituting the front lines, and that it was only bit by bit that German participation in the protests increased.[166] Later German publications and memoirs would look quite different, and would judge Berlin's 68 to be simply a part, however significant, of the German student movement. These discrepant memories should not be understood merely as differing points of view of a single event, but rather as the first indication of the contradiction in the modern history of Western Europe that would impact Echeverría's future theoretical activity: while trying to analyse the world hastily from the European point of view, with a universalising gesture and pretension, one's own history is reduced, at the same time, to a merely local history.[167]

Echeverría considered the friendship and theoretical-political discussion that he began with Rudi Dutschke (and Bernd Rabehl) in Berlin to be 'a kind of dialogue between the Third World and the European centre, or something of the sort'.[168]

---

in the Faculty of Philosophy and Arts of the UNAM, cassette I, side A, pos. 018–23 [cited hereafter as Fifth interview with Bolívar Echeverría].)

Gretchen Dutschke, the widow of Rudi Dutschke, confirmed in 1996 that as far as she knows, none of Rudi Dutschke's published texts mention Bolívar Echeverría. She justified the fact that Echeverría does not appear in his most recent biography, which she published, by saying that there existed 'better documents' for other histories relative to Dutschke's work on the Third World, and that it was necessary to select texts. (Gretchen Dutschke, letter to the author. Berlin, 6 September 1996. See, moreover, Dutschke 1996).

166 First interview with Bolívar Echeverría, side A, pos. 372–81.
167 The explanation that Echeverría gave for the deliberate concealment of the importance of foreign comrades, at least at the outset of the Berlin student movement, in practically all German publications, sets out from this local narrow-mindedness. To the question of why such omissions occur in German historiography, including that of the left, he formulates this response: 'I believe that such matters are not grasped in their full importance because they do not correspond to local history' (First interview with Bolívar Echeverría, side A, pos. 388–90).
168 First interview with Bolívar Echeverría, side A, pos. 261. The corresponding passage from the interview is reproduced in full on page 64 of this book. Gretchen Dutschke recalled in 1996 the friendship between Dutschke and Echeverría: 'Rudi appreciated Bolívar. They frequently engaged in discussions.... I had the impression that they agreed in their evaluation of the situation and revolutionary possibilities in Latin America.... I met Bolívar in Berlin, he was a friend of Rudi's.... What was his importance in these discussions in Berlin? I would say that it was only within Third-World circles and with refer-

In 1964, Echeverría meets Horst Kurnitzky, a Berlin native, who studied for several years in Frankfurt and had just returned from there.[169] Together, they edit a short volume on *The Critique of Bourgeois Anti-Imperialism*.[170] Echeverría drafted the introduction to a book prepared by Kurnitzky, consisting of a collection of texts by Che Guevara, on the occasion of his murder.[171] This text, written by Echeverría in German, with the language corrected by a friend at his request, expresses unequivocally the fascination he has felt for Che since his last years in Quito. It begins as follows:

> ... 'Next time I will send a call, a newspaper, and some mines that we are preparing right now – 9 November 1957. Che'. Revolutionaries in Latin America and the world over will no longer receive news like this ..., because the man who wrote them, Comandante Guevara, has died. He fell injured in combat, 'in one of the many battles he led'. Afterward, they murdered him. They mutilated his corpse, buried it, dug it up, burned it, and buried it again. They made it disappear. The complex equilibrium of minerals that were held together in his body was forever broken. That special project ceased to exist, that outstanding initiative, that man with a 'first and last name' who knew how to respond to the concrete demands of Latin American revolutionary movements and who was thereby transformed into that historical person called 'Che Guevara'.
> Ernesto Guevara is dead, and his death weakens the revolution.[172]

Alongside this admiration for the most well-known Latin-American *guerrillero* of the 1960s, Echeverría's text, written at the age of thirty-three, also shows

---

ence to the problems of the Third World' (Gretchen Dutschke, letter to the author, Berlin, 6 September 1996).

The letter from Mrs. Dutschke ends with a formulation that is worth reproducing here because of its description of the prevailing atmosphere among the circles of 'student rebels' that might later be considered to be very liberal: 'I feel that I cannot help further [with the various questions regarding Bolívar Echeverría]. The way things were then, men had little to do with women (unless they had an affective relationship), and so I could only observe Bolívar from a distance'.

169   First interview with Bolívar Echeverría, side A, pos. 61 and 370.
170   Frank et al. 1969.
171   Echeverría 1968.

Kurnitzky's double interest in the Frankfurt School and in national liberation movements in Latin America is expressed in one other book he edited during this period: Kurnitzky and Kuhn 1967.

172   Echeverría 1968, pp. 7f.

his interest in Marxist theory when he says: 'For communist revolutionaries in Latin America, who consciously and by practical necessity reinvent Marxist theory, the loss of Comandante Guevara does not annul the influence that he exercised at the heart of the revolutionary movement, but merely transforms it, stripping it of the concrete'.[173]

As late as Echeverría's last years in Quito, Karl Marx was more or less insignificant both for him and for his local political debating circle of friends. For them, he was 'a sort of wise man who provided the basis for all these stupid things that the bureaucrats [of the Ecuadorean Communist Party] were saying... we read fabulous, excellent phrases by Marx, but nothing else.... No one read *Capital* because no one understood it, I imagine'.[174]

These old reservations toward Marx's writings were based on reservations toward the 'bureaucrats' of the Communist Party who 'said they were waiting for the objective conditions for the revolution', 'when in reality they were waiting for orders from Moscow'.[175]

Echeverría's introduction to the Che Guevara book contains, moreover, a sort of self-definition, when the author speaks of the 'revolutionary communists of Latin America'[176] or of the 'new communists of Latin America'.[177] In the same place, Bolívar Echeverría gives between the lines the impression that he considered the foremost task to be the development of a 'new theory' of

---

173   Echeverría 1968, p. 8.
174   Third interview with Bolívar Echeverría, cassette 1, side A, pos. 430–5.
175   Third interview with Bolívar Echeverría, cassette 1, side A, pos. 425–7. The passage cited here says in full:

'We therefore [with the Cuban Revolution, S.G.] understood that things needed to change and change radically. But those with a monopoly on political activity were the Communist Parties, which were a terrible thing, a bunch of men there, bureaucrats, dogmatic, sectarian, drunks, useless, the worst. They were the ones who gave the orders, the ones who said yes or no, and the ones with the tactics and strategies. What disgusted us was that when in reality they were waiting for orders from Moscow, they said they were waiting for the objective conditions for the revolution [laughs]. So we said: "what conditions?" So they brought in Marx and half the world to show that the objective conditions did not exist and we would wait'.

'This was why, when the Cuban Revolution appeared, we said "there it is!" What objective conditions? None! So we were very voluntaristic, but that was that'.

'In this sense I told you: for us Marx was a sort of wise man who supported all these idiocies that the bureaucrats said. Of course, we read fabulous, excellent phrases by Marx, but nothing more than a few phrases. We had no idea. No one read *Capital* because no one understood it, I imagine' (pos. 418–35).

176   Echeverría 1968, p. 12.
177   Echeverría 1968, p. 14.

radical social transformation for the non-dogmatic Left, be it in Latin America or the 'metropoles'.[178]

When he simultaneously observes that the (theoretical) collaboration between 'revolutionary communists in Latin America' and 'their comrades in the metropoles' 'is not as close as would be desirable',[179] this could be understood as the first published formulation of an intention that, with all the modifications of this 'new theory' and its contents, would determine a substantial part of his later activities up to the early 1990s: to be a unifying nexus on the theoretical level between Latin America and the so-called First World, and particularly Europe.[180]

This introduction to the book on Che Guevara already demarcates a force field within which – great variations notwithstanding – many of Echeverría's later texts would move. On the one hand, we find already a critique of the idea of 'national unity' above the limits of class in the so-called Third World, whose inhabitants, so they say, suffer together under imperialism 'from elsewhere', and who should therefore fight imperialism together;[181] on the other hand, we

---

178 Echeverría 1968, p. 12.
179 Ibid. The complete sentence says: 'These central statements by Che – nuanced, expanded, systematised – have become part of the new theory, that revolutionary communists are developing in Latin America (in conjunction, although not as closely as one might like, with their comrades of the metropoles)'.
180 See, in this regard, for example, the speech 'Le marxisme et la sémiologie', University of Picardy (France), 1981; the course 'Barock als Kulturform', Freie Universität Berlin, September–October 1990; the roundtable 'Democracy between realism and utopia', 11 International Political Philosophy Meeting, Mérida (Spain), April 1993; the roundtable 'Marxism and history in the 1990s. The crisis of Marxism', International Congress Historia a Debate [History in Debate], Santiago de Compostela, July 1993; the speech 'Die Moderne außerhalb Europas: Der Fall Lateinamerika', Johann Wolfgang Goethe University in Frankfurt, November 1994; the roundtable 'The baroque in America', Colloquium: *Barrocos y Modernos*, Lateinamerika-Institut, Freie Universität Berlin, December 1994 (from his unpublished 1996 CV).

From 1998 onwards at the Faculty of Philosophy and Arts at the UNAM, Echeverría gave an annual undergraduate course on the topic of *German philosophical texts*, which discusses texts by Heidegger, Horkheimer, Adorno, and Benjamin. Moreover, until the 1990s he maintained contact with Horst Kurnitzky in Berlin (see p. 78 of this biography), and in the journal *Cuadernos Políticos* he was charged, as a member of the editorial board, with maintaining foreign contacts (see p. 72 of this biography). On Echeverría's discussion of European authors in his works, as well as the German and French translations he carried out, see the bibliography of Bolívar Echeverría in the appendix.
181 'The reformist thesis ... that the interests of the "national bourgeoisies" [in Latin America] are anti-imperialist ... is false, and it means a subordination of Marxism to liberal-bourgeois ideology' (Echeverría 1968, p. 13).

find a critique of the idea that Latin America and its Left is, with respect to Europe and its Left, merely an incomplete and backward copy, in urgent need of development.[182]

By contrast, what is characteristic of Echeverría in this period of development, but would be formulated inversely in later texts – as a non-explicit self-criticism – is his concept of the revolution as a total rupture with what preceded it, a revolution that emerges from a 'new man', as he puts it in the final line of the introduction: 'In Cuba ... the current state of the new man, that of the internationalist revolutionary'.[183]

To conclude, with regard to the theoretical-political position expressed in the *'Einführung'* ['Introduction'] it bears mentioning that Echeverría, though he here maintains his aforementioned rejection of the 'Latin American pseudo-communists'[184] from whom he distances himself, and strongly criticises their 'reformist, legalistic, and dependent politics',[185] it is clear that with regard to the Soviet Union itself he is more prudent in his critique. In the text, he does not mention it directly, but alludes to it in a passage as a model to follow, in a manner that could be interpreted as wholly affirmative.[186] In the context of an almost euphoric certainty, guided by the axiom 'The socialist revolution is possible in Latin America!',[187] drawn from "praxis" more than theory, Echeverría wrote in 1968 on the occasion of Che Guevara's death: 'Soon, the Latin-American revolution will have learned all the lessons of its "1905" '.[188]

This allusion to the crushing of a peaceful demonstration in St. Petersburg by Tsarist troops in January of 1905 – which served as a trigger for the first

---

182   'The Latin American proletariat cannot be described as an incomplete copy of the European proletariat of a century past' (ibid.).

183   Echeverría 1968, p. 18. Elsewhere, Echeverría expresses with no less euphoria his certainty of the potential spread of the Cuban revolutionary movement across all of Latin America, in speaking of the 'establishment, on the island of Cuba, of the first beachhead of the Latin-American revolutionary movement'. Echeverría 1965a, p. 13.

184   Echeverría, 1968, p. 14.

185   Ibid.

186   In 1996, when Echeverría was asked about this passage, he would indicate retrospectively that in that period he was 'very Leninist', but in the sense of the 'Lenin of the revolution', which should evidently be understood as distinguishing him from Lenin the statesman. Here, he said, he was once again interested in the radicality in this case incarnated in Lenin. But this admiration for the revolutionary ended after reading the biography Isaac Deutscher wrote about Lenin around 1974. (Fifth interview with Bolívar Echeverría, cassette I, side A, pos. 140–82). In the interview, Echeverría says that he had read Deutscher's book in German, shortly before the Mexican edition appeared. See Deutscher 1970.

187   Echeverría 1968, p. 10.

188   Ibid.

democratic-bourgeois revolution in Russia, the precursor to the October Revolution – has a double content: on the one hand, the hope that the death of Che Guevara might be able to unleash a great leftist movement, and on the other hand, an implicit celebration of what occurred in the Soviet Union, during and after the October Revolution, as a 'successful revolution'.

From this we can see that the *young* Bolívar Echeverría, despite his later assertion that he was never an orthodox Marxist,[189] nevertheless shared a weakness with a large section of the heterodox Latin American Left: that their criticism of local (Stalinist) Communist Parties is aimed above all at their 'subordination *vis-à-vis* Moscow'. The central motive tends to be the fact that different conditions predominate in Latin America than in Europe or the Soviet Union and that, therefore, leftist politics should be different and independent. The idea of criticising the (internal) politics of the Soviet Union as such, from Latin America, did not occur to even the most critical spirits at that time. This applies as well to practically the only Latin-American Marxist who is well-known, at least superficially, in Germany: José Carlos Mariátegui.[190] This Peruvian theorist and political leader has the reputation of having been a persistent critic of Stalinism, but his break with 'Moscow' resulted not from his critique of internal Soviet politics, but rather from his ambition of theoretically planning (albeit with certain practical consequences, especially with regard to party politics) an autonomous socialist path for Peru, without counting on the approval of the Politburo of the CPSU.[191]

---

189   First interview with Bolívar Echeverría, side A.
190   Mariátegui's *Siete ensayos de interpretación de la realidad peruana* has been translated into English: *Seven interpretive essays on Peruvian reality*. [Note to the English-language edition: This self-limitation of the Latin-American (anti-Eurocentric) Left, which consists in criticising *subordination* to European or US-American theoretical and political models, without directing this critique towards the reality and theories of the so-called First World *itself*, persists still today in discussions and publications. What is necessary is a radical critique of the universal reality and theory, starting from the so-called Third World, without any self-limitation. There exists still a – much too big – respect for the falsely supposed ability of self-understanding and self-organising by the societies, people and theories of the so-called First World. (From the author of the book, S.G., as well as all subsequent 'notes to the English-language edition'.)]
191   Mariátegui's conflict with the Third International resulted from his differing conception of communist/socialist politics. His conviction that the rural Peruvian population and its partially pre-Hispanic traditions should play a significant role in the struggle for a communist/socialist Peru came up against fierce opposition in the Comintern. By contrast, we do not know of any explicit critique that he made of what occurred in the Stalinist Soviet Union, and nor does José Aricó – who proclaims Mariátegui to be the original founder of a non-dogmatic Marxism in Latin America – reveal any such critique by him. Mariátegui

This position, widespread in Latin America among those on the Left critical of the local Communist Parties, would only change after the disappearance of the Soviet Union and can be explained, among other things, by the background of the United States seeing Latin America as its sphere of influence, and directly influencing the central political-social decisions of the southern part of the American continent.[192] Thus, the Soviet Union, while it existed, was seen by a large part of the Latin American Left as a necessary counterweight to the United States, and a too harsh critique of it would be seen as harmful to the interests of the countries of the so-called Third World.

Let us return to Bolívar Echeverría in Berlin, who during these years was a member of the editorial board of the journal *Pucuna* in Quito, in which he published several articles.[193] How did this shift or transition on the theoretical-philosophical terrain from partisan of Heidegger to 'revolutionary communist' occur? What happened to him such that, in a sort of philosophical adventure, he left his Andean city acquiring a scholarship without speaking a word of German and landed in West Berlin with its atmosphere of a battle front: in other words, from the Third World he threw himself not only into the so-called First World, but precisely into the location of its fiercest tensions with the so-called Second World?

At the risk of repeating something that has been said already, allow us to again cite Bolívar Echeverría's mature recollection in a 1994 interview with this author:

> Regarding what you ask me about the importance of my time in Berlin... it is the following: I began in Berlin to roll out – you could say – all of my functions: vital, intellectual, corporeal. So there I connected a lot with Rudi Dutschke, but in a kind of dialogue between the Third

---

let Stalin be Stalin, published Stalin's texts in his most important intellectual project – the journal *Amauta*, which he founded and published; but, moreover, he hoped that Stalin would let Mariátegui be Mariátegui, which did not happen.

Regarding the Latin American debate surrounding Mariátegui, see the introduction to Aricó 1990 as well as Cueva Dávila 1986.

192 Here, we could give a list (which could fill entire books) of loose examples, with one of the best known being its total support for the Pinochet coup against the Chilean President Salvador Allende on 11 September 1973. In the present day, one of the most striking examples is the Cuban blockade, which is in open violation of international law. In this regard, see Galeano 1973.

193 His friend and companion during these first months in the German Federal Republic, Luis Corral, is also a member of the board. The texts published there are Echeverría 1965b; 1965c.

World and the European centre, or something of the sort [laughs]. So we, some Latin American *compañeros* and I, started the Association of Latin American Students in Germany, the AELA. I was at one time president of the AELA. We had meetings where we read literature, like for example Frantz Fanon's *The Wretched of the Earth*, or works by Marcuse presented by Rudi Dutschke or Bernd Rabehl, who was also in the group. So it was a sort of internal seminar.[194]

In the mid 1960s, the AELA had twelve to eighteen members, because at that time, in contrast to later years, there were very few Latin American students in the German Federal Republic.[195] Its headquarters in West Berlin were located on the Carmerstrasse, near Savigny-Platz.[196] The association edits a journal by the simplest printing means, under the title *Latinoamérica*.[197] In that journal, Echeverría published a first text entitled 'Intellectuality in Latin America'.[198] This was a presentation given in one of the AELA seminars, 'which was devoted to the study of three forces in Latin American social dynamics: the Church, the Armed Forces, and intellectuality'.[199] The text concludes with a review of the 1963 Brazilian film *Os Fuzis* ['The Rifles'], by Ruy Guerra.[200] The cover of the journal, designed in half-letter size, represents, printed in black and red on light paper, a schematised map of Latin America in red – from the northern border of Mexico to Tierra del Fuego – with black letters curving upward and to the left. 'Latin Americans, unite' is the slogan that appears here, as an evident paraphrase of Marx's 'Proletarians of all countries, unite'.[201] In the introduction to the projected series of articles – which begins with Echeverría's article mentioned above – there is an optimistic expression of the journal's theoretical-political orientation, which sets out from the certainty of 'an event

---

194 First interview with Bolívar Echeverría, side A, pos. 255–75. See Fanon 1991.
195 Third interview with Bolívar Echeverría, cassette II, side A, pos. 420ff.
196 First interview with Bolívar Echeverría, side A, pos. 275–95.
197 See *Latinoamérica*, Association of Latin American Students in West Germany (Göttingen), from 1965.
198 See Echeverría 1965a.
199 Echeverría 1965a, p. 8.
200 This film review appeared in another location as well as an independent text: Echeverría 1965c.
201 The description from the cover of the journal comes from no. 2 (1965). According to what can be deduced from the comments of a reader on the first issue, the cover of number 1 had a very similar design. See Cabrera 1965, p. 45. Cabrera notes that the slogan of the journal should be discussed in later issues.

that is knocking at the doors of Latin America: revolution'.[202] Its claim to disseminate not only theory is expressed clearly in the editorial from the same issue, in phrases like: '*Compañero*, how will you react to the concrete challenge that presents itself to you?'[203]

Let us return in more detail to our prior discussion of the theoretical transition from a Heideggerian to someone who wonders how 'communist revolutionaries in Latin America' might be able to 'reinvent Marxist theory', with the presentation of the context of the history of his life in a 1994 interview:

> *Were you and Rudi Dutschke friends?*
>
> Of course. It was with him, for example, that we attended a seminar by professor Lieber. This is interesting because he is the first who dared to discuss Marxist topics in the seminars of the Freie Universität, because Berlin was totally anti-communist...
>
> So he prepared a seminar on *History and Class Consciousness* ... and Rudi Dutschke and I intervened with papers and all that in those discussions. It was from there that the idea of a completely different Marxism, which other participants in the seminar liked, began to circulate. It was there that at least Marxism began to be spoken of openly, because it was impossible to mention Marx's name: 'They are guys from the GDR [German Democratic Republic] or the Sowjetzone [Soviet zone]', like they used to say [laughs a bit]. This was an emphatically anti-communist atmosphere everywhere, in the U-Bahn [the metro] on the S-Bahn [the suburban train], in the stores, everywhere. It was impossible, militantly anti-communist.
>
> So, in order to speak of Marx there, one had to do a series of things, and as a result our meetings were nearly clandestine ... it was a fabulous group.... Of course, this is also delightful for a young person, the opportunity to meet, to discuss interesting things, important [things] that connected with my country insofar as they spoke about revolution and the Cuban Revolution and all that. And to come across Germans who were concerned with and informed about Latin America was fascinating, it was a good point.... In general they are xenophobic and poorly-informed.[204]

---

202   'Serie', in *Latinoamérica*, no. 2, p. 7.
203   'Editorial', in *Latinoamérica*, no. 2, p. 6.
204   First interview with Bolívar Echeverría, side A, pos. 296–336. As concerns the first ever seminar on Marxism in the history of the Freie Universität Berlin, Bolívar Echeverría mentions, moreover, an edition of Marx in several volumes by the director of the seminar, professor Lieber. This is: Karl Marx, *Werke, Schriften, Briefe in 7 Bänden (8 Teilbände)*.

In his text from this period on 'Intellectuality in Latin America', Echeverría describes why it is that 'revolutionary intellectuality' in Latin America, of which he considered himself a part – being a reader of Heidegger and a partisan of the Cuban Revolution – 'feels inevitably attracted to Marxism':

> Revolutionary intellectuality thus needs to abandon the European-bourgeois principles and ideology, to complete philosophically the definitive process of decolonisation, which is demanded practically by the dominated classes. For such intellectuality, notions like 'human nature,' 'metaphysical individuality,' 'preconceived order,' 'linear evolution,' etc. disappear. Its task becomes one of elaborating a theory that arises from the principles implied by the radically revolutionary interests of the subjected classes. This explains why this intellectuality feels inevitably attracted to Marxism – the philosophy of workers' struggle, the culmination and overcoming of all other metaphysical European traditions.[205]

In this passage, what is noteworthy is the effort to connect Heideggerianism with Marxism, when Karl Marx – as in the case of Heidegger – is not considered to be the last great representative of (European) metaphysics, but rather he who surpassed it – something that Heidegger, in turn, considered to be his own mission.[206] It was also in this period that the first theoretical discussion between Echeverría and Adolfo Sánchez Vázquez occurred. In 1994, Echeverría would recall that:

> ...within the AELA study circles in Berlin, in which we dialogued with comrades like Rudi Dutschke and Bernd Rabehl, among others, who

---

By Lieber there also exists, among others: *Marx Lexikon. Zentrale Begriffe der politischen Philosophie von Karl Marx*: Lieber (ed.) 1988.

The shock with which Echeverría viewed the exaggerated anti-communism and anti-Marxism of West Berlin in the 1960s should not be relegated to the past. As late as 1997, researchers arriving, for example, from Mexico can scarcely believe the degree to which anti-Marxism continues to exist as a sort of Pavlovian reflex in German academic life.

205 Echeverría 1965a, p. 14.
206 In this early phase, we can already sense Bolívar Echeverría's ambivalent relationship with Heidegger. He oscillates between a fascination with the latter's 'philosophical radicalism,' and doubts regarding his errors (which are expressed in the political realm, without being simply political and extra-philosophical). Later, Echeverría would attempt to explain Heidegger's wrong turn largely through his stubborn refusal to understand and discuss Marxism.

were sensitive to the problematic of the Third World, there was little to nothing, aside from Mariátegui's essays, that we Latin Americans could offer within a theoretical line preoccupied with reconstructing Marxist discourse. For this reason, I remember in a very special way the occasion in which, exceptionally, I was able to proudly present a text by a Latin American who could cope with these demands. It was an essay by Sánchez Vázquez on Marxism and aesthetics, which had just been published in a journal in revolutionary Cuba, which already sketched out his later effort to reground Marxism on the basis of the 'theory of praxis'.[207]

During his period in West Berlin, Echeverría travelled frequently to the Eastern part of the city and also to the rest of the German Democratic Republic (GDR) in order to get to know that society. He considered his experiences, especially with the border crossings, horrifying.[208] Bolívar Echeverría became increasingly politically active and his life increasingly nomadic. Beginning around 1966, he oscillated between Latin America and Berlin. One of his missions is to serve as a messenger between the Berlin comrades and those Latin Americans close to Ernesto *Che* Guevara, among others. Through detours, he transported letters and packages of whose content he was unaware. One layover on those travels was, around April 1966, Mexico City.[209]

Once his scholarship for the Federal German Republic was no longer renewed,[210] remaining in Berlin became increasingly difficult for him. With a friend's salary tax card, he attempted to remain afloat by working the night shift in a Philips factory assembling phonographic record players, but he only lasted two months in this job.[211]

---

207 Echeverría 1995b, pp. 78f. Bolívar Echeverría presented this text as a speech at the UNAM on 21 January 1994 at the series of events 'Setenta años de la Facultad de Filosofía y Letras [Seventy years of the Faculty of Philosophy and Arts]' (see 'Procedencia de los texto' in Vargas Lozano (ed.) 1995, especially p. 631. See, moreover, Echeverría 1995c.
208 Third interview with Bolívar Echeverría, cassette II, side A, pos. 388f.
209 Third interview with Bolívar Echeverría, cassette II, side B, pos. 232, and Fifth interview with Bolívar Echeverría, cassette I, side A, pos. 035–040.
210 In a conversation with the author in 1995, Echeverría commented that if his scholarship was not extended, this was due to the fact that his activities had been focused on the student movement in Berlin.
211 Third interview with Bolívar Echeverría, cassette II, side A, pos. 408.

From the Divided City to the Mexican Capital

In mid-July of 1968, Bolívar Echeverría definitively ended his residency in Berlin and went to Mexico City with his girlfriend Ingrid Weikert. The decision to move there was motivated largely by Weikert, who was interested in Mexico due to the focus of her studies, namely the history of pre-Hispanic art. Echeverría was not sure where he should go, and he would have also been interested in living somewhere like Buenos Aires, the capital of Argentina.[212] He could not return to Ecuador, as he was considered *persona non grata*; all his friends from there had either gone abroad or into clandestinity, for example joining the guerrilla struggle. Following the July 1963 coup d'état, after which power ended up in the hands of a military junta composed of the generals Ramón Castro Jijón, Luis Cabrera Sevilla, Marcos Gándara Enrique, and Guillermo Freile Posso, the political situation of the country became characterised by an extreme hostility toward the Left. The replacement of the junta in 1966 by an interim civilian president (Clemente Yerobi Indaburu, imposed by the military leadership) did not fundamentally change the situation, despite the restoration of the right to strike and the reopening of the University of Quito, which had been closed by the junta. On 1 September, José María Velasco Ibarra took charge of the government as president-elect; on 22 June 1970 he dissolved the Congress and the Supreme Court, governing from that point on through openly dictatorial decrees.[213]

When Echeverría decided to go to Mexico, it was also because he had already established contacts there, particularly during his stopover in 1966, when he spoke to a representative of the journal of the Universidad Nacional Autónoma de México,[214] to whom he later sent book reviews discussing Sartre, and with Arnaldo Orfila from the publishing house Siglo XXI, for whom he translated Adolf Kozlik's *El capitalismo del desperdicio. El milagro económico norteamericano* [*Wasteful capitalism. The North American economical miracle.*][215] In the Mexican capital, he taught a course in logic at a college, for which he was, however, never paid at all, due to administrative confusion. Shortly after settling in Mexico City, he made contact with Adolfo Sánchez Vázquez, who invited him

---

212   Third interview with Bolívar Echeverría, cassette II, side B, pos. 153, and Fifth interview with Bolívar Echeverría, cassette I, side A, pos. 024–031. In regard to the academic side, we could note that while Echeverría attended all the required seminars for the Master's Degree in Philosophy and, therefore, fulfilled the prerequisites to write his master's thesis, he did not do so, as a result of his abrupt departure. (Third interview with Bolívar Echeverría, cassette II, side A, pos. 390.)

213   See Cueva Dávila 1974.

214   Bolívar Echeverría, in conversation with the author on 10 July 1996 at the Faculty of Philosophy and Arts of the UNAM.

215   Kozlik 1968. See, moreover, Echeverría 1967a, 1967b.

to work as an adjunct professor. Later, Echeverría would recall that while he was never a 'disciple' of Sánchez Vázquez in the strictest sense of the word, he agreed fully with his critical vision of Marxism and received from him all the support necessary to begin his academic work in the Faculty of Philosophy and Arts [Facultad de Filosofía y Letras] at the UNAM.[216]

Echeverría does not get directly involved in the student movement – which was enjoying a moment of great upsurge during his first months in Mexico, and which reached a first peak (a few days after his arrival in Mexico City) in the great demonstration of 26 July 1968 – but he maintains close contact with two important figures of that political movement: Roberto Escudero and Carlos Pereyra. Roberto Escudero, who was at that time Sánchez Vázquez's assistant, was detained after the slaughter of 2 October 1968 in the Plaza de las Tres Culturas (Tlatelolco),[217] which marked the beginning of a wave of repression of the student movement, and after his release departed as an exile for Chile. Immediately thereafter, in December of 1968, Echeverría travelled to Berlin to report at the Freie Universität on events in Mexico and to establish contacts for solidarity with those detained and tortured in official and secret Mexican jails (with most of the latter located on military bases without any contact with the outside world). 'Most of the solidarity expressed by those in Berlin for the [Mexican] movement' went through his mediation, as he later recalled.[218] During that trip, he married Ingrid Weikert in Berlin.[219]

---

216 Third interview with Bolívar Echeverría, cassette I, side B, pos. 053f. In Spanish, there exist two words for what is understood in German as 'Schüler': 'alumno' which is simply a participant in a course, and 'discípulo,' which refers to the student who is a follower and supporter of a teacher, in the sense, for example, of a philosophical or theoretical education. Bolívar Echeverría emphasises that he was never in the latter category vis-à-vis Sánchez Vázquez, since he was already developed on a philosophical/theoretical plane when the two first met. 'I was already very old when I arrived in Mexico', he would recall, laughing, on another occasion; 'I was already made when I got to Mexico. So it is a parallel question, I have never been a disciple of Sánchez Vázquez' (First interview with Bolívar Echeverría, side B, pos. 463f).

217 See also our biography of Adolfo Sánchez Vázquez, p. 36.

218 Third interview with Bolívar Echeverría, cassette II, side B, pos. 200. Echeverría continues on this point: 'We did some things: many of the creative artists there made some Plakats [posters] for the movement in Mexico, beautiful ... very nice ... and interviews with the leaders here, translations so they would come out in Germany. And as a part of this work I went to Germany at the end of '68 to give talks and explanations to build solidarity with the Mexican political prisoners. ... I went, I believe it was in December, to Berlin ... to the FU ... to give presentations ... because it was solidarity with the recently imprisoned and tortured prisoners' (pos. 201–20).

219 Third interview with Bolívar Echeverría, cassette II, side B, pos. 153.

During the 1970s, Bolívar Echeverría intensified his collaboration with Sánchez Vázquez, and around 1973 our author came to be his assistant in the Faculty of Philosophy and Arts at the UNAM, providing support for Sánchez Vázquez in organising the seminar on Aesthetics. The two philosophers also collaborated in editorial tasks, with the former student in Berlin translating various texts and fragments by Bertolt Brecht into Spanish for the anthology *Aesthetics and Marxism*, which appeared in 1970.[220] Sánchez Vázquez published Karl Marx's *Economic and Philosophic Manuscripts of 1844* for the first time in Spanish in 1974 through Ediciones Era in Mexico.[221] Echeverría translated these, while the editor provides the introduction.[222]

In 1974, Echeverría formally completed his studies with a bachelor's degree [*licenciatura*] in Philosophy from the Faculty of Philosophy and Arts of the UNAM. His thesis deals with Marx's *Theses on Feuerbach*, of which he made a new Spanish translation in this work, dividing them into four 'thematic groups';[223] In this same year, he is granted a half-time professorship in Philosophy, with which he is no longer Sánchez Vázquez's assistant.[224] A year later, the theorist from Ecuador, fluent in the language of Marx, is granted a full-time professorship in the Faculty of Economics at the UNAM.[225] During this period, reading *Capital* over five semesters was part of the official curriculum for the UNAM's bachelor's degree in economics;[226] at this high point in

---

220 See Sánchez Vázquez (ed.) 1970. The following translations of texts and fragments by Bertolt Brecht in this anthology were done by Bolívar Echeverría: in Volume I, 'La efectividad de las antiguas obras de arte [The effectiveness of antique artworks]' (p. 330); 'El formalismo y las formas [Formalism and forms]' (pp. 230–3); and 'El Goce Artístico [Artistic enjoyment]' (p. 210); in Volume 2: 'Novedades formales y refuncionalización artística [Novelties of form and artistic refunctionalisation]' (pp. 161f); 'Del realismo burgués al realismo socialista [From bourgeois realism to socialist realism]' (pp. 250–5); "Sobre el modo realista de escribir ['On the realist way of writing'] (pp. 59–73).

221 See Marx 1974.

222 Sánchez Vázquez, 'Economía y humanismo' in Marx 1974, pp. 11–97.

223 See *Apuntes para un comentario de las Tesis sobre Feuerbach*, undergraduate [licenciatura] thesis presented by Bolívar Echeverría Andrade, defended on May 14, 1974 at the Faculty of Philosophy and Arts of the UNAM. This text was later published various times under various titles: 'La revolución teórica comunista en la Tesis sobre Feuerbach', in *Historia y sociedad*, Vol. II, no. 6, pp. 45–63; 'El materialismo de Marx', in Echeverría 1986, pp. 18–37; and *Sobre el materialismo. Modelo para armar* (Echeverría 1990a).

224 Third interview with Bolívar Echeverría, cassette II, side B, pos. 86.

225 Third interview with Bolívar Echeverría, cassette II, side B, pos. 90.

226 The 1974 study plan for this degree entered into force in 1975. The political economy assignment comprised five semesters of detailed lectures on the three volumes of *Capital*; during the sixth, theories of imperialism were discussed; and in the seventh, the 'socialist

the study of Marx, Echeverría's courses on *Capital* were so successful that during discussions of the second volume the classroom overflowed with up to 150 participants.[227] During this period at the Faculty of Economics of the UNAM, Bolívar Echeverría deepened his knowledge of Marx and published various studies on Marx's writings.[228]

Collaboration on the Journal Cuadernos Políticos

Some of his scientific essays from that period first appeared in a journal that Echeverría would mark with his own stamp, and by which he would be marked in turn: *Cuadernos Políticos*, first appearing in September of 1974, after a year of 'incredibly complicated meetings' by the editors.[229] The founding board of this quarterly publication by Ediciones Era was comprised of Carlos Pereyra, Ruy Mauro Marini, Ronaldo Cordera, Arnaldo Córdova, Adolfo Sánchez Rebolledo, Bolívar Echeverría, and the head of the publishing house, Neus Espresate.[230] Espresate, who had up to that point run the leftist Ediciones Era, was born in 1934 in Canfranc, a town in the Spanish Pyrenees. In 1946, as a young woman of 12, she arrived in Mexico when her parents left Spain as refugees from the Civil War.[231] The publishing house, run by 'the heir of this generation of great [Spanish] exiles',[232] counts among the most creative and intrepid independent publishers in Mexico.

The first two issues of *Cuadernos Políticos* made no mention of those members of the editorial board who did not have Mexican citizenship (Ruy Mauro Marini and Bolívar Echeverría), such as to avoid problems with the immigration authorities. Article 33 of the Constitution – which, as a historical product of colonial and postcolonial experiences, has still gone largely unquestioned by the Mexican Left – provides for the possibility of immediate expulsion, without appeal, of all foreigners engaged in the internal political affairs of the

---

economy'. A first effort in 1989 to eliminate or at least reduce the reading of *Capital* in the Faculty of Economics of the UNAM failed against the resistance of a group of economics students known as *El Colectivo* [The Collective].

227 Third interview with Bolívar Echeverría, cassette II, side B, pos. 112.
228 See, for example, Echeverría 1977a, 1977b, 1977c, 1977d, 1977e. (See moreover the attached bibliography of Bolívar Echeverría, where we indicate all the reprints of the texts mentioned here in their first publication.)
229 Neus Espresate, in Villegas and Uribe 1975, p. 75.
230 Ibid. Adolfo Sánchez Rebolledo is the son of Adolfo Sánchez Vázquez.
231 Poniatowska 1995, p. 11.
232 Poniatowska 1995, p. 14. On the meaning of refugees from the Spanish Civil War for the (leftist) cultural and intellectual development of Mexico, see pp. ff of the biography of Sánchez Vázquez.

country. Nevertheless, these two names do appear as part of the editorial committee beginning with the third issue.

As Ediciones Era, since its founding in 1960, played a significant role both for Bolívar Echeverría (who published his first important book there) as well as for the non-dogmatic Mexican Left as a whole,[233] allow us to go into some length on the topic. The five founders, Neus Espresate, her brothers Jordi and Francisco, Vicente Rojo, and José Azorín, named the publishing house using the initials of their surnames.[234] During those years, the father of the Espresate siblings, Tomás Espresate, owned the small Madero Press in Mexico City, and was from the outset supportive of the goals of the publishing house. All of the press's founders were already known for their activity in the JSU, originally from Republican Spain.[235] Of the later personalities who were central to the press, aside from a single exception all had come from Spain, often as children, as a result of the Civil War and the defeat of the republicans by the Francoists. Héctor Manjarrez, who worked with Era beginning in 1972, would later describe the situation as follows: 'Now that I think about it, with the exception of Estela Forno – who is Guatemalan ... – this was a territory of Spanish republicans ... people with the very clear idea that some things needed to be done for the good of humanity, by way of the book. Franco was a curse for Spain, but a blessing for Mexico. This is well-known'.[236]

The publishing house is born shortly after the Cuban Revolution, and its first book – *La batalla de Cuba* [*The Battle of Cuba*], by Fernando Benítez (print run:

233 Sánchez Vázquez also publishes a series of his books in Ediciones Era: *Las ideas estéticas de Marx. Ensayos de estética marxista* (Sánchez Vázquez 1965b); *Estética y marxismo* (Sánchez Vázquez 1970); *Del socialismo científico al socialismo utópico* (Sánchez Vázquez 1975a); he also published through the same press, with his own introduction, Marx 1974.

   Likewise, he wrote prologues for the following books by European Marxists published by Ediciones Era: Karl Korsch, *Marxismo y filosofía* (Korsch 1971) and Palmiro Togliatti, *Escritos políticos*, translated by A. Rossi (Togliatti 1971).

   In the journal *Cuadernos Políticos*, from the same publishing house, Sánchez Vázquez published the following articles: 'El teoricismo de Althusser: notas críticas sobre una autocrítica', (no. 3, January–March 1975, pp. 82–99); 'La filosofía de la praxis como nueva práctica de la filosofía' (no. 12, April–June 1977); 'Marx y la democracia' (no. 36, April–June 1983, pp. 31–9); 'Once tesis sobre socialismo y democracia' (no. 52, October–December 1987, pp. 82–8); and 'Cuestiones marxistas disputadas', an interview by Vjekoslav Mikecin with Adolfo Sánchez Vázquez (no. 42, January–March 1985, pp. 5–19).

234 Poniatowska 1995.

235 Vicente Rojo, in Villegas and Uribe 1995, p. 61. On the history of the JSU, see also our biography of Sánchez Vázquez, pp. 21ff.

236 Héctor Manjarrez, in 'Son gente muy rara. Entrevista con Héctor Manjarrez' in Benítez 1995, pp. 41–9, here: p. 43.

5,000 copies) – deals precisely with that historical event.[237] Despite its courageous commitment, even in periods of open repression, the publisher was never openly prosecuted by the Mexican government, and nor was Spanish exile Sánchez Vázquez. Against the backdrop of the hundreds of political prisoners who were 'disappeared', tortured, and who after 1968 were forced to leave the country for political reasons, this is worthy of mention. (One reason for this, along with the fact that most Spanish exiles lived in the capital, which was a bit 'more secure', could lie in the fact that, even among governing circles, there was a certain degree of respect for 'the representatives of the other, non-colonialist and non-bourgeois Spain'.)

But, to return to the *Cuadernos Políticos*, issue 41 – published on the occasion of the journal's tenth anniversary – described the circumstances and intentions with which the journal was founded in 1974 in the following terms:

> That was a very particular moment in Latin American life. The increase in military coups, which began in Brazil in 1964, would reach its height in the year prior to the founding of *Cuadernos Políticos*, with the overthrow of the Chilean government of Popular Unity, and would even expand during the years that followed. Popular movements would suffer a string of defeats, country by country.... The climate of anxiety that this created could not but be reflected in the Latin American Left, which became polarised between those whose despondency led them to preach an alleged realism, occasionally bordering on capitulation, and those who opted for the more stubborn path when faced with the lessons of life, and who assumed a poorly-understood orthodoxy as their last resort.
>
> It was in Mexico that this situation emerged with greatest force. Political exiles arrived here every day, bringing with them their experiences and reflections, and often, their fears and internal disputes as well. This occurred in a country which – unlike the Southern Cone – recovered from the impact of 1968 and where the Left forged the means to re-channel its activities – in the universities, in the media, and later in political organisations – while the popular movement rose up once again, with the encouragement of insurgent unions. It was natural for intellectual activity to be intense and for initiatives on this plane to multiply.[238]

The 'increase in military coups' and resulting defeat of the left in South America brought with it the suspension of a number of leftist theoretical-political

---

237   See Benítez 1960.
238   Anonymous 1984 p. 2.

journals. Neus Espresate would later recall that this was an important reason for the birth of the *Cuadernos Políticos*, since a critical voice, at least in the form of a journal, needed to exist somewhere in Latin America.[239]

In the same period that the plans to release the *Cuadernos Políticos* were begun, significant military units rose up in Chile against the Popular Unity government, which was democratically elected and headed by president Salvador Allende Gossens. The coup let by Augusto Pinochet with United States support was followed by a repressive wave against all possible opponents, which affected tens of thousands.[240] On exactly that day, 11 September 1973, the last issue of *Punto Final*, a bimonthly journal that had been published in Santiago de Chile since 1965, appeared.[241] Shortly after the appearance of the first issue of *Cuadernos Políticos* in September of 1974,[242] came the final issue of the Uruguayan leftist weekly *Marcha*, which had been founded in 1939.[243] Likewise, the Argentinean leftist journal *Pasado y Presente* was no longer published in the aftermath of the coup of 24 March 1976. Another example

---

239 Neus Espresate, conversation with the author on 11 July 1996 in the headquarters of Ediciones Era in Mexico City (written notes). Espresate mentioned the journals: *Punto Final, Pasado y Presente*, and *Pensamiento Crítico*. Elsewhere, she made a similar indication regarding the context of the birth of *Cuadernos Políticos*, speaking of of *Pasado y Presente* and *Marcha* (see Benítez 1995, p. 75).

240 The best known victims of the Pinochet régime were the deposed President Allende and the musician Victor Jara. After the coup, Jara would play the guitar and sing for the more than ten thousand politically motivated detainees in the stadium in Santiago de Chile. His captors would then smash both of his hands to pieces. When Jara continued to sing unaccompanied in the stadium, the Pinochetists destroyed his tongue, causing his death.

The massive US support for Pinochet – motivated in particular by the Popular Unity government having nationalised the largest copper deposits in the world and thus removing them from immediate capitalist access, which was clearly unforgivable – was perhaps a reason behind the Latin American Left distancing itself, towards the end of the 1980s, from the parliamentary democracy so celebrated in the United States.

It is also important to grasp, as we have said previously, the fact that in Mexico the critique of Stalinism appeared late or not at all. The blunt support of the United States for all repressive Latin American régimes and, in part, its support for the coups that brought these governments to power, led the government in Washington to lose all credibility with its talk of democracy.

241 The dates of the final issue are: *Punto Final*, year 7, no. 192 (Santiago de Chile: 11 September 1973).

242 The dates of the first issue are: *Cuadernos Políticos*, year 1, no. 1 (Mexico, July–September 1974).

243 See *Marcha*, year 1, no. 1 (Montevideo: Prensa Latina, 23 June 1939). Suspended 22 November 1974, with year 36, no. 1676.

was Cuba, where there was no bloody coup, but where the growing internal difficulties – which also had an impact on cultural policy – lead to the suspension of a critical periodical; as early as June 1971, publication of the well-known nondogmatic leftist journal *Pensamiento Crítico* ceased, after four years of publication.[244] Against this political-social background, sketched out for Mexico and Latin America, the editorial board formulated the theoretical-political objectives of the *Cuadernos Políticos*, which they would retrospectively see, upon the tenth anniversary of the journal's birth, as being: 'the project of an independent Marxist journal. Independent *vis-à-vis* the state, of course, but also *vis-à-vis* political parties; but above all, independent of those currents of opinion which, from within the Left, sought to convert Marxism into a narrow and sectarian doctrine or – worse still – to make it faceless, to the point of degrading it to be a useless and boned philosophy'.[245]

The purpose was, in other words, 'taking up Marxism as a space for work – to promote a broad reflection on Latin American and Mexican problematic, without losing sight of the global framework that over determines them'.[246] With regard to the new situation at the moment of the tenth anniversary, the editors proposed: 'The plan for *Cuadernos Políticos*, in sum, corresponds to a moment in the theoretical and political development of Mexico, of Latin America, and of Marxism. This moment is characterised by the fragmentation of the Left and the need to formulate responses to problems both new and old'.[247]

Echeverría, a member of the board, understood the purpose of the *Cuadernos Políticos* as follows: 'neither strictly orientated towards day-to-day politics, nor super theoretical, nor academic, nor journalistic... [but instead] a discourse of reflection on politics'.[248] Later, with regard to the realisation of this longed-for combination of theory and praxis in the thematic spectrum of the *Cuadernos Políticos*, Echeverría recalled:

> I believe that at particular moments we did succeed in doing that. But afterward we fell precisely into one or the other.... We fell into either analyses, which were orientated too directly towards day-to-day politics, or very abstract studies.... [The original project] was in some ways connected to a certain upsurge that occurred in the workers' movement

---

244   See *Pensamiento Crítico*, year 1, no. 1 (Havana: Centro de Estudios Latinoamericanos, 1 February 1967). Suspended in June 1971, with year 5, no. 53.
245   Anonymous 1984.
246   Anonymous 1984.
247   Anonymous 1984, p. 3.
248   Third interview with Bolívar Echeverría, cassette II, side B, pos. 252–6.

here [above all in the independent unions] with regard to the electricians. This was a very interesting, and very workerist, very proletarian moment...So, while this existed, the period was also good, and good things were produced. Then when this [passed], we turned into sociologists, a bunch of studies of the working class in, I don't know, the seamstress of northern Mexico, the...these boring sociological studies, and theory – grand theory [said ironically]. We imported articles, translations from *New Left Review*, from here and there.[249]

The format of the journal, almost square, was 'Cuban-inspired'[250] and recalled that of the island's post-revolutionary journals, such as *Casa de las Américas*, which since 1960 has been published by the cultural organism of the same name.[251] The pages of the *Cuadernos Políticos*, generally numbering 120, were filled with texts discussed exhaustively in the weekly editorial sessions at the home of Neus Espresate.[252] Bolívar Echeverría, 'present from the first day to the last', was, for Espresate, 'the theoretical head of the board, with a very good general vision of contemporary theoretical discussions in Mexico, Latin America, and Europe'. Echeverría was, moreover, in charge of foreign contacts, and specifically with Europe.[253] Neus Espresate recalled this in the following terms in 1996: 'For the generation of those who are now in the middle or toward the end of their fifth decade of life, the generation of '68, the journal was very important as a point of departure for their thought and discussions.

---

249 Ibid. The actions of the electrical workers that Echeverría mentions here occurred at the beginning of the 1960s and culminated between late 1975 and early 1976. They were organised by the Democratic Tendency within the Electrical Workers' Union of the Mexican Republic, which separated from the vertical control of the Mexican Confederation of Workers, a union strictly faithful to the government. These acts followed the actions of the railworkers' union in 1958–9 and managed some large mobilisations, even outside of the electricians' circles.

Echeverría published various articles under the pseudonym 'Javier Lieja' in the Electricians' Union journal *Solidarity* between 1969 and 1970. See the 'Bibliography of Bolívar Echeverría'.

250 Echeverría 1995d, p. 36.
251 See *Revista Casa de las Américas. Órgano de la Casa de las Américas*, year 1 (Havana 1960).
252 Neus Espresate, conversation with the author. Espresate's formulations are reproduced here according to the author's written notes.
253 Ibid.

In many university seminars at the time, for example, articles from it were a fundamental part of the required reading'.²⁵⁴

The journal was equally or even more important for Bolívar Echeverría than it had been for Mexico and Latin America. Discussions among the editorial board, to which the most signifcant leftist authors belonged, were for him, over the years, the only place for the continuous analysis of 'more political, social, and economic approaches' without which 'I would be lost in ... objects of pure theory'.²⁵⁵

'... [T]he journal's greatest merit' – the board wrote in 1984 on the tenth anniversary of its establishment – 'is having known how to overcome that fragmentation and demonstrating that differences do not prevent us from seeking answers through fraternal dialogue and the practice of solidarity'.²⁵⁶ At the time that these lines were written, the board had already changed with regard to its original constellation in virtue of internal political-theoretical differences. Rolando Cordera, and later Adolfo Sánchez Rebolledo and Arnaldo Córdova, left the board of *Cuadernos Políticos*. Cordera would move closer – in his positions and institutional linkages – to the governing Institutional

---

254   Ibid.
255   Third interview with Bolívar Echeverría, cassette II, side B, pos. 335–8. In the 1996 interview, I asked Echeverría:

   '*Was this participation important for your own political-theoretical development?*'

   'In *Cuadernos Políticos* yes, because it was the only place that I had a connection to more political discussions and all that. For me it was very important, because if not for that I would be lost in my purely theoretical things. But there [it was] good: I discussed and read all sorts of articles, because we read all the articles, we discussed article by article. It was a very serious journal. The articles were distributed to everyone and we had a session discussing every article. This was very good. So I read all kinds of things there. It was very important for me, because it kept me tied a bit to more political, social, and economic themes, because I tend to be more ...

   '*So this allowed you to avoid falling into the same situation as Heidegger?* [In allusion to a previous passage in the interview, in which Bolívar Echeverría explains Heidegger's participation in National Socialism with, among other reasons, the fact that the latter left aside the real world in his studies and analysis.]

   'The antidote [laughs].

   '*And what do you do these days ... ?*

   '[Laughing] Now we have the Zapatistas, now we have the Subcomandante [Marcos's] communiqués ...' (pos. 333–50).
256   Anonymous 1984.

Revolutionary Party (PRI)[257] and join the journal *Nexos*,[258] which consisted of intellectuals close to the PRI.[259]

With the double issue 59–60 on the topic *1989: Twelve months that changed Eastern Europe*, the journal ceased publication in August 1990 after sixteen years of uninterrupted publication.[260] Bolívar Echeverría provided a detailed introduction for the issue[261] without falling into tearful sentimentality and without following many ex-leftists in their turn toward the celebration of capitalism. He attempted, instead, in light of the news of mass fleeing – then underway – by the inhabitants of those countries characterised as 'actually existing socialism', to highlight everyday ways of escaping the consequences of the capitalist mode of production. Echeverría, in this piece, understands both social forms as, in the final instance, two variants of the European version of modernity. A decisive weakness of this text, however, lies in the fact that his critique of the blind jubilation at the collapse of actually existing socialism (and the concomitant consolidation of an even more powerfully unified global capitalist system) is limited almost exclusively to the economic realm and he does not dedicate a single word to something central to the symbol he is analysing: while it is true that he analyses the so-called 'fall' of the wall between East Berlin, capital of the GDR, and West Berlin through symbolic and ideology critique, what escapes our Latin American author – who spent a significant portion of his life in West Berlin – is the central motive for the jubilation at

---

257   The political system of the governing party in power in Mexico during most of the twentieth century knew how to combine with precision selective repression and the cooptation of parties and individuals critical of the régime. In particular, president Carlos Salinas de Gortari (1988–94) was able to attract to government ranks a good number of leftist intellectuals, like those coming out of the *Movimiento de Acción Popular* [Popular Action Movement]

258   In the 1990s, the journal *Nexos* had, moreover, its own weekly political talk show on the state television channel (Channel 13 of Imevisión) directed by Rolando Cordera, former member of the *Cuadernos Políticos* editorial board.

259   Third interview with Bolívar Echeverría, cassette II, side B, pos. 313–33.

 Adolfo Sánchez Rebolledo was, alongside Neus Espresate, the initiator of the *Cuadernos Políticos* journal project. When it was founded he was director of the leftist politics journal *Punto Crítico*. (See Espresate, in Villegas and Uribe 1995, pp. 74ff, and also Echeverría 1995d, p. 35 – here, Echeverría characterises *Punto Crítico* as a 'radical journal of the Left'. Moreover: Third interview with Bolívar Echeverría, cassette II, side B, pos. 313–33, where Bolívar Echeverría, referring to the year 1974, suggests that Adolfo Sánchez Rebolledo was part of the Mexican Left, with a 'Leninist' orientation).

260   *Cuadernos Políticos*, no. 59/60 (Mexico City, January–August 1990), special issue: *1989. Twelve months that changed Eastern Europe*.

261   See Echeverría 1990b. This essay is included under the title '1989' in Echeverría 1995a, pp. 13–23.

the 'attack' (which was state-sanctioned, but allegedly a spontaneous action of the masses) on the 'anti-fascist protective wall' (in the language of the government of the GDR). The Berlin Wall owed its existence indirectly to National Socialism and, therefore, constituted a sort of unwanted monument to the millions of Jews, gypsies (Sinti and Roma), and others who were murdered, as well as to the millions of war dead in the countries which were attacked, especially the Soviet Union. So it is surprising how Echeverría – who during his Berlin period was perfectly well-aware of the survival of Nazi myths in everyday life – at the very moment in which the elimination of checkpoints between the two Germanies (which ultimately did not interest anyone in the FRG) gave rise to hysterical celebration, forgot one of the primary motives inspiring Germans on both sides: namely, the definitive forgetting of the unpunished crimes committed under National Socialism by many more people than tends to be suggested, and to which large portions of the population gave their consent, if not support.[262]

To return to the cessation of the publication of *Cuadernos Políticos* in 1989, the motive did not lie in sales statistics, since the demand for the *Cuadernos* remained constant, but rather – as Neus Espresate understands it – in a 'great silence by the Left', related to its fright at the rapid disappearance of the Soviet Union.[263] Five years later, Bolívar Echeverría would explain the end of a journal, which was so important for him, in the following terms, also expressing his current point of view with regard to the relationship between theory and praxis:

> The extinction of *Cuadernos Políticos* is inscribed within a larger fact that had already begun to develop prior to the collapse of the Soviet system and its 'actually existing socialism': the end of the period of existence of this very specific form of publications represented by theoretical-political journals that were both critical and leftist. This is truly a question of the end of all kinds of theoretical-political discourse; a discourse that set out

---

262 On more recent investigations of the topic, see Goldhagen 1996, for example, pp. 3ff. After studying voluminous archives, Goldhagen concludes, 'tens of thousands of ordinary Germans... became genocidal killers' (p. 4).

We will return to the problem Echeverría sketches out regarding the opening of the intra-Berlin borders in the subchapter: 'An Example of the Limitations of the Concept of *Ethos*', p. 331 of this book.

263 Neus Espresate, conversation with the author on 11 July 1996. In the discussion, Espresate recalled that there were no longer even many texts that could have been published, since in 1990 the existing leftist political culture came to an end. The journal 'died a natural death'. The internal conflicts within the editorial board, which resulted (according to Espresate) from everyone looking hard for different escapes from the crisis of the Left, played a subordinate role.

from the assumption of a spontaneous double harmony; the belief, in the first place, that a certain relationship of complementarity exists between the academic and the public, the scientific and the militant, theory and praxis; and the conviction, secondly, that a natural affinity if not an identity prevails between the rationality of discourse and the 'logic' of revolutionary classes, between Enlightenment and Revolution. With the illusion of this double harmony dispelled by historical experience, and with an insurmountable contradiction between discourse and praxis and between reason and revolution exposed – often brutally – in its place, all editorial projects which, like *Cuadernos Políticos*, attempted to express this theoretical-political discourse found itself in need of radically reconsidering its own constitution.

The conviction that it is possible and necessary to awaken and explore both this complementarity and this affinity cannot disappear from a theoretical-political discourse that sets out from the recognition that, despite everything, revolution and democracy are situated on the horizon of the desirable and the possible; that capitalist modernity and its destructive consequences are not an ineluctable destination, and that the will to radically transform it is already there, clearing the way from the very bases of the social body. But the situation within which such a conviction must be affirmed has become substantially more difficult than in previous periods.

A project to interactively connect rational discourse with the practice of radically transforming the established social reality should be today – when the reason of technocratic modernisation and the regressive practice that opposes it seem to agree on the pursuit of catastrophe – more urgent than ever. However, despite the fact that their conjunction would be the only guarantee that civilised life is still possible, critical discourse and the practice of critique neither coincide nor join together spontaneously. Unlike previously, their coincidence and union can no longer serve as the natural starting point for political theory and practice; they are, to the contrary, something that remains to be found, which must be sought and invented.

The form of theoretical-political discourse expressed in *Cuadernos Políticos* was, as is everything, a historically limited and finite form. But it was the form of a project that, nevertheless, has not ceased to be valid and necessary, and that seeks a new and different form, one that is more keeping with contemporary times.[264]

---

264 Echeverría 1995d, pp. 38–40.

At the beginning of the 1990s, various voices – inspired by a similar concern – would bring to Ediciones Era the request that *Cuadernos Políticos* or a comparable journal be reinitiated, but this has not happened.[265]

Back to Philosophy

On 1 November 1976, Ingrid Weikert gave birth to her son Andrés, who grew up bilingual with his Spanish-speaking father and German-speaking mother. Among other things, Weikert taught German classes at the Goethe Institute of Mexico and the Department of Modern Languages and Literatures at the UNAM; she would later be a full-time professor of German philology at the Faculty of Philosophy and Arts of the UNAM. In the early 1980s, Echeverría separated from his wife and later lived with Raquel Serur, born in Mexico City and daughter of Jewish exiles from South-Eastern Europe. On 6 October 1984 and 16 June 1986, she gives birth to their children, first Albert and then Carlos.[266] Serur studied for her master's degree in Literature in England in the early 1980s.[267] She would later be a full-time professor in the Department of Modern Languages and Literatures at the Faculty of Philosophy and Arts at the UNAM. Echeverría regularly visited Ecuador and his family there, occasionally giving courses at universities in that country.[268] His articles were published

---

265   Neus Espresate, Conversation with the author, 11 July 1996.
266   Raquel Serur, Interview with the author, 4 July 1996.
267   Ibid. Serur also experienced the fact that there does not always exist in Europe the great tolerance that Latin Americans sometimes like to expect from the 'old continent'. Overnight, both the original evaluator of her M.A. thesis on Jorge Luis Borges as well as other scholars consulted in 1982 refused to accept it as a thesis, because in light of the Malvinas War (April–June 1982) it was impossible for them to see themselves in contact with an Argentine writer. (Conversation with Raquel Serur in early January 1996 in Mexico City).
268   Thus, for example: monographic course on the theme of 'Reproducción social y cultura material [Social reproduction and material culture]', IADAP, Quito, Spring 1979; master's course on the topic 'Seminario sobre *El Capital* [Seminar on *Capital*]', Spring 1980; monographic course on the topic 'Revisión de *El Capital* [Revisions to *Capital*]', School of Sociology, Universidad Central del Ecuador, Spring 1980; monographic course on the theme 'Cultura, Sociedad e Historia [Culture, society, and history]', Casa de la Cultura Ecuatoriana, Quito, Summer 1985; monographic course on the topic 'El Mestizaje y la Sociedad Criolla [*Mestizaje* and *criollo* society]', Casa de la Cultura Ecuatoriana, Quito, Summer 1986; master's course on 'La cultura política en América Latina [Political culture in Latin America]', Summer 1991; monographic course on 'La cultura política en las sociedades andinas [Political culture in Andean societies]', CIESE, Quito, Summer 1991; master's course on 'La modernidad en América Latina [Modernity in Latin America]', Universidad Andina Simón Bolívar, early 1996 (see Echeverría 1996a, pp. 8, 12–14).

and often republished in various Ecuadorian journals, for example in *Nariz del Diablo*, run by his brother Julio Echeverría.[269] And nor did he abandon his contact with Berlin, visiting his most important friends there every two or three years, central among these being Horst Kurnitzky.[270]

In 1986, Bolívar Echeverría published through Ediciones Era his first important book, entitled *El discurso crítico de Marx* [*Marx's Critical Discourse*].[271] The following year, he was given a full-time professorship in the Faculty of Philosophy and Arts at the UNAM, thereafter resigning from his position in the Faculty of Economies at the same university.[272] In 1991, he graduated as Maestro [Master] in Economics with a thesis on the topic: *Apunte crítico sobre los esquemas de la reproducción esbozados por Karl Marx en 'El Capital'* [*A critical note on the outlines of reproduction sketched by Karl Marx in* 'Capital'].[273]

From 1991 to 1993, he coordinated a research project at the Faculty of Philosophy and Arts, '*El concepto de mestizaje cultural y la historia de la cultura en la América Española del siglo XVII* [The concept of cultural *mestizaje* and the history of culture in seventeenth-century Spanish America]', and beginning in

---

269 'Nariz del Diablo' is the name of a mountain peak in Ecuador. Bolívar Echeverría also published in the following journals in Quito: *Pucuna, La Bufanda del Sol, Revista Latinoamericana, Letras del Ecuador* (ed. Casa de la Cultura Ecuatoriana), *Procontra*, and *Palabra Suelta*. His essay 'Discurso de la revolución, discurso crítico [Discourse on revolution, critical discourse]', which appeared in 1976 in *Cuadernos Políticos*, was simultaneously published in Quito in a volume edited by Agustín Cueva. See the attached bibliography of Bolívar Echeverría.

270 Kurnitzky, for his part, travelled regularly to Mexico and introduced the German public to contemporary Mexican culture. See: Beck and Kurnitzky 1975, 1982.

In part of their publications, an animated exchange occurs between the two authors, above all in relation to the theme of use-value as well as the correlative relationship to economics, culture, and (internal) nature; see in this regard the following books by Kurnitzky: *Versuch über den Gebrauchswert* (1970); *Triebstruktur des Geldes. Ein Beitrag zur Theorie der Weiblichkeit* (1974); *Museum des Geldes. Über die seltsame Natur des Geldes in Kunst, Wissenschaft und Leben. Eine Ausstellung* (1978a); *Ödipus. Ein Held der westlichen Welt. Über die zerstörerischen Grundlagen unserer Zivilisation* (1978b); *Der heilige Markt. Kulturhistorische Anmerkungen* (1994).

271 Echeverría 1986.

272 Third interview with Bolívar Echeverría, cassette II, side B, pos. 090.

273 Tutor: Pedro López Díaz. Defended on September 12, 1991 to the Division of Postgraduate Studies of the UNAM Faculty of Economics. The final master's thesis was published twice, after light revisions: *La circulación capitalista y la reproducción de la riqueza social. (Apunte crítico sobre los 'Esquemas de Reproducción' esbozados por K. Marx en 'El Capital')* (Echeverría 1992), and *Circulación capitalista y reproducción de la riqueza social. Apunte crítico sobre los Esquemas de K. Marx* (Echeverría 1994a).

1994, as a continuation, the research project '*El concepto de cultura política y la vida política en América Latina* [The concept of political culture and political life in Latin America]',[274] in whose sessions and discussions Horst Kurnitzky also frequently participated. The concept of 'cultural *mestizaje*' referred to the process, present with especially great force in Mexico, in which pre-Hispanic traditions – or the remains thereof – join together with Spanish and European tradition. This concept would play a central role in Echeverría's later work, and its translation into English as 'cultural mixture' is not the most adequate – and the same could be said of the racist proposals of certain Spanish-English dictionaries, which translate the term as 'crossing of races',[275] as a result of which we have decided to maintain the Spanish term *mestizaje*.

What is meant by the concept of cultural *mestizaje* is completely visible in everyday Mexican culture, for example in food: there are tacos on every street corner, which have as their basis the pre-Hispanic corn tortilla, but with a filling almost always including as a central component beef or pork, which were only used in Mexico after colonisation. The primary condiment is, almost without exception, a very hot sauce made from chillies, which is also derived from pre-Hispanic tradition. Such processes are observed to a greater degree in Mexico than in many other Latin American countries. In Guatemala, for example, a middle-class urban inhabitant would not understand by 'tortilla' the corn variety, and much less would he or she exchange the latter for the Spanish tortilla made of egg and potato. One cause of these differences lies in the Mexican Revolution of 1910, in which, at least in specific spaces and classes, the racial segregation that continues to be widely practiced across much of the American continent and the world, was punctured. Another cause of this Mexican particularity – which should also not be underestimated and of which the Zapatista uprising of 1 January 1994 would serve as a reminder – is the Mexican independence movement of the early nineteenth century, which itself already contained, more so than other such movements in Latin America, more social elements which were moreover oriented against the 'separation of the races'. The previously mentioned objects of culinary investigation, which might seem hardly theoretical to some philosophers, constitute the material for the discussions in the mentioned research projects. Consider, in this regard, the following passage from one such discussion:

---

274   Echeverría 1996a p. 11.
275   See Cuyas 1956, p. 364. See also *Wörterbuch der spanischen und deutschen Sprache* 1975, p. 739, where the term, in a similar way, is translated as 'Rassenkreuzung' ['racial crossbreeding'].

Raquel Serur: ... on another occasion we had mentioned the need to pose culinary *mestizaje* as a form of cultural *mestizaje*. I said then, for example, that in the usage of chilli in Mexican cooking there exists a complex game between the chilli as an enhancer of flavours and as a saboteur of flavours. Here, the conflict of culinary practice represents a conflict on another level, on the deeper plane of understandings and misunderstandings between different cultural identities...

Bolívar Echeverría: ... Culinary art is also a very important semiotic field. In the case of the formation of Mexican food, of *mestiza* food, we can discover a veritable war of position between two codes – that which is imposed and that which resists – which is taking place in the kitchen, on the table, or even on the plate itself. Pre-Hispanic culture (which already at that moment existed only as a series of cultural ruins) engages in a veritable siege with the chilli on the one side and the tortilla on the other; it mounts a pliers operation, within which practically all flavours could fit. It is in the middle of this that the Europeans then introduce an element, which seeks to open it, to break the gustatory encirclement that has been set against them; it is there that they introduce the element of meat.[276]

It is from these research projects that the anthology *Modernidad, mestizaje cultural, ethos barroco* [*Modernity, cultural* mestizaje, *baroque* ethos] emerged, appearing in 1995.[277] That same year, Echeverría's second important book appeared (comprised entirely of his own texts): *Las ilusiones de la modernidad* [*The illusions of modernity*],[278] which was originally supposed to carry the title

---

276   Echeverría, Kurnitzky, and Serur 1993, p. 26 and pp. 28ff. This small volume (Echeverría and Kurnitzky 1993) also contains contributions from Horst Kurnitzky, Carlos Aguirre, and María Alba Pastor.

277   See Echeverría (ed.) 1994b. This collected volume contains texts from some outstanding Mexican intellectuals, like the historian Antonio García de León and the writer Carlos Monsiváis. The latter writes on the topic of 'The neo-baroque and popular culture' (pp. 299–309). The prestigious art historian Teresa del Conde also contributes (see also our 'Bibliography of Bolívar Echeverría').

The nucleus of the research group for this first project comprised María Alba Pastor, Carlos Aguirre, and Raquel Serur. Other collaborators included: María Massa, Eduardo Peñaloza, Tania Mena, Karla Zurián, and Marco Aurelio García Barrios (pp. 8ff). The most important participants in the second research project are: Pedro Joel Reyes, Antonio García de León, Patricia Nettel, Raquel Serur, María Alba Pastor, and Marco Aurelio García Barrios (Echeverría 1996a, p. 11).

278   See Echeverría 1995a.

Modernidad y capitalismo [*Modernity and capitalism*],[279] but due to the wishes of the publisher[280] now carried a 'less Marxist' title. With the publication of these books in 1994–5 and an interview in the nationally circulated newspaper *La Jornada* in June 1996,[281] Echeverría comes to be known and recognised not only (as he already was) in Mexico City, but also beyond it. This resulted in invitations, like that by Immanuel Wallerstein to carry out research for a year at the Fernand Braudel Center in Binghamton, New York,[282] and the bestowal in 1998 of one of the most important Mexican prizes for the philosophical and social sciences, the *Premio Nacional* [National Prize] of the UNAM. Already several years earlier, there were few public launches for (non-dogmatic) leftist books to which he was not invited as a speaker. For more than just one new project for a critical journal, it was now a question of including him as an author as well.[283]

To his role as one of the most outstanding intellectuals on the non-dogmatic Mexican Left, Bolívar Echeverría would need to respond in a form that the majority of faculty members, and not only in Mexico, would have preferred to forget and disapprove of, with all tranquility of consciousness, as inopportune. On 1 January 1994, the day that the free trade agreement between Canada, the United States, and Mexico (NAFTA, the North American Free Trade Agreement) entered into force, an armed indigenous rebellion broke out in the South-East of Mexico, in the Lacandón Jungle and the Los Altos region of the state of Chiapas. The EZLN, which now became known to Mexico and later to the world, through its praxis and its declarations broke down the wall of

---

279   In the notes on the authors of the previously mentioned anthology, the book is still announced with this title and is described as 'in print': see Echeverría 1994b, p. 390).
280   Bolívar Echeverría, conversation with the author in 1995, Mexico City.
281   See Alberto Cue, 'Por una modernidad alternativa. Entrevista con Bolívar Echeverría', in *La Jornada Semanal*, Mexico City, 2 June 1996, pp. 10f.
282   Bolívar Echeverría, by invitation of Immanuel Wallerstein, spent the period from Summer 1998 to Summer 1999 in this research center at SUNY-Binghamton. [Note to the edition in English: on 20 March 1997, Echeverría obtains the title *Doctor en Filosofía* (PhD in Philosophy) from the Faculty of Philosophy and Arts of the UNAM with a thesis 'Lo barroco y la historia de la cultura [The baroque (way of being) and the history of culture]', with Carlos Pereda as adviser, published with some minor changes as book: *La modernidad de lo barroco*, Echeverría 1998a. The principal change in the book is that the main sections have been reordered. The second part of the thesis ('II. En torno al ethos barroco [On the baroque ethos]', pp. 97–202) became the similarly-titled but unnumbered first part of the book (pp. 17–118); after that comes the rest of the thesis, generally in the original order.]
283   See, for example, the first issue of the journal *Viento del Sur* (Mexico City). Founded by Adolfo Gilly, it was inspired by the Zapatista rebellion, and first appeared in April 1994. There, in the section 'Ideas', we find Echeverría 1994c, 'Postmodernidad y cinismo'.

silence and forgetting[284] that had been built around indigenous peoples and their (generally extreme) poverty.[285] In early July 1996 in San Cristóbal de las Casas, Bolívar Echeverría participated (as an advisor to the EZLN) in the Special Forum for State Reform called by the Ejército Zapatista de Liberación Nacional [Zapatista Army of National Liberation], giving a presentation in the session dedicated to the topic 'Transición a la democracia en México [Transition to democracy in Mexico]'.[286]

This forum was, with regard to domestic Mexican discussions with the Zapatistas, the most important event since the great leftist assembly called by the EZLN at the first 'Aguascalientes'[287] constructed beside the village of Guadalupe Tepeyac (Chiapas) in the summer of 1994. Formally, he was an integral part of the EZLN's negotiations with the Mexican government, and the outcome of the final resolutions was sent to Congress for debate. The 'democra-

---

284 The best-known member of the Zapatista Army for National Liberation understands their war as a struggle against oblivion. See, in this regard: 'The government's position says that it wants to eliminate the causes that made us an oppositional force so that we can become part of the government. We say that this is a lie, because they aren't going to be able to solve the causes or resolve the demands of the communities for health, land, work, housing, food because they don't have money, they are in a crisis and aren't willing to invest. They only put money where they will get more, with the mentality of businessmen. The governors cease to govern and set themselves to the administration of a business. Mexico ceases to be a country and becomes a business with parts that are profitable and others that don't yield a profit. The indigenous people are the ones who don't produce a profit. If you don't produce a profit you're fired, but since they can't fire them from the country, they need to annihilate them with bullets, with oblivion. They simply begin to make decisions as though they didn't exist. This is the fundamental origin of the Zapatista uprising. It is a war against oblivion'. Subcomandante Marcos, cited in Francoise Escarpit, 'El gobierno, sin una línea clara de negociación, asegura Marcos', in La Jornada (Mexico City, 27 December 1995).
285 On the background and details of the Zapatista rebellion, see, for example, Largend 1995.
286 The basis of this speech is Echeverría's essay 'Postmodernidad y cinismo' (or alternatively 'Postmodernismo y cinismo') (Bolívar Echeverría, conversation with the author, Mexico City, 9 June 1996). See Echeverría 1994c. The same essay appears under the title 'Postmodernidad y cinicismo' in Echeverría 1995a, pp. 39–54. For a German translation by Stefan Gandler, see Echeverría 1996b.
287 'Aguascalientes' is what the Zapatistas call the meeting places they have established on various occasions in the Lacandón Jungle, which house thousands of people with meager means. The name refers to the capital of the Mexican state of Aguascalientes, where the 'Aguascalientes Convention' was held during the Mexican Revolution, in which the bases were established for a new, post-revolutionary constitution, with the participation of the two most radical Mexican revolutionaries: Emiliano Zapata and Pancho Villa. [Note to the edition in English: for some recent reflections on the work and life of Bolívar Echeverría, see: Gandler 2010.]

tisation' of the state was held by the Mexican government (and supported not only by its own partisans) to be intimately related with the 'modernisation' of the country. What this means is often confusing. It certainly suggests modernisation in the technical-industrial sense, but in reality this is not the case, since the neoliberal (or *laissez-faire*) policies applied since the 1980s have resulted in a tendency toward the de-industrialisation of the country. 'Modernisation', praised by many, in reality means, above all, the unshakable validity of capitalist mechanisms, which up to this point still coexisted with regulative state intervention, practiced in part according to the model of actually existing socialism. 'Modernisation', according to this view, means, for example, the shrinking of the state. We can also see as part of this actually existing 'modernisation' the *de facto* suspension of Article 27 of the Constitution, which originated during the Revolution and which prohibits the sale of large portions of arable agricultural lands (especially that of the *ejidos*, which are communally cultivated). But large sectors of the population and many of those critical of the government understood 'modernisation' to mean putting an end to state corruption and the old power elites. It is hoped that by 'looking like the First World' these sectors' 'modern political culture' will make its appearance in Mexico, thereby resolving old problems. It is in the context of these prevalent debates, one on democracy and the other on modernisation, that Echeverría's theoretical position can be located.

The concept of revolution, similarly subjected to general critical analysis by Echeverría in his theory, is, in Mexico, in the majority of political contexts, much more frequently used than is the case in Germany. Something similar occurs with the concept of the nation, which is also on everyone's tongue and often refers to national independence *vis-à-vis* the United States. In general, the need for 'national unity' is thus elevated in order to, so the argument goes, stand strong against attempts at foreign intervention. Internal differences, for example of a linguistic nature, are seen by practically all political currents as a danger to 'national unity', and as a result, the more than fifty existing languages aside from Spanish are understood as an unavoidable evil. And this situation was not transformed much either by the EZLN's armed rebellion or the countless rounds of conversation, assemblies, and so on, with the (majority urban) Spanish-speaking Left, who lack interest in the problems created by ignoring the *de facto* existence of a multilingual Mexico. Up to the present, most act as though this were a problem that will be resolved by the purported gradual disappearance of the other languages.

Echeverría's theory is one of the few to emerge in Mexico, which – without redefining the question as though it were ethnological – enters into these contradictions.

CHAPTER 3

The 'State of Art'

a   On Social Philosophy in Latin America

In setting out upon the present study, we followed the plan of spanning the entirety of social philosophy in Latin America. It soon became clear that to do so would be excessively audacious for a single person and that, moreover, despite the best intentions, this was based on a Eurocentric idea, as though the formation of social-philosophical theory in Latin America were so limited as to be possible to condense into such a text on the basis of a few years of research. Nevertheless, allow us to look briefly at the results obtained in the first such inquiries, and especially as regards the situation of the literature written in Europe and the United States on this topic.

First of all, we must indicate that a large part (and in some countries, the majority) of writings appearing in Europe on Latin American (social) philosophy have come from the pen of authors themselves born in Latin America. Many came to the 'old continent' to study for a degree or their doctorate; others, as exiles or the children of exiles. The latter is the case above all in the cases of France and Spain;[288] the former, above all in Germany.

In the United States, there likewise exist several works on the topic, written by immigrants from Latin America or their descendants, which are complemented by translations of texts, which appeared, or were at least written, in Latin America.

With regard to the reflection of Latin American Marxist philosophy in Europe, we can note that there exists an incalculable fixation on dogmatic authors. Some of José Carlos Mariátegui's writings seem to be the exception, although it is debatable to what degree his theory constitutes a true critique of Soviet Marxism or merely a 'Latin Americanised' way of reading it.[289] Both bourgeois and Marxist-Leninist authors set out, as if it were the most natural thing in the world, from the idea that Marxist and Marxist-Leninist theories were the same thing. Thus, non-dogmatic Marxist texts – in both philosophy

---

288   See the attached 'Selected bibliography on Marxist philosophy in Latin America' (and in particular, Mexico).

289   See, in this regard, the marginal notes on José Carlos Mariátegui on p. 59 of this book. Studies on Mariátegui, however, have in their overwhelming majority appeared in Latin America. See the selected bibliography cited in the previous footnote.

and other sciences – pass unnoticed,[290] or are merely considered as exotic footnotes in the development of bourgeois or Marxist-Leninist theories. This simplistic manner of viewing things can be observed not only in research on Latin American social philosophy carried out in Europe or in the United States, but also in synoptic works produced in Latin America itself. In this way, non-dogmatic Marxist authors are always allocated, by the representatives of one of the two theoretical camps, precisely to the opposite one. It seems as though neither side is very fond of them.

b On Adolfo Sánchez Vázquez and Bolívar Echeverría

Two clear examples of this attitude appear with regard to Adolfo Sánchez Vázquez's work. We refer to two theses ('*Dissertation A*') written during the last eleven years of the GDR's existence. The first is from the year 1988 and was written at the Karl Marx University in Leipzig by the Cuban Jorge Luis Acanda González.[291] He formulates his thesis on the basis of a dogmatic Marxist position; while recognising a 'progressive intent' in Sánchez Vázquez,[292] he nevertheless condemns his philosophy for containing 'in the end an erroneous idealist interpretation of the practical life process'.

The following formulations by Acanda González also clearly express this way of understanding Sánchez Vázquez's work: 'the principal element of praxis is of a subjective nature, that is, an effect of consciousness';[293] and also: 'despite his ... declarations in opposition to subjectivism and anthropologism, Sánchez Vázquez assumes these same positions'.[294] According to Acanda González's interpretation, Sánchez Vázquez, in formulating his *Philosophy of Praxis*, makes poor use of central concepts like 'materialism' and 'objectivity', in order to finally arrive at the horrifying 'principal objective' of this 'incorrect use of terms': 'the interpretation of Marxism as Marxism-Leninism is stubbornly rejected by the author throughout his work'.[295]

But what the Cuban doctoral candidate in Leipzig especially laments is the fact that Sánchez Vázquez, with his *Philosophy of Praxis*, 'in any case throws

---

290 See, for example, GRAL 1979, Carr 1991 and Liss 1991. (In all three cases, the authors understand Marxism only in its dogmatic form).
291 Acanda González 1988.
292 Acanda González 1988, appendix: 'Thesen zur Dissertation A', p. 10.
293 Acanda González 1988, p. 85.
294 Acanda González 1988, p. 88.
295 Acanda González 1988, p. 93.

the Leninist positions of his previous works overboard',[296] which is precisely what constitutes the importance of his work as one of the cornerstones of non-dogmatic Marxism in Latin America. Acanda González comes to see this in a certain sense, but he immediately limits its importance: 'his search for an anti-dogmatic Marxism leads him to extreme positions', which are expressed in the 'complete rejection of almost all philosophy originating in the socialist countries'.[297] What precisely this 'complete rejection'[298] means is something that the author leaves up in the air.

If this work gives the impression that the author has certain general ideas about contemporary Marxist philosophy, his commentaries on Sánchez Vázquez – to whom he dedicates the last of four chapters, after an introduction to 'Marxist-Leninist philosophy as a philosophy of praxis', a discussion of Gramsci, and the Yugoslav theoretical group 'Praxis' – are, by contrast, rather weak.[299] These commentaries neither facilitate the understanding of Sánchez Vázquez's theories, nor do they point in the direction of a more extensive critique of his work. In the end, Acanda González's presentation of Sánchez Vázquez's work exhausts itself in a highly non-dialectical oscillation between recognition of 'progressive intent' and condemnation of 'an erroneous idealist interpretation of the practical life process'.

It is symptomatic of that stage in the history of dogmatic Marxism that, ten years later, Acanda González no longer wished that the positions expressed in his thesis be remembered. Thus it happened that in an interview with Manuel Vázquez Montalbán, the current philosophy professor at the Universidad de La Habana, the Spanish writer begins with the words: 'I am here with the representative of Gramsci in Cuba'.[300] Vázquez Montalbán, who does not know the biography of his interviewee in detail, follows this direction in his interview, in which Acanda González presents the broad strokes of dogmatic Marxism in Cuba, above all since 1971, in a form that would not in the least suggest to the reader that the interviewee himself had engaged in this same dogmatic reading.

In his own exposition, he only appears once as a subject of history, in the passing mention that he had once lived in the GDR. But he does not talk about his highly dogmatic thesis at Leipzig on philosophical Marxism, merely

[296] Acanda González 1988, appendix, p. 2.
[297] Acanda González 1988, appendix, p. 9.
[298] Acanda González seems to like this term so much that he uses it repeatedly. See also Acanda González 1988, p. 86.
[299] Acanda González 1988, Chapter 4: 'Die Philosophie der Praxis bei A. Sánchez Vázquez', pp. 78–105. Regarding Acanda González, see also p. 168.
[300] Vázquez Montalbán 1998, in particular pp. 375–91, here: p. 375.

mentioning that 'I discovered Bahro',[301] 'he was considered a revisionist and as a result was not read', and nor was he mentioned a single time in his own thesis. But this does not seem sufficiently interesting to Acanda González to pester Vázquez Montalbán, who was more interested in the history of Cuban theory, with it.[302]

We can observe apparent blunders in various details if we compare the quoted interview with the 1988 text. While Acanda González maintains to Vázquez Montalbán in 1998, speaking critically, that, in the Cuba of the 1970s and '80s, 'Eurocommunism was seen simply as a right-wing phenomenon',[303] in 1988 he still saw that sort of critical position toward Moscow as the cause of Sánchez Vázquez's central philosophical errors.[304]

Here, we are not attempting to deny the possibility of correcting one's individual intellectual trajectory, but it is only possible to do so seriously if one does not silence the limitations and errors of the prior period, instead subjecting them to critical reflection. If Jorge Luis Acanda González is interested in overcoming the weaknesses that he evidently shared with dogmatic Marxism in his 1988 thesis ('*Dissertation A*'), this would require a theoretical argument justifying this changing position. Otherwise, the reader versed in both of Acanda González's theoretical periods would remain in doubt as to whether the first or the second period, the dogmatic or the non-dogmatic, or perhaps both at the same time, were the result of philosophical opportunism.

Of course, his thesis contains a defence of Gramsci against the dogmatic critiques made against him (critiques that Acanda González then reproduces in turn). However, in order to understand the development of Gramsci's reception in Cuba after the 1970s, and debates on the island regarding Marxism more generally, it would have been very useful for us to understand up to what point Acanda González's condemnation of Adolfo Sánchez Vázquez's *Philosophy of Praxis* and the extensive critique of Gramsci in his dissertation resulted from a simple ideological concession to those giving the money and the orders, or

---

301   Acanda González, cited in Vázquez Montalbán 1998, p. 385.
302   Ibid.
303   Vázquez Montalbán 1998, p. 382.
304   'Forgetting the profound differences between Western Europe and Latin America, Sánchez Vázquez uncritically appropriated all these ideas [from Eurocommunism]. Sánchez Vázquez's transition to praxisology [*sic*] is essentially linked to the elaboration by necessity of a theoretical foundation that allows him to deny the importance of Lenin's political and philosophical legacy, and present some simultaneously practical and spontaneous conceptions of the revolution, alongside ideas – typical of Eurocommunism – on the organisation of the vanguard party and of democracy in socialism as though these were "truly Marxist" '. (Acanda González 1988, p. 104.)

whether historical and intellectual events – beyond all opportunism – had obliged him to correct his theoretical positions.[305]

In his interview with Vázquez Montalbán, Acanda González mentions a series of non-dogmatic Marxists currently relevant in Cuba, but he does not say a single word about Sánchez Vázquez, the author discussed in his thesis, despite the fact that since the Revolution, Sánchez Vázquez had been and continued to be a regularly invited guest to philosophical and even political events, and that a significant number of his works have been published there. One such presentation of this sort in Cuba occurred in January of 1999, as a part of the workshop 'The Cuban Revolution 50 years after 1950', in which some thirty intellectuals from Latin America and around twenty intellectuals and functionaries from the Cuban government – among them, Fidel Castro – participated. According to Sánchez Vázquez's own account,[306] he was the only one to suggest critically in this working meeting that during the 1970s and '80s dogmatic Marxism prevailed on the theoretical terrain just as actually existing socialism did on the political terrain, whereas the general tone of this closed-door meeting was quite different. According to the view which predominated, dogmatic Marxism and actually existing socialism in particular were phenomena, which were limited to the Soviet Union and Eastern Europe, and for which there was no room in Cuba. Sánchez Vázquez's position – which was already well-known among Cuban intellectuals prior to the 1999 event – requires a serious self-critical reflection on the recent history of Cuba, which might paradoxically explain why Acanda González refrained from mentioning him in his laudatory references to non-dogmatic Marxists.[307]

The second example of the false identification of Marxist theory in general with Marxism-Leninism, in this case from the bourgeois-conservative side, is the work of the Mexican Rubén Capdeville García, begun at the Humboldt University in Berlin during the period of the GDR and completed in May of 1992, after the so-called reunification of the two German states.[308] This text

---

305   In no part of the interview (which spans seventeen pages of the book), does Acanda González clarify if he himself during the 1980s belonged to the 'more conservative, that is, more orthodox ideological platform, more dedicated to a Marxist nomenclature' in Cuba; if this was not the case, why then did he present a highly dogmatic master's thesis in Leipzig? If this was indeed the case, when and why did he break with this 'platform'? (See Acanda González, cited in Vázquez Montalbán 1998, p. 379).

306   Adolfo Sánchez Vázquez, conversation with the author, Mexico City, 8 May 1999.

307   In the interview, Acanda González mentions as important non-dogmatic Marxist thinkers Herbert Marcuse, Georg Lukács, and Antonio Gramsci (in Vázquez Montalbán 1988, p. 382), as well as Adam Schaff (p. 390).

308   Capdeville García 1992.

is written from a bourgeois-conservative position which does not recognise important differences at the heart of Marxism, since from this perspective all Marxism should be considered Marxism-Leninism, and thus in the last instance, it is not possible to distinguish between authors as varied as Lenin, Marcuse, Bloch, and Sánchez Vázquez. Thus Capdeville García characterises Sánchez Vázquez's work in the following terms: 'Underlining the concept of praxis after a theoretical approach to Lenin is therefore the essential characteristic of his *Philosophy*'.[309]

The existence of two tendencies so different from one another within Marxism is so inconceivable for this author that it requires very little effort of him to turn everything on its head. Precisely the concept that Sánchez Vázquez uses to criticise the philosophy of Marxism-Leninism and distance himself from Lenin's theory is what Capdeville characterises as the consequence of an 'approximation to Lenin'. It would be difficult to say anything more false about the role played by the concept of praxis in the theoretical development of the author of *The Philosophy of Praxis*. On another occasion, he implicitly refers to Sánchez Vázquez and Herbert Marcuse as 'Marxist-Leninists'[310] and unproblematically incorporates their works into that theoretical orientation.[311]

Sánchez Vázquez's work is also dealt with in passing in this text. After a rapid tour through the 'Latin American philosophy' of nearly all orientations since the nineteenth century, his critique of Sánchez Vázquez exhausts itself in two points: 'at no point do we come across concrete references to the reality of, say, Latin America',[312] as well as what he, horrified, characterises as a 'negative discourse'. Capdeville García expresses, finally: 'but (and this "but" plays a significant role here) to establish a conception of the world also requires positive elements, positive concepts that cannot be found in Marxism as "critical theory". Theorists like Sánchez Vázquez and Marcuse share this methodological problem'.[313] This quotation contains the central problem of the work – aside from the fact that it hardly enters into Sánchez Vázquez's theory at all. It is an abstruse mixture of typical formulations of actually existing socialism with a total rejection, beyond any differentiation, of all Marxist thought.[314]

---

309   Capdeville García, p. 121.
310   Capdeville García, p. 112.
311   Capdeville García, p. 113. 'The Marxism-Leninism and [the Marxism] of Sánchez Vázquez has two major characteristics'.
312   Capdeville García, pp. 35f.
313   Capdeville García, p. 112. The entire work is impregnated with such solemn wisdom.
314   This is evidently closely related to the situation of radical change then taking place of the universities of the former GDR.

Despite the vast limitations that we have ascertained in the work of Jorge Luis Acanda González, there is a pleasant difference between him and Capdeville García, the latter being distinguished by a high degree of confusion and an absolute lack of knowledge with regard to Marxist philosophical debates. In the case of the latter, we might even doubt that he knows Sánchez Vázquez's work at all, which is evident in countless passages in his discussion, for example when he hurries to put him in the same theoretical sack as Marcuse and does not pause to clarify how it is that Sánchez Vázquez, in the first edition of his *Philosophy of Praxis*, is still very critical of Marcuse.[315]

Beyond this, there exist in Mexico as well as in Europe various articles and a monograph about the work of Adolfo Sánchez Vázquez, which we will return to at a more pertinent point.[316] Certainly, more than a few of these texts suffer from the defect of criticising Sánchez Vázquez in a banal fashion or celebrating him unconditionally.

With regard to Bolívar Echeverría, whose work has only in recent years achieved some degree of dissemination, until now there only exist a few reviews of his books, whose argumentative force, however, is limited.[317]

As regards bibliographies for both authors, it is worth noting that until now no bibliography has been published for Echeverría. Three bibliographical indices already exist for Sánchez Vázquez, two published and one presented as a bachelor's thesis in Library Science at the UNAM. The three are highly incomplete and imprecise. On the basis of the information contained in said bibliographies, many texts could only be found after a prolonged search. All entries in our accompanying bibliographies of Sánchez Vázquez and Bolívar Echeverría, and which we consider complete with regard to primary sources, were confirmed by having the publications themselves in our possession, with the exception of a few works published in journals which were difficult to access, for example, those published in other Latin American countries. [Note to the edition in Spanish: for the updated bibliographies corresponding to the period from 1999 to June of 2005, we have not been able, in all cases, to check bibliographic entries on the basis of the original publications. In these cases, various bibliographical databases and library catalogues were used, which were compared in cases of the incomplete or incorrect information that these sometimes contain.]

---

315 See in this regard pp. 183ff. of this book. In the end, both works, insofar as they correspond to Sánchez Vázquez, should be seen as articles.
316 See the 'Bibliography of Adolfo Sánchez Vázquez' in the Appendix of this book.
317 See the 'Bibliography of Bolívar Echeverría' in the Appendix of this book. One exception is a brief critical article by Aureliano Ortega Esquivel on a short essay by Echeverría: see p. 331.n.398 of this book.

PART 2

Adolfo Sánchez Vázquez: Praxis and Knowledge

∴

CUERPOS XI

CHAPTER 4

The Concept of Praxis

In the following pages, we will examine Sánchez Vázquez's approach to the concept of praxis. After all, in the contemporary praxis of social emancipation, there exist contradictions, flaws, and aberrations, which indicate that an immediatist and spontaneous 'just do it' approach hostile to theory will not suffice. At the same time, contemporary Western theoretical debate regarding social relations has moved away from all serious, practical (and radical) attempts at intervention to such a point that, also for this reason, it seems necessary again to deal with a theorist who is interested in understanding the relationship between theory and praxis – including transformative and emancipatory praxis – and, in so doing, to develop a critique of both social action divorced from theory as well as theory divorced from political and social praxis.

a   The Term 'Praxis' in Various European Languages

Adolfo Sánchez Vázquez begins his research in his first principal book, *Philosophy of Praxis*,[1] with a first definition of praxis and this definition, in turn, sets out from the position occupied by the corresponding terms in various European languages, as well as their history. Alongside the word 'praxis', a transliteration of the Greek word πραξιζ, which means 'action' in the most immediate sense, Sánchez Vázquez's language also makes use of the parallel expression 'práctica'. In Spanish, both terms ('praxis' and 'práctica') can be used synonymously, but the latter is common in colloquial and literary language, whereas the former 'resides only – and not even always – in a philosophical vocabulary'.[2] Italian similarly possesses two terms: 'prassi' and 'pratica'; in

---

1   Sánchez Vázquez 1980b (first edition 1967). On the differences, which are occasionally substantial, between the first and second editions of the book, see the chapter 'The Philosophy of Praxis: Two Versions' (pp. 183ff of this book.) [Trans. – In what follows, we have consulted and cited where possible the existing English translation, which appeared as *The Philosophy of Praxis*, trans. M. Gonzalez (New Jersey: Humanities Press, 1977), but since this was based on the first edition of the book, it was occasionally necessary to translate passages directly from the Spanish.]
2   Sánchez Vázquez 1980b, p. 19.

French the term 'pratique' is used almost exclusively,[3] and in everyday Russian and English only пра́ктика (práktica) and 'practice' are used, respectively. German, according to Sánchez Vázquez, is an exception, since it knows only the transcription of the Greek word, that is, 'Praxis', and unlike the other languages mentioned lacks its own linguistic development in this regard.

On this point, of course, we cannot simply agree with the author, since in today's German the term 'Praktik' exists in expressions like 'Sexualpraktiken' [sexual practices] or 'Verhörpraktik' [interrogation practice]. We can, therefore, wonder how he comes to make such a claim. In the Spanish-German dictionaries consulted, 'Praktik' is not mentioned as a possible translation for 'práctica', but rather, for example, 'Übung, Gebrauch, Praxis' [exercise, use, practice].[4] But in the German retranslation, 'Praktik' is mentioned and 'práctica' is given as a Spanish translation.[5] German dictionaries mention the word 'Praktik' and its orthography as originating in the early high modern German, 'practic, practik', and, among other things, provide the following descriptions: 'Art der Ausübung (einer Tätigkeit), Verfahrensweise, Handhabung'[6] [mode of exercising (an activity), manner of proceeding, handling]. Regarding the plural 'Praktiken' it suggests that it is used pejoratively and indicates the influence of the medieval French and French expression 'pratiques "Ränke, Umtriebe"' [machinations, intrigues].[7] Either Sánchez Vázquez errs in stating that German only knows the word 'Praxis' and lacks its own linguistic development in this

---

3   It is worth noting that in French the term '*praxis*' is also used by authors referring back to philosophical texts written in the German language.
4   Cited according to *Langenscheidts Taschenwörterbuch der spanischen und deutschen Sprache. I: 'Spanisch-Deutsch'* 1985, p. 401. In *Wörterbuch der spanischen und deutschen Sprache* 1975, we find the following proposed translations for 'práctica': 'Anwendung, Praxis, (Aus) Übung, Erfahrung, erlernte Fertigkeit, Ausführung, Gewohnheit, Gebrauch, Kniff, Kunstgriff, Verfahren, Methode, Manier' (see *Wörterbuch der spanischen und deutschen Sprache* 1975, p. 859).
5   See *Langenscheidts Taschenwörterbuch der spanischen und deutschen Sprache. II: 'Deutsch-Spanisch'* 1985, p. 841.
6   See *Etymologisches Wörterbuch des Deutschen* 1989, Vol. 2, p. 1309.
7   Ibid. Note, moreover, 'The word [*Praktik*] tends to be used pejoratively and in the plural: commercial practices, economic practices, 'tricks, deals'; to not shrink from certain practices': *Wörterbuch der Sprachswierigkeiten* 1989, p. 383. And, moreover, 'The commissioner knows the practice of interrogation' (ibid.). He who pilots boats into port is called a 'práctico' in Spanish and in German '*Praktik*' also means 'permission granted a boat to enter port for commercial ends'. *Meyers Kleines Konversationslexicon* 1908, Vol. 5, p. 423.

respect, or else he is referring to the fact that in the sphere of social debates in Germany the word 'Praktik' is not commonly used.[8]

Regarding the etymology of the word 'praxis', Sánchez Vázquez makes the following observation: 'praxis' in ancient Greek denotes an action aimed toward achieving something, but an action which has its objective within itself and does not allow anything outside the agent or his activity to emerge. Here, Sánchez Vázquez refers to Aristotle and his concept of 'moral action', which is for him 'praxis', as is all action that does not have effects outside itself.

This is why, for example, the activity of the artist (which certainly produces something outside him- or herself) is not praxis, but is instead designated as ποιησις (poiesis), something which literally means both making and doing. 'In this sense, the artisan's work is *poetic* rather than *practical*'.[9] In this respect, Sánchez Vázquez observes that, in strict consonance with the original meaning of these words, philosophy, whose fundamental concepts he seeks to clarify, should be called 'Philosophy of poiesis'. But, given the fact that in Spanish (as in German) this Greek word continues to exist in expressions like 'poetry', 'poet', and 'poetic' (which, while referring to productions, is nevertheless a very limited meaning), this word is of no use to Sánchez Vázquez, since the object of his research is much broader. He thus selects praxis as the central concept of his analysis, in order to designate 'conscious objective activity' in its broadest sense.[10]

Sánchez Vázquez's concept of praxis thus shows, even in his very justification for choosing the term, a simultaneous desire for exactness and generalisation. This points toward a double demarcation, *vis-à-vis* both the implications of the contemporary restriction of the word 'poiesis' to the poetic and literary, and the reduction of 'the term *practice*' to its everyday and utilitarian sense.[11]

---

8   The author, in any case, does not find 'Politische Praktik' ('political practice') to be a normal formulation. Here, we could add the question: why has praxis, as a political term, remained foreign to Germany?

9   Sánchez Vázquez 1977a, 'Introduction. From ordinary consciousness to the philosophical consciousness of praxis', pp. 1–38, and here p. 1.

10 Ibid. At this point, we are not looking for a critical reflection on Sánchez Vázquez's reception of Aristotle; rather, on the basis of this reception, we attempt to proceed by giving primary focus to the development of his theory. [Note to the edition in English: This quotation is translated directly from the original edition in Spanish of the book *The Philosophy of Praxis*, because the published English translation is not correct: 'la actividad consciente objetiva' appears incorrectly in that translation as 'that human activity which produces objects'. See Sánchez Vázquez 1980b, p. 20 and Sánchez Vázquez 1977a, p. 2 (S.G.)]

11 Sánchez Vázquez 1977a.

b The Terms 'Praxis' and 'Práctica' and the Problem of Their Translation

The previously discussed circumstance that Spanish has two parallel terms, 'praxis' ['praxis' in the English translation of *The Philosophy of Praxis*] and 'práctica' ['practice' in the same translation], entails in the texts by Sánchez Vázquez here analysed certain problems which could create confusion and complicate their translation into German. We have distinguished three planes of the problem: first, the various terminological definitions that Sánchez Vázquez establishes in different works; second, the discrepancy between the introductory exposition in his book *The Philosophy of Praxis* and the real use of those terms in his work; and finally, the difficulty inherent in the distance between the two languages.

First: in large sections of *The Philosophy of Praxis*, the author uses 'praxis' and 'practice' as synonyms. It would seem as though the decision to use one or the other word has little importance for its content, and that the author – who was originally educated as a journalist and poet – has allowed himself to be guided by questions of style.[12] The only exception is the chapter headings, all of which – except one ('Unidad de la teoría y la práctica [Unity of theory and practice]') – refer to 'praxis'.[13] In a 1977 lecture, Sánchez Vázquez makes, to the contrary, a strict distinction between the two terms: there, 'práctica' ['practice'] means 'activity or exercise in general' and is rigorously distinguished from 'praxis', which only designates a very specific form of human activity, namely, that which he understands as praxis.[14] The distinction between 'activity in general' and 'praxis' that Sánchez Vázquez develops in *The Philosophy of Praxis* (where, as we have said, praxis is referred to not only as 'praxis' but also as 'practice') is specified in the aforementioned lecture, 'La filosofía de la praxis como nueva práctica de la filosofía [The philosophy of praxis as a new philo-

---

12 Jaime Labastida emphasises that Sánchez Vázquez is also interested in literary beauty in his work, while at the same time showing the dryness and repetition of passages in the book. He compares the subchapter 'Grandeza y decadencia de la mano [Supremacy and decline of the hand]' with the 'literary beauty ... [of] the best passages from the "economic-philosophical manuscripts of 1844" ': Labastida 1967, p. 56.

13 Note, for example, that Sánchez Vázquez uses as a subtitle for his interpretation of the second thesis on Feuerbach 'Praxis as a criterion of truth', and in the section bearing this title, writes: 'The criterion of truth may be found in practice' (Sánchez Vázquez 1977a, pp. 120 and 121).

14 The precise difference between 'activity in general' and 'praxis (in particular)' will need to be developed throughout this section of the book. A first introduction to the concept of 'praxis' is found in the next subchapter.

sophical practice]',[15] through the distinction between the concepts of 'practice' and 'praxis'. Thus two terms which were used almost synonymously in the first text become in this second text[16] concepts which are clearly delimited from one another.[17]

Second: the discrepancy of the real use of the terms 'praxis' and 'practice' with regard to his introductory exposition in *The Philosophy of Praxis*. In contrast to the nearly indiscriminate use of the terms in question throughout his book *The Philosophy of Praxis*, Sánchez Vázquez insists: 'Without completely ruling out the predominant word in ordinary language, we have preferred to use in our research – and despite its limited use – the term "praxis" '.[18] The reason he gives is that he is interested in freeing the concept in question from the limited and utilitarian meaning that it has in expressions like 'practical man', 'practical results', 'a very practical profession'.[19] But we do not, in fact, observe this 'preference' for the term 'praxis'. Seen in terms of frequency of usage, the

---

15 Sánchez Vázquez 1983b (Lecture given at the Eleventh Interamerican Philosophy Congress in Caracas, Venezuela, June 1977. First published in *Cuadernos Políticos* no. 12, Mexico 1977). We are quoting according to the book version; in the textual variations we have noticed, we rely on the textual version of the first edition, which coincides moreover with the French translation (Sánchez Vázquez 1977b).

16 The elaboration of the second text (first appearing in 1977) falls temporally between the first edition in Spanish of *Filosofía de la praxis* (1967), published in English translation as *The Philosophy of Praxis*, and the second, broadly corrected and expanded edition (1980) of *Filosofía de la praxis*, which has never been translated into English.

17 This difference becomes exceptionally clear in Sánchez Vázquez's critique of Althusser's concept of '*pratique théorique*'. In *Filosofía de la praxis*, our author still makes clear that Althusser's ' "theoretical practice" ... corresponds in large part ... to what *we have called theoretical activity*' (Sánchez Vázquez 1977a p. 166, n. 21, italics by S.G.).

By contrast, he expresses things differently in another text: 'In the present work "practice" means activity or exercise and in accordance with this *we speak of* "philosophical practice" (as a form of "theoretical practice") to refer to the way of making, cultivating, or exercising philosophy. But this is a practice which is not in itself praxis' (Sánchez Vázquez 1983b, p. 36).

18 Sánchez Vázquez 1980b, p. 19. [Note to the Edition in English: The introduction of *The Philosophy of Praxis*, with the title 'From ordinary consciousness to the philosophical consciousness of praxis' begins with the subchapter 'A note on terminology', which is called in the Spanish original text 'Precisiones terminológicas'. This first subchapter was partly rewritten – more than translated – for the Edition in English of *The Philosophy of Praxis*. For this reason, the quoted sentence does not exist in the English translation and must be translated here form the Spanish original text. Compare Sánchez Vázquez 1977a, p. 1: S.G.]

19 Sánchez Vázquez 1980b, p. 20.

term 'practice' is the one which instead dominates throughout the text of *The Philosophy of Praxis*.

Third: the difficulty prompted by the distance between Spanish and German. The parallel terms which exist in Spanish and in German ('praxis/práctica' and 'Praxis/Praktik') show that their habitual usage is different in everyday and philosophical linguistic usage. While 'práctica' predominates in Spanish, 'Praxis' does in German. But if one wants to preserve this difference in a translation, the best thing to do would be to translate 'praxis' as 'Praxis' and 'práctica' as 'Praktik'. Both the utilitarian tone resounding in the respective second term of both languages as well as the evident linguistic proximity of both terms coordinated with one another would support such an approach; but due to the aforementioned asymmetrical distribution of the frequency with which the thus generated terms are used, there emerges the problem that the German-speaking reader may expect a special motive for using the word 'Praktik', which would not at all be the case with the word 'práctica' in the original Spanish.[20]

Finally, this problem also could not be clarified entirely in conversations with Sánchez Vázquez. Therefore, we will observe the following way of proceeding, bearing in mind the reservations formulated above: we generally translate [in the original, German edition of this book] 'práctica' as 'Praktik' and 'praxis' as 'Praxis'. Of course, translation is also interpretation, as expressed more broadly in other European languages than in German,[21] but the reader of these lines will sense in the quotations themselves what happens when someone attempts to discuss with Sánchez Vázquez by splitting hairs.

Put differently, the translator must, of course, attempt to resolve for himself the problems of the text in question, but must at the same time draft the translation in such an 'innocent' way that others might also discover the problem and perhaps resolve it better.

c   General Introduction to the Concept

Before continuing with Sánchez Vázquez's argumentation in *The Philosophy of Praxis*, we are going to sketch out in advance the conception of praxis that he formulates. In so doing, we will follow the previously mentioned article, 'La

---

20   In this respect, see moreover that the well-known Spanish translator of Marx, Wenceslao Roces, in the translation of the second thesis on Feuerbach, renders the German word 'Praxis' as '*práctica*' [practice]. See Marx 1987, p. 666.
21   Thus, for example, French uses 'interpréter' in addition to 'traduire' and Spanish 'interpretar' in addition to 'traducir', to grasp the mediation between different languages.

filosofía de la praxis como nueva práctica de la filosofía [The philosophy of praxis as a new philosophical practice]',[22] in which Sánchez Vázquez, however provisionally, attempts explicitly to define the concept of praxis.

To do so, he refers to Karl Marx's first *Theses on Feuerbach*, in which Marx criticises the anthropological materialist in the following terms: 'he does not conceive human activity itself as objective [*gegenständliche*] activity ... he does not grasp the significance of "revolutionary", of "practical-critical", activity'.[23] Sánchez Vázquez cites this affirmatively as a definition of 'praxis' and speaks of 'human activity as objective activity' and 'critical practical ... revolutionary activity'.[24]

The author – in the first interpretation of Marx's concept of praxis in the *Theses on Feuerbach* – grants a special value to the two moments of praxis: on the one hand, following its objective side, praxis consists of the true transformation of the world as it exists now (and which often presents itself to us as overwhelming); in this sense the concept of praxis refers just as much to palpable things, to nature, as to the relations which exist between humans and nature and also between humans and humans, whose totality constitute society. On the other hand, the subjective side of praxis constitutes the active moment, initiative, the aspect of the human being as an actor in history, who focuses consciously on objectives and attempts to realise them. In this sense, Sánchez Vázquez understands praxis as 'activity ... oriented toward the end of transforming an object (nature or society), devised by the conscious and active subjectivity of men'.[25] The activity that he understands as praxis is, 'consequently, activity – in indissoluble unity – objective and subjective at the same time'.[26] He understands the particularity of Marx's concept of praxis as that of the *unity* of those two moments. 'What is determinant in this practical process is neither objective transformation (separated from subjectivity) nor

---

22 Sánchez Vázquez 1983b.
23 Marx 1978b, p. 143.
24 Sánchez Vázquez 1983b, p. 36. Sánchez Vázquez does not note the precise citation here, but we could assume that he is referring to the same Spanish translation of the *Theses on Feuerbach* that he cites in *Philosophy of Praxis* (namely, that of Wenceslao Roces). See Sánchez Vázquez 1980b, p. 22. Omissions belong to Sánchez Vázquez. The quotation marks in Marx's original text do not appear in Sánchez Vázquez).

On the problem of how to translate the German word 'gegenständlich', which in German is not the same as 'objektiv', despite both being translated into Spanish as 'objetivo,' see our chapter 'The *Theses on Feuerbach*', subchapter 'Interpretation of the *Theses on Feuerbach*'.
25 Sánchez Vázquez 1983b, p. 36.
26 Ibid.

subjective activity (separated from objectivity), but rather the unity of both moments'.[27]

Marx formulates this unity through his double critique of two different unilateralising philosophies: 'hitherto existing materialism – that of Feuerbach included' which only grasped the objective side in the form of contemplation, and idealism, which of course reflects the side of human activity neglected by 'hitherto existing materialism', but which could only arrive at a concept of praxis as ideal, intellectual, and not 'real, sensuous'.[28] Therefore, in Marx's concept of praxis the immense achievements on the theoretical terrain of both previous materialism and idealism find their place; following Sánchez Vázquez, we could boldly ask if this concept does not simultaneously transcend, maintain, and suspend (in the Hegelian sense of 'aufheben') the entire dichotomy between materialism and idealism. Understood in this way, the seriousness of the second part of the eleventh thesis on Feuerbach begins to take shape: 'the point is to change it [the world]', which, pronounced too quickly on more than one occasion, only serves to 'justify' our own distress in observing the philosophical giants upon whose shoulders we all stand.

---

27 Ibid.
28 Marx 1978b, p. 143.

CHAPTER 5

Everyday Consciousness of Praxis[29]

a   The Critique of the Everyday Consciousness[30] of Praxis, or, What Is a Theoretical Knowledge of Praxis Good For?

Sánchez Vázquez introduces his critique of everyday consciousness of praxis through reference to the latter's philosophical conception: the philosophy that has praxis as its central concept, as its cornerstone, is Marxism. Now, the philosophical concept of praxis does not develop on its own, but rather draws support from a long history of humanity and its intellectual doctrines (theories), and so we cannot conclude that it reaches its conclusion with the philosophy of Marx. In order to arrive at a true understanding of the relationship between theory and praxis, it is necessary to overcome the mystifying concept of praxis found in German idealism, in which praxis is always grasped only as human intellectual activity.

In terms of overcoming the 'level reached by German idealism',[31] Marxism entails both a more developed consciousness of praxis as well as a more

---

29 This chapter was written for this *philosophical* study for two reasons. In the first place, because our author also develops his work *The Philosophy of Praxis* (to which we refer most directly) on the basis of a double critique of two forms of self-sufficiency: the 'practical' and the 'theoretical'. In the second place, our book should be of interest not only to philosophers, and as a result should not only refer to discussions among philosophers ('why does knowledge need praxis?'), but must also be directed toward those who are not philosophers, toward friends and comrades in the struggle on the path toward an emancipated society, and thus we should not spare our critiques regarding this aspect either (hence: 'why does praxis need knowledge?').

30 The concept of 'conciencia ordinaria' that Sánchez Vázquez employs can be translated not only as '*gemeines Bewusstsein*' [ordinary consciousness] but also as '*Alltagsbewusstsein*' [everyday consciousness]. As a general rule, we use the second variant, which is slightly freer but also more common in German, and in favour of which Sánchez Vázquez also speaks with regard to the meaning of the concept of the everyday (see p. 107n55). For a similar reason, his expression 'ordinary man' [literally, '*der gemeine und gängige Mensch*'] can be translated as '*Alltagsmensch*' [everyday man]. In free expressions, the author of this book also used the terms '*Alltagsverständnis von Praxis*' [everyday understanding of praxis] and '*Alltagsverstand*' [everyday reason / common sense].

31 Sánchez Vázquez 1980b, p. 21. [Note to the English-language edition: in the English version of *The Philosophy of Praxis*, these words are simply translated as: 'Having gone beyond German Idealism' (Sánchez Vázquez 1977a, p. 2.)]

powerful theoretical connection to it. So we must overcome idealism, but this does not mean a return to the immediate and naïve perspective of everyday consciousness. This is not a question of returning to a pre-philosophical state or to a 'vulgar or metaphysical materialist philosophy' – to some degree stuck to ordinary and run-of-the-mill conceptions of the human being – and which 'preceded the more developed expositions of Idealist philosophy (in Kant, Fichte, and Hegel)'.[32] A developed concept of praxis is obligated, from a historical-philosophical perspective, to pass through and transcend its idealistic formulation.[33]

In order to overcome philosophical idealism, we thus need a more broadly-developed 'philosophical theory' and not 'a dose of "common sense"'.[34] To the contrary, such a theory would distinguish itself even more from everyday consciousness than does idealism. This is not just any philosophy, however, but precisely that which – based on its theoretical analysis of what praxis is – demonstrates the conditions that make possible the transition from theory to praxis.[35] The importance of idealism in world history has been underestimated, as the theoretical foundation for a Marxism which has broken radically with it, but which has been heavily enriched by this same idealism.[36] This underestimation is one of the reasons why, in various sectors, Marxism has found itself reduced to 'the old materialism fertilised by dialectics on the one hand, or a materialist metaphysics which is little more than an inverted Idealism'.[37]

In internal Marxist debates, what interests Sánchez Vázquez is rescuing 'a true conception of praxis', which has been lost as much in 'Hegelian deformations of Marxism' as in 'mechanistic, scientistic or neopositivist interpretations of Marx's work'.[38] But this rescue cannot occur through reference to everyday consciousness of praxis, but by destroying even the attitude that the latter determines;[39] this is necessary not only to achieve a developed theoretical-philosophical conceptualisation of praxis, but also to propel every-

---

32   Sánchez Vázquez 1977a, p. 2.
33   Ibid.
34   Sánchez Vázquez 1977a, pp. 2f.
35   Sánchez Vázquez 1977a, p. 2.
36   See, in this book, the section 'Praxis as the Basis for Knowledge (Thesis I)' (pp. 134ff).
37   Sánchez Vázquez 1977a, p. 3.
38   Ibid.
39   Sánchez Vázquez 1977a, pp. 2ff. The 'abolition' discussed here refers above all to the *attitude* of everyday man. His consciousness, as Sánchez Vázquez says later, must be 'overcome' (ibid. In this regard, see the following extensive quotation in our main text).

day political praxis and elevate it to a higher level, which means, for Sánchez Vázquez: to make it creative.[40]

The Spanish-Mexican philosopher, who elsewhere in this work still situates the proletariat as an at least potentially revolutionary subject[41] (something which would be modified in later of his statements),[42] nevertheless considers – in opposition to more than one Marxist author – that the consciousness of the proletariat in itself is in no sense more developed than, for example, idealistic German philosophy.

> In this sense, the abolition of the standpoint of ordinary consciousness as well as a dialectical negation of the mystified consciousness of praxis are necessary preconditions of the development of an objective, scientific perspective upon man's practical activity. Only in this way can thought and action be united in consciousness. And only when the framework of ordinary consciousness is transcended can the philosophical consciousness of praxis and the elevation of reiterative, spontaneous everyday praxis to a higher, creative, level be achieved.... The theory of revolutionary praxis requires that the instinctive and spontaneous point of view of ordinary proletarian consciousness be overcome, and that for both

---

40 Ibid.
41 See, for example, Sánchez Vázquez 1977a, Part Two: 'Some philosophical problems of praxis', Chapter VII, 'Spontaneous and reflective praxis', subchapter 'The historical mission of the proletariat in our time' (pp. 234–7) and the subchapter 'Marxism as a philosophy of the proletariat' (pp. 241–3). In these passages, Sánchez Vázquez also explains that it is not possible, on the basis of the objective situation of the proletarian class, to come to direct conclusions regarding its specific consciousness, but theoretical effort, among other things, *is* absolutely essential to its development.
42 At least as regards the proletariat of industrialised countries, Adolfo Sánchez Vázquez later became increasingly sceptical, and he recognised their *partial* identity of interests with the ruling classes when attempting to preserve the existing global relationship (for example, the 'North-South conflict').

In this respect, see Sánchez Vázquez's statements at the Seminar on Marxism and the State Question, summer semester of 1989, UNAM, Faculty of Philosophy and Arts, and his lecture 'La razón amenazada', given in 1984 at the Universidad Autónoma de Puebla (Mexico), on the occasion of being presented a doctorate *honoris causa* by that institution, and which was published in his book *Escritos de política y filosofía* (Sánchez Vázquez 1987), where he asserts that 'in this period... we must bear in mind a series of facts:... The displacement of the fundamental social antagonism (bourgeoisie-proletariat, according to classical Marxism) onto that of imperialism-Third World' (Sánchez Vázquez 1987, p. 135).

theoretical and practical reasons, it be countered by a correct understanding of praxis.[43]

(These words are directed against the absence of theory within emancipatory organisations and movements – an absence that exists not only in Mexico and Spain – as well as against various petrifications of Marxism, for example, in its Stalinist form,[44] and point toward the same thing that we hope to emphasise in this part of our study: why it is that Sánchez Vázquez is considered by many to be one of the first and most outstanding non-dogmatic Marxists in Mexico and Latin America.)[45]

Nevertheless, the development of the philosophical consciousness of praxis, which is supposed to overcome everyday consciousness of the latter, begins – and this is worth observing – from that same everyday consciousness[46] or, as Sánchez Vázquez says repeatedly, from the consciousness of 'the ordinary man'.[47] Everyday consciousness believes itself to be in direct connection with the world of praxis and, precisely as a result of the self-postulated circumstance of not being stained by any theoretical reflection, believes that in the realisation of everyday tasks such reflection would be more a hindrance than a help. A similar practicalist hostility to theory can be found occasionally within Marxist-oriented circles. It is worth noting that this posture could evidently be based on formulations by Marx such as the following: '[Men] begin, like every animal, by *eating, drinking*, etc., hence not by "standing" in a relation, but by

---

43   Sánchez Vázquez 1977a, p. 4.
44   It is true that there was an ostensible production of theory under Stalinism, but it was more a question of legitimating the established state apparatus than a critical theory of 'revolutionary praxis', which is Sánchez Vázquez's topic here. But, on the other hand, our author discusses ideas common to everyday consciousness and to that dogmatic theory, for example, in the critique of ingenuous realism. (See, for example, our next subchapter: 'Revolutionary Praxis and Everyday Consciousness').
45   'Sánchez Vázquez's philosophical work ... [is] without a doubt ... one of the greatest of all Latin American Marxism: anti-dogmatic, constantly reconsidering its initial questions, dialoguing with European Marxisms, and open to new social problems': Morales 1985, p. 133.

   'In the 1979 preface to the re-publication of the already classic *Filosofía de la praxis*, Adolfo Sánchez Vázquez insisted on the urgent "need to overcome the dogmatism and sclerosis that for many long years had dulled Marxism's critical and revolutionary edge". His own work is an incredibly important contribution to this task, posing as it does the centrality of revolutionary praxis in the Marxist worldview': Löwy 1985, p. 387.

   See, likewise, K. Nair's preface to the French translation Sánchez Vázquez 1977b, p. 141.
46   See, for example, Sánchez Vázquez 1977a, p. 4.
47   See, for example, Sánchez Vázquez 1977a, p. 6.

relating themselves actively, taking hold of certain things in the external world through action, and thus satisfying their need[s]. (Therefore they begin with production.)'[48]

Alfred Schmidt, who more or less at the same time as Sánchez Vázquez – but in the intellectual, historical, and geographical context of the Frankfurt School – was also developing a critical and non-dogmatic interpretation of Marx's theory, observes with regard to such affirmations that 'these formulations are not to be understood in the sense of practicist enmity toward theory'. Schmidt continues, with reference to historical praxis (which for Sánchez Vázquez constitutes the central concept in Marx): 'Historical practice is in itself "more theoretical" than theory, as indeed it was in Hegel (although in his case of course it was determined in the last analysis as a mode of knowledge). Practice has already accomplished the mediation of Subject and Object before it becomes itself the theme of reflection'.[49]

In other words, a fully *atheoretical* world does not exist, and this assessment unites Sánchez Vázquez with Alfred Schmidt. However, the former bases this point on two elements, without referring – as does Schmidt – to the history of philosophy. As against the belief that everyday consciousness is not tainted by any theoretical reflection, he criticises not only the fact that this neglects the 'prejudices, mental habits and commonplaces' that influence it, but moreover that – whether we like it or not – theories sediment within such consciousness.[50] Equally, the real human being, who possesses this consciousness, which is purportedly not influenced by the history of ideas, is a social being, incapable of subtracting himself from the historical framework in which he finds himself. 'The day to day character of his life, as well as the vision that he has of his own practical activity, are historically and socially determined'.[51]

So the human being who wants to see things simply as they are, without any major interpretation, without gossip, without philosophy and this whole

---

48   Marx 1996, p. 235.
49   Schmidt 1971, p. 194. [Note to the English-language edition of this book: In the German original, Schmidt writes here about 'historische Praxis', which would have been better translated as 'historical praxis', for the reasons Sánchez Vázquez mentions for the use of the term 'praxis' in Spanish, even when in both languages (English and Spanish) this term is less usual than the term 'practice'/'práctica'. (Compare Schmidt 1974, p. 204.) This edition of the book is identical – including the pagination – to the 1993 edition, with the only difference that the last one includes a new prologue from Schmidt, paginated with Roman numerals (pp. i–xvii). The same applies for the whole book: where Schmidt writes in German 'Praxis' in the English translation there always appears 'practice'.]
50   Sánchez Vázquez 1977a, pp. 4ff.
51   Sánchez Vázquez 1977a, p. 5.

nebulous mess, he who believes more in solid proof rather than Aristotelian ones, in a word, the unrepentantly practical, will be frustrated by Sánchez Vázquez, who always grants such importance to praxis. According to this Marxist philosopher, our 'practical' friend, who observed long ago that philosophers are the last people to expect anything from,[52] will not be able to find what it is that is most relevant to him: the naked fact.[53]

Is this a fresh trick by the philosophers? Could it be that, now that no one trusts them and everyone ignores them, they now send forth a Marxist colleague with the message that, up to this point, philosophy has done anything but change the world, but that now we again need a philosophical theory for effective radical emancipation? This is as far as our taking the side of 'ordinary consciousness' against Sánchez Vázquez's devastating explanations can go. But the latter still does not provide an answer as to how, *in detail*, the transition from everyday consciousness to critical consciousness will occur, a question that became central with the experience of National Socialism and fascism, in other words, with the collective participation of mass sectors of the population in a social engagement as far from emancipatory as could possibly be imagined. Only in a later passage does Sánchez Vázquez enter into this problem, which he had left unconsidered up to this point.[54] We will need to see, then, how he situates himself *vis-à-vis* the three common recipes for overcoming everyday consciousness, namely: first, everyday consciousness becomes more critical through education; second, 'the Party is always right'; and third, it is only in struggle that consciousness can develop.

To everyday consciousness – with its suspicion of talk of helping to overcome it or even destroy it, that is, its fear that another ideology is already pre-

---

52   Our interpretation of Sánchez Vázquez's text is ultimately too optimistic. Philosophers can very well 'be of some use' to the practical person. Just think, for example, about the close cooperation that currently exists in various genetic research institutions with philosophers who directly oversee the 'ethical harmlessness' of the most recent discoveries in the natural sciences, and once giving this certification of non-objection, know how to defend it (philosophically) against insatiable critics. Here, the best possibility of enlightenment has emerged from the debates surrounding Peter Singer, who emerged from the animal rights movement and is the ideologue of scientifically-grounded human selection (not the ideological version, as with the Nazis, who were profoundly hated by scientists and, above all, by philosophers, as has been repeatedly reaffirmed since 1945).

53   Sánchez Vázquez 1977a.

54   See, in this regard, our section on the interpretation of the third thesis on Feuerbach: 'Revolutionary praxis as the unity of the transformation in human beings and in circumstances' (pp. 143ff), and the subchapter 'Critique of Certain Marxist Conceptions of Knowledge' (pp. 134ff).

pared to disfigure the simple and natural thought of the human being who lives in the world of practice – Sánchez Vázquez responds that the consciousness of the ordinary human 'is never called upon to confront a naked fact, for each fact is assimilated by him into an ideologically determined perspective generated by the particular social and historical situation of his daily life'.[55]

In this point of the discussion of everyday consciousness, Sánchez Vázquez does not explain how we should understand in detail the end of the quoted phrase, for example, how the current 'historical situation' engenders a specific 'ideologically determined perspective'. Setting out from Marx, we could explain these formulations in the sense that, under given social relations, a specific ideological consciousness can be facilitated in humans insofar as, in all their contradictions, such relations slow or impede their correct knowledge. Marx explains this in *Capital*, and especially in the subchapter 'The Fetishism of the Commodity and Its Secret'.[56] He shows the effects provoked by the double character of human labour, which simultaneously generates *use-value* (concrete and useful, created by 'private individuals')[57] and *value* (abstract and socially mediated). This double character of human labour prevents or makes it difficult for humans to see its second side, as a result of which *value* does not appear as a social relationship, but, instead, as something almost inherent in the nature of the commodity. The false consciousness that the human being develops, here, does not result simply from a deceptive theoretical development, but from the objective appearance of the commodity, which 'automatically

---

55 Sánchez Vázquez 1977a, p. 5. Sánchez Vázquez does note the fact that the theme of the everyday and everyday consciousness receives special attention in 'contemporary bourgeois philosophy', and in this respect he mentions Edmund Husserl, Karl Jaspers, José Ortega y Gasset, and Martin Heidegger, but the topic is scarcely mentioned in Marxist debates 'despite Marx's extremely valuable discussion of the topic'.

This is why those studies which exist on the topic despite everything are especially important, among which he mentions the following authors: Karel Kosík, György Lukács, Henri Lefebvre, and Agnes Heller (Sánchez Vázquez 1977a, p. 34, n. 4. Compare also: Sánchez Vázquez 1980b, p. 24, n. 3, where the complete list of the aforementioned authors appears.).

Elsewhere, he refers to Antonio Gramsci as an author who dealt critically with the problem of everyday consciousness (Sánchez Vázquez 1977a, Part II: 'Some philosophical problems of praxis', Chapter V: 'Unity of theory and practice', section: 'The "common sense" point of view: pragmatism', pp. 169ff. and p. 195, n. 2).

56 *Capital* Volume I, Chapter One, Section Four: 'The Fetishism of the Commodity and Its Secret': Marx 1976a, pp. 163–77. On the discussion of this section of *Capital*, see also pp. 315ff of this book.

57 Marx 1976a, p. 165.

conceals' its social character.[58] This, in turn, leads necessarily to errors in economic theories, the critique of which is the central objective of Marx's main work.

On the question of everyday knowledge – which here concerns us principally in relation to theoretical conceptions and its dependence on them – Sánchez Vázquez concludes that everyday consciousness is influenced by ideas that 'are present in the very air [the human being] breathes'.[59] Consequently, everyday consciousness is not completely free of a certain 'theoretical basis' in which it carries theories, albeit in a simplified and degraded way.[60]

Sánchez Vázquez develops the character of the double dependency that everyday consciousness has on both 'infiltrated' theories and real social relations, on the basis of his understanding of two specific forms of creative praxis: revolutionary and artistic.

b   Revolutionary Praxis and Everyday Consciousness

The individual activity of a revolutionary cannot be understood in general by the everyday human being in his social or class dimension, who thus considers it to be something 'fruitless, foolish or irresponsible [... that will] never lead to the transformation of the world in its present state'.[61] But this disdain toward practical transformative activity on the terrain of social relations fits seamlessly within a generalised pessimistic atmosphere which is characterised by the underestimation of the active, social, and transformative elements[62] of the human being.[63] Schopenhauer openly defends this same attitude in the philosophical-theoretical sphere, with his 'pessimistic and irrationalist philos-

---

58   Ibid. See also the subchapter: 'Contribution to the Reconstruction of the Concept of Ideology in the Critique of Political Economy', pp. 245ff of this book. On the translation of Marx's concept of *'gegenständlicher Schein'* ['objective appearance'] see there p. 317.
59   Sánchez Vázquez 1977a, p. 5.
60   Ibid.
61   Ibid.
62   '... [M]an as a social, active, and transformative being ...' (Sánchez Vázquez 1980b, p. 25). This is different in the English-language edition: 'the active role of men in transforming society' (Sánchez Vázquez 1977a, p. 5). Sánchez Vázquez does not let slip such anthropological determinations.
63   This underestimation of transformative practical activity returns again in certain Marxist orientations. See, in this regard, for example, our chapter: 'Critique of Some Marxist Conceptions of Knowledge', subchapter a): 'Critique of Certain Conceptions of Marxism in General'.

ophy', which 'walks hand in hand with those contemporary philosophies that deny socio-historic progress and rob both history and human action of any and all significance'.[64]

Here, the critique of everyday consciousness begins to emerge. For Sánchez Vázquez, it is not a question of privileging philosophical consciousness as better developed and truer than everyday consciousness *per se*, but of demonstrating the intersections and connections between a widely disseminated orientation of the latter and influential tendencies among the former. Everyday consciousness should, therefore, not be transferred to a philosophical and therefore rational plane through a theoretical-pedagogical mechanism, but instead critical analysis must uncover the contradictions of all predominant types of thinking (both everyday and theoretical). But to do so, a particular foundation is essential, another theoretical basis which understands the human being as social, historical, and active.[65]

This is one of the questions to which the Marxist theory of knowledge owes its relevance. But here we would like to return to a more precise investigation of everyday consciousness. The fact that the latter is infiltrated with theoretical ideas, which it collects unconsciously does not in any way entail that everyday understanding assumes a theoretical attitude toward praxis. What is lacking for it to do so is the conscious relationship of consciousness to its object.[66] The everyday human being, who perceives himself to be a 'practical man, ... living and acting in a practical way',[67] has, of course, a conscious relationship with his actions – he cannot carry them out without reflecting – but at the same time 'he does not separate or stress practice as his proper object in such a way that that separation occurs first of all in consciousness as a theoretical attitude'.[68] It is as a result of this that, as Sánchez Vázquez explains, everyday

---

64   Ibid. On Sánchez Vázquez's understanding of the 'meaning of history', see our observations on his critique of Hegel on pp. 150f.

65   But why is everyday consciousness not oriented, as a result, according to *this* philosophical consciousness? Why is it that it does not allow itself to be infiltrated by it, rather than this being merely occasional, as stated above? Is Schopenhauer simply more astute than Marx, does he have better 'public relations'? Or is it because the man from Trier, since his burial at Highgate Cemetery on 17 March 1883, has died over and over again in recent years with increasing frequency and greater commotion? (And what, then, would Lazurus – one of the few figures who, according to tradition, died *twice* – say of this immoderate competitor?)

66   Sánchez Vázquez 1977a, p. 5.

67   Sánchez Vázquez 1977a, p. 6.

68   Ibid.

consciousness does not develop a theory of praxis (and nor could it do so, as will need to be shown).[69]

Sánchez Vázquez's critique of everyday consciousness of praxis has, therefore, raised, through a contrast with revolutionary praxis, two problems: in the first place, its concrete determination, namely, its immanent *pessimism*, which fails to grasp the human being in all its importance as a subject of history, and in the second place, its general conception, which he has determined to be *atheoretical* and which, in the absence of the reflexive moment, 'can never nurture a true revolutionary praxis'.[70] He continues his critique on the basis of three other concrete determinations of the everyday consciousness of praxis: its inherently 'ingenuous realism', its 'objectivism', and its 'utilitarianism'.[71]

Ingenuous realism, insofar as everyday consciousness assumes that things 'are ... known in themselves, irrespective of their relation to human activity', whereby when speaking of human intervention, Sánchez Vázquez evidently refers to the act of knowing.[72]

The *objectivism* characterises the everyday consciousness insofar as, through the assumption that things are known in themselves, it additionally implies that their importance, their meaning, and their significance are given to the human being almost as if by nature. That is to say, the ordinary man ignores 'the fact that because they have a practical significance practical acts and objects exist only *for* and *through* men. The characteristic of ordinary consciousness is that it regards the practical world as a world of things and meanings *in themselves*'.[73]

Sánchez Vázquez speaks here, above all, of that aspect of the cognisant subject, which is underestimated by everyday consciousness: the *active* subject who recognises things and gives them meaning. But it seems that, at the same time, this is present in a hidden way in the other side of the subject, which also produces those things, which are already implicitly present in the 'critique of pessimism'. A formulation in the final line of the 'critique of objectivism' in the introduction to *The Philosophy of Praxis* would seem to speak to this

---

69   Ibid.
70   Ibid.
71   Ibid.
72   Ibid. With regard to the concept of ingenuous realism, as well as later on, when Sánchez Vázquez sharpens and explains over and over again his analysis through the example of art as human praxis, we should recall his close relationship with aesthetic debates. On his critique of realism, see, moreover, our subchapter: 'Praxis as the Basis for Knowledge (Thesis I)' (pp. 134).
73   Sánchez Vázquez 1977a, p. 6. In this regard, see Part Three: 'Bolívar Echeverría: Use-Value and *Ethos*,' the chapter 'Reproduction and Communication,' especially p. 234 of this book.

broader interpretation: 'this objectivism which disregards the human, subjective aspect, and maintains the separation between the practical object and the subject'.[74]

Aside from this objectivism, which, as we have seen, constitutes part of ingenuous realism, our author also critiques everyday consciousness of praxis for its *utilitarianism*, which it is similarly not conscious of and which implies that it 'reduces the practical to a single utilitarian dimension, whereby a practical action or object is one which has material utility or which produces profit or advantage; that which lacks that direct or immediate utility, is impractical'.[75]

Here, Sánchez Vázquez takes an interesting turn when he relates this aspect of everyday human consciousness to the economic reality in which it is located as well as respective economic theories. While he does not suggest that the latter represent the immediate material foundation of this consciousness, in any case he indicates that 'ordinary consciousness and the standpoint of capitalist theories of economics and production coincide', as was the case with earlier economists and their theories, such as classical political economy, for example.[76] The utilitarian understanding of the concept of praxis in everyday consciousness maintains a discrete but definite relationship with the capitalist mode of production in which the law of value dominates. What other authors would understand as a clear *dependency*, Sánchez Vázquez describes as *simultaneity*, a concept that he makes broad argumentative use of in various texts (while it is true that the grammatical construction of simultaneity is, as far as we know, used more in Spanish than in German, a language in which the *causal* construction insatiably and jealously demands its rightful place): 'For ordinary consciousness what is productive is by definition practical; from the point of view of capitalist production the practical is defined as whatever produces new value or surplus value'.[77]

Sánchez Vázquez's critique of everyday consciousness of praxis, to summarise what we have explained up to this point, the following aspects which we have emphasised in the search for a general understanding of everyday consciousness and its concrete determination: an *atheoretical* conception, as well as its concrete determination as pessimistic, ingenuous realistic, objectivist, and utilitarian.

---

74   Sánchez Vázquez 1977a, p. 7.
75   Ibid.
76   Ibid.
77   Ibid.

Practical Politicism and Practical Apoliticism

'Everyday (or ordinary) practical consciousness', which we address in this section, is criticised by Sánchez Vázquez not only for its insufficient transcendence for radical, emancipatory, and revolutionary transformation of existing social relations – as we have argued thus far – but also because, in particular cases, it even *directly* stabilises these relations. To the critique of its passive non-emancipatory character, we add a critique of its active side. Sánchez Vázquez simultaneously grasps this aspect with the concepts ' "practical" politicism and "apoliticism" that is encouraged and sustained for "practical" reasons'.[78] Both can find themselves favoured by specific behaviours of the ruling power [*el poder*].

Practical politicism sets out from the seeming integration of the ordinary human being into political life, 'but in fact on the condition that he restricts himself exclusively to its "practical" aspects, that is politics as a career'.[79] In contrast, for those who remain outside this integration, politics reduced to this practical content understandably acquires a negative connotation. It becomes impossible for those who hope to intervene politically despite all this to see another dimension of politics – one which is not that of 'romanticism, idealism, or Utopia'[80] – beyond this 'practical' politicism.

Practical apoliticism, like practical politicism, feeds off the attempt 'to satisfy the "practical" aspirations of ordinary men', which can lead to depoliticisation.[81] On this point, Sánchez Vázquez does not formulate precisely how this depoliticisation is generated. But we can conclude that he has in mind, on the one hand, the aforementioned secondary effects of practical politicism and, on the other hand, the phenomenon that via small 'concessions', apparent or real, the impression can be generated that being quiet and waiting for gradual improvement through an automatic process or the activity of others promises more possibility of success, as we read in the following passage: 'The attempt to satisfy the "practical" aspirations of ordinary men can also take another form, much favoured by those in power, whose object is to suppress any awaken-

---

78   Ibid., p. 7. [Note to the English-language edition: 'politicismo' is translated in the Edition in English of *The Philosophy of Praxis* as 'politics'. We prefer the translation 'politicism'. We will also make this correction in other quotations, without further mention. Compare: Sánchez Vázquez 1980b, p. 27.]
79   Sánchez Vázquez 1977a, p. 7.
80   Ibid.
81   Ibid.

ing of a clear political consciousness, however slight, and to maintain ordinary people in a totally apolitical state.'[82]

c   Artistic Praxis and Everyday Consciousness

The position of everyday consciousness *vis-à-vis* artistic praxis is only analysed by Sánchez Vázquez with regard to its dependence on real (social) relations, and not, as we just saw in relation to revolutionary praxis, with regard to its dependence on 'infiltrated' theories. Everyday consciousness stamped with utilitarianism perceives artistic praxis as 'unproductive or impractical activities par excellence', since from the angle of immediate personal interest, it produces nothing more than aesthetic pleasure (just as revolutionary praxis produces only 'hunger, misery, and persecution'). As a result, since this form of praxis does not produce anything 'solid' or directly usable, it is, for the everyday man, a 'parasitic activity'.[83]

d   Concluding the Critique of Everyday Consciousness

To conclude, Sánchez Vázquez observes in the course of his critique of everyday consciousness of praxis in the introduction to *The Philosophy of Praxis*[84] that the picture sketched there of the ordinary human being and its everydayness is that of a historical human being whose everyday character cannot be separated from a determinate 'social structure'.[85] What today's everydayness represents is, therefore, not the quintessence of human history nor the end of time. The boredom of the everyday – Adolfo Sánchez Vázquez might add – so easily confused with eternity, is not itself secure from decadence or destruction.

Summarising: human praxis, whose forms are mentioned at the end of the introduction to *The Philosophy of Praxis* as including 'labour, art, politics, medicine, education, etc.'[86] and described elsewhere as 'experimental scientific

---

82   Ibid.
83   Sánchez Vázquez 1977a, p. 8.
84   Sánchez Vázquez 1977a, pp. 1–38. Title of the introduction: 'From ordinary consciousness to the philosophical consciousness of praxis'.
85   Sánchez Vázquez 1977a, p. 9.
86   Sánchez Vázquez 1977a, p. 10.

activity' that 'qualifies as praxis',[87] is not grasped in all its 'anthropological, cognitive, and social dimension' by everyday consciousness.[88] This abandonment of those three dimensions of praxis coincides with an understanding of the latter as 'utilitarian', 'self-sufficient (atheoretical)', and 'individual'.[89]

That is to say, the error of 'common sense' is that it is in no way capable of understanding praxis 'in its social and historical totality' which is expressed in various forms, some already mentioned, and in 'the activities specific individuals and groups, as well as their varied products'.[90] This broad understanding of praxis in its totality is the object of a certain consciousness. Sánchez Vázquez explains in relation to this specific form of consciousness: 'Historically it is possible to trace the development of that perspective from the ingenuous, empirical conception of praxis to the philosophical consciousness that finds expression, though not yet a complete or absolute expression, in Marxism'.[91]

But this developed philosophical consciousness (of praxis) is not accomplished in our era as something immanent to theory, or based on a particular stroke of genius, but, instead, can only be achieved in the historical process

---

87 Sánchez Vázquez 1977a, Part Two: 'Some philosophical problems of praxis'; Chapter IV: 'What is praxis?'; subchapter: 'Forms of praxis', pp. 156–61, here p. 159.

   The question of whether or not scientific experimentation constitutes a form of praxis is controversial in the literature. While Engels sees the only possible demonstration of causality inherent in nature 'in human activity, in experimentation, in labour' (Engels 1955, p. 244) the opposite is the case – as Alfred Schmidt emphasises – in Lévi-Strauss and in structural ethnology more generally: 'Dialectical materialism... is distinguished from structural ethnology since (like the early Lukács) it calls into doubt the character of the objective praxis of experimental knowledge in the natural sciences'. (Schmidt 1969a, pp. 254ff.)

   Schmidt describes Lévi-Strauss' manner of understanding experimentation through his 'Feuerbachianism': 'Lévi-Strauss falls back into Feuerbachianism when he isolates the category of the legality [regularity] of things from that which social production (however modest it may be) undertakes in each one of those things' (Schmidt 1969b, p. 254).

   Merleau-Ponty also calls into doubt the character of experimental praxis and 'insists that experimentation is merely a mode of knowledge that industry also relies on. Merleau-Ponty's interpretation has its gaps insofar as, to determine Marx's concept of praxis, it refers only to the Theses on Feuerbach': Schmidt 1973, p. 1137 n205. Schmidt refers here to Merleau-Ponty 1968, p. 60.

88 Sánchez Vázquez 1977a, p. 9. The gnoseological dimension of praxis, already mentioned here by Sánchez Vázquez, will need to be discussed in more depth by both him and by us during the course of this book, as a central point in research concerning his work.

89 Ibid.

90 Sánchez Vázquez 1977a, p. 10.

91 Ibid.

when human praxis itself makes this step of knowledge necessary and possible; *necessary*, because at this real historical point the human being 'can no longer continue to act upon and change the world creatively, that is in a revolutionary way, without first gaining a true philosophical consciousness of praxis'; and *possible*, 'when the necessary theoretical premises have been allowed to mature through the history of ideas'.[92] Consequently, in order to continue developing the concept of praxis, we must refer critically to both real history and the history of ideas and follow the footprints of human praxis and its concept in this history of humanity grasped in this double form.

It would be obviously too much to demand that everyday consciousness overcomes, using only its own forces, its 'spontaneous and unreflective conception of practical activity',[93] if we consider this need of a double recourse to its own buried historical and intellectual foundations. But the theorist and philosopher Sánchez Vázquez does not make this suggestion maliciously, such that, satisfied with himself and his discipline, he might sit happily in elevated philosophical consciousness and ponder about everyday consciousness, untainted by the latter and distancing himself from it. Rather, he seeks – as we understand it – to break with the helplessness of 'ordinary consciousness' and intervene in the development of a 'true philosophical conception of praxis',[94] as an urgently necessary development in real history. To do so, Sánchez Vázquez attempts to explain the reciprocal dependency that exists between the two mentioned historical developments, in the subchapters 'Towards a history of the philosophical consciousness of praxis'[95] and 'Towards a full vindication of human praxis',[96] in the introduction to *The Philosophy of Praxis*, where he discusses this interdependent relationship by looking at it, above all, as one in which the concept depends on the state of the real and material development of the respective historical forms of society and praxis.

---

92   Ibid.
93   Ibid.
94   Ibid.
95   Sánchez Vázquez 1977a, pp. 10–23.
96   Sánchez Vázquez 1977a, pp. 23–31.

CHAPTER 6

The Relationship between Philosophy and Praxis in History

In his investigation of the development of the concept of praxis in the history of thought, which he presents through an analysis of some of its 'fundamental milestones',[97] Sánchez Vázquez turns his gaze toward the philosophical traditions that Karl Marx also had before him: namely, those predominant in the West.[98] He sets out, then, from ancient Greek sources (Plato and Aristotle),[99] advances onward to the Renaissance (for example, Leonardo da Vinci and his opinions with regard to the theory of art, Leon Battista Alberti, Giordano Bruno, Niccolò Machiavelli, as well as two utopians of renaissance humanism, Tomasso Campanella and Thomas More);[100] he then moves on to bourgeois 'consciousness of productive praxis'[101] (Francis Bacon, René Descartes, and the Encyclopedists) and touches upon Jean-Jacques Rousseau's negative consciousness of praxis, to finally arrive – through a triple path that passes through classical English political economy to Adam Smith and David Ricardo; on the philosophical terrain by German Idealism (Georg Wilhelm Friedrich Hegel, and, in passing, also Johann Gottlieb Fichte) and anthropological materialism (Ludwig Feuerbach), as well as briefly referring to the influences of early French sociology (Claude Henri Saint-Simon) – to the classics of the 'philosophy of praxis', Marx and Engels.[102]

As for Marxism, Sánchez Vázquez's historical sketch covers Nikolai Bukharin, Georg Lukács, Karl Korsch, Adam Schaff, Karel Kosík, Mikhail N. Rutkevisch, Gaidukov, G. A. Davydova, and F. Eles, as well as the Yugoslavian 'Praxis' group.[103]

---

97 Sánchez Vázquez 1980b, p. 30 [this phrase does not appear in the English translation – translator].
98 Sánchez Vázquez 1977a, p. 11.
99 Sánchez Vázquez 1977a, pp. 10–17.
100 Sánchez Vázquez 1977a pp. 17–21.
101 Sánchez Vázquez 1977a pp. 22ff.
102 Sánchez Vázquez 1977a, pp. 23–30.
103 Sánchez Vázquez 1977a, pp. 30–3, above all p. 30, notes 42–4. The following people belonged to this 'Praxis' group: Gajo Petrović, Mihailo Marcović, Predrag Vranicki, Rudi Supek, Danko Grlić, and Milan Kangrga. Sánchez Vázquez, whose work has been translated several times in Yugoslavia and who participated in a wide range of theoretical debates there, mentions, on this topic, Karel Kosik's *Dialéctica de lo concreto*, prologue by Adolfo Sánchez Vázquez

He discusses Lenin,[104] Antonio Gramsci, and Louis Althusser in more detail.[105] After completing this brief introductory tour of the history of the theory, Sánchez Vázquez enters into more detail in the first part of his book – entitled 'Fundamental philosophical sources for the study of praxis' – into analysis of the concept of praxis in Hegel,[106] Feuerbach,[107] Marx,[108] and Lenin.[109]

In our study, we will follow Sánchez Vázquez's introductory sketch of the history of the philosophical concept of praxis, taking only as examples his explanations concerning Greek antiquity in order then to turn in more depth to his analysis of the Marxian concept of praxis through the relationship between praxis and knowledge, especially in the *Theses on Feuerbach*.

a   Antiquity

Sánchez Vázquez traces the following sketch of the philosophical concept of praxis in Antiquity: in ancient Greece, prevailing philosophy 'ignored...the practical world'[110] or avoided a more detailed discussion as well as the contact with praxis, precisely because it did not perceive in it anything more than the everyday consciousness that we just subjected to critique, but rather only

---

(Kosik 1967). The English translation appeared as *Dialectics of the Concrete: A Study on Problems of Man and World* (Kosik 1976). Sánchez Vázquez also mentions another book, in its German version: *Revolutionäre Praxis. Jugoslawischer Marxismus der Gegenwart* – Gajo Petrović (ed.) 1969.

104   Sánchez Vázquez 1977a, pp. 28–9.
105   On Sánchez Vázquez's discussion of Gramsci and Althusser, see in this book the chapter: 'Critique of Some Marxist Conceptions of Knowledge' (pp. 153ff).
106   Sánchez Vázquez 1977a, pp. 40–69.
107   Sánchez Vázquez 1977a, pp. 70–91.
108   Sánchez Vázquez 1977a, pp. 92–147.
109   Sánchez Vázquez 1980b, pp. 193–242. On the genesis of the chapter on Lenin in *Filosofía de la praxis*, see the chapter: '*The Philosophy of Praxis*: Two Versions', pp. 183ff of this book. [Note to the edition in English: Sánchez Vázquez's chapter on 'The concept of praxis in Lenin' is not included in the English-language edition of *The Philosophy of Praxis*, as this translation is based on the first edition of *Filosofía de la praxis*, in which the Lenin chapter is not included.]
110   Sánchez Vázquez 1977a, p. 11. It is not entirely correct to say that the practical world was 'ignored' in ancient Greek philosophy. Despite later clarifications made by Sánchez Vázquez (see p. 119n116 in this book), it is worth recalling, for example, Plato's manifestations in the *Politeia* regarding administration and life in a large city. See Plato, *Politeia*, 372c–373d.

its 'practical-utilitarian character'.[111] Practical activity, and above all productive praxis[112] – that is, labour – is considered by the predominant thought of ancient Greece to be something unworthy of free men [*freie Menschen*][113] and as the innate destiny of slaves.[114] What is of paramount interest is 'the transformation of social matter, of man', in order to create with it a decisive 'innovation' of antiquity, the *polis*.[115] Its development, the conscious transformation of the human as a social being, as a *Zoon politikon*, is especially important for the predominant form of thought in antiquity. The transformation of things and

---

111 Sánchez Vázquez 1977a, p. 11.
112 In his analysis of the consciousness of praxis in ancient Greece (Sánchez Vázquez 1977a, pp. 10–17), Sánchez Vázquez uses the term 'praxis' according to its meaning *today*, despite its partial deviation from the meaning of the terms '*praxis*' and '*poiesis*' in ancient Greece, which we mentioned previously; this could have led him into some difficulties. (See our chapter: 'The Concept of Praxis', subchapter: 'The Term "Praxis" in Various European Languages').
113 The formulation '*hombres libres*' ['free men'] in Sánchez Vázquez's discussion of the strict division of labour in ancient Greece, could also be translated [into German] as '*freie Männer*' ['free male persons'], since Spanish, like other Romance languages, does not distinguish between '*Mensch*' and '*Mann*' (aside from auxiliary constructions like 'human beings' ['*seres humanos*'], which are occasionally used to make this distinction clear in certain cases). In any case, the German formulation 'freie Männer' would suggest, here, that Sánchez Vázquez also includes the topic of gender among the relations of oppression and exploitation in ancient Greece. But since he does not do so in the text even when discussing later social formations, the formulation 'freie Männer' [free men] would surreptitiously make the text appear to be more critical and perspicacious than it really is.
    In any case, allow us to suggest for the disappointed reader that while Sánchez Vázquez, as far as we know, certainly does not take up this relationship in a more profound manner, both in the aforementioned Seminar on Marxism and the State Question in 1989 and in later texts he recognised the importance of the feminist movement, which, as is well-known, is not free of controversy even among self-defined leftist academics and political actors. Note, for example: 'Just as we cannot ignore the pre-Marxist (principally anarchist) contribution to the image of a new society and the awakening and mobilisation of consciousness in favor of it, nor can we similarly ignore that today we must take into account social movements (environmental, feminist, and pacifist ones in the West and Christian movements in Latin America) which even if they do not all claim socialism as their own, and even less Marxism, nevertheless act and struggle objectively toward its realisation' ('Reexamen de la idea del socialismo', in Sánchez Vázquez 1987, pp. 163–82, here: p. 164).
114 Sánchez Vázquez 1977a, p. 11. On the description that Sánchez Vázquez gives here of ancient society as one that was merely divided between free and slaves, see pp. 121f of this book.
115 Sánchez Vázquez 1977a.

of nature, which is to say, 'productive material praxis', is granted a secondary position.[116] In this way, what is not seen is the combination of the transformation of the human being as a social being, of society, and the transformation of things.[117]

The idea of the human who 'elevates himself... liberating him from all practical, material activity, from practice, and isolating him in the realm of theory', finds its most marked expression in Plato and Aristotle.[118] In Plato, the *bíos theoretikós*, or 'theoretical life',[119] acquires an outstanding significance that it never had before. The observation of pure, immutable, and eternal ideas can only become contaminated by contact with the material world. 'Life, properly speaking, was contemplation'.[120] Sensuality, corporeality, these are not vital expressions of the human being in the strict sense. Therefore, Plutarch says that for Plato, the practical application of theoretical distinctions debases the latter, as occurred for example in the practical application of geometry. Art, for example sculpture and painting, in crafts and manual labour, has a suspiciously intimate level of contact with imperfect matter.[121] How, then, to bring together the human being with the perfection of the idea?

For Aristotle, practical material activity, productive praxis, is considered to be below the dignity of the free – and thus true – human being, and what is necessary is to establish a distance between the two.[122] In this regard, Sánchez Vázquez cites the following passage from Aristotle's *Politics*: 'A state equipped with an ideal constitution... cannot have its citizens living the life of mechanics or shopkeepers, which is ignoble and inimical to goodness. Nor can it have them engaged in farming; leisure is a necessity, both for growth in goodness and for the pursuit of political activities'.[123]

---

116   Ibid. Notice: Sánchez Vázquez has already transformed his original formulation about ignoring the practical world into another regarding the underestimation of *productive* praxis in thought.
117   'The idea that man makes and elevates himself as a human being as a direct result of his practical activity, his labour, which transforms the material world is one that was alien to the Greek world' (ibid.).
118   Ibid.
119   Ibid.
120   Ibid.
121   Sánchez Vázquez 1977a, p. 12.
122   Ibid.
123   Aristotle, *Politics*, Book VII, 1328b–1329a. (We quote here according to the translation used by Sánchez Vázquez 1980b, p. 32). In other translations, we find the term 'tasks of government' instead of 'political activities'. The formulation employed by Sánchez Vázquez, by

In Aristotle, however, just as in Plato, political praxis (which in this passage obviously has a higher value than productive praxis, and is even compared to the achievement of virtue) remains subordinated to the contemplation, observation, and conception of theory. Sánchez Vázquez notes that: 'In the ancient world, theory never lost its supremacy, however important a role political activity might fulfill'.[124]

Faced with political praxis and above all the relationship between politics and theory, the Spanish-Mexican philosopher mentions a notable difference between Aristotle and Plato: 'Plato did recognize, however, that theory had to be practical, that thought and action would have to maintain a unity which was located on the realm of politics'.[125]

That unity of theory and praxis in politics is, according to Plato, however, extraordinarily difficult to establish and is unilateral. Political praxis scarcely has its own foundation, and should be based entirely on theory; or put more precisely: 'That unity is maintained by allowing ideas to become practical in themselves'.[126] The chasm that Plato opens between theory and praxis is bridged in the relationship between philosophy and politics by a person who unites both aspects in himself: the philosopher king. 'Theory and practice, philosophy and politics merge in the person of the philosopher king'.[127]

But even in this 'solution' of the theory-praxis problem on the political terrain, there persists the aforementioned unilateral relationship: 'Plato's attitude...simply prefigures future Utopian conceptions of the transformation and organisation of society. He admits that theory can become practice, and even accepts the possibility of political praxis, but only to the extent that this implies the application of the absolute principles set out in his theory'.[128]

But how is this relationship developed in Aristotle? His marked sense of reality leads him to consider the unity of theory and political praxis – which Plato clearly recognised as a necessity, but presented only in an idealist and unilateral form – to be impossible. As a result, he must also reject the direct influence of theory over praxis. The separation of theoretical life from practical life,

---

contrast, does not canonise the state in advance as the only sphere for organisation and discussion of the social. See, for example, Rolfes's translation: Aristotle 1948, p. 255.
124   Sánchez Vázquez 1977a.
125   Ibid.
126   Ibid.
127   Sánchez Vázquez 1977a, p. 13.
128   Ibid. The text cited continues: 'Praxis, therefore, must be philosophical; its value derives from its rational theoretical content. So the Platonic unity of theory and practice simply represents the dissolution of practice in theory'.

praised by Plato, cannot simply be overcome on the terrain of politics through the construction of a philosopher king. Sánchez Vázquez interprets Aristotle as follows: 'The philosophers could not be kings, nor the kings philosophers'.[129]

The suspension of the direct subordination of praxis to theory does not mean that theoretical and practical life have nothing to do with one another, but that both 'merge and complement one another once their differences and hierarchies have been recognised'.[130] Thus political activity in Aristotle is not essentially irrational, but is, instead, guided by another sort of reason, 'the reason that inspires it, which is practical reason, has as its object not pure essence but human acts'.[131]

In this sense, we find in Aristotle a 'theory of praxis' on the plane of practical public affairs, in the sense of an 'art of directing public affairs in practice'.[132] Therefore, while political praxis is still granted some theoretical recognition by Aristotle and his teacher Plato (in different ways, as we have seen), such recognition is completely denied to productive praxis.

Before leaving the introduction that Sánchez Vázquez provides to the concept of praxis in Plato and Aristotle, we will lastly return to that contempt for productive praxis that he attempts to clarify from a different angle with the help of Marx, and above all with his analysis of value and reference to the 'giant thinker... Aristotle' in *Das Kapital*.[133] The predominant form of thinking in ancient Greece featured this contempt for productive praxis. This attitude is understandable in relation to the low level of development of the mode of production in slave society and the sufficient availability of slave labour to satisfy practical necessities.[134] In considering the labour process, what was of interest was only the slave's (final) product, and not its active subject, the producer.

Sánchez Vázquez expresses this by way of Marx's economic conceptualisations, and ventures to claim that in ancient Greece 'use-value [and not exchange-value] was the only criterion of value'.[135] This would mean that ancient society was based upon a purely subsistence economy, without exchange of commodities or extensive foreign trade, commercial capital, and suchlike. Evidently, this *lapsus* has to do with Sánchez Vázquez's presentation of ancient Greece, which divides the latter simply into 'free' and 'slaves',

---

129 Ibid.
130 Ibid.
131 Sánchez Vázquez 1977a, p. 14.
132 Ibid.
133 Marx 1976a, p. 175, n. 35.
134 Sánchez Vázquez 1977a.
135 Ibid.

leaving out completely, for example, the day labourers or craftspeople who were neither 'free' nor 'slaves' and who were forced to freely sell their capacity to labour.[136] His lack of precision with regard to exchange-value in ancient Greece is explained when we continue to read this chapter of *The Philosophy of Praxis*. The circumstance we refer to is that the *concept of value* as the value of labour (in the Marxian sense) was still not known in antiquity; what was already known, conversely, was the *value-form*, which Sánchez Vázquez here erroneously equates with it.[137] This slippage, which is more than terminological, refers back to the lack of precision in the presentation of ancient society, and is corrected without comment by Sánchez Vázquez himself when he goes on to speak of Aristotle's reflections on value and Marx's observations in this respect:

> Aristotle, who Karl Marx describes as 'the great investigator who was the first to analyse the value-form, like so many other forms of thought, society and nature',[138] 'did ... perceive', in the words of Sánchez Vázquez, 'the need to stabilize commodity production in order that they could be exchanged, but as Marx points out, he could never discover how these relations of equality might be assessed'.[139] But what is common, what is shared among all human products,

---

136   See Aristotle, *Politics II*, Book III, 1278a.
137   The formulation in question is the following: 'In Greece, work was seen as a function of the product, and the product in its turn as a function of its utility or capacity to satisfy a concrete human need. *Exchange value, or the value of a commodity in relation to other commodities where all are regarded as equivalent expressions of general human labour, is of no interest*' (Sánchez Vázquez 1977a, italics by S.G.). It is true that value and exchange-value are used synonymously in *Capital*, but not knowing the *concept of value* does not automatically mean that human beings do not know and do not apply *exchange-value as a form*. Thus, exchange-value 'counts' without having been penetrated intellectually, or as Marx says in *Capital: they do not know it, but they are doing it*.
       One possible explanation for this difficulty with the concept of value can be extracted from Melvin Cantarell Gamboa's review of the original Spanish-language edition of *The Philosophy of Praxis*: 'the book ... suffers from forgetting, not ignoring, works as fundamental as Marx's *Capital*, ... where there exist rich references to praxis and from which we believe he did not squeeze enough juice, in contrast to the exaggerated emphasis on the works of Marx's youth'. See Cantarell Gamboa 1967, p. 29.
       In this regard, see also the observations in Part Three: 'Bolívar Echeverría: Use-Value and *Ethos*', subchapter 'Differences vis-à-vis the Concept of Praxis in Sánchez Vázquez', above all p. 202, in this book.
138   Marx 1976a, Chapter One, Section Three 'The Value-Form or Exchange-Value, III: The equivalent form', p. 151.
139   Sánchez Vázquez 1977a, p. 15. He refers here to the following passage in the Spanish-language edition of *Capital*: Marx 1964, p. 26.

is precisely the fact that the human labour employed in their production is objectified in them. Aristotle's difficulty in discovering the concept of value must be considered as at one with his contempt for human labour, for productive praxis.

But while Karl Marx, in *Capital*, 'only' sees this weakness of 'Aristotle's genius' as based on 'the historical limitation inherent in the society in which he lived' and which prevented him from 'finding out what "in reality" this relation of equality consisted of',[140] Sánchez Vázquez speaks in simpler and sharper terms: the concept of praxis in ancient Greece (including that of Aristotle) 'was central to the ruling ideology'[141] that 'corresponded... to the interest of

---

140   Marx 1976a p. 152ff. The cited passage from Marx says in its entirety:

'However, Aristotle himself was unable to extract this fact, that, in the form of commodity-values, all labour is expressed as equal human labour and therefore as labour of equal quality, by inspection from the form of value, because Greek society was founded on the labour of slaves, hence had as its natural basis the inequality of men and of their labour-powers. The secret of the expression of value, namely the equality and equivalence of all kinds of labour because and in so far as they are human labour in general, could not be deciphered until the concept of human equality had already acquired the permanence of a fixed popular opinion. This however becomes possible only in a society where the commodity-form is the universal form of the product of labour, hence the dominant social relation is the relation between men as possessors of commodities. Aristotle's genius is displayed precisely by his discovery of a relation of equality in the value-expression of commodities. Only the historical limitation inherent in the society in which he lived prevented him from finding out what "in reality" this relation of equality consisted of' (pp. 151f).

In this passage, Marx refers to Aristotle's *Nicomachean Ethics*. See, for example: 'In all friendships between dissimilar people, as we have said, it is proportion that produces equality and preserves the friendship; for example in political friendship the shoemaker receives in return for his shoes what they are worth, and so do the weaver and the rest. In these cases, a common measure is provided in the form of money, and so everything is referred to this and measured by it' (Aristotle 2000, p. 164). See Marx 1975a, p. 848, editorial note 24.

[Note to the edition in English: Fowkes's translation 'fixed popular opinion' for Marx's German expression 'Volksvorurteil' [literally: 'popular prejudice'] is very 'free'. It obscures the Marxian critique of the idea of 'human equality', which is expressed more systematically in his *Critique of the Gotha Programme*. This is not a secondary question, as – in a very problematic way – a substantial proportion of today's Marxists (and also anti-Marxists) think naively that Marx's philosophical and economical work is a *integral* part of modern, ingeniously 'rational thought' and enlightenment thinking. It is, and at the same time it is not. See also, on this, note 188 in Part Three of this book. Compare Marx 1976a, p. 152, with Marx 1975a, p. 74.]

141   Sánchez Vázquez 1977a, p. 14.

the ruling class'.[142] But at the same time, in discussing these thinkers, Sánchez Vázquez uses a more circumspect formulation, one which recalls Marx's discussion of Aristotle: 'the impotence of the mode of production based on slavery coupled with the capacity of a servile labour force to satisfy all the practical needs... *led to* a debasement of the value of human labour, which appeared as a routine and demeaning activity whose product alone was of importance'.[143]

Sánchez Vázquez concludes his presentation of the concept of praxis in Greek antiquity by turning to some voices 'who disagreed with this disdainful attitude'.[144] He cites as an example Hesiod, who in his text *Works and Days* attributes to human labour a greater importance than the veneration of the gods and the possibility of achieving riches, independence, and glory.[145] The Sophists, who came out against slavery, similarly had a dissenting concept of productive praxis; in this regard, he cites Antiphon[146] and Prodicus of Ceo.[147] Moreover, he mentions the 'cynic Antisthenes', who also attributes great significance to human labour.[148]

---

142   Sánchez Vázquez 1977a, p. 16. Sánchez Vázquez, in relating the predominant philosophy of antiquity to the economic form of slave society and the 'interests of the dominant classes', continues the central tendency of his *Philosophy of Praxis*, which is characterised precisely by emerging gracefully from situations without comfortable simplifications. In this regard, see Berel Lang's comments in his review of the book: 'Vázquez, who usually avoids clichés, relates this idea of contemplative knowledge to the Greek distaste for manual labour and acceptance of slaveholding; so much, one might say, for the Sparta which proposed no such leisurely view of knowing – which flourished, in fact, without philosophy at all...': Lang 1978, p. 30.

143   Sánchez Vázquez 1977a, p. 14, italics by S.G. Sánchez Vázquez speaks here of the 'value of human labour' obviously in the normative sense. Seen economically, human labour has no value, but rather *creates* value. What *has* value is the human labour-power. (See also Marx 1976a, Chapter One, 'The Commodity', pp. 125–77).

144   Sánchez Vázquez 1977a, p. 16.

145   Ibid.

146   Antiphon sees productive praxis not as a simple residual of the natural, as if foreign to the 'man as such'. For him, 'fame never arrives by itself, but is instead accompanied by pain and fatigue'. Marx's quoted statement, according to which the concept of human equality is necessary for a developed concept of productive praxis, seems to be completed here. For Antiphon, all human beings are equal 'by nature'. See Antiphon, frag. 44 d D. See also, Lexicon der alten Welt 1965, pp. 433ff.

147   Sánchez Vázquez refers here to Plato's testimony regarding Prodicus and cites, according to Plato, *Charmides*, 163 a d.

148   Sánchez Vázquez 1977a. Here he cites the compilation of fragments of Antisthenes by Diogenes Laertius, *Book VI*, 2.

To conclude, Sánchez Vázquez suggests that in the 'industrial and commercial cities of Ionia ... the mechanical arts did undergo some development' and that another attitude toward the unity of science and technology (in this case, an approving one) prevailed at the time, in contrast with Athens and other Greek cities of the same period.[149] In sum, Sánchez Vázquez affirms with respect to the predominant tendencies of ancient Greece: 'It was the material conditions of life in Ancient Greece which was characterised by a slave-holding mode of production, which determined the rupture between theory and practice, held back technical progress and "blocked" that progress both socially and ideologically, in part as a result of its negative attitude towards productive physical labour'.[150]

Discussions surrounding the concept of praxis in ancient Greece cast an initial light on the winding paths that the development of this concept had to take in the history of philosophy. The force field between Plato and Aristotle – between the view of the need for the unity of theory and praxis, and the recognition of the almost insurmountable obstacles existing to this unity among relations which were up until now antagonistic – already demarcates a significant part of the framework within which it was necessary to struggle theoretically for centuries. The importance, which Sánchez Vázquez highlights, of the material relations underlying these respective formulations (even where there is a concept with higher esteem for praxis), indicates another line of demarcation in the history of thought.

In the aftermath of the enormous transformations, expansions, and limitations suffered by the concept of praxis in the course of history, a philosophy appears which grants this concept a completely new weight.

b   The Philosophy of Praxis

Let us turn, then, to the thinker whose doctrine is understood by our author as a *Philosophy of Praxis* and who, by virtue of this particularity, deserves his

---

This adversary of Plato is seen in the literature, of course, as a precursor to the Cynics (through his disciple, Diogenes of Sinope), but he himself is not characterised as a Cynic, but as a Socratic. His philosophy shares with the Cynics the doctrine of the absolute absence of necessity, but not their appreciation for the lack of shame (see, for example, Lexicon der alten Welt 1965, pp. 1657ff).

149   Sánchez Vázquez 1977a, p. 17.
150   Sánchez Vázquez 1977a, p. 17. Sánchez Vázquez mentions in this regard Magalhaes-Vilhena 1962.

greatest attention: Karl Marx. Adolfo Sánchez Vázquez defines Marx's concept of praxis as the 'central category of his philosophy', 'which began with the *Theses on Feuerbach*'.[151] What is revolutionary about Marx's work does not lie in some internal theoretical novelty or innovation, and is not a simple shift in paradigms or something of the sort, but, instead, consists in the explicit turn toward praxis as the locus in which true and false are distinguished. Philosophy, which had throughout millennia (as the elevation of the spirit above the vileness of the world) understood praxis as a necessary evil which was more or less avoidable, and centred its efforts on being affected as little as possible by it,[152] receives with Marx the function of making the world accessible to thought, precisely to help human activity, which is practical and transformative, to acquire conscious forms.

Up to this point the objective, contradictory, and imperfect world had been a heavy burden on theory (philosophy), which aspired to full force and perfection, a burden that must be repeatedly shaken off. That objective world is now in question. Its contradictions must no longer be left aside, but must instead explicitly become the principal topic of analysis and the object of real transformation. Thus, the force field between reality and intellectual reflection on that reality cannot simply be 'resolved' through the repeated modulation of reflection, but must instead be transformed through a revolution of reality *itself*.

Therefore, Marxian theory does not come to rest after a process of intellectual maturation, but cannot desist while human society is not emancipated, while the exploitation of human by human persists. Sánchez Vázquez thus approaches this theory not due to the insufficiencies of prevailing philosophy (and its history), but rather on account of the adversities of social relations themselves.[153]

---

151   Sánchez Vázquez 1977a, p. 96.
152   As in the previous section, here we are speaking primarily of productive praxis.
153   To illustrate this, we will cite as a footnote a small anecdote: when the author of this book asked Adolfo Sánchez Vázquez at the UNAM about his assessment of the development of Marxism in Latin America, he answered that this was above all a question of political praxis and not a scholastic one that could be answered within a merely theoretical framework. The author had a similar experience over and over again in a philosophy seminar (!) at the same institution, in which he was exhorted repeatedly to not make theoretical debates so academic or to consider these in isolation from concrete political praxis. For the author, who had only always heard exactly the opposite at the University of Frankfurt, this was an incredible theoretical-political experience.

CHAPTER 7

The *Theses on Feuerbach*

Sánchez Vázquez analyses the relationship between praxis and knowledge in Marx primarily on the basis of the *Theses on Feuerbach*. In this text, which was written immediately after the *Paris Manuscripts* and at almost the same time as *The German Ideology*, the essential elements of a 'true "philosophy of praxis"' already appear clearly.[154]

But he does not consider this early Marxian text to be separate from Marx's complete works, referring at various points to *The German Ideology* in order to help interpret it. Moreover, for understanding the relationship between praxis and knowledge, he refers to *Capital*, for example, the subchapter on 'The Fetishism of the Commodity and Its Secret', which is of such great significance to Western Marxism.[155] This manner of approaching Marx's work already allows us to glimpse the fact that our author considers it to be one whole. Now, to understand with greater precision the position that the *Theses on Feuerbach* occupy in Sánchez Vázquez's general interpretation of Marx, and, in connection with this, in the structure of his chapter on *Marx's conception of praxis*,[156] as well as the position he takes regarding the problem of continuity and rupture in Marx's work, we will look at this proposal in greater detail.

a   The Position of the *Theses on Feuerbach* in Marx's Work

In the aforementioned chapter on Marx, the author presents the development of the concept of praxis on the basis of a discussion of 'Marx ... in his early work'.[157] In the structure of his book, he follows the chronological order in which these texts were written: 'Introduction to the Critique of Hegel's Philosophy of Right' (late 1843 to January 1844, a text which Sánchez Vázquez

---

154 Sánchez Vázquez 1977a, Part I: 'Philosophical sources of the study of praxis', Chapter III: 'The conception of praxis in Marx', subchapter: 'Praxis and knowledge: the "Theses on Feuerbach"', pp. 115–17, here: p. 115. See, moreover, Part II: 'Some philosophical problems of praxis', Chapter V: 'The unity of theory and practice', pp. 169–98.
155 See, for example, Sánchez Vázquez 1977a, p. 189.
156 Sánchez Vázquez 1977a, Part One: 'Philosophical sources of the study of praxis', Chapter III: The conception of praxis in Marx', pp. 92–147.
157 Sánchez Vázquez 1977a, p. 97.

discusses in his subchapter 'Philosophy and action');[158] *Economic-Philosophical Manuscripts of 1844* (April to August of 1844); *The Holy Family or Critique of Critical Criticism. Against Bruno Bauer and Company* (coauthored with Engels, September–November 1844); *Theses on Feuerbach* (Spring 1845); *The German Ideology: Critique of Modern German Philosophy According to Its Representatives Feuerbach, B. Bauer and Stirner, and of German Socialism According to Its Various Prophets* (with Engels, 1845–6), and the *Manifesto of the Communist Party* (with Engels, December 1847 to January 1848).

Here, we find accentuated the question of when 'Marxism began to assert itself as such' (since Sánchez Vázquez understands Marxism as 'a theory clarifying praxis and providing a basis and a guide for practical, revolutionary transformation'). In his theoretical development, Marx's 'point of departure was a speculative conception of the world, and from there he progressed beyond the confines of the Left Hegelians to arrive finally at a fully elaborated philosophy of praxis',[159] but this does not mean that he underwent a 'definitive break'[160] and that a specific text can be identified unequivocally as marking the birth of Marxism. Rather, Marx's work 'should be seen as a process that is both continuous and discontinuous, of which each work forms a part'.[161]

Sánchez Vázquez mentions a series of texts which various authors suggest mark the point at which 'Marxism began...as such'. The difference between this enumeration and the previously presented list stems from the

---

158   Ibid. The word 'action', which is used repeatedly by Sánchez Vázquez in formulations like 'theory of... revolutionary action' (ibid.) could also be translated into German in other passages as 'Tat' or 'Handlung'. Here, with support from Marx's formulation in the *Pariser Manuskripte*, the term 'Aktion' was chosen. Note, for example, 'Um den *Gedanken* des Privateigentums aufzuheben, dazu reicht der *gedachte* Kommunismus vollständig aus. Um das wirkliche Privateigentum aufzuheben, dazu gehört eine *wirkliche* kommunistische *Aktion*': Marx 1985a, p. 553.

   In the translation of this passage to Spanish, which is cited by Sánchez Vázquez, Marx's formulation 'wirkliche kommunistische Aktion' is reproduced as 'acción real del comunismo' ['real action of communism'] (cited from the Roces translation, in Sánchez Vázquez 1980b, p. 143: see Marx 1962a, p. 96). Compare this with the full translation of this passage [from the edition in English, in which the given phrase appears instead as '*actual* communist action' – Trans.]: 'In order to abolish the *idea* of private property, the *idea* of communism is completely sufficient. It takes *actual* communist action to abolish actual private property' (Marx 1978a, p. 99).

159   Sánchez Vázquez 1977a, p. 96.
160   Sánchez Vázquez 1977a, p. 97.
161   Ibid. Notice, however, that Sánchez Vázquez, despite all his critiques of the idea of a 'definitive break', here poses the question of the 'beginning of Marxism'. We will return to this problem at the end of this section.

fact that *Critique of Critical Criticism* disappears and the 1859 prologue to the *Contribution to the Critique of Political Economy* is added.[162] In so doing, Sánchez Vázquez emphasises that 'determining in which work or at what stage of his thought Marx broke with previous philosophy depends upon the question which is deemed to be the point of separation'.[163]

Sánchez Vázquez explains this in the introductory part of this chapter with two examples: the first is that of Galvano della Volpe, who in his *Rousseau and Marx*[164] situates that rupture on the terrain of the philosophy of law and the state and locates it in the text 'Introduction to the Critique of Hegel's Philosophy of Right' (1843). This determination can be explained by the fact that Della Volpe is interested in casting light on Marx's clear rejection of idealist Hegelian philosophy, which 'represented a mystification of the reality that was to be transformed'.[165] In this regard, Sánchez Vázquez observes that in this text Marx's rupture with prior philosophy 'is still not a radical one', since while 'his critique did expose reality to the eye, ... the point, however – as he was to put it later – was not to transform its mystifications, but to transform the reality itself'. He had still not reached the point from which it is possible 'to envisage a philosophy that was both theory and guide to action'.[166]

Sánchez Vázquez does not document the second example by mentioning any author concretely, but, on the basis of its content, it is clear that he is alluding to Althusser and his scientistic interpretation of Marx:

> If... it is asserted that Marx broke with all ideology before going on to elaborate the theory of scientific socialism, the break would correspond to the replacement of an ideological mode of thought – that is, an unreal, false, illusory mode of thought in accordance with his own class conditioning – by scientific thought, then it would be justifiable to regard *The German Ideology* as being impregnated with ideological elements. In that case the true, scientific conception of society, based on the discovery of the contradiction between productive forces and the relations of production, could only be elaborated once the cardinal principles of the materialist conception of history had been laid down.[167]

---

162   Sánchez Vázquez 1977a, pp. 96ff.
163   Sánchez Vázquez 1977a, p. 142, n. 6.
164   Della Volpe 1978.
165   Sánchez Vázquez 1977a, p. 142, n. 6.
166   Ibid.
167   Ibid.

In discussing the *Paris Manuscripts*, Sánchez Vázquez clarifies to which author he is referring. He explicitly criticises Althusser's *Pour Marx*,[168] in which the latter argues that Marx breaks with Feuerbach's anthropologism in *The German Ideology* and that his preceding early works can be seen simply as an extension of the theory of 'human nature' to political economy.[169] And he continues with a critique of Althusser's approach: 'Such an interpretation burns all the bridges between the two works, but leaves unanswered the question as to how ... Marx was able to move (or rather leap) from the speculative or ideological Feuerbachian perspective of the *Manuscripts* to the new scientific method of the work of 1845'.[170]

Sánchez Vázquez, on the contrary, insists that the discontinuity of Marx's theoretical development is not 'radical' and shows this through the concept of *alienated labour*, which for Althusser – we should note – characterises precisely the Hegelianising phase which still had not been overcome in this phase of Marx's work. This concept, according to Sánchez Vázquez, is already contained in the *Manuscripts* as a 'fundamental premiss of all human history'. In this sense, 'the *Manuscripts* constitute a decisive contribution to the formation of Marx's thought'.[171]

Sánchez Vázquez criticises Althusser for not granting, in his theory, a sufficiently important position to the concept of praxis. Certainly, he does recognise that we can speak of something like a 'transition from ideology (or Utopia) to science', but he insists that what is new about Marxism is not a paradigm shift internal to the theory, but rather the fact that it was born 'as a scientific theory of the revolutionary praxis of the proletariat'.[172]

So Sánchez Vázquez rejects the supposed radical rupture in Marx's development, and, to the contrary, makes clear that this 'process that is both continuous and discontinuous' reached maturity in the *Communist Manifesto*, since it was in this latter text that the encounter between theory and action was established,[173] even though it might seem a little strange to attribute such a key position precisely to the text which is considered to be most problematic in Marxist debates. The response probably lies in the fact that this text, more than many others, is directly related to his political praxis. Marx, along with

---

168 Althusser 1965a.
169 Sánchez Vázquez 1977a, p. 109.
170 Ibid.
171 Ibid.
172 Sánchez Vázquez 1977a, p. 143 n6. This quote was corrected using the Spanish original: Sánchez Vázquez 1980b, p. 121 n8.
173 Sánchez Vázquez 1977a, p. 97.

Engels, was commissioned by the second congress of the Communist League in London of November–December 1847 to lay out its programme, and the result is the *Manifesto of the Communist Party*.

But in the same breath, he establishes one of those very breaks that he has criticised – not only for their exact location, but also on principle – and declares that the *Manifesto* represents the true moment of Marxism's birth: 'Marxism can only be said to exist as a philosophy of praxis after the publication of *The Communist Manifesto*'.[174] As though having a premonition of these objections, or through the hope that his own presentation should not lead to a rigid definition of the 'beginning of Marxism', he adds, qualifying: 'Marxism becomes a philosophy of praxis with the *Manifesto*, where a process with no foreseeable end is set into motion'.[175]

In the end, this passage by Sánchez Vázquez on the 'beginning of Marxism' (as a philosophy of praxis) leaves some room for doubt. On the one hand, he rejects the establishment of divisions, while at the same time attempting to do the same. The fact that he does not give this attempt much importance is clear in the fact that he indicates, as a point of inflection, the *Theses on Feuerbach* on one occasion, at another point the *Paris Manuscripts*, and finally the *Manifesto*.

Our author, when questioned on the topic, would show his disinterest by turning away from the topic, reproaching its scholastic nature, suggesting that in the end such questions must be discussed and clarified with praxis and in praxis, and immediately entering into a virulent political confrontation in Nicaragua to discuss the topic of 'revolution and democracy' on a theoretical level with the Sandinistas themselves, *à propos* of the then upcoming general elections of 1990.[176]

But let us return to Sánchez Vázquez's theoretical text. Summarising, we could sketch, congruently, his exposition of the development of the Marxian concept of praxis in the following fashion: the concept of praxis is already delineated in the early works; in the *Paris Manuscripts* it gains its full content by the addition to the concept of political praxis that of productive praxis; and

---

174 Ibid.
175 Ibid.
176 Sánchez Vázquez speaks in all seriousness when referring to the relationship between theory and praxis. He does not merely play with the idea and nor does he play with politics. In the period in question, the topic of parliamentary elections in Nicaragua was one of the most explosive for the Latin American Left. On this terrain, his research moved in the force field that existed between the experiences of the Soviet Union after Lenin's dissolution of the constituent assembly and the Nazis' rise to power in Germany, through the parliamentary elections of 1933. (Sánchez Vázquez 1989).

in the *Theses on Feuerbach* it becomes the central concept, which 'culminates'[177] in the *Communist Manifesto*. In Marxist debates, this concept should continue to develop in a 'process with no foreseeable end.'[178]

b   Interpretation of the *Theses on Feuerbach*

This philosopher, emerging from his anti-Francoist praxis, summarises in an introductory manner what is decisive about the *Theses on Feuerbach*: 'In the *Theses*, Marx formulated a conception of objectivity founded on praxis, and defined his philosophy as the philosophy of the transformation of the world'.[179]

These two aspects are inseparable. The material world can only be recognised along with the concept of its transformation. When Marx locates the practical and transformative activity of human beings at the centre of all human relations, this cannot but have serious consequences on the terrain of knowledge. The praxis/knowledge relation is represented in three ways in the *Theses*:

1. Praxis as basis of knowledge (Thesis 1);
2. Praxis as criterion of truth (Thesis 2); and
3. Praxis as the end of knowledge.[180]

As has already been asserted, 'the intervention of praxis in the process of knowledge leads to the overcoming of the antithesis between idealism and materialism', which is to say, the antithesis 'between the understanding of knowledge as knowledge of objects produced or created by consciousness and the conception that sees that knowledge as the mere ideal reproduction of objects in themselves'.[181] It is necessary to overcome both positions: we cannot persist in either an idealist theory of knowledge or in 'a realist theory like that of traditional materialism, which had done little more than elaborate upon the standpoint of ingenuous realism'.[182]

Sánchez Vázquez indicates, here, that different interpreters of Marx derive different conclusions from the introduction of the concept of praxis to the problem of knowledge, mentioning three positions in this regard:

---

177   Sánchez Vázquez 1977a, p. 97.
178   Ibid.
179   Sánchez Vázquez 1977a, p. 116.
180   Ibid.
181   Ibid.
182   Ibid.

1: 'the fact that praxis is a factor in our knowledge does not mean that we cannot know things in themselves';

2: 'the admission of the decisive role of praxis as an indication that we can never know things in themselves, outside their relation to man, but only things humanised through praxis and integrated thus into a human world' (Gramsci's view);

3: 'maintain[ing] that without praxis, or the creation of socio-human reality, knowledge of reality is itself impossible' (Kosík's position).[183]

The difference between the second and third positions is not immediately obvious. On the basis of the entirety of *The Philosophy of Praxis*, it is possible to sketch in broad strokes the differences between the three, as well as Sánchez Vázquez's own evaluation of them. While the first position recognises, albeit underestimating it, the epistemological relevance of human praxis, the second position moves in the opposite direction and grants human praxis such importance that, beyond its influence, no reality exists.[184] The third position, like the second, appreciates the irreplaceable epistemological relevance of praxis, but, diametrically opposed to the second position, does not make this into an ontological claim, and, as a result, shares with the first position the recognition of the primacy of the object.

In what follows, the author here analysed would need to explain why it is that he understands the third position to be correct. To do so, he returns to Marx's original text to investigate its 'actual meaning', which, at first, becomes problematic for him since the text lends itself to opposing or even contradictory interpretations.[185] But, in order to understand how Sánchez Vázquez goes into more depth in the three mentioned aspects of praxis in the process of knowledge – praxis as basis for knowledge, as criterion of truth, and as the end of knowledge – we will follow him in his interpretation of the *Theses on Feuerbach*.

---

183   Sánchez Vázquez 1977a, pp. 116f.
184   Elsewhere, Sánchez Vázquez characterises Gramsci's position with the latter's own words, as 'absolute immanentism', 'absolute historicism' and 'humanism' (Sánchez Vázquez 1977a, p. 33. This quote was changed using the second edition of the Spanish original: Sánchez Vázquez 1980b, p. 56.). In this regard, see also our next chapter: 'The Critique of Some Marxist Conceptions of Knowledge'. There, in the first subchapter ('Critique of Certain Conceptions of Marxism in General'), we deal with Sánchez Vázquez's critique of Gramsci.
185   Sánchez Vázquez 1977a, p. 117.

Praxis as the Basis for Knowledge
(*Thesis 1*)

In the following paragraph, the author of *The Philosophy of Praxis* provides us with an interpretation of the first thesis on Feuerbach and refers us to the original text:

> The chief defect of all hitherto existing materialism – that of Feuerbach included – is that the thing [*Gegenstand*], reality, sensuousness, is conceived only in the form of the object [*Objekts*] or of *contemplation* [*Anschauung*], but not as *human sensuous activity, practice* [*Praxis*], not subjectively. Hence it happened that the *active* side, in contradistinction to materialism, was developed by idealism – but only abstractly, since, of course, idealism does not know real, sensuous activity as such.
>
> Feuerbach wants sensuous objects [*Objekte*], really distinct from the thought objects, but he does not conceive human activity itself as *objective* [*gegenständliche*] activity. Hence, in *Das Wesen des Christentums*, he regards the theoretical attitude as the only genuinely human attitude, while practice [*Praxis*] is conceived and fixed only in its dirty-judaical manifestation. Hence he does not grasp the significance of 'revolutionary,' of practical-critical, activity.[186]

The German terms '*Gegenstand*' and '*Objekt*' can only be translated into Spanish as '*objeto*', but the distinction between these two words is of great importance in Marx, which is easy to see in this case. Therefore, Marx's translators tend to place the respective German word ('*Gegenstand*' or '*Objekt*') in parenthesis after 'object', and the same can be said for the adjectives '*gegenständlich*' and '*objectiv*' ['objective']. Wenceslao Roces, the celebrated Spanish translator of Marx and whose translation of *Theses on Feuerbach* Sánchez Vázquez utilises, also makes use of this.

Sánchez Vázquez emphasises this translation difficulty in his discussion of the first thesis on Feuerbach and explains the different meanings of both

---

186 'Theses on Feuerbach': Marx 1978b, p. 143. (Sánchez Vázquez uses the Spanish translation of the 'Theses' by Wenceslao Roces: Marx 1987, pp. 665–8.)

Sánchez Vázquez does not think it necessary to enter into Marx's formulation regarding the 'dirty-judaical form [of praxis]'. Like the vast majority of Marxist authors, he jumps unproblematically over this problematic expression. We are planning later to present a more detailed study of this problem, which in Marx's main work places his theoretical focus (diametrically opposed to anti-Semitism) face-to-face with the anti-Semitic allusions or formulations in *Capital*.

German terms on the basis of the Marxian critique of 'hitherto existing materialism – that of Feuerbach included':[187] 'In the original he used two words to designate the object – *Gegenstand* and *Objekt* – in order to distinguish between the object as theoretical and practical objectification (*Gegenstand*) on the one hand, and the object itself, external to man and his activity (*Objekt*)'.[188]

According to this, the German word '*Objekt*' designates 'the object itself', which is 'external to man and his activity'.[189] But the German word '*Gegenstand*' was already understood in the previous quotation as 'theoretical and practical objectification'.[190] This distinction is already the first step toward understanding the Marxian critique of traditional materialism, whose concept of the cognoscitive relationship of the subject with the world of objects Marx also seeks to 'negate' in this thesis on Feuerbach, just like that of idealism.[191] Now, this double negation already prepares the terrain in which its overcoming can occur: 'a conception of human activity as real, objective, sensual activity, or practice [praxis]'.[192] To illustrate Marx's critique of 'hitherto existing materialism', our author continues with his interpretation of the German term '*Objekt*': 'This latter is opposed to the subject, for it is a given, existing *in* and *for* itself, and not a human product; thus the form of relation between subject and object in this case is one in which the subject is passive and contemplative'.[193]

Sánchez Vázquez's interest in aesthetics, and above all his dispute with 'socialist realism',[194] is visible, here, as in so many other parts of the book when he continues with his interpretation of the Marxian critique of traditional materialism: 'the subject ... restrict[s] itself [in traditional materialism] to receiving or reflecting reality. Here knowledge is simply the result of the actions of the objects in the external world and their effects upon the sense organs'.[195] And he takes up again the distinction between the concepts '*Gegenstand*' and '*Objekt*': 'The object is *objectively* grasped, rather than *subjectively* as the product of practical activity'.[196]

---

187   Marx 1978b, p. 143.
188   Sánchez Vázquez 1977a, p. 117.
189   Ibid.
190   Ibid.
191   Ibid.
192   Ibid.
193   Sánchez Vázquez 1977a, pp. 117–18.
194   On Sánchez Vázquez's abandonment and critique of socialist realism, see our biographical introduction.
195   Sánchez Vázquez 1977a, p. 118.
196   Ibid.

Human knowledge is not directed at things that are totally foreign to it. The world as presented to us today is produced by previous generations; it is, therefore, the product of human praxis.[197] When a human being looks upon the world, he does not see just any accumulation of matter, which in turn gives off just any electromagnetic waves – which is to say, light – entering his retinas through his open eyes, but, instead, confronts the product of his own activity and that of his contemporaries, as well as his forebears. The rays of light that stimulate his optical cells – continuing with this idea – are not in any way a merely natural phenomenon, but are, instead, socially and historically conditioned. Even the light of distant stars that we see today, even though they could have been extinguished before there were even humans on this Earth, do not reach our eyes in a 'pure' or untouched fashion (and this is not to even speak of the telescope, through which such light is channeled, and which also does not come out of nowhere). The air over Frankfurt, like that of many of the world's cities, is becoming increasingly cloudy, according to the complaints of the scientists at the old Observatory at the Senckenberg Museum, and this again is a result of the overwhelming nature of human praxis.

This is what pre-Marxist materialism fails to see or 'forgets' when it does not include in its reflections praxis as the basis for knowledge. Marx does not examine in greater detail the problematic of human praxis as the basis for knowledge in this text of 'noteworthy brevity' (Bloch); Sánchez Vázquez, therefore, instead refers to *The German Ideology*, 'written almost at the same time',[198] citing from this text the following passage regarding Feuerbach:

> He does not see how the sensuous world around him is, not a thing given direct from all eternity, remaining ever the same, but the product of industry and of the state of society; and, indeed, in the sense that it is an historical product, the result of the activity of a whole succession of generations, each standing on the shoulders of the preceding one, developing its industry and its intercourse, modifying its social system according to the changed needs. Even the objects of the simplest 'sensuous certainty' are only given him through social development, industry and commercial intercourse.[199]

---

197 Sánchez Vázquez 1977a, p. 119.
198 Sánchez Vázquez 1977a, p. 97.
199 Marx and Engels 1978a, p. 170.
      The passage cited concludes in the original with the well-known passage about the cherry tree: 'The cherry-tree, like almost all fruit-trees, was, as is well known, only a few

In contrast to traditional materialism, idealism has focused subjective activity on the process of knowledge (the active side). 'The subject [in idealism...] did not grasp objects in themselves, but as products of his activity'.[200] In this sense, therefore, it is superior to 'hitherto existing materialism'. Sánchez Vázquez mentions, on this point, that Marx is thinking of Kant's idealist conception of knowledge, and that 'it was to Idealism's credit, in Marx's view, that it had underlined the active role of the subject within the subject-object relation'.[201]

But idealist philosophy has another weakness in its understanding of knowledge: it knows the active and creative subject only as something conscious, thinking, but in which its practical, sensuous, and real activity is excluded.[202] Thus, Marx sees the need for a double overcoming: of traditional materialism and of idealism, the overcoming of the theoretical negation of human praxis – with which natural forces become eternal and absolute – and the overcoming of the neglect of the material force inherent in praxis and the latter's reduction to thought.

> Marx's position, therefore, constituted an overcoming of both the contemplative attitude of traditional materialism and the Idealist, speculative conception of activity. True activity is revolutionary, practical-critical activity, which is revolutionary because it transforms reality, and at the same time critical and practical, that is theoretico-practical, because theory is no longer conceived as mere contemplation but as a guide to action, while practice is action guided by theory. Criticism, or theory, cannot exist, therefore, without reference to practice [praxis].[203]

In summary: human praxis is the foundation, the basis for knowledge, since it has first created the objects that will be recognised (against traditional materialism), but it is not an isolated question of spirit, but tangible, since with material interventions it creates an objective, real, sensuous reality (against idealism). Regarding the first aspect of the critique of the ingenuous understanding of nature as already given, prior to human history, the author adds that with this Marx does not deny the existence of a nature beyond human praxis, but merely insists that what confronts our knowledge today is hardly

---

centuries ago transplanted by commerce into our zone, and therefore only by this action of a definite society in a definite age it has become "sensuous certainty" for Feuerbach'.
200   Sánchez Vázquez 1977a, p. 118.
201   Ibid.
202   Ibid.
203   Sánchez Vázquez 1977a, p. 119.

this '*virgin nature*'.²⁰⁴ 'Thus Marx accepts the ontological priority of a nature outside praxis whose ambit is progressively reduced as it becomes humanised nature'.²⁰⁵

In this part of his interpretation of the first thesis on Feuerbach, Sánchez Vázquez also cites *The German Ideology*, in which Marx explicitly explains what we have said: 'Of course, in all this the priority of external nature remains unassailed ... For that matter, nature, the nature that preceded human history, is not by any means the nature in which Feuerbach lives, it is nature which today no longer exists anywhere (except perhaps on a few Australian coral-islands of recent origin) and which, therefore, does not exist for Feuerbach'.²⁰⁶

Sánchez Vázquez argues that Marx takes up again here his understanding of the human-nature relationship developed in the *Paris Manuscripts*.²⁰⁷ In his interpretation of the first thesis on Feuerbach, it has become evident that the author, as previously indicated, leans toward the last of the three possible exegeses of this brief text: Marx does not here deny the existence of a reality of things which is fully independent of human beings; however, he does reject the idea that 'knowledge could be mere contemplation unrelated to practice. Knowledge exists only in practice as knowledge of objects integrated into practice and of a reality that has already lost or is in process of losing its immediate existence to become a reality mediated by man'.²⁰⁸

Praxis as a Criterion of Truth
(Thesis II)

With the help of the second thesis on Feuerbach, Sánchez Vázquez explains to what degree human praxis is not only, as we have said, the basis for knowledge (insofar as it creates its object), but, moreover, the criterion for the truth of knowledge. Recall Marx's thesis: 'The question whether objective truth can

---

204 'Marx does not deny the existence of a nature outside praxis or prior to history; the nature that actually exists for him [man], however, is given *in* and *through* practice' (ibid.).
205 Ibid.
206 Marx and Engels 1978a, p. 171. See also Sánchez Vázquez 1977a, pp. 145ff n52.
    Before this passage, our author again cites the following in order to document and illustrate his interpretation: 'but where would natural science be without industry and commerce? Even this "pure" natural science is provided with an aim, as with its material, only through trade and industry, through the sensuous activity of men. So much is this activity, this unceasing sensuous labour and creation, this production, the basis of the whole sensuous world ...' (Marx and Engels 1978a, p. 171).
207 Sánchez Vázquez 1977a, p. 119.
208 Sánchez Vázquez 1977a, p. 120.

be attributed to human thinking is not a question of theory but is a *practical* question. Man must prove the truth, that is, the reality and power, the this-sidedness of his thinking in practice. The dispute over the reality or non-reality of thinking which is isolated from practice is a purely *scholastic* question'.[209]

While it was possible to read the first thesis on Feuerbach with a degree of calming distance, from the perspective of an intra-philosophical force field – suspended between idealism and traditional materialism – the second thesis, by contrast, is a slap in the face to any respectable philosopher. The problem of the reality or non-reality of thought, which has left this 'mother of all sciences' breathless for so long and on so many occasions, and which the latter – of course – attempted to resolve within its sacred salons (where else?): was this merely a scholastic problem? For modern philosophy, which believed itself to be an opponent of scholasticism, which it considered itself to have overcome, this reproach is certainly an insult. But let us see how our Marxist philosopher handles this torrent unleashed at the discipline itself.

Sánchez Vázquez insists that, according to this thesis, 'truth does not exist in itself'.[210] A thought, a theory, cannot be certain in and of themselves; their truth cannot be verified within the theoretical terrain. Here, as a result, the truth of a thought, a theory, is understood as its 'this-sidedness [*terrenalidad*]'. It is only when the idea applied in praxis is crowned with success that we have a basis for the verification of this idea with regard to pre-existing reality.[211] Sánchez Vázquez observes that the second thesis on Feuerbach is the result of the one that precedes it:[212]

---

209 Marx 1978b, p. 144.

Marx's cited formulation, 'the truth, that is, the reality and power, the this-sidedness of his thinking', shows that he is not interested in an abstract concept of truth that floats in the air, as is generally associated with the German term 'Wahrheit'. The Spanish term 'verdad' [truth] does not generally carry that heavy significance, but can also be understood by the terms 'Richtigkeit' [being correct] or 'Wirklichkeit' [reality]. This question – which we here describe as specific to the Spanish language and of its German translation, as well as one pertaining to Sánchez Vázquez's texts – is also present in Marx's original text. Studies on the topic note that 'two concepts of truth coexist in the second Thesis on Feuerbach'. Alfred Schmidt distinguishes between truth as ' "objective truth": pertinent knowledge' and truth as the ' "reality", "power", and "this-sidedness" of human thought' (Schmidt 1973, p. 1129).

210 Sánchez Vázquez 1977a, p. 120.
211 Sánchez Vázquez 1977a, p. 121.
212 Sánchez Vázquez 1977a, p. 120.

If praxis is the foundation of knowledge, that is if man knows the world only to the extent that it is the *product of his activity*, and activity aimed at the transformation of the real world, it follows that the problem of objective truth, or whether our thought accords with those things existing prior to it, is not a problem that can be resolved theoretically, *merely* by setting our concept against the object in a theoretical way, or setting my thoughts against the thoughts of others. The foundation of truth, in other words, is to be found outside the sphere of knowledge itself.[213]

This understanding of truth, we could add, reminds us of the modern natural sciences, which are oriented toward application: a law of the natural sciences is recognised as such at the moment in which it produces the desired results in experiments and in technical application.[214] An emphatic notion of truth – like that which Sánchez Vázquez also claims – as the coincidence of the idea with the reality existing outside of that idea,[215] is not (or almost never) found in the natural sciences. Nor is this logic uncomfortable with the recognition of reciprocally contradictory theories as valid – at least at a specific level of scientific development – as is the case with the ondulatory and corpuscular theories of light. In each case, the theory which promises the best path to success is simply applied.

With reference to social theory – which is what most interests us here – it is thus worth asking whether Marx formulates an empiricist or a pragmatic concept of truth. Is the social or political theory which gives rise to the greatest political success therefore the most correct one? Is the one which we manage to impose more easily the right one? In the final instance, it would be possible to ask the following with regard to human praxis: is imposed praxis correct praxis? Which would imply: are stable systems of domination, by principle and thanks to the force of their imposition, the truest ones, which would therefore need to be placed outside any radical and systematic critique? Adolfo Sánchez Vázquez rejects such a pragmatist interpretation of the *Theses on Feuerbach*: 'At the same time we must be wary of interpreting this relation between truth

---

213 Ibid., italics by S.G.
214 See, in this respect, Sánchez Vázquez's following formulation in his interpretation of the second thesis on Feuerbach: 'If the ends pursued are achieved through action, this means that the knowledge out of which those ends can be elaborated is true knowledge.... if we base our hope for the achievement of certain ends on a given judgment about reality, and those ends are not achieved, it follows that our judgment was false' (Sánchez Vázquez 1977a, p. 121).
215 Ibid.

and success, or falsehood and disaster, in a pragmatist way, as if truth or falseness were determined by success or failure'.[216]

In praxis, the human being *is obliged to demonstrate* the truth of his reasoning, as Marx says in the thesis in question. He needs to demonstrate it there, but this does not mean that success constitutes truth or that praxis automatically confirms, so to say, the truth of a theory applied successfully. Sánchez Vázquez formulates this relationship between praxis and truth as follows: 'If a theory can be successfully applied, it is because it is true; the reverse, however, is not necessarily also true'.[217]

The success of a praxis, then, should not be compared to the truth of the theories upon which it is based. The power or this-sidedness of reasoning is not the essence of its truth, but rather merely an indication thereof. To express our understanding of Sánchez Vázquez's interpretation of Marx in the language of formal logic: the this-sidedness of thought is the necessary but not sufficient condition for its truth; since this condition must not be understood in the sense of formal logic as an *attribute*, but rather in the chemical sense as an *indicator*. Or, as Sánchez Vázquez puts it: 'Success does not constitute truth; it simply reveals the fact that thought can adequately reproduce reality'.[218]

This 'reveals' or 'makes visible' should be understood in relation to what has been said and quoted before, in the sense that success makes visible the truth of the theory that serves as its basis because it is also true independently of it. Success, then, is an indication of truth, but is not sufficient for its knowledge, while the absence thereof denotes that there is something that requires revising in the thought in question. After this critique of a possible erroneous interpretation of the concept of truth in the second thesis on Feuerbach – an interpretation which Sánchez Vázquez calls 'pragmatist' – our author indicates another interpretive problem which points implicitly toward an empiricist focus. This second aspect is both complementary to the first as well as offering the possibility of understanding what is necessary, alongside the 'success' of a given praxis, in order to follow the trail of the truth of the corresponding thought.

The 'making visible' of a theory's truth through praxis should not be understood to mean that it suffices to merely open one's eyes and simply read truth

---

216 Ibid. Translation corrected. Adolfo Sánchez Vázquez speaks here – as in general in his book – about the 'pragmatist [pragmatista]' conception of knowledge and not about a 'pragmatic [pragmático]' one, as Mike Gonzalez wrongly translates it. (Compare: Sánchez Vázquez 1980b, p. 159.)
217 Sánchez Vázquez 1977a.
218 Ibid.

in praxis. If praxis is the criterion for a theory's truth, this does not mean, according to our author, that the search for truth is exempt from all theoretical feedback: 'Practice does not speak for itself; practical facts must be analyzed and interpreted, since they do not reveal their meaning to direct and immediate observation nor to intuitive apprehension'.[219]

In order to make praxis effective as a criterion for truth, a theoretical relationship to it is necessary. The dependent relationship between theoretical knowledge and praxis, as we again see demonstrated here, is bilateral, extremely close, and intertwined.[220] In order to document this understanding of the concept of praxis contained in the second thesis on Feuerbach as a criterion of truth, Sánchez Vázquez refers, for assistance, to the eighth thesis, from which he cites the following: 'All mysteries which mislead theory to mysticism find their rational solution in human practice and *in the comprehension of this practice*'.[221]

For Sánchez Vázquez, this is how we establish the unity of theory and praxis in the second and the eighth *Theses on Feuerbach*, namely: in a 'double movement; from theory to practice (*Thesis* II) and from practice to theory (in *Thesis* VIII)'.[222] In so doing, Marx – in the concept of the unity of theory and praxis – turns against two conceptions of knowledge which are incapable of understanding this double movement as a result of their unilateralising optic: on the one hand, against an idealist understanding of the truth of knowledge 'whereby theory contains within itself the criterion of its own truth', and, on the other hand, an empiricist approach 'according to which practice provides the criterion for judging the truth of theory in a direct and immediate way'.[223]

---

219 Ibid.
220 'The criterion of truth may be found in practice, but it is only discovered within a properly theoretical relation with practice itself' (ibid.).
221 Marx 1978b, p. 145. Italics according to Sánchez Vázquez 1977a, p. 121.
222 Sánchez Vázquez 1977a, pp. 121–2.
   Another note, perhaps a *pedantic* one: we are not citing here from the second edition, which we have used in other cases, but from the first edition (Sánchez Vázquez 1967b, p. 130). This is due to an error in the second edition: in the phrase cited above, 'thesis II' suddenly becomes 'thesis I'. We have allowed ourselves to correct this error, one that is obvious in context. With regard to the unity of theory and praxis, Sánchez Vázquez always speaks only of theses II and VIII, but not thesis I. [Note to the edition in English: the English translation also includes a mistake, corrected above, when mentioning the numbers of the theses here referred to: instead of 'thesis VIII', the translator of *The Philosophy of Praxis* put 'thesis III' (ibid.)]
223 Sánchez Vázquez 1977a, p. 122.

Sánchez Vázquez would like to make known the role of praxis as the criterion of truth of significant generality, without being restricted to the sphere of the sciences, which he discusses in greater detail, making note of the fact that this criterion for truth can assume different forms in the different sciences. But, at the same time, he indicates that this criterion for truth finds limitations in its application 'which prevent it [praxis] from becoming an absolute criterion of truth'.[224]

Revolutionary Praxis as the Unity of the Transformation in Human Beings and in Circumstances
(Thesis III)

Sánchez Vázquez says that in this thesis, unlike the first and second, praxis does not appear as a 'cognitive category', but instead here 'becomes a sociological category';[225] however, in discussing it he comes to speak various times about the relationship between praxis and knowledge. From the aforementioned double movement in the unity of theory and praxis, after studying up to this point principally the movement from theory toward praxis (what does praxis mean for theory as its basis and criterion of truth?), we now turn to the other movement, namely that from praxis toward theory (what does theory mean for praxis?). The problem of the role of the process of knowledge with regard to a world-changing transformative praxis is dealt with in this third thesis on Feuerbach, through a discussion of the meaning of the power and limitation of knowledge or understanding acquired through education. Let us turn to Marx's thesis:

> The materialist doctrine that men are products of circumstances and upbringing, and that, therefore, changed men are products of other circumstances and changed upbringing, forgets that it is men who change circumstances and that it is essential to educate the educator himself. Hence, this doctrine necessarily arrives at dividing society into two parts, one of which is superior to society.

---

224   Ibid. The reader who was hoping for a clear and final answer to the possibility of establishing a definitive truth will respond with disgust. Where, in the end, does this leave the advanced position of knowledge as compared with idealism and empiricism? Here, once more, we see the results of a non-dogmatic interpretation of Marx: great disgust and insecurity, but little knowledge that can be applied. How to build a state on this?
225   Sánchez Vázquez 1977a, p. 125.

The coincidence of the changing of circumstances and of human activity or self-change can be conceived and rationally understood only as revolutionary praxis.[226]

In this formulation, Marx is thinking about Enlightenment philosophers and thinkers and about eighteenth-century materialists, whose thought Feuerbach and the nineteenth-century utopian socialists 'carried on'.[227] According to this understanding, the human being is essentially marked by two influences: circumstances and education. Voltaire places more emphasis on the first aspect, philosophers of the German Enlightenment the second; they understand the transformation of humanity as a 'vast educative enterprise'.[228] The foundation of this view of education is the idea of the human as a rational being. According to this view, human progress can be driven by the destruction of prejudices and the dominion of reason. 'In order for man to progress, enter the age of reason and live in a world constructed according to rational principles, all that is required is that consciousness be illuminated by the light of reason'.[229]

This process of enlightenment occurs through the labour of the educator, who frees human beings from superstition and brings them from obscurantism to the realm of reason. And who are these noble educators? They are the Enlightenment philosophers and the 'enlightened despots' who follow their advice. But this understanding contains precisely the division of humanity that Marx mentions, into an active part and a passive part. Nothing remains for the rest of society (the non-educators) but to allow their consciousness to be shaped from without.[230] The human being, then, is considered 'passive matter

---

226 Marx 1978b, p. 144. Original: Marx 1962b, pp. 5f.

In Engels's first publication of this text in 1888, he modified it considerably, which is most noticeable in this third thesis. Thus, in this point, 'revolutionary praxis [revolutionäre Praxis]' becomes simply 'transformative praxis [umwälzende Praxis]'. See Marx 1962b, p. 534. See, moreover, p. 547 n1.

The Spanish-language translation of the *Theses*, which Sánchez Vázquez cites, is based on Marx's original version: see, for example, the translation of the third thesis in Sánchez Vázquez 1980b, p. 161. This edition in Spanish is in Marx 1959a, pp. 633–5. The Spanish translation in this book is identical to that which Sánchez Vázquez uses.

[Note to the edition in English: the quoted translation of the *Theses* into English also needed a correction: Marx's important expression 'revolutionäre Praxis [revolutionary praxis]' was wrongly translated as 'revolutionizing practice'].

227 Sánchez Vázquez 1977a, p. 122.
228 Ibid.
229 Sánchez Vázquez 1977a, p. 123.
230 Ibid.

which can be molded by the environment and by other men'.[231] Sánchez Vázquez reconstructs in three steps Marx's critique of this idea of the human being and its possible transformation by the '*simply* pedagogical', and not the practical revolutionary, route.[232]

a) The circumstances, which undeniably influence the human being, are treated as external and immutable instances, and the fact that they are produced by human praxis is ignored.[233] Following the ideas of our author, we could say that this step follows the focus of a critique of reified consciousness, which does not understand the degree to which the things we confront are in themselves the expression and result of a historical social situation and of relations of production which are in turn created by human hands. The

---

231   Ibid. Here we had planned a chapter on the topic of *praxis and violence*, but despite the contemporary importance of this topic, given our new era of offensive wars by Europe and the United States, we will have to deal with this theme elsewhere.

   On this topic, what interests Sánchez Vázquez is, among other things, the various forms of violence applied in politics and art. In the latter case, this violence falls on passive material, for example, the stone to be carved, but in the first the action is exercised upon active beings, toward whose creation of consciousness it is directed and which in a given case can generate a counter-violence. Here we will quote a central passage from this chapter to allude to the force field in which our author is roaming: 'Indeed violence has been so clearly linked to all historical production or creation, that many commentators have seen violence as the very motor force of historical development – for example those who, like Dühring and Gumplowicz, have tried to find a theoretical justification for racism or fascism'. Sánchez Vázquez 1977a, Part II: 'Some philosophical problems of praxis', Chapter VII: 'Praxis and violence', pp. 305–36, here: p. 308.

   This final chapter from *The Philosophy of Praxis*, which, moreover, has been the only one published separately, is very widely remarked upon in the secondary literature and interpreted in very different ways. While Cantarell Gamboa and Labastida see it as the fundamental crystallisation point of the work, in which the great importance of violence (seen as an exclusively human capacity) for social and artistic creation has been developed, Cogniot sees it as 'without a doubt the least convincing chapter.' See Cantarell Gamboa 1967, p. 30; Labastida 1967; and Cogniot 1968, pp. 146ff. Cogniot critiques Sánchez Vázquez as being excessively abstract and ahistorical with the argument: 'the peaceful transition to socialism is presented as a "possible, but exceptional" path.... The problem is not discussed with the spirit of renovation and creativity that animates the work as a whole; it is not posed in concrete terms, according to the current situation of the world and the specific situation of such a country or group of countries. This discomfort is palpable'. (The chapter was published separately in *Casa de las Américas*: see Sánchez Vázquez 1967c).

232   Sánchez Vázquez 1977a, p. 123, italics by S.G.

233   Ibid.

circumstances studied thereby acquire the character of a thing, they appear as 'objective' [*objektiv*], which is to say, untransformable, as a thing-in-itself, which rises intact amid the swell of history. Or as Marx puts it in *Capital*: in the world of commodities, products of human hands – like the products of the mind in the 'misty realm of religion' – appear as 'autonomous figures endowed with a life of their own, which enter into relations both with each other and with human beings'.[234]

b) The educators must also be educated. Marx here criticises the presumption typical of the revolutionary bourgeoisie of the eighteenth century, which considers itself the single driving force of the historical process and, at the same time, deems it unnecessary for this process to continue developing. To the dualism of educators and those who are to be educated Marx counterposes the 'idea of a continuous praxis in which both subject and object are transformed'.[235]

To explain the third thesis on Feuerbach, Sánchez Vázquez cites the following passage from Marx's main work (*Capital*) on the effects of human labour: 'Through this movement he acts upon external nature and changes it, and in this way he simultaneously changes his own nature'.[236] He discusses a process of 'self-transformation' which 'is never completed', thereby excluding the existence of educators who, in turn, would not need to be educated.[237]

c) The aspects mentioned in the two previous points, the circumstances which transform humans and are in turn transformed by humans, and the educator who educates other humans and must in turn be educated, can be combined in thought with the idea that only the human being is capable of transforming both his circumstances and himself. Those transformations can only be understood as a joint and simultaneous task, as revolutionary praxis.[238] This unity of the transformation of the human being through understanding,

---

234 Marx 1976a, p. 165. Regarding this central section, see also the section on 'Contribution to the Reconstruction of the Concept of Ideology in the Critique of Political Economy', in this book, pp. 313ff.

[Note to the edition in English: the fantasy of the translator of *Capital*, Ben Fowkes, must have been very active, when he translated 'Menschen [human beings]' as 'human race'. We corrected it in the quotation. (Compare: Marx 1975a, p. 86.)].

235 Sánchez Vázquez 1977a, p. 124.
236 Marx 1976a, p. 283.
237 Sánchez Vázquez 1977a, p. 124.
238 '... [C]hanges in circumstances cannot be separated from changes in man, just as the changes that occur in him as circumstances and human activity, or rather of the transformation of circumstances and the self-transformation of man, can only be achieved *in* and *through* revolutionary practice' (ibid.).

education, and the transformation of circumstances, as well as the manner that the author has of interpreting these, can be understood as an emphatic formulation of what is meant by the inalienable meaning and importance of the unity of theory and praxis more generally.

Sánchez Vázquez interprets that unity to which the third thesis on Feuerbach refers as a double negation. Here, he again takes up the model of the critique of two forms of unilateralising a process which is only conceivable in the unity of two moments: on the one hand, he rejects the 'Utopian conceptions' that consider the self-transformation of human beings through education to be sufficient, 'irrespective of the circumstances of his life', to accomplishing a radical transformation. At the same time, and on the other hand, he rejects a 'rigorous determination' which considers it sufficient to transform the conditions of life 'without reference to the changes in his consciousness resulting from the labour of education', in order to transform the human being.[239] But what both conceptions have in common is that they underestimate the importance of a unity between the subjective transformation of consciousness and the transformation of objective social relations; in other words, the relevance of revolutionary praxis.

From the Interpretation of the World to its Transformation (Thesis XI)

After interpreting the first three *Theses on Feuerbach*, during the course of which he also introduced the eighth, our philosopher moves directly to discussing the final thesis, which is by far the most famous, and not only for being the shortest. The eleventh thesis on Feuerbach, one of the best-known phrases of Marx's entire body of work, can be understood as an extremely concise summary of what Marxists like Sánchez Vázquez understand to be the German exile's great theoretical revolution: the entrance of praxis as a fundamental category of theory, which had previously opposed it with a greater or lesser degree of scepticism. Let us once again examine the phrase that, chiseled in large letters, today adorns the gravestone of its author: 'The philosophers have only *interpreted* the world in various ways, the point is to *change* it'.[240]

---

239 Ibid.
240 Marx 1978b, p. 145. [Note to the edition in English: translation corrected, based on the German *original* text of the *Theses*, written by Marx. It seems that the translator of the English-language edition of the *Theses* used here was taking its cue from the problematic German version published by Engels. It mistakenly separates the two parts of the sentence by a semicolon and confronts them with the added word 'however', both non-existent in Marx's handwritten original. In consequence, the translator writes erroneously: 'The

To the reader of the Spanish [and English] edition of this book, whom we have always spared the original text of the passages cited up to this point, we here offer this one: 'Die Philosophen haben die Welt nur verschieden *interpretiert, es kömmt drauf an, sie zu verändern*'.[241]

If we analyse more closely the Spanish translation of the *Theses on Feuerbach*, we will see that the translator tends toward an understanding of the eleventh thesis that is lenient towards the philosophers. If Marx says concisely: '*haben nur ... interpretiert*' [have only interpreted], the translation by Wenceslao Roces says 'they have limited themselves to *interpreting*'. That 'nur' [only] becomes 'limited themselves to', which in German is equivalent to '*sich beschränken auf*' [restrict oneself to].

There is an old dispute over how this 'nur' ought to be interpreted, whether as a disparaging observation about philosophy – which ought, therefore, to be abandoned entirely – or as a reference to a limitation, one that naturally recognises the importance of philosophy, but indicates its dependence upon the real transformation of the world, on praxis. The Spanish translation of the eleventh thesis has already passed sentence on this dispute. Roces, by opting against a concise translation of 'nur' as 'only [*solamente*]' and in favour of the more content-laden variant, takes the wind out of the sails of the Spanish reader, who, with a different translation, might have understood this thesis, in his own way, as a critique of philosophy.[242]

Sánchez Vázquez here trusts completely the translation carried out by his companion in exile, a translation that is very much in line with his understanding of the final thesis on Feuerbach and of Marxian philosophy as a whole as a *Philosophy of Praxis*. He understands the thesis in the context of those

---

philosophers have only *interpreted* the world, in various ways; the point however is to *change* it'. (Ibid. Compare, on this question, the following original quote of the sentence, as well as footnote 242 in this chapter.)]

241 Marx 1962b, p. 7.
242 Engels also made, in his first publication of the *Theses on Feuerbach*, a 'clarificatory intervention' – albeit in the opposite direction – by inserting a small 'but', with serious consequences. The thesis thus says: 'The philosophers have only interpreted the world in various manners; but the point is to transform it' (Marx 1962b, according to the text published by Engels in 1888, p. 535. The original reads: 'Die Philosophen haben die Welt nur verschieden interpretiert; es kommt aber darauf an, sie zu verändern').

Engels decides on the pejorative interpretation of this 'only' by counterposing the first and second parts of the phrase through the insertion of the 'but', something that in Marx was sufficiently open to provoke debate. The semicolon between the two parts of the phrase merely formally confirms the clear separation between 'interpreting' and 'modifying'.

discussed previously,[243] meaning that this thesis must be established in the force field between the two aspects of revolutionary praxis: of an 'action on circumstances and consciousness carried out in unity'.[244]

The author we are here analysing understands Marx's critique 'of philosophers' as a critique of the *previous* philosophy, or in other words, a critique of the idealism and traditional materialism mentioned in the first thesis, but never as a reproach toward philosophy as such and not, of course, of that which might be developed in the future.[245] 'Marx rejects those theories which are mere interpretations isolated from praxis, and support a view that accepts the world as it is'.[246] Or in other words, Sánchez Vázquez considers *previous* philosophy to be reprehensible, not only for not having clarified its relationship with material human praxis, but precisely for having ideologically supported in its own way (in the sense of 'forms in which men become conscious

---

243   Thus, Sánchez Vázquez says, with regard to the eleventh thesis on Feuerbach: 'This response is perfectly congruent with the earlier theses, and particularly with theses II and III (see above)'. (Sánchez Vázquez 1977a, p. 125) [English translation: based on the first edition of *Filosofía de la praxis*, Sánchez Vázquez 1967b, and altered in concordance with the generally used second edition of *Filosofía de la praxis* (Sánchez Vázquez 1980b, p. 164.)]

In the first edition, by contrast, he makes reference to – instead of 'thesis II and III' as is the case here – 'thesis I and II' (Sánchez Vázquez 1967b, p. 133).

How can we explain this change? The author of this book does not know, but it does not seem very important to us, since in reality the first three theses on Feuerbach had already all been analysed in detail by Sánchez Vázquez and, moreover, they all aid our understanding of the eleventh thesis. Like the other place we have mentioned in which there is confusion in the numerical designation of the theses, we could suppose this was a simple printing error, one that is possibly easy to make whenever Roman numerals are used.

244   Sánchez Vázquez 1977a, p. 125.

245   'Thesis XI does not entail the diminution of the role of theory, and even less its rejection or exclusion' (Sánchez Vázquez 1977a, p. 126.)

When Sánchez Vázquez says 'theory' here and not 'philosophy,' this does not reflect the distinction that some Marxist currents make between the two. Here, as a general rule, he uses both terms synonymously, as in other parts of *Filosofía de la praxis* (insofar as he speaks of the theory or philosophy of praxis). Thus, in the passage prior to the one cited above, in which he speaks of that philosophy or theory that must not be rejected:

'... practical philosophy, which did regard the world as the object of praxis. In this sense his is a theory of praxis, an interpretation of the world that makes its transformation possible' (ibid.).

246   Ibid.

of this conflict and fight it out')[247] the persistence of ruling relations, namely the exploitation of human by human.

As the 'most complete expression' of such an apologetic philosophy, Sánchez Vázquez cites Hegel, for whom he dedicates not a single kind word in this passage.[248] He considers Hegel to be a thinker for whom 'the world *was as it ought to be*' and whose position is that of the identity of thought with being.[249] For this reason, there is no place in his philosophy for a reality that is an object of transformation by human beings.[250] Sánchez Vázquez is here referring, no doubt, to formulations like 'the state is the actuality [*Wirklichkeit*] of the ethical idea',[251] as Hegel wrote of the bourgeois state.

Evidently, Sánchez Vázquez has a contradictory relationship with Hegel: on the one hand, the Hegelian influence is patent when in various passages in *The Philosophy of Praxis* he offers a teleological image of history in his rejection of certain philosophies that 'rob both history and human action of any and all significance',[252] or when he speaks of 'more developed [philosophical] expositions',[253] although he does not let Hegel's name slip in this context. On the other hand, however, in a later text, he subjects Hegel's teleological understanding of history to critique,[254] and criticises the great dialectician in a more head-on way than tends to be the case, for example, among Hegelian Marxists. Marcuse, for example, attributes great importance to Hegel's conception of reality, in a manner very different from the author studied here. In *Reason and Revolution*,[255] Marcuse distinguishes emphatically between Hegel's concept of reality [*Wirklichkeit*] and 'effectivity' [*Tatsächlichkeit*] as formulated in *The Philosophy of Right*. When Hegel speaks of the reality [*Wirklichkeit*] of the bourgeois state, he does not refer to its effective condition, but to the principles established in the idea, which must be developed in effectivity and which, moreover, can be developed on a fundamental level. Marcuse, no doubt, would look sideways upon Sánchez Vázquez, who does not make such a distinction,

---

247 'Author's preface' in Marx 1904, p. 12.
248 Sánchez Vázquez 1977a, p. 126.
249 Ibid.
250 Ibid.
251 Hegel 1991 §257, p. 275. Original: 'Der Staat ist die Wirklichkeit der sittlichen Idee' (Hegel 1970, § 257, p. 398).
252 Sánchez Vázquez 1977a, p. 5.
253 Sánchez Vázquez 1977a, p. 2.
254 'La razón amenazada': Sánchez Vázquez 1987, p. 134.
255 Marcuse 1955.

here.[256] In another passage from *The Philosophy of Praxis*, he speaks of Hegel in a more differentiated manner and analyses in detail his contribution to the development of the concept of praxis, for which he also refers back to Marx.[257]

The philosopher Sánchez Vázquez consequently understands the eleventh thesis on Feuerbach as a radical critique of previous philosophy, above all German Idealism, which 'culminat[ing] in Hegel and Feuerbach was just such a philosophy of interpretation'.[258]

We are dealing – as we have just seen – with a profound rupture with *this* philosophy, but at the same time and through this same rupture, there is an effort to save philosophy – in a new sense – as a highly developed theory of the revolutionary transformation of existing social relations. When Marx, in this famous thesis on Feuerbach, criticises earlier philosophers for limiting themselves to *interpreting* the world, this is also synonymous with the affirmation that 'they have accepted and sought to justify it, but have not contributed to its transformation'.[259]

The transition from interpretation to transformation implies a 'theoretical revolution' that Marxism must carry out and which is inseparable from the 'revolutionary praxis of the proletariat'.[260] Sánchez Vázquez turns his interpretation of the final thesis on Feuerbach in the direction of a manifesto for the unity of revolutionary theory and praxis, against the two attitudes which see only one side of the coin, and which bypass this unity entirely: unreflexive spontaneism and academic Marxism. Regarding the first of these attitudes (Sánchez Vázquez does not use either of the two terms mentioned), he emphasises that it is 'an interpretation of the world that makes transformation possible'.[261] On the second, he insists that to reduce Marxism to mere interpretation means no less than to do exactly what Marx denounces in the

---

256 On Sánchez Vázquez and Marcuse, see, moreover, the section on '*The Philosophy of Praxis*: Two Versions', pp. 183ff of this book.

257 Sánchez Vázquez 1977a, Part I: 'Philosophical sources of the study of praxis', Chapter 1: 'The conception of praxis in Hegel', pp. 40–69.

258 Sánchez Vázquez 1977a, p. 126.

259 Ibid.

260 Sánchez Vázquez 1977a, p. 127. For his interpretation of the eleventh thesis on Feuerbach, Sánchez Vázquez refers here to the last line of Engels's text, 'Socialism, Utopian and Scientific': 'To thoroughly comprehend the historical conditions and thus the very nature of this act, to impart to the now oppressed proletarian class a full knowledge of the conditions and of the meaning of the momentous act it is called upon to accomplish, this is the task of the theoretical expression of the proletarian movement, scientific Socialism': Engels 1907, p. 87.

261 Sánchez Vázquez 1977a, p. 126.

eleventh thesis on Feuerbach: to persist in remaining enclosed within the limits of theory.[262]

Epilogue to the *Theses on Feuerbach*

To conclude the interpretation of the *Theses on Feuerbach* by the Marxist philosopher, we will permit ourselves a small political-theoretical observation. The contradiction between traditional materialism and idealism that Marx attempted to overcome, which was mentioned in the first thesis and which reappears here, seems to continue to be present in debates within German organisations oriented toward emancipatory politics. In more than a few of the conflicts fought out there, occasionally quite vehemently, we can detect two currents, which follow the respective steps of argumentation.

On the one hand, a naively sensuous current attempts to determine political action by setting out directly from lived experience, individual involvement, and in part from felt desires. In so doing, this current loses its connection to the social and historical determination of that reality, which is understood as immediately and directly graspable.

On the other hand, another current with a serenely distanced attitude which, from a more or less neutral and certain vantage-point, knows the dynamic of the process in which we are all immersed and, therefore, does not think simply that the 'untouched sensuousness' is a path which gives direct access to the correct analysis of the situation. But, at the same time, it hides behind this judgement; as a critical commentator its only enemy is the false concept, and it gradually loses the possibility for the materially-transformative and objective conscious intervention into this reality, which is at least verbally recognised as historically and socially conditioned (and, therefore, as transformable in its very foundations).

Without a doubt, it is not possible to equate these two currents with 'traditional materialism' or 'idealism', respectively, but there seems to exist a certain parallel in their problematic and their errors, such that we can ask ourselves if present debates and actions (the emancipatory praxis) have fallen far behind Marx, or if while he recognised the problem – and despite the immense effort that he no doubt carried out – he was still not in a position to resolve it.

---

262 Ibid.

CHAPTER 8

Critique of Some Marxist Conceptions of Knowledge

In his interpretation of the *Theses on Feuerbach*, Sánchez Vázquez has already criticised explicitly two philosophical understandings of knowledge in general: on the one hand, an idealist conception, according to which theory carries its criterion of truth within itself, and on the other hand, a pragmatist or empiricist conception, according to which praxis constitutes the truth criterion for theory directly and immediately.[263] As a first approach to the critique that the author makes of some Marxist conceptions of knowledge, we will cite here a passage in which he clarifies the border distinguishing two understandings of knowledge: the Marxist view, understood in the sense he supports, and the pragmatist view:

> Knowledge is useful to the degree that it is true, but it is not true to the extent that it is useful as the pragmatists maintained. For Marxism, utility is not the basis or essence of truth, but its consequence; the pragmatists, on the other hand, subordinated truth to utility, or the efficacy or success of the actions of men, conceived as subjective, individual acts rather than as objective, material, transforming activity.

And a bit further on, Sánchez Vázquez writes, with regard to Marxism and pragmatism, of the

---

263 Sánchez Vázquez 1977a, pp. 121f. Regarding Sánchez Vázquez's critique of a pragmatist understanding of knowledge, see moreover his Part II: 'Some philosophical problems of praxis', Chapter V: 'Unity of theory and practice', subchapter: 'The "common sense" point of view: pragmatism', pp. 169–72.
   In his critique, Sánchez Vázquez mentions William James as an example of a pragmatist author, and his works: *Philosophical conceptions and practical results* (1898); *Pragmatism: a new name for some old ways of thinking* (1909, later edition, London, 1928); and *The Meaning of Truth* (1909, later edition in *The Works*, 1975, Vol. II, 'The meaning of truth'). (Sánchez Vázquez 1977a, pp. 170f. and 194 n3).

distinction between their respective criteria for truth.... Both, it is true, locate the law of truth in practice itself, but that apparent coincidence is given the lie by the very different understanding of practice characteristic of one and the other. In the one case, practice is simply individual, subjective action designed to satisfy individual interests; in the other, it is objective, transforming activity responding to social interests which consists, from the socio-historical point of view, not only in the production of a material reality, but in the creation and unfolding of a human world.[264]

Within the theoretical development of Marxism, the author also critiques several approaches to knowledge. This critique should be understood on the basis of his general position regarding Marxism's various theoretical orientations, setting out from the central importance that it assigns to the concept of praxis.

a   Critique of Certain Conceptions of Marxism in General

When Sánchez Vázquez called his first major work *The Philosophy of Praxis*, he did so somewhat in allusion to Gramsci, but with a degree of critical distance. Within Marxist debates, the concept of praxis has suffered various deformations, that is, erroneous analyses, whose foundation can be located in the concrete historical situation of each case. As two focal points in Marxist debates, Sánchez Vázquez presents the following with regard to Gramsci and Althusser:

Gramsci judges praxis to be the principal unifier of the various spheres of Marxism and as a central philosophical category. Thus, he opposed Second International Marxism (at the end of the nineteenth century), which, 'impregnated with scientifistic, objectivist, and positivist conceptions' left no space for revolutionary praxis, as well as materialist metaphysics in the style of Bukharin, 'which reinstates the old materialism, dressing it up with the dialectic'.[265] Gramsci, in any case, only manages to save (revolutionary) praxis at the expense of abandoning the reality that lay beyond that praxis and, simultaneously, the scientific analysis of social relations not in agreement with that praxis. Sánchez Vázquez characterises the implications of this concept of praxis, in Gramsci's

---

264   Sánchez Vázquez 1977a, p. 171.
265   Sánchez Vázquez 1980b, p. 56 [these passages do not appear in the English translation – trans.]. Sánchez Vázquez cites Gramsci's *Il materialismo storico e la filosofia di Benedetto Croce*, translated to English as *Historical Materialism: A System of Sociology* (Sánchez Vázquez 1980b, p. 52), and also his 'La rivoluzione contro il "Capitale"' (Sánchez Vázquez 1980b, p. 57).

own words, as 'absolute immanentism', 'absolute historicism', and 'humanism': 'For Gramsci praxis is... the only reality (hence his "absolute immanentism"), a reality which is likewise subject to a constant becoming, for which reason he identifies it with history (hence also his "absolute historicism"). Finally, since that history is the history of man's self-production, Gramsci characterises his philosophy as *humanism*'.[266]

The fact that Gramsci designates Marxism as the 'philosophy of praxis' must be understood on the basis of this understanding of praxis as its support point, a naming which was erroneously reduced by some authors to a word arrived at by chance in order to circumvent prison censorship.[267] So, while Gramsci rightly sought to navigate his way around a powerful contemporary current in the reception of Marx, one defined by 'the crudest kind of opportunist reformism',[268] he ran aground in the shallow waters of an underestimation of the decisive importance of objective factors ('which the opportunists had converted into absolutes'), and, with this, 'forgets' the scientific character of Marxism.[269]

It was precisely this scientific character that Louis Althusser, Jacques Rancière, Pierre Macherey, Étienne Balibar, and Roger Establet sought to reestablish as a weapon of critique in their *Reading Capital*, in an era of the dogmatisation of Marxism and the Communist Party chiefs's absolutist pretensions of defining truth. (This emphasis on the 'scientific character of Marxism' meant – it is worth adding to what Sánchez Vázquez says – erasing from Marxist science all 'ideological elements', and thereby opposing what was then the 'rediscovery' of humanism in Marx's writings.) Their call to read *Capital* sought to return 'the attention of Marxists to the determinant role of objective factors like the mechanism and structures of capitalist relations of production, and analyzing them with the conceptual rigour and objectivity demanded by the scientific character of Marxism'.[270]

---

266   Sánchez Vázquez 1980b, p. 56 [these passages do not appear in the English translation – trans.].
267   Sánchez Vázquez 1977a, p. 32.
268   Sánchez Vázquez 1977a, p. 33.
269   Ibid. Moreover, he refers to 'Gramsci's purpose in underlining the role of practical revolutionary activity at a time when most of the leaders of European social-democracy had dismissed it altogether. This legitimate preoccupation, however, led him to underestimate the determinant role of objective factors which the opportunists had converted into absolutes' (ibid.).
270   Sánchez Vázquez 1977a, p. 38 n50. Sánchez Vázquez refers to Althusser's critique of Gramsci in *Lire le Capital*, Althusser *et al.* 1965b, pp. 82ff, pp. 144–9, pp. 248f, and pp. 276f (see Sánchez Vázquez 1980b, for example, pp. 30ff), and Althusser's own position in *Pour*

These authors, in any case, also paid a high price for defending the scientific character of Marxism: 'the forgetting of praxis' in the theory itself. If, like Sánchez Vázquez, we understand praxis to be the central concept of Marx's theory, this price is, of course, too high.

In this presentation of the dispute internal to Marxism regarding the importance of social/revolutionary praxis, the author under consideration stresses the fact that the two 'concerns' sketched above were, each in their own moment, 'as legitimate' as the other was 'praiseworthy'.[271] It is true that not only in selecting the term 'philosophy of praxis', but also in the insistence with which he deplores the errors of both approaches, we can recognise that Sánchez Vázquez is closer (theoretically) to Gramsci than to Althusser and the other authors of *Reading Capital*. However, he is not interested in pedantically handing out the points won and lost, as though he were some sort of umpire. Sánchez Vázquez instead seeks to insert himself into the process of struggling for the formation of the theory necessary for human emancipation.

His desire is, in avoiding the defects of both positions, to rescue the 'richness of meaning with which Marx invested' the category of praxis; a rescue 'to which Marxist researchers from different countries today contribute, and to which I aspire to contribute the present work'.[272]

b   Critique of Certain Marxist Conceptions of Knowledge

On the particular problem of knowledge, Sánchez Vázquez criticises in particular two different theoretical orientations within Marxism, and, in so doing, some moments of the critique of the pragmatist or empiricist conception of knowledge once again emerge.

Knowledge as the Direct Result of World-Transformative Praxis

The point of departure for this critique is the observation that theory not only satisfies the demands and needs of an already existing praxis, but also those of a potential future praxis. Were this not the case, theory would not be able to influence praxis in its process of development. But, with the investigation of

---

Marx, in the chapter 'Sur la dialectique materialiste', (Althusser 1965a, pp. 161–224). So, too, Althusser 1965c (Sánchez Vázquez 1977a, p. 37 n41).

271   Sánchez Vázquez 1977a, p. 38 n50.

272   Sánchez Vázquez 1977a, p. 33 [the second passage does not appear in the English translation – trans. Compare: Sánchez Vázquez 1980b, p. 58. In the English translation, the quote ends: 'that is the objective of the present work' (Sánchez Vázquez 1977a)].

this relationship between theory and a still non-existent praxis, the analysis of the relationship between praxis and knowledge reaches a new level. When the human being sees the need to develop new forms of transformative praxis but lacks the theoretical instruments to do so, there arises the peculiar situation that the necessary theory is determined by a praxis on which it cannot yet feed in any way.[273] Praxis, here, determines the theory as its end, or more precisely as its 'project or ideal anticipation'.[274]

As examples of a theory that greatly precedes its corresponding praxis, Sánchez Vázquez mentions 'cosmic practice [praxis]',[275] or in other words, the audacious human enterprise of appropriating not only Earth but also 'neighboring' space; he refers also to Einstein's general theory of relativity and Lobachevsky's non-Euclidean geometry.[276] This situation in which praxis determines theory, not only as its basis, source, and criterion of truth, but also as its end, shows 'that the relation between theory and practice cannot be discussed in simplistic, mechanical terms, as if every theory were based in a direct and immediate way on practice'.[277]

The author limits these statements on the relationship between theory and praxis a bit, since 'there clearly are specific theories that bear no direct relation to practical activity'.[278] But, above all, he is interested in the theory-praxis relationship the historico-social process, which has its theoretical and practical sides. On the basis of what he has established, Sánchez Vázquez criticises a proposal that abstractly divides human history into a history of theory and a history of praxis, in order then to attempt to find a direct and immediate relationship of dependency between the theoretical and practical parts of that history. But that relationship is in no way direct and immediate – instead, it develops in the course of 'a complex process that sometimes moves from practice towards theory, and sometimes from theory to practice'.[279]

For Sánchez Vázquez, the relationship between theory and praxis is not direct and immediate, since, on the one hand, there exist theories which are born to resolve directly the difficulties and contradictions of others and, on the other hand, praxis is only 'in the final instance' the source and end of theory, and it is only such as a *part* of a vast historico-social process. This process

---

273 Sánchez Vázquez 1977a, pp. 186f.
274 Sánchez Vázquez 1977a, p. 186.
275 Sánchez Vázquez 1977a, p. 187.
276 Sánchez Vázquez 1977a, p. 191.
277 Sánchez Vázquez 1977a, p. 187.
278 Ibid.
279 Ibid.

cannot be split into parts that run parallel and isolated from one another, as a result of which theory is therefore a part, among others, of practice.[280] The 'relative autonomy' of theory *vis-à-vis* praxis, as explained here, does not simply place these on a level in which both coexist in reciprocal independence. Our author holds on, moreover, to a primacy (however mediated) of praxis over theory, albeit one which is only realised in the unity of theory and praxis.[281]

Sánchez Vázquez's affirmation that theory does not depend directly and immediately on praxis leads to the critique of the idea that, in abolishing existing relations and their inherent objective appearance, in abolishing the commodity production and with it the commodity fetishism inherent in it, the entire mystery will be solved, and thus social praxis will render theory superfluous, having already led to communism. One interpreter of Marx who understands him in this way, according to Sánchez Vázquez, is Kostas Axelos.[282] The relation between theory and praxis thereby becomes completely unilateral: praxis grounds theory without the latter in turn grounding praxis. As a result, sciences come to be little more than a 'reflection of practice'.[283] Accordingly, in this other society the supremacy of praxis is such that human praxis and the 'comprehension' of praxis[284] coincide, that is, there is no longer any difference

---

280   Sánchez Vázquez 1977a, p. 188. Here, the critique of Althusser's conception of 'pratique théoretique' as one form of praxis among others, which we will deal with in the next section, resonates.

281   Ibid. 'The dependency of theory on practice, and the role of the latter as the final object of theory demonstrate the primacy of practice, seen as total human praxis. Far from implying that practice provides a counterpart to theory, however, this conclusion confirms the intimate connection between the two'.

282   Sánchez Vázquez 1977a, p. 197 n23–4. Adolfo Sánchez Vázquez here mentions Axelos 1961, particularly pp. 254–8.

283   Sánchez Vázquez 1977a, p. 189. Sánchez Vázquez's terminology once again demonstrates here the great influence that his break with the aesthetic theory of 'socialist realism' has had on his discussion. [Note to the English translation: Sánchez Vázquez speaks here about a direct reflection, and not its intellectual 'reflection'. The first is expressed by the word he uses: 'reflejo', the second would be 'reflexión'. In the English translation, the important difference between the two forms of reflection: immediate/physical, on the one hand, and mediated/intellectual, on the other hand, is lost. Compare Sánchez Vázquez 1980b, p. 293: 'reflejo de la práctica' (S.G.)].

284   Sánchez Vázquez 1977a. Sánchez Vázquez here refers to the eighth thesis on Feuerbach, and in particular to its final line, in order to oppose Axelos's understanding of Marx. In this regard, see also our analysis of the interpretation of the second thesis on Feuerbach in the section 'Interpretation of the *Theses on Feuerbach*', in this book (pp. 138ff).

between intellectual and material production. 'In a word, praxis would necessarily be of itself theoretical'.[285]

Adolfo Sánchez Vázquez, who in his epistemological research unfolded the unity of theory and praxis – but, at the same time, their non-identity[286] – cannot of course allow the affirmation of such an absolute primacy of praxis to pass, even if limited to a society which is presented as an 'association of free men [*Verein freier Menschen*]' ('working with the means of production held in common, and expending their many different forms of labour-power in full self-awareness as one single social labour force').[287] The borders between theory and praxis are mobile and relative, and the relationship between the two extraordinarily powerful, but both demand – in order to be able to develop – a relative degree of reciprocal autonomy. Therefore, the border between them can never disappear completely. On the basis of the determining role of praxis for theory as the basis, end, and truth criterion of knowledge, we cannot arrive at Axelos's conclusion, which totalises praxis as automatically leading to general knowledge, without the intervention of theory and as a direct consequence of social liberation.[288]

Here, we can understand Sánchez Vázquez in the following way: the confluence of theory and praxis in a communist society would mean something like the end of human social development, which prospers in the force field between these two vital expressions of the human being (its theoretical capacity and its practical capacity). Consequently, in positions like that Sánchez Vázquez criticises in Axelos, communist society is seen, ultimately, as an entity in which there are no longer any fundamental problems. But this contradicts Marx's view, which did not link the proletarian revolution to the end of history but, properly speaking, to its *beginning*. This revolution would not resolve at a stroke all human problems, but would only eliminate that fundamental

---

285   Sánchez Vázquez 1977a. Sánchez Vázquez does not go into the socio-political background of Axelos's conception of knowledge. On the background of Gramsci's theory, which is similar to that of Axelos, stressing the primacy of praxis to excess, see the preceding section, 'Critique of specific conceptions of Marxism in general'.

      Here, our author does not go into the exact epistemological implications of Gramsci's theory, with one exception: in the critique of William James's pragmatist approach to knowledge, which Sánchez Vázquez begins with a critique of everyday consciousness, he briefly mentions Gramsci in a positive fashion, by praising the latter's discussion of contemporary everyday consciousness (Sánchez Vázquez 1977a, pp. 169–72, and in particular pp. 195ff n2).

286   Sánchez Vázquez 1977a, p. 191.
287   Marx 1976a, p. 171. Original: Marx 1975a, p. 92.
288   Sánchez Vázquez 1977a, p. 190.

antagonistic contradiction which prevents a serious solution to many other problems. With the conclusion of the 'prehistoric stage of human society',[289] human beings should enter precisely into the conscious organisation of their social form. With the overcoming of the commodity – and with it, its fetishism – a colossal barrier to knowledge is taken out of the way; but nowhere does Marx speak of the kind of automatic process we have mentioned, which, in the end, would make even thought itself superfluous. A simple return to some natural state – almost as if knowledge were automatically evoked by instinct – was not what Marx desired.

In this context, there can be no debate – and so, too, for the author here under analysis – that science and philosophy[290] – which Sánchez Vázquez, unlike 'positive science', did not want to leave behind – should transform themselves in another society, for example by getting rid of their authoritarian, vain, and narrow-minded distancing of themselves from non-specialists.

Knowledge as Something Achieved Exclusively in Theory

The rejection of the suppression of the relative autonomy of theory – namely, disapproving of the presumption that praxis is the sole generator of theory, which would, at least in the long term, render theory (or philosophy) superfluous – can, nevertheless, lead to an equally false 'solution' of the theory-praxis problem, a solution which has something in common with what was earlier criticised: namely, that also in this view the unity of theory and praxis is understood as a simple *identity*. But in the aforementioned approach to knowledge, which is almost empiricist, that identity is produced by making the primacy of praxis nearly absolute; that is, if theory – where it is more than mere theoretical technique – gradually becomes superfluous through progressive (and especially revolutionary) praxis, then, in the presumption we are here subjecting to critique, the primacy of praxis is destroyed; theory becomes autonomous of it, not only relatively but fully so. This conception reaches such a point that theory, which itself boasts its own truth criterion, crosses the border of praxis to itself become that praxis. As a result, the problem of the basis, end, and truth criterion of theory being located outside that theory is no longer posed.

If, in the previously criticised formulation, theory was 'gobbled up' by praxis, in this case the former nibbles away at the latter, itself becoming a form of praxis among others with which it can coexist. Sánchez Vázquez mentions the

---

289 Marx 1904, p. 13.
290 Sánchez Vázquez 1977a.

French Marxist Louis Althusser as one author who maintains such a position with regard to knowledge.[291]

In order to be able to follow Sánchez Vázquez in his critique of the Althusserian conception of knowledge, it is worth pointing out that both theorists developed different concepts of praxis and, therefore, different concepts of theory. Our author criticised the concept of theoretical praxis, or as he calls it here, 'theoretical "practice"'.[292] It is true that theoretical activity[293] – this concept being more appropriate, according to Sánchez Vázquez – transforms ideas and concepts, creating 'specific products called hypotheses, theories, laws, etc.'; but what is also necessary is the material side of primary matter, of activity, and of the result, which essentially corresponds to praxis.[294] Therefore, says Sánchez Vázquez, 'theoretical activity cannot be considered to be a form of praxis'.[295] The differences between theory – understood as the production of objectives and knowledges – and praxis, impedes the introduction of such a conceptualisation.

For what is distinctive in theoretical activity, which may produce ends and knowledge, is the specific nature of its *object, its medium, and the results* that stem from it. Its object, or material, are sensations or perceptions – psychic objects that have a subjective existence only – or concepts, theories, representations or hypotheses which have only an ideal existence. The immediate *purpose* of theory is to transform its material at the level of the ideal, not at the level of actuality, with the aim of producing theories that can explain an actual reality, or models that prefigure its future shape or development.[296]

---

291 On Sánchez Vázquez's critique of Althusser's conception of knowledge, see especially the following sections: Part II: 'Some philosophical problems of praxis', Chapter IV: 'What is praxis', subchapter: 'Theoretical activity', and 'Philosophy and praxis', pp. 161–8.

See also Sánchez Vázquez 1978b, especially pp. 61–72 and pp. 154–64. There also exists a more recent 1983 Grijalbo edition of this book with an interview carried out by Bernardo Lima with Sánchez Vázquez as its prologue, as well as his correspondence with Étienne Balibar in an appendix. On Sánchez Vázquez's critique of Althusser, see also his 'El teoricismo de Althusser. Notas críticas sobre una autocrítica' (Sánchez Vázquez 1975b). The only existing monograph on Sánchez Vázquez refers to the mentioned discussion: González Rojo 1985.

292 Sánchez Vázquez 1977a, p. 162.
293 Ibid.
294 Ibid.
295 Ibid.
296 Ibid., italics by S.G.

This theoretical activity is of indispensable importance for world-transformative praxis, insofar as it drives the knowledge necessary for it and sketches out objectives that anticipate this transformation in ideal form. But despite this, theoretical activity leaves existing reality intact.[297] It is true that theoretical activity also transforms something, but its *object* is not reality in itself: rather, it carries out ideal transformations (which also determines its *result*). 'Theoretical activity can transform a hypothesis into a theory, or one theory into another, more sophisticated and developed one'.[298]

Its means of transformation are, equally, distinct from what Sánchez Vázquez understands as praxis. Its operations are 'mental operations: abstraction, generalisation, deduction, synthesis, prediction etc.'[299] These operations, while presupposing a 'physical substratum' and the functioning of a nervous system, continue to be, despite all this, subjective or psychological, 'whatever the objective manifestations they may have'.[300]

Here, the question arises of what exactly the author means by 'objective manifestations': is he referring to the lines of ink on the paper with which theories are established in written form, or to the sound waves with which they are communicated to contemporaries, or is he referring to other forms of propagation, for example the publishing and distribution of a political-theoretical journal?

As he distances himself from the concept of 'theoretical praxis', Sánchez Vázquez rejects the idea that the elaboration and later development of theories can be understood in and of itself as 'praxis'; but where exactly, in the necessary mediating steps between theory and praxis, does he see the border separating the one from the other? He himself insists on the need for such intermediary and mediating steps when he writes: 'There intervenes between theory and practical, transforming activity, the task of educating and raising consciousness, organizing the material means and the concrete programmes of action, which constitute essential preconditions for effective activity'.[301]

But to which are these intermediary steps allotted – to theory, or to praxis? Or, if they are allotted to a third party, this would only apparently resolve the problem of the precise distinction between theory and praxis, by transferring

---

297 Ibid.
298 Ibid.
299 Ibid.
300 Ibid. [Translation corrected, the term 'manifestaciones objetivas' was imprecisely and problematically translated by Mike Gonzalez as 'objective consequences'. Compare Sánchez Vázquez 1980b, p. 262 (S.G.)].
301 Sánchez Vázquez 1977a, p. 165.

it to the recently emerged double problem of where the borderlines of this intermediary element are to be found, and, in turn, in what precise relation they lie *vis-à-vis* theory and praxis, and whether introducing this element does not lead to a greater distancing of them from one another.

The question that we see, here, for Sánchez Vázquez could be formulated as follows: how did this philosopher understand his own role, his own activity, when, for example, he wrote political-theoretical articles for a Mexican newspaper, when he coordinated a book series whose subjects were sociological and philosophical, or when during the Spanish Civil War he edited the newspaper of the Communist Youth in Madrid, as well as a newspaper for soldiers on the front – which, aside from the drafting of texts, also implies a permanent search for a publishing outlet in each new location? Is this a question of theory (which for him, as we have said, touches on practical objectives aside from the production of knowledge) and its inherent 'physical substratum' and 'objective manifestations',[302] or is it praxis; or is it a question of the intermediary steps which he does not, however, discuss in any more detail?

So, while Sánchez Vázquez is critical, on the one hand, of the concept of 'theoretical praxis', setting out from his conceptual distinction between theory and praxis and concluding that theory can only be conceived as a form of praxis when the latter is stretched 'to the point where all the specific differences between theory and activity in general disappeared',[303] he also criticises this questionable concept from the other side. He refers directly to two of Marx's texts in order to provide a basis for his rejection of a 'theoretical praxis': the *Theses on Feuerbach* and the *General Introduction to the Critique of Political Economy*.

In the first thesis on Feuerbach, Marx criticises Feuerbach for limiting himself to the contemplative relationship between the human being and reality and neglecting the practical side. Hence Sánchez Vázquez interprets Marx as establishing a counterposition between contemplation, what we could call theory, and praxis, establishing a border between the two.[304] So, in the eleventh thesis on Feuerbach, Marx distinguishes between a philosophy oriented toward transformative praxis and one limited to the pure interpretation of the world. The author in question also concludes, on this basis, that Marx understands theory and praxis as two clearly distinguishable forms of human behaviour: 'Marx counterposed theoretical, or contemplative, and practical

---

302   Sánchez Vázquez 1977a, p. 162. (See footnote 300 in this chapter.)
303   Sánchez Vázquez 1977a, p. 163.
304   Ibid.

relations ... Clearly, then, Marx did not regard theory as a form of praxis, but saw them in fact as opposed to one another'.[305]

In the *General Introduction to the Critique of Political Economy*, Marx establishes a distinction between the real concrete and the thought concrete, and characterises theoretical-intellectual activity as the process of rising from the abstract to the concrete.[306] This process occurs in thought and contains the 'spiritual reproduction of the real object in the form of concrete thought'.[307] Marx clarifies unequivocally that in this activity, in this intellectual reproduction, we are dealing with a production that does not create anything real, which is to say, it does not transform reality.

Here also, Sánchez Vázquez again sees a clear distinction in Marx between thought and 'practical material activity, adequate to ends, that transforms the world' (that is, between theory and praxis;[308] a differentiation, then, that categorically prohibits any mention of something like 'theoretical praxis'.

The concept of theoretical praxis under critique comes accompanied by an understanding of knowledge that, even though it was defended by Marxist authors at the time, Sánchez Vázquez designates as the 'old Idealist thesis'.[309] This approach to knowledge, apart from the aforementioned parallel, commits exactly the opposite error of the previously criticised, *quasi*-empiricist, conception within Marxism that grants revolutionary praxis an absolute character as the creator and basis of knowledge and underestimates or denies entirely the importance of the emancipatory theory that accompanies revolutionary praxis. This Marxist but *quasi*-idealist conception denies praxis as the criterion of truth. Our author rejects such an approach as being an exaggerated reaction against the underestimation of theory within Marxism and the communist parties. 'Practice alone cannot determine whether something is true or false,

---

305 Ibid.
306 See, for example, 'Hegel fell into the error, therefore, of conceiving the real as the result of self-coordinating, self-absorbed, and spontaneously operating thought, while the method of advancing from the abstract to the concrete is but a way of thinking by which the concrete is grasped and reproduced in our mind as a concrete. It is by no means, however, the process which itself generates the concrete'. Marx 1904, pp. 293–4.
307 Sánchez Vázquez 1977a.
308 Sánchez Vázquez 1977a, p. 262. [This formulation is not included in the English-language edition of Sánchez Vázquez's book, which is based on its first edition in Spanish. Compare Sánchez Vázquez 1980b (S.G.)].
309 Sánchez Vázquez 1977a, p. 191.

that is without a mediating theory. This does not mean that it is not, in the final analysis, the criterion of truth...'[310]

The sort of approaches here criticised end up seeking their truth criterion through a review of theoretical processes themselves, in the internal constitution of the theory or in its logical coherence. This is, of course, the idealistic form of seeking truth, a form that does not grasp the factor of objective praxis as elemental in the process of knowledge itself.[311] That was exactly the position that Marx sought to reproach by granting the central role in his work to praxis.

Sánchez Vázquez here formulates his critique of the concept of 'theoretical praxis' in a general manner, but in his footnotes, as we have already said, he mentions Althusser repeatedly as the theoretician at whose conceptualisation the critique is aimed.[312] As such, the accusation of idealism that he has levelled against the approach to knowledge here being investigated, must necessarily be understood with reference to Althusser. In another footnote, however, Sánchez Vázquez attenuates this critique of Althusser. He concedes to his contemporary that his theory can be distinguished from idealist approaches in that Althusser is conscious of the fact that ideas or theory by themselves do not occasion transformations of the real world.[313] In this vein, he refers to a text by Althusser published in Cuba.[314] Sánchez Vázquez underlines, here, that Althusser is interested in highlighting the peculiarities of what he calls 'theoretical praxis', which 'corresponds in large part, though not totally, given that it also includes the production of ends, to what we [that is, Sánchez Vázquez] have called theoretical activity',[315] without any intention of comparing it to material, objective praxis.

---

310 Sánchez Vázquez 1977a, pp. 190f. But here we can note, for our part, that the expression 'in the final analysis' which is used here, very common in Marxist literature and originating with Engels, has led over and over again to the most serious vagaries, imprecisions, and confusions with precise regard to the question – one not far from our present problem – of the 'dependence of the superstructure on the base'. (See Engels 1961, p. 463.)
311 Sánchez Vázquez 1977a.
312 See, for example, Sánchez Vázquez 1977a, p. 197 n26. For the texts of Althusser to which Sánchez Vázquez refers in his general critique of the author, see the previous subchapter, in which we refer above all to Althusser's conception of knowledge, citing the following texts: *Pour Marx* (Althusser 1965a) pp. 167 and 175; *Lire le Capital*, (Althusser et al. 1965b), Vol. I, p. 85; and 'Teoría, práctica teórica y formación teórica. Ideología y lucha ideológical' (Althusser 1965c), pp. 13–17 (Sánchez Vázquez 1977a, p. 168 n21).
313 Sánchez Vázquez 1977a.
314 See Althusser 1965c (Sánchez Vázquez 1977a.).
315 Sánchez Vázquez 1977a.

But with this, he has not withdrawn his critique, but has only modified it: the author whom we have thus far been discussing closes this important footnote with a new formulation of his critique of the concept of 'theoretical praxis': 'Thus in our view, the use of the term "practice" where that objective transformation does not occur, only serves to confuse the issue, despite the time expended on distinguishing between its specific forms'.[316]

---

316 Ibid. The phrase quoted is preceded by this: 'Nevertheless, the extension of the term "practice" to cover every type of relation to or appropriation of the real world, including not only the theoretical and ideological relation, but also the ethical and the religious relation, leads him to deny the essential character of praxis, which Marx correctly underlined, as the real, effective and concrete transformation of a real object, in contrast to an "idealism of praxis", which reduces praxis to a theoretical or moral activity' (ibid.).

CHAPTER 9

Once Again on the Problem of Knowledge and Praxis

The theory of knowledge represents a central problem in Marxist philosophical debates. As we have explained, it contains questions as fundamental as that of the relationship between idealism and (pre-Marxian) materialism and that of the – ultimately – materialist character of a praxis-orientated interpretation of Marxism.[317] These theoretical problematics had and continue to have far-reaching consequences, insofar as within them is found the balancing act that any critical Marxist philosophy and theory must constantly dare to realise; a balancing act to which this philosophical tendency owes a great deal of its allure and importance, but which simultaneously represents an internal philosophical reason that this theoretical current does not enjoy much sympathy in the current political context.

Bourgeois thinkers and actors took pleasure in casting against this current the allegation that it was allied with dark forces in the Soviet Union, a reproach which still finds adherents after the end of the experiment of actually-existing socialism. Among Marxist theorists and activists, on the other hand, this theoretical current – known as *Western* Marxism – always awakened the suspicion that it might contain a 'bourgeois' softening of the Marxist critique of the ruling capitalist relations of production and bourgeois society. With the end of the Soviet Union, the majority of dogmatic Marxists have also disappeared from the face of the Earth. Now, old dogmatic Marxists who suddenly recall that they were always good bourgeois democrats, together with untiring anti-communists, unleash insults against any persisting efforts to develop Marxist

---

317   See also: 'The fact that the point of departure for dialectical materialism is of a specifically epistemological character is due to the circumstance that Marx and Engels accept Hegel's critique of Kant without being able to simultaneously accept his speculative foundation. With Hegel they affirm the possibility of knowing the essence of phenomena, and with Kant (certainly without referring to the *Critique of Pure Reason*) they insist on the non-identity of form and matter, subject and object of knowledge. It comes in such a way – albeit without expressing it openly – to a materialist reformulation of the problem of constitution': Schmidt 1969c, pp. 10f.

theory, and affirm with relief that at least one thing has remained constant in their thought: their rejection of a non-dogmatic interpretation of Marx.

This first way of avoiding self-reflection on one's own theoretical weaknesses at a previous moment – that of projecting one's own defects in interpreting Marx onto others who were always suspicious of them – is complemented by a second way. Some formerly dogmatic Marxists are now convinced that they have always been critical, non-dogmatic Marxists. Through this reconstruction of their own theoretical history, they avoid, in their own way, the pending self-criticism. An example of this second form of conduct is the mentioned Cuban philosopher Jorge Luis Acanda González, who has recently presented himself, without any kind of reflection on his own philosophical past,[318] as someone who has always interpreted Marx critically.

The philosopher from Frankfurt, Alfred Schmidt, is one of those theorists who, already long before the end of the Soviet Union, was developing an autonomous and non-dogmatic interpretation of Marx in contrast to state philosophers, and after the end of the experiment in actually-existing socialism does not want his own philosophical production during that period to disappear into oblivion.[319] In light of the fact that Schmidt has made decisive contributions to the non-dogmatic debates surrounding Marxism, above all on the terrain of the theory of knowledge, it would be beneficial to place some of his reflections alongside Sánchez Vázquez's philosophy of praxis.

a   Materialism and Idealism

As concerns the relationship between praxis and knowledge, Alfred Schmidt, like his Spanish-Mexican contemporary, upholds the third of the positions mentioned in the chapter regarding the discussion of the *Theses on Feuerbach*.[320] As we have already observed, Sánchez Vázquez describes this position in the following terms: 'Finally others, like Kosík, maintain that without praxis, or the creation of a socio-human reality, knowledge of reality is itself impossible'.[321]

---

318   See also, in this regard, pp. 85ff of this book.
319   Alfred Schmidt, for example, expressed years ago that he continued to defend the positions put forth in his book *The Concept of Nature in Marx*. Evidently alluding to the treatment that Max Horkheimer gave his own previous writings after having returned to Frankfurt in 1947 from his exile in the United States, Schmidt said that he would not lock his early writings up in the basement (personal communication, c. 1993).
320   See the chapter 'Interpretation of the *Theses on Feuerbach*', pp. 132ff of this book.
321   Sánchez Vázquez 1977a, pp. 116f.

While Sánchez Vázquez recognises the primacy of matter, but insists that external reality is only *recognisable* by human beings insofar as they have entered into a practical relationship with it, Alfred Schmidt formulates a similar idea but in three different variants. The material being, which no doubt exists independently of human subjects, only 'acquires meaning' in a first formulation – ontological, if you will – after having passed through human praxis: 'It is true that material being precedes every form of historical practice as extensive and intensive infinity. But in so far as it is meaningful for men, this being is not the abstractly material being presupposed in its genetic primacy by any materialist theory, but a second being, appropriated through social labour'.[322] In a second formulation, the author from Frankfurt says, moreover, that the existence of natural material objectivity, the precursor to human praxis, only comes to be 'pronounceable' once it has become, at least partially, an object of human praxis:

> The social subject, through whose filter all objectivity passes, is and continues to be a component of the latter. No matter how much man, a 'self-conscious natural thing', goes beyond the immediacy of 'natural substance' found in each case, in transforming it through an ideal anticipation of his ends, the natural context [*Naturzusammenhang*] won't be ruptured in this way. Faced with this natural context (and in this Marx also follows Hegel's 'logic') purposeful doing can only assert itself by cunningly meshing with the process of the internal laws of matter. The fact that these laws exist 'in-themselves', independent of all praxis (and its theoretical implications) is, of course, *pronounceable* only insofar as the objective world has become a world 'for us'.[323]

This second formulation grasps the problem on the philosophical-linguistic level. Like the first, it includes the broader problematic that a materiality external to the immediate sphere of influence of human praxis can only be grasped by subjects in counterposition to matter already formed by praxis. This reaches the point that even the very term of the 'being untouched' of external nature can only be created by human beings who already practice a

---

322   Schmidt 1971, p. 194. He puts it similarly elsewhere: 'Like all materialism, dialectical materialism also recognizes that the laws and forms of motion of external nature exist independently and outside of any consciousness. This "in-itself" is however only *relevant* in so far as it becomes a "for-us", i.e. in so far as nature is drawn into the web of human and social purposes' (pp. 58f, italics by S.G.).
323   Schmidt 1973, p. 1117, italics by S.G.

massive domination over nature, and, therefore, know precisely what it means to not leave nature intact, but instead to 'touch it' violently. 'Even those objects which have not yet fallen into the sphere of human intervention depend on man insofar as their *being untouched* can only be formulated with relation to the human being'.[324]

Schmidt gives a reason for not referring, in this context, to the cognoscitive relationship between subject and object, one to which Sánchez Vázquez refers above all. 'The question of the unity and difference between subject and object loses its supra-temporal and "cognoscitively" limited character; it shows itself to be one of the unity and difference – determined in different forms in each case – of history and nature'.[325]

In another passage, the philosopher from the Frankfurt School tradition of critical theory indicates that the romantic yearning for the 'beautiful nature of God' is established historically at the precise moment in which the industrial development of a specific region or nation – with its consequent domination of nature through heavy machinery – has reached a certain level of development, as has the destruction of nature. Thus it was that it would occur for the first time to a few bourgeois gentlemen from the English industrial cities of the dawn of capitalism, dressed in their chequered shirts, to scale the Alps, a desire that they declared to be irresistible.[326] The native population could only be astounded by such a commotion. Their distance from extra-human nature was

---

324 Ibid. On the linguistic plane, this circumstance can be observed above all in literary activity, in which virgin nature is discovered at the same moment that its definitive conquest appears as the order of the day. Thus, the English poet Percy Bysshe Shelley describes Mont Blanc in 1816, in his poem of the same name, as 'Remote, serene, and inaccessible' after its summit had been reached five times by groups of climbers in the twenty years following its first ascent in 1786. Percy Bysshe Shelley, 'Mont Blanc, Lines Written in the Vale of Chamouni', (Shelly 1989, line 97).

325 Schmidt 1973. He continues: 'Both are mutually interpenetrating, without of course becoming identical; men always have the experience of a "historical nature" and of a "natural history"'. Schmidt refers here to the German edition of the *German Ideology*: Marx and Engels 1969, p. 43.

326 The first ascents of high mountains, above all the Alps, are an excellent example of the relation between external untouched nature or materiality, on the one hand, and subjectivity or praxis, on the other. The idea of a untouched nature has, from a certain moment of its potential, imaginable *tangibility* on, an incredible force of attraction, and thereby, this intangibility – which is from the beginning linked with the imagination of its potential tangibility – turns into the reality of already having been touched. The first high peak to be climbed by humans, according to the historical register, is Mont Blanc, the highest in Europe. This first great alpine ascent took place three years prior to the French Revolution. It is not only industrial development, but ideological development as well,

not sufficiently great to make it an object worthy of appeal, or even to perceive it as such.

In a third formulation – in terms of philosophy of consciousness – the material world, in its form of movement corresponding to the laws of nature, in no need of the subject in itself, is only 'recognisable' or becomes mentally 'certain' if it has already been the object of human praxis. This third formulation, evidently, comes close to Sánchez Vázquez's position as mentioned previously: 'The *dialectical* element of Marxist materialism does not consist in the denial that matter has its own laws and its own movement (or motion), but in the understanding that matter's laws of motion can only be recognised and appropriately applied by men through the agency of mediating practice'.[327]

In another passage, Schmidt formulates a similar idea in describing the relationship between materialism in general and 'dialectical materialism': 'The fundamental materialist tenet could be summed up as follows: the laws of nature exist independently of and outside the consciousness and will of men. *Dialectical* materialism also holds to this tenet, but with the following supplement: men can only *become certain* of the operation of the laws of nature through the forms provided by their labour-processes'.[328]

In the moment of productive activity, human beings collide with the borderlines of the transformability of matter, and thereby recognise its subordination to the laws of nature. It is only by recognising this regularity that they can, in turn, modify the barriers of nature where its objective content makes it possible. The double movement of praxis toward theory and theory toward praxis, which Sánchez Vázquez indicates, is also visible in Schmidt's considerations. With reference to Marx's and Hegel's reflections on 'labour's purposes',

---

that provokes and makes possible the yearning to reach the apparently unreachable parts of external nature.

The first to climb Mont Blanc, the guide Jacques Balmat and the medical doctor Michel Paccard, while they were inhabitants of Chamonix, responded to the call of the natural scientist Horace Bénédict de Saussure, who had offered a prize for climbing Mont Blanc. One year later, De Saussure himself reached the summit with eighteen carriers during the course of several days. Equipped with a variety of measuring instruments, a table, and a chair, he spent four and a half hours at the summit, carrying out among other things hygrometric experiments like those of the boiling point of water and taking notes of the effects of the elevated altitude on his own body: Horace Bénédict de Saussure 1979.

327 Schmidt 1971, p. 97. [Note to the edition in English: in the English translation of Schmidt's book, the following footnote is included after 'motion': ' "Movement" and "motion" are alternative renderings of the German word "Bewegung", both of which are required by the English context at different points' (p. 220 n17a).]
328 Schmidt 1971, p. 98, second italics by S.G.

among which productive praxis stands out, Schmidt proposes the following idea: 'Anticipatory knowledge presupposes practical action which has also been completed and from which this knowledge proceeds, just as, inversely, it forms the precondition of any such activity'.[329]

Now, for the two authors considered here, it is very important to insist that this reciprocal interdependence between praxis and knowledge does not simply put both on the same level. The mutually dependent relationship does not lead to a suspension of the primacy of matter *vis-à-vis* the subject and its capacity for knowledge and decision. But, at the same time, in Marxism this 'priority of external nature' is not static, but mediated:[330] 'Nature was for Marx both an element of human practice and the totality of everything that exists'.[331]

These reflections are much more than philosophical subtlety. The path across the tightrope that a philosophy of praxis must walk, as we mentioned at the beginning of this subchapter, is paraphrased by Alfred Schmidt in the following terms:

> These considerations are less trivial than they might seem, since if the concept of praxis is tightened excessively as it is by Fichte (as also in the early Lukács, who transforms historical materialism almost into an idealism of 'creation' in sociological clothing), it is toned down and becomes a concept of mere contemplation. 'Pure and absolute activity which is nothing more than activity' thus finally ends up in the 'illusion of "pure thought"'.[332]

We could make the following comment regarding this line of argumentation: this illusion of pure thought and pure activity leads, in political praxis, to the presumption that ideal processes determine material processes. To judge a specific policy within this logic, one merely examines the argumentative strategies of the agents and their followers in search of the internal coherence of the reasoning (for example, in its moral argumentation), instead of wondering about the real motives of those policies. In consequence, the effects of that

---

329 Schmidt 1971, p. 100. 'Labour's purposes' is, in the German original, 'Die bei der Arbeit verfolgten Zweck-Inhalte' (compare Schmidt 1974, p. 99).
330 'Marx, like Feuerbach, wrote of "the priority of external nature", although with the critical reservation that any such priority could only exist within mediation' (Schmidt 1971, pp. 26–7, Alfred Schmidt cites Marx here according to Marx and Engels 1969, p. 44).
331 Schmidt 1971, p. 27.
332 Schmidt 1973, p. 1117. Schmidt cites here according to Marx and Engels 1969, pp. 452f.

policy are not considered and valued in and of themselves, but always with respect to whether these effects were desired or not.

In Marxist theoretical debates, at the same time, the concept of praxis is indispensable in order to be able to confront the objectivist tendencies of both the reformist and Stalinist Lefts. Despite their considerable theoretical differences, one important parallel between the revisionist and dogmatic Lefts consists in the fact that both tend to understand the transition to socialism as an inevitable process. The reformist position is based on the idea that this transition will occur through a *passage*, as smooth as possible, through capitalism and a gradual transformation (which can only be sped up through reforms) of capitalist structures into socialist ones. The orthodox Marxists, by contrast, invoke the idea that a radical rupture must be reached at some particular moment. Despite this difference, they have something in common: both tendencies fear nothing so much as the spontaneous rebellion of the oppressed and exploited beyond the bounds of the party and organisational structures they are given.

But to grant praxis such a central position in their theories as do Sánchez Vázquez and Alfred Schmidt in their respective philosophical investigations, throws these objectivist understandings of politics and history radically into doubt. The concept of praxis, which is fundamental for Marxist theory, contains an element of rebellion against all those who, from their desk, from the Party headquarters, or from the *workers' fatherland*, aspire to lead the activities of the rebels of all countries. Since the concept of praxis already contains within itself the mediation of theory and activity, and, speaking more generally, of subject and object, and since it shows in theoretical reflections that the straight separation of the two (contained in the conception of *leading the masses through the Party*) leads to utter absurdity, this concept resists the authoritarianism of both the reformists and the orthodox. Given that both currents, confronted with the spontaneous rebellion of the masses, take pleasure in arguing that these masses lack theoretical knowledge and preparation, with the goal of taking charge of them again, the *philosophy of praxis*, which pleads the case of praxis on a highly theoretical level, is a splinter which is not very easy to remove. The cadres (who claim to be theoretically superior to the masses) are confronted on a terrain that they claim to be their own. But this does not at all mean simply to take the side of spontaneous and non-reflective action, practicism over theory. Both Adolfo Sánchez Vázquez and Alfred Schmidt are more interested in showing via their interpretations of Marx that theoreticism (and stubborn insistence on one's own theoretical training, as against those who do not formally possess it) is not necessarily any closer to the process of theoretical knowledge than is praxis in the fullest sense of the word.[333] It should thus be understood that Schmidt, like Sánchez Vázquez, insists on the fact that 'historical practice is in itself "more theoretical" than theory'.[334]

These references to the reformist and orthodox Lefts may, for more than one reader, seem anachronistic. And, in reality, they are, at first glance, since the 'orthodox' Left has disappeared since 1989 and the reformist Left has transformed itself, in parallel, into a political scaffolding that, while claiming control over several European governments, at best has only its name in common with the original project. While at the beginning of the twentieth century, and in part even during the first years after the Second World War, European social-democratic parties understood the need and possibility for a *transition to socialism* – and *reformism*, for them, did not mean calling this end into doubt, but merely questioning the path leading to it, as against the classical Marxist position – things are very different today. When reforms are pushed today, it is no longer as an alternative to socialist revolution, but instead as the surest way to guarantee the persistence of capitalism, in attempting to mitigate the consequences of its absurd contradictions with methods that could just as well have come from enlightened conservatives.[335]

---

333 Brecht expresses a similar idea when, in his *Flüchtlingsgespräche* [*Refugee Dialogues*], the character of the intellectual confesses to the character of the proletariat: 'I always think of the philosopher Hegel. I have taken some of his books out of the library so that you will not be behind, *philosophically* speaking' (Brecht 1961, p. 76, italics by S.G.). In any case, this should only be understood negatively, i.e., as an ironic critique of theoreticism and not as a banal cult of the proletariat. As a disdainful allusion to the conceptual capacities of the working class, amateurishly praised, which finds its expression in the substitution of classics by *textbooks* by a part of the communist party, the character representing the proletariat adds shortly thereafter, referring again to Hegel: 'They gave us extracts of his works. In him, as in crabs, one must focus on the extracts'.

[Note to the edition in English: There exists in English a published adaptation of the text for theatre performance: 'Conversations in Exile', adapted by Howard Brenton from a translation by David Dollenmayer, in Brecht 1986.]

334 Schmidt 1971, p. 194.

335 This is not a malicious assumption, but merely a summary of the most recent party and government programmes of European social democracy. We would scarcely find a social democrat today who would continue to question the claim that such programmes are pro-capitalist.

With regard to the Green Party, which has reached the ranks of government positions in the German Federal Republic, we would be best advised to say nothing, since – as a party – even in the best of times they did not achieve the sharpness of the social theory previously claimed, despite everything, by social democracy.

Despite everything, these reflections continue to be of great importance when the problem of the relationship between theory and activity, between subjectivity and objective relations, and between cadres and *party base* are posed to us with an urgency that has not decreased. It remains valid today to insist that emphasising the meaning of praxis does not mean to simply take the side of subjectivity against the importance of objective relations. In the critical-philosophical concept of praxis, what is more interesting is grasping the dialectical relationship between these two instances, which can only be counterposed so simply on the terminological level, and to understand the importance of this relationship. Thus we should follow Alfred Schmidt when he indicates that simple objectivism and simple subjectivism should in no way be identified as unequivocal opposites, but rather that – in specific ideologies or forms of political action – both tend to coexist. With regard to the problem of the relationship between praxis and knowledge, as we have explained in detail as a central philosophical problem for Sánchez Vázquez, Schmidt writes: 'On the terrain of *conceived praxis* the bad abstraction of a purely mental subject "lacking a world" is highlighted, as is that of a world "lacking a subject", which exists in itself. Praxis as effective realisation teaches us how empty these alternatives are which are fixedly determined as *points of view* "in the theory of knowledge"'.[336]

So, following both Sánchez Vázquez and Alfred Schmidt, we could say that both positions under critique – that of the dogmatic Left as well as its reformist variant – contain a peculiar combination of mechanical materialism and idealism. This does not mean that the defenders of those positions truly understand it in this way. It is precisely in the not-comprehended (or even unconscious) combination of these two philosophical traditions that the theoretical problem is buried.[337] Marx's contribution (and we thus return to Sánchez Vázquez's interpretation of the *Theses on Feuerbach*) consisted in critically – which is to say, through reflection – contrasting the epistemological contributions of mechanical materialism to those of idealism, in order to thereby arrive at the developed concept of praxis. Schmidt emphasises that, for Marx, the question

---

336   Schmidt 1973, p. 1115.
337   In this regard, see also: 'Marx does not "combine" (which would be a pure eclecticism) reflective motives rooted in idealism and materialism, but rather puts forth the idea (which had appeared in different shades from Kant to Hegel) that the immediate is already mediated, against its previously idealist formulation' (Schmidt 1969c, p. 11).

... given the unavoidable historic tasks of humanity, is no longer one of arguing – on the basis of higher principles of being and knowledge (for which it matters little whether their interpretation is spiritual or material) – but rather one of setting out from the 'materiality' of the human living conditions – a materiality which is anything but ontological – which are '*practical* from the outset, that is, relations established by action': productive and class relations.[338]

b   Political and Productive Praxis

As we have already indicated, there is a difference between Sánchez Vázquez's and Schmidt's studies of the concept of praxis, and this difference consists in the fact that the latter understands human praxis as most centrally economic, whereas the former, in contrast, when he touches upon specific forms of praxis, mentions political and artistic praxis in particular. This difference is accompanied by the different way in which each author locates the centre of gravity of his reading of Marx. While Sánchez Vázquez refers principally to Marx's early works, granting *Capital* little importance, Alfred Schmidt sets out from the observation 'that Marx was by no means at his most philosophical when he made use of the traditional, scholastic language of the philosophers'. Therefore, in his book on Marx's concept of nature, he warns the reader from the beginning that 'his middle and later, politico-economic writings will be consulted much more than is customary in interpretations of Marxist philosophy. Particular attention has been paid to the *Grundrisse der Kritik der politischen Ökonomie (Rohentwurf)*, the preliminary draft of *Capital*, which is of the utmost importance for understanding the relation between Hegel and Marx, and which has so far hardly been used'.[339]

Although in his aesthetic writings Sánchez Vázquez certainly does occasionally refer to Marx's intermediate and mature politico-economic writings,

---

338   Ibid. Schmidt cites here from Marx 1996, p. 235, Marx's emphasis.
        Schmidt continues here by referring to Mao: 'These reflect in each case not only the degree to which society has already achieved true power over nature, but they also determine the what and the how of human knowledge, of the general horizon in which it moves' (Schmidt 1969c, p. 11).
339   Schmidt 1971, pp. 16–17.

above all the *Rohentwurf* (the *Grundrisse*) and *Capital*,[340] his texts regarding the philosophy of praxis focus above all on Marx's early writings. This orientation, however, should not be directly connected to the tendency 'fashionably and mistakenly, to reduce the strictly *philosophical* thought of Marx to what is written in those texts, namely to the anthropology of the Paris Manuscripts of 1844'.[341] Rather, Sánchez Vázquez shares Schmidt's critique in relation to the period in which the latter composed his book on the concept of nature:

> In those years, the decades of the 1940s and 50s, the young Marx – before the astonished gaze of Marxists – became almost the exclusive property of bourgeois thought..., many sought to discredit the mature Marx in the name of the young Marx, and in this sense, interpretations and critiques in many ways became ideological and even political weapons. The transformation of the young Marx into the true Marx... affected not only the *Manuscripts* but also its relation to the mature works and its position within the process of formation and constitution of Marx's thought.[342]

Distinguishing himself vehemently from Althusser's Marxism, Sánchez Vázquez insists that Marx's work is indivisible.[343] Though he draws principally on Marx's early and middle works for his philosophical analyses of the concept of praxis, this is not necessarily because he considers this Marx to be 'more philosophical', but because the topic of artistic and political praxis in these works is more foregrounded than in the critique of political economy, in which, Marx is discussing, above all, the reproductive form of praxis which sustains the human world. This privileged position that creative and, particularly, political-revolutionary praxis enjoys above other forms of praxis in Sánchez Vázquez's work *The Philosophy of Praxis* should be understood more as a result of his own life history than for internal reflections of pure theory. When he is engaged with the study of the writings of Marx, this is above all due to the political activity of his early youth.

---

340 See, for example, Sánchez Vázquez 1974, especially Chapter 14: 'Wage Labor an Artistic Activity', pp. 202–8, and Chapter 17: 'Production and Consumption. (Creation and Enjoyment)', pp. 223–9.
    Spanish original: Sánchez Vázquez 1965b.
341 Schmidt 1971, p. 16.
342 Sánchez Vázquez 1982, p. 227.
343 See also the subchapter 'Knowledge as Something Achieved Exclusively in Theory', pp. 160ff.

A change of countries imposed for political reasons (so, too, for Sánchez Vázquez) gives rise to a permanent and almost unavoidable presence of the political in the everyday lives of exiles. Like it or not, the consequences of their own political praxis play a determinant role in the lives of exiles, and for the hustle and bustle of everyday life, these can be more imperative than those which emerge directly from reproductive praxis. The latter, by contrast, determine the everyday life of individuals who were never forced to change countries for political reasons, more so than their (own) political praxis and its consequences. This is why the fact that Sánchez Vázquez turns more toward political than reproductive praxis in his philosophical analysis is not a matter of purely internal theoretical motivation, but rather one that develops out of political praxis itself.[344]

This result of the reflection as to why Sánchez Vázquez, despite his critique directed towards Althusser as regards the unity of Marx's work, leaves Marx's later contribution almost completely out of his philosophical analysis of praxis, seems to fit in harmony – so to say – within the context of this part of the book where the bilateral relationship between praxis and knowledge is our central object.

However, we are left with a doubt, and it is more than a methodological one. Did we arrive at this conclusion – from praxis to theory – too quickly? Is not, perhaps, one of the important results of Sánchez Vázquez's interpretation of the eleventh *thesis on Feuerbach* that this phrase, the best-known of all Marx's work, loses its undeniable meaning if it is pronounced too quickly? Does our answer not reduce philosophy to a form of thought which depends too directly on everyday life, except for being more systematic? While it is, of course, pleasant when a text appears to justify itself quickly, caution is advisable as to avoid sinking into banal self-affirmation. If not, theory would become like political propaganda, which knows truth only as a means: 'propaganda ... falsifies truth simply by taking it into its mouth'.[345]

As we have suggested previously, there is another place where Sánchez Vázquez deals more closely with the late Marx, and this is in his first book *Marx's Aesthetic Ideas*. But what is peculiar is that, in his later works, he practically ceases to mention *Capital* and the *Grundrisse*. What could have been

---

[344] Bertolt Brecht also sees a direct relationship between emigration and the form of creating theory: 'The best school of dialectics is emigration. The most acute dialecticians are refugees. They are refugees as a result of changes, and they study nothing but changes. Out of the tiniest signs they conclude the greatest events. When their opponent wins, they calculate how much the victory cost, and for contradictions they have a refined eye'. Brecht 1961, p. 79.

[345] Horkheimer and Adorno 2002, p. 212.

the motives for such a shift? Our argumentation on the basis of his life history could, of course, explain the different centres of gravity according to which Schmidt and Sánchez Vázquez select the forms of praxis they investigate, but this history would be hard-pressed to make understandable a theoretical shift that takes place more than 25 years after the beginning of his exile. So we must go more closely into the internal theoretical aspects of this problem. Sánchez Vázquez himself values his book *Marx's Aesthetic Ideas* as the first expression of a certain magnitude of his break with dogmatic Marxism.[346] In particular, he is interested in questioning an immediate relationship of dependency between artistic developments and those of a social nature: 'the history of art and literature shows that changes in aesthetic sensibility do not come about spontaneously, which explains the persistence of aesthetic criteria and values in contradiction to profound changes in other spheres of human life'.[347]

With this he poses the need for the independent – revolutionary – development of art, even in a society which has just undergone a revolution, as was the case in Cuba during the 1960s. 'A new sensibility, a new audience, a new aesthetic attitude have to be created; they are not fruits of spontaneous processes'.[348]

Although in this book Sánchez Vázquez breaks in many senses with dogmatic Marxism, and in particular with the ahistorical fixation on socialist realism as the only art form adequate to socialism, it is nevertheless the case that this work – which was written prior to *The Philosophy of Praxis* (the principal topic of our study)[349] – maintains a whole lot of residues of that orthodoxy. For example, Sánchez Vázquez writes the following in a footnote:

> But the revolutionary proletariat, guided in its public and private actions by consciousness of its class interests and its historic role (a consciousness which it develops to the extent that it assimilates its class ideology, Marxism-Leninism), can successfully resist the *massifying* endeavors of professional consciousness-manipulators. The proletarian himself, in the alienating conditions of capitalist society, grasps himself as a subject, as an active, creative subject, with the power to bring about not only his own emancipation but also the emancipation of all mankind.[350]

---

346 In this regard, see the biographical discussion of Sánchez Vázquez, p. 35.
347 Sánchez Vázquez 1974, p. 228.
348 Ibid.
349 In his *The Philosophy of Praxis* he thus completes his break with Soviet Marxism.
350 Sánchez Vázquez 1974, p. 250 n4. Luis Villoro could be referring to these expressions of Sánchez Vázquez when he writes: 'Sánchez Vázquez shares a Marxist-Leninist

Beyond the naïve cult of the proletariat and praise for Marxism-Leninism, this passage contains, moreover, the manipulation thesis, according to which ideology is above all the result of the activities of 'professional consciousness manipulators'. These three formulations generally went hand-in-hand with economism, according to which it was assumed that, for Marx, all social phenomena depended directly on economic development. Although Sánchez Vázquez, as we have already set out, insists that the artistic development of a country should not be directly attributed to development in general, namely including economic development, one possible explanation for Sánchez Vázquez's later reticence to refer to Marx's mature work is this: in his process of distancing himself increasingly from both the Soviet Union and dogmatic interpretations of Marx, Sánchez Vázquez hoped to avoid at any cost any indication that this rupture might be incomplete, therefore preferring to refer as little as possible, as a philosopher, to Marx's critique of political economy.

No matter how much proof Alfred Schmidt provides that Marx can be more philosophical in the writings that are generally classified as 'economic' than in the early works, which are generally understood as 'philosophical', he points out regardless that this interpretation is far from the predominant one. As Sánchez Vázquez, in the recently cited passage, still utilises some dogmatic elements – despite having conceived of this book (*Art and Society*) as a break with Marxist dogmatism – and moreover, considering the fact that since his youth he was a member of the PCE, which remained faithful to Moscow, it is possible, to continue in this line of thought, that it was more urgently necessary for him than for Alfred Schmidt to categorically avoid the reproach of economism. From this may emerge the peculiar circumstance that Adolfo Sánchez Vázquez, while emphasising repeatedly the importance of Marx's main work[351] and defending the indivisibility of his work as a totality, does not again return to discuss in greater detail *Capital* or the *Rohentwurf* after his *Art and Society*.

Without being able to clarify definitively if these motives played or continued to play a decisive role in Sánchez Vázquez's extensive abstinence in employing Marx's main work for his philosophical interpretation, it would nevertheless be worthwhile to enter again into this variant of the explanation, since still now some people assume that a strong reference to economic facts in clarifying problematics that are not directly of an economic nature, leads to an *economistic* (that is, in the end, dogmatic) reduction of reality. Toward this

---

understanding of the world' (Villoro 1995, p. 577). In speaking in this way, Villoro neglects the fact that Sánchez Vázquez experienced a decisive theoretical development after 1965. Later, Villoro would partially correct this position in other interventions.

351 See, for example, Sánchez Vázquez 1984, p. 194.

end, the third of the three elements of dogmatic Marxism which emerge in the previously reproduced paragraph by Sánchez Vázquez is of special interest.

While the cult of the proletariat and the glorification of Marxism-Leninism have largely disappeared from the face of the Earth, the manipulation thesis persists in the most diverse of circles. Sánchez Vázquez refutes this indirectly in his interpretation of the third of Marx's *Theses on Feuerbach*:[352] just as there can be no educators who are above society, leading it from the outside toward a freer consciousness, we could add that the same applies to the formation of human consciousness which is harmful to the cause of emancipation. Both the absence of enlightened consciousness as well as the process of its formation can only be rationally represented as grounded in social processes.

While Sánchez Vázquez, in his book *The Philosophy of Praxis*, clearly sees the just mentioned problem in relation to the difficulties that exist in the process of the formation of emancipatory consciousness – setting out from the *Theses on Feuerbach* – in the earlier text just cited he does not perceive this problem in relation to the processes which generate presumptions harmful for human self-liberation. Although the manipulation thesis was generally accompanied, in the history of dogmatic Marxism, by broadly economistic explicative emphases, the two are nevertheless very different things. In a more painstaking analysis of the *critical* Marxian concept of ideology – and especially as this emerges from the critique of political economy – we must bear in mind that only the consideration of economic factors can cancel out the banal thesis of manipulation within Marxist debates. If, in various passages, Marx refers ingenuously to the purportedly irrepressible power of the proletariat,[353] it is

---

352 See pp. 143ff of this book.
353 Expressions such as these are to be found not only, as tends to be assumed, in the *Manifesto*, but also in Marx's main work, where, as political expressions, they contradict the theory, which is otherwise basically critical. In a passage in *Capital*, Marx upholds, in passing, 'the inevitable conquest of political power by the working class' (Marx 1976a, p. 619), later adding: 'Along with the constant decrease in the number of capitalist magnates, who usurp and monopolize all the advantages of this process of transformation, the mass of misery, oppression, slavery, degradation and exploitation *grows*; but with this there also grows *the revolt of the working class, a class constantly increasing in numbers, and trained, united and organised by the very mechanism of the capitalist process of production*... The knell of capitalist private property sounds. The expropriators are expropriated' (p. 929, italics by S.G.).

Note, moreover, the *Communist Manifesto*: 'What the bourgeoisie, therefore, produces, above all, are its own gravediggers. Its fall and the victory of the proletariat are equally inevitable. Of all the classes which confront the bourgeoisie today, the proletariat alone is a really revolutionary class'. Marx cites these passages in *Capital*, Vol. 1: Marx 1976a, p. 930 n2.

precisely in *Das Kapital* that our eyes are opened. In a subchapter which has proven central for Western Marxism, 'The Fetishism of the Commodity and Its Secret', conceptual foundations are developed which are useful for keeping a tight rein on the manipulation thesis. Fully to grasp the critical Marxian concept of ideology thus developed means, consequently, abandoning the naïve cult of the proletariat, since the German exile asks insistently why the consciousness of *all those* who are immersed in capitalist relations (and today no one could deny that they are included in this) has been blinded by the objective appearance of the society of commodity producers: an appearance that functions as a generator of ideology.

It is thus paradoxical that the manipulation thesis, the usual companion of economism, can be overcome through reference to the Marxian critique of political economy, rather than by turning one's back on that critique. Economism consists precisely in an uncritical – which is to say, positivist – misunderstanding of the Marxian phrase according to which the economy is the anatomy of bourgeois society. This polemically critical description of the dominant social relations has led, occasionally, to the false conclusion that everything can be explained directly on the basis of the economic constellation of each case. According to this view, for example, the consciousness of a specific subject is derived from his class situation; whereas, according to the critical Marxian concept of ideology, consciousness is formed, rather, through a mediated process which is partly determined by economic factors but is not immediately deducible from these factors.

Overcoming economism does not mean throwing the critique of political economy overboard, but rather avoiding such simplifications through truly understanding that critique. In general, it was not those who were most knowledgeable of Marx's main work that saw it in such a trivial manner, but instead those who only received it through the telescope of those handbooks which made a *critique* of political economy into a positive framework of the entire social relations. Economism did not subsist on an excess of economic knowledge, but rather on the nostalgic desire to summarise the three Marxian volumes in twenty theorems and thereby explain the world.

Frightened by their own economistic simplifications, many formerly dogmatic Marxists have turned their backs on economic theory entirely and now search for the origin of ideology, be it in the mass media, in *ancient ethnic or religious conflicts*, or in similar instances. Now oriented theoretically according to disparate perspectives, they often tend to fall, nevertheless, into a flat theory of manipulation that grasps, in its own reductionist form, the powerfully mediated process of the formation of consciousness and, in the end, resembles their old dogmatism more than might seem to be the case at first glance.

CHAPTER 10

The Philosophy of Praxis: Two Versions

The difference that stands out most between the two versions of *The Philosophy of Praxis* [as they exist in the original versions in Spanish] consists in the intensification of the book's critical discussion of Lenin. The chapter on Lenin was only formulated for the second edition, which was published in 1980 and is the edition that we have used here. It is, therefore, absent from the English translation, which was published in 1972 with the title *The Philosophy of Praxis*.[354]

In the 1980 version, some subchapters of the first 1967 edition have been deleted. In the second part, 'Some philosophical problems of praxis', Chapter VII, 'Spontaneous and reflective praxis', the following four subchapters were deleted: 'Flashes of consciousness and class consciousness',[355] 'From spontaneous to reflective praxis',[356] 'The Leninist conception of socialist consciousness',[357] and 'The Party as a "collective intellectual" '.[358] Moreover, in the same seventh chapter, Sánchez Vázquez rewrites, expands, and changes the name of the subchapter 'The problem of the transition from theory to action', which is now called: 'The problem of the transition from theory to action in the "Manifesto" '.

By contrast, the entirety of Chapter V – 'Class consciousness, organisation, and praxis'[359] – has been added, in which, in discussing in particular Lenin, Stalin, Rosa Luxemburg, Trotsky, and Althusser's critique of the French

354 See Sánchez Vázquez 1967b, and 1980b, pp. 193–242, as well as Sánchez Vázquez 1977a. See, moreover, Sánchez Vázquez 1979, pp. 46–61.

355 Sánchez Vázquez 1977a [as mentioned, this translation is based on the first edition of *Filosofía de la praxis*, Sánchez Vázquez 1967b, pp. 237f. [Note to the English-language edition: The numeration of the chapters is changed in the English version of *The Philosophy of Praxis*, because the translator uses a continuous numeration, but in the Spanish original the numeration of the chapters starts again with 'I' in the second part of the book. In the English-language edition of the present work, we refer to the numeration used in the English translation of *The Philosophy of Praxis*. In the above-mentioned case of Chapter VII, 'Spontaneous and reflective praxis', this has the number 'IV' in the Spanish original of the first edition of the book. (S.G.).]

356 Sánchez Vázquez 1977a, pp. 238f.

357 Sánchez Vázquez 1977a, pp. 239–41.

358 Sánchez Vázquez 1977a, pp. 253–8.

359 Sánchez Vázquez 1980b, pp. 353–78. [Note to the English-language edition: as concerns the numeration of this new chapter 'Conciencia de clase organización y praxis' in the

Communist Party (PCF), Sánchez Vázquez studies the question of the Party as an organisational form and, assessing the significant role of Lenin in the Russian Revolution, he asserts the 'impossibility of a model of the revolutionary party – that of Lenin or any other imaginable form – that would be universally valid'.[360] Without having followed in detail each of the modifications that we mention between the second edition of *The Philosophy of Praxis* and the first, we can assume that specific ideas of Lenin which were included more implicitly in the first version – above all regarding the 'organisational question' – become an explicit theme of the second edition and are thereby subjected to critical analysis. Therefore, the previous quotation is representative for the new draft of these passages: Lenin's theory is not merely thrown out, but is, instead, grasped according to its historical limitations. A similar change can be seen in the deletion of a footnote about Marcuse, who Sánchez Vázquez criticises robustly in the first edition due to his critical attitude toward the party-form. One part of this deleted footnote originally read: 'A clear example of this distortion of Marx's thought can be found in Herbert Marcuse (*cf. Soviet Marxism*, New York, 1958, pp. 24–26), who claims that the Leninist doctrine of the party is opposed to Marx's original conception, since in it the proletariat becomes the object and not the subject of the revolution'.[361]

While Sánchez Vázquez, in deleting this footnote, does not convert directly to Marcuse's perspective, in any case his words in the second edition of *Philosophy of Praxis* which we have reproduced here as regards the Leninist theory of the party demonstrate a *rapprochement* with the positions that he had previously rejected vehemently. It is not clear to what degree a direct influence of Marcuse played a role. But there was certainly an indirect influence, since in the student movement of 1968 Marcuse, who spoke in various Mexican universities, was enthusiastically received and Sánchez Vázquez did explain, for his part, that this movement influenced him on a theoretical level.[362]

---

second edition of *Filosofía de la praxis*, which does not exist in English, see above, footnote 355.]

360   Sánchez Vázquez 1980b, p. 372.
361   Sánchez Vázquez 1980b, p. 372. Sánchez Vázquez 1967b, p. 145 n77. Georges Cogniot would no doubt be disappointed with Sánchez Vázquez if he knew that the latter had scratched out this note about Marcuse, since he celebrates it as an expression of an *'esprit militant'*: 'His study of the conception [of human praxis] in Marx is extremely rich... and is animated by a militant spirit. Sánchez Vázquez polemicizes for example with all those who, like Herbert Marcuse and Maximilien Rubel, deform the problem of the passage from theory to action in Marx, falsely claiming that he did not provide the basis for a workers' party, that it was only Lenin that did so, etc.' (Cogniot 1968, p. 147).
362   In this regard, see in Part One of this book, 'Life and Work of Adolfo Sánchez Vázquez', in the section, 'The "new theoretical and practical posture"', especially pp. 34ff. [Note to

The alterations that we have indicated between the first 1967 edition and the second 1980 edition of *The Philosophy of Praxis* [in its Spanish original, *Filosofía de la praxis*] should be understood as part of Sánchez Vázquez's theoretical-political development, which we have already studied in detail in his biography: from a politicised youth during the Spanish Civil War, integrated firmly into the structures of the Stalinist PCE, passing through an independent development among exiled PCE members in Mexico against the Party central located in Paris, until arriving at the beginning of the rupture in 1956, after the CPSU's Twentieth Congress, at a non-dogmatic Marxist orientation increasingly grounded in theory. After the experience of the Cuban Revolution in 1959 – which at the beginning did not correspond at all to orthodox ideas – he then developed the theoretical perspective described in *The Philosophy of Praxis*, but which, as we have said, remained orthodox in certain respects. The events of the Prague Spring, the Mexican student movement of the summer of 1968, and the 1979 Sandinista Revolution (which was condemned also by the Nicaraguan CP) certainly did influence the alterations reflected in the second edition of the book. Sánchez Vázquez's theoretical-political trajectory can be understood as the effort to free himself of the errors – in part the cause of immense sufferings – of a Marxist Left, without thereby falling into an apologia for existing relations of exploitation and oppression or forgetting the radical critique of everything existing which would be unthinkable without Marx. This is an effort which, as we can observe with greater intensity in recent years, almost no one dares to undertake and which, nevertheless, represents the only opportunity to continue formulating a critical theory of society, the premise for the transition from the prehistory of humanity to what is, properly speaking, *its own* consciously developed history.

---

the edition in English: Marcuse not only spoke in the two Mexican universities relatively near to San Diego, California, in Tijuana and Mexicali, but also, in the first months of 1968, at the Faculty of Political and Social Sciences of the UNAM. (José Anaya Vicente, personal information, January 8, 2012, Coyoacán. The Mexican poet was present at Marcuse's conference at the UNAM.) Compare also, for example: 'In the 70s, the at that time director [of the Faculty of Social and Political Sciences], Víctor Flores Olea, started an international theoretical opening, inviting outstanding intellectuals of the period, with the objective to discuss the most important problems of that time; Herbert Marcuse, [Charles] Wright Mills, Erich Fromm, Jean Whal, Maurice Duverger, Karel Kosík, Ralph Miliband, Eric Hobsbawm, Rossana Rossanda, K.S. Karol, István Mészáros... in other times came Marcuse, today we are inviting people like Manuel Castells,... explains the director [Fernando Castañeda]'. (Alida Piñón, 'Facultad de Ciencias Políticas y Sociales de la UNAM, seis décadas de crear pensamiento crítico', *El Universal*, Mexico City: 13 August 2011.)].

CUERPOS VII

PART 3

Bolívar Echeverría: Use-Value and *Ethos*

∴

We now move on to the presentation and interpretation of our second author. While we do not in any way consider Bolívar Echeverría's work to be merely a subsequent development of the philosophy of Adolfo Sánchez Vázquez, it can nevertheless be considered on many points to represent a decisive contribution to deepening the non-dogmatic interpretation of Marx that was initiated in Mexico by Sánchez Vázquez.

In the course of what remains of this book, the following order of presentation has been chosen: in a first step, the question is to present Echeverría's effort to concretise the concept of praxis in the contemporary context. At the beginning some indications are given about certain differences or parallels to Sánchez Vázquez's concept of praxis, which is considered by Echeverría to be too abstract. In so doing, we will place at the centre of our investigation the two topics which constitute the core of Echeverría's social philosophy: on the one hand, his analysis of the concept of *use-value* – the natural form of the social process of production and consumption – as the centre of the process of material and semiotic exchange, and on the other, his investigation, based on the first element, of the four *ethe* of capitalist modernity. The latter are not merely four basic moral attitudes, but rather four ways of bearing what is unbearable in ruling relations, including the various types of production and consumption of use-values.

As to the first topic: the concept of use-value, the serious analysis of which interests Echeverría, of course occupies a central position in Marx as a pillar for the creation of value, and Marx did not tire of showing that, under capitalist relations of production, the dynamic of the production of use-values is increasingly dominated by the apparently autonomous dynamic of the production of value. But the founder of the critique of political economy did not enter deeply into the culturally diverse details of these use-values produced under capitalist conditions (and the way that they continue to exist despite the increasingly perfect real subsumption to value).[1] To put it in the language of Marx's 1859 prologue: *Capital* concentrates especially on the 'anatomy' of bourgeois society: political economy. In so doing (to expand the medical terminology), it takes into account, moreover, psychology and neurology, and this is the critique of ideology; but what remains outside it is what corresponds to the ear, nose, and throat specialist and to internal medicine. The latter correspond

---

1 Marx does, of course, enter into the details of the deterioration of use-values in general within the ruling economic system; for example, in *Capital* he notes that the bread eaten by English industrial workers in the period in question consisted of an ever higher proportion of ingredients that have nothing in common with cereals, salt, spices, yeast, water, or milk, which is to say the traditional components of bread (See Marx 1976a, p. 278 n14).

to the study of the various use-values and the respective modes by which they are consumed, enjoyed, and digested, as well as how they are produced, with different techniques and work instruments according to the given case.

To analyse – without falling into social relativism – the various ways in which humans arrange their lives under capitalist relations of production, Echeverría resorts to a detailed investigation of the Marxian conception of use-value, confronting it conceptually with Ferdinand de Saussure's linguistic theory. In order to resolve this tangle, we need to distinguish different sign systems, according to how Echeverría conceives the production and consumption of *different* use-values, accentuating at the same time what these share, namely, the capacity to develop these vast sign systems. The distinction the founder of modern semiotics makes between, on the one hand, different languages [*langues*], and on the other, the unifying language capacity [*faculté de langage*], must play the role of midwife in this effort to birth a concrete universalism, in opposition to the falsely abstract – which is to say, Eurocentric – universalism which today prevails.

This, then, brings us to the second central theme of Bolívar Echeverría's work, which consists of the specific way of approaching a fundamental question for Western Marxism: how is it possible that the capitalist mode of production, which is so obviously unbearable, as well as the bourgeois society that accompanies it, are perceived by the subjects of that society to be inevitable, bearable, and perhaps even reasonable?

Despite sharing this question with Western Marxism, in the answer Echeverría offers he diverges notably from its research path. In some cases, he does so with the explicit intention of pursuing it autonomously, enriching it with subsequent theoretical contributions. This critical and autonomous 'continuation' of Western Marxism outside of the geographical sphere commonly understood as 'the West', which Echeverría carries out with explicit (albeit partially distanced) reference to György Lukács, Karl Korsch, Walter Benjamin, Theodor W. Adorno, and Max Horkheimer, differs from these authors in two respects.

On the one hand, the critical perspective of ideology is broadened, and, although it is not abandoned, it is noticeably modified through this broadening. On the other hand, Echeverría attempts to take seriously a postulate that he reads between the lines of Frankfurt School texts, and proposes to confront it with the problem of Eurocentrism. The postulate in question is a matter of rescuing the singular and the particular against the conceptual and real attack by the (apparently) general, without throwing overboard general concepts and the quest for universal emancipation. As we will need to demonstrate later, it is no coincidence that such an effort is made precisely in Latin America, which is to say, outside the simultaneously real and apparent centre of the contemporary world.

This is to say, Echeverría proposes to demonstrate that the various forms adopted by everyday life, the conceptions existing therein as well as the production of specific use-values within capitalist relations of production, should not be understood as steps within a linear process of historical development, but that there exist instead, *at the same time*, different capitalist modernities (although one of these increasingly tends to dominate the rest). Consequently, Walter Benjamin's theses 'Über den Begriff der Geschichte' ['On the concept of history'],[2] which are of profound importance for Echeverría, are taken up again because the simply progressivist conception of history must be discarded and – here following Benjamin quite literally – we must 'brush history against the grain'.[3]

It is worth noting that Echeverría attempts to undertake this 'brush ... against the grain' not only by exploding the 'continuum of history',[4] as Benjamin proposes, but instead by interrupting, from another side, the apparently linear development of history. He is interested in escaping from the idea – which also pertains to the linear image of history – that a determinate historical development must originate at a certain point and then gradually spread across the rest of the planet and that, therefore, there must always exist territories whose development is more advanced than that of others. Put differently: while Benjamin wants to brush the continuum of history against the grain above all in temporal (or chronological) terms, Echeverría attempts to do so in spatial (or geographical) terms.[5]

---

2 Benjamin 1968, pp. 253–63. Original: Benjamin 1978, pp. 693–704.
3 Benjamin 1968, Thesis VII, p. 257. Echeverría refers to Benjamin in his essay 'The baroque *ethos*', when in referring to the 'American seventeenth century', he writes: 'The peculiarity and importance of this century only truly appear when, following Benjamin's advice, the historian returns to the historical continuity that has led to the present, but examining it "against the grain" ' ('El ethos barroco', in Echeverría 1994b, p. 29).
4 Benjamin 1968, Thesis XIV, p. 261.
5 Walter Benjamin is, of course, fully conscious of the impossibility of seeing a spatial continuum in history, as the progressivism he is criticising always claims to do. In this respect, see the following passage from Benjamin: 'Dreams vary according to where you are, what area and what street, but above all according to the time of year and the weather'. (Benjamin 1999, p. 830.) Original: 'Es träumt sich sehr verschieden nach Gegend und Straße, vor allem aber ganz unterschieden nach Jahreszeiten und nach dem Wetter' (Benjamin 1982, p. 996.). Echeverría cites this passage at the beginning of his essay 'La compression y la crítica. Braudel y Marx sobre el capitalismo', in Echeverría 1995a, pp. 111–31.

The central concept in this effort is that of the modern *ethe*, of which Echeverría distinguishes four basic types. In this conception, Bolívar Echeverría is interested – without calling it out – in a critique of (philosophical) Eurocentrism. He proposes not only to investigate the effects of commodity production on the process of knowledge in general terms, but also to highlight the differences that exist according to region. This focus entails a critique of ingenuous universalism and naïve progressivism. Both tend toward ethnocentrism insofar as *a particular form* of the capitalist mode of production – which, present in north-central Europe, and under predominantly Protestant influence – as well as its corresponding social relations and ideological manifestations, is declared, on the basis of a presumed *universalism*, to represent the *only* developed form of this historical stage and, according to the dictates of *progressivism*, all other regions must follow, long for, and slavishly copy *this* form.

Echeverría's concept of historical *ethos* includes, in this context, not only ideological forms in the first Marxian sense – formulated in the 1859 prologue to the *Contribution to the Critique of Political Economy* as the 'legal, political, religious, aesthetic, or philosophic – in short ideological forms in which men become conscious of this conflict and fight it out'[6] – but also extends beyond these and includes forms which Marx considers part of the economic structure of society, above all those of producing and consuming the various sorts of use-values.

The political importance of this differentiation of *different ethe*, and with it, of *different modernities*, resides in the fact that countries pertaining to the real and apparent periphery need not await 'modernisation' nor to hurry up and run along behind it in an effort to become participants in the marvelous aspects of capitalist productive relations. For Echeverría, those countries are, instead, already – and have been since long ago – in a situation of full capitalist modernity, but merely in another *form* of that modernity. In contemporary Mexican political and theoretical debates, this argument is not an unimportant one, since not only the federal government,[7] but also many of its declared adversaries, speak ceaselessly of the need to 'modernise' the country. Such calls implicitly contain two presumptions: on the one hand, Mexico is a pre-modern country, and on the other, everything will be better once Mexico becomes modern, almost all political groups with significant social presence

---

6 Marx 1904, pp. 9–15, here: p. 12.

7 Especially that of Carlos Salinas de Gortari, who governed Mexico between 1988–94, which is to say, during the period in which Bolívar Echeverría's theory of *ethos* was developed most intensely.

understanding this to mean what Echeverría calls the 'realist modernity'. His theory attacks both presumptions as totally erroneous.

To do so, Echeverría distinguishes four basic types of capitalist modernity. Each has a particular way of managing that the unbearable of these social formations is perceived as bearable, sometimes as explainable, and in extreme cases even as reasonable. Echeverría refers to these four basic forms as the four 'modern *ethe*', or more precisely, the '*ethe* of capitalist modernity'. Each predominates in a determinate region: while the 'realist *ethos*' prevails in territories where Protestant culture predominates, the 'baroque *ethos*' does so where Catholic culture predominates.

This conception of historical *ethos* (such is the generic term) explains the aforementioned first difference *vis-à-vis* Western Marxism. It goes beyond the concept of ideology, since it goes further than the second Marxian concept of ideology as necessarily false consciousness. The concept of *ethos*, as we said before, comprises, moreover, forms of everyday praxis which include the production and consumption of *different* use-values. This subsumption of such distinct aspects which exist in the lives of humans under a single concept is possible because the production and consumption of different use-values are conceptualised as semiotic forms, since every production of use-values also contains the emission of a sign, and their consumption – according to Echeverría – contains their 'interpretation'.

However, Echeverría does not juxtapose Marx and Saussure in this way in order to soften the materialist theory of society by way of linguistics, but rather to give linguistics more material content, and to expound the fact that the most fundamental sign systems developed within human societies are those of the different use-values and the different ways and manners in which these are produced and consumed. We must move beyond non-dogmatic Marxist theory insofar as we hope to investigate not only the formal and real subordination of use-value to value, with the consequences this entails, but also to make an effort to analyse and classify the diverse forms in which this subordination takes place.

Use-value cannot easily and completely be destroyed by value (this, following Marx, is Echeverría's starting point), but value requires at least the rudimentary residues of use-value in order to sustain its own existence. The specific forms in which deformed use-value subsists, to put it this way, are of an extraordinarily varied nature. With the aforementioned concept of the four modern *ethe*, what Echeverría attempts is to investigate and classify these varied forms.

Just as use-value necessarily subsists as the basis for the value that rules over it, there also subsist under capitalist relations of production – albeit in a similarly subordinated and adapted condition – pre-capitalist and pre-bourgeois social forms. These processes of survival and adaptation occur in the most varied forms, and, moreover, the most diverse of pre-capitalist social forms are subsisting in the basement of capitalist relations of production and the corresponding social forms. This is the difference that must be grasped with the concept of the four modern *ethe*. These remain, in the last instance, very schematic and too generalising, but they allow, nevertheless, a first step toward a more differentiated analysis of the social formation that practically predominates today on a global level.

Next, we will contrast Echeverría's theory with the concept of ideology which emerges from Marx. The central point of this contrast is the absence in Echeverría's theory of a critique of the process of knowledge, which is, without a doubt, the price he pays to reach some of his most important theoretical contributions. As we will need to demonstrate, here, it is only at the cost of abandoning some of his central theoretical conquests that Echeverría accomplishes the momentous contribution of an interpretation of Marx which is less falsely generalising and, as a result, less Eurocentric – and for the same reason, less subjected to the dominant logic.

In a final step, we will look more closely at one result of his claim to carry out his studies on the basis of concrete everyday reality, which coexists with that of nonetheless being a philosopher of general ideas. This claim moves Echeverría to approach the interpretation of current social events more than Sánchez Vázquez was accustomed to do in his philosophical texts. Given the weaknesses of the text entitled '1989', which analyses the fall of the Berlin Wall in that year, we will attempt to clarify what consequences might result from the limitations of his concept of *ethos*; on this matter it is worth indicating that his important effort to found a 'concrete universalism' on the basis of Marx (unfolded in the struggle against Eurocentrism) can lead in its concrete application to distorted interpretations.

CUERPOS I

CHAPTER 11

Praxis and Use-Value

a Theory of Use-Value and Critique of the Abstract Concept of Praxis

In the article 'Postmodernidad y cinismo' ['Postmodernity and Cynicism'],[8] originally published in 1994, Echeverría develops a detailed critique of some of the basic ideological elements of capitalist modernity, whose entirety he characterises as a 'mythical complex'[9] and each one in particular as a 'modern myth'.[10] In this text, he gives the 'modern political culture'[11] of those societies which secure their material existence under capitalist relations of production – with special reference to 'western states at the end of this century'[12] – the name 'realist political culture'.[13] In this text, there seems to be present a critique by Echeverría of the concept of praxis as formulated by Sánchez Vázquez, setting out from Marx, and with one of the three modern myths to be subjected to critique being that of revolution.

Echeverría's reflection, summarised succinctly, is the following: the socialist idea that all human relations can be overturned through a revolution is not only a poor copy of bourgeois revolutionary assumptions (as emerged, for example, in the French Revolution of 1789) – in which everything ought to begin anew, this even being emphasised with a completely restructured calendar – but was, ultimately, merely a congruent continuation of the 'experience of the market as the privileged *locus* of socialisation',[14] a fundamental experience for modern society. In the market, (exchange) value controls the

---

[8] The text was originally published under the title 'Postmodernismo y cinismo', in *Viento del Sur*, April 1994: Echeverría 1994c. The following year it was reprinted twice with slightly different titles: 'Posmodernismo [*sic.*] y cinismo', in Aguilar Rivero (ed.) 1995 and as 'Postmodernidad y cinismo', by Echeverría himself in his second book with wide circulation, Echeverría 1995a, pp. 39–54. The text appeared in a German translation, slightly abbreviated, by the author of this book: Echeverría 1996b. On the history of the text, see, moreover, the chapter 'Life and Work of Bolívar Echeverría', especially pp. 8off.
[9] 'Postmodernidad y cinismo' in Echeverría 1995a, p. 42.
[10] Echeverría 1995a, p. 43.
[11] Echeverría 1995a, p. 42.
[12] Echeverría 1995a, p. 40.
[13] Echeverría 1995a, p. 42.
[14] Echeverría 1995a, p. 43. The italics here as in what follows, if not otherwise indicated, pertain to the original text.

occurrence of 'socialisation', not the use-value that is also in play. But value is the dimension which is exclusively determined by the human factor, which is to say, the average labour time socially necessary for its production. It is in this way that the impression is born that the forms of socialisation are determined exclusively by the human being.[15] Echeverría implicitly suggests that in this formulation here subject to critique, the human factor is conceived as a conscious factor.[16] So, the revolution is falsely seen as a unique rupture, consciously provoked, the simple playing out of the 'materialisation of an ideal generated by political discourse'.[17]

What would seem at first glance to be a general rejection of the concept of the subject, is instead a critique of the concept of the human subject as one which is fully free to make decisions, that is to say, a critique of certain idealistic understandings of the subject. However, as will be demonstrated throughout this part of the book, in his determination of the limitations of the freedom of the subject, Echeverría moves beyond Marx, who sees this limitation in the objective appearance of the self-sufficiency and independence of commodities, in relations to one another and toward human beings. In his theoretical formulation, Bolívar Echeverría focuses on another determination of human beings when taking decisions, one that, though mentioned by Marx, is scarcely the object of his major elaborations: the natural form of social reproduction.

That natural form is not only found in what Marx calls the 'natural basis' for surplus value,[18] which is to say, in the 'natural conditions' to which 'the productiveness of labour' remains tied[19] – in other words, the 'naturally

---

15 See Echeverría 1995a, pp. 43ff.
16 On the broad implications for a theory of knowledge and the problems that this assumption entails, see the chapter '*Ethos* and Ideology' in this book.
17 Echeverría 1995a, p. 44. See, in this regard, the following passage: 'The activity that crystallises as value and is realised as exchange-value appears as the human activity *par excellence*. The man who objectivises, possesses and realises the values of commodities, becomes through this very act the subject which creates the reality of the concrete bodies of the those commodities. The very concretisation of social life, which is defined according to what it produces and consumes, labours and enjoys, thus seems to turn on the fact of the formation and realisation of value. The *experience* of the ontological hierarchy of this fact, which occurs in a diffuse and imperceptible manner in everyday commercial life – and which converts the human being into the *hypokeimenon* on whose activity the entire qualitative consistency of the real rests, and which just as it creates this, it can also take it away or modify it – is precisely the experience that the myth of the revolution thematises in its own way under the form of a single, legendary act which concentrates the exercise of that absolute sovereignty in a single decisive moment' (pp. 43f).
18 Marx 1976a, p. 647.
19 Marx 1976a, pp. 647–8.

conditioned productive forces' of labour[20] – but also in the determination of the specific qualities of use-values, as well as in social formations themselves, for example, in the work tools employed, the primary productive materials employed, and so on. These factors are not determined so simply by the law of value, but are, instead, simultaneously subjected to an inherent dynamic that could be understood as a cultural one (and here, culture is not to be understood in the idealist sense of mere intellectual tradition, but in the sense of material culture).[21] In this dynamic, the concrete use-value determinations and the exact properties of the social formation in each case are intimately linked to one another. In other words: Echeverría's critique of the idealist concept of the subject is also directed against a concept of subject which also exists at the heart of certain Marxist tendencies. The defenders of those tendencies believe that by determining a social formation to be 'capitalist', they have already expressed what is decisive and, as a result, they see the eventual geographical and cultural differences as purely secondary phenomena. Moreover, this manner of viewing things is naïvely progressivist, because, as a general rule, in examining different capitalist social formations, it can only understand their differences on the basis of the distinction between a 'developed' and

---

20   Marx 1976a, p. 651.
21   This very broad concept of culture that Echeverría mentions here is the theme of a book that was in its final stages in 1999 and, according to its author, had as its topic 'a theory of culture and the problem of anthropology', and was to be based upon certain central conceptions of his text 'La "forma natural" de la reproducción social', which we analyse later. (Fifth interview with Bolívar Echeverría, cassette I, side A, pos. 227–30).

Despite the importance that we could suppose this investigation would have in the complete works of Echeverría, it cannot be taken into account in this book. This 'book on culture' is, according to his own formulation, 'an extension' or 'a sort of expansion of the concept of the "natural form" ' and, moreover, 'the problematisation of the natural form' alongside an 'opening toward the question of modernity'. Since this is one of Echeverría's two decisive contributions to Marxist debates, in what follows we will dedicate special attention to his text on the *natural form* which serves as the starting point of this as-yet unpublished book (see Fifth interview with Bolívar Echeverría, cassette I, side A, pos. 217–25).

The concept of culture that Echeverría here takes as his basis and intends to continue developing is more common to Mexico than to Germany. In the Museum of Anthropology of the Mexican capital, for example, in order to represent the diverse cultures that exist in Mexico today, what is exhibited more than anything else is their forms of production and the means of production employed in those forms; then, their forms of housing and clothing as well as dietary habits. They then move on to musical instruments, language, and dance, without giving the latter any priority over the others in the sense of being somehow 'superior'.

'underdeveloped' level of the same form which – apart from this difference – is understood as single and homogeneous.

Echeverría's interest in the cultural aspects of 'capitalist modernities' should not be understood, therefore, as an idealist dilution of the Marxian analysis of society,[22] but rather as an effort to develop a radical critique of the powerful idealist and ethnocentric residues and naïve faith in progress that exist among various currents of contemporary Marxist and materialist thought. In so doing, he attempts to save Marx (by making reference to passages which focus on this problematic, in the *Grundrisse* for example)[23] from such interpretations.[24] This attempt at a materialist concretion of the concept of use-value production, determined in each case according to cultural differences, and the concomitant critique of the pseudo-universalist concept of the subject – which is, *de facto*, ethnocentric[25] – cannot but entail consequences for the concept of praxis. Human praxis, too, must be understood in each case within its historical, cultural, and geographical context; it cannot really be understood within the framework of a form of thinking which apparently remains universal.[26]

---

22 In this regard, see Echeverría's response to Juan Villoro's critique of his text 'El *ethos* barroco' (presented at the launch of Echeverría's book *Modernidad, mestizaje cultural, ethos barroco*, in which that text of Echeverría's is included). In this launch, held on 18 April 1995, Villoro criticised Echeverría for perceiving the cultural to be predominant over the economic and, in so doing, drawing closer to Max Weber and moving away from Marx. To this, and responding also to other critiques by Villoro, Echeverría argued: 'What most enrages me and mortifies me in a narcissistic sense in Juan Villoro's interpretation is the claim that I have abandoned the Marxist camp and passed over to the other side. This is not true. Since the 1920s there has existed a non-orthodox Marxism within which very good work has been done ... Think of the decisive influence of Max Weber on Georg Lukács and his formulation of the concept of alienation, which is unimaginable without Weber'. (Bolívar Echeverría, contribution to the book launch for *Modernidad, mestizaje cultural, ethos barroco*, 18 April 1995, Mexico City, written notes in German by the author).
23 Marx 1993.
24 We cannot hide the fact that Marx and Engels themselves on various occasions formulated ideas that encourage such an ethnocentric and progressivist interpretation of their work and of the ruling relations. In this regard, see, for example, the previously indicated declarations by Engels about the annexation of a large part of then-Mexican territory by the United States, an event which he greeted enthusiastically and which has never been forgiven to this day in the land of the oldest urban cultures of North America, to which much of Mexico pertains, despite the ignorance of most Europeans.
25 This ethnocentric pseudo-universalism is, under the ruling global relations, Eurocentric.
26 ' "... [T]hat is a very problematic concept, because it is too general, too abstract. That is to say, praxis is counterposed to theory", "what is fundamental is not theory, but praxis ...", not the symbolic but the real, not the superstructure but the base". The concept of praxis should be understood in the polemic with spiritualism: "it is not spirit but matter". This

b   Differences *vis-à-vis* the Concept of Praxis in Sánchez Vázquez

After this first introduction to Echeverría's critique of the abstract concept of praxis, we will now enter in greater detail into that which we mentioned at the outset, on the possibility of understanding this as an implicit critique of Adolfo Sánchez Vázquez's concept of praxis.

Right away, it is worth noting that there has never been an open philosophical discussion between Adolfo Sánchez Vázquez and Bolívar Echeverría. It is only in one philosophical text that Echeverría, in a footnote, cites a text by Sánchez Vázquez, indicating that he had consulted six pages of the latter's *Filosofía de la praxis* for a section comprising two and a half pages of his own text on Marx's *Theses on Feuerbach*. 'In our examination of these Theses we have borne in mind, above all, Sánchez Vázquez's analysis of them in pp. 130–135 of his book *Filosofía de la praxis*'[27] (although Echeverría only refers to the first edition of this text).[28]

It has not been possible to document whether or not Echeverría would take note, equally, of the second edition of Sánchez Vázquez's main work (given the vast differences between the two editions indicated in the chapter '*The Philosophy of Praxis*: Two Versions', which would be of no small account for a possible evaluation of its author by Echeverría). In a 1994 discussion with the author of this book, Sánchez Vázquez refers to the problem that many theorists have only known the first edition, and not the considerable changes registered in the second.[29]

In an speech celebrating the seventieth anniversary of the Faculty of Philosophy and Arts at the UNAM, a speech of a more political and historical nature, Echeverría recalls his first theoretical encounter with Sánchez Vázquez at the beginning of the 1960s, and in retrospect he does not hesitate to

---

is a sort of materialist orientation that is behind all this. But the problem for me is then: how do we determine praxis? What is praxis? What is practice or the practical life of the human being?' (Third interview with Bolívar Echeverría, cassette I, side B, pos. 132–71).

27   'El materialismo de Marx' in Echeverría 1986, p. 35 n9.

28   Sánchez Vázquez 1967b, in English Sánchez Vázquez 1977a. Echeverría refers here to Chapter III: 'The conception of praxis in Marx', and especially to two of the five subchapters on the *Theses on Feuerbach*, namely: 'Revolutionary praxis as the unity of the change in man and the change in circumstances (Thesis III)' (Sánchez Vázquez 1977a, pp. 122–5) and 'From the interpretation of the world to its transformation (Thesis XI)' (pp. 125–7). In the second Mexican edition of the book (Sánchez Vázquez 1980b), which we have used, these subchapters are found on pp. 160–4 and pp. 164–6, respectively.

29   However, the two subchapters to which Echeverría refers were included, largely unchanged, in the second edition. One minor change is mentioned in note 243, page 149 of this book.

characterise him as the 'best Marxist we have ever had'.[30] For his part, Sánchez Vázquez only mentions his 'colleague and friend' Bolívar Echeverría twice in his texts. In an encyclopedia article, he thanks him in a footnote for his 'suggestions and critical observations',[31] and in a book review he makes a marginal reference.[32]

In light of this dearth of more extensive written notes by Echeverría about Sánchez Vázquez's theory, we will resort, here, to the corresponding passages of interviews carried out with him. In the decision to give space to the interviews conducted with Bolívar Echeverría, we allowed ourselves to be guided by, among other things, Brecht's phrase in the 'Legend of the Origin of the Book Tao-Te-Ching on Lao-Tsu's Road into Exile': 'a wise man's wisdom needs to be extracted'.[33] To the question of whether or not his theory can be understood as a critique of Sánchez Vázquez's concept of praxis, Echeverría makes this clear: 'Of course, Sánchez Vázquez's affirmation is without a doubt a reaffirmation of what Marx proposes. But I believe precisely that the problem lies in the fact that Marx does not have a definition of what the practical life of the human being consists'.[34]

This practical life of the human being is composed, precisely, of concrete forms of the production and consumption of use-values, forms which – even at the very heart of a single mode of production – differ vastly from one another. Marx, of course, clearly grasps the importance of use-value, but he does not develop a 'definition of what he calls the "metabolism between man and nature". That is a phrase but it is not a definition, it is not a theory'.[35] Echeverría is determined to develop this theory, for which task he seeks a decisive foundation in some of Marx's own suggestions. Marx 'speaks of "the natural form" of the process of social reproduction, which is to say of this metabolism that assumes a natural form ... I believe that this constitutes the concept of praxis. If we want to define "praxis" we would need to define this: what is the natural form of human behaviour, its practical-natural form?'[36]

Returning to the question of Sánchez Vázquez, Echeverría continues: 'So Marx doesn't have that theory and I believe that Sánchez Vázquez makes certain contributions but that he doesn't have a structured theory of what this

---

30 Echeverría 1995b, pp. 78ff.
31 Sánchez Vázquez 1997.
32 Sánchez Vázquez 1998.
33 Brecht 2003, p. 69.
34 Third interview with Bolívar Echeverría, cassette I, side B, pos. 150–3.
35 Ibid.
36 Third interview with Bolívar Echeverría, cassette I, side B, 154–9.

process is either ... The concept of praxis is so general that we would need to see first what we are talking about and what is the history of praxis'.[37]

Echeverría attempts to develop what is present in rudimentary form in the Marxian concept of the natural form of social reproduction. He does this above all in his article 'La "forma natural" de la reproducción social' ['The "natural form" of social reproduction']'[38] to which he explicitly refers in this context in the cited interview.[39] Our second author is not interested in discarding the concept of praxis but, instead, hopes to situate it in its historic dimension and thereby to reveal how to criticise the anthropocentrism that exists in 'modern praxis', which is to say the 'anthropolatry' which is frequently present in this concept.[40]

Echeverría undertakes the attempt to liberate the concept of praxis from the false generality, that it has in his estimation in Sánchez Vázquez, particularly on the economic terrain, which is to say productive praxis. Here, he already distinguishes himself from our first author insofar as the Spanish exile philosopher develops his concept of praxis – despite his declared intention to understand it as broadly as possible – above all through political praxis (specifically, revolutionary and artistic). If there is already in Sánchez Vázquez an emphasis on seeing in everyday life a central object of philosophical research, Echeverría goes much further, since every human being is forcibly implicated in reproduction – although, in some cases, this is only on the side of consumption, revolutionary praxis, by contrast, is not everybody's thing. Naturally, we could say that in some sense political praxis includes everyone, since even non-political behaviour has political consequences and, consequently is, in a broader sense, in itself a form of political praxis; however, it seems to us that Echeverría, to a greater degree than Sánchez Vázquez, places the centre of gravity of his research on ordinary everyday life, which in turn constitutes the material basis for his understanding of culture.

---

37 Third interview with Bolívar Echeverría, cassette I, side B, pos. 160–2 and pos. 168–71.
38 Echeverría 1984.
39 'This [seeing what praxis is and what its history is] is something that I do attempt ... in an essay that I have on "The *natural form* of social reproduction" ['La *forma natural* de la reproducción social']. ... For me, this is one of the best things I have written' (Third interview with Bolívar Echeverría, cassette I, side B, pos. 171–9).
40 Third interview with Bolívar Echeverría, cassette I, side B, pos. 192–8. See moreover: 'Modern praxis is a praxis that poses ... in terms of an anthropolatry, a sort of self-idolatry of praxis: "we, human beings, we are super powerful, we do what we want with anything, including with ourselves". This idea that we are the raw material of our own will, this would be an exaggeration of the self-comprehension of praxis' (pos. 200–8).

In these distinct ways of situating their respective centres of gravity we can see, moreover, one of the decisive reasons why Echeverría has a more cautious and sceptical concept of praxis, since he understands as praxis, first of all, the current capitalist form of reproductive praxis, whereas Sánchez Vázquez concentrates in his theories on that praxis which seeks to abolish precisely that praxis which our second author looks upon with horror; a praxis which is exceedingly destructive. Put differently: while Echeverría foregrounds philosophically that praxis which constitutes the world, Sánchez Vázquez foregrounds that which transforms the world. Echeverría describes this in the following terms: 'There we find a problem with Sánchez Vázquez, because Sánchez Vázquez sings the praises of praxis. But if we pose praxis in historical terms, this praise would not accommodate the praxis of capitalist modernity, which is a totally excessive praxis, a praxis that we could therefore deem "monstrously autistic"'.[41]

In looking at Marx, Sánchez Vázquez refers in the first place to his early work, and in our research his interpretation of the *Theses on Feuerbach* is taken into special account. Although he does not see any radical rupture in Marx's theoretical development, special attention is attracted by the near total lack of references to Marx's main work, what culminates in formulations like the one above, in which 'value' appears as a purely moral category.[42] Echeverría, who similarly rejects the idea of a *'rupture épistémologique'* in Marx's work as a whole (and in general makes common cause with Sánchez Vázquez in condemning Althusser's interpretation of Marx),[43] refers to a broad spectrum of Marxian texts which stretches from the *Theses on Feuerbach*, passing through the *Grundrisse*, before arriving at *Capital*.[44] The examination of the concept of praxis that we are analysing here finds its support largely in the latter two texts.

---

41 Third interview with Bolívar Echeverría, cassette I, side B, pos. 208–13.
42 See also p. 124 of this book, including note 143.
43 The rejection of 'Althusserianism', a significant current on the Mexican Left during the 1970s and '80s is, in fact, one of the elements that unifies the two authors dealt with here. In April of 1993, only recently arrived in Mexico City to research this book, its author accepted an invitation to the home of Sánchez Vázquez in the southwestern part of the Mexican capital. Upon arriving there, Bolívar Echeverría was already seated, having also been invited by our host. Thus we had one of the few encounters among the three of us. There, when the author asked about the various Marxist theoretical currents present in Mexico, a rare moment of unanimity between the two philosophers could be observed, which consisted of the two describing in a lightly jocular tone the rise and fall of Mexican 'Althusserianism', which was generally seen in this conversation as an outmoded academic phenomenon.
44 In this respect, see Echeverría's many years of activity in the Economics Faculty of the UNAM, where he gave courses with a particular emphasis on *Capital* (see, in the chapter on the 'Life and work of Bolívar Echeverría', p. 67).

Now then, this difference in choosing a centre of gravity for research does not result from a simple difference of focus; instead, it constitutes, in and of itself, an expression of the previously mentioned doubts regarding the omnipotence of human praxis, in even its political and revolutionary guises. Echeverría advocates, then, a concept of history that does not crush the powerful dynamic proper to tradition and which, as a result, is conscious of the importance of the sturdiness of those forms of everyday praxis which similarly are not *automatically* modified by the transformation of the political, social, and economic constitution.

> This is the reason for the critique of the myth of revolution. The myth of revolution which is the myth of this omnipotence of the human being. 'The human being is able to change whatever, whenever he wants'. So for example, with regard to his own traditions, his own cultural forms, the modern human being believes that these have no density and that he can make and unmake [with ease – SG] the social substance, the historical-social substance.[45]

But this should not be understood in the sense of throwing overboard the idea of a fundamental transformation of social relations, but rather quite the opposite. Bolívar Echeverría is interested in saving the *concept* of revolution through a radical critique of the *myth* of revolution, in other words a totally wrong-headed understanding of revolution which simultaneously glorifies it.[46] Giving concrete character to the concept of praxis requires that we pass through a demonstration of the difficulties of a possible revolutionary transformation

---

45   Third interview with Bolívar Echeverría, cassette 1, side B, pos. 215–21. When Echeverría speaks of the *myth* of revolution, as a general rule, he is *not* referring to Marx's theories.

46   This banality of sticking the concept of revolution in the same sack as the myth of revolution is something that certain leftist circles, above all the dogmatic ones, share with conservative circles. Echeverría criticises this elsewhere on the basis of certain political statements by the deceased organic intellectual of recent Mexican governments, Octavio Paz. Alongside these two positions, which equate the myth with the concept of revolution in order to no longer need to hear anything more of the latter, there can still exist those other positions – as residues – which Echeverría himself in certain moments upheld: present in groups that occasionally place extreme trust in their fantastic imaginations, in order to not become discouraged too early on and thus to bring the concept of revolution closer to realisation. Despite similarities to the former position in terms of the equation of the concept of revolution with the myth, we should not forget that this latter orientation is diametrically opposed to the former. Bolívar Echeverría himself, in an interview, agreed that a certain degree of self-stimulation via fantastic and exaggerated elements is necessary in order to bear the load of a revolutionary action.

while at the same time revealing its true possibilities, which have been up to this point hidden. In the current sociopolitical context of Mexico, where things today turn out to be an apparent submission to the government, but against a background of rebellion,[47] this is expressed as follows:

> – Is this a critique of a concept of praxis which is emptied of its historical content?
> – Yes, exactly.
> – So we could say, simplifying, that while Sánchez Vázquez is constantly looking forward, you want to look back as well?
> – Yes, yes, or: he only looks upward and in general terms, and I on the other hand tend to look downward at the whole swamp [laughs] that we're trying to swim through.
> – Could we say then that ..., on the theoretical level, you are a pre-1994 Zapatista?
> – Yes, this is why I like very much what the Zapatistas say, because they realise that the question is not purely one of the political game, that is to say: 'let's replace the politicians and with that we have already decided that history goes that way'. They say: 'no, it's not that easy, the problems are much older, much heavier. How are we going to change all of this if, just because we simply take Los Pinos [the seat of the presidency] or the Government Palace and decide that beginning tomorrow Mexico is no longer this but that?' Like they say: 'no, no, that's not how it is, that isn't possible, there is a knot of historical conflicts here that needs to be awakened first, so that it itself can begin to generate its own solutions', and not: 'we came from the mountains of Chiapas and we say that this is the solution'.
> They are revolutionaries who are relativising very much their own power, to such a degree that the only thing that they say is 'we don't even

---

47 Already during the Mexican Revolution, which began in 1910, a peculiar contradiction was present in the country according to which, even in everyday life, it was only an invisible line that separated a calm bordering on apathy from violent forms of expression, with intermediate forms less present than, for example, in Frankfurt. Under the dictatorship of Porfirio Díaz, Mexico was considered to be one of the most stable countries on Earth, when the Revolution suddenly exploded. In a similar way, almost no one foresaw the Zapatista rebellion that began on 1 January 1994, which began, moreover, in a region in which the governing PRI party always registered certain electoral victory, to the point that the following political joke circulated in Mexico: 'Isn't it curious that a rebellion began precisely in the Lacandón Jungle, in Chiapas, where the PRI always won 105 percent of the votes?'

struggle to survive because they are killing us, that is a fact, we are dying and all we are doing is dying in a way that seems more elegant to us', they say, don't they? In reality, the Zapatistas' most profound message is this. It is a very terrible message, because it isn't optimistic, it isn't luminous like the October Revolution: the upward gaze and the horizon of the rising sun and such things, no; instead it's a terrible view, because they say: 'we are corpses, they are killing us, our people are dying, while I am here speaking my people are dying, and I myself am dying as well'.

So: 'our movement exists only to affirm', what they call 'our dignity, to die with dignity ... We don't care about Muñoz Ledo or Camacho, if they get rid of Salinas and replace him with someone else, it is not worth a bean. It is a murderous machinery that is killing us' – and a bit in the way of thinking of Horkheimer and Adorno [laughs]: 'it would be good if things were different, hopefully it wouldn't be like this.'

Here we do indeed find ... these rare connections between the apparently elitist discourse of Horkheimer and Adorno and that of the Indians of Chiapas. Because what they say is a little like this. You aren't going to find historical optimism, but to the contrary, they see a machine and say: 'If only it weren't like this'.[48]

Sánchez Vázquez, for his part, as a veteran of the Spanish Civil War and an anti-dogmatic Marxist today, does not stand at an insuperable distance from the Zapatistas either, but he would nevertheless need to make considerable theoretical leaps in order to conceptually approach neo-Zapatista praxis and doctrine. At first glance, the combination of radical and reformist leftist elements with apparently 'pre-modern' ideas and traditions is highly unusual.

---

48   Third interview with Bolívar Echeverría, cassette I, side B, pos. 236–87. To explain the context: shortly before the interview, Bolívar Echeverría participated as an advisor to the Zapatistas in the 'Special Forum on State Reform' that the rebels organised and which included various discussion tables, each presided over by a Zapatista representative. The cited phrases were obviously stated recalling what the rebel representatives from the Mexican southeast had said. In this respect see the chapter 'Life and Work of Bolívar Echeverría', especially pp. 79ff.

Porfirio Muñoz Ledo was the leader of the left-reformist PRD party (Party of the Democratic Revolution), the only party in Mexico with parliamentary relevance, which was not situated to the right of the governing PRI party. Manuel Camacho was the representative of the Mexican federal government during the first peace negotiations with the Zapatistas and, in that period (1994), was a close confidant of the then president, Carlos Salinas de Gortari. In 1996 he abandoned the PRI, and stood as another bearer of hope for the reformist Left.

This combination is, departing from Echeverría's approach, doubtless more understandable, since he makes an effort to follow the tracks of the survival of ancient traditions and those conflicts which are aggravated under the capitalist modernity that is presently dominant. Hence, Adolfo Sánchez Vázquez, in the document prepared for the 'Foro especial sobre la reforma del Estado' ['Special Forum on State Reform'][49] does of course enter into questions of democracy and human rights (which are of extreme importance for the Zapatistas), but he stops before engaging in the necessary analysis of *different* forms of democracy (for example, the parliamentary form on one hand, and on the other hand the communal form that is practiced in many parts of Chiapas under Zapatista control) and the various understandings of what exactly 'human dignity' is or ought to be. Here, Sánchez Vázquez remains within the classic 'Western' ideals inherited from the French Revolution.

c   Historical Limitations of the Marxian Concept of Use-Value

The question that arises before entering into Echeverría's theory of use-value is: how does he explain the fact that Marx, who he repeatedly invokes as one of his principal theoretical sources,[50] never managed to fully grasp the importance and meaning of use-value, despite having provided their preliminary outline? Why does Marx not take this step toward a precise analysis of praxis in its concrete forms, that is, the production and consumption of determinate use-values? Why does Marx remain abstract and linger in his analysis over general observations regarding praxis, according to Echeverría's critique? The latter does not explain it by the limitations of the German exile in London, nor by his supposed economism (observe: it is just those who do not aspire to anything more than to dominate the world through economic power, that reproach Marx for economism). Rather, Echeverría explains it by the fact that in Marx's time use-value in general, even that in the political economy he subjected to critique, was not yet a relevant topic, and this because 'the definition

---

49   See p. 39 and pp. 81ff of this book.
50   In the earliest of Echeverría's texts like 'La "forma natural" de la reproducción social' ['The "natural form" of social reproduction'], or his book on *El discurso crítico de Marx* [*Marx's Critical Discourse*], this is palpable. But also in his late texts – in which he partly uses a terminology that could, at first glance, point to a distancing from Marx and an increasing return to topics which could seem to be 'not materialist at all' – Echeverría refers explicitly to Marx's main work. In this respect, see p. 258 of this book for a quote in which he declares *Capital* to be no more and no less than the point of departure for his theory of the 'modern *ethe*'.

of use-value only appears as a problem in real life when capitalist development everywhere shatters the ancient local balance'.[51] During Marx's time, of course, the problem of the destruction of nature already existed in practice, and within this the problem of the apparently limitless possibilities of increasing value, as well as the simultaneous, consequent loss of its foundation – use-value – was especially visible. However, this had not yet reached the planetary magnitude with which it today confronts us. As such, Marx does deal with the topic, but not with the due intensity.

To these considerations by Echeverría, we could add the following: Marx himself, who begins *Capital* with an analysis of the commodity – since it appears as the 'elementary form' of the 'wealth of societies in which the capitalist mode of production prevails' – opens his presentation of the critique of political economy by considering use-value.[52] But after something more than a page, he passes from use-value to value, which from this moment on would be at the centre of his main work. In his short introductory words on use-value, there are two allusions to the fact that use-value *does not* represent the purely natural side of the commodity (in the sense of a naïvely mechanistic materialism), since 'satisfies human needs of whatever kind', for which it is irrelevant that these needs 'arise, for example, from the stomach, or the imagination'.[53] On the other hand, Marx locates the historical dimension of use-value: 'The discovery of these ways and hence of the manifold uses of things is the work of history'.[54] In two passages in the first volume of *Capital*, Marx returns to analyse in some detail the process of production as it refers to use-value. This occurs, on the one hand, in the first chapter, second subchapter, entitled 'The Dual Character of the Labour Embodied in Commodities',[55] and on the other hand, in the seventh chapter, 'The Labour Process and the Valorisation Process',

---

51 Echeverría 1984, p. 34 n4.

52 *Capital*, Vol. I, Chapter 1 'The Commodity', section 1, 'The Two Factors of the Commodity: Use-Value and Value (Substance of Value, Magnitude of Value)': Marx 1976a, p. 125.

53 Ibid. Here already appears a problem that would later play an important role in particular parts of Marxist debates: what product truly satisfies a need? Is the consumption of a product a sufficient argument in favour of the existence of the need to consume that thing, or is there also consumption without need, or even needs, which are not 'properly' needs at all? The latter is clearly central to the critique of consumer society, but it cannot be resolved simply with Marx, since while he considers the question of whether a thing is 'useful' or not to be decisive in deciding if it is a use-value, he does not cede this decision – as we mentioned – to the vulgar materialists when he places fantasy alongside the stomach on equal terms at the origin of needs.

54 Marx 1976a, p. 125.

55 Marx 1976a, pp. 131–7.

in the first subchapter, 'The Labour Process'.[56] In his analysis, Echeverría refers explicitly to the second of these passages.[57]

In the last quote, we find an indication in Marx, which grants the utmost importance to production with reference to use-value, which is to say, its natural form. In this observation, Marx maintains something quite distinct from the fixation, commonly attributed to him, on the decisive importance of the *relations* of production – which cannot be determined on the basis of concrete and material productive differences – but, instead, on the basis of *property relations*[58] and on the basis of forms of social organisation in their totality, above all the production of value: 'It is not what is made but how, and by what instruments of labour, that distinguishes different economic epochs'.[59]

But Marx, as we have said, does not continue to develop these barely-insinuated hints,[60] which is perhaps explained by what he says at the beginning of the subchapter on commodity fetishism in *Capital*, where he asserts, with regard to the commodity, that 'so far as it is a use-value, there is nothing mysterious about it', and, therefore, the properties of the commodity as use-value are 'absolutely clear'.[61] Things are much more complicated for the product of labour in regard to value which, as soon as it appears as a commodity, becomes

---

56 Marx 1976a, pp. 283–92. [Trans. – this is the fifth chapter in the German edition].
57 Echeverría 1984, p. 35 n5; p. 38 n16; and p. 41 n22.
58 See also: '... the material productive forces of society come into conflict with the existing relations of production or – what is but a legal expression for the same thing – with the property relations' (Marx 1904, p. 12).
59 Marx 1976a, p. 286.
60 In the place we have just cited, Marx continues: 'Instruments of labour not only supply a standard of the degree of development which human labour has attained, but they also indicate the social relations within which men work' (ibid.). At first glance, it could seem as though Marx wants to derive the instruments of labour used in each case in an immediate manner from every historical period and its respective social relations. On the one hand, the instruments of labour used are merely *indicators* of their respective ruling social relations, not their necessary consequence. In terms of formal logic: specific instruments of labour are a sufficient but not a necessary condition of specific social relations. In other words, specific social relations can be deduced from the existence of specific instruments of production, but the reverse is not the case. This maintains the possibility, so crucial for Echeverría, of different models of use-value existing at the heart of a particular relation of production, namely, capitalism.

On the other hand, Marx writes that instruments of labour '*also* indicate the social relations', which even further increases the openness of the cited passage (ibid. italics by S.G.).
61 Marx 1976a, p. 163.

'a thing which transcends sensuousness'.[62] This 'mystical character of the commodity does not therefore arise from its use-value',[63] but from its value. Since Marx has proposed a rational analysis of the capitalist mode of production, he must set out by overcoming those mysticisms which necessarily disfigure knowledge, which as a result renders the detailed analysis of use-value seemingly superfluous, or at the very least, secondary.

But Echeverría is not satisfied with Marx's self-assessment, and embarks upon another path in order to explain the origin of his limited vision of use-value. Alongside what we have previously mentioned, he draws attention to the fact that Marx's theory is a critical one, meaning that it does not seek to extract from itself and develop a pure concept of the being of things, but is, instead, a theory which sets out explicitly from a confrontation with the most serious theoretical analyses of its era. But classical political economy, to which Marx refers in his main work with the subtitle *A Critique of Political Economy*, was not, in its theoretical aspect, and particularly in the economic sciences, devoted to a detailed study of use-value.[64] It is in this respect that Echeverría insists: 'Marx's discourse is a critical discourse: it operates on the positive or ideological discourse that modern society spontaneously generates. In his time, the concept of use-value to be critiqued had only an incipient formulation, that of political economy; it was possible to trace the general contours of a critical concept of "natural form" or use-value, but it was not yet time for its developed elaboration'.[65]

This act of coming to Marx's defence against his critics reminds us a great deal, in its argumentative structure, of the way and manner in which Marx explained that a 'giant thinker like Aristotle'[66] was incapable of developing the concept of value. According to Marx, this 'greatest thinker of antiquity'[67] failed in his analysis of the commodity, which had already reached the expression of value and an inherent relationship of equality, in running up against the objective relations of his time: 'Aristotle's genius is displayed precisely by his discovery of a relation of equality in the value-expression of commodities. Only the

62   Ibid.
63   Marx 1976a, p. 164.
64   This interpretation by Echeverría of Marx's work as critique and not as a positive theoretical model is already expressed in the title of his first major book: *Marx's Critical Discourse* (see Echeverría 1986).
65   Echeverría 1984, p. 34 n4.
66   Marx 1976a, p. 175 n35. Marx says here: 'If a giant thinker like Aristotle could err in his evaluation of slave-labour, why should a dwarf economist like Bastiat be right in his evaluation of wage-labour?'
67   Marx 1976a, p. 532.

historical limitation inherent in the society in which he lived prevented him from finding out what "in reality" this relation of equality consisted of'.[68]

d   The Aristotelian Concept of Use-Value as Interpreted by Marx

Marx, who refers repeatedly to Aristotle in *Capital*, also does so when speaking of the concept of use-value, which Echeverría chooses as the central object of his analysis. This is of interest, among other reasons, because Aristotle had already sketched out the relationship between use-value and the natural form of production and consumption (which Marx established, and which Echeverría studied in depth) when he spoke of the 'natural way' of using products;[69] the latter is, for Marx, precisely 'use-value in the original meaning', and thus not in the sense of 'use-value ... as a bearer of exchange-value, and consequently, a means of exchange'.[70] This advice is necessary because it presents a parallel between Aristotle and Echeverría, so it seems to be strange that the latter never refers to the former, or even to Marx's many references to Aristotle in *Capital*, for the elaboration of his theory. Thus, for example, the distinction that Aristotle makes between chrematistic (the theory of money) and economic science and the related distinction between commerce for the purpose of commodity exchange and commerce whose only objective is to earn

---

68   Marx 1976a, p. 152. Marx's argument at this point, right before the passage cited, is the following: 'However, Aristotle himself was unable to extract this fact, that, in the form of commodity-values, all labour is expressed as equal human labour and therefore as labour of equal quality, by inspection from the form of value, because Greek society was founded on the labour of slaves, hence had as its natural basis the inequality of men and of their labour-powers. The secret of the expression of value, namely the equality and equivalence of all kinds of labour because and in so far as they are human labour in general, could not be deciphered until the concept of human equality had already acquired the permanence of a fixed popular opinion. This however becomes possible only in a society where the commodity-form is the universal form of the product of labour, hence the dominant social relation is the relation between men as possessors of commodities' (Marx 1976a, pp. 151–2).

69   ' "For twofold is the use of every object ... The one is peculiar to the object as such, the other is not, as a sandal, which may be worn and is also exchangeable. Both are uses of the sandal, for even he who exchanges the sandal for the money or food he is in need of, makes use of the sandal as a sandal. But not in its natural way. For it has not been made for the sake of being exchanged" (Aristotle, *Republic*, I, i, c. 9)'. [Trans. – cited from the English translation in Marx 1976a, p. 179 n3].

70   Marx 1976a, p. 179.

money,[71] share much with Echeverría's reflections on the non-capitalist market, which is overwhelmed by the capitalist market and tends toward destruction, as against the chatter about the 'free-market economy', which generally alludes to nothing other than the realisation, in the most unrestrained form possible, of the capitalist mode of production.

Equally instructive is the parallel between the two thinkers when Aristotle speaks of the fact that use-values and their consumption ought to make the 'good life' possible.[72] Such a formulation is as foreign to Marx as the accentuated importance it implicitly concedes to consumption. Echeverría's theory of the four 'modern *ethe*' – the four fundamental ways of dealing with the otherwise unbearable everyday life under the capitalist mode of production – also examines the 'baroque *ethos*', which, even knowing the impossibility of this audacious enterprise of wanting to do justice to use-value *vis-à-vis* value, nevertheless seeks out the good life in the bad, to put it colloquially. The question of the exact meaning of this parallel between Echeverría and Aristotle remains latent. Marx himself, in a passage from *Capital*, provides a commentary that could help to clarify it:

> Political economy, which first emerged as an independent science during the period of manufacture, is only able to view the social division of labour in terms of the division found in manufacture, i.e. as a means of producing more commodities with a given quantity of labour, and consequently of cheapening commodities and accelerating the accumulation of capital. In most striking contrast with this accentuation of quantity and exchange-value is the attitude of the writers of classical antiquity, who are exclusively concerned with quality and use-value.... If the growth of the quantity produced is occasionally mentioned, this is only done with reference to the greater abundance of use-values.[73]

In any case, if on the basis of this passage we wanted to conclude that Echeverría develops determinate theories which concede significant importance to use-value because he comes from a so-called 'developing' country – in the previously discussed contemporary sense of a country which has been *left behind* in terms of general human-historic-civilisational *development* – this would be to fall again into the naïve and progressivist Eurocentrism we have previously

---

71 Aristotle, *Republic*, Chapters 8–9, cited according to Marx 1976a, p. 253 n6).
72 'True wealth... consists of such use-values; for the amount of property which is needed for a good life is not unlimited' (ibid.).
73 Marx 1976a, pp. 486–7.

challenged. Echeverría himself, according to what we have discussed above, sees the situation as the reverse: that Marx *could not yet see that far*,[74] because in his time the problem of the destruction of nature (and with it, discussions of this topic) did not present themselves to the degree that they do today. In other words, concrete knowledge of use-value should be understood as the third, and at present, the last step in the development of the theory after Aristotle and Smith. This knowledge can be developed within a Marxist theoretical framework, always with reference to the fact of the subjection of use-value to the dominant relations. Pursuing Echeverría's observations on the history of this theory further, we would say that if Aristotle – and also Plato in a more naïve fashion, according to Marx[75] – grants great importance to use-value, he achieves this only at the expense of remaining unable to grasp the content of the concept of value. Meanwhile, while classical political economy discovers the concept of value (but not that of surplus value), in so doing it largely obscures the importance of use-value.

To return to Echeverría's own thoughts, we would say that Marx – in his critique on this point – for the most part follows the classical political economists, while already alluding in his formulations to the importance of use-value, its subsumption, and resulting tendency to be destroyed by value. Only the generalised and perfected form of this destructive tendency situates a theoretical-concrete analysis of use-value as the first item on our agenda.[76] At this point of

---

74 We see that not even Echeverría can avoid entirely some minimal imagination of historical progress.

75 See also: 'Hence both product and producer are improved by the division of labour. If the growth of the quantity produced is occasionally mentioned, this is only done with reference to the greater abundance of use-values. There is not a word alluding to exchange-value, or to the cheapening of commodities. This standpoint, the standpoint of use-value, is adopted by Plato, who treats the division of labour as the foundation on which the division of society into estates [Stände] is based, and also in Xenophon ... Plato's Republic, in so far as division of labour is treated in it as the formative principle of the state, is merely the Athenian idealisation of the Egyptian caste system, Egypt having served as the model of an industrial country to others of his contemporaries' (Marx 1976a, pp. 487–9).

76 With this background it is worth mentioning, anticipating our indication on p. 219 regarding the concept of progress implicit in Echeverría, which is different from a naïve apologia. It is true that Echeverría sets out from a possible advance in the *development of theory* but, insofar as this refers to *social praxis*, he has a non-glorified concept of progress, something like that of Walter Benjamin (an author he refers to more than to Critical Theory), who describes this view in an unparalleled manner in his ninth thesis on history: 'A Klee painting named "Angelus Novus" shows an angel looking as though he is about to move away from something he is fixedly contemplating. His eyes are staring, his mouth is open, his wings are spread. This is how one pictures the angel of history. His face is turned

the analysis we could say, following Echeverría, that the causal nexus between his everyday experience (in which his place of residence is also determinant) and his theory, consists of the fact that the 'baroque *ethos*' appears forcefully in Mexico. Among other things, the presence of this baroque *ethos* means that the subjection of use-value to value is also, of course, a constitutive foundation for the formation of this specific society, something which is generally valid for capitalist productive relations, but which on the ideological and everyday plane is neither celebrated by the subjects nor carried out in a tragic suffering manner (but with determination nonetheless), as occurs with other '*ethe*'. The simple fact that other *ethe* distinct from the baroque prevail in the most industrialised countries does not mean in and of itself that such countries pertain to a 'higher stage of general human development'. On the contrary, it is worth repeating, the degree of industrialisation does not express the degree of presence of capitalist productive relations. Here, following Rosa Luxemburg – to whose works in Spanish he provided the prologue – Echeverría sets out from the fact that the global capitalist system must necessarily include countries with different degrees of industrialisation in order to function, but that all these countries should be understood as capitalist regardless. Moreover, as we said in the chapter on Echeverría's life and work, we can observe here a constant in Echeverría's thought, which stretches from his youthful days in Berlin to the present. For example, he put it as follows in those early years:

> Latin America cannot 'enter' the bourgeois era, because it has already been there since the Iberian conquest; its underdevelopment results from neither its persistence in a pre-capitalist mode of production nor the 'immaturity' of local capitalism, but rather from the structural deformation of its colonial and neocolonial economy, which is the effect of its function which has been oriented toward the outside, subjugated, and specialised, which was imposed on it by the capitalism of the metropolis and the self-destructive system of imperialist production.[77]

toward the past. Where we perceive a chain of events, he sees one single catastrophe, which keeps piling wreckage upon wreckage and hurls it in front of his feet. The angel would like to stay, awaken the dead, and make whole what has been smashed. But a storm is blowing from Paradise; it has got caught in his wings with such violence that the angel can no longer close them. This storm irresistibly propels him into the future to which his back is turned, while the pile of debris before him grows skyward. This storm is what we call progress' (Benjamin 1968, pp. 257–8).

[77] Echeverría 1968, p. 13. The cited passage is preceded by the following: 'The reformist thesis which implies the following assumptions is false: Latin America "is located between the Middle Ages and the bourgeois period of its history"; its underdevelopment results from

The Marxian conception of history speaks of three major phases of human development: primitive classless societies, which remained dependent upon nature; later, the era of domination of nature, which was only possible at the expense of the domination of human beings by other human beings – which is to say, the class society in which we find ourselves today – implying the oppression of internal nature and the tendency toward destroying external nature; then, the possibility of a third phase of freedom in a broader sense, meaning, freeing ourselves from immediate, omnipotent, and totally external forces of nature, and at the same time from social and individual oppression itself. Following on from this Marxian understanding, Echeverría traces the following parallel in the field of philosophy and social theory: in antiquity there was a powerful conception of use-value, but which was conceived in direct relation to the natural, without a real understanding of its social, which is to say subjective, aspect, and without a developed concept of value. In modernity, we find the progressive development of the concept of value, but this comes at the price of systematically underestimating use-value and the tendency toward its destruction. With his concept of surplus value, Marx gives critical content to the concept of value, and thereby, of course, takes the first steps toward the overcoming of this limitation, while remaining partly trapped by the bourgeois fixation on value. Echeverría does not manage to take this decisive step either, but he takes important intermediate steps toward a third rung on the ladder, which ought to be that of a complete and simultaneous analysis of both value and use-value.

As speculative as this last idea may be, it shows nevertheless that a critical focus on Eurocentrism like that attempted in this book is not the result of a sentimental or simply moralising impulse, but rather seeks to (and is able to) break down the barriers to knowledge associated with Eurocentrism. Had we made our arguments from within a purely Eurocentric perspective, it would be easy to answer the question of why the 'Latino' Echeverría situates use-value so centrally and, in so doing, reminds us of the economic thought of antiquity: both would be falsely conceived to be obsolete and only the collective narcissism of the inhabitants of certain latitudes would have been satisfied.[78]

---

the "dual" (which is to say, feudal and capitalist) character of its form of production; its proletarian class "has still not developed fully"; the interests of the "national bourgeoisies" are anti-imperialist, and; the revolutionary perspective standing before them is that of completing the "democratic-bourgeois revolution", and it is false because it means a subordination of Marxism to liberal-bourgeois ideology' (ibid.).

78 Which would be no small accomplishment, however. This is valid, nevertheless, with the limitation that among *critical* or humanistic circles this Eurocentrism would be expressed with the requisite tone of lamentation, always ready to help, which is to say, compassion-

e   Marx as the Founder of the Critical Concept of Use-Value

In the text analysed here – 'La "forma natural" de la reproducción social' ['The "Natural Form" of Social Reproduction'] – Echeverría goes even further in his defence of Marx. As against two critics[79] of the latter, Echeverría vehemently emphasises Marx's decisive contribution to a theory of use-value. Beyond merely explaining the absence of a full conceptualisation of use-value, its production, and its consumption, as we just demonstrated, our task, here, is to clarify the fact that Marx could even be considered as the founder of the *critical* theory of use-value, or – as Echeverría also puts it in Marx's own words – of the 'natural form' of social reproduction. We refer to his manner of approaching use-value as 'critical' because it does not simply affirm the existing production of use-value – as was common in earlier theories – but, instead, conceives use-value from the perspective of its own destruction, provoked by the dynamic of value production.

Alfred Schmidt, who would formulate the first systematic analysis of Marx's concept of nature, also considers Marx among the first scientists to include in his theory a reflection on the tendency inherent in the production of value toward the destruction of use-value. In his self-critical prologue to the French edition of his doctoral thesis, Schmidt writes:

> On the other hand, in Marx and Engels we find, however rarely and in dispersed contexts, some approaches of an *'ecological'* critique of the destructive aspect of modern industrial development. The fact that human intromission can do considerable damage to the *natural equilibrium* [*Naturhaushalt*], constituted a problem for them before it did for the biologist Ernst Haeckel, whose *Generelle Morphologie* (1866) introduced the term *'ecology'* [*'Ökologie'*] into scientific discussion.[80]

This book by Schmidt, published more than two decades prior to Echeverría's text, follows an emphasis similar to that of the Latin American philosopher discussed here, but with a different orientation. A 'philosophical interpretation

---

ately, and a smile toward the South (a donation of sixteen euros to charity and a flyer for the Zapatistas).

79   Foucault and Baudrillard. See, in this book, two subchapters below: 'The Critique of Political Economy as a Critique of Modernity'.

80   See the author's preface to the French edition of *The Concept of Nature in Marx*: Schmidt 1994, pp. 2f. In the strict sense, we are quoting here the German manuscript for this prologue to the French edition. In the prologue to the new 1993 German edition ('Für einen ökologischen Materialismus') this phrase does not appear: see Schmidt 1993, pp. i–xvi.

of Marx' also interested Schmidt, and both refer extensively for such an interpretation to the critique of political economy (above all, *Das Kapital* and the *Grundrisse*, texts not generally considered to be especially 'philosophical'). In this context, Schmidt emphasises, as does Echeverría, the importance of the concept of use-value and of the natural form: 'The natural form of the commodity, called by Marx its use-value, only appears in the analysis of the process of creating value in so far as it is the "material substratum, the depositary of exchange-value". Here, on the contrary, we are concerned primarily with the philosophical elements of Marxist theory, and the process of production will be considered above all in its historical movement, as a labour-process bringing forth use-values'.[81]

Given that Echeverría, in his essay on 'La "forma natural" de la reproducción social', seeks a panoramic view of contemporary discussions of the topic,[82] and so does not skimp on references to other authors, it is curious indeed that he says nothing of Schmidt's essay. Alongside a quick *explanation* of this situation by the general existence of a reciprocal 'philosophical distrust between Frankfurt and Berlin' (effective perhaps for Echeverría's long years spent studying at the Freie Universität Berlin), there is an important difference between the two approaches that could help clarify the situation. In his introduction, when Schmidt explains the plan of his book, it is striking that in the passage cited above – beside the parallels with the position of Bolívar Echeverría – Schmidt places at the centre of his observations the importance of use-value above all in relation to its *production*, and not so much to its *consumption*, which Echeverría almost always mentions in the same breath as production. This is clearly related to another decisive difference between the approaches of Echeverría and Schmidt, which consists of the fact that the former situates the process of communication in an intimate relationship to the process of production, therefore conceiving communication as a sub-form of production/consumption, a topic not broached by Schmidt.

Schmidt realises perfectly well the unity of production and consumption in Marx's theory, but setting out from the primacy of production, as we see clearly, for example, in the following formulation: 'Marx, like Hegel, regarded productive activity as consumption as well, which used up both the material worked on and the activity of work'.[83]

---

81   Schmidt 1971, p. 15.
82   Note, in this respect: 'The concept of the "natural form" occupies a central position in Marx's discourse.... The following notes seek to bring together for the first time a series of ideas, almost all of which are commonly used in contemporary Marxist debates, which can facilitate their adequate formulation' (Echeverría 1984, p. 34).
83   Schmidt 1971, p. 71.

Schmidt understands this 'dialectic of consumption and production'[84] in terms of Marx's formulation of 'productive consumption' in *Zur Kritik der politischen Ökonomie* (*Contribution to the Critique of Political Economy*). In other words, all productive acts already contain a consumptive one. Echeverría, who as a general rule appreciates Marx's Hegelian inheritance while not accentuating it as strongly as does Schmidt (who is more deeply rooted in the tradition of Western Marxism), perceives the unity of these two distinct processes as tendentially external rather than internal, as is the case with Schmidt, in the sense of the unity of opposites. This understanding is a constitutive component of Echeverría's comparison of the processes of communication and production. In situating the production and consumption of a use-value in two different people, we can detect between them a form of communication that is produced because the consumer of the use-value necessarily has to interpret the use-value as a sign in order to be able to enjoy it.

The divergent valorisation of Marx's theoretical relationship to use-value that we find in Echeverría and Schmidt could be understood as follows: Marx's two tendencies, contradictory at first sight, namely of recognising, on the one hand, the importance of use-values and thereby understanding very early on the danger of their destruction, while on the other hand referring to use-values systematically only in terms of a 'material substratum ... bearers of exchange-value',[85] are not two totally divergent tendencies within Marxian thought, but rather both the expression of a single situation.

Just as Herbert Marcuse, in his *Reason and Revolution*, views Hegel's affirmative expressions with regard to the existing social formation (for example toward the monarchy or war) as directly related to his ideas critical of bourgeois society, so, too, can we, by analogy, rationally conceive and understand this contradiction within Marx. Thus, when Hegel glorifies war as something as beneficial for society as the storm is for the sea, freeing it of stagnation by stirring it up, this is on the one hand the most shallow affirmation of the existing, but it is at the same time one of his most critical formulations, one which could also be understood to mean that this social formation would collapse if not for war since, as Hegel puts it in another passage, bourgeois society's reason ends at the border of the nation state.[86]

With reference to the problem at hand, we could then say: Marx's limitation in referring systematically to use-value – the natural form of the commodity – only in connection to the analysis of the production of value, is on the one hand a genuflection toward classical political economy studied in the present,

---

84 Schmidt 1971, p. 214 n44.
85 Marx 1976a, p. 293.
86 Hegel 1991, §324. See also Marcuse 1955, especially pp. 220–3.

but simultaneously and in the same sense, this theoretical limitation is nothing other than the account of the full subordination of use-value to value as manifested in the capitalist mode of production. This latter side is radicalised even further because Marx analyses use-value in relation to value, above all in its tendency to be destroyed by value. To celebrate use-value would not have provided any better solution to the actually-existing problem, and nor would it have contributed a bit to resolving it. To return to the parallel with Marcuse's critique of Hegel: just as the naïve musings on perpetual peace and the idea of being able to create and guarantee it within the framework of existing social relations and through international peacekeeping institutions[87] ultimately run off course and miss the central problem, so too a naïve fixation on the use-value side of production and consumption always runs the risk of being less critical than Marx's proposal on this point, which seems at first glance to be uncritical. Hegel's occasionally frightening realism – which makes him sound so cynical and at the same time often so understanding – is also present in part in Marx's work.

The reflection is on the knife's edge. Doubtless, we should not remain within Marx's undeveloped reflections on use-value, on the natural form of social reproduction, but here we run up against a question which is more than merely scholastic: how can we take this step today, when the formation of society is not *in principle* different from what it was in Marx's times, without losing the realism that led him to his highest reflections, which in large part have still not been surpassed?

Is it really enough, as Echeverría and Schmidt each stress in their own way, that the destruction of nature is more advanced and even more evident than it was in Marx's time?[88] Can this break down the barriers to knowledge that caused this 'theoretical giant' to stumble? Without falling into a naïve adoration of Marx, we can ask ourselves if we do not find in the arguments of his critics some faith in progress, however negatively formulated, which is to say from

---

87 Hegel reproaches Kant for this *philosophical* eyewash: 'Perpetual peace is often demanded as an ideal to which mankind should approximate. Thus, Kant proposed a league of sovereigns to settle disputes between states, and the Holy Alliance was meant to be an institution more or less of this kind. But the state is an individual, and negation is an essential component of individuality. Thus, even if a number of states join together as a family, this league, in its individuality, must generate opposition and create an enemy': Hegel 1991, §324, addition, p. 326.

88 From this, Schmidt does not draw the conclusion that the analysis of use-value stumbles on fewer barriers to knowledge than in Marx's era. Rather, he limits himself to developing, in the aforementioned self-critical prologue, the critique of the fixation – occasionally bordering on naïveté – on the omnipotence of human praxis.

the destructive side?[89] Was it not Marx himself who, horrified by the destruction of human existences, of children, of the populations of entire regions, picked up his pen and wrote *Capital*? Can all his moderation, his frequently cynical scorn toward the vileness of the capitalist mode of production, can this fool us into forgetting that this human being, in every line of his critique of political economy, had in the back of his mind the reports of the English factory inspectors which hardly fell short of Dante's description of Hell? But when Marx describes how poor working mothers would give their three-year-old children opiates so they would be quiet, was he talking about anything other than the destruction of use-values, of the natural form of social reproduction?[90] When, in *Capital*, Marx debates in the utmost detail on the so-called theories of 'overpopulation' (which are now present more or less openly in UN conferences), is this not a question of use-value and its destruction? Is the question only about the law of value, when Marx observes the following?

> In fact, not only the number of births and deaths, but the absolute size of the families stands in inverse proportion to the level of wages, and therefore to the amount of the means of subsistence at the disposal of the different categories of worker. This law of capitalist society would sound absurd to savages, or even to civilized colonists. It calls to mind the boundless reproduction of animals individually weak and constantly hunted down.[91]

Capital is full of this sort of formulation and a meticulous analysis of the text would demonstrate that more than half of Marx's main work consists of developments with this sort of 'empirical' content. But what is surprising is that the majority of writings about *Capital* leave them out of consideration. If, in any case, this is justified, it is done with the argument that they are mere illustrations and as such should be disregarded – a quite materialist method, this ignoring of the low everyday working life!

Paraphrasing Alfred Schmidt,[92] we could say that Marx is not at his most theoretical (and in the end, nor is he at his 'most philosophical' in the emphatic sense) where he makes use of the traditional method of determining

---

89   In this respect, see also note 76 on p. 212 of this book.
90   Marx 1976a, p. 522.
91   Marx 1976a, pp. 796–7.
92   In the introduction to his volume, Schmidt says the following about his method of writing: 'In the conviction that Marx was by no means at his most philosophical when he made use of the traditional, scholastic language of the philosophers, his middle and later,

concepts – which remain relatively 'uncontaminated' by empirical details – as in the first chapters of *Capital*, but rather where he rescues these concepts from the fate of being mere definitions and converts them into concepts in the rigorous Hegelian-Marxist sense, filling them with their real historical content. Therefore, a philosophical interpretation of Marx cannot have as its foundation only the theoretical-economic reflections in their most mature form, as they appear at the outset of the first volume of *Capital* (and which, as is known, represented the last step of analysis in the course of his research), but must also proceed in a materialist form and subsequently carry out Marx's reasoning as a whole, traveling with him through all the depravity of the history of English industrial legislation, and so on. To stop short of this would be to remain a philosopher in the worst sense of the word.

Returning to the problematic of use-value, this means: the most important and fundamental use-value for the human being is the human being itself. The first 'natural form' that humans encounter is their mother, and they later come to be increasingly conscious of the use-value of their own bodies and, later, that of all other humans. Marx himself also says that labour power is a fundamental use-value, and in a certain degree the most important, since it is the only commodity that creates value (and with it, surplus value). Seen in this way, use-value is even more central to Marx's analysis than value, not only quantitatively (with regard to the number of pages devoted to it), but also in terms of its fundamental focus. This focus evidently sets out from the massive destruction and gradual annihilation of the human life of the English working class, which – on account of the factory inspectors, who were often brave and committed[93] – represents one of the best-documented cases of the capitalist

---

politico-economic writings will be consulted much more than is customary in interpretations of Marxist philosophy' (Schmidt 1971, pp. 16f.).

[93] 'The social statistics of Germany and the rest of Continental Western Europe are, in comparison with those of England, quite wretched. But they raise the veil just enough to let us catch a glimpse of the Medusa's head behind it. We should be appalled at our own circumstances if, as in England, our governments and parliaments periodically appointed commissions of inquiry into economic conditions; if these commissions were armed with the same plenary powers to get at the truth; if it were possible to find for this purpose men as competent, as free from partisanship and respect of persons as are England's factory inspectors, her medical reporters on public health, her commissioners of inquiry into the exploitation of women and children, into conditions of housing and nourishment, and so on. Perseus wore a magic cap so that the monsters he hunted down might not see him. We draw the magic cap down over our own eyes and ears so as to deny that there are any monsters' (Marx 1976a, p. 91).

destruction of use-value.[94] But this speech for the defence in support of Marx has not been inserted here in order to distract the reader from the limitations that Alfred Schmidt and Bolívar Echeverría diagnose in his treatment of use-value, but instead to indicate a danger that we see in the way that many today follow the fashion of referring to ecology and use-value (Schmidt's text was written long before this, as was Echeverría's, leaving a certain distance in time between the flourishing of such discourse in Latin America).

Marx has been criticised for not having analysed use-value, the natural form of social reproduction, sufficiently within his theory. This critique largely neglects the fact that the destruction of 'human use-value' – especially in the form of the proletarian and the members of his family – occupies a central position in Marx's main work. The failure to recognise this could have a double meaning. Either it sets out from the belief that the destruction of *external* nature in Marx, as the destruction of natural forms alongside the *internal* (that proper to human beings), should be discussed in more detail; or, alternatively, it sets out from the belief that the very destruction of human nature *itself* is no longer a topic for discussion, because in its extreme form such destruction has been transferred from Europe to other continents, and in the (ostensible) mother continent of the capitalist mode of production the destruction of external nature, at least at first glance, has become the most urgent problem. If the second variant were the case, then Marx's focus is surely closer to the truth than those ecological propagandists who see nothing more in the deforestation of virgin forests than the loss of 'our' collective lungs and who do not know – and much less want to know – what happens in the affected region when these forests are destroyed, and who do not care at all that the inhabitants of those forest regions were destroyed long before the holes in the ozone layers over the polar caps were discovered. It is this false ecologism,[95] which represents little more than the highest stage of pseudo-humanist Eurocentrism, of those who remember basic human needs only when their necks burn or they find spots on their own skin, that we must beware. It is very interesting to note that

---

94 In the end, simply emphasising the importance of use-values does not eliminate the problem that external or internal nature are only understood – to use Kant's language – as a *means* and not an end. This relates to the economist's view of social relations, a view which Marx adopts not because he finds it especially convincing but because he is interested in analysing a society in which human beings can live, if at all, only because they possess the use-value of creating value. But, in the end, Marx is interested in something more than an 'economy oriented toward use-value'. Without using Kant's language, there is in every description of the living conditions of the English working class a resonance of what interests him but which he very rarely dares to state: a society in which, as Brecht says, 'man is no longer a wolf to man'.

95 In this regard, see also Dittmar 1995.

such a view fits much less comfortably within Marxian theory than with the conceptions of those who seek to overcome the aforementioned limitations in Marx solely through an act of will or a mere redefinition of the problem. In general, growing distress is not sufficient for the resolution of a problem, and it would only be so if the solution had failed to arise only for lack of will power. In this sense, we can understand Echeverría's explanation, intended as well-meaning, of Marx's limitation with regard to the analysis of use-value, as well as the expression of his own insufficiency with respect to the critique of knowledge and ideology.

In other words, is Bolívar Echeverría's attempt to develop the Marxian analysis of use-value and overcome its limitations a radicalisation of his analysis of commodity-producing society (in which the value and surplus values which Marx analyses first play a central role), or are we dealing implicitly with a watering down of Marx's approach, of diluting his radical critique of the capitalist mode of production, of generalised commodity production? This question will accompany us (albeit latently) throughout the whole of the rest of this book, for example, in the following investigation of Echeverría's concept of 'modern *ethos*' and his reflections on the relationship between capitalism and modernity, in which he conceptually pursues a non-capitalist modernity. It is interesting that, as Echeverría understands it, a fundamental characteristic of all imaginable modern societies is generalised *commodity* production. This is to say, a non-capitalist modernity would have a non-capitalist economic form in which commodity production would be a predominant characteristic.

Here, the same question will come up again: does Echeverría radicalise Marx, or does he outwit himself with this (apparent) radicalism while in reality only minimising the problems that emerged through the analysis of value, and which were not merely contradictory concepts, but instead the becoming visible of unspeakable misery as the basis of the capitalist mode of production, the tracks of what Marx calls the 'capitalised blood of children'?[96]

---

96 Marx 1976a, p. 920. Marx makes such observations at various points in *Capital* with detailed data on child labour, with even children younger than five being forced to work. As is known, child labour is common even today in the majority of countries adhering to a capitalist mode of production (which is not the same as the category of highly industrialised countries).

The fact that the capitalist mode of production in the so-called First World depends directly on conditions in the Third World was clearer to Marx than to many contemporary 'critical thinkers': 'In fact the veiled slavery of the wagelabourers in Europe needed the unqualified slavery of the New World as its pedestal' (Marx 1976a, p. 925).

Regarding the 'capitalised blood of children', Marx speaks on the next page of *Capital* about 'the necessity of childstealing and child-slavery for the transformation of

f   The Marxian Concept of *Natural Form* and the Theory of *Ethos*

According to Marx, social reproduction has a 'double form': the 'value form' and the 'natural form'.[97] The concept of natural form is accompanied by that of use-value. The commodity, in Marx's words, has a double-objectivity: the 'objectivity of commodities as values' versus their 'sensuous objectivity'. It is precisely its 'double' way of existing as something that converts this specific historical product into a commodity. It is this 'plain, homely natural form', as Marx calls it [*'hausbackene Naturalform'*][98] – which, in opposition to the value form, does not only appear in bourgeois forms of production, but in all forms of production throughout history – from which research into the Marxian concept of nature must set out.[99] Bolívar Echeverría sees the possibility of applying the Marxian concept of natural form not only to the 'sensuous objectivity of commodities as physical bodies', but also to other aspects of production not directly related to the capitalist mode of production, but which are older and which could even outlast it.

In order to do so, he thinks above all about regional traditions, peculiarities, and preferences, as well as about culturally caused differences in how human products are made and consumed. It is certain that Echeverría, in the framework of his theory, argues for the necessity of this conceptual expansion, but he does not document – on the basis of Marx's texts, and with detailed arguments – up to what point his interpretation of the natural form of social reproduction could be justified by a Marxian conceptualisation.

The fundamental question on this topic could be put as follows: does Marx's concept of natural form refer exclusively to non-human, external nature, or also to the activity of humans and manner in which they live? Echeverría's interpretation of Marx would only be convincing on this point if the latter were the case, since Echeverría relates the concept of the natural form of social reproduction to the human *ethe*, with forms for the everyday configuration of

---

manufacturing production into factory production and the establishment of the true relation between capital and labour-power', referring to the then-common practice in England of literally enslaving children from orphanages (and often from Christian churches) and exploiting them to the maximum, frequently resulting in their death and not uncommonly in their suicide (Marx 1976a, p. 922).

97   Marx 1976a, p. 138.
98   Ibid. (Original: Marx 1975a, p. 62.)
99   Compare, for example, Schmidt 1971, p. 66: 'If exchange-value is a "non-natural characteristic" typical of the bourgeois form of production, in the use-value the commodity confronts us in its "plain, homely natural form". The present investigation is particularly concerned with the latter form of the commodity'.

society. Moreover, he does not in any way consider these *ethe* as something given exclusively according to the conditions of external nature.

Alfred Schmidt offers a relevant observation for this problematic: such a formulation could only emerge with certain reservations, since in Marx's theory – as a dialectical theory – external nature cannot be strictly separated from the human influence exercised over it.

> But as far as the world of experience as a whole is concerned, the material provided by nature cannot be distinguished from the practico-social modes of its transformation. The question of the quantitative and qualitative share of man and the material nature in the creation of the product of labour is one to which there is no general answer for Marx. The fact that this relation cannot be fixed formally is an indication of the dialectical nature of the process.[100]

This is to say that the concept of natural form, however much it comes from the natural character of the objects and instruments of labour, cannot be reduced to a merely external nature. Just as was emphasised in the discussion of the concept of praxis in Marx and Sánchez Vázquez, the concept of a nature which is external to the human being is no longer possible, imaginable, or expressible outside its connection with the radical appropriation of that nature. But, as soon as human praxis confronts external nature, the latter – as 'humanised nature'[101] – ceases to be strictly external.

In any case, this should not be misunderstood as trivial idealism in the sense that external nature becomes humanised to the point of being degraded to almost an extension of the humans. Schmidt insists on this dialectical relationship of human intervention with nature and nature's ultimately irrevocable external immediacy. 'The immediacy of nature asserts itself at ever higher stages of the process of production, though now humanly mediated through men'.[102] In the reciprocal interpenetration of external nature and human praxis, the results of this process become as external to human beings as the immediate natural material. 'Once created, the world of use-values

---

100 Ibid. Here, Schmidt adds: 'If labour is the formal "creator of value", the stuff of nature is its material creator. Hence, through what we have already said of the character of labour, the division of natural material and labour cannot be absolute. At the level of the individual use-value, it may *in abstracto* be possible to make a distinction between what derives from labour, i.e. from the activity of men, and what is provided by nature as the "material substratum" of the commodity'.
101 Ibid.
102 Schmidt 1971, p. 67.

compounded of labour and natural material (i.e. humanised nature) confronts men as something objective, existing independently of them. The material of nature itself confronted men in the same way in its first immediacy, when it had not yet been penetrated by men'.[103]

Nature and human activity reciprocally interpenetrate one another in productive praxis in such a way that it may be comprehensible to use the concept of the natural form of social reproduction for the analysis of the specific forms of this interpenetration in production and consumption. Above all, in reference to the material results of the culturally conditioned everyday processes that Echeverría analyses, his use of the Marx's concept of the natural form of social reproduction is substantially justified. The 'historical *ethos*', one of whose central characteristics consists of the special forms of production and consumption of use-values, not only influences the specific forms of those use-values, but also becomes part of them in the process of its realisation. For Echeverría, then, Marx's concept of the natural form of social reproduction represents not only his point of departure in the search for a materialist theory of culture, but will also return – upon the completion of his ambitious theoretical project – as the final point of his analysis.[104]

This concept of 'historical *ethos*', which Echeverría stresses as the principal object of his research in the 1990s can, therefore, be understood simultaneously as the foundation and the result of the dialectical relation that exists between human subjectivity and all that exists independently of consciousness. The primacy of matter can be understood to be confirmed, interpreted in this way, by Echeverría's application of the concept of natural form to the modes of subjective human behaviour in the production and consumption of use-values, and not – as a first reading of his texts may occasionally suggest – as idealistically toned down. Schmidt interprets the relationship between human productive force and natural substance in a similar fashion: 'Human productive forces stamp the material of nature intellectually and practically. This process however completely confirms nature's independence of consciousness rather than destroys it'.[105]

---

103 Schmidt 1971, p. 66. It is from this understanding that both the theory of alienation and, in the final instance, the critique of ideology as well set out in Marx and in Western Marxism.

104 This is why the fact that Bolívar Echeverría takes up once again one of his oldest theoretical texts – the text we discuss here on 'La "forma natural" de la reproducción social' (Echeverría 1984) – fourteen years after its original publication, republishing it in a slightly retouched form in a recent book, can be understood as something more than a simple recourse to previous work. See Echeverría 1998b, pp. 153–97.

105 Schmidt 1971, pp. 66f.

We wonder whether Echeverría's application of the concept of natural form to human modes of behaviour relativises the materialist concept of matter in the style of the theory of action, or if, on the contrary, he is instead filling the generally idealist theory of culture with materialist content. As we have seen, this is a very difficult question to answer. Resolving it, in the end, will depend on nuances, but these nuances can only be truly grasped when we have developed his theory more than we have thus far.

g   The Critique of Political Economy as a Critique of Modernity

In highlighting the fact that Marx, despite all the limitations, had already sketched out a critical concept of use-value, Bolívar Echeverría hoped to show that Marx should not be simply classed as belonging undoubtedly to modern thought, as is generally done. In so doing, he did not merely set himself apart, as we have mentioned, from his old 'preceptor' Heidegger, but also from other contemporary authors. This affirmation is not fully graspable at this point in our investigation, since Echeverría's concept of modernity has a different content at different moments. In the text under discussion here,[106] our author evidently uses the concept of modernity in the sense of Western, enlightened civilisation; but elsewhere he grants the concept of modernity a much broader meaning, distinguishing different modes of capitalist modernity, some of which do not fit in the dominant vulgar sense of the term, or at best as 'immature, early forms', and he moreover sees the possibility (in principle) of a non-capitalist or a post-capitalist modernity.[107] Thus we can understand why Echeverría insists, on the one hand, that 'the concept of use-value, which Marx contrasts with modern thought, explodes the horizon of concepts within which the latter moves',[108] and at the same time, in later writings, like the central text in his book *Modernidad y capitalismo*, conceptually engages with the possibility of a 'non-capitalist modernity'.[109]

---

106   Echeverría 1984.
107   On the concept of modernity in Echeverría, see pp. 278ff.
108   Echeverría 1984.
109   Note the following: 'The theses put forth in the following pages attempt to detect in the field of theory the possibility of a modernity which is different from that which has been imposed until now, a non-capitalist modernity' (from 'Modernidad y capitalismo', in Echeverría 1995a: citation from p. 137).

    Some observations regarding the history of this central article of Echeverría: the book *Las ilusiones de la modernidad* [*The illusions of modernity*] was originally supposed to bear the title *Modernidad y capitalismo* [*Modernity and capitalism*] – at least this was the name of the manuscript that Echeverría completed some two years prior to its appearance. But

The other aforementioned contemporary authors, to whom Echeverría directs his findings about Marx's critical attitude toward 'modern thought', are Michel Foucault and Jean Baudrillard. To the question: 'does Marx have something to contribute to contemporary discussions on the foundations of revolutionary political activity?'[110] – which is equivalent to asking if Marx broke in principle with 'modern Western thought' – these two authors would respond 'no', because a far-reaching 'lack of understanding'[111] prevents both of them from grasping Marx's theoretical contributions with regard to use-value and his concomitant break with the customary 'modern thought'. But this 'lack of understanding' of Marx's thinking, according to Echeverría, results from very different causes.

In Foucault, it results from a simple lack of understanding of Marx's main work,[112] which impoverishes his otherwise magnificent body of work. Echeverría laments the fact that Foucault arrived at the erroneous conclusion that Marx's critique of political economy was little more than a 'storm in a teacup',[113] one which in reality does not represent a 'real break' with nineteenth-century thought.[114] Bolívar Echeverría seems to refer in this passage to a slightly different metaphor about water to which Foucault refers in *Les mots et les choses*, and which in the words of the French philosopher sounds this

---

at the last moment the word 'capitalism' disappeared, leaving in its place the softer term 'illusions'. The new title of the book is doubtless critical of modernity, but what is specific to Echeverría's theoretical approach is lost entirely, and on the basis of this title we could take the book to be 'yet another one of those postmodern books'. But this is precisely what Echeverría does not propose: he wants to save modernity without conserving its capitalist variant; he wants, then, to empty the dirty bathwater of the capitalist mode of production without allowing the baby of modernity to fall on the ground. Here, there is a parallel with the Frankfurt School, if we set out from the fact that Echeverría understands by 'modernity' something similar to what the latter understand by 'Enlightenment'. In this regard, consider the following passage: 'Enlightenment itself, having mastered itself and assumed its own power, could break through the limits of enlightenment': Horkheimer and Adorno 2002 (Chapter 'Elements of Anti-Semitism') p. 172.

The essay on 'Modernidad y capitalismo' ['Modernity and capitalism'] had a long history and appeared various times prior to its final version, which is used here, in drafts that were retouched each time: 'Diecinueve tesis sobre modernidad y capitalism,' in *Cuadernos de la DEP*, March 1987 (Echeverría 1987); 'Quince tesis sobre modernidad y capitalismo', in *Cuadernos Políticos*, September–December 1989 (Echeverría 1989); 'Quince tesis sobre modernidad y capitalismo', in *Review*, Fall 1991 (Echeverría 1991).

110   Echeverría 1984, p. 34 n4.
111   Ibid.
112   '... [T]he distance between this author [Michel Foucault] and the text of *Capital*' (ibid.).
113   Echeverría 1984, p. 34 n4. Echeverría refers here to Foucault 1988, pp. 272–5.
114   See Echeverría 1984, p. 34 n4.

way: 'Le marxisme est dans la pensée du XIXème siècle comme un poisson dans l'eau: c'est-à-dire que partout ailleurs il cesse de respirer'. ['Marxism exists in nineteenth-century thought like a fish in water: that is, it is unable to breath anywhere else'.][115]

In Baudrillard, on the contrary, things are very different, according to Echeverría. Here, the 'lack of understanding' with respect to Marx's theory of use-value is of the highest calibre, a 'voluntary lack of understanding'.[116] The intention of Baudrillard – who Echeverría characterises as 'one of the most shrewd contemporary theorists of exchange, production, and consumption'[117] – is to appear smarter than Marx, that is to say, to make his own an understanding which had already previously been formulated in crucial respects. Echeverría describes this method, one not entirely unusual in philosophy or in science, in the following terms as concerns the case of Baudrillard:

> Baudrillard...resists distinguishing between the abstract utility or exchange value of an object and its concrete utility or use-value, which is always by necessity collectively and individually symbolic. In an effort to reserve for himself the 'originality' of exploring the latter in its 'symbolic exchange', he overlooks Marx's affirmation of the concrete singularity and 'incommensurability' of the use-values, allotting him instead the flattest of utilitarianism and disqualifying all that could be said – beyond Marx but in line with him – regarding a use-value whose theoretical comprehension necessarily transcends Western metaphysics.[118]

With this, Echeverría imposes limits on the Heideggerian Baudrillard, while simultaneously and discretely subjecting his own phase of naïve Heideggerianism to critique.[119] In any case, it is worth noting this difference between the two: Echeverría, during his phase as an unshakeable partisan of the philosopher from Freiburg, was practically unaware of Marx's writings; his attitude, therefore, while seemingly limited when seen today, did not come about intentionally.

---

115 Foucault 1988 p. 274 [in English: Foucault 1970, p. 262].
116 Echeverría 1984, p. 35 n4.
117 Ibid.
118 Ibid. Here, Echeverría refers to the following text: Baudrillard 1972, pp. 154–63.
119 See in the chapter 'Life and work of Bolívar Echeverría', pp. 47ff.

CHAPTER 12

Concretisation of the Concept of Praxis

a   Reproduction and Communication

As we read Echeverría's texts, we conclude that he set himself a task that cannot be resolved easily. He wanted to provide a concrete content to the concept of praxis, and thereby to grasp it in its historical dimension. According to all indications, the problem consists of the following: if the concept of praxis is inseparably linked to the concept of the (autonomous) subject who freely decides, then how can this be understood as something determinate, with concrete content? How can we theoretically reproduce this complex ensemble of *particular subjective* decisions on the basis of historical-concrete conceptual determinations, which must necessarily seek out the *general*?

Or, to put it differently, and more closely in line with the materialist theory of culture toward which Echeverría aspires: how is it possible to understand a specific cultural determination of human praxis, especially the productive (and consumptive) one, without falling into ethnologising human subjects in their respective everyday forms of reproduction, or even construct biological fixations? Echeverría, who, as we have said, does not limit human culture to its 'elevated' forms – for example, art at a gallery – and bases his analysis, rather, in the precise manner of material reproduction (as the unity of production and consumption), finds an adequate image of this relationship between freedom and tradition, between individuality and a historically- and geographically-determined collectivity. This image lies in human languages and their innumerable speech acts and in a science that studies the relation of interdependence among them: semiotics, founded by Ferdinand de Saussure. To do so, he refers to authors like Roman Jakobson and Louis Hjelmslev.[120]

---

120 Bolívar Echeverría emphasises the importance of these two authors in his study of the natural form: 'To a certain degree I approximated above all Jakobson and Hjelmslev, they are the two that I treat as crucial in questions of semiology and linguistics' (Fifth interview with Bolívar Echeverría, 11 September 1996, in the Faculty of Philosophy and Arts of the UNAM, cassette I, side A, pos. 247–50 [cited hereafter as Fifth interview with Bolívar Echeverría].)

In so doing, he draws support from Jakobson 1960, Jakobson 1971 and Hjelmslev 1971, p. 55. See Echeverría 1984, pp. 42, 3, and 40).

In contrast to the majority of his other published texts, here he gives multiple bibliographical references regarding his theoretical sources and texts used. With a modesty that

In the article we are discussing here – 'La "forma natural" de la reproducción social' – he does so through the use of not only text, but also, on average every two pages, graphics with schematic representations of the processes of communication and reproduction which, no doubt, allow us to grasp their similarity visually. We should not overlook his affinity for Saussure's figures, although Echeverría's are much more complex and can only be understood after a meticulous study of the primary text in question.[121] Here, what is crucial is the fact that Echeverría does not refer to semiotics in order to grasp all reality as a mere sign and thereby to see history only as an 'unfinished text', but the opposite. Not only does he want to demonstrate that the first and fundamental human sign system is, in every case, that of the various forms of producing and consuming use-values, but he wants to show even more than this: for Echeverría, the communication process is a dimension of the process of reproduction.

does not correspond at all to his previously cited self-assessment of the text as 'one of the best things' he had written (note 39 on p. 201), in this article he states that it is an effort 'to bring together for the first time a series of ideas, almost all of which are commonly used in contemporary Marxist debates, which can facilitate their adequate formulation' (Echeverría 1984, p. 34).

Beyond those already named, he refers in the text to the following authors, which we merely mention to give a certain idea of from which direction the wind of his theoretical influences blows: Aristotle, Roland Barthes, Georges Bataille, Walter Benjamin, Émile Benveniste, Roger Callois, Martin Heidegger, André Leroi-Gourhan, Claude Lévi-Strauss, Georg Lukács, André Martinet, Maurice Merleau-Ponty, Charles Kay Ogden, Ivor Armstrong Richards, Jean-Paul Sartre, and Karl August Wittfogel.

121 Seven years prior to his text on the natural form, Bolívar Echeverría had published an (annotated) series of 'Esquemas gráficos para el estudio del capítulo quinto de *El Capital*' ['Graphic diagrams for the study of the fifth chapter of *Capital*']. In looking at these diagrams, and above all the last and most complex among them, the reader is spontaneously reminded of the circuit of an electronic apparatus. Looking more closely at the explanation and the manner in which he labels the images and documents their elements with loose letters or combinations of letters, something came to the mind of the author of this book that Bolívar Echeverría had told him on one occasion: in his school days what most interested him was mathematics and precisely their most developed form. He hoped to study 'pure mathematics', but this was not offered at the University of Quito, only applied maths. Thus it was that he arrived at philosophy.

To show with mathematical rigour the results of Marx's analysis of the labour and the valorisation process does not in any way mean that the critical impulse of his main work is lost. What is, instead, clarified by Echeverría's various economic texts (see the attached bibliography) is that he cannot be counted among those interpreters of Marx who never subjected *Capital* to a serious – which is to say, a critical – reading as well. See Echeverría 1977e.

'So I make visible a parallel between the process of reproduction and that of communication.... That is to say, the latter (the process of communication) is an aspect, a dimension of the former [which is to say, the process of reproduction]';[122] that is, the process of reproduction can be compared to the process of communication not because the world as a totality can only be grasped as a complicated combination of 'texts' and 'ways of reading', but the reverse; communication, as the unity of the production and consumption of signs, is in itself one among many productive and consumptive acts that human beings must undertake in order to be able to organise and maintain their lives, but it is in no way the fundamental form and always has an inevitable materiality as its foundation.

'Speech [el lenguaje][123] in its basic, verbal realisation is also a process of the production/consumption of objects. The speaker presents to the listener a transformation of nature: his voice modifies the acoustic state of the atmosphere, and this change, this object, is perceived or consumed as such by the ear of the other'.[124]

Bolívar Echeverría is concerned with explaining the process of producing and consuming use-values through reference to the theoretical contributions of semiotics, but without denying the primacy of nature and the primacy of the material as the inalienable foundation of the ideal. Here, we find an essential difference *vis-à-vis* a series of contemporary approaches which are caught up in the concept of communication (or related conceptions, for example that of 'articulation'), and who see in it the most diverse forms, real or imagined, the explanation, and, at the same time, the salvation of the world.

---

122   Fifth interview with Bolívar Echeverría, cassette 1, side A, pos. 264–7.
123   Evidently, by 'lenguaje' ['speech'] Echeverría understands what Ferdinand de Saussure (who he cited at various points in the text here analysed) calls '*langage*'. Saussure also uses this term as a synonym for '*faculté de langage*, and explains': '*l'exercice du langage repose sur une faculté que nous tenons de la nature*'. Ferdinand de Saussure 1979. English translation: 'the use of speech is based on a natural faculty': Saussure 1966, p. 9.

   Saussure already indicates here that we should understand by '*langage*' ['speech' in English, 'lenguaje' in Spanish] not only the languages ['langue' in French, 'lengua' in Spanish] spoken, but also the totality of all *possible* forms of expression or also of forms of exteriorisation; it should be used to refer to any systematisation or homogenisation of any forms of expression. Note: 'Whereas speech is heterogeneous, language, as defined, is homogeneous ... Language, once its boundaries have been marked off within the speech data, can be classified among human phenomena, whereas speech cannot' (Saussure 1966, p. 15) Compare also: 'faculty of speech' (p. 10).
124   Echeverría 1984, p. 45. Echeverría refers here to Troubetzkoy 1970, p. 38.

While Saussure subordinates linguistics to semiotics [*sémiologie*][125] and realises that knowledge of the 'true nature of language' is only possible if it is correctly classified under the most general field of 'all other systems of the same order [tous les autres systèmes du meme ordre]'[126] which semiotics studies, Echeverría seeks to classify semiotics (understood by him as the production and consumption of signs) under the even broader field of production and consumption in general. It is clear that Saussure and Echeverría differ notably from one another, since Saussure considers semiotics to be embedded within social psychology, and this, in turn, within psychology in general, while Echeverría's system of reference is the critique of political economy.[127] We can find a parallel between the two, since in order to study the most general object, that which is necessary for the understanding of particulars, they both set out from the most complex among particular objects. Hence Saussure writes: 'Signs that are wholly arbitrary realize better than the others the ideal of the semiological process; that is why language, the most complex and universal of all systems of expression, is also the most characteristic; in this sense linguistics can become the master-pattern for all branches of semiology although language is only one particular semiological system'.[128]

Here, what attracts our attention – despite all of the differences – is a degree of similarity with Marx's methodological procedure, clearly summarised in the phrase: 'The anatomy of the human being is the key to the anatomy of the ape'.[129]

---

125 'Linguistics is only a part of the general science of semiology; the laws discovered by semiology will be applicable to linguistics, and the latter will circumscribe a well-defined area within the mass of anthropological facts' (Saussure 1966 p. 16).

126 Note: 'But to me the language problem is mainly semiological, and all developments derive their significance from that important fact. If we are to discover the true nature of language we must learn what it has in common with all other semiological systems' (Saussure 1966, p. 17).

127 '*A science that studies the life of signs within society* is conceivable; it would be a part of social psychology and consequently of general psychology; I shall call it *semiology* (from Greek *sēmîon* "sign")' (Saussure 1966, p. 16). Elsewhere he speaks not of 'social psychology' but 'group psychology' (Saussure 1966, p. 78). Note that Saussure implicitly understands social psychology as a science whose object is '*society*' ['*la vie sociale*'].

So what interests Saussure is to establish the semiotics he has founded within the social sciences, with the only limitation being that he here thinks about above all social psychology, which is to say, he seems to see society first of all determined by one aspect of those dynamics that Marx calls 'ideological forms', distinguishing them from the 'economic conditions of production, which can be determined with the precision of natural science' (see Marx 1904, p. 12).

128 Saussure 1966, p. 68.

129 Marx 1904, p. 300.

Formulated differently: Saussure's method reminds us of the Marxian distinction between the trajectory of research and the trajectory of explanation, which, for example, in the case of *Capital*, move to a large extent in opposite directions. Echeverría, who as we have seen wants to link Marx with semiotics, also seeks to employ a similar method in his research. For the analysis of the general fact of the production and consumption of objects, he refers largely to the production/consumption of signs. He does not choose this approach because the latter are more important than other forms of production/consumption, but quite simply because it is in these that we can grasp something general, and moreover because the production/consumption of anything, and above all with reference to use-value, always contains a production/consumption of signs.

Once this has been clarified, we must state the fact that there is a broad presence of communicative elements in material reproduction itself. On this point, one could feel tempted to say lightly: 'naturally, since to organise the process of reproduction it is necessary to communicate, it is necessary to discuss projects, to resolve problems orally and to carry out other linguistic acts'. While this is correct, it is not the central aspect of Echeverría's understanding of how similar and interwoven reproduction and communication are. Rather, he sees in the very production and consumption of these use-values an act of 'communication',[130] and possibly the most decisive communicative act for

---

130   Already in his earliest works, Echeverría suggests the importance of other types of 'languages' distinct from commonplace ones. However, in so doing he does not refer to economic praxis, as in his more recent works, but rather to political praxis, and above all its revolutionary form. See, in this regard: 'The guerrilla speaks in his own way, and his word, unlike all the others, is understandable: he prefers to speak the language of violence; his allocutions are armed actions against the enemy. For the guerrilla discursive propaganda is essential, but this arrives afterward, when it can fall upon fertile soil.

'The revolutionary communists have learned from historical materialism that to speak on the stage of the class struggle is something more than exchanging words, flyers, or insults; that all social institutions to which spoken language pertains form a system of persuasion, structured in a single direction: toward an apologia for relations of production which represent the apologia of the class that has created those relations and maintains their functioning; that, even if the action undertaken is totally negative for the existing social order, it is enough to recognize the validity of the institutional system for the effort to be lost and aligned with the general apologia. Revolutionary communists know that this ideological system of bourgeois institutions grounds the force of their conviction regarding the violent repression of the communist social project, toward which the productive forces aspire and which is concretised in the interests of the proletarian class. They know that this reactionary violence manifests in different forms and with varying intensity. They see that the "argument" of violence is the only one capable of

social life itself. For example, to prepare a meal and the following act of eating it is, at the same time, to produce a determinate sign and to interpret it.

> To produce and consume objects is to produce and consume meanings [*significaciones*]. To produce is to communicate [*mitteilen*], to propose a use-value of nature to someone else; to consume is to interpret [*auslegen*], to validate this use-value that another has found. To appropriate nature is to make it meaningful [*significativa*].[131]

A brief mention of Sánchez Vázquez would be appropriate here. In his reflections on the relationship between praxis and knowledge, he shows that knowledge of objects is only possible insofar as these have already come into contact with human praxis. If we set out from Echeverría's analysis of the process of 'making something meaningful', which is to say, the act of granting things meaning, this is not something which is discretionary or arbitrary; but if the meaning given to the objects has to do directly with their natural constitution, then this 'making something meaningful' can be conceived in a form similar to the 'recognition of an object'.[132] A point in favour of the interpretation that Echeverría does not grasp this 'giving meaning' as an arbitrary act – as is the case in some tendencies of discourse theory – is his insistence on the primacy of matter. For Echeverría, this 'giving meaning' is a fundamentally material process, one that contains precisely the transformation of an object of nature into an object, which is important *vis-à-vis* human needs. But this transformation

---

    correcting the destructive effects of imperialist-bourgeois institutions on the proletariat of oppressed countries. They draw the conclusion that revolutionary violence is the only "counter-argument" which, in destroying bourgeois society, can "convince it" of its historic ineffectiveness' (Echeverría 1968, pp. 16f).

    It is clear that these formulations are separated by a chasm from the idea of a 'coercion-free discourse' or anything of the sort. While Echeverría criticises in other texts the 'myth of the revolution' and, in general, does not allow himself to be carried away with such incendiary formulations, the parallel with his current ideas is clear: 'spoken language' is not the only or even the determinant language for understanding, at least while humanity is not free.

131 Echeverría 1984, p. 42. Here, Echeverría refers to the following text: Leroi-Gourham 1964, p. 163.

132 In this regard, see for example Part Two: 'Adolfo Sánchez Vázquez – Praxis and Knowledge', the chapter 'Revolutionary praxis and everyday consciousness', and above all Sánchez Vázquez's critique of the objectivism linked to everyday consciousness, which contains the idea that the *meaning* of things is given to human beings almost by nature, p. 110 of this book.

cannot occur as an arbitrary act, since it must always necessarily take account of the natural constitution of the object. A cook, to keep this example, can only prepare a meal on the basis of *determinate* natural things, despite all the freedom he may have in that action, since if he truly wants to create a use-value he is obligated to prepare the piece of meat and not the plastic packaging that today almost always encases it.

Otherwise – and this can already be mentioned as a step toward Echeverría's other reflections – we find here an important difference with regard to the production of value, which tendentially can leave aside the real satisfaction of human needs, if only the creation of value and with it surplus value remains guaranteed. The catch lies in the fact that, after all, the production of value cannot completely refrain from the production of use-value, which is its 'natural' foundation. It is from this point, for Echeverría, that the possibility of overcoming the apparently eternal capitalist mode of production emerges. In his theories, Marx based his hopes for putting an end to the ruling relations – without the disappearance of the subjects who uphold them – on the fact that the current social formation cannot exist without proletarians, and yet they are the potential revolutionary subject. In contrast with this view, Echeverría is not fixated exclusively on production. His point of departure lies more in the unity of production and consumption, and with it, in the unity of the production of value and the production of use-value, since it is only in consumption that we can determine if an object effectively has use-value and with it value as well (which Marx formulates succinctly when he says that a product must realise its value in the market).[133] It is only a product's use-value that makes it possible for it to be really consumed and, therefore, to be bought in the first place. Thus, Echeverría, inspired by Marx, takes as his starting point the fact that the production of value does not proceed without the production of use-value, but rather that it simultaneously and by necessity controls, oppresses to an increasing degree, and tends toward the destruction of that use-value. This antagonistic contradiction inherent to the capitalist mode of production gives him some indication of a possible way out. Dogmatic, Soviet-style Marxism presumed that the way out lay in simply overcoming shortages of working-class consumer products, to be accomplished through a massive and

---

133 'Hence commodities must be realised as values before they can be realised as use-values.
    'On the other hand, they must stand the test as use-values before they can be realised as values. For the labour expended on them only counts in so far as it is expended in a form, which is useful for others. However, only the act of exchange can prove whether that labour is useful for others, and its product consequently capable of satisfying the needs of others' (Marx 1976a, pp. 179–80).

continuous increase in the productive forces, which in theory entailed a narrow productivism, a naïve progressivism, and the most brutal methods for increasing productivity under Stalinism.[134] Echeverría, like the majority of the thinkers of Western Marxism, believed that in quantitative terms, the question of supplying all human beings is one which was long since easily accomplishable through the deployment of a relatively limited amount of labour. According to him, the problem lies not in the quantitative, but in the qualitative: *what* is produced and *how* it is produced, or in other words, the question of production and consumption insofar as these refer to use-value: 'Only the reconstruction of the critical and radical concept of use-value can demonstrate the absence of a basis for that identification of Marxism with Western productivism, the economistic progressivism of capitalism, and bourgeois political statism'.[135]

In this passage, two themes are touched when Echeverría makes a critique of the 'identification of Marxism with Western productivism'; in the first place, he indicates the need for a critique of Eurocentrism, something which mostly has not be surmounted on the Left, even in important sectors of the non-dogmatic Left. Even the terminology of 'developed' and 'underdeveloped' countries – naïvely taken up all too often – expresses a deeply-rooted economistic productivism which underhandedly elevates the productive forces and its technical-industrial perfection (in the sense of being competitive under capitalist conditions) to the characteristic of 'development' in general. At the same time, this includes the presumption of a 'natural' need for a constant further development of the productive forces in the previously indicated sense (moreover, in very determined ways), which, however, is an unavoidable necessity exclusively under ruling social conditions. In the framework of this

---

134 Observe also, in this respect, the powerfully Eurocentric tendency of Stalinism, in which the scarce efforts (by Lenin, above all) in the first post-revolutionary years to eliminate or soften racist oppression toward the non-Russian inhabitants of the Soviet Union (efforts which materialised as a degree of sovereignty, in particular autonomous regions under the banner of different nationalities), were practically abandoned, restoring the Tsarist model of Russian control over the entire territory.

   Otherwise, it is very significant in this context that critiques of the Soviet Union – be they from conservative or leftist positions – the theme of racism is very rarely present, and in the case of the first position, the USSR is designated unhesitatingly as 'Russia', not with an air of critical irony but of Tsarist Eurocentrism.

135 Echeverría 1984, p. 34 n4. The cited phrase continues: '[an identification] that led K. Korsch in 1950 ... to raise again, for the second half of the century, the theme, vulgarised in the 70s, of the inadequacy of Marxist discourse for the requirements of the new historical form of the revolution'. Echeverría is here referring to '10 Thesen über Marxismus heute': Korsch 1965, pp. 89–90.

logic, then, some countries are 'more developed' than others, but the resulting hierarchisation of the world acquires a life of its own and continues to function even in the heads of critics of the capitalist mode of production. (In a certain sense, Eurocentrism is more problematic on the Left than in conservative theory. For conservatives, Eurocentrism emerges necessarily from their uncritical reflection on power relations; on the Left, on the contrary, it can only be explained as an ideological remnant of cultural chauvinism).[136]

Secondly, this passage cited from Echeverría contains, moreover, an implicit response to a philosopher whose work kept our author occupied during many years of his youth. When Echeverría insists that Marx does not constitute an integral part of 'Western' thought, but that the concept of use-value 'necessarily moves beyond Western metaphysics',[137] we are dealing with an unequivocal rejection of Martin Heidegger's assertion that Karl Marx is the ultimate representative of Western metaphysics.

---

136 In this Echeverría can be distinguished – despite all the similarities – from Western Marxism and the Frankfurt School. Thus, for example, while the critique and analysis of *Dialectic of Enlightenment* admittedly mentions 'European civilisation' as the central object of the investigation, its ethnocentric character is not taken as a theme (Horkheimer and Adorno 2002, p. 9). Neither in its scientific behaviour nor in its interests has the Frankfurt School been able to remove itself from common Eurocentric prejudice, and it has largely ignored authors from the so-called Third World.

But despite these circumstances, this theoretical focus has elements that can be useful for a critical theory of Eurocentrism and racism. We could realise this in various seminars given in Mexican universities where, for example, reading the chapter about 'Elements of Anti-Semitism' of the aforementioned book provoked revealing discussions regarding internal racism within Mexico – almost always targeting indigenous people – which duplicates the effects of Eurocentrism in the country, and as a result the text has been taken as a theoretical foundation for research on this topic. There are, of course, serious differences between anti-Semitism and racism against indigenous people, but combining a critique of the naïve belief in enlightenment with an analysis of the causes of the persecution of Mexican minorities is so stimulating precisely because also in Mexico the idea is very widespread that an application of the ideals of the French Revolution can resolve all the country's ills almost miraculously. But if we recognise that it is not an 'incomplete modernity' that stokes racism, but, instead, that this racism brings modernity to its perfect expression in its own contradiction, this could help us to avoid errors in Mexico before they are committed with the same perfection as they were in Europe. This aspiration to imitate the errors of 'European civilisation' is actually the common denominator of both the Left and of conservatives in Mexico, and is described as the 'modernisation' and 'democratisation' that is demanded and sometimes celebrated by all.

137 Echeverría 1984, p. 35 n4.

b   Use-Value and Signs

With regard to the question of how we can think the relationship between subject and object as profoundly marked by determination (by the laws of nature, for example), as well as and at the same time by human freedom, we can sketch out Echeverría's effort to approach the question in the following terms. As indicated, it is possible to trace the parallel between the processes of reproduction and communication without de-materialising the former or reinterpreting it idealistically. But in the process of communication we find the peculiarity of this same singular coexistence of freedom and new creation in each speech-act and the simultaneous determination by the language in which the communication occurs in each case. It is only because in each moment a new speech act with a certain degree of freedom is created that the speaker can more or less correspond to each constellation that he should capture. But at the same time, he only can make himself understood to another, because he moves within the respective language and broadly accepts its rules.

Something similar can be said of the production and consumption of use-values. The producer cannot simply fabricate anything whatsoever if he wants it to be recognised by others as a use-value, which is to say, to be purchased. Here, it is not merely the biological capacity of the human organism to consume determinate products that is decisive. It is precisely here that the decisive difference between humans and animals lies. In the human being, the process of distinguishing between a useful and a useless thing, which is to say between use-value and non-use-value, is largely influenced by historical factors. Marx already indicates as much in the previously cited passage: 'The discovery ... of the manifold uses of things is the work of history'.[138] In Echeverría's exposition of Marx's theory of use-value, the concept of history additionally includes geographical 'asynchronies' (in the sense that place, and not only time, also enters into historical factors).

In the comparison of reproduction with communication, it is of great importance that in both processes we find those instances that the founder of semiotics distinguishes as 'signified' and 'signifier', whose unity is represented

---

138   Marx 1976a, p. 125. [Note to the Spanish-language edition: Where 'the work of history' appears in the Spanish-language edition of *Capital*, Scaron translates 'geschichtliche Tat' as 'hecho histórico' ['historical fact'], which comes too close to positivist jargon. Considering the significant harm that the positivist influence has provoked in Marxism, especially in its dogmatic orientation, we decided to translate the phrase as 'acto histórico' ['historical act'], which restores the concept of praxis implicit in Marx's formulation: S.G. (See Marx 1975a, pp. 49f, and Marx 1975b, p. 44.)]

by the sign. In language, the first represents the 'concept' and the second the 'acoustic image'. The pure concept, however, contains just as few as the pure image; both are, thrown back on their own resources, lost, or to put it more precisely, not imaginable as isolated from each other. So, for example, Saussure suggests that the presumption of a pure concept, without an image, contains the thought that there can exist mature ideas prior to their linguistic expression,[139] a view that he clearly rejects.

Before again broaching the comparison with the production of use-values, we must moreover keep in mind the fact that Echeverría, in referring to Walter Benjamin, takes as his point of departure the fact that human beings express themselves and make themselves understood not only *through* languages but also *in them*, which should be understood to mean that languages are not fixed systems which are merely employed as means of communication, but are created anew and modified with each communicative act.[140] Echeverría interprets Benjamin's claim as one, which is valid for all sign systems,[141] but just

---

139   Echeverría 1984 p. 97.
140   Echeverría refers here to Walter Benjamin's 'Über Sprache überhaupt und über die Sprache des Menschen': Benjamin 1966, pp. 10f. See Echeverría 1984, p. 44 n31.
141   Echeverría 1984, p. 44. 'Like the instrumental field to which it pertains, the code has a history because the process of communication/interpretation is not only fulfilled *with* it but also *in* it; because in serving on the evident level, it is itself modified on the profound level. In principle, every time the code is used in the production/consumption of meanings, its project of meaning is put into play and can be at risk of ceasing to be what it is. The project of meaning, which is the establishment of a horizon of possible meanings, can be transcended by another project and move on to constitute the *substantial stratum of a new establishment of semiotic possibilities* [*posibilidades sémicas*]. In truth the history of the code takes place as a succession of layers of patterns for meaning, resulting from the refunctionalisation – more or less deep and more or less broad – of earlier projects for new meaning-granting impulses' (pp. 44f).

In this regard, see moreover a similar reference to the same text by Benjamin elsewhere: 'In Benjamin's essay *On Language in General and Human Language in Particular* an idea predominates which has been central to the history of twentieth-century thought... human beings do not only speak *with* a language, using it as an instrument, but, above all, speak *in* that language... In principle, in all singular speaking it is the language that is expressed. But also – and with an equal hierarchy – all singular speaking involves that language as a totality. The entire speech [lenguaje] is in play in every individual act of expression; what each of those acts does or ceases to do alters that language in an essential way. The specific language is nothing less than the totalisation of all of these speakings' (from 'La identidad evanescente', in Echeverría 1995a, p. 60).

The text in question was publicly presented for the first time in February of 1991 in the form of a speech at the First Hispano-American Encounter of Essays and Literature, in

as every speech-act or speaking ['*parole*' in Saussure] calls into question the language as a totality ['*langue*' in Saussure], the same occurs in the production and consumption of use-values.

According to our explanation above, Echeverría understands the unity of the production and consumption of use-values in the same way that semiotics understands *langage* [speech], as the faculty of speech, or, in other words, the capacity to make oneself understood in a way that, is not chaotic, but nevertheless free. Not free in the sense that completely new signs can be invented at any moment out of nothing, because in this case, in the end, the very functioning of the sign system would be put into doubt,[142] but at least free enough for us not to communicate merely as animals, according to forms of stimulus and reaction which are fixed by the biological, in the instincts.[143]

So, in the act of producing a use-value, we simultaneously find the production of a sign, and its consumption, its interpretation. Here, we also have a signifier and a signified, which, together, constitute a sign. Echeverría does not tell the reader in a totally unambiguous way which is the signifier and which is the signified in the sign contained in the use-value. But in one place, he

---

the Faculty of Philosophy and Arts of the UNAM (see Echeverría 1995a, p. 199). Echeverría here confuses concepts when he suddenly speaks of 'lenguaje' ['speech'] when what we can determine unequivocally from the context, and above all the preceding phrase, is that he means to say 'lengua' ['language'].

142 Saussure says in this regard: 'Language is no longer free, for time will allow the social forces at work on it to carry out their effects. This brings us back to the principle of continuity, which cancels freedom. But continuity necessarily implies change, varying degrees of shifts in the relationship between the signified and the signifier' (Saussure 1966, p. 78).

But the moment of the absence of freedom, which Saussure emphasises, only applies to the specific language, the *langue*, and not to the ability of speaking in its totality (*langage* or *faculté de langage* in Saussure's original text in French, *speech* or *faculty of speech* in the English translation of Saussure's text, *lenguaje* or *facultad de lenguaje* in the Spanish translation of Saussure's text and in Echeverría's article), which, as we will see below, of significant importance for Echeverría's reflections.

143 For the process of production, Marx formulates this difference between animals and humans in the following famous passage: 'A spider conducts operations which resemble those of the weaver, and a bee would put many a human architect to shame by the construction of its honeycomb cells. But what distinguishes the worst architect from the best of bees is that the architect builds the cell in his mind before he constructs it in wax. At the end of every labour process, a result emerges which had already been conceived by the worker at the beginning, hence already existed ideally. Man not only effects a change of form in the materials of nature; he also realizes [*verwirklicht*] his own purpose in those materials. And this is a purpose he is conscious of, it determines the mode of his activity with the rigidity of a law, and he must subordinate his will to it' (Marx 1976a, p. 284).

observes that raw materials tend to come nearer to the signified, and the used instruments of labour nearer to the signifier, but without pigeonholing them definitively.[144] Rather, it would seem that both raw materials and instruments of labour can possess both functions, but that the second element plays a predominant position in the generation of signs in general.[145]

But the instruments of labour (tools) are distinguished because their effectiveness, in most cases, is not exhausted in a single combined act of production/consumption, as occurs with those use-values which are immediately consumed as food. This tendency toward durability in the instrument of labour[146] draws us much closer to a solution to our previously mentioned doubt, since here the parallel with other sign systems becomes clearer, a parallel which up to this point perhaps remained in a degree of obscurity. Just as we do not speak *through language* but rather *in it*, so we produce not only through an instrument of labour, but rather in it. On the one hand, in many cases these are of a durable nature but, on the other hand, they are exposed in most cases to the possibility of a constant transformation. In mentioning this, we are not referring only to their wearing out, but to the constantly emerging need (or also the desire arising in the subject) to transform them. As a result, we can broaden the parallel to Saussure's semiotics in the sense that every singular act of production (and also of consumption) of a use-value is a *parole*, or speaking, but

---

144 'Among the means that intervene in productive consumption there are some that only offer it an indication of form for themselves: raw materials or objects of labour; there are others, by contrast, that open up before labour itself an entire set of possibilities for giving form, between which labour can choose for transforming raw materials: these are *instruments*' (Echeverría 1984, pp. 40f, italics by S.G.).

145 'The most completed form of the social object is without a doubt that of the *instrument*. In it, the two tensions that determine all objective forms – the pretension of a form for the subject and his disposition to adopt it – remain in a state of confrontation, in an unstable equilibrium that can be decided differently in each case. The proposition of a formative action on raw materials, inscribed in the instrumental form as a technical structure, not only allows – as in all social objects – but also demands, to be effective, a formative will to action that takes it up and makes it concrete. The general transformative dynamic that the instrument entails must be completed and singularised by labour' (Echeverría 1984, p. 41).

Echeverría refers, here, to the following passage in *Capital*: 'Living labour must seize on these things, awaken them from the dead, change them from merely possible into real [*wirklich*] and effective [*wirkend*] use-values' (Marx 1976a, p. 289.) Original: 'Die lebendige Arbeit muß diese ergreifen, sie von den Toten erwecken, sie aus nur möglichen in wirkliche und wirkende Gebrauchswerte verwandeln' (Marx 1975a, p. 198).

146 On the problem of the durability of the instrument, see the following subchapter, and above all the reflections on the concept of the tool in Hegel, pp. 247ff in this book.

the totality of these acts in a particular society,[147] under particular conditions and in a particular historical epoch, can be understood as *langue*, as language.

c Marx's Theory of Tools

The problem in the previous reflections (on the question of the 'signified' and 'signifier') which has not been completely resolved – regarding the relationship between the instrument of labour and the object of labour,[148] and, therefore, also of the relationship of the tool to raw materials – points to the need to refer to Marx's 'theory of the tool'.[149] For Marx, all that which humans find pre-existing on Earth and on which they can work can be considered an 'object of labour'. Therefore, the Earth in its totality constitutes an 'object of labour' for the human beings who inhabit it.[150] Here, Marx distinguishes between 'objects of labour spontaneously provided by nature', which humans merely 'separate from immediate connection with their environment', and 'raw material'.[151] The 'raw material' is differentiated from the 'object of labour' in that it has already

---

147 This concept should be clarified precisely, since within a single society there can exist various codes at the same moment. Echeverría speaks elsewhere of 'a subjective-objective being, provided with a particular historic-cultural identity..., the historico-concrete existence of the productive and consumptive forces, that is,...the substance of the nation' (from 'El problema de la nación desde la "Crítica de la economía política"', in Echeverría 1986, pp. 192f.)

　　With this, he could be speaking of the subsystems of a society in which, in each case, codes predominate that are more or less unified. But since this concept of the 'substance of the nation' (transformed elsewhere into that of the 'natural nation') is problematic to us, we do not want to use it here without a critical introduction. Here a problem emerges which is generally present in Echeverría's theory. On the one hand, it is suitable for indicating the internal differences within a society and also within the social system today organised on a global level and to make of these objects of investigation, but it pays the prices of returning to highly dubious conceptualisations like that of the 'substance of the nation', which fall short with relation to the general concept of society. [Note to the edition in English: Compare also on the translation of Saussure's term 'parole': 'I shall call the executive side *speaking* (*parole*)': Saussure 1966, p. 13.]

148 'The simple elements of the labour process are (1) purposeful activity, that is work itself, (2) the object on which that work is performed, and (3) the instruments of that work' (Marx 1976a, p. 284).

149 See, in this regard, Schmidt 1971, pp. 99–107, here: p. 103.

150 Marx 1976a, p. 284. Today even the Moon and outer space have begun to serve as objects of labour for humans, albeit only in an experimental stage at this point.

151 Ibid.

undergone a treatment which goes beyond mere detachment from nature as a whole, 'for example, ore already extracted and ready for washing', which has thus already been 'filtered through previous labour'.[152] Hence, the concept of the object of labour is broader than that of raw materials.[153] Evidently, for Marx something analogous happens with the conceptual pairing of 'instrument of labour' and 'tool': 'An instrument of labour is a thing, or a complex of things, which the worker interposes between himself and the object of his labour and which serves as a conductor, directing his activity onto that object. He makes use of the mechanical, physical and chemical properties of some substances in order to set them to work on other substances as instruments of his power, and in accordance with his purposes'.[154]

But Marx understands the instruments of labour, which have already been transformed by human labour, as 'tools'.[155] This concept of the tool as an already-produced instrument of labour can also be found in Benjamin Franklin's definition of the human being as a 'tool-making animal'.[156] Marx does not make this distinction between instruments of labour in general and those which are produced – that is, tools – as unequivocally as the previously mentioned distinction between objects of labour in general and those which have been worked, which is to say, raw materials. In any case, Marx repeatedly

---

152 Ibid.
153 'All raw material is an object of labour [*Arbeitsgegenstand*], but not every object of labour is raw material; the object of labour counts as raw material only when it has already undergone some alteration by means of labour' (Marx 1976a, pp. 284–5).
154 Marx 1976a, p. 285.
155 Compare: 'As soon as the labour process has undergone the slightest development, it requires specially prepared instruments. Thus we find stone tools [*Werkzeug*] and weapons in the oldest caves' (ibid.)
156 Benjamin Franklin, cited according to Marx 1976a, p. 286.

Elsewhere in *Capital*, Marx contrasts this definition to that of Aristotle's definition, according to which the human being is 'by nature a citizen of a town'. While this is 'characteristic of classical antiquity', Franklin's definition is 'characteristic of Yankeedom'. This should not be understood to mean that, in Marx's opinion, Franklin's definition is only valid for the United States, but merely that it goes hand-in-hand with the ideology of that society (Marx 1976a, p. 444 n7). Marx, generally quite succinct in his use of reflections on 'human nature', makes use of both authors on this question, albeit with the limitation that 'man, if not as Aristotle thought a political animal, is at all events a social animal' (Marx 1976a, p. 444). We can observe a certain distance between Marx and the authors in question, due to the ideological tendency of the latter, which expresses something about the problem forcibly confronted by critical theory when it attempts to formulate assertions regarding 'human nature'. (Some years ago, the first systematic study of this problem in Herbert Marcuse appeared: Bundschuh 1998).

observes the particularity which characterises the 'instruments [of labour] [*Arbeitsmittel*]...which have already been mediated through past labour' from those pre-existing instruments of labour which are used just as they were found.[157]

One explanation of the fact that Marx uses the term 'tool' rarely, employing instead 'instrument of labour', can consist in the fact that, effectively, today there exist fewer instruments of labour that have yet to be transformed by humans than there exist objects of labour which are still untransformed. Also, in the history of humanity – for example, in the material remains of extinct civilisations – it is easier to demonstrate the use of the latter than the former. While in unelaborated instruments of labour it is possible that, in dropping them after use, they leave no or little trace of that use, it is a different matter with objects of labour which have not been previously worked-upon, since in most cases these form a material part of the final product. In strictly logical terms, it is also correct to substitute the term tool for that of instrument of labour, since 'tool' is a subcategory of 'instrument of labour', and consequently, every tool is also always an instrument of labour. The problem here is that the readers could get confused and create the impression that Marx used the two terms 'instruments of labour' and 'tool' synonymously.[158]

The consequences of this problem are not immediately serious because Marx, in his analysis, does not study closely those instruments of labour which are not themselves procured through labour, but instead refers almost always in his examples to those which have been produced.[159] In discussions of the

---

157 Among other things, Marx distinguishes between instruments of labour 'in general' and those 'already mediated by labour,' referring to the subcategory of those which, without intervening directly in the labour process, are nevertheless its unconditional premise: 'Once again, the earth itself is a universal *instrument* of this kind, for it provides the worker with the ground beneath his feet and a "field of employment" for his own particular process. *Instruments* of this kind, which have *already been mediated through past labour*, include workshops, canals, roads, etc.' (Marx 1976a, pp. 286–7, italics by S.G.). [Note to the edition in English: Fowkes here translates Marx's concept of 'Arbeitsmittel' simply as 'instrument'. In other cases, mentioned above, he translates the same term more precisely as 'instrument of labour' (Compare Marx 1975a, p. 195).]

When Marx separately mentions the use and construction of instruments of labour' he equally indicates the conceptual difference between instruments of labour in general and their elaborated form, which is to say, tools: all instruments of labour are used, but only tools are fabricated (Marx 1976a, p. 286).

158 Alfred Schmidt also refers to 'the instrument of labour, which was for Marx identical with the tool' (Schmidt 1971, p. 103).

159 See, for example, Marx's mention of the oldest known human instruments of labour, in which he emphasises their character as a tool, that is, their having been made available previously through human labour: 'domesticated animals, i.e. animals that have

relationship between labour and external nature in Marx's work, some maintain the thesis that Marx himself, in granting primacy to the analysis of value in *Das Kapital*, implicitly discarded use-value as secondary – which is to say, the process of production and reproduction with reference to the natural – and thereby fostered the destruction of nature, practiced by or at least rarely criticised by actually-existing socialism and different forms of Marxism.[160] This argument does not withstand close inspection if we take into account the high esteem in which Marx holds external nature, which has not been mediated by labour.

According to Alfred Schmidt, Marx's theory of the tool in *Das Kapital* is that of 'the existing, the materialised mediator between the labourer and the object of labour [*Arbeitsgegenstand*]'.[161] In saying this, he stresses the importance of tool-making for the entirety of human development, and above all the development of human intellectual capacities: 'There can be hardly any doubt that the most basic abstractions have arisen in the context of labour-processes, i.e. in the context of tool-making'.[162]

In this sense, Echeverría's attempt to see a parallel between the processes of production and communication stands in the non-dogmatic Marxist tradition, above all if we bear in mind the fact that after the 'linguistic turn' in idealist and related philosophies, the concept of spirit or reason was generally substituted by that of communication or discourse. To the question of whether or not Echeverría's attempt makes him an idealist philosopher, we could respond that in such matters a separation cannot always be established with the kind of clarity we find in the textbooks of dogmatic Marxism. In this context, it is worth emphasising the close consistency between Hegel and Marx regarding the theory of the tool. In this respect, Schmidt underlines Hegel's contribution

---

undergone *modification by means of labour*, that have been bred specially, play the chief part as instruments of labour along with stones, wood, bones and shells, which have *also had work done on them*' (Marx 1976a, pp. 285–6, italics by S.G.).

160 On this discussion, see moreover Alfred Schmidt's prologue to the most recent edition of his book on the concept of nature in Marx (Schmidt 1993, pp. I–XVII.). Likewise, see the subchapter 'Marx as the Founder of the Critical Concept of Use-Value', pp. 215ff of this book.

161 Schmidt 1971, p. 103. [Note to the edition in English: Fowkes here translates (in 1971) 'Arbeitsgegenstand' as 'subject of labour', as it was used in the English translation of *Capital* published in Moscow. Fowkes revises that in 1975, when elaborating his own English version of *Capital*, and translates 'Arbeitsgegenstand' now more precisely as 'object of labour', as quoted several times above. (Compare: Schmidt 1971, p. 102; and Marx 1954, pp. 125ff.)]

162 Schmidt 1971, p. 102.

to understanding the tight relationship between the development of tools and the human capacity for communication:

> Hegel, as well as Marx, was aware of the historical interpenetration of intelligence, language and the tool. The tool connects man's purposes with the object of his labour. It brings the conceptual element, logical unity, into the human mode of life. Hegel wrote in the *Jenenser Realphilosophie* [the Jena manuscripts]: 'The *tool* is the existent rational mean, the existent universality of the practical process; it appears on the side of the active against the passive, is itself passive in relation to the labourer, and active in relation to the object of labour'.[163]

It is precisely in Hegel's linking of the processes of production and communication in his formulations on the tool that Schmidt sees Hegel's importance for historical materialism.[164] Incidentally, this importance of Hegel for the Marxian theory of the tool is recognised by Marx himself. In his discussion of the tool in *Capital*, Marx cites Hegel's understanding of the 'cunning of reason' in an effort to understand philosophically the 'cunning of man' in the use of tools,[165] as Schmidt describes it in summarising Marx. The human being – Marx writes – 'makes use of the mechanical, physical and chemical properties of some substances in order to set them to work on other substances as instruments of his power, and in accordance with his purposes'.[166] In a footnote inserted at this point in *Capital*, Marx immediately quotes the following well-known phrase from Hegel's *Logic*: 'Reason is as cunning as it is powerful. Cunning may be said to lie in the intermediative action which, while it permits the objects to follow their own bent and act upon one another till they waste away, and does not itself directly interfere in the process, is nevertheless only working out its own aims'.[167]

---

163 Ibid. Here Schmidt cites Hegel 1932, p. 221.
164 Schmidt notes: 'Lenin stated correctly that Hegel was a precursor of historical materialism because he emphasised the role played by the tool both in the labour-process and in the process of cognition' (Schmidt 1971, p. 105).
165 Ibid.
166 Marx 1976a, p. 285.
167 Hegel 1986, §209, appendix, p. 365. Cited according to Marx 1976a, p. 285 n2.
  Compare, moreover, Hegel's observations which precede his reflections on tools in the *Logic*: 'That the end relates itself immediately to an object and makes it a means... may be regarded as *violence*... But that the end posits itself in a *mediate* relation with the object and *interposes* another object *between* itself and it, may be regarded as the *cunning* of reason'. Hegel 2002, p. 746.

Despite this direct reference by Marx to Hegel in the context of his theory of the tool, we must note an important difference between the two philosophers. Alfred Schmidt draws attention to the fact that 'Marx had a far lower estimation' of the tool than did Hegel.[168] The latter viewed the ends of production as subordinated to its means, since the end is finite, and, therefore, 'it is not an absolute, nor simply something that in its own nature is *rational*'.[169] The tool, on the contrary, as the '*means* is *superior* to the *finite* ends of *external* purposefulness: the *plough* is more honourable than are immediately the enjoyments procured by it and which are ends'.[170] On the contrary, for Marx the tool is not something completely extrinsic to the product, and nor does he subordinate the latter to the former in terms of its capacity to immediately satisfy human needs, as does Hegel; while for Hegel the presumed durability of tools situates them on a higher level *vis-à-vis* those products which are extinguished in consumption,[171] Marx – here moving completely within the materialist tradition, which was generally far from asceticism and opposed to it – 'had no intention of deriving any arguments against the satisfactions of the senses from their transitory nature'.[172]

Moreover, the relative durability of tools, a trait which according to Hegel distinguishes them from products, is not always a given. Alfred Schmidt understands the Marxian definition of the tool as a 'mediator between labour with a definite aim and its object', and setting out from this, he distinguishes 'three forms of tool':[173] 'The tool can maintain itself in its identical form, it can enter materially into the produce of labour and, finally, it can be completely consumed, without becoming part of the product of labour'.[174]

---

168 Schmidt 1971, p. 104. See also, on Marx: 'He was wary of fetishizing the tool in relation to the immediate use-values created with its help, as Hegel had done' (ibid.).
169 Hegel 2002, p. 747.
170 Ibid. [Note to the edition in English: the immediate philosophical relationship between Hegel's *Logic* and Marx's *Capital* gets lost for the reader in English on account of the different ways in which the German term 'Mittel' is translated: in the *Logic*'s case as 'means', and in *Capital* as 'instrument', for example in the case of the central Marxian concept of 'Arbeitsmittel' translated by Fowkes as 'instrument of labour', instead of 'means of labour', as mentioned above.]
171 'The *tool* lasts, while the immediate enjoyments pass away and are forgotten. In his tools man possesses power over external nature, even though in respect of his ends he is, on the contrary, subject to it' (ibid.).
172 Schmidt 1971, p. 104.
173 Schmidt 1971, p. 103.
174 Ibid.

It is evident that of these three types of tool, Hegel knows only the first. If Schmidt understands this as a limitation of the dialectical idealist's understanding of the tool, he clarifies that 'it had an element of truth in it, in that most tools remain the same in use, and are foreign to their product'.[175] In this respect, Hegel has limited his philosophical reflection to the predominant form of tool. In any case, we can see the degree to which the materialist Marx grasps reality better than Hegel, moreover, in the fact that he understands just how relative the conceptual determinations of these various objects with regard to their position in the labour process are.[176] This is no small thing, since their durability and perishability are also merely relative qualities with reference to other components of the labour process, and are not absolute as Hegel suggests with his categorical judgement that those components which do not constitute tools 'pass away and are forgotten'.[177]

At this point, we can return to Bolívar Echeverría's studies on the role of use-value in the process of reproduction and on the possible application of the semiotic categories of 'signifier' and 'signified' to this process and its objects. The above-mentioned vagueness as to whether the tool constitutes the signifier and the raw material the signified should be discussed as follows. At first glance, the response to this question would be the following: the tool is the signifier, the raw material the signified. But with this we would come too close to Hegel's concept of the tool, not only in his tendency to establish a hierarchy between tool and raw material, but moreover the danger of favouring a static assignment (which we just criticised) of specific components of the process of reproduction to some pre-given role.

Certainly, we could say that the Hegelian conception could grasp these components again at any moment of production, and that insofar as his philosophy is dialectical, he ought to be able to understand conceptually the double form of objects. However, Hegel's emphatic discourse on the tool as the 'more honourable' and his disparaging valorisation of consumption indicate a static element in his theory. The concept of 'productive consumption',[178] which is

---

175 Ibid.
176 'Hence we see that whether a use-value is to be regarded as raw material, as instrument of labour or as product is determined entirely by its specific function in the labour process, by the position it occupies there: as its position changes, so do its determining characteristics'; and 'Again, a particular product may be used as both instrument of labour and raw material in the same process. Take, for instance, the fattening of cattle, where the animal is the raw material, and at the same time an instrument for the production of manure' (Marx 1976a, pp. 288–9).
177 Hegel 2002.
178 Marx 1976a, p. 290.

central for Marx and indicates precisely the difficulty of fixing determinate elements of reproduction on one factor and in one static form, as does Hegel, is unfamiliar to the great dialectician, who, in his turn, gave Marx important indications for his theory of the tool.

The fact that Echeverría scarcely touches on the question of signifier and signified in social reproduction (and in the end, leaves this question unresolved) could, therefore, be interpreted as follows: Echeverría perceives the concomitant danger of an idealist reduction of the Marxian theory of the tool and of reproduction. He wants to enrich or make more comprehensible the Marxian theory of use-value through the semiotic approach, while simultaneously avoiding the possibility of an idealistic softening of the Marxian critique.

d Concept of Concrete Universalism

At this point, the reader might be asking him- or herself: and all this, what is it good for? What does this confrontation of the production and consumption of use-values with semiotics clarify that could not be clarified in some other manner? To such a question, we see two possible responses: on the one hand, Echeverría's recourse to the semiotic approach should be understood as polemical. In understanding the production and consumption of use-values as the most fundamental of semiotic systems, he is taking the wind out of the sails of those theoretical currents which, without the least consideration, declare spoken language to be the most important of human sign systems. We must, then, liberate semiotics from the slavery into which it has fallen, *after Ferdinand de Saussure*, at the hands of linguistics, and as the mere supplier of the latter:

> ... do you see it like these 'radical' discourse theorists, for whom the only thing that exists is discourse?
> No, to the contrary; precisely against this tendency of the most radical structuralism, I tried to disconnect semiotics from structuralism as far as possible and integrate it into Marx's conceptual apparatus.[179]

On the other hand, we could give the following answer to the same question: through the combination of Marxian theory with Saussure's semiotics, Echeverría seeks to oppose a specific interpretation of the former. According to this interpretation, what is decisive in the relations of production is the

---

179 Fifth interview with Bolívar Echeverría, cassette 1, side A, pos. 258–65.

value side of production; on the basis of this, we can explain and evaluate everything else, which is to say, including the use-value side of production. This view results in the fact that the use-values produced in the framework of a society in which there exists a relatively high degree of industrialisation will lead them to be automatically conceived as 'more developed' than others. And, moreover, since it is known that use-values are in every case connected with the cultural constitution of a country, one can draw the conclusion that particular cultural forms are 'more developed' than others merely because they are found in a region in which a higher degree of industrialisation reigns than in other regions. Even if there are ever fewer theories explicitly defending such a view in an aggressive manner, this is, nevertheless, implicitly the prevailing view in everyday life as in the sciences. The fact that it is not proclaimed all the time does not for a moment undermine its almost absolute omnipresence between the lines.

One example from everyday life in Mexico would be the predilection of the urban middle class for white bread, above all sliced bread for toasting ['*pan bimbo*']. From a medical and nutritional perspective, such bread has an incomparably inferior use-value to corn tortillas, which are more common among the poor population in fulfilling the same function of accompanying meals. But as white bread is identified with a culture that has become predominant due to a more powerful development of productive forces (and with these, weaponry as well) and due to its empires – who with this development were thus in a position to dominate more than one continent – the middle class set out from the idea that nothing beats white bread. Even though the motives that are explicitly formulated for this choice may be different on any given occasion, that does not in the slightest degree alter the foundation of this preference.[180]

But we can also observe the same mechanism on the theoretical and political planes. Since the term 'underdeveloped countries' came under critique, these are now referred to as 'developing countries', or very fashionably as 'emerging countries'; however, it remains clear in which direction their aspiration points and to what they are aspiring, namely the threshold that must be crossed with the utmost haste: that leading to the 'first world', which also implies subordination to the cultural forms that prevail there. All of this terminology is not typically Marxist, although it also appears frequently at the heart of Marxist debates. In this form – lightly concealed – what prevails is the idea that sooner or later all human beings should live as the inhabitants of Europe and the United States live today, and that this will represent true 'development'.

---

180 'It's just that white bread tastes better', they say, which is true for some reason; many things taste better when in the vicinity of the powerful.

A fixation on the production and consumption of values, alongside a naïve progressivism, form an ideological breeding ground in which Eurocentrism is unlikely to cease to flourish.

It is even the case that political groups which consider themselves to be very much above such discussions, tend to be stuck up to their neck in them, although without wanting to realise it. But this becomes evident when their members arrive in peripheral countries and immediately protest when things move differently in local leftist organisations than they do in their country of birth, quickly suspecting that the level of local discussion has not flourished to the same extent as in the refuge of truth: Europe. The same can be said, in reverse, for Latin America, where for example many people on the Left yearn for nothing more than to travel to Europe in order to get to know as closely as possible the projects, theories, and discussions underway there. At the same time, the Mexican Left, for example, for the most part attempts – just as do the other national political currents – to imitate with the utmost perfection those European political tendencies to which they are similar, and in the best of cases to 'apply' their projects and ideologies to Mexico.[181]

On the contrary, the serenity with which Saussure places the many existing languages side-by-side, without undertaking the effort to establish hierarchies between them, is without a doubt what Echeverría appreciates in his work. And Echeverría imagines something similar for use-values: a sort of analysis which does not begin by considering some better than others merely on account of having emerged within the framework of a more industrialised form of value creation. In this context, it would also be interesting to study, without establishing hierarchies, the various existing regional forms of living and moving about intellectually in capitalist everydayness.

The application of Ferdinand de Saussure's semiotics to the theory of use-value therefore has the following facet: alongside *langue* [*language* in English, *idioma* in Spanish], that is to say, the totality of multiple productions and consumptions of use-values in a particular historical constellation, there exists moreover the general *langage* or *faculté de langage* [*speech* or *faculty of speech* in English, *lenguaje*, or *capacidad de hablar* in Spanish]. This is the fundamental point. What is specifically human – that is the question in Echeverría's article 'La "forma natural" de la reproducción social', and it is *not langue* (a particular language) but rather *langage*, the faculty of speech in and of itself.

---

181   The fact that the most diverse set of political tendencies have inscribed 'nationalism' on their flags does not change in the least their mimicry of the political models of the so-called First World. Nationalism itself is a typically European invention.

What distinguishes human beings and their self-creation is not a specific form of use-values that are made and used, but the very capacity to do so at all.

With the distinction of language from speech (faculty of speech) and the application of this distinction to the sphere of production, we can no longer arrive so easily at the conclusion that a determinate constellation of use-values exists in a state of 'superior' or 'inferior' development. Similarly, if we compare, for example, French to German, we cannot reasonably say that one is 'superior' to the other. So, in Saussure's theory, the things discussed are ones in which Marxist theories do not feature. Thus the Swiss Saussure speaks with an almost insurmountable naturalness about the 'differences among languages and... the very existence of different languages'.[182]

For him, there is absolutely no possibility of discussing whether a language is more valuable than another, or something of the like. Such questions absolutely do not exist for him.[183] This is what Saussure's semiotics and linguistics can teach us: what unifies humans is not their common language, but rather the common faculty of speech they share. Or, better put, their capacity to understand one another through signs, and in this speech is but one of many forms, the fundamental form being the production and consumption of use-values.

So Echeverría's interest in Saussurean semiotics can be understood as a theoretical auxiliary for combating 'false universalism', which is nothing more than the self-elevation of one existing particularity to the status of 'general' (for example, the self-elevation of European culture to the status of human

---

182   Saussure 1966, p. 68.
183   Here we will not go into where Saussure's position comes from. What is surprising, both in the cited passage as in others, is that as a general rule he derives his examples from French and German. In the history of Switzerland, we witness a process uncommon in Europe in the stability of its multilingual system which has not seen successful attempts to raise one language (French, Italian, Romansh, or German) into a position of dominance over the others, on the basis of it being purportedly 'better' or 'more developed'. The friends of 'purity' and enemies of the 'prisons of peoples [*Völkergefängnisse*],' a name that many like to give to multilingual states today, have not yet dared to propose the partition of Switzerland. It would seem as though Wilhelm Tell did not frighten them as much as Tito.

(Moreover, we must recognise the Swiss confederates [*Eidgenossen*] that were not as rebellious under Nazism as were the Yugoslav guerrillas, which can naturally only lead to a 'prison of peoples,' and this clarifies the meaning of the term, which designates an instance closed to the 'völkisch' [of the people, but in the racist sense of the National Socialists]. When Yugoslavia was called a 'prison of peoples,' what was meant is that it could be an instance restraining the free development of the racist and exclusionary idea of the 'people').

culture in general), and to do so without falling into a general whatever-ism. This is not to say that no universal exists, as many tend to argue today;[184] a universal factor that unites human beings does, indeed, exist, but it is one which allows within itself the most diverse of forms. This is the faculty of speech in its broadest sense, as discussed above, with the possibility that this entails (and realises) of the formation of the most diverse sign systems, which is to say, in other words, the most diverse ways of organising everyday life, assuring reproduction through the most diverse sorts of use-values.

Elsewhere, in the article 'La identidad evanescente' ['The Evanescent Identity'] Echeverría formulates a similar idea with regard to the non-Eurocentric approaches of Wilhelm von Humboldt, the founder of comparative philology, in the sense that beyond false and abstract Eurocentric universalism there can also exist a 'concrete universalism' in which subjects – individual as well as collective – are fully conscious of the need for the 'other', be it inside or outside themselves. The 'concrete universalism of a humanity which is at the same time unitary and unconditionally plural',[185] which is possible in principle in modernity, has, nevertheless, been impossible, due to the previous and present capitalist form of modernity and due to the 'artificial scarcity' which it necessarily produces.[186] This concrete universalism is already delineated in the

---

184 This seemingly 'plural' argument tends to serve as the basis for what in recent research on racism is called differential racism [*differentieller Rassismus*], which is distinct from racism of superiority [*superiorer Rassismus*], which was predominant, for example, in National Socialism or in classical colonial policy. The former is distinguished from the latter, since in it, the 'differences' of various 'cultures' – this tends to be the terminology – are emphasised, fixed, and celebrated, and all are claimed to be equal in value. But this fixing of differences brings with it a politics of 'maintaining the purity' of the different cultures, and thereby of keeping them separate. The absolute absence of critical moments then fixes the actually-existing inequalities in the social, economic, and political situation of the various countries as something almost pre-established by nature. In light of this, this ideology is equally racist as the reality it affirms. See Müller 1990.

This does not in any way contradict in principle the so-called postmodern search for difference, etc. See 'Modernidad e identidad' in Gandler 2009, pp. 118–27, in German: 'Moderne und Identität', in Gandler 2013b, pp. 115–24.

185 Echeverría , 'La identidad evanescente' in Echeverría 1995a, p. 59.

186 Ibid. Echeverría refers explicitly to Marx here, and writes: 'from an instrument of abundance, the technical revolution becomes, in the hands of capitalism, a generator of scarcity' (ibid.). This is necessary to maintain the capitalist mode of production, which functions only on the basis of exploiting the labour of others and, in turn, requires a general scarcity that, according to Marx, and followed on this point by Echeverría and other serious economists, under current technical conditions can only be guaranteed artificially

history of European theory, but only in the 'self-critical dimension of European culture'.

Echeverría writes: 'Humboldt's *Sprachphilosophie*...sought the general human [*lo humano*] more in the very capacity for symbolisation or "codification"...than in a specific result of certain particular symbolisations'.[187] Here, the vast gulf separating Bolívar Echeverría from the central tendencies of so-called postmodern theories becomes obvious. He is not interested in a simple condemnation of the concept of universalism, but rather a critique of the prevailing false universalism, which is abstract in nature, in favour of a 'concrete universalism' that takes as its point of departure that which all humans hold in common and which thus represents the possibility of their coexistence, while recognising at the same time the various different cultures and forms of life, without falsely (which is to say, abstractly) establishing hierarchies in that universalism in the sense of less or more developed forms of some general human culture – which is always, of course, that of the conquerors.

At this point, it would be worth asking, certainly, why it is that Echeverría does not refer to Marx himself for this critique of false universalism. Is it not possible to deal with the Eurocentric interpretations of Marx – as dominant as these may be within Marxism – on the basis of Marx himself, if we understand his critique of the capitalist mode of production as precisely a critique of the false universalisation that stands as its foundation? On the one hand, all human beings are themselves equated in the act of equating their products (for the purpose of being freely interchangeable); but, in any case, this is transformed into the root of the greatest form of inequality, that which exists between those who own the means of production and those who have nothing to sell except their labour power.[188]

(see ibid.). In this respect, *Capital* Vol. I, Chapter 15, 'Machinery and Large-Scale Industry': Marx 1976a, pp. 492ff.

187   Echeverría, 'La identidad evanescente' in Echeverría 1995a, p. 57 ['*Sprachphilosophie*' means 'philosophy of language'].

188   Marx emphasises his critique of the concept of equality in the 'Critique of the Gotha Programme', which could be read here as a critique of what Echeverría calls 'abstract universalism':

'In spite of this advance [in the proposals of the Gotha programme], this equal right is still constantly stigmatised by a bourgeois limitation. The right of the producers is *proportional* to the labour they supply; the equality consists in the fact that measurement is made with an *equal standard*, labour.

'But one man is superior to another physically, or mentally, and supplies more labour in the same time, or can labour for a longer time; and labour, to serve as a measure, must be defined by its duration or intensity, otherwise it ceases to be a standard of measurement.

The problem here is the following: even when the Eurocentrism of 'bourgeois stupidity' provokes disgust in Marx,[189] neither he nor Engels are always free of it, for example, when they say that countries like Mexico could experience nothing better than an occupation by the United States since this would finally make them a participant in a certain kind of *development* (which is, of course, 'universally human'). Just as in the problem of anti-Semitism, here we can find a contradiction internal to Marx's work. From his basic approach, his work is extremely critical toward the bourgeois abstract conception of equality, and he analyses not only the mendacity expressed in the bourgeois ideology of equality, but also the problematic of the idea of equality in general (which is also expressed in his rare mentions of communism, in thinking that an emancipated society is precisely that in which everyone receives according

---

This *equal* right is an unequal right for unequal labour. It recognizes no class differences, because everyone is only a worker like everyone else; but it tacitly recognizes unequal individual endowment, and thus productive capacity, as a natural privilege. It is, therefore, a right of inequality, in its content, like every right. Right, by its very nature, can consist only in the application of an equal standard; but unequal individuals (and they would not be different individuals if they were not unequal) are measurable only by an equal standard insofar as they are brought under an equal point of view, are taken from one definite side only – for instance, in the present case, are regarded *only as workers* and nothing more is seen in them, everything else being ignored. Further, one worker is married, another is not; one has more children than another, and so on and so forth. Thus, with an equal performance of labour, and hence an equal in the social consumption fund, one will in fact receive more than another, one will be richer than another, and so on. To avoid all these defects, right, instead of being equal, would have to be unequal'.

Marx's critique of the adoption by social democracy of bourgeois presumptions of equality and justice then leads up to the phrase, his most famous aside from the eleventh thesis on Feuerbach, on the possible slogan for a 'higher phase of communist society': 'From each according to his ability, to each according to his needs!' Marx 1970, pp. 13ff.

189   On Marx's rejection of bourgeois ethnocentrism, see his critique of Jeremy Bentham, or as he refers to him, 'that soberly pedantic and heavy-footed oracle of the "common sense" of the nineteenth-century bourgeoisie': 'Bentham does not trouble himself with this. With the dryest naïveté he assumes that the modern petty bourgeois, especially the English petty bourgeois, is the normal man. Whatever is useful to this peculiar kind of normal man, and to his world, is useful in and for itself. He applies this yardstick to the past, the present and the future. The Christian religion, for example, is "useful", "because it forbids in the name of religion the same faults that the penal code condemns in the name of the law". Art criticism is "harmful" because it disturbs worthy people in their enjoyment of Martin Tupper, etc. This is the kind of rubbish with which the brave fellow, with his motto "*nulla dies sine linea*", has piled up mountains of books. If I had the courage of my friend Heinrich Heine, I should call Mr Jeremy a genius in the way of bourgeois stupidity' (Marx 1976a, pp. 758–9 and n51).

to his needs and gives according to his capacities, with which the very idea of human equality perishes). But in isolated cases, remnants of bourgeois thought do occasionally raise their head, including some of Eurocentric orientation.

As it is also the case with anti-Semitism, it is worth noting here how sharply certain parts of the Left – above all, its dogmatic forms – have chosen and brought together precisely those leftovers of bourgeois thought still stuck to the Marxist approach, much as pieces of shell stick to baby chicks who have just broken out of the egg, in order thereby to justify their own ideas 'in a Marxist fashion'. For many Marxists, Marx was too huge, and his thought too radically counterposed to prevailing thinking, to be truly grasped after having read a fifteen-page handbook; or it was too radical to be easily convincing outside of a revolutionary situation. In order to escape this awful tradition (and this is our second explanation), Echeverría attempts to take up again other theories as well, for example semiotics.

CHAPTER 13

Modernity and Capitalism

a   The Critique of Actually-Existing Modernity and the Critique of Actually-Existing Postmodern Thought

Echeverría's distancing himself from so-called postmodernity consists not only of his aspiring toward a 'concrete universalism' that contradicts postmodernism (both conceptually and ultimately also practically), but also involves something more. Despite the first impression that the sermon on the overcoming or abolition of modernity and its concomitant universalism may provoke in us – in the sense that from now on, anything is possible and nothing is prohibited, 'anything goes', which constitutes a large part of the attraction of this tendency – here Echeverría wants to recognise exactly the opposite. Since, along with modernity, so, too, are its (self) critical elements (even if these have often been repressed or buried in modernity) left behind, 'postmodern thought' ends up in nothing better than the oldest Eurocentrism, which is logical in a way, since it does little more than repeat in theory what is in reality imposed every day with greater or lesser degrees of violence. 'We could say that to the "fall of grand narratives" that Lyotard identified as a principal characteristic of the "postmodern condition", the actually-existing postmodernism spirit responds more and more with a (re)lapse into grand prejudices.'[190] Shortly before this, Echeverría specifies which prejudice it is that deserves particular attention, which is at the same time 'one of the most characteristic traits of actually-existing modernity: its Eurocentrism'.[191]

Also, and beyond this, Echeverría notes that postmodernity is opening the way for anything but the promised suppression of the 'modern' adversities resulting from its 'abstract universalism'. Instead, he sees in postmodernity a growing tendency toward something which does not in any way resemble the desired overcoming of the contradictions of 'actually-existing modernity', but which even incites him to an allusion to that obscurantist institution that was for modernity always opposed to its own luminous project: the Holy Inquisition. As against all the hot air about a new confusion [*neue Unübersichtlichkeit*],

---

190   Echeverría 1995a, p. 63.
191   Echeverría 1995a, p. 62. See: 'Postmodernity has stumbled – and the strife exhausts and disrupts it – on the impossibility of questioning one of the most characteristic elements of actually-existing modernity: its Eurocentrism' (ibid.).

an ever-increasing plurality, and so on, he diagnoses a powerfully dogmatic inclination in postmodernity, one which, moreover, is aimed above all against decisive texts which are critical of 'actually-existing modernity':

> Which contradiction of the modern epoch must specifically be dissolved? From what must we 'take refuge', against what must we 'arm ourselves' in modernity? It is not possible to attempt to respond to this question without consulting one of the first texts critical of this modernity (although it stands at the head of the neoliberal and postmodern *Index librorum prohibitorum*): Marx's *Capital*.[192]

To summarise, Echeverría's theoretical project could, therefore, be formulated as follows, distinguishing it from all postmodern approaches. He is interested in developing a radical critique of 'actually-existing modernity', as he says with evidently ironic reference to the name given to the social system of the Soviet Union and its dependent states (whose social system he understands as 'state capitalism' which 'was never more than a cruel caricature of liberal capitalism').[193] Now, for Echeverría, this critique cannot be an indeterminate and abstract negation: rather, the task is to develop a concrete negation of this actually-existing modernity. This should not be understood as a flattening of the critique of the ruling modernity, but as its radicalisation. Overcoming the errors of the ruling modernity is only possible after having analysed its content precisely; but as we have seen, this analysis leads Echeverría to a double result. In accord with this, the two fundamental errors of the ruling modernity are not universalism in general as such, but on the one hand Eurocentrism, which abstractly (which is to say, falsely) universalises 'European' criteria, traditions, cultures, and so on; on the other hand, the abstract universalisation of the

---

192 'El ethos barroco', in Echeverría 1994b, p. 18.
193 'El ethos barroco', in Echeverría 1994b, p. 16. The question of whether the concept of 'state capitalism' is not a '*contradictio in adiecto*', as Franz Neumann for example explains it in the framework of his discussion of National Socialism, will be discussed on another occasion.

'The very term "state capitalism" is a *contradictio in adiecto*', Neumann says, and continues by citing Rudolf Hilferding: 'The concept of "state capitalism" cannot bear analysis from the economic point of view. Once the state has become the sole owner of the means of production, it makes it impossible for a capitalist economy to function, it destroys that mechanism which keeps the very processes of economic circulation in active existence'. 'Such a state', Neumann continues, 'is therefore no longer capitalistic. It may be called a slave state or managerial dictatorship or a system of bureaucratic collectivism – that is, it must be described in political and not economic categories'. Neumann 2009, p. 224. Here, Neumann cites Hilferding according to Macdonald 1941, p. 213.

current form of social reproduction (namely, the capitalist form) as the only one imaginable, is also false and so must also be overcome.

Now, the fact that Echeverría formulates these critiques in the form of critiques of the ruling modernity, is something more than a simple repetition of particular fashionable terminological phenomena. Instead, what interests him is scrutinising the complex intertwining of specific economic structures with cultural processes, in order to understand the difficulties of escaping *this* modernity while *at the same time* seeking approaches for its possible overcoming. He does not want to fall into the error that he believes to have found in Lukács. From the radical analysis the latter offers for understanding the difficulties in achieving consciousness, given the powerful rootedness of questions of knowledge in ruling social conditions, he consequently arrives at a 'theoretical hopelessness', which can only be overcome in messianic visions of salvation. Lukács, who our author appreciates for his radical critique of dogmatic Marxism, understands and attempts to solve – erroneously, according to Echeverría – the problem of the 'world of modernity' in the following way:

> 'The modern world as a totality, as the interpenetration of the qualitative or concrete dynamic with quantitative or abstract logic, turns out to be incomprehensible. Its totalisation can only exist *in an isolated way and instantaneously*: that of the moment of the revolution, that of the act of salvation in which the proletariat reactualises its capacity for concrete synthesis in reappropriating the synthetic activity that had existed – abstractly reified – in capital.[194]

b   The Term 'Actually-Existing Modernity'

The term 'actually-existing modernity' ['*modernidad realmente existente*'][195] plays a central role in Echeverría's theory. Along with the previously mentioned and obviously polemical and ironic meaning with regard to the Soviet Union and the so-called 'socialist' countries, it has another meaning as well.

This second meaning is more complex and will become more important throughout the course of our discussion of Bolívar Echeverría's theory, but it

---

194   From 'Lukács y la revolución como salvación', in Echeverría 1995a, p. 109. We will enter in greater detail into the question of Lukács's interpretation of the concept of fetishism in Marx and Echeverría's critique of Lukács in the chapter '*Ethos* and Ideology'.

195   Echeverría 1995a, p. 62, and 1995a, p. 143. Echeverría frequently speaks of capitalist modernity as the 'actually-existing world' (1995a, pp. 144 and 164). Elsewhere, Echeverría speaks of the 'actually-existing postmodern spirit' (1995a, p. 63).

must be understood in terms of the confrontation with the failed experiment of these countries. Just as 'actually-existing socialism' affirmed itself as the *only* possible version of socialist society and successfully convinced not only its supporters but also its adversaries of this, so, too, does actually-existing modernity affirm its status as the only possible form, likewise convincing supporters as well as critics. Therefore, if non-dogmatic Marxism and the non-dogmatic Left played and continue to play the role of pointing out the possibility of a different form of socialist or communist society than that which with the deepest conviction[196] was called 'actually-existing', Echeverría considers it his role to point out theoretically the *possibility* and even (albeit repressed, concealed, or negated) the *reality* of *other* modernities. From Echeverría's point of view, 'actually-existing modernity' is not the only one which really exists, but is, instead, the one which dominates, and moreover from whose perspective the presence or possibility of other modernities is looked upon with disapproval: it simply denies their existence and attempts to crush them in praxis.

In the case of the 'actually-existing socialism, the problem is not limited to the circumstance that it was not the one and only version of socialism that could exist, but rather it was never a version of socialism at all. As we have said, Echeverría understands this extinct social system as 'state capitalism.' Setting aside the positions we may have toward this concept, it is clear that Echeverría does not understand it to be socialism. Elsewhere, he expresses this through a leading question: 'Or is it the case that *real socialism* has consisted of a systematic repression of the same [the revolutionary (*Marxist*) version of socialism], and that its current *débâcle* constitutes its liberation?'[197]

Thus Echeverría's formulation regarding 'actually-existing modernity' can also be interpreted in the sense that the expression 'real existence' not only tends to obscure or obscures the possibility of other forms of existence, but that it should likewise be understood as detached from *reality* (in the Hegelian sense). Or, put differently: could it be that the concept of 'real existence' describes merely the momentary appearance of a thing, and not the potential for development that it bears within itself?

In support of this understanding of the concept of actually-existing modernity (an interpretation which goes much further than the explicit discussion in our author's texts), we could mention the fact that – as mentioned

---

196 Of course, the duplication present in this expression already contains a degree of doubt. What reality does not exist, and what existence is not real? This propagandistic *terminus technicus* clearly does not refer to the possible philosophical differentiations of this concept.

197 From 'A la izquierda' in Echeverría 1995a, p. 35.

above – Echeverría sees one important characteristic of the ruling form of modernity in its false and abstract universalism, and this he opposes in turn to a concrete universalism. These conceptions similarly evoke Hegel's philosophy, which considers the present appearance of a thing as remaining abstract, and that by contrast its reality [*Wirklichkeit*] – in this sense – is concretised in time. In support of this 'Hegelianising interpretation' of Echeverría's conceptualisation, we can cite the following reference of this Ecuadorian-Mexican philosopher to the Swabian-Prussian: 'the revolution, if it is to be true, must be, as Hegel indicated, a "determinate negation" of the existing'.[198]

Here, Echeverría's effort to connect himself with Hegel's dialectical method is very apparent, which supports our exegesis of Bolívar Echeverría's concept of 'real existence' as objective appearance [*gegenständlicher Schein*] (Marx). The determinate negation of abstract universalism is, therefore, in his terminology, the aspiration toward a concrete universalism, while the indeterminate negation is the naïve postmodern condemnation of all universalism, alongside the equally naïve presumption of having solved once and for all the difficult problem of reconciling the general, the particular, and the individual.[199]

This has important consequences for the discussion of modernity. If 'actually-existing modernity' is understood as merely the momentary manifestation of real modernity, then this means that it carries within it possibilities

---

198   Echeverría 1995a, p. 37. Also, in the essay 'La "forma natural' de la reproducción social' (Echeverría 1984, p. 35 n6) he refers approvingly to §§255–9 of Hegel's *Philosophy of Nature*. One of the rare citations of Marx that Echeverría makes in this essay points toward Hegel's concept of reality through the synonymous use of the expressions 'wirklich' [real] and 'wirkend' [being effective/acting]. See the quotation from Marx in footnote 145, p. 241 of this book.

199   Many 'postmodern' thinkers avoid, on this point, the fact that universalism does not emerge from the head of philosophers, but from reality itself. Under ruling relations, the equalisation of all human labour forces is an unavoidable constitutive condition and is evidently a *real* universalist premise (in the sense of an abstract universalism). We cannot ignore the fact that this practically negates the differences among human beings, but this is not the fault of the theory that reflects upon it.

   Universalism and its consequences, some of which are dreadful, can only in the end be abolished in praxis, which is to say, by constructing a society in which human freedom is guaranteed without requiring the bourgeois equality that exists in reality and in concepts. The (theoretical) problem does not change in the least because a large part of the Left inscribed the slogans of equality on their flags at a moment in which bourgeois society no longer believed in itself and only understood equality as '(capitalist) equality of the conditions of exploitation' (see p. 253 n184 of this book).

   About the Marxian concept of '*gegenständlicher Schein*' ['objective appearance'] and its translation, see p. 317 n358 of this book.

for development that have not yet been taken advantage of; but we must not forget that we are attempting to extract the dialectical content of Echeverría's thought. Here, this means that when one seeks to exhaust the possibilities for development in real modernity in theoretical as well as practical terms, this does not mean that the modernity of today (or, as Echeverría also says, the modernities) is (are) an 'unfinished project' and should be pushed a bit more toward its (their) completion. It could very well be the case that the passage from a thing's abstract form of presence toward its realisation entails crossing enormous ruptures in the Hegelian sense. Those ruptures could even be so massive as to be characterised, without exaggeration, as revolution.

But – and this is decisive for Echeverría's approach – as radical as these ruptures may be, they will not deceive us regarding the connection that exists between what there is before and what remains after them. Abstract, 'actually-existing' modernity [*realexistierende Moderne*] is, on the one hand, very distant and separated by a vast and almost insurmountable gulf from real, concrete modernity (in which, therefore, the old postulates of modernity are realised), while being at the same time the only palpable sign, the only material basis that exists for that 'real modernity' [*wirkliche Moderne*]. It is in this way that we should understand the last part of Echeverría's statement on Hegel cited above: 'the revolution, if it is to be true, must be, as Hegel indicated, a "determinate negation" of the existing, *committed to what it negates, dependent upon it for the concrete posing of its novelty*'.[200]

The dialectical relationship that exists between the momentary forms of manifestation [*gegenwärtige Erscheinungsformen*] of modernity and the reality [*Wirklichkeit*] to which they should aspire and which is possible in principle, consists, as we have sketched out and summarised, in the unity of continuity and rupture. On this basis, moreover, it becomes possible to understand the contradictory relationship between reform and revolution, with which we finally return from our critically Hegelianising interpretation[201] to the original text. In various places throughout the whole of his work, Echeverría makes

---

200 Echeverría 1995a, p. 37, italics by S.G.
201 The necessity for such interpretations, 'told at great length,' owes to the fact that Echeverría's work occasionally seems obscure at first glance and requires a broad interpretation in order to be approachable. Note to the edition in Spanish: when we speak of 'real modernity' [*wirkliche Moderne*] or 'reality of modernity' [*Wirklichkeit der Moderne*], we do so in the Hegelian sense. Therefore, this has nothing to do with the formulation of the 'realist *ethos*' [*realistisches* Ethos] or 'realist modernity' [*realistische Moderne*], conceptions formulated by Echeverría which refer to naïve notions of 'reality' [*Realität*] present in 'realism' as it is known, for example, in art history.

observations on the relationship between reform and revolution, all of which point in the direction that we just sketched and can illuminate through this optic Echeverría's understanding of actually-existing modernity and that (real) modernity toward which we should aspire, and the relationship between the two. Hence, for example, in the essay in question we read the following:

> It is true that there is no continuity between the revolutionary resort and the reformist solution. As Rosa Luxemburg liked to say, revolution is not an accelerated accumulation of reforms and nor is reform a revolution in small doses.... However, while these are totally different from one another – and even hostilely counterposed – revolutionary and reformist perspectives are mutually necessary within the political horizon of the Left.[202]

In the essay 'Postmodernidad y cinismo' ['Postmodernity and cynicism'] mentioned at the outset of our discussion of Bolívar Echeverría, he expounds on the same topic in the following terms:

> If a political theory that starts from the concept of 'reification' accepts that there exists the possibility of a politics *within* alienation, that society – while deprived of the possibilities of its sovereignty – is neither politically demobilised nor paralysed nor condemned to await the messianic moment in which its political liberty will be returned to it, the problem that is posed consists in establishing points of contact at which the reformist search for an appropriate democratic game for the conversion of civil interests into the citizens' will comes into contact with the revolutionary search for a substantial broadening of the scale according to which society is capable of making decisions with regard to its own history.[203]

Such affirmations could seem a bit reformist, but in the current Mexican context they are the opposite, and have been confirmed – at least in today's perspective – by the Zapatista rebellion, which is not suffering the full military violence of the Mexican federal army, in part due to the fact that reformist forces protest and act against it with their own specific (reformist) methods.[204]

---

202 Echeverría 1995a, p. 36.
203 Echeverría 1995a, p. 94.
204 As a practical tool for more easily discovering the 'points of contact' between reformist and revolutionary politics, Echeverría proposes the capacity for self-irony and a more

In any case, it is worth adding that if Echeverría's political positions (which are totally congruent with his theoretical work) can be counted among the most critical there are in the contemporary context of the country in which they developed, this should not mean that his theory unconditionally stands above any and all critique. Such a way of viewing his theoretical work would also not have pleased Echeverría himself,[205] who repeatedly stressed the need for critical thought.

c Actually-Existing Modernities as Basis for a Non-Capitalist Modernity

We will now attempt to close the circle. As we have indicated, actually-existing modernities are necessarily the basis for another, a non-capitalist modernity. As a result, in order to drive the indispensable *determinate negation* of capitalist modernity or modernities on the theoretical terrain, we need a precise analysis of these existing modernities, one which allows us to glimpse what should not in any case be saved in the transition to a non-capitalist modernity, and which ought to be the first points of departure for this other real, concrete modernity. This latter point should not be understood as philosophical speculation, but as the materialist search for elements existing within capitalist modernity, which do not at all fit its primary destructive tendency. For Echeverría, however, the development of a *method* for this search must precede the concrete search for such elements.

This method is to be found in his attempt described above to enrich Marx's analysis of capitalist reproduction with knowledge gained through semiotics. Through this method, Echeverría arrives at an analysis of the *various* present capitalist modernities which, despite the 'claim to be the sole legitimate representative' of 'the modern' by one of its variants, nevertheless coexist with this one. Toward this end, he introduces the concept of *modern ethos*, or to be more

---

critical attitude toward the 'spirit of seriousness' (meaning, lack of a sense of humour), since the latter leads to dogmatism and censorship: 'there is something that could be learned from the *brother enemies* of the Left: there is little that is healthier than dumping a bit of *irony* on one's own certainty. The same spirit of seriousness that leads to absolutising and dogmatising, whether for revolutionary or reformist truths, leads also to the need for censorship, discrimination, and the oppression of the one by the other' (Echeverría 1995a, p. 37).

205 Echeverría, in conversations with the author, expressed that he was not pleased by an uncritical attitude toward his work and his teaching.

precise, that of the *modern ethe* (plural) which will be the object of our study in the following chapters.

At this point in our study of Echeverría's theory of the four modern *ethe*, we must return to the connection between Echeverría and Hegel (and here, Walter Benjamin comes into play as well) in order to clarify, when all is said and done, that this connection is also present in the critical impulse against the positivist element contained in Eurocentrism of all political stripes.[206] The dominant *ethos*, according to Echeverría, is the 'realist', as will be shown in detail in what follows. This designation has some extremely ironic and polemical content, and thus – and not without reason – echoes the previously discussed term 'actually-existing modernity'. In his critique of this dominant *ethos*, Echeverría takes up again the recently mentioned critique of a fixation, a petrification to death, on the 'factual', which is naïvely equated with the 'only real' in the sense of 'the only truly possible'. He is interested in 'losing respect for the factual', and here we must always remember that by 'the factual', Echeverría is always referring to capitalist modernity, in which Eurocentrism is a principal characteristic. This Eurocentrism must be condemned not only because in the past and in the present it was and is inseparably accompanied by unspeakable suffering in the so-called underdeveloped countries, but also because it blocks recourses to possible indications toward other forms of configuring modernity. In order to avoid passing over these other possibilities – which are perceptible in the hidden 'scars' of history if we look or touch carefully – despite the dominant and hasty ethnocentric ignorance, it is necessary to 'touch or look over the back of historical continuity against the grain', just as Echeverría explains, with obvious reference to Walter Benjamin's formulation discussed previously.

> The back of historical continuity offers an impeccable line to the touch and to the sight; but it conceals scars, the remains of mutilated limbs and even still bloody wounds which are only visible when the hand or the gaze which passes over it does so against the grain. It is, therefore,

---

206 This positivist fixation of Eurocentric stereotypes and realities is, of course, also to be found in Hegel's works, as more generally in almost all of the minds (even the most critical and dialectical) from the so-called First World, *because* – as Brecht's character the Pirate Jenny would respond to them with a smile (were she in Echeverría's place), when these minds are laughing about the fact that it is precisely from the furthest corner of the really divided world that there would come a practical approach, as well as the corresponding theoretical reflection, towards *another* modernity – '*And you never guess to who you're talkn*'. Compare: Ute Lemper interpreting Brecht's 'Pirate Jenny', at <http://www.youtube.com/watch?v= iorZEEbAC4U>. (See also Brecht 1949).

advantageous to lose respect for the factual; to doubt that rationality which bows down before the 'actually-existing' world, not only as the better one (due to its reality) but as the only possible world, and to trust in another less 'realist' and officious world, one which is not at odds with freedom. To show that that which is has no more 'right to exist' than that which was not but could have been; that beneath the established project of modernity, the opportunities for an alternative project ... have not yet been exhausted.[207]

But the method for discovering these 'opportunities for an alternative project' of a non-capitalist modernity (possibilities hidden 'beneath the established project of modernity') is exactly the method described above for the comparative study of use-value and the sign. On this topic, we must again bear in mind (as we move to the next theme) the fact that Echeverría, in introducing the semiotic method into terrains traditionally reserved for economics or the social sciences, did not attempt in the least to exaggerate the importance of language. Rather, he attempted to grasp the totality of social life as something which becomes possible through a complex combination of sign systems, for which the fundamental form – or as Marx would say, the base – is that sign system which has its place in the production and consumption of use-values, in the natural form of social reproduction. These sign systems are vastly varied among themselves, but do not raise insuperable barriers between one another, and nor is there any reason to consider them 'pure' in any sense. To the contrary, it is instead the common capacity of all human beings to generate signs (or to develop systems of signs or languages, *langues*), the faculty of speech in the broad sense of Ferdinand de Saussure, *langage* [speech], which makes understanding among everybody possible in principle, as well as a linking, a combination, a blending, a reciprocal enrichment, and so on, of various sign systems – and in the final instance, for Echeverría, this means material cultures – with one another.

Echeverría calls the specific aspect of these sign systems, which makes possible the organisation and reproduction of everyday life '*ethos*', and these will be the theme of the next chapters. This search for 'hidden possibilities' will come to discover that one of the four '*ethe*' of capitalist modernity which Echeverría grasps theoretically, namely the 'baroque *ethos*' which exists in Latin America, stands out positively from the rest in its connection to the reciprocal enrichment of such social sign systems (in which, as we have said, one central aspect is the production and consumption of use-values), and this largely for historical

---

207   Echeverría 1995a, pp. 143f.

reasons. In the discussion of this 'baroque *ethos*' it should thus become definitively clear why Echeverría makes the effort to connect Marx with semiotics; such a connection is necessary to overcome the limitations that Echeverría has detected in the Marxian concept of use-value or, at the very least, to try to do so, not with the end of putting forth yet another concept for academic debate, but to pull Marx once and for all away from one of the darkest aspects of modernity, and, at the same time, throw him against it: its Eurocentrism.

CHAPTER 14

The Concept of Historical *Ethos*

The central concept in Bolívar Echeverría's recent theoretical production, which is also his most original concept, is that of 'historical *ethos*',[208] which we will present in the following chapters.

---

208   See 'El *ethos* barroco', in Echeverría 1994b. Alongside this text by Echeverría, his extensive essay 'Modernidad y capitalismo (15 tesis)' ['Modernity and capitalism (15 Theses)'] is also important for his conception of historical *ethos*, and especially thesis 7: 'El cuádruple ethos de la modernidad capitalista' ['The quadruple *ethos* of capitalist modernity']. The text of this thesis, however, was largely included and reformulated in 'El *ethos* barroco', and as a general rule, we follow the latter version (See Echeverría 1995a, pp. 163–7). Thesis 6 ('Las diferentes modernidades y las diferentes maneras de existencia del capitalismo' ['The different modernities and the different manners of capitalist existence']) and thesis 8 ('El occidente europeo y la modernidad capitalista' ['The European West and capitalist modernity']) deal with similar questions (Echeverría 1995a, pp. 161–3 and 167–81).

Finally, there exist other important explanations of the concept of historical *ethos*, especially the baroque *ethos*, in the book *Conversaciones sobre lo barroco* [*Conversations on the baroque*], (Echeverría and Kurnitzky 1993). There we find included the transcriptions of five discussions on the baroque that took place in 1991 within the framework of the research project directed by Bolívar Echeverría at the UNAM, with the participation of Horst Kurnitzky, as well as two short texts by Echeverría on the same topic. The problem with these *Conversations on the baroque* is that they are just that, conversations, more than debates in the strict sense of the term. That is, they bring out a series of interesting ideas one after the other without seeing to what degree they are complementary or mutually contradictory. At first glance, these *Conversations* give the appearance of general harmony, almost as if a single idea had been distributed among various speakers to be formulated by them through an exchange. It is only by looking more closely at them that the suspicion of some differences arises, and between the lines the participants in the conversation criticise each other. But if we hope to recognise this more precisely, it is almost necessary to psychologically analyse the smallest details of the formulations chosen in each case. This limits a bit the possibility of easily citing the *Conversations* to document Echeverría's position, since the ideas crystallise between the participants without, as we have said, leaving a clear indication of who thinks what. Thus, for a scientific work that needs to move in the world of easily identifiable 'discursive' subjects, which are always self-identical, this type of text poses a problem. In this book, as a result, we will make only occasional use of the *Conversations on the baroque*.

a   On the Term *Ethos*

The term *ethos* refers etymologically to the Greek word τὸ ἦθος. It originally meant, first of all, 'habitual place of residence' and 'domicile' for people, in animals: 'grazing land' and 'stable', as well as the 'position' of the Sun. Secondly, it means 'habit,' 'use,' as well as 'custom,' and thirdly, refers to 'character,' 'way of thinking,' 'mentality'.[209] Bolívar Echeverría uses the term in the second and third senses. The ambiguity of the Greek term in the coexistence of these two more recent meanings makes it suggestive for Echeverría's formulation of the concept. 'The term *ethos* has the advantage of its ambiguity or double-meaning... It brings together the concept of "use, custom or automatic behaviour"... with the concept of "character, individual personality or mode of being"'.[210]

The first of these two meanings expresses, in his judgement, something 'defensive or passive'; the second, by contrast, something 'offensive or active'.[211] In the passive meaning as 'custom', there is 'a presence of the world in us, which protects us from the need to decipher it at every step'; by contrast, in the active meaning, 'character' refers to 'a presence of ourselves in the world, which obligates it to treat us in a certain manner'.[212] This ambiguity between active and passive in the term *ethos* is already present, according to Echeverría, in its first and original meaning. 'The term *ethos*... invites to combine, in the basic meaning of "residence or shelter", what in it refers to "refuge"... with what in it refers to "weapon"'.[213]

Finally, Echeverría values the double meaning of the term '*ethos*' due to the fact that the two meanings described can be understood as determinations of objective as well as subjective circumstances. 'Located equally in the object as in the subject,... the *historical ethos* can be seen as an entire principle for the construction of the lifeworld'.[214]

---

209   See Gemoll 1965, p. 360.
210   'El *ethos* barroco', in Echeverría 1994b, p. 18. Following the tradition of Latin countries, Echeverría gives only the Latin orthography of the Greek word. In so doing, he sets aside the difficulty that arises from the ambiguity of the Greek term in two words written differently: τὸ ἔθος, with the meaning 'habit, custom, use', alongside the version already mentioned (see Gemoll 1965, p. 241).
211   Ibid.
212   Ibid.
213   Ibid.
214   Ibid.

Translation Problems

In translating Bolívar Echeverría's conceptualisation into German, the following problematic arises. Unlike Spanish, in which non-academic speech does not contain the term '*ethos*' which he uses,[215] the word '*ethos*' is quite usual in German. As early as the eighteenth century, German writers had taken it from the Greek, but in Germany from the twentieth century on, the term would acquire a strongly limited meaning compared to the original one, in the sense of 'moral norms of members of a specific social group, accepted as a driving force of one's own behaviour'.[216] As a result, the lightness with which Echeverría refers to the word '*ethos*' with the ambiguity contained in the Greek term puts the German-speaking reader or listener much more on alert than those who speak Spanish, for whom the term '*ethos*' has no such capacity within specific philosophical debates, and even there only among those who have taken it up from German literature, above all in the nineteenth and first half of the twentieth centuries.

The question of why also the term '*ethos*' has, starting from the originally broad meaning which followed the Greek (still mentioned in 1908 in an encyclopedia),[217] finally acquired the idealist orientation typical of contemporary German, cannot be clarified here.[218] From '*Sitte* [custom/common decency], *Brauch* [use], *Gewohnheit* [habit]' only '*Sitte* [custom/common decency]' emerged, and is now only understood in the moral sense; from '*Charakter* [character]' emerged '*moralische Gesamthaltung eines Menschen* [a man's global moral attitude]'.[219]

---

215 In this regard, see the reference texts on the Spanish language in which this term does not appear, for example in *Diccionario ideológico de la lengua española* 1990; *El pequeño Espasa* 1987; and *Wörterbuch der spanischen und deutschen Sprache* 1975.

216 See *Etymologisches Wörterbuch des Deutschen* 1989, Vol. I, pp. 381ff.

217 See '*Ethos*' in *Meyers Kleines Konversationslexikon* 1908, Vol. II, p. 666. Alongside the two meanings of '*ethos*' in Greek, '*Sitte* [custom/ common decency]' and at the same time '*Charakter* [character]', *Meyers Kleines Konversationslexikon* refers the reader to the following related terms: Ethologie [ethology], Ethographie [ethography]: Charakter- oder Sittenschilderung [description of character or custom]; Ethograph [ethographer]: and Sittenschilderer [describer of customs].

218 This is a broad field, as is elegantly said, but is at the same time a very interesting question which always occurs to the author of this book in both everyday life in Mexico and in reading Spanish texts interchanged with German ones.

219 In recent reference texts the signifier '*Charakter* [character]' does not appear, and moreover the acceptance of '*Sitte* [custom/ common decency]' in the sense of '*Brauch* [custom]' is excluded by formulations that interpret the term '*ethos*' as assignable to pure ethics, although within this both the objective and subjective sides are grasped. The

It is worth observing that Echeverría does not refer to the predominant meaning of the term '*ethos*' in German, which is limited to the moral, but rather to its general Greek meaning.[220] The plural, which Echeverría renders as '*ethe*' in a direct transcription from the corresponding Greek form, and which in German usually does not exist for '*ethos*', we reproduce [in the German text] as '*die Ethen*', drawing our support from cases of similar construction (for example, *das Epos, die Epen*).[221]

b   Determination of the Concept of 'Historical *Ethos*'

The concept of historical *ethos*, which Echeverría introduces, if we are to define its content, sets out from the real subordination of the production of use-value to the production of value, which has been discussed repeatedly throughout this work. Also in conceptual terms, the studies on *ethos* follow those on use-value, for example, when the latter is repeatedly characterised as the 'natural form'[222] and, in the investigations about *ethos*, the production and consumption of use-values is understood as the ' "social-natural" process of reproduction'.[223]

In the final instance, the capitalist mode of production tends toward the destruction of all use-values, which are sacrificed on the altar of its destructive logic. The fact that the production of value simultaneously requires a minimum of use-value production to ensure its own sustainability does not necessarily mean that this process has a natural barrier, and nor does it mean that

---

Fremdwörterbuch describes the following translations of the word '*Ethos*': 'General moral attitude, moral principles of life of a human being or a society, which form the basis for desiring and acting; totality of ethico-moral norms, ideals, etc., as the basis for subjective motives and internal guidelines' ('*Ethos*', in *Fremdwörterbuch* 1974, p. 220).

220 In the most common formulation in which the term *ethos* appears in German, this reduction to the moral aspect also appears; when one speaks of the 'professional *ethos*' of a guild, what this indicates above all is what is considered to be the decent way of practicing the profession, and not necessarily the reality of this profession.

221 This was also recommended by the Service for Lexicographic Information when we asked for advice from the highly recognised Mannheim Bibliographical Institute (Lexikon-Auskunftsdienst, Bibliographisches Institut & F.A. Brockhaus AG, Mannheim, letter of 17 December 1996 to the author of this book). [In the Spanish-language edition of this book we use, following Echeverría's example, '*ethe*' to express the plural of '*ethos*'. Similarly, in the English-language edition of this book, we use '*ethe*' to express the plural of '*ethos*'.]

222 'El ethos barroco', in Echeverría 1994b, p. 20.

223 'El ethos barroco', in Echeverría 1994b, p. 19.

this destructive tendency which is immanent in capitalist conditions will at some point turn fatally against the relations themselves, as Marx still assumed at various points in his work. Rather, there exist the possibility and the risk, already enunciated by Rosa Luxemburg in her famous phrase 'Socialism or barbarism', that the self-destruction could be of humanity as a whole. Stated in economic terms: if use-value were to disappear definitively, with it value and surplus value would also disappear, and with that, the exploitation of human beings by other human beings. But all this would be no cause for celebration, since while repressive capitalist relations of production would, of course, have disappeared from the face of the Earth, human beings themselves would be gone as well, since without use-values, which is to say, without the means to satisfy needs, they cannot live a single day. What we must evidently deal with is overcoming the subordination of use-value to value while at the same time safeguarding the production of use-values. This, as such, is nothing new. But what should be seen in the preceding passages is the fact that, from the perspective of Echeverría's social philosophy, this urgent need to liberate the production of use-value from the production of value is no game, and nor can it be resolved absolutely through a single 'messianic act'. Historically, the production of use-value and the production of value are so intertwined that it seems to be an impossible task to think this liberation, or indeed to bring it about.

Echeverría's focus on this dilemma – one which has occupied, in different ways, generations of non-dogmatic Marxists – is the following: he attempts to set out from the existing. Nor is this anything new: Marx himself erects his theory largely as a critique of existing capitalist relations. Echeverría, however, goes further beyond the sphere of production than Marx usually does, and tries to gather moments of everyday life into his analysis. This is nothing new either, since in various currents of non-dogmatic Marxism, above all in what is known as 'Western Marxism', this had already been carefully attempted. Thus, for example, György Lukács, in his momentous book *Geschichte und Klassenbewusstsein* [*History and Class Consciousness*], dedicated a great deal of attention to the question of ideology and to wondering why, despite the presence of objective conditions, the subjects of history do not take the step forward to escape 'prehistory' (Marx).

But Echeverría, according to his self-understanding, moves beyond this as well, understanding in his analysis not only ideology, but considerably more forms of everyday life. He attempts to grasp all that makes otherwise unbearable ruling relations bearable. Unlike the Lukács of *History and Class Consciousness*, for Echeverría not merely simple ideological forms awake the false objective appearance, that what exists is not so unbearable, that it is even acceptable and moreover fundamentally inalterable, but that beyond this, there are also forms of behaviour, social institutions, and other things which render the unlivable livable. The heart of the question, according to what we have sketched out in preceding chapters, lies in the fact that those forms of everyday life cannot be understood and analysed simply on the basis of commodity form of production (that is, the value relation), but must also be understood through the concrete form of use-values produced and consumed in each case.

The totality of these forms of everyday life – which vary according to region and epoch – whose social function is to make ruling social relations tolerable, relations which tend toward the destruction of use-value, and which are thus intolerable, are what Bolívar Echeverría refers to as 'historical *ethos*',[224] and he says: 'structural social behaviour, which we can call *historical ethos*, can be seen as an entire principle for the construction of the lifeworld. It is a behaviour which attempts to make the unlivable livable'.[225]

A bit later on, he speaks of a determinate historical *ethos* as '[that] peculiar way of living with capitalism',[226] and in another text he understands the various *ethe* as foundations for 'the different complex *spontaneities*' that constitute the 'lifeworld made possible by capitalist modernity',[227] or as '[a] form of naturalising capitalism'.[228] Historical *ethos* is the totality of uses, social institutions, forms of thinking and acting, tools, forms of producing and consuming use-values which make it possible to live as a human being or as a society under actually inhuman capitalist relations of production, without having to continually invent a solution to the problems resulting in each case from these relations. Therefore, the various *ethe* appear as differing foundations of increasingly differentiated 'complex spontaneities', since it is through them that specific forms of behaviour are predefined, forms which not only make it possible to tolerate the intolerable contradictions of existing relations, but which moreover even make these seem like something automatic, to put it that way, something instinctive and even spontaneous.

Only an analysis of historical *ethos* in its various formations allows a complete recognition of the exact situation of the problem of ruling social relations, which is necessary for grasping why it has not yet been possible to overcome this destructive social formation. In the best of cases, the points of departure necessary for this overcoming could emerge from such an approach.

---

224 'El ethos barroco', in Echeverría 1994b, p. 18.
225 Ibid. Italics in original.
226 'El ethos barroco', in Echeverría 1994b, p. 20.
227 Echeverría 1995a, p. 164.
228 Ibid.

Practical life under actually-existing modernity must develop in a world whose objective form is structured around a dominant presence, that of the reality or the *fact of capitalism*. We are dealing, here, in essence, with a reality which is a permanent contradiction between the counterposed tendencies of two simultaneous dynamics which are constitutive of social life: that of social life itself, insofar as this is a process of labour and enjoyment referred to use-values, on the one hand, and that of the reproduction of its wealth, insofar as this is a process of 'valorisation of abstract value' or accumulation of capital, on the other. We are dealing otherwise with a conflict in which, repeatedly and ceaselessly, the former is sacrificed and subjected to the latter.[229]

However, within the logic of that historical *ethos*, which is today the predominant one under capitalist relations, the contradiction between use-value and value simply does not exist. Unbearable existing relations are assimilated in order to make them bearable by conceiving them as the 'second nature' of humans, and, therefore, as impossible to question or transform. That which is irreconcilable is thereby converted, as quickly as possible, into harmony. In such formulations, Echeverría's close relationship with Western Marxism is strikingly visible, and not only on a terminological level: 'Capitalist reality is an inevitable historical fact', he says, 'from which no escape is possible, and which, therefore, must be integrated into the spontaneous construction of the lifeworld'. 'Capitalist reality', Echeverría continues, 'must be transformed into a second nature by the *ethos* which assures the indispensable "harmony" of everyday existence'.[230]

But what sounds like a parallel with Western Marxism's ideology critique should not be allowed to obscure the decisive differences between the concept of historical *ethos* in Bolívar Echeverría and the concept of ideology. The concept of *ethos* is broader, spanning many more forms than the concept of ideology, and at the same time claims to contain more internal differentiations. These two differences maintain an intimate relationship with the fact that György Lukács and Bolívar Echeverría both set out toward these conceptualisations from the double character of the commodity, but with different perspectives. To simplify, we could say that the former attempts to solve the problem starting from the value side of commodity production, and the latter starting from the use-value side. Lukács sets out from the value side of the commodity, which expresses nothing but a social relation – but one which shows

---

229 'El ethos barroco', in Echeverría 1994b, p. 19.
230 Ibid.

the producers the objective appearance of a commodity, which is granted a life of its own. He sees the social character of production captured in the value side of the commodity, but this character is removed from immediate knowledge by the appearance of the commodity as a mere use-value, which, for Lukács, instead relates to the private aspect of production, which is equally present in the not-understood double character of the commodity. What interests Lukács is, above all, explaining how it is that ideology necessarily emerges from the fact that production is developed under the commodity form, in order then to explain why in his epoch, despite the given objective conditions, the necessary and awaited revolutionary subjectivity has not yet developed.

For the Latin American author, it is a different matter, and this is not least related to their different historical experiences. For Lukács, as for the whole of Western Marxism, the central question was: how is it possible that reified forms of consciousness can exist also among oppressed classes, above all among the proletariat; or, in a word, how can the proletariat – that is, the potential revolutionaries – have a counter-revolutionary consciousness (which, with the rise of fascism and National Socialism, becomes more acute as a simultaneously theoretical and practical problem)? For Echeverría, the problem appears in a slightly different form.[231] Latin America did not experience to any large degree mass desertions from traditional leftist organisations toward fascist or Nazi movements; a desertion which made Lukács's text *Die Verdinglichung und das Bewusstsein des Proletariats* ['Reification and the Consciousness of the Proletariat'] so important within Western Marxism,[232] for example, in the origins of the Frankfurt School. It was, instead, a different problem which occupied the critical left in Latin America for several decades and which in part continues to do so today (insofar as such a Left continues to exist): Eurocentrism, which impacts large sections of the Left. This Eurocentrism is problematic, not because it implies (as is often claimed today in ostensible but very trivial critiques) an 'absence of national self-esteem' or similar aberrations, but because it has led to and continues to lead to grave political errors, above all in the politics of cross-class alliances. From the parallels purportedly observed between Latin American reality in the twentieth

---

231 See, in this respect, the fact that Echeverría himself, speaking of his generation in Latin America, writes: 'This generation of leftist intellectuals, grew up more with the heterodox impulse of the Cuban rebels than with the memory of the antifascist struggle...' (Echeverría 1995b, p. 78). This constitutes, moreover, an important biographical difference vis-à-vis Adolfo Sánchez Vázquez, which is doubtless expressed in theoretical divergences similar to those discrepancies sketched between Echeverría and Lukács.
232 'Reification and the Consciousness of the Proletariat' in Lukács 1971, pp. 83–222.

century and European feudalism, it is concluded, on the basis of very little conceptual effort, that the continent remains in the feudal epoch. From this the conclusion is distilled, consequently, that the next revolutionary step will be that of the bourgeois revolution, to then afterwards carrying out the socialist or communist revolution as the protocol indicates. The politics that was and is justified by such an argument is that of ingratiating oneself to the national bourgeois class while simultaneously condemning any collaboration with the 'backward' classes, like, for example, the impoverished rural population, the landless farmers, the *campesinos*, and – less imaginable still – the indigenous population, which is conceived as *even more* backward and even as *pre-feudal*.[233]

The problem, then, was not and is not that of the desertion of large portions of the traditional Left to organisations and ideologies on the far Right, but rather that of ingratiating oneself to the national capitalist bourgeoisie while simultaneously rejecting the creation of alliances with organisations representing the most marginalised social classes of those countries, who, moreover and as a general rule, were and are much more rebellious than the local industrial proletariat. To attack this problem with the resources of theory – a problem, which is provoked on the theoretical plane largely by Eurocentrism – Echeverría develops the concept of *ethos*, in order to make visible the *diversity* of forms, which the self-deception and the enduring of ruling social relations assume in each case. However, we will attempt to show that he achieves this step on some occasions more by emphasising the *diversity* of these *ethe* than their *falseness*. (The four *ethe of capitalist modernity* are false because they make tolerable something which cannot and should not be tolerated, which is to say, they make possible not only human survival under capitalist relations of production, but also the 'survival' of those existing social relations themselves).

So, while it is true that Echeverría undoubtedly goes beyond Marx, particularly in Lukács's reading, which in broad strokes is similar to that of Adolfo Sánchez Vázquez,[234] it remains necessary in any case to turn to that interpretation of Marx typical of Western Marxism in order to avoid relapsing unnecessarily into a limited analysis.

---

[233] This Eurocentrism in the Latin American Left was favoured, moreover, by the influence of Moscow, a European city, on communist parties across the entire world, an influence which resulted not only from the success – as it seemed – of the Russian Revolution, but also from the material and logistical support (which was often considerable) from the old Tsarist city. On this and the meaning of this problematic in the origin of Bolívar Echeverría's political and social-philosophical thought, see pp. 55f in this book.

[234] This *despite* the fact that Sánchez Vázquez did not come into contact with Lukács's texts until after he had elaborated his central ideas.

But before returning to the Marxian concept of ideology (in Lukács's sense) and contrasting this to Echeverría's concept of *ethos*, we must first enter with greater detail into the latter. The concept of *ethos* is broader than that of ideology, since, as we have explained, it embraces *with a vast scope* both the subjective as well as the *objective* side of the social process,[235] and with it, goes far beyond the broadest Marxian understanding of ideology (ideology in the sense of 'legal, political, religious, aesthetic, or philosophic – in short ideological forms').[236] Thus, for example, a central aspect of the historical *ethos* is the previously discussed production of use-value, which differs in each case and which transcends these 'ideological forms'. As a result, the concept of *ethos* can be understood as a continuation of Echeverría's analysis of the relationship between use-value and the sign. With this, it should be clear that Echeverría's concept, despite the common understanding of the term '*ethos*' in German, has nothing to do with a theory of ethics. To the contrary, like the concept of ideology, it seeks to take up, for example, the moral ideas of human beings, which appear to 'float freely' and place these in the context of the ruling social and cultural situation. But the latter has as its foundation and as its 'sign system' that of the specific mode of the production and consumption of use-values, from which perspective the proximity of Echeverría's concept of *ethos* and the Marxian concept of praxis becomes palpable.

In comparison with the Lukács of *History and Class Consciousness*, it should be highlighted that the latter sees the social character of production principally in its value side, and does not have as a theme the social (and cultural) determination of use-values, while Echeverría also sees a powerfully social aspect in the production *and* consumption of use-values (as such). The aspect of consumption, moreover, has much less theoretical relevance to Lukács than it does to Echeverría. In the concept of historical *ethos*, more differences are established within his object of study than is the case with the concept of ideology. The concept of historical *ethos* may not stop at the moment of being specifically determined as a 'historical *ethos* of capitalist relations of production', but, instead, requires another still more specific determination. The concept of historical *ethos*, central to Bolívar Echeverría's work, arrives at its theoretical end only upon distinguishing its four principal forms: 'The different possibilities that are offered for living in the world of capitalism would thus, in principle, be four; each of these would imply a peculiar attitude – be it

---

235   'The *historical ethos* [is] located both in the object and in the subject' ('El ethos barroco', in Echeverría 1994b, p. 18).
236   Marx 1904, p. 12.

of recognition or ignorance, of distancing or participation – toward the contradictory fact that capitalist reality constitutes'.[237]

In order to tackle these 'four possibilities', it is necessary, firstly, to examine another recurring concept in Echeverría's work, that of *modernity*.

c Concept of Modernity

Although the central theme of Echeverría's work in the 1990s is that of modernity, with the particularity that – against the majority of other theorists dealing with the topic – he conceives of the existing modernity as *capitalist*, nowhere in his work does he systematically explain what exactly he means by the concept of modernity; although he does mention three aspects of modernity that can serve as fundamental components for a general description of the concept. In a passage from his introduction to the book *Las ilusiones de la modernidad* [*The illusions of modernity*] he states that there are two principal factors, which represent 'a challenge for human capacity of civilisation', where 'modernity can be understood as the multiple response that human society has been able to give to this challenge throughout history'.[238] These are: a 'rational technology' and 'exchange of commodities', both of which are accompanied by 'the advent of a new age of productive forces, whose antecedents date back to the classical era'.[239]

On the topic, elsewhere in the same book he sees that 'just until the revolution of modernity' is the possibility opened up of 'perceiving the other in his own "selfness", and not as the narcissistic image of the one who perceives him'.[240] The concept of modernity includes, for Echeverría, aside from a rationalised technology and constantly expanding exchange of commodities, an opening of local cultures and societies to others. But Echeverría immediately warns those naïve friends of the predominant modernity that this opening occurred 'perversely', because it was immediately replaced by the self-closure that the 'capitalist counterrevolution' provoked.[241] This opening was perverse because it took place in that early modernity which could only continue to develop through this 'capitalist counterrevolution'.[242] Even if this latter aspect of

---

237 'El ethos barroco', in Echeverría 1994b, p. 19.
238 Echeverría 1995a, p. 10.
239 Ibid.
240 Echeverría, "La identidad evanescente" in Echeverría 1995a, p. 56.
241 Ibid.
242 Ibid. Both here as well as in other places in Bolívar Echeverría's work, a certain degree of proximity to Critical Theory is evident. Horkheimer and Adorno, for example, in their

modernity (being the overcoming of the local narrow-mindedness and mechanisms of sealing a certain society off from others) could only be affirmed and developed with certain difficulties, it is nevertheless central for Bolívar Echeverría, and, as we will demonstrate, it is the motive for his rejection of a simple condemnation of modernity itself (for example, in the fashion of postmodernity).

Regarding generalised exchange of commodities as a characteristic of modernity, we should add that this is accompanied by another characteristic of the same: the market in 'modern social life' becomes the 'privileged *locus* of socialisation'.[243] This, taking Echeverría's idea even further, could be seen as one of the reasons that make it necessary, and also to some degree possible, to overcome localistic closure, since it is only in this way that the market is able to function in the end. This 'fundamental experience' of everyday life in modernity leads to one of the three principal erroneous conceptions that are born in modernity and which Echeverría, in contrast to Western Marxism, does not call 'ideologies' or 'ideological conceptions', but rather 'myths' or 'modern myths'.[244]

The overcoming of local closure, of closure in general, and with it the recognition of the 'other', becomes not merely necessary under modernity but moreover *possible*. Through the 'qualitative leap' in the development of the productive forces at the origins of modernity, when 'the productive forces ... seem finally to install Man, according to the promised hierarchy, as "lord and master" of the Earth',[245] it occurs that

> ... an old suspicion then came to arise again – this time on the basis of increasingly trustworthy data – that scarcity does not constituted the '*sine qua non* curse' of human reality; that the warlike model that had inspired all projects for the historical existence of Man, becoming a strategy which sees one's own survival as conditional upon the annihilation or exploitation of the Other (of the human or non-human Nature), is not the only one possible; that without being an illusion, a different model is imaginable, in which the challenge toward the Other instead follows the model of *eros*.[246]

Dialectic of Enlightenment, emphatically indicate that those factors conducive to and which contribute to the self-destructive tendency of the Enlightenment are intimately linked to those which constitute its emancipatory side.

243 Echeverría 1995a, p. 43.
244 In this regard, see the text that we just quoted.
245 Echeverría 1995a, p. 141.
246 Echeverría 1995a, p. 142.

Echeverría formulates the chronological determination of the beginning of modernity with regard to its material base as follows: 'The *foundation* of modernity is found in the unstoppable consolidation – first slowly, in the Middle Ages, later accelerated, beginning in the sixteenth century, and even explosive, from the Industrial Revolution to the present – of a technological shift which affects the very root of the multiple "material civilisations" of the human being'.[247]

In conclusion, to Echeverría's concept of modernity we could add the point that if modernity and capitalism have had a common historical development up to the present, this does not mean that they are inseparably intertwined. On the contrary, Echeverría is interested in following the theoretical tracks of the possibilities for a non-capitalist modernity. To do so, he sets out not from their common traits, but precisely from the differences existing inside modernity, or between its different shapes.

d   The Terms 'Realist', 'Romantic', 'Classic', and 'Baroque *Ethos*'

Echeverría specifies the four most important basic forms of the contemporary historical *ethos* to be the 'realist, romantic, classic, and baroque *ethos*'.[248] At first glance, it might seem strange that he uses terms from the history of art to describe *social* phenomena.[249] He justifies this, *à propos* of the baroque *ethos*, as 'an already irreversible fact: the concept of the baroque has emerged from the history of art and literature in particular and established itself as a category for the history of culture more generally'.[250]

Another Mexican author (whose stance toward Echeverría is otherwise critical) supports his position on this point. Jorge Alberto Manrique, a recognised Mexican art historian and ex-director of the Museum of Modern Art in Mexico City, suggests that 'in fact, after defining stylistic forms in the arts and in literature, the following step was taken: to understand "the baroque" as defining an epoch.... The term made the mortal leap from being one limited

---

247   Echeverría 1995a, p. 141.
248   'El ethos barroco', in Echeverría 1994b, pp. 19ff.
249   A similar critique was expressed in the discussion following a speech by Echeverría at the University of Frankfurt, an event organised by Alfred Schmidt and the author (Speech: 'Die Moderne außerhalb Europas: Der Fall Lateinamerika' ['Modernity outside Europe: the case of Latin America'], 10 November 1994. Department of Philosophy at the Johann Wolfgang Goethe University in Frankfurt am Main; in this regard, see p. 42 of this book.
250   'El ethos barroco', in Echeverría 1994b, p. 13.

to defining an architectonic style in the history of art, to become a historical term'.[251] Manrique indicates, in this regard, that there is nothing new about detaching the concept of the baroque from its narrow ascription to the history of art and literature, and to use it as a general concept in the history of culture, something which was already openly discussed as early as 1952: 'The famous Venice colloquium of 1952, "Rhetoric and the baroque", already assumed this position; any aspect of the baroque epoch (still not very well defined temporally) could be a matter of discussion, including thought, forms of life, city planning, and so on'.[252]

Echeverría takes as a starting point that – in general, and not only in the case of the baroque ethos – the art of a society and an epoch puts the historical *ethos* in evidence, which also justifies the use of this terminology.[253]

e   The Concept of the Four *Ethe* of Capitalist Modernity as a Contribution to a Materialist History of Culture

One of the principal theoretical objectives of Bolívar Echeverría from the 1980s onwards was to lay the foundations for a materialist theory of culture. The concept of culture should be understood here, in its broadest sense, as the totality of human manifestations. It matters little if these are more or less material, of an everyday nature or pertaining to 'high culture'. Thus, Echeverría goes beyond the broadened use of the concept of the baroque as described by Manrique. Even if Echeverría attempts to transcend abstract universalism but grants the concept in question a highly differentiated concreteness, in any case he continues to be a philosopher and limits himself to laying the conceptual groundwork for that materialist history of culture. 'Our intention [is] more reflexive than descriptive', he says.[254] 'It is, above all, a question of proposing a theory, a viewpoint'.[255]

In publishing his book *Modernidad, mestizaje cultural, ethos barroco*, Bolívar Echeverría leaves empirical and historical research in the hands of

---

251   Manrique 1994, p. 235.
252   Ibid.
253   'In this case [of the baroque *ethos*], as in the other modalities of the modern *ethos*, the artistic presence of the *ethos* is exemplarily clear and developed, since it is precisely – at the same time – the task of art to put the *ethos* of a society and a period into evidence' ('El ethos barroco', in Echeverría 1994b, p. 27).
254   'El ethos barroco', in Echeverría 1994b, p. 14.
255   Ibid.

other authors.[256] This collection contains studies by sixteen other authors on the theme of 'the baroque'.[257] The majority of these essays consist of specialised studies of the development of the baroque (in a broad sense) in Latin America, in contrast to Echeverría's own essay, which we are concerned with, which takes a more theoretical-philosophical form and is situated as the first chapter of the book. Within this collective volume, the range of the concept of the baroque is gradually modified. While it is true that none of the authors have a narrow understanding of the concept in the sense of being limited merely to art history, but not all share Echeverría's concept of culture, which is so broad as to embrace even the most everyday forms of production and consumption. Another difference between these essays is the fact that the concept of the baroque as accepted in art history is understood in different ways. Thus Manrique (one of the eighteen contributors to the book) reproaches Echeverría for not distinguishing 'baroque' from 'mannerism' in the history of art and for erroneously subsuming the latter to the former.[258]

But Echeverría is not interested in making possible, through a mere broadening of art history, a classification of various socio-cultural formations in order to smooth the way for an extremely broad antiquarian history of culture with a materialist appearance, but rather he also seeks a critical concept of history in which the present itself finds its place, as an undetachable element: 'In our case, the need felt by the historiography to construct the concept of a baroque epoch connects with a different need, which appears in the field of critical discourse regarding our present epoch'.[259]

f   The Theoretical Positioning and Explosive Force of the Concept of *Ethos*

The theoretical effort that Bolívar Echeverría undertakes in order to develop this materialist theory of culture does not result from a shallow culturalism,

---

256   'El ethos barroco', in See Echeverría 1994b.
257   On the background of the genesis of the book mentioned above and the research project that gave rise to it, see pp. 80ff of this book, and in particular, note 277.
258   Regarding Echeverría's essay 'Sobre el barroco romano y la Roma de Bernini' (published in Echeverría and Kurnitzky 1993, pp. 75–85), Manrique writes: 'Here I would like to draw attention to certain ambiguities ... that do not help our understanding of either art or historical phenomena. Of course, for me the central issue is the confusion between mannerism and baroque' (Manrique 1994, pp. 238ff).
259   'El ethos barroco', in Echeverría 1994b, p. 14.

but has its cause immediately in social praxis. After the collapse of the Soviet Union and its satellite states, whose social formation – as we expounded – Echeverría understood to be state capitalism, there has not remained even the appearance of an alternative to the capitalist model of socialisation. Nevertheless, the search for an alternative is now more urgent than ever, since the destructive tendencies of the ruling relations continue to have their effects, without anyone stopping them.

'The signs are weak that the modernity which prevails at present is not an ineluctable destination – a programme that we must fulfill until the very end, until the not improbable apocalyptic scenario of a return to barbarism amid planetary destruction – but these signs cannot be ignored'.[260]

What Echeverría means by 'return to barbarism' is clarified when he characterises the twentieth century as an 'era of unprecedented genocides and ecocides'.[261] With this, while correcting the common but false formulation of a 'return', the quoted phrase nevertheless strangely compares the destruction of external nature to genocide. In previous texts, he found more cautious formulations on this topic. In his 1984 introduction to his first book, Echeverría was still reluctant to declare the twentieth century as simply a century of barbarism, and in the framework of a still less developed pessimism, he abstains from making this sort of hasty judgement in a formulation of Auschwitz:[262]

> Just one fact prevents us from speaking of the twentieth century as a period of barbarism. It is not a matter of the existence of a nexus, which, in uniting one barbarity with another, grants them some transcendental significance: a category of necessary evils along the path toward an ultimate good. This one fact is the existence of the Left: a certain community of individuals, a certain fraternity, compact at times, diffuse at others, which has lived this barbaric history as the negation of another desired and possible history which must be reached through revolution.... Because the Left was there, *Auschwitz* was not merely an

---

[260] 'El ethos barroco', in Echeverría 1994b, p. 16.
[261] Ibid.
[262] The fact that the devastation of external nature and the destruction of European Jewry, as well as other twentieth-century genocides, might *in the final instance* have common causes, is one thing; it is another question entirely if we hastily make solemn formulations that understand the multifaceted reality as a single incident, thereby making it too-easily digestible for pseudo-critical hot air about the 'cruelties of modernity', when opposing this is precisely the end of Echeverría's investigations into the relationship between capitalism and modernity.

accidental holocaust provoked by a madman; it was the result of a failure of the Left itself; the excessive sacrifice to be paid by the social body for the triumph of the anti-communist counter-revolution in the Europe of bourgeois civilisation.[263]

What this assertion shares with what Echeverría would later argue in his book about the *ethe* is his hesitance to consider the general tendency toward destruction to be irrepressible. But the difference between the two positions consists in the fact that, in the earlier case, he still ascertains a 'certain' (political) subject, namely 'the Left', which interrogates this tendency in praxis, while this determination is absent in his later position, and Echeverría instead searches for moments of a 'ray of hope' in the absence of a *cultural*[264] uniformity of modernity.[265] In the internal differentiation of capitalist modernity, which he analyses with the help of the concept of the four *ethe*, Bolívar Echeverría attempts to find signs of the transitory character of the seemingly everlasting, for what the capitalist mode of production and its inherent social formations appear today.

It seems that there is a dislocation of the possible point of departure for overcoming the existing social falseness, and therein lay the reason why Echeverría, in his theory of the four *ethe*, completely sidestepped the question of social classes. These four distinct forms for the 'naturalisation' of the capitalist mode of production are carried out not only by the dominant classes, but also by the dominated classes. The different *ethe* of capitalist modernity span (at least potentially) all social classes of the society in question. The exploited, too, can perfectly well follow these paradigms with great fervour, orienting toward them their entire manner of producing and consuming use-values. For Echeverría, this is so obvious that he does not explicitly mention the possibility for these *ethe* to transcend class borders, but rather implicitly leads us to believe that in all of the described differences between the four *ethe* the question of social class does not factor, and he thus limits himself to historical,

---

263 'Presentación' in Echeverría 1986, pp. 11ff.
264 At the risk of boring the reader, we will attempt once again to eliminate any confusion: 'cultural' is again used here in the *broadest possible sense*, as already mentioned several times.
265 'It is an undeniable fact that the dominance of the established modernity is neither absolute nor uniform; as is the fact that it is not a monolithic reality, but is instead composed of innumerable different versions of itself, versions that were defeated and oppressed by another version in the past but which, dominated and subordinated, have not ceased to exist in the present' ('El ethos barroco', in Echeverría 1994b, pp. 16ff).

geographical, and cultural determinations. But the fact of turning his back on the concept of social class or that of the 'left' does not result from an intention on Echeverría's part to conform to the ruling (self-destructive) social formation, but instead he wants to pursue the anti-capitalist project of the Left despite its repeated failures and considerable tendency toward disappearance in the present.[266]

In this sense, the following quotation can be understood as a programmatic statement that this studied author makes with regard to his central concept of *ethos*, and especially the concept of the baroque *ethos*:

> Our interest in investigating the social consistency and historical relevance of a *baroque ethos* thereby appears on the basis of a concern for the contemporary crisis of civilisation and responds to the desire, already trained by experience, to think post-capitalist modernity as a realisable utopia. If baroquism in social custom and in art finds its roots in a *baroque ethos* and if the latter effectively corresponds to one of the capitalist modernities that preceded the current one, surviving within it, we could then think that the exclusionary self-affirmation of the realist and puritan capitalism that predominates in contemporary modernity is ephemeral, and we can also indirectly infer that it is not true that it is impossible to imagine as attainable a modernity whose structure is not established according to the capitalist arrangement of production, circulation, and consumption of social wealth.[267]

---

266 The 'New Left', to which Echeverría himself belonged to some degree from his time in Berlin, is included here. Its efforts to overcome the errors of the old Left have failed completely, as shown by, for example, the speed – which greatly surpassed that of German Social Democrats – with which the German 'Green' Party, which emerged from the New Left and is today supported by many of its old leftist critics, became a bourgeois institution. With the argument of maintaining power, all relevant differences vis-à-vis the conservative political opponent are eliminated, thereby tossing shovelfuls of dirt onto its own political grave. It is apparently this course of events, which has accelerated since 1989, that explains why Echeverría does not say a single word about the New Left as a possible solution. His experiences during the 1960s in Berlin, with the regionalist and Eurocentrist narrow-mindedness of the New Left, its almost always superficial internationalist orientation notwithstanding, made him more careful than many of his contemporaries/ comrades in struggle not to harbour false hope in this political movement. Also, this fact allows us to grasp Echeverría's relevance for the contemporary German debate.

267 'El ethos barroco', in Echeverría 1994b, p. 17.

Echeverría here puts forth four important theoretical theses whose political consequences should not be underestimated.

Form of Civilisation Versus Mode of Production (for Martin Heidegger)

In the first place, the current crisis is understood not only as that of a mode of production, as understood as a general rule in orthodox Marxism, but as a crisis of 'civilisation'. The latter can be understood as one of the basic constants in Echeverría's thought since his younger Heideggerian phase, in which he already saw the Cuban Revolution to be much more radical than the Soviet one, because he interpreted the former as a practical interrogation of not only economic relations (as he saw in the Russian Revolution), but moreover as the point of departure for a 'global transformation of civilisation as such', a 'radical global process of revolution' which 'goes beyond modern, European culture and all that'.[268]

The Finite of the Dominant Modernity and of All Capitalist Modernities (for Karl Marx)

In the second place, Echeverría has clarified the fact that the four different modern *ethe* and their four corresponding modernities are, in their totality, capitalist. It is true that the birth of some modernities comes prior to that of others, but they all exist today and none can be deemed pre-modern in form due to its age, as the 'currently dominant modernity' does to others in its 'exclusionary self-confirmation'.[269]

Moreover, by setting out from the internal differentiation of capitalist modernity, Echeverría seeks to arrive at an 'indirect' conclusion regarding the transitory character of all modernities. While in *Capital* Marx recalls the prior existence of various *pre*-capitalist forms of production in order to mock the bourgeois assumption that the capitalist mode of production is the only imaginable form, one almost innate to humans,[270] Echeverría is not satisfied with this critical thought and, evidently hoping to discover a positive manifestation

---

268 Bolívar Echeverría: Third interview with the author on 10 July at the Faculty of Philosophy and Arts of the UNAM in Mexico City. Tape recording. In the chapter on Echeverría's life and work, we go into greater detail about the positions of that period, and there we reproduce a longer passage from the interview cited above (see p. 48).

269 'El *ethos* barroco', Echeverría 1994b. This idea is also prefigured in Echeverría's early political thought.

270 *Capital*, Vol. I, 'The Fetishism of the Commodity and Its Secret': Marx 1976a, pp. 163–77, here: 169. In this respect, see also pp. 321f of this book.

in the *internal* differentiation of 'capitalist modernity', finds an indication of its surmountability. While he himself characterises this conclusion as 'indirect', this does not change in any way the fact that it has feet of clay. As much as the author of this book sympathises with the result of this 'conclusion' (the claim that a non-capitalist modernity is imaginable), the *conclusion* is not convincing as necessary. Echeverría also fails to say how this will come about 'indirectly'.

Of course, one could reason that, given the lack of uniformity in capitalist modernity, Echeverría deduces possible lines of rupture and the possibility that these might break out into a process of dissolution from within capitalist modernity itself, but there are two objections to this. Such a process could, in the worst of cases, mean the self-destruction of humanity, something that surely does not fit within the concept of non-capitalist modernity. As mentioned above, Echeverría in the same text suggests this possibility, but leaves it out of this point in his reflections. To this author's doubt, one could respond that Echeverría, in his reasoning, works with a double negation. Strictly speaking, he does not discuss the possibility of a non-capitalist modernity, but only the *falseness* of the claim that 'it is *not* possible to imagine a (non-capitalist) modernity as feasible',[271] which means that there is no irrefutable argument against the establishment of a post-capitalist social formation, but nor is there any certainty at all that this will take place.

Our second objection is more serious still. Is it not the case that the internal differentiation – and even eventually the inner turmoil – of capitalist modernity could also be a factor in its stability? Is it true that a homogenous social formation is automatically more firmly in the saddle in history than a heterogeneous one?[272] But even if this heterogeneity were to generate one crisis

---

271 'El ethos barroco', in Echeverría 1994b, p. 17.
272 A series of historic examples seem instead to point toward the opposite, at least if we take as our measure of history not 'forms of civilisation' as a whole, as Echeverría would say, but religious or state *institutions*. Thus, for example, the incredible stability of the Catholic Church owed no doubt to its capacity to preserve its unity and, at the same time, to allow a multitude of internal, for example, local, differences. This contradiction, which is expressed in the unity of declared monotheism and the practiced polytheism of the cult of the saints and above all Mary, is no doubt one of the secrets of its power throughout the centuries. One example in the history of empires would be the Habsburg monarchy, which fully allowed a cultural and linguistic multiplicity under the dominance of Germany without becoming weaker in the least as a result. A final example would be the Mexican PRI, the party that held uninterrupted power longer than any other on Earth, because it knew how to bring into itself – to an astonishing degree – the most diverse oppositional currents without demanding their full adaptation to a homogeneous whole, but only primarily their subordination and reverence for the president – and, in addition,

after another, would this really mean a quicker end or merely a long period of 'internal peace'? Could it not be the case that precisely a happy combination of 'small' crises could stave off the decisive, revolutionary crisis? Echeverría himself discusses this latter idea in another essay, when he speaks of a 'state intervention' whose mission consists of the 'social translation or functionalisation of the effects of an economic dynamic that does not attempt to overcome the crisis affecting it in a nearly chronic manner, or even to 'ride it out', but rather to live with crisis and even make it profitable'.[273]

These objections seem important to us, since Echeverría – despite his acute critiques of 'postmodern' theories – occasionally demonstrates a tendency to celebrate 'heterogeneity' as the bearer of hope, without detailing exactly what this hope is based on. But at this point our objection ends – and it is one which touches merely tangentially upon Echeverría's central argumentative thread (which we have detected to be the most interesting) without cutting it. In the end, Echeverría is interested less in demonstrating that the internal differentiation of capitalist modernity points toward its transitory character,[274] than finding points of departure for the possible configuration of a post-capitalist society which cannot emerge from nothing, but only from the ruins of what comes before (and, as a result, cultural formations which are subordinate in the present gain a special importance).

Christianity and Capitalism (for Max Weber)
In the third place, the above-mentioned 'programmatic' quotation expresses the fact that two of the four *ethe* lie at the centre of Bolívar Echeverría's interest: the baroque *ethos* and the realist *ethos*. The baroque *ethos* corresponds 'to

---

skillfully combining an extreme internal *plurality* with the simultaneous *centralisation* of power. Statements regarding 'civilisations' as a whole are, in essence, more difficult to formulate due to the indeterminacy of the concept, but nor are there, here, unequivocal indications that the most homogeneous are automatically more stable than others. The so-called 'highly developed civilisations' ['Hochkulturen'] are in general distinguished, rather, by their capacity to learn from other forms of culture or civilisation and adopting for themselves elements of those forms in a permanent fashion.

Precisely the capacity to allow diverse cultural elements to enter and to blend them is something that Echeverría mentions positively with regard to the baroque *ethos*. Here, however, a confusion appears which could arise from the fact that history is always written by the victors; therefore, a so-called superior culture, in order to feel its own superiority, tends to proclaim as 'perennially innate' the voluminous legacies it has collected from the cultures it has conquered, thereby creating an objective appearance of homogeneity.

273   Echeverría 1995a, p. 83.
274   For this, one could refer to the classic arguments of Marx.

one of the capitalist modernities which preceded the current one and survives within it',[275] albeit dominated by 'realist, puritan capitalism',[276] which pertains to the realist *ethos*. The baroque *ethos* is closer to Catholicism and the realist *ethos* closer to Protestantism. At first glance, it could perhaps seem that, in relating Protestantism to the question of capitalist relations of production, there is a certain degree of agreement between Echeverría's theory of *ethos* and Max Weber's thought. In this sense, Echeverría's theory also comes under criticism from Juan Villoro.[277] Echeverría himself, by contrast, emphasises the differences with Weber's approach, in which the Protestant ethic is seen as the closest to the spirit of capitalism, therefore giving rise to an unmistakable hierarchy *vis-à-vis* other non-Protestant forms of capitalist modernity, which are thus only conceivable as subordinate or less developed.[278]

> Max Weber's formulation, according to which there is some biunivocal correlation between the 'spirit of capitalism' and the 'Protestant ethic', associated with the assumption that it is impossible to have a modernity which is not capitalist, offers arguments toward the conviction that the only imaginable way of giving order to the modern revolutionising of the productive forces of human society is precisely that which is outlined according to this 'protestant ethic'.[279]

Echeverría, on the other hand, is interested in showing that there exist, moreover, *other* forms of capitalist modernity apart from that which coincides directly with the 'Protestant ethic'. He understands his theory of the four *ethe* of capitalist modernity, and above all the emphasis on the baroque *ethos*, not as a faithful continuation of Weber's theory, but, instead, as an 'attempt to respond to the theoretical dissatisfaction that [Weber's] conviction awakens in all critical perspectives on contemporary society'.[280]

The disciplining element contained in the 'Protestant ethic (in its puritan Calvinist version)' is certainly functional for the development of the capitalist mode of production, as a result of its 'individual technique of productivist

---

275 'El ethos barroco', in Echeverría 1994b, p. 17.
276 Ibid.
277 In this regard, see note 22 on p. 198 of this book.
278 We should additionally note the fact that the concepts of 'ethic' and '*ethos*', despite having some elements in common, are very different, and above all in that the latter is substantially broader than the former.
279 'El ethos barroco', in Echeverría 1994b, p. 17.
280 Ibid.

self-representation and sublimated self-satisfaction',[281] but the 'spirit of capitalism' cannot be reduced to this. Echeverría records the fact – and not in the utopian sense, but in the non-ethnocentric, descriptive sense – that in the reality of ruling social relations, 'to live *in and with* capitalism can be something more than to live *by and for* it'.[282]

Despite this difference between Echeverría and Max Weber, there is a slightly hidden connection between the two. In the final instance, both authors see a connection between the 'spirit of capitalism' (or in Echeverría's case, the four *ethe* of capitalist modernity) and Christian religiosity. Echeverría combines his *ethe* with either the Protestant or Catholic version, whereas Weber – with respect to the 'spirit of capitalism' – does so with a preference for the former. This combination of capitalist ideology with Christian doctrine is not mentioned by either in a direct manner, but appears implicitly in both. Here, there is a similarity with Karl Marx who, at various points in *Capital*, refers ironically but with all seriousness to the intimate relationship between 'political economy and Christianity'.

Excursus: Marx on 'Political Economy and Christianity'
Marx writes, mockingly:

> Oh those heathens! They understood nothing of *political economy and Christianity*, as the learned Bastiat discovered, and before him the still wiser MacCulloch. They did not, for example, comprehend that machinery is the surest means of lengthening the working day. They may perhaps have excused the slavery of one person as a means to the full human development of another. But they lacked the *specifically Christian qualities* which would have enabled them to preach the slavery of the masses in order that a few crude and half-educated parvenus might become 'eminent spinners', 'extensive sausage-makers' and 'influential shoe-black dealers'.[283]

This sort of observation by Marx regarding the 'specifically Christian qualities' which are necessary to propel the capitalist mode of production to its most absurd excesses tend to be bypassed in analyses of his main work, despite their

---

281   'El ethos barroco', in Echeverría 1994b, p. 18.
282   Ibid. In this regard, see moreover: 'El ethos barroco', in Echeverría 1994b, p. 22.
283   Marx 1976a, pp. 532–3, italics by S.G.

undeniable presence in it.[284] In Echeverría, too, we observe the curious circumstance of his not dedicating a single word to Marx's observations on this relation, though he himself had already situated that relation at the very centre of one of his most important formulations. We might be tempted to explain this by recalling the fact that Marx did not systematise his observations on the topic and that, in the majority of cases, these formulations took an ironic form. But could this explanation possibly be sufficient for an author who, for his part, laments the lack of humour on the Left? Moreover, in the subchapter on fetishism in *Capital*, there is a passage on the same topic in which Marx explains in prosaically conceptual form the connection between Christianity – above all its Protestant version – and generalised commodity production (in other words, the capitalist mode of production) through the (abstract) concept of equality that serves as the foundation for both:

> *For a society of commodity producers*, whose general social relation of production consists in the fact that they treat their products as commodities, hence as values, and in this material [*sachlich*] form bring their individual, private labours into relation with each other as homogeneous human labour, *Christianity with its religious cult of man in the abstract*, more particularly in its bourgeois development, i.e. in Protestantism, Deism, etc., is the most fitting form of religion.[285]

---

284 In some way, this is relatively easy to understand in the case of authors whose intention it is to establish a proximity between Marx and Christianity, like for example Enrique Dussel in his book *Las metáforas teológicas de Marx* (Dussel 1993).

285 Marx 1976a, p. 172, italics by S.G. On the economic significance of Protestantism, see also: 'However, in so far as the asceticism of the hoarder is combined with active industry, he is rather a Protestant by religion and still more a Puritan' (Marx 1904, p. 173).

In Volume III of *Capital*, Marx again indicates the difference between Protestantism and Catholicism in relation to the capitalist mode of production (see: 'The monetary system is essentially Catholic, the credit system essentially Protestant. The Scotch hate gold. As paper, the monetary existence of commodities has a purely social existence. It is *faith* that brings salvation. Faith in money value as the immanent spirit of commodities, faith in the mode of production and its predestined disposition, faith in the individual agents of production as mere personifications of self-valorizing capital. But the credit system is no more emancipated from the monetary system as its basis than Protestantism is from the foundations of Catholicism'. This passage would also be relevant for Echeverría's theory of *ethos*, since Marx attempts to grasp here the connections between particular forms of consciousness and everyday life in capitalism with respect to the Catholic and Protestant versions of Christianity (Marx 1981, p. 727).

Bearing in mind that this idea is interwoven in the most intimate way with the argumentative structure of not only the subchapter on fetishism, but also with the totality of *Capital*, the fact that it was 'skipped over' by Echeverría (who for many years gave courses on *Capital* in the Economics Faculty of the Universidad Nacional Autónoma de México) makes us wonder: is what we are seeing here the same mechanism for which Echeverría reproaches Baudrillard, according to which, as we said previously, he is careful not to mention too many of Marx's formulations on a certain thematic in order to not diminish his own contribution as a critical Marxist? Another explanation could be that he does not wish to foreground Marx's critique of commodity production too much, since he himself is drawn to the utopia of a non-capitalist society of commodity producers.

Whatever it is, the importance of the relationship between the Christian religion and the capitalist mode of production cannot be ignored if we look more closely at Marx's main work. Here, we are not referring only to the above-mentioned allusions to the 'specifically Christian qualities',[286] or the 'Christian character of primitive accumulation',[287] but also to his critical observations on Platonism, which in a popularised version had managed to slip into Christian doctrine. Thus Marx makes no secret of his disdain for Plato, whose defence of slavery he understands to be totally distinct from that of Aristotle. He suggests that the latter 'dreams', at least, of a society without slavery and justifies its existence only on account of the low level of development of the productive forces of the period, citing as proof the following phrase: 'if every tool, when summoned, or even by intelligent anticipation, could do the work that befits it, just as the creations of Daedalus moved of themselves, or the tripods of Hephaestus went of their own accord to their sacred work, if the weavers' shuttles were to weave of themselves, then there would be no need either of apprentices for the master craftsmen, or of slaves for the lords'.[288]

Against Plato, on the contrary, Marx writes, mockingly, that: 'the same Platonic idea recurs in the protest of the English bleachers against the clause in the Factory Act providing for fixed meal-times for all workers'. He is referring

---

286 Marx 1976a, p. 533.

287 Marx 1976a, p. 917. 'The treatment of the indigenous population was, of course, at its most frightful in plantation-colonies set up exclusively for the export trade, such as the West Indies, and in rich and well-populated countries, such as Mexico and India, that were given over to plunder. But even in the colonies properly so called, the Christian character of primitive accumulation was not belied' (ibid.).

288 Marx here quotes according to Biese 1842, p. 408 (See 'Machinery and Modern Industry': Marx 1976a, p. 532).

here to the following 'idea' found in Plato: 'If the work, says Plato, has to wait for the labourer, the critical point in the process of production is often missed and the article spoiled'.[289]

This scolding of Plato, which Marx closes with the phrase *'Le platonisme où va-t-il se nicher!* [Where will Platonism be found next!]',[290] should in no way be mitigated by reducing it to a mere 'philosophical remnant' in *Capital*. Instead, it represents part of an entire series of observations Marx makes in his main work on the relationship between economics and ideology. It is true that these lack academic systematisation and are dispersed, but in no case are they accidental, and when seen in terms of their substantial content, they demonstrate a surprising vigour. So Marx's flank attack against Plato and Platonism should be seen in relation to various other observations on the importance of Christian doctrine for capitalist development. In the previously cited passage on Aristotle's 'dream', Marx continues: 'And Antipater, a Greek poet of the time of Cicero, hailed the water-wheel for grinding corn, that most basic form of all machinery, as the liberator of female slaves and the restorer of the golden age. Oh those heathens!'[291]

With which we return to the point of departure for our brief excursus. To conclude, the fact is to be recorded that Juan Villoro's critique of Echeverría – according to which, with the concept of *ethos*, Echeverría distanced himself far away from Marxist discussions and fell into Weber's clutches – cannot be accepted as such, since, as we have seen, Marx himself judged that particular ideologies and behaviours, tied to Christian doctrine, maintained a close relationship to the capitalist mode of production.[292]

Puritanism and Realism

In the fourth place, in the quote above which we have deemed 'programmatic', it is worth observing the following: in the formulation of a 'realist, puritan capitalism', it is clear that the realist *ethos* is granted a puritan element. With respect to the question of use-value, discussed previously, the qualifier 'puritan' should be understood in the sense that the consumption of use-values

---

289 'Division of Labour and Manufacture': Marx 1976a, p. 488 n57.
290 Ibid.
291 Marx 1976a, p. 532.
292 It is difficult to determine here and without formulating it clearly whether or not Villoro's critique of Echeverría is due to an economistic reading of Marx's work by the former, or if he perceives a simplification of Marx's critical concept of ideology, since his critique has only been presented verbally and we have access to nothing more than our brief written notes. On Villoro's critique and Echeverría's response, see p. 198, note 22.

plays a subordinate role *vis-à-vis* their production, and that moreover, there exist preordained manners of consumption which are very determined, self-restricted, and the enemies of pleasure. Under Puritanism, consumption is harnessed to bad conscience, while productive labour is in close proximity to the religious hope for salvation. Consequently, the importance of production over consumption is exaggerated. On the theoretical level, this is not without its consequences either. As we have demonstrated, in his theory of use-value, Echeverría maintains a close relationship between production and consumption, and in so doing, does not establish any sort of hierarchical relationship between the two. Here, we can already note a degree of proximity or sympathy that Echeverría has for the baroque *ethos*, in which consumption plays a much more central role than in the realist *ethos* which predominates today on a global level.

CHAPTER 15

The Four *Ethe* of Capitalist Modernity

The four *ethe* of capitalist modernity, according to Echeverría, are born historically out of four 'distinct epochs of modernity, that is to say, with reference to distinct successive impulses of capitalism – the Mediterranean, the Nordic, the Western, and the Central-European'.[293] The first impulse in this historic succession, namely the Mediterranean, is the one that accompanies the baroque *ethos*.[294] The last, the Central-European, is the one related to the romantic *ethos*. What Echeverría does not indicate explicitly is whether the classic *ethos* maintains a relation with the Nordic impulse and the realist *ethos* with the Western, or if the opposite is the case. But we can suppose that the first is the case. Their sequence in time would support this view: for Echeverría, the Nordic impulse arrives prior to the Western one, and in art history classicism establishes itself before realism. What again obscures the question, raising the possibility that Echeverría himself is not entirely clear on how to establish this pairing, is his formulation in another passage of a 'realist North-West',[295] in which the realist *ethos* can suddenly enter into relation with both the Nordic and Western 'impulses'.

a   The Realist *Ethos*

Naïve and militant fascination for the valorisation of value. (Value is acclaimed, without observing that use-value is sacrificed.)

Echeverría begins his presentation of the four *ethe* of capitalist modernity with the 'realist *ethos*', the predominant one on the global scale today, since it predominates above all in those countries which, in turn, are dominant. The contradiction, which is typical of the capitalist mode of production, between the unavoidable necessity of producing and consuming use-values and the tendency toward their destruction by the production of value, is flatly denied in this *ethos*, and not only in theory, but also practically, in a downright fighting spirit. Just as in all other *ethe*, the realist *ethos* is not, then a simple way of

---

293   'El ethos barroco', in Echeverría 1994b, p. 21.
294   Ibid.
295   Echeverría 1995a, p. 167.

seeing the relationship between use-value and value, but rather the taking of a position with material implications. Ruling social relations are held in high esteem, not only due to their 'insuperable efficiency and goodness', but also due to the '*impossibility* of an alternative world'.[296]

> A first way of converting into immediate and spontaneous the capitalist fact, is that of the behaviour which develops within an attitude of affirmative and militant identification, with the pretension of creativity that the accumulation of capital has, with its pretension not only to faithfully represent the interests of the 'socio-natural' process of reproduction – interests that in reality it represses and deforms – but also of being at the service of the quantitative and qualitative empowerment of the same. The valorisation of value and the development of productive forces would be, within this spontaneous behaviour, more than two coinciding dynamics, one and the same, unitary and indivisible. This elemental *ethos* may be called *realist* for its affirmative character of not only the insuperable efficiency and goodness of the established or 'actually-existing' world, but, above all, of the *impossibility* of an alternative world.[297]

A brief insertion: here, as is generally the case in his texts, Bolívar Echeverría speaks neither of the capitalist mode of production nor of capitalist relations of production, as these are commonly formulated in Marx, but instead of the 'capitalist fact' and elsewhere of 'capitalist reality',[298] or he describes these as simply 'the capitalist [thing] [*lo capitalista*]'.[299] This evidently has to do with his interest in not only relations of production but, generally, in specific qualities of a historic form of the organisation of social life. Regardless, it is worth asking here why it is that Echeverría does not employ the term (common in this context) of 'bourgeois society'.

Another possible explanation for his terminology, which is quite unusual among Marxists, could be that he wants to avoid a direct identification of his work with Marxism. Similarly as in the case of other non-dogmatic Marxist authors, we can ask if this discrepant terminology indicates a degree of caution so that the generalised rejection of Marx's work (in these days in which capitalist relations of production are celebrated in almost all quarters as insuperable) might not drag him into the abyss of collective damnation, or if we are dealing with a conceptual difference with regard to earlier Marxism, which in Mexico

---

296 'El ethos barroco', in Echeverría 1994b, p. 20.
297 'El ethos barroco', in Echeverría 1994b, pp. 19ff.
298 'El ethos barroco', in Echeverría 1994b, p. 20.
299 'El ethos barroco', in Echeverría 1994b.

was, above all, dogmatic. But this alternate explanation does not go any further, since it still cannot explain why Bolívar Echeverría, as we have said above, continues to refer explicitly in his most recent writings to *Capital* as one of the decisive foundations for understanding the modern world.

Another possible interpretation could be that he does not use the concept of 'bourgeois society' because he considers it to be part of a rigid image of history (an 'obsessive idea of a linear progression of history'),[300] one responsible for many failed interpretations of history and of the present in Latin America, according to which the continent must first 'enter' into the bourgeois epoch.[301]

b The Romantic *Ethos*

Deceptive fascination for use-value. (Use-value is acclaimed, thereby overlooking that it is not this, but value, which is favoured.)

Echeverría refers to the second *ethos* of capitalist modernity as 'romantic'. This second *ethos* also overlooks (if it does not deny outright)[302] the fact that the dynamic of producing value is not in any way identical to that of producing use-values, with the difference being that, in contrast to the realist *ethos*, it is not the dynamic of value that is extolled as the single bearer of happiness, but instead that of use-value. Therefore, it sets out from the idea that the social organisation of production and consumption always revolves around use-value. Such a view does not admit any contradiction with the 'needs' of the valorisation of value. The 'life' of capital is conceived as a great adventure, and the capitalists transformed from mere administrators into true heroes. In this *ethos*, Echeverría alludes to the everyday language that we all know and to the propaganda language of corporations, in which we can find many adequate expressions of the romantic *ethos*. For example, capitalists become

---

300   Echeverría and Kurnitzky's foreword to Frank *et al.* 1969, p. 9.
301   'Latin America cannot "enter" the bourgeois epoch because it has been in it since the Iberian conquest', Echeverría wrote as early as 1968, and we could assume that today he continues to subscribe to this early position. (See Echeverría 1968, p. 13. In this regard, see also p. 213 of this book.)
302   Echeverría says that the romantic *ethos* denies the contradiction inherent to the capitalist mode of production. We must consider that in Spanish, the term 'negar' [to deny – trans.] is also used in the psychoanalytic sense of *'verdrängen'*. In Echeverría's formulations regarding the romantic *ethos*, it is never entirely clear which of the two meanings of the word he refers to, whether to an active negation of this contradiction which is more or less conscious, or to an unconscious displacement of the same – but it is possible to set out on the basis of the assumption that he has both aspects in mind simultaneously.

'entrepreneurs', or in other words, *men* who supposedly undertake something exciting, collective economic projects become 'joint ventures'. Moreover, the boardroom masters – surrounded by a swarm of security and various facilities with air conditioning, and protected by the most expensive medical insurance, if necessary covering their immediate transport from any point on Earth to the best possible hospital existing in any given case – like nothing more than to speak of the great 'risk' they have run, by which they are almost always referring to the risk of those who depend on a salary, and who, if something goes wrong in the 'adventure', will be thrown out on the street. At least Odysseus was alongside his men when they were put to the test by all the dangers. Today's exploiters, who would not survive an hour in *The Odyssey*, speak as though the hero of Antiquity were a poor, easily frightened devil compared to them. This is the romantic *ethos*. In every transfer of capital everything is on the line, but this is supposedly always a question of the production and consumption of use-value, with everything else a mere appendage.

> A second way of naturalising the capitalist thing [*lo capitalista*], as militant as the first but completely counterposed to it, also implies the confusion of the two terms, but not within an affirmation of value but precisely of use-value itself. In this view, 'valorisation' appears as fully reducible to the 'natural form'. As a result of the 'entrepreneurial spirit', valorisation itself would thus be nothing more than a variant of the realisation of the natural form, since this 'spirit' would be, in turn, one of the figures or subjects which makes of history a permanent adventure, on the level of the human individual as on that of collective humanity. In what is likely a perverse mutation, this metamorphosis of the 'good' or 'natural world' into the 'hell' of capitalism would not cease to be a 'moment' of the 'miracle' that is Creation itself. This peculiar manner of living with capitalism, which is affirmed insofar as this social form is transfigured into its opposite, pertains to the *romantic ethos*.[303]

This way of 'naturalising' the capitalist mode of production is accomplished not only by the dominant classes, but also by the dominated. As previously mentioned, this theoretical lack of differentiation between antagonistic social classes is also valid for the other three *ethe* of capitalist modernity.

---

303   'El ethos barroco', in Echeverría 1994b, p. 20.

c   The Classic *Ethos*

Tragic fulfilment of the capitalist way of things. (With all heartfelt pain, use-value is sacrificed to value.)

In the classic *ethos* of capitalist modernity, the contradiction between value and use-value – inherent to the capitalist mode of production – is not denied (in contrast to the first two *ethe*, which each do it in their different ways), but here also it is assumed that a political practice against it would be impossible, as well as no militant support for existing relations is proposed, as this would be equally superfluous. The established social relations seem untransformable, and the predominant attitude here is one of the 'tragic fulfilment' of the social process, destined beyond the influence of human subjectivity. In the classic *ethos*, the existing is not glorified, and nor are its contradictions are brushed under the table, as occurs in both the realist and romantic *ethe*, but all (more radical) rebellion is held to be senseless.[304]

Going beyond Echeverría, in the present context we could, instead, compare this *ethos* of capitalist modernity with the political attitude of social democracy, in those periods in which it was still at least reformist and did not celebrate capitalism as inevitable. In principle, it admitted the existence of problems, which emerge, necessarily from capitalist relations of production. But, at the same time – above all when in power – its proponents pointed to the 'necessities derived from political realism' [*Sachzwänge*/material constraints] which unfortunately only allow for reforms within narrow limits (and, moreover, only when no capitalist feels too affected and the 'general situation of the economy' allows for it). The Marxian critique of ideology, in the interpretation of György Lukács, is doubtless applicable to this *ethos* with even greater force. While it is true that this *ethos* holds up the will to change something, it simultaneously insists on the impossibility of altering with human hands something created by humans, which is a posture typical of 'reified consciousness'.[305] The classic *ethos* is accompanied by 'the distancing and equanimity of a stoic rationalism', according to which view all 'attitudes for or against what exists, which

---

304   Ibid. 'The classic *ethos*, in turn, does not erase ... the contradiction of the capitalist fact; it clearly distinguishes this contradiction, but allows it to live as something given and unchangeable, with regard to which there is no room for the militant attitude either for or against' (Echeverría and Kurnitzky 1993, pp. 68ff).
305   In this regard, see also the subchapter 'Contribution to the Reconstruction of the Concept of Ideology in the Critique of Political Economy', in this book.

is a militant attitude in its enthusiasm or in its lamentation' seem 'pointless and superfluous'.³⁰⁶

To conclude, let us examine Echeverría's formulation regarding the third *ethos* of capitalist modernity, which, after these clarifications, ought to be digestible:

> To live the spontaneity of capitalist reality as the result of a transcendental necessity, that is to say, as a fact whose detestable traits are compensated in the final instance with the positivity of effective existence, which is beyond the limit of action and valuation that corresponds to the human, is the third manner of doing so. This is the manner of the *classic ethos*; distanced: not committed against a negative purpose, which is perceived as incontestable, but rather, acting understandingly and constructively within the tragic fulfilment of the course of things.³⁰⁷

d   The Baroque *Ethos*

Paradoxical combination of sobriety and rebellion. (Use-value is to be saved by passing through its clearly seen destruction.)

The baroque *ethos* shares with the classic *ethos* the fact that it neither erases nor conceals the contradiction between use-value and value under the capitalist mode of production, as occurs under the realist *ethos*, and nor does it ignore this contradiction, as does the romantic *ethos*. But the difference *vis-à-vis* the classic *ethos* stems from the fact that the baroque *ethos* does not adopt a tragic attitude toward this contradiction.³⁰⁸ It recognises existing relations in the sense of a knowledge-act, but does not do so in the sense of a decision-act. As a result, it represents a paradoxical attitude:³⁰⁹ knowing that use-value is fully

---

306 Echeverría 1995a, p. 165.
307 'El ethos barroco', in Echeverría 1994b, p. 20.
308 'El ethos barroco', in Echeverría 1994b, p. 21.
309 See 'El ethos barroco', in Echeverría 1994b, p. 26, and see also p. 31. On the concept of the paradoxical as a less irrational posture, in an unreasonable world, than the apparently logical one, see also Horkheimer and Adorno 2002, p. 147, where the authors discuss the 'paradoxical Christians' as the only Christians who managed to avoid Christianity's anti-Semitic tendency.

In order to grasp Echeverría's reasoning regarding the baroque *ethos*, which is occasionally obscure (for example, when he speaks of saving oneself from destruction through destruction), it can be useful to refer to the ideas of the Frankfurt School which, on more

subjugated to the dynamic proper to the law of value, and knowing that this social relation cannot simply be abolished/overcome [*aufheben*], the baroque *ethos* attempts nevertheless to live the true within the false. This *ethos*, like the other three fundamental *ethe*, belongs to *capitalist modernity*. Thus it does not contain any anti-capitalist tendency, but nevertheless entails the incessant attempt to break the rules of capitalist relations of production. Now, this is not toward the higher end of achieving better social relations; but in every individual case there is an attempt, despite everything, to save use-value and with it enjoyment. As an example, we could think here of the great festivities in which, even amid a situation of suffering and repression, participants find moments of undeniable happiness. The fact that such happiness is not possible in-itself and for-itself within the existing order is grasped with clarity and good sense, in contrast to the realist *ethos* (which is not concerned directly with human happiness) and the romantic *ethos* (which specialises in negation/repression in psychological terms [*Verdrängung*]). But the fact that this happiness should simply exist in the here and now (not as a result of the logic of history, but because everything would be in vain otherwise) counterposes the baroque to the classic *ethos*, the latter of which delights in the semblance of wise suffering. According to this view, the baroque *ethos* is 'a strategy which accepts the laws of mercantile circulation..., while simultaneously refusing to conform to them and subjecting them to a play of transgressions which refunctionalises them'.[310]

In the baroque *ethos* of capitalist modernity, we find a 'conflictual combination of conservatism and non-conformity'.[311] It is conservative because it does not rebel against capitalism, although it is against the latter's tendency toward the destruction of use-values; it is also conservative because, in general, it holds on to the existing social relations, also with regard to culture, but it is precisely the case that the latter is already part of its non-conformism, since, in the end, the baroque *ethos* is not satisfied by the destruction of use-values and resulting sign systems, as discussed in previous chapters. While Echeverría does not, in these theoretical texts, refer directly to everyday politics, on this

---

than one point, come into contact with those of Echeverría. Thus, Horkheimer's following phrase from the year 1940 can be interpreted as one which formulates a paradoxical idea, as could be typical for the baroque *ethos* which – despite dissolving into absurdity when confronted with formal logic – says more about current history than many 'congruent' phrases did. 'As long as world history follows its logical course, it fails to fulfill its human destiny' Horkheimer 1982, p. 117.

310 'El ethos barroco', in Echeverría 1994b, pp. 26ff.
311 'El ethos barroco', in Echeverría 1994b, p. 26.

point we could mention the fact that he considers the Zapatista uprising, which has since 1994 torn off Mexico's appearance of social stability, to be heavily invested with the baroque *ethos*.[312] Here, we find this same peculiarly conflictive combination of conservatism and non-conformity, which has not yet been truly captured by any analyst. The Zapatistas come from one of the furthest corners of the country, where leftist politics are less well-known than all the soda brands; they live in ways that can occasionally strike us as archaic, and they speak languages that in modern Mexico are held to be residues of long-extinct epochs, whose disappearance – according to this ideology – is a necessary component of the country's 'modernisation'. In negotiations with the government, their representatives wear clothing that would make any Western European anti-authoritarian shudder, and, nevertheless, they have something that no one would dare to doubt: a rebellious and almost revolutionary pulse which, in a world in which history had supposedly come to an end, was only imaginable as an illusory daydream.

Returning to Echeverría's text, we can say that the paradoxical attitude of the baroque *ethos* is expressed through the fact that use-values are constituted *within* and *through* the dynamic of their own destruction: 'That [specific] way of being modern is baroque, which allows one to live the destruction of the qualitative – a destruction produced by capitalist productivism – by converting this destruction into access to the creation of another, provocatively imaginary, dimension of the qualitative'.[313]

Thus the destructive tendency of the current social formation is not denied (romantic *ethos*), nor is it implicitly celebrated (realist *ethos*), and nor is it mourned (classic *ethos*), but rather what is attempted is to turn it 'on its head'; in a certain way, to misuse or deceive it, using it for ends which are totally alien to it.

If we take a step back and look upon the topic from a distance, we may find out that there is a parallel in this way of thinking to the hope that Karl Marx maintains imperturbably in his work. Marx sets out from the idea that the capitalist mode of production and its corresponding bourgeois social formation are already producing their own gravediggers. In the moment of greatest desperation, then, he sees a ray of hope, emerging from the very causes of that desperation. In the baroque *ethos*, however, this whole contradictory process occurs *within* the capitalist mode of production; the rays of hope do not point directly toward something post-capitalist. This is one of the biggest differences from the Marxian conception.

---

312   In this regard, see pp. 204f of this book.
313   'El ethos barroco', in Echeverría 1994b, p. 21.

To explain this peculiarly paradoxical *ethos*, Echeverría compares it to eroticism, following Georges Bataille's definition. 'Bataille's idea of eroticism, which he called the "affirmation of life (chaos) even within death (the cosmos)" can be transferred, without too much violence (or perhaps even correctly), to the definition of the baroque *ethos*'.[314]

This parallel between the baroque *ethos* and eroticism – we could say, interpreting Echeverría – points toward a central aspect of this fourth *ethos* of capitalist modernity. In eroticism, it tends to be precisely *the Other*, which is attractive. In contrast to those 'theories' which proliferate everywhere today and offer a supposed explanation for racism – re-baptised as 'xenophobia' – to fear or even to hate the 'other' is *not* a natural characteristic of the human. Rather, we can find the exact opposite in an element of human behaviour and feeling which is of no small importance, that is, in eroticism. Echeverría considered this to be something characteristic of the baroque *ethos*, just as it comes accompanied by cultural *mestizaje*,[315] which he understands as 'codigophagia [*códigofagia*]',[316] which is to say, a mutual devouring of social sign systems (in the broadest sense, described above, which has use-value as its basis).[317]

This capacity for '*mestizaje*', which is distinctive to the baroque *ethos* and congruent with its paradoxical attitude (since it is paradoxical to accept the other, despite everything, in competitive society), largely exists in Latin America, as does the baroque *ethos*.[318] But this does not result from the fact that perhaps better humans lived there, but simply from a historical situation which, according to Echeverría's analysis, continues to provoke consequences in the present. In the sixteenth century, the two existing forms of culture in Spanish America, and the collective subjects supporting them, were in danger of extinction. The rest of the pre-Hispanic societies found themselves in a

---

314   Ibid.
315   On the concept of 'cultural *mestizaje*', see the indications on pp. 79f of this book.
316   'El ethos barroco', in Echeverría 1994b, p. 32.
317   Given the manner in which Echeverría describes this 'cultural *mestizaje*', we can see why he considers it useful to incorporate semiotics into his theory: '*Mestizaje*, the natural way of life of cultures, does not seem to be comfortable either in the chemical (the juxtaposition of qualities) or biological forms (the intersection or combination of qualities) in which it is generally understood. Everything suggests that this is instead a *semiotic process* which we could deem "codigophagia"' (ibid., italics by S.G.).
318   'It is possible to say, then, ... that the strategy of cultural *mestizaje* particular to the Ibero-American tradition is a baroque strategy which coincides perfectly with the behaviour characteristic of the baroque *ethos* of European modernity and with the baroque attitude of the post Renaissance facing the classical canons of Western art' ('El ethos barroco', in Echeverría 1994b, p. 36: see, moreover, pp. 27–36).

process of generalised decomposition. Of the original inhabitants of the continent, 90 percent had died as a result of the European conquest (through excessive labour, deficient nourishment, maltreatment, murder, new illnesses, and a long list of other reasons). The Spanish-born inhabitants were also in danger. In that period, their mother country abandoned them and they were forced to figure out how to save themselves. In that situation, the only salvation for both sides was to get involved with a cultural *'mestizaje'*. They did this not out of magnanimity or a high degree of tolerance, but purely for the need to survive.[319] It was in this historical situation that both 'cultural *mestizaje*' and the powerful presence of the baroque *ethos* in the southern part of the American continent were born.

This aspect of the baroque *ethos*, which gives it, in principle, more possibilities of openness toward other cultures, and thereby makes it less directly inclined to aggressive racism than the other *ethe*, is a key reason why Echeverría dedicates so much space to its analysis. If the baroque *ethos* (like the other three *ethe* described) is inserted within capitalism, it nevertheless has something intrinsic to it, which could eventually be rescued and transferred to a post-capitalist society: namely, its relatively meager proclivity toward racism, in comparison to the other *ethe* of capitalist modernity.[320]

Among the other historical reasons that the baroque *ethos* gained particular force in Latin America, Echeverría discussed the historical presence of the Jesuits, above all during the seventeenth and early eighteenth centuries, and the projects they attempted here. He sees them as executors 'of the Catholic Church's effort to create its own, religious modernity which would revolve around the revitalisation of the faith – posed as an alternative to the individualistic and abstract modernity that revolved around the vitality of capital'.[321]

Echeverría considered it justified to speak experimentally of a 'Jesuit modernity' that was attempted, for example, in the Paraguayan 'Reductions'.[322] These

---

319 'El ethos barroco', in Echeverría 1994b, pp. 36f.
320 None of this is to suggest in any way that there is no racism in Latin America, which would be an absurd claim. The 1994 Zapatista rebellion that we have mentioned was born, among other things, precisely as a movement against the racist oppression of indigenous peoples, which exists throughout Latin America. Here, our end is only to compare the various capitalist modernities and to describe, moreover, what constitutes, according to Echeverría, the baroque *ethos*, which determines everyday life in Latin America in only a partial manner, since here, as in other cases, there exists a combination of the basic forms of *ethe* of capitalist modernity. In this combination of *ethe*, just as is the case everywhere today, also in Latin America the predominant form is the realist *ethos*.
321 'El ethos barroco', in Echeverría 1994b, p. 29.
322 Echeverría (intervention in debate), Echeverría and Kurnitzky 1993, p. 43.

indigenous communities, organised into small societies by Jesuits in various regions of Paraguay, experimented with forms of economics and socialisation in which, while a market did exist, the capitalist dynamic was not supposed to reign. Given that, as we have seen above, Echeverría considered production for the market (that is, the commodity production) to be one of the decisive characteristics of modernity, and since the Paraguayan Jesuits attempted a system of commodity production without capitalism, we have, here, an early form of an attempt to construct a non-capitalist modernity. The fact that the Jesuits failed in their project and were expelled from Paraguay (and from all of New Spain) in 1767, with which the Reductions were dissolved, does not reduce Echeverría's interest in this historical attempt, since what he is looking for is a contemporary theoretical proposal for a non-capitalist modernity.[323] In his estimation, the Jesuits in Paraguay had a clear understanding of the laws of the capitalist economy: 'They saw, from the outset, that the free laws of the market lead necessarily to monopoly, and they therefore believed that what was important was to combat monopolies through the presence of the state or, better put, a religious state entity'.[324]

The Jesuit project for modernity, borne of the attempt to present an alternative to Protestantism and its concomitant *form* of modernity, is more than a simple counteroffensive against the Reformation and should not be misunderstood as an anti-modern project or a mere reformulation of earlier forms of Catholicism.[325] What is specific to this project of 'Jesuit modernity' is the claim to bring together two things, which, according to Echeverría, do not harmonise in reality: political economy and justice.[326] But how is this contradiction to be

---

[323] 'It was therefore a very peculiar utopia that they [the Jesuits] attempted to implant; that of production for the market, but for a "domesticated" market, for a market dominated by a political-religious distributive process. This project ... is no doubt a modern one, but it is not modern-capitalist' (ibid.).

[324] Ibid.

[325] '... [T]his other proposal, that of Ignacio de Loyola, is not merely a defence, an attempt to regain territory that the Church lost with the Reformation, but one that instead claims to be more powerful than the latter': Echeverría (intervention in debate), in Echeverría and Kurnitzky 1993, p. 36). Shortly before this, Echeverría suggests: 'What the Jesuits attempted was to introduce a dynamism into this drama, to light up the everyday life of the Christian, "to modernise it". To make it not a question of waiting for a future life (life in heaven) but of conquering Blessedness' (p. 35).

[326] Ibid. Here, Echeverría does not go into the problem that, according to Marx, in the ruling political economy of capitalism a form of justice prevails as a general rule, and this justice is precisely that of the exchange of equivalents. With this, he rejects exactly those theories and practices which set out from the idea that all that is necessary is a bit more moral

overcome? Precisely through a typically 'baroque' method, that of the 'confusion of opposites': 'the risky (and in many cases even insane) claim of substituting the "subjective" action of the believer for the "objective" action of capital can only be accomplished by working on the plane of the imaginary, through the secularisation – or even popularisation – of mysticism, of vertiginous experience, systematised by baroque art, of the confusion of opposites'.[327]

This tendency toward 'insanity' is characteristic of the baroque *ethos*, since it attempts something which is completely insane, namely, as we have said, to make the salvation of use-value possible *through* its destruction. In the case of the Jesuits in Latin America, this insanity, for Echeverría, is also expressed in the desire to give general access to a *secret* doctrine, mysticism, which is evidently absurd. The 'predominance' of the baroque *ethos* in Latin America during the seventeenth and eighteenth centuries was 'central and open' and is by today only 'marginal and subterraneous'.[328]

e   **Non-existence of the Historical *Ethe* in Pure Form**

How is this 'marginal predominance' we have just discussed imaginable? The explanation of Echeverría's slightly strange expression stems in part from the idea that the realist *ethos* predominates today on the world scale, but is nowhere present in pure form, instead always appearing as mixed with the other three *ethe* of capitalist modernity. But, as a general rule, one of these other three *ethe* becomes, in turn, *predominant* among the *marginal ones*.[329] Hence our point here is to suggest, after our brief presentation of Echeverría's classification of the four *ethe* of capitalist modernity, that these are ideal types,

---

behaviour and less fraud for the brutality of existing conditions to cease. For Marx, the problem is much more complex, in discovering that surplus value and, with it, exploitation as well are possible without 'fraud', through the certain difference between the value of the commodity labour-power and the value it creates in labour (through its *use*).

Marx already outlines the essentials of a critique of the bourgeois concept of justice, which is problematic because it sets out from equality among human beings. But the concept of equality is already questionable in itself, as has been studied in, for example, Horkheimer and Adorno's *Dialectic of Enlightenment*, as being not only a theoretical and practical weapon against previously-given conditions of oppression and exploitation but also, at the same time, their very foundation in the present (see p. 255, note 188 of this book).

327   Echeverría (intervention in debate), Echeverría and Kurnitzky 1993, p. 32.
328   'El ethos barroco', in Echeverría 1994b, p. 28.
329   'El ethos barroco', in Echeverría 1994b, p. 22.

which thus do not appear in a pure form in reality. This is not the case only because, as we have just mentioned, the realist *ethos* is practically always the predominant one and the other *ethe* can only coexist as subordinate, but moreover because as a whole, and therefore also in other times, the reality of the historical *ethe* is always much more complex than can be grasped with a simply fourfold classification: 'It is worth adding ... that none of these four elemental strategies of civilisation offered by capitalist modernity can effectively emerge in isolated, and much less exclusive, form. Each one always appears, in the effective life of the different historical "world constructions" of the modern epoch. The way of these combinations with the others is different in each case, according to the circumstances'.[330]

These constraints on the conception of the four *ethe* of capitalist modernity are important in the sense that they do not emerge in reality in the previously described forms. Their concepts can serve only as a connecting thread for understanding the different forms that modernity takes today in different places, and this point is also important because Echeverría does not in any way attempt to fix particular national characteristics or anything of the sort; rather, he decidedly rejects this. The folklorisation of Latin Americans as 'baroque' or 'magical realists' seems to Echeverría to be, in the final instance, nothing more than a part of the strategy of the dominant *ethos* to rid itself of the baroque *ethos* by banishing it to the 'non-world of pre-modernity'.[331] The baroque *ethos* is not something directly visible and nor does it pump in the 'blood' of Latin Americans, and nor can it be easily fixed in multicoloured masks of the devil or in *exotic* funerals, but rather, as was explained at the outset of the discussion of Bolívar Echeverría's theory, this *ethos* is installed in the basic forms of producing and consuming use-values as the foundation of the entire social sign system; thus, it is installed in the very foundation of the real economic structure of the respective societies and, as a result, is as far from folklore as it is from genetics.

f   Textual Variations of the Concept of *Ethos*

In the previously expressed sense, it is worth observing a radicalisation of the critical, non-affirmative aspect of Echeverría's theory of the *ethe*, insofar as in recent texts he opposes the presumption of 'pure' historical *ethe* with greater decisiveness than he had in earlier works. In the text 'Modernidad y

---

330   Ibid.
331   'El ethos barroco', in Echeverría 1994b, pp. 28f.

capitalismo (*15 Tesis*)', which appeared in 1995 but was written in 1992, and whose seventh thesis is taken up again in his essay on 'The baroque *ethos*'[332] (published in 1994 but clearly written after the '15 Theses'), he says:[333] '[Each of the four *ethe*] can, however, play a dominant role in that composition, organise its combination with the others, and force these to translate themselves into its terms in order to become manifest. It is only in this relative sense that we can speak, for example, of a "classic modernity" *vis-à-vis* a "romantic" one, or of a "realist mentality" in contrast to a "baroque" one'.[334]

The newer formulation of these lines puts it this way: 'What happens is that the *ethos* which has come to play the dominant role in this composition, the realist *ethos*, is the one which organises its own combination with the others and forces them to translate themselves into its terms in order to become manifest. It is only in this relative sense that we can speak of capitalist modernity as a scheme of civilisation which requires and imposes the use of the "Protestant ethic"'.[335]

Let us note briefly the differences between the two formulations. To start, what is surprising in the first is the term 'mentality', which Echeverría is still using there. In the second formulation this term no longer appears, which is congruent with the framework of his theory of *ethe* and the insistence on use-value as the foundation for these *ethe*. A certain idealistic tendency, which as a general rule sneaks easily into such studies, is also expressed here, something which Echeverría seems to want to correct and improve by eliminating the term. Regardless, the term 'mentality' is not to be found anywhere else in his work.

The other difference consists in the fact that the emphasis is displaced from a comparison of the four *ethe* (with the four considered to be powerfully present up to the present) toward the judgement that today there can be no such thing as a 'classic modernity' or 'romantic modernity' or, it would seem, a 'baroque' modernity either, in contrast to what remains insinuated in the first quotation. According to the new formulation, now only realist modernity

---

332 This peculiar inversion of the order of printing, vis-à-vis the order in which the drafts of the texts in question were completed, is no rarity in Mexico, and is related to the characteristics of the publishing system in this country, in which long periods can pass from when a text is finished and when it is finally published. Note, moreover, that the two texts appeared almost simultaneously, since one came out at the end of 1994 and the other in early 1995.

333 In the text of the '15 Tesis', this passage is slightly different from what appears in the most recent version of 'El *ethos* barroco', but this change is not relevant here.

334 Echeverría 1995a, p. 166.

335 'El ethos barroco', in Echeverría 1994b, p. 22.

exists, in which the realist *ethos* is also dominant; the other three *ethe* can now only exist insofar as they are 'translated' into the realist *ethos*, that is, only insofar as they manage to express their own logic according the sign system of the latter. We should not underestimate the importance of this displacement of emphasis. In his '15 Theses' on modernity and capitalism, Echeverría was greatly concerned to arrive at the conclusion that not only did diverse forms of modernity exist in the past, but that these survive today as well, at least in particular places and spaces of social life. By contrast, with his formulation in the book *Modernidad, mestizaje cultural, ethos barroco* [*Modernity, Cultural Mestizaje, Baroque Ethos*], this position is partially retracted. Now all that is emphasised is that *there were* other modernities in the past and that these effectively constituted modern, and not pre-modern, forms of socialisation. Immediately, he indicates that these *ethe* – which correspond to those past modernities – survive as dominated ones, but not completely destroyed, within the current, realist modernity.

This reformulation resolves, moreover, a problem found in his book *Las ilusiones de la modernidad* [*The Illusions of Modernity*]. While in this book, as we have said, he upholds (in the '15 Theses') the existence of *various* modernities, in a more recent essay – included in the same book – there appears a critique of the three fundamental 'modern myths' (these are: the myth of the revolution, the myth of the nation, and the myth of democracy)[336] without specifying to which modernity this alludes. It is clear that one paragraph features the observation that the predominant 'political culture' of the current modernity is 'realist',[337] but there is no mention of the possibility of a political culture or modernity, which is baroque, classic, or romantic. This problem is

---

336 See 'Postmodernidad y cinismo' in Echeverría 1995a.
337 Referring implicitly to Heidegger's critique of humanism, Echeverría speaks of the predominant political culture of today, the same which, among other things, he calls the 'humanist political culture': 'The humanist political culture reaffirms the human being of modernity in the illusion it is living, that it is the *maître et possesseur de la nature*, and does so because it is in a position to define the modern human being as the creative subject of a "harmonious" social world, one based on "material well-being". This is a *realist political culture* to the degree that it goes hand-in-hand with the expansion of capitalist wealth, with the in principle unlimited growth of the new productive forces which capitalism instrumentalises along with its capacity to produce abundance. It is thus a realist political culture, as all data contradicting its claim to build the utopia of the shining city can be interpreted convincingly as "problems" that this political culture and Progress will solve "in the future". The *"realism" of modern political culture*, its capacity to "translate" the positivity of the "life" of capital to the level of the everyday, rational activity of social individuals, is accomplished through the construction of a *mythical complex* that combines

resolved through the new formulation of the passage discussed above, once it is completely clear that Echeverría's studies of contemporary modernity refer in theoretical form and with critical intention to realist modernity.

A question remains in the air: where did this shift, which is already outlined in the book *Las ilusiones de la modernidad* [*The Illusions of Modernity*], come from? On the one hand, this is, no doubt, an expression of Echeverría's own theoretical development, but we can also suppose that important stimuli emerged from the research project headed by Echeverría, as well as from the colloquia organised by this project.[338]

---

three different myths: that of the revolution, that of the nation, and that of democracy' (Echeverría 1995a, p. 42, italics by S.G.).

338 See in this regard p. 79 of this book.

CHAPTER 16

Ethos and Ideology

a   Limitations of the Concept of *Ethos*

We will now turn to a reflection on the limitations of the concept of historical *ethos* in Bolívar Echeverría. We are not interested in criticising the minutiae of his descriptions of each of the four modern *ethe*, which no doubt could be formulated (from a sociological, historical, or art-historical perspective) regarding various aspects or inaccuracies of Echeverría's theory, as does, for example, the well-known art historian Manrique who we have discussed above. The latter highlights a fixation on the Jesuits in Echeverría's presentation of the baroque *ethos* in Latin America, while according to Manrique, there were other Catholic orders which were at least equally important in the stamp they left on the everyday culture of the continent today (for example, the Franciscans).[339]

But all this critique of details, while no doubt instructive, is not what most interests us here, since it would require in the first place a more detailed exposition of Echeverría's theory than we have provided, and would require that we undertake vast and specialised studies on the controversial points; none of this would affect Echeverría himself much at all, since for him, the demonstration of one or another inaccuracy in his historical references or in art history does not in any way mean that his theory of the *ethe* as such is cast into doubt.[340]

Here, what we are doing is something more: to ascertain whether or not his theory of the four *ethe* of capitalist modernity contains weakness of principle,

---

339 'The importance of the Jesuits in the enterprise of the new Catholic affirmation and in the creation of the baroque is undeniable, but they were far from the only ones, either in Europe or in the Americas. The *propaganda fide* [diffusion of Catholicism through the *ad hoc* Roman congregation] was a Franciscan, not a Jesuit, affair' (Manrique 1994, p. 241).

On the technical papal term '*propaganda fide*', note that the *Diccionario ideológico de la lengua española* indicates for the word 'propaganda', as its first meaning: 'congregation of cardinals of the Roman Curia, responsible for spreading the Catholic religion' (*Diccionario ideológico de la lengua española* 1990, p. 683).

340 This could also be one of the reasons why Echeverría was able (seemingly without serious problems) to include in the collective volume he edited, *Modernidad, mestizaje cultural y ethos barroco* [*Modernity, cultural* mestizaje, *baroque ethos*] the cited text by Manrique, which contains a fairly sharp critique of several errors of detail by both Echeverría and some of the other participants in the research project.

or to put it differently, to determine whether or not to arrive at the highest degree of understanding this theory does not end up paying too high a price.

Let us, then, present a brief recap of the advances offered by Echeverría in his theory of the *ethe*. His objective is, firstly, to oppose the Eurocentric presumption that only the modernity which predominates today, is a 'true' modernity, and that all other forms are merely proto-forms or poor copies of it. With these differences internal to capitalist modernity established, he then seeks to establish the possibility of a post-capitalist modernity.[341] Returning to the critique of Eurocentrism, we can say that Echeverría must, in order to analyse the various forms of (capitalist) modernity, proceed with a certain degree of agility in his presentation of the corresponding *ethe*. In so doing, he is conscious of the fact that these contain much that is false and that they include forms of self-deception, since they must make tolerable that which is in reality intolerable. But what is decisive is where it is that Echeverría locates precisely the origin of this falseness of the *ethe* of capitalist modernity. In the end, this lies in what he calls 'capitalism' or 'the capitalist thing [*lo capitalista*]' or 'the fact of capitalism', which he carefully separates off from the society of commodity producers, which is, for him, modern society *per se*, which he hopes to hold on to in principle.

The critique that Echeverría is able to formulate of the *ethe* of capitalist modernity is thereby limited in its own radicalism. It does not seek, for example, to radically interrogate the possibility of knowledge in the society of commodity producers, as did György Lukács in *History and Class Consciousness*, on the basis of the Marxian critique of commodity fetishism. And this, as we have said, has a double motive: on the one hand, the comparison of the *ethe* of capitalist modernity should not be impeded by asking too quickly if these are true or false, but we should, instead, allow them to develop in their own right *before* posing the question of what is true or false in one or another *ethos*. On the other hand, however, this is why Echeverría does not understand his theory as a mere critique and analysis of the existing, but that it seeks moreover to make a theoretical contribution to 'the possibility of a politics *within* alienation'.[342] The problem with this view is that all-too radical theoretical critique toward the current process of knowledge apparently suffers, as a consequence, no longer being able to provide clues for a 'politics within alienation'.

Here, Echeverría himself, who on other occasions laughs at solemn seriousness and holds the baroque *ethos* with its paradoxical attitude in high esteem,

---

341 We have already offered one critique of this conclusion, and it should be of no further interest.
342 Echeverría 1995a, p. 176.

finds himself in a bad mood. With a slightly stern expression, he seems to say: 'Enough joking, we are going to put our feet on the ground so that our critique gives us results for politics *now*'. To put it in his own words, he hopes to prevent that, as a result of a too-radical theory of reification, one might only be able, in the final instance, to imagine the solution to the problem in a messianic form, as he perceives in Lukács of *History and Class Consciousness*.[343]

To better present Echeverría's argument and the limitations that we think we see in him and his theory of the *ethe*, we must insert here an excursus on the concepts of ideology, fetishism, and reification in Marx and Lukács, since in discussions today we cannot assume that these are even known – and much less grasped – with clarity.

b   Contribution to the Reconstruction of the Concept of Ideology in the Critique of Political Economy

In order to present the Marxian concept of ideology in the critique of political economy, we take here as our point of departure two fundamental texts: the 1859 preface to the *Contribution to the Critique of Political Economy*[344] and the subchapter 'The Fetishism of the Commodity and Its Secret', in the second edition of the first volume of *Capital*.[345] In the said texts, what is formulated is not an academic concept of ideology, and in the second, the word 'ideology' does not even appear. To what degree, however, it contains a concept of ideology, one of great importance for the theory of knowledge, is something that we will discuss in this excursus.

1859 Preface to the Contribution to the Critique of Political Economy
This text sets out from a critical review of Hegelian legal theory: juridical relations and state forms should *not* be understood either in themselves or through 'the so-called general progress of the human mind' but, rather, are based on the material relations of human life.[346] Hegel calls these relations as a totality 'bourgeois society'; its anatomy is political economy. Human beings enter into relations of production (whose juridical concept is 'property relations'), which are *necessary*, which is to say, independent of their will. The totality of those

---

343   See also 'Lukács y la revolución como salvación', in Echeverría 1995a, pp. 97–110, especially p. 109.
344   'Author's preface' in Marx 1904.
345   *Capital*, Vol. I, 'The Fetishism of the Commodity and Its Secret': Marx 1976a.
346   Marx 1904, p. 11.

relations of production constitutes the economic structure of society, its real basis.

On top of this real basis, a juridical/political superstructure is erected to which definite *social forms of consciousness* correspond. The exact relationship between base and superstructure is shown when a necessary 'period of social revolution' arrives.[347] Thus arrives, first, a transformation in the economic conditions of production, and in the second place, a transformation of the 'legal, political, religious, aesthetic or philosophic – in short *ideological forms* in which men become conscious of this conflict and fight it out'.[348]

The transformation mentioned in the second place – that of the (ideological) superstructure – is explained by and depends on the first, albeit not in an immediate and direct way. This occurs sooner or later according to the transformation of the economic base.[349] Thus, while for Marx it is clear that for human beings 'their social existence determines their consciousness',[350] he nevertheless recognises, as we have seen, a certain temporal lag, or in other words, something like a (limited) 'inherent dynamism of traditions'. But this does not reverse the causal relation. Such a period of economic transformation cannot be explained nor determined by its corresponding consciousness. This is the first concept of ideology (ideological forms/superstructure).[351]

The second is that of ideology as *false consciousness*, from which we must separate ourselves; in the 1859 preface this is only briefly mentioned when Marx writes with reference to himself and to Friedrich Engels: 'we decided to set forth together our view as opposed to the ideological one of German philosophy'.[352] This second concept of ideology is that which is present in

---

347 Marx 1904, p. 12. This 'period of social revolution' necessarily arrives because the relations of production in a particular moment no longer correspond to the productive forces, which continue to develop and enter into contradiction with the relations of production, which no longer foment their development but hinder it.
348 Ibid. Italics by S.G., as with those that follow in this subchapter.
349 Ibid.
350 Marx 1904, pp. 11–12.
351 Also, in a remote part of *Capital*, Marx deploys a similar concept of ideology when he speaks of 'the "ideological" groups' among which he mentions 'members of the government, priests, lawyers, soldiers, etc.' (Marx 1976a, p. 574).
352 'Preface to a Contribution to the Critique of Political Economy': Marx 1976b, p. 4. [For this quotation we do not use the 1904 Chicago edition of this text, as the translation is erroneous. The translator changes 'ideological one of German philosophy' into 'the idealism of German philosophy'. Compare: Marx 1904, p. 13. Compare also the German original: 'die ideologische der deutschen Philosophie' (Marx 1985b, p. 10).] Here, in what follows in the paragraph cited, there would appear to be an indication of how the two concepts of ideol-

Capital, and its development is the objective of the following reflections. With regard to the formulation in the 1859 preface of the 'interested prejudices of the ruling classes'[353] the following question arises: to what point does this understanding fit in one of the two mentioned concepts of ideology, or in a third version, or perhaps in none? This will not be answered through the preface, but we will, instead, take it up again in our discussion of *Capital*.[354]

The Text: 'The Fetishism of the Commodity and Its Secret'

To explain this fourth and final subchapter of the first chapter of *Capital* ('The Commodity'), we will recount briefly the argumentation preceding it. The text begins with a presentation of the double character of the commodity (use-value/value), in which value constitutes a social dimension, namely, the median socially necessary labour time for the commodity production. This implies the double character of labour represented in commodities. To the commodity producers applies the following: on the one hand, they are private workers, they are free, and they possess special knowledges and capacities, and with these they create various use-values; on the other hand, their labour is socially mediated, and in this sense they are also producers of value and, for the same reason, tied to the average of socially necessary *labour time* for the production of a commodity.

Commodity producers, then, are also chained, albeit without literal chains, to the relations of production through the average socially necessary labour time; therefore, they must work with a certain intensity, albeit without the lash of the whip, if they do not 'want' to sell their product for less than the corresponding value,[355] because it has taken too long, that is, they have wasted too

---

ogy they have distinguished might converge despite everything, perhaps in the sense that to stop at an analysis of the superstructure – that is, purely ideological and philosophical forms (ideology I), instead of studying the real economic base – is also ideological in the second sense (that is, ideology II as 'false consciousness'). When Marx and Engels propose 'to settle our accounts with our former philosophic conscience' (ibid.), they thus say goodbye to ideology (I, pure superstructure) at the same time that they escape ideology (II, false consciousness).

353 Marx 1904, p. 15.
354 In this regard, see the section 'On the Relation between "Necessity" and "Interest" in the Formation or Perpetuation of Ideologies' on pp. 324ff of this book.
355 The expression 'commodity producers do not want to sell their products below their value' should be understood thus: they cannot do anything else, because were they to do so, sooner or later, they would lose the very basis of their existence; or as Marx puts it, citing bourgeois apologists: the capitalist employment of machinery 'sets the workers free from their means of subsistence' (Marx 1976a, pp. 565ff, here: p. 566).

much time. The private labourer is, therefore, and against all appearances, also a social producer.

On the basis of the general measure of average necessary labour time for their production (abstractly human labour time), all commodities become commensurable, which is to say, they become indiscriminately exchangeable. This is a fundamental disposition of the developed commodity-producing society. In such a society, there must be an abstraction from the qualitative differences between different works; qualified labour is 'paid off', to put it that way, as multiplied simple labour. For the implementation of the commodity exchange, a general and stable equivalent 'is established', one which is divisible for whatever need and which can be exchanged in an unlimited way for all other commodities: money. In all value relations, then, a social relation is expressed, namely how much abstractly human labour is necessary for the production of commodity A in relation to the production of commodity B.

In a word: value is a social relation, and the commodity, the bearer of value, is the product and expression of that social relation. In the value of the commodity are expressed both the level of development of the productive forces as well as the results of social struggles, for example, over the length of the working day, the conditions of labour, and the quantity and quality of the means of reproduction of workers (that is, the level of salaries). The commodity is, therefore, a thing with a powerful social content: qualitative insofar as its generalised existence necessarily presupposes the developed society of commodity producers (which sounds trivial but is not obvious), and quantitative insofar as its value – as we have shown – is socially determined.

The Fetishism of the Commodity

What we are interested in discussing here is precisely the phenomenon that the commodity, in itself, possesses the property of concealing its social and historical dimension that we have described. To its producer, the commodity appears as something natural, eternal, immutable, given, and divine (from whence 'fetish') or, as Lukács would put it, it appears as a 'thing-in-itself',[356] standing on its own feet intact against the assault of history. What is important

---

356 'Reification and the Consciousness of the Proletariat' in Lukács 1971, for example p. 199: 'it is clear that from the standpoint of the proletariat the empirically given reality of the objects does dissolve into processes and tendencies; this process is no single, unrepeatable tearing of the veil that masks the process but the unbroken alternation of ossification, contradiction and movement... This insight alone puts us in a position to see through the last vestiges of the reification of consciousness and its intellectual form, the problem of the thing-in-itself'.

is that whoever accepts this finds his critique immediately limited within the limits of bourgeois society (as a developed society of commodity producers). Let us return, then, to Marx and to his concept of ideology – despite the fact that this word does not figure in the text that we are discussing.

The fact that the commodity appears to its producer in mystified form does not result from some stupidity or bad will on their part, but to the double character of the commodity and, with it, the double character of the labour that fabricates it. This double character of the commodity is not noted, and since – according to Marx – it is 'a very strange thing, abounding in metaphysical subtleties and theological niceties',[357] in the blink of an eye it occurs that all that is perceived is its superficial '*gegenständlichen Schein* [objective appearance]'.[358]

The *objective appearance* of the double character of producers is that of being simple private producers, since 'the specific social characteristics of their private labours appear only within this exchange [of the products of their labour]'.[359] In this process, the producers exchange commodities whose objective appearance is that their value corresponds to them 'by nature' and not by the social character of labour they conceal. In the moment of exchange, the social relation expressed by value has already petrified – meaning, it has become reified[360] to the point that for the moment it is not visible as such. The

---

On the problem of the thing-in-itself, Lukács speaks at length and with great detail in part II of that essay: 'Antinomies of Bourgeois Thought' (Lukács 1971, pp. 110ff) and again at various moments in the previously cited part III: 'The Standpoint of the Proletariat' (Lukács 1971, pp. 149f): 'Thus the knowledge that social facts are not objects but relations between men is intensified to the point where facts are wholly dissolved into processes' (Lukács 1971, p. 180).

See also in this respect note 385 on p. 325f of this book.

357   Marx 1976a, p. 163.
358   Marx 1975a, p. 88. [Note to the edition in Spanish: we do not agree, here, with the translation into Spanish of *Capital* – which we have generally used – where this is written as: '*apariencia de objetividad*' ('appearance of objectivity'): Marx 1975b, p. 91.)] [Note to the edition in English: in the edition in English of *Capital* here used, the translator does not understand the dialectical connotation of Marx's expression and writes down: 'semblance of objectivity' (Marx 1976a, p. 167). Some pages later, when Marx again uses the same term, the translator formulates it correctly as 'objective appearance' (Marx 1976a, p. 176: compare Marx 1975a, p. 97).]
359   Marx 1976a, p. 165.
360   This concept of reification, which becomes a central concept for Lukács in *History and Class Consciousness*, was not, as is often claimed, 'imposed by Lukács in a *Hegelianising* manner onto Marx's theory'. Marx himself uses this concept in relation to the fetishism of the commodity, for example, when he writes: 'this economic trinity as the connection between the components of value and wealth in general and its sources, completes the

false consciousness the producer has toward his product, the commodity, is a *necessarily false consciousness*, insofar as the value form of the commodity already obscures the relation between humans, by reifying it.[361] A social relation adopts the *form* of a relationship between things (commodities), thereby becoming eternal and immutable.

For Marx, however, it is *ideological* to remain stuck on the form of relations instead of analysing their real foundation. This means that only the analysis of the relations of production underlying the value form of the commodity can clarify the objective content of value relations, and not a presumably 'non-ideological' manoeuvre with supply and demand curves, on the basis of which the value of commodities is to be determined. To remain on the plane of objective appearance (here, for example, simply on the quantitative plane of value, or in this case, of prices), means evidently to produce ideology, or in other words, *necessarily false consciousness*. Marx puts it like this:

> Whence, then, arises the enigmatic character of the product of labour, as soon as it assumes the form of a commodity? Clearly, it arises from this form itself. The equality of the kinds of human labour takes on a physical form in the equal objectivity of the products of labour as values; the measure of the expenditure of human labour-power by its duration takes on the form of the magnitude of the value of the products of labour; and finally the relationships between the producers, within which the social characteristics of their labours are manifested, take on the form of a social relation between the products of labour.
>
> The mysterious character of the commodity-form consists therefore simply in the fact that the commodity reflects the social characteristics of men's own labour as objective characteristics of the products of labour themselves, as the socio-natural properties of these things. Hence it also reflects the social relation of the producers to the sum total of labour as a social relation between objects, a relation that exists apart from and outside the producers.[362]

In this context, we should also consider Marx's assertion elsewhere in *Capital* that material reproduction always means, moreover, the reproduction of existing social relations. With each product, the producer creates again an object

---

mystification of the capitalist mode of production, the reification of social relations, and the immediate coalescence of the material relations of production with their historical and social specificity': Marx 1981, p. 969.

361   Marx 1976a, p. 164.
362   Marx 1976a, pp. 164–5.

that expresses and fixes existing relations.³⁶³ In this way, consciousness rooted in the objective appearance of the product is reinforced. Marx compares *commodity fetishism* with phenomena from 'the mist-enveloped regions of the religious world', in which 'the products of the human brain appear as autonomous figures endowed with a life of their own, which enter into relations both with each other and the human race'.³⁶⁴ In the world of commodities, it is not the products of the human mind, but rather those of the human hand, that adopt the form of such independent figures and which are 'evidently' endowed with a life of their own.

Here, we can understand what Marx means with the *concept of 'objective appearance'*:³⁶⁵ appearance is not external to the object, but is, instead, inherent to and inseparable from it. So, on the one hand, commodities effectively enjoy something like 'a life of their own'. Existing relations are so imposing that they are presented to the producer as 'laws of nature', such that the producer is demoted to being a passive object of these laws and sees the commodity set up in the category of acting subjects. But, on the other hand, this is a false appearance insofar as, according to what we have said, the relations of commodities among one another and even the commodities themselves are nothing more than *reified forms* of the social relation between human beings, or in other words, of relations of production. What reinforces the objective appearance described above is the fact that the producers, in the exchange of commodities, lack full consciousness of what they are doing and, therefore, effectively lean in the direction of being passive objects without consciousness. The value relation of commodities is imposed behind the producers' backs:

> Men do not therefore bring the products of their labour into relation with each other as values because they see these objects merely as the material integuments of homogeneous human labour. The reverse is true: by equating their different products to each other in exchange as values, they equate their different kinds of labour as human labour. They do this without being aware of it.³⁶⁶
>
> The value character of the products of labour becomes firmly established only when they act as magnitudes of value. These magnitudes vary continually, independently of the will, foreknowledge and actions of the exchangers. Their own movement within society has for them the form of

---

363   Marx 1976a, pp. 763f.
364   Marx 1976a, p. 165.
365   Marx 1975a, p. 88 (see note 358 in this chapter).
366   Marx 1976a, pp. 166–7.

a movement made by things, and these things, far from being under their control, in fact control them.³⁶⁷

Here, we again see the political force of the commodity fetishism: the (active) subjects of history, in their necessarily false consciousness, lower themselves to being mere passive objects of their own social life-process (that is, of history). Necessarily false consciousness coincides, as we have seen, with objective appearance.

This all means that what is false in false consciousness refers, therefore, to the 'falseness of relations' more than the ignorance of those 'caught up in the relations of commodity production'.³⁶⁸ This is the concept of ideology in its full force.

The Historical Dimension of the Fetishism of the Commodity, or Knowledge as a Political-practical Process

The double character of the commodity emerges with relevance when goods are produced for exchange, when direct consumption (and with it their aspect of being use-values) is no longer the principal objective of things to be produced; but the character of value comes to be considered as the principal aspect only in the developed society of commodity producers, which is to say, in capitalism.³⁶⁹

---

367 Marx 1976a, pp. 167–8.
368 'The belated scientific discovery that the products of labour, in so far as they are values, are merely the material expressions of the human labour expended to produce them, marks an epoch in the history of mankind's development, but by no means banishes the [objective appearance] possessed by the social characteristics of labour. Something which is only valid for this particular form of production, the commodity production, namely the fact that the specific social character of private labours carried on independently of each other consists in their equality as human labour, and, in the product, assumes the form of the existence of value, appears to those caught up in the relations of commodity production (and this is true both before and after the above-mentioned scientific discovery) to be just as ultimately valid as the fact that the scientific dissection of the air into its component parts left the atmosphere itself unaltered in its physical configuration' (Marx 1976a, p. 167; original Marx 1975a p. 88: see note 358 on p. 317 of this chapter).
369 'As the foregoing analysis has already demonstrated, this fetishism of the world of commodities arises from the peculiar social character of the labour which produces them.... It is only by being exchanged that the products of labour acquire a socially uniform objectivity as values, which is distinct from their sensuously varied objectivity as articles of utility. This division of the product of labour into a useful thing and a thing possessing value appears in practice only when exchange has already acquired a sufficient extension and importance to allow useful things to be produced for the purpose of being

The 'mysticism of the world of commodities' – which, especially in its finalised form (the *money-form*), conceals rather than reveals the social character of private labours – coincides with 'forms of thought which are socially valid, and therefore objective, for the relations of production belonging to this historically determined mode of social production, i.e. commodity production'.[370] For this reason, with the disappearance of the world of commodities disappears as well the fetishism inherent to it. This should be sought not only in the historical process of overcoming commodity production ('an association of free men'),[371] but can also already be represented conceptually by directing our gaze to other forms of production.[372] As examples of forms of production distinct from the commodity production, Marx mentions the following:

1) [*Robinson Crusoe*]: All the relations between Robinson and these objects that form his self-created wealth are here so simple and transparent that even Mr. Sedley Taylor [a vulgar economist] could understand them. And yet those relations contain all the essential determinants of value.[373]
2) [*The medieval Europe, shrouded in darkness (general dependency)*]: The *corvée* can be measured by time just as well as the labour which produces commodities, but every serf knows that what he expends in the service of his lord is a specific quantity of his own personal labour-power ... the social relations between individuals in the performance of their labour appear at all events, as their own personal relations, and are not disguised as social relations between things, between the products of labour.[374]
3) [*The patriarchal rural industry of a peasant family (natural [naturwüchsig] division of labour within the family)*]: The fact that the expenditure of the individual labour-powers is measured by duration appears here, by its very nature, as a social characteristic of labour itself, because the

---

exchanged, so that their character as values has already to be taken into consideration during production. From this moment on, the labour of the individual producer acquires a twofold social character' (Marx 1976a, pp. 165–6).

370 Marx 1976a, p. 169.
371 Marx 1976a, p. 171.
372 'The whole mystery of commodities, all the magic and necromancy that surrounds the products of labour on the basis of commodity production, vanishes therefore as soon as we come to other forms of production' (Marx 1976a, p. 169).
373 Marx 1976a, p. 170, italics by S.G. [trans. – Gandler cites the Spanish translation which evidently takes the original German as its source, since the passage names 'Mr Max Wirth' instead of Sedley Taylor (who was substituted by Engels)].
374 Marx 1976a, p. 170, italics by S.G.

individual labour-powers, by their very nature, act only as instruments of the joint labour-power of the family.[375]

4) [*Ideal representation of an emancipated society*]: *an association of free men*, working with the means of production held in common, and expending their many different forms of labour-power in full self-awareness as one single social labour force. All the characteristics of Robinson's labour are repeated here, but with the difference that they are social instead of individual.[376]

As humans produce, in this case, consciously in society, which is to say, not as private labourers, the double character of labour which produces commodity fetishism and, with it, fetishism itself, are abolished: The social relations of the individual producers, both towards their labour and the products of their labour, are here transparent in their simplicity...[377]

The historicity of commodity fetishism must be understood in such a way that the relation of production, which generates this fetishism, is conceived as a rung in the development toward rational (in an emphatic sense) relations of production and, with that, toward an emancipated society. The question is not to mourn the loss of older and more transparent productive relations,[378] but, instead, by recalling bygone forms of production, the transitoriness of today's ruling forms of production is made visible.

The heart of Marx's ideological (in the first sense) struggle for the concept of fetishism lies in that his analysis of capital demonstrates that while the antagonistic contradictions of the bourgeois productive organism are not visible at first sight (according to which society reconciles general interests with particular and individual interests), by unveiling the superficial appearance of

---

375 Marx 1976a, p. 171, italics by S.G.
376 Ibid.
377 Marx 1976a, p. 172. On the topic of 'the fetishism of economic relations in the different historical modes of production', see also Marx 1981, p. 970.
378 'Those ancient social organisms of production are much more simple and transparent than those of bourgeois society. But they are founded either on the immaturity of man as an individual, when he has not yet torn himself loose from the umbilical cord of his natural species-connection with other men, or on direct relations of dominance and servitude. They are conditioned by a low stage of development of the productive powers of labour and correspondingly limited relations between men within the process of creating and reproducing their material life, hence also limited relations between man and nature. These real limitations are reflected in the ancient worship of nature, and in other elements of tribal religions': Marx 1976a, pp. 172–3.

the exchange of equivalences, it turns out that bourgeois society is also one in which the exploitation of human being by human being serves as its constitutive base. In other words, while *'Liberté, Égalité, Fraternité'* removed the nobility from power, bourgeois society is much further away from the universalist claim of freedom, equality, and solidarity among all human beings, than what it would be able to admit, even in dreams.

But bourgeois society should not be understood as progress *vis-à-vis* feudal society merely for having inscribed human rights upon its banners, but especially for having created the material bases for the form of society[379] that it itself claims to be: that of human beings who are conscious of their acts, or in other words, an enlightened society that has constructed a bridge across the crack which exists between social and individual interest.

The stumbling block for human consciousness of the fact that it is necessary and possible to take advantage of this foundation now set for a society different from the bourgeois version lies, unfortunately, in the fact that the latter, more than any of its predecessors, reproduces the false appearance that it already represents the peak of history, or at least 'in principle', the 'best imaginable world'. As a result, the critique of political economy that Marx provides in the three volumes of *Capital* should be understood as a *critique of fetishism*, one which presents step-by-step the contradictions inherent to the capitalist mode of production, in light of the contradictions and deficiencies of bourgeois economic theories.[380]

Beyond this possibility of the theoretical critique of fetishism as the point of departure for overcoming reified consciousness, Marx's work indicates, consequently, that the fetishisation of relations of exploitation – which appear on the surface as free interactions among free human beings under conditions of fair exchange – only vanish at the moment in which relations of exploitation give way to rational, which is to say free, forms of production, which are consciously understood and organised as social. This means that knowledge is understood *as a political-practical process*.

Fetishisation, the reification of relations, objective appearance, and necessarily false consciousness 'vanish only when the practical relations of everyday life between man and man, and man and nature, generally present themselves

---

379   For the 'process of material production ... [to] become ... production by freely associated men ... however, requires that society possess a material foundation, or a series of material conditions of existence, which in their turn are the natural and spontaneous product of a long and tormented historical development' (Marx 1976a, p. 173).

380   In this regard, see note 387, p. 326 and note 388, pp. 326f of this book.

to him in a transparent and rational form'.³⁸¹ That is: ideologies can only be overcome, only come undone in a free society, organised according to reason, with corresponding relations for the reproduction of the conditions of life. The difference from the common sense understanding of 'ideology' could hardly be formulated more strikingly: 'The veil is not removed from the countenance of the social life-process, i.e., the process of material production, until it becomes production by freely associated men, and stands under their conscious and planned control'.³⁸²

On the Relation between 'Necessity' and 'Interest' in the Formation or Perpetuation of Ideologies

In our discussion of the preface to the *Contribution to the Critique of Political Economy*, we already touched briefly upon the question of the relationship which exists between the 'interested prejudices of the ruling classes'³⁸³ and *necessarily* false consciousness, one which is posed once again when Marx, in referring to 'political economy', writes of: 'These formulas, which bear the unmistakable stamp of belonging to a social formation in which the process of production has mastery over man, instead of the opposite, appear to the political economists' bourgeois consciousness to be as much a self-evident and nature imposed necessity as productive labour itself'.³⁸⁴

Thus we also find here an approach to the concept of ideology: the form of consciousness which in a particular epoch is expressed as the dominant form, whose example here is bourgeois consciousness, is ideological because it grasps the existing social formation as the conclusion and culmination point of the historical process and, setting out from this, reinterprets the contradictions which are present (or theoretical confusions) as something 'natural', in order to thereby escape from critique and critical analysis. But here, we are confronted with another question: to what degree is this ahistorical and self-overestimating *bourgeois consciousness* also *'necessary'*? In this regard, Alfred Schmidt's suggestion is important: the Marxian concept of ideology is a *polemical and combative*, and *not an academic* one. This means that the interest of acting subjects is, of course, also an aspect of the formation or, and where appropriate, the preservation of an ideological consciousness. The political concept of 'bourgeois consciousness' and the affirmation regarding the 'formulæ, which bear it stamped upon them', which is to say, forms which do not

---

381   Marx 1976a, p. 173.
382   Ibid.
383   Marx 1904, p. 15.
384   Marx 1904, pp. 174–5.

hide behind an objective appearance, and, despite this, are fetishised, all point toward this interpretation.[385]

The formation of ideological 'consciousness' should, therefore, be understood as the product *both* of an *'interested knowledge'* and *also* of the *'necessarily false appearance'*. Thus, when we say that the Marxian concept of ideology is not an academic concept, it should be understood without a doubt that Marx did not distinguish rigidly between these two components. In turn, this is due to the fact that both components emerge from the same: from the society which is antagonistic in itself and in which there necessarily exist contradictions not only between 'appearance' and the 'true relation',[386] but also between the interests of the different classes.

Since Marx was not interested in 'true consciousness' in the abstract, but rather in the scientific analysis of the intrinsic contradictions of bourgeois society, this is for him part of the struggle against that social formation and its hunger for eternity; therefore, it is not necessary for him to separate these two planes in a rigid way (ideology as a problem in the theory of knowledge or as a direct spawn of the political struggle).

Capital as a Critique of Fetishisms

Now, before anything we should clarify that Marx did not in *Capital* elaborate an academically-developed concept of ideology (and nor did he present such a

---

385   It is worth noting moreover that Marx speaks of something like 'the interested prejudices of the ruling classes' when he distinguishes between classical economics and vulgar economics. The representatives of the latter feel 'completely at home' in the 'configurations of appearance'; their formula thus engendered 'corresponds to the self-interest of the dominant classes, since it preaches the natural necessity and perpetual justification of their sources of income and erects this into a dogma'. Classical political economy, on the other hand, has at least partly dissolved 'this false appearance and deception ... this personification of things and reification of the relations of production, this religion of everyday life ... ' But there even its best representatives 'remained more or less trapped in the world of illusion their criticism had dissolved', and the reason for this lies not only in politically-motivated 'prejudices' or exclusively in internal theoretical reasons, but rather that, from the 'bourgeois standpoint', a coherent overcoming of this barrier to knowledge is not possible: Marx 1981, p. 969. (On Marx's distinction between classical and vulgar economics, see, moreover, Schmidt 1972, pp. 39ff.)

   This idea is also pursued by Lukács, who says that the reification of the existing relations, objective appearance, and necessarily false consciousness can (only) be eliminated according to the criterion of the proletariat (that is, by the proletariat itself). (See *History and Class Consciousness*, and in particular the section 'The Standpoint of the Proletariat': Lukács 1971, pp. 149ff.)

386   Marx 1976, p. 107 n38.

concept of the fetishism). This is contained, instead, in the way that Marx had of developing and representing the critique of political economy. For this reason, it is not sufficient to refer only to the subchapter on commodity fetishism. It is, instead, the structure in its totality – that is, the organisation of *Capital*'s exposition – as well as the argumentation in each case where Marx subjects to critique ideological conceptions and fetishisms, as well as his *specific way of criticising bourgeois economic science*, which means at the same time criticising the reality this science describes,[387] that must be considered as the foundation upon which to formulate and present the Marxian concept of ideology.[388]

---

387   A circumstance, understood as such in the debates surrounding *Capital*, in general corresponding to the method of investigation and to a certain degree also to the manner of exposition. Marx himself wrote in his letter to Ferdinand Lasalle of 22 February 1858 regarding *Capital*: 'The work I am presently concerned with is a Critique of Economic Categories or, if you like, a critical exposé of the system of the bourgeois economy. It is at once an exposé and, by the same token, a critique of the system': Marx 1983a, pp. 268–71. (In this regard, see also Schmidt 1972, p. 36.)

There are debates regarding whether Marx, in speaking of the 'system of bourgeois economics', was referring only to the scientific system or also to the system existing in reality, that is, to the relations of production. For this, see a previous expression of his from the *Economic-Philosophical Manuscripts of 1844* (section XXII: 'Alienated Labour'): 'We have proceeded from the premises of political economy.... On the basis of political economy itself, in its own words, we have shown that the worker sinks to the level of a commodity and becomes indeed the most wretched of commodities; that the wretchedness of the worker is in inverse proportion to the power and magnitude of his production;... Political economy starts with the fact of private property; it does not explain it to us.... It does not *comprehend* these laws': Marx 1959b, p. xxii.

388   The Marxian critique of political economy can be understood as a progressive analysis of fetishisms, one which reveals the latter from their simplest to most complex forms (commodity, dual character of labour, value, value-form, money, money-form, capital, absolute and relative surplus value, wages, accumulation, circulation, circulation time of capital, profit, rate of profit, average profit, commercial capital, interest and profit of enterprise, banking capital, money capital, credit system, ground-rent, differential rent, rent of buildings, rent of mines, price of land – which represents the broad strokes of the course of the exposition in the three volumes of *Capital*). See, in this regard, Brentel 1989, and especially 'Einleitung', point 2, 'Soziale Form und die Theorie des Fetischismus: die Ansätze einer kritischen Kategorienlehre', pp. 14–18. Brentel asserts that: 'The totality of the three volumes of *Capital* is, therefore, organised as an economic-social theory of forms, in the manner of an analysis of the fetishism of economic categories. To each of these economic categories under critique, to each level of the presentation, there correspond ... notions of consciousness, which, on the basis of the specific character of economic relations, are imposed on the subjects that act within them. There, the fetishism of the categories of

On this last point, it is especially important to notice that the critique of reality through the critique of (economic) theories of that society already presupposes the concept of the *necessarily false consciousness*. How else would this linkage be possible? If ideologies were simply erroneous presumptions or if particular flaws or blunders in economic theories could be attributed only to the casual 'stupidity' of the theorist, and if the contradictions in the theories did not suggest contradictions in reality, then how would it have been possible on the basis of an analysis, and with it a critique, of those theories, to enter into an analysis, and with it a critique, of existing social relations? (Which, as is known, was Marx's method of investigation, and which comes to be present again on occasions in the very presentation of its scientific results.)[389] Thus should be understood the fact that Marx defended the classics of political economy against the reproach that they 'have been considering production as an end in itself, too much to the exclusion of everything else. The same has been said with regard to distribution'. And he continues his defence: 'as though it were the text books that impress this separation upon life and not life upon the text books'.[390]

Seen thus, then, the Marxian concept of ideology or of fetishism is constitutive for his critique of political economy, considering the latter not as a 'pure' contribution to the history of theories, but also as the work of a committed champion of the struggle to overcome the exploitation of human by human.

---

political economy is the result of the double nature of economic-social objectivity as a peculiarly dual social form (form I and form II): specifically social behaviour (of men in their work) that acquires an objective character and is then presented as a property of things' (pp. 16f).

To which we add: this progressive critique of fetishism from its simplest and most general forms to the most complex and concrete is based on the fact that the more concrete the forms, the greater is the chasm between conceptual content and visible form. On this, Marx says: 'As the commodity-form is the most general and the most undeveloped form of bourgeois production ... its fetish character is still relatively easy to penetrate. But when we come to more concrete forms, even this appearance of simplicity vanishes' (Marx 1976a, p. 176).

It is this that Lukács refers to when he speaks of the 'fine elucidation of the different stages' of fetishised forms that is found in the chapter on the 'trinity formula'. (Lukács 1971, p. 220 n50. Lukács is here referring to *Capital* Vol. III, Marx 1981, pp. 965–70).

389 On the relationship between method of investigation and method of exposition in Marx, see Schmidt 1972, pp. 37f.

390 Marx 1904, p. 274. Marx ends by exclaiming: as if it were a matter of 'a dialectical balancing of conceptions and not an analysis of real conditions' (ibid.).

Here is located the *explosive political-theoretical force of the assessment of the Marxian concept of ideology*. By recognising the concept of ideology as necessarily false consciousness, in which 'some economists are misled by the fetishism attached to the world of commodities, or by the objective appearance of the social characteristics of labour',[391] the previously discussed 'theory-praxis relation' is simultaneously assimilated. This means that all those who accept this concept of ideology have left behind the strict separation between science and political struggle, or rather, the separation between science and society, or finally, reason as purely instrumental (evident in the conceptions of reason as external to history and the process of human development).

That is to say, whoever does so has already recognised the Hegelian 'legacy' that exists in *Capital*, in the sense that reality is, in principle, accessible to reason, and also in principle, it can be configured by that reason, or in other words, that the conciliation of general with particular interests is possible, equally in principle, and that the process of development of the human beings who make history tends (or could tend) toward this.

c The Concept of *Ethos* as a Toned Down Critique of Ideology

While Echeverría grants a central importance to the concept of reification and to fetishism for understanding current social relations, he nevertheless understands these differently from how we have explained them here. And nor does he do so with the radicalism of Lukács in *History and Class Consciousness* (although the young Echeverría was always interested in 'radicalism' – this is how he explains his attraction to Heidegger).[392] Echeverría takes as his point of departure the fact that Lukács could only think in this way because, at the moment that he wrote his essay of such central importance to Western Marxism, 'Reification and the Consciousness of the Proletariat', he was convinced – on the basis of the historical situation of the period – that revolution 'was the order of the day'. According to this view, Lukács could allow himself such a radical critique of knowledge thanks to his conviction that the capitalist relations of production deforming that knowledge – and the corresponding reified consciousness – were, in any case, nearing their end.[393]

---

391 Marx 1976a, p. 176.
392 In this regard, see pp. 47ff of this book.
393 See also 'Lukács y la revolución como salvación' in Echeverría 1995a, p. 105.

In this regard, it is worth observing that if Lukács's concept gained importance in Western Marxism it was precisely because it helped to explain what left orthodox Marxism largely speechless: the innumerable desertions of former members of the old mass parties of the Left, who passed to the camp of the European fascists or Nazis in the 1930s (and even from the end of the 1920s). In his article on Lukács, however, Echeverría does not enter into this question at all. Instead, he situates the radicalism of Lukács's critique of knowledge as the simple consequence of the purported imminence of the communist revolution in various European countries at the beginning of the 1920s. In Echeverría's logic, National Socialism arrived as a historical event that, *a posteriori*, rendered Lukács's theory of reification obsolete due to its 'lack of contemporary relevance'.[394] Here, Echeverría completely ignores the fact that, for example, the analyses carried out by the Institute for Social Research in Frankfurt during the 1930s and 1940s more than once took as their central point of reference the Marxist concepts of fetishisation, reification, and ideology which were interpreted and developed by Lukács, and that in these analyses *History and Class Consciousness* played a not inconsiderable role.

Echeverría's error here consists in insisting that in Lukács's assessment that revolution was the order of the day, without taking into account the fact that Lukács was attempting to determine why it was that the subjects of history *were not aware* that this was the order of the day (and this is why he turns to the critique of knowledge), that is, why they did not transform the objective imminence of the revolution into their subjective aspiration.[395]

---

394 'Lukács's book lost its *political contemporary relevance* at the very moment it was published. Drafted in the immediate postwar period, within this exalted spirit of apocalyptic inspiration, for which the "storming of heaven" was "the order of the day"; when the "contemporary relevance of the communist revolution" [*"actualidad de la revolución comunista"*] seemed to have reached its highest point in European civilisations, the publication of *History and Class Consciousness* coincided nevertheless with the rapid decline of this revolutionary contemporary relevance [*actualidad revolucionaria*] and with the overwhelming channeling of this spirit in a decidedly messianic direction, both toward its bureaucratisation in the service of the "construction of socialism in one country" and its counter-revolutionary outbreak, which would turn it into the destructive and suicidal impulse of National Socialism.

'Lukács's theoretical proposal was thus discredited for the lack of contemporary relevance [*falta de actualidad*] of the political conclusions that its author derived from it': Echeverría 1995a, p. 105).

395 While it is true that Lukács emphasises the need for a revolution to overcome reified consciousness, and while in his own way of formulating this need its possibility is also implicitly present (as a residue of the dogmatic Marxist thought which lacks the concept

As we have indicated, there are two reasons that Echeverría might have distanced himself from Lukács's radical materialist theory of knowledge: first, he wanted to adopt this theory only insofar as it was useful for his *description* of the existing *ethe* and not necessarily for a critical examination of their contents;[396] secondly, he could not accept a critique of ideology that understands the form of commodity production and the inherent double character of the commodity as the foundation of false consciousness, and this is because he is interested precisely in establishing a new (non-capitalist) form of commodity production.[397]

In this sense, the fact that Echeverría mitigates the (radical) critique of ideology developed by Western Marxism is in keeping with his general theory. It is undeniable that with this theoretical posture, he arrived at proposals that had not been achieved within that theoretical current, above all, with regard to his studies of *other* forms of modernity in *other* regions of the planet. He attempts

---

of reification), the concept of reification is, at the same time, the central element of a powerful doubt surrounding the possibility of this revolution and lays the bases for the understanding that this is not as simple as was perhaps assumed.

Even if the revolution is understood as a rupture with reified consciousness, this concept recovers what Marx emphasised in the *Theses on Feuerbach* and which dogmatic Marxism ignored and rejected: that this process (!) should be simultaneously that of the transforming of circumstances (ruling relations) and of human beings themselves (that is, of their consciousness as well). Although Marx himself writes in the *Theses on Feuerbach* that this unity can only be rationally understood as *revolutionary praxis*, this should not necessarily be understood as a 'messianic rupture' of the sort Bolívar Echeverría attributes to Lukács (and, in a certain way, to Marx as well). In this regard, see also Sánchez Vázquez's research on Marx's conception of praxis, above all his reflections on the third thesis on Feuerbach: pp. 124ff of this book.

396 'The concept of reification – this is the conclusion that we can derive both from Lukács's decisive theoretical proposal and from the limitations observed in its development – allows us to think of a reality that perhaps most essentially characterises modernity: that of the existence of the social subject as a subjectivity which is conflictively distributed between man and things. In order to affirm itself as an abstract subject, self-valorising value needs to realise itself as a concrete project; it needs human beings and the *election of the* – civilisational, cultural – *form* that they make in working on nature' (Echeverría 1995a, p. 110).

397 Note: 'It all occurs as though Lukács, who acutely grasps the effects of the historical phenomenon of reification under the form of a dialectic of decomposition and re-composition of social life, was nevertheless unable to manage to adequately define this dialectic and nor to therefore discover the way in which it acts when the reification that manifests in it is not simple, purely mercantile reification, but rather its more complex, mercantile-capitalist version' (Echeverría 1995a, p. 106).

to overcome one of the largest blind spots of that theoretical school to which Echeverría, despite whatever critique he might have, feels committed; this blind spot is its Eurocentrism. But the price he paid for this was having ridded himself of the instruments of a far-reaching analysis – and with it, critique – of the various *ethe* or social sign systems and, above all, of the concrete ideas transmitted within them. With this, his theory runs the risk that, while able to elaborate the *differences* between the various historical *ethe* and thereby confront any false hierarchisation of these *ethe*, his analysis of each one of these *ethe* remains stuck on the plane of immediate appearance. In other words, he can weigh the *ethe* against each other and examine their reciprocal relationship, but when it is a question of each particular *ethos* he must trust its self-conception, since he himself has removed the right to radical doubt and the capacity of having such a doubt.[398]

d   An Example of the Limitations of the Concept of *Ethos*

The following example of the possible consequences of the limitations of the concept of *ethos* in contrast to the (critical) concept of ideology does not seek to demonstrate that Echeverría has made a mistake in an *isolated case*; instead, it should be understood as an illustration of the self-limitation (described in the previous chapter) that Echeverría imposes upon his own theory of the *ethe*.

In his essay entitled '1989',[399] Echeverría compares the years 1989 and 1789. 'Everything seems to indicate – he writes – that the year 1989 will, as with the exemplary case of 1789, also come to be the sign of an era'.[400] Here, of course, Echeverría uses the word 'seems' in a critical sense, since, as he later indicates,

---

398   This self-limitation could also be related to a critique of Echeverría in one of the few relevant studies about his work. Aureliano Ortega Esquivel argues that in the essay 'Postmodernity and Cynicism' there is 'an excessive confidence in the possibility of constructing a general anti-capitalist will under the *real* conditions of the moment'. Such confidence could naturally be disturbed quite easily by a too-radical critique of ideology. We could also see as evidence in favour of such an interpretation the fact that Echeverría keeps silent with regard to the most reactionary *volonté générale* documented in history, at the precise moment when the majority tries to erase it from collective memory, as can be seen in the next subchapter. See Ortega Esquivel 1995, p. 43.
399   '1989', in Echeverría 1995a, pp. 13–23. On the history of this essay, and in particular its first publication and a first critique by ourselves, see pp. 74ff of this book.
400   Echeverría 1995a, p. 13.

he sees the *'fall of the Berlin Wall'* as a 'symbol "in abeyance"'.⁴⁰¹ But what is the reason for this critical position, which does not wish to simply participate in the chatter and the clamour surrounding a 'historic moment' and suchlike? Echeverría's argument appears critical, but in the end remains on the surface of things. First, he unquestioningly believes in the dominant ideology, before immediately going on to criticise it. He goes no deeper, and does not manage to take the step toward a radical critique of ideology. Why he fails to do so would be difficult to explain here, but we should state that this position fits impeccably well with his theory of the *ethe* and his limited critique of ideology.

Let us look at the question in more detail. Echeverría's argument for why the so-called fall of the Berlin Wall on 9 November 1989 constitutes a 'symbol "in abeyance"' rests above all on economic structures: 'It is possible that one day, when the distance from the facts allows us to see its full magnitude, we could say that the failure of actually-existing socialism was truly nothing more than one of the different complementary figures in which the "reluctant historical decline" of capitalism took place'.⁴⁰²

A lovely idea, certainly, but too beautiful once we compare it with ideological reality. What Echeverría seems not to perceive is the other symbolic meaning that the Berlin Wall also had, aside from its 'official' character as dividing line between 'East' and 'West', between actually-existing socialism and capitalism, a line which was difficult (or impossible, depending on the person) to cross. This meaning was known everywhere and was also mentioned subtly in many declarations regarding the opening of the Berlin border crossings. But, unlike the Bastille (whose assault Echeverría grants a symbolic character similar to that of the 'fall of the wall'), the Berlin Wall symbolised not only the régime, which ordered its construction and used it for its ends, but moreover symbolised something else.

This other thing is something that in Germany is mentioned reluctantly, and which even in other countries is recalled in a very ideologised form, that is when it does not become completely *taboo*. We are referring to an event that was also symbolised, albeit indirectly, by the Berlin Wall.

Without exaggeration, we could say that the *memory* of this historical event, not the event in itself, was on average more hated among the German population than the GDR régime itself (German Democratic Republic, 'socialist' Germany). Moving further, it is worth wondering if the régime of the GDR

---

401 Echeverría 1995a, p. 15.
402 Echeverría 1995a, p. 17.

was not hated precisely for having held this memory high, over and over again, albeit in a dogmatic and simplified form. The hatred of the Berlin Wall and the concomitant symbolic meaning of its 'fall' have referred, in the end, as much to this historical event as to actually-existing socialism, and arguably more to the first than to the second.

Echeverría does not dedicate a single word to this.[403] What is more, although in his essay he speaks a great deal about historical symbols and symbolism, he does not include the slightest observation regarding the possible meaning of the fact that the border controls between East and West Berlin were abolished exactly fifty-one years after the so-called *Reichskristallnacht* or Night of the Broken Glass (which had occurred on the exact same date in 1938), a decision which, as is known, did not emerge from any street battle or anything of the sort, but which was taken administratively. Whoever was responsible for this decision, and whatever their motives, one thing became clear on that day: on 9 November in German territory there are *more important* things than to bore oneself with whatever type of commemorative act regarding the genocide committed against European Jews, as had occurred one year previously (in 1988) with major ceremonies marking the fiftieth anniversary.[404]

Western Marxism's critique of ideology had historically as one of its principal objects the question of the causes for the desertion of many members of traditional leftist organisations, who crossed over to the ranks of fascism or Nazism, as we have mentioned. Echeverría sets aside this critique, or at least weakens its radicalism. This gesture is accompanied, as we see in the '1989' essay discussed here, by a decrease in the importance attributed to these historical events. But the problem is the following: whenever in the Federal Republic of Germany, be it the old or the supposedly new, one speaks of the 'normality' that would be so desirable to achieve (which was on everyone's tongue, as concerned the aforementioned abolition of border controls), this means nothing more than extinguishing the memory of what happened immediately prior to the establishment of the *two* German states.

What use is this whole theory of *ethe*, with its implicitly included intention of helping the oppressed *ethe* and, as a result, helping the oppressed collectivities to gain their theoretical, and in the end, practical right, if in so decisive a moment we move in reverse? But, and this is the pressing question: is not the price paid for the advances of the concept of historical *ethos* precisely

---

403   In this regard, see moreover what we have said in the chapter 'Life and Work of Bolívar Echeverría', especially pp. 74ff.
404   See Gandler 1990.

that in a moment of greatest theoretical helplessness – namely, when what is necessary is to determine why specific groups were and are oppressed and physically exterminated, beyond all directly economic logic – it produces a great silence?[405]

---

405   Here, Echeverría is too close to rather than too far away from the majority of contemporary German philosophers. With few exceptions, they prefer to silence or tone down the history of German philosophers under National Socialism, who were in their majority the teachers of the most *prestigious* thinkers in Germany today. It is no coincidence that two decisive studies in this respect were carried out by foreigners, Latin Americans to be specific, indeed acquaintances of Echeverría's: Zapata Galindo 1995 and Orozco 1995. See, moreover, Farías 1987. See as well p. 57, note 159 of this book.

   Echeverría's silence is perhaps related to his desire to understand the oppressed not only as victims but also, at the same time, as the potential point of departure for the overcoming of social misery. With this, he once again appears to have some similarity to Marx.

CHAPTER 17

Utopia: A Non-Capitalist Society of Commodity Producers

In Echeverría's '15 Theses' on *'Modernidad y capitalismo [Modernity and Capitalism]*',[406] one of his central questions deals with the relation between the market economy and capitalism, which are generally taken to be identical. For Echeverría, however, while these are indeed historically coincident forms, the second tends toward the destruction of the first through the establishment of monopolies. This question is important, because his theoretical project of a non-capitalist modernity is accompanied by his concept of modernity, according to which the highly developed global market is a central basis of modernity in general. This leads necessarily to the formulation of a non-capitalist form of production oriented toward the market, which is to say production developed under the commodity-form. What Echeverría leaves up to his readers is the explanation of how to manage that the generalised commodity production – which, seen historically, necessarily led to the capitalist mode of production – ceases to do so now in its second attempt, or in what instances it can be prevented from doing so without falling into an authoritarian or only apparently non-capitalist society.[407]

This author spent some two and a half hours interviewing Echeverría on his utopia of a non-capitalist society of commodity producers[408] and its possible internal contradictions;[409] but the complexity of this topic would have required a more detailed treatment, one outside the scope of this book.[410] However, as a step toward a possible later discussion, we can sketch out here what seems

---

406 See 'Modernidad y capitalismo' in Echeverría 1995a, especially thesis 14: 'La modernidad, lo mercantil y lo capitalista', pp. 192–195.
407 Aside from Marx, Bolívar Echeverría also refers frequently to Fernand Braudel for these reflections (see 'La comprensión y la crítica. Braudel y Marx sobre el capitalismo', in Echeverría1995a pp. 111–31). On p. 111, he refers to *Civilization and Capitalism, 15th–18th Century*: Braudel 1992.
408 See in this regard the citation in note 397 on p. 330 of this book.
409 B. Echeverría, fourth interview with the author, Mexico City, UNAM-FFL, 28 June 1996 (audio recording).
410 The author preferred to allow this extremely interesting interview to rest in his audio archive, to be worked on at another opportunity, rather than dealing here lightly and in a reductionist way with its controversial theme.

to us to be the central problem in Echeverría's utopian understanding of a non-capitalist commodity production: this comes into contradiction with a circumstance that he himself also demonstrates, and which Joachim Hirsch, for example, formulates as follows: 'The market economy, however, means first of all private production and exchange, and consequently carries within it the seed for the development of capitalist structures'.[411]

Echeverría and Hirsch have the same point of departure for their reflections: they are aware of the *need* to overcome the ruling capitalist relations of production with the simultaneous restraint regarding the true political *usefulness [Brauchbarkeit]* of Marx's utopia in the *Critique of the Gotha Programme*: 'From each according to his ability, to each according to his needs!'[412] Both are interested in discovering the possibility of an 'anti-capitalist politics *within* alienation'.[413] Also in the disillusionment that preceded this restraint, there exists a similarity between the two authors, who were both shaped by the experience of the West German student movement of the 1960s. Hirsch formulates this with the following words: 'First of all it is necessary to realise that a highly technologically developed economy according to the current state of knowledge and experience cannot be managed without functioning *market regulation*'.[414]

But the difference is already indicated in this last formulation. Whereas Hirsch, in a dryly materialist fashion, qualifies his assessment as being based on 'the current state of knowledge and experience,' Echeverría goes further, as we have mentioned, and sees the market as a basic constant of modernity. At first glance, Hirsch is much more modest than Echeverría in proposing a possible concrete definition of ends for leftist politics in the present. While Echeverría insists on the overcoming of capitalism (maintaining commodity production) as a concrete end for contemporary emancipatory thought, the author from Frankfurt states tersely: 'At this moment we cannot deal with anything more than the end (in fact, a modest one) of a *better* regulated *capitalism in political and social terms*. This, in any case, does not entail a reformist politics with no perspective.'[415]

We will not go any more deeply into the question of which of the two authors is more radical, but one thing should be said: Hirsch's provisional political modesty is less distant from serious emancipatory aspiration than Echeverría's

---

411   Hirsch 1990, pp. 178f.
412   Marx 1970.
413   Echeverría 1995a, p. 176.
414   Hirsch 1990, p. 178.
415   Hirsch 1990, p. 181.

'market without capitalism', due to the fact that the latter converts at certain moments his implicit defense of the commodity-form of production into an anthropologising determination, and thereby cuts the last theoretical thread connecting this theory to a communist society. 'The commodity-form of production' implies in the final instance the bourgeois understanding of equality, which is the basis for the exchange of equivalents. This leads to a very peculiar impression, since Echeverría has as one of his points of critique of 'capitalist modernity' the latter's 'false universalism'. While it is true that the problematic of this false universalism is tied to forms which are culturally conditioned (for example, historical *ethe*), it is also nevertheless deeply tied to the *equality of all men and, above all, with that of their labour power*.

How can we overcome Eurocentrism, that form of expression of bourgeois false universalism which so occupies Echeverría, if he is going to eternalise precisely its economic foundation: the commodity? Is the accentuation of diverse use-values sufficient to do so? In any case, the self-directed irony opened by Joachim Hirsch's epilogue regarding proposals to 'ride the capitalist tiger'[416] would benefit Echeverría and his attempts to domesticate the non-capitalist commodity tiger:

> There was a young lady of Riga,
> Who rode with a smile on a tiger,
> They returned from the ride
> With the lady inside
> And the smile on the face of the tiger.
>   (By an unknown but extremely perceptive author)[417]

---

416   Hirsch 1990, p. 189.
417   Hirsch 1990, p. 191.

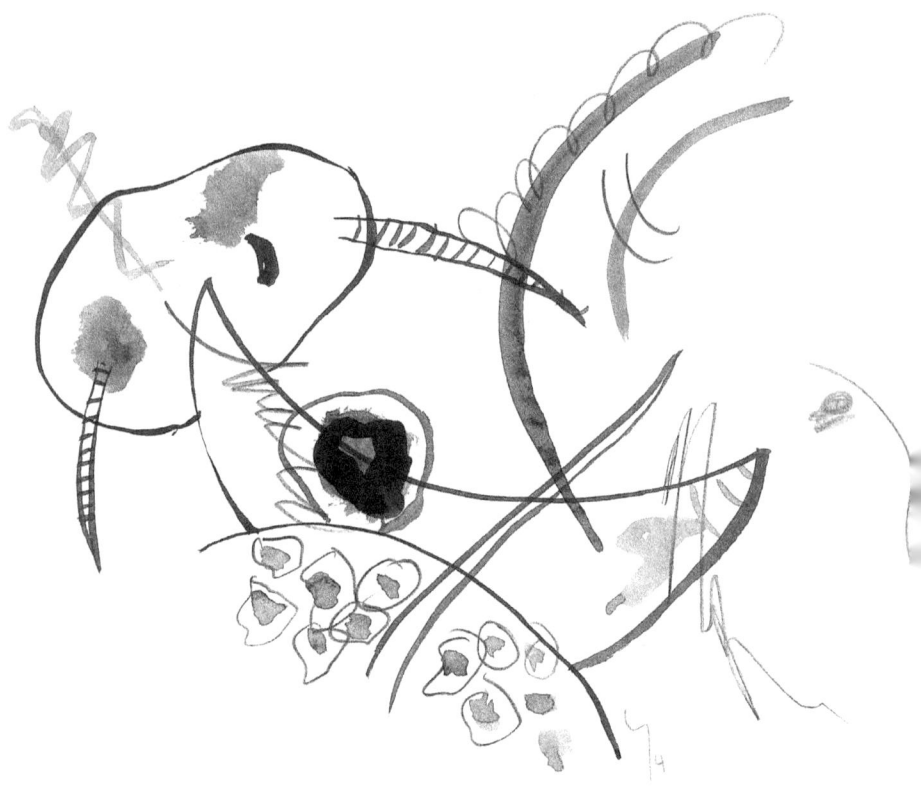

CUERPOS VI

PART 4

On the Relationship between Praxis and *Ethos*

This investigation has had a double objective: on the one hand, to demonstrate that outside the so-called First World there are also philosophers worthy of study, even by inhabitants of the alleged philosophical motherlands; on the other hand, on the basis of our theoretical examination of the selected authors, the critical discussion of their works and the conceptual comparison with one another, as well as the philosophical confrontation with debates discussed in Germany, we thought to make a contribution to the development of social philosophy.

Limitations of the present text and its approach, which is critical towards Eurocentrism. If we bear in mind that this process of formation of a critical social philosophy can today only be carried out on the global level, then the two purposes of this study are inseparable. But the current level of debate in Europe (and especially in Germany) regarding philosophical Eurocentrism is very low, such that it was not possible to presume awareness of this need as a component of general academic knowledge, not even at the heart of the theoretical current which is the one with the fewest provincial attitudes[1] between the philosophical traditions in Germany: non-dogmatic Marxism. It is in large part due to this that we have occasionally privileged the exposition of the philosophies of Sánchez Vázquez and Echeverría over critiques of them. The project of productively disregarding philosophical Eurocentrism cannot steer clear of the pitfalls of the object of its critique, which due to its omnipresence simultaneously constitutes the very context of investigation. We have also presented here the problem of all critical self-reflection insofar as one is simultaneously the subject and object of critique.[2] The *philosophical* critique of the Eurocentrism at the heart of philosophy can only target an already existing audience, which due to the circumstance here under critique carries with it

---

1 'Provincial' is used here in its figurative, not literal, sense. In today's economic and political metropolises, social theory tends to be more provincial than the social ideas originating from the most remote provinces, as demonstrated not only by the Zapatista rebels in the Lacandón jungle of the Mexican south-east. Their declarations helped to grasp current social relations more clearly than the tonnes of increasingly ideologically one-dimensional academic journals of the metropolises. The degree of this ideological one-dimensionality was manifest, above all, at the outset of the war by the German Federal Republic, the United States, and other NATO member states against the Federal Republic of Yugoslavia (1999).

2 Despite the author's effort in this book to confront philosophical Eurocentrism – not only discursively but also in the theoretical activity itself – it is evident that he is more trapped within ruling social conditions than a person with moments of free and critical thinking would desire. It would seem that even a change of residence, in this case to Mexico, is insufficient to open up closed perspectives, to escape a localist narrowness of viewpoint; something which flourishes increasingly within the framework of a frenetically advertised globalisation.

not only a total ignorance but also, as a general rule, unconscious prejudices against theorists from the so-called Third World. In order to be able to confront this situation, the author, in his presentation, must approach through elemental questions, which are not common among philosophical studies. This circumstance perceptibly limits the potential for our investigation to enter more deeply into possible critiques of the analysed works of the two authors in Mexico. On the other hand, in light of the fact that in Germany there is generally little knowledge of the context – in its broadest sense – it becomes necessary, in the case of possible doubts about the authors and their conceptualisations, to first avoid possible misunderstandings, resulting from gaps in the readers' knowledge or even by limited information from the author of this book on the complex philosophical, social and political actual situation and history in Mexico and Latin America. Finally, the author has the profound conviction that even those thinkers consciously determined to overcome Eurocentrism are incapable, on a subconscious level, of simply stripping off the old arrogant and aggressive European tradition. In this sense, we need to sail permanently against the current in order to make possible an adequate understanding of the selected authors. The fact that these considerations can also result in an indulgent-paternalistic perspective and that this, in the final instance, is part of what must be overcome, constitutes the great difficulty of the project and one of the reasons why, until this point, such efforts were scarce or never managed to break the ancient thread of Eurocentrism.

On the first purpose of the investigation. With regard to the first of the two purposes of this study that we have sketched out, it is worth stating the following: if the readers have arrived willingly up to this point in the text, we could assume that they share the following conclusive assessment toward our first purpose. The fact that we have studied Adolfo Sánchez Vázquez and Bolívar Echeverría has served to demonstrate that philosophical discussion (in this case social philosophy [*Sozialphilosophie*]) will be enriched in Europe, no doubt, with the elimination of the barriers to the reception of ideas generated in the South. In the author's judgement, in Europe and the rest of the so-called First World, in a context of social stagnation, a generalised paralysis in the development of relevant social philosophies has emerged,[3] which is to say, philosophies which contribute to the process of emancipation of the human being from oppression and exploitation by other humans. This paralysis could

---

3   There are exceptions, for example, in the development of feminist theory. This study has an affinity with the latter due to the fact that, in both cases, what is at stake is to undermine the pseudo-rational mechanisms operating in the service of the defence of existing structures of domination and science.

possibly begin to be overcome through discussion with the two here analysed and other relevant authors from the so-called Third World.

On the second purpose of the study. In what follows we will attempt to summarise and, at the same time, provide a conceptual synthesis of the possible partial results obtained in the study of Adolfo Sánchez Vázquez and Bolívar Echeverría. To this end, they will also be contrasted with one another, and with philosophical non-dogmatic Marxism in Germany. The tasks to be addressed are the following: the question concerning a concept of praxis which is eventually too optimistic; the question of the ideological naturalisation of social relations which simultaneously obstructs our gaze toward external nature and our own nature; as well as, connected with the two first questions, finally the question as to the possibility or the difficulty of breaking with Eurocentric tradition and with the naïve faith in progress as inevitable, which are present even in leftist and Marxist philosophies.

CHAPTER 18

Affirmation or Critique of Praxis?

One of the decisive differences between the two authors examined in this work seems to reside in the distinct mode of referring to human praxis. Bolívar Echeverría's point of departure is that Adolfo Sánchez Vázquez has a concept of praxis, which is too optimistic. He even perceives in the philosopher of Spanish origin an apology for praxis.[4] Echeverría situates Sánchez Vázquez within a posture that has not broken sufficiently with Marxian tradition, which he seeks to improve on this point.[5] Are the two authors as radically different as the younger would have it? If so, where does this difference come from? And if not, what is Echeverría's understanding of this difference based on? In order to respond to these questions it is necessary to refer to Marx and to Western Marxism.

Alfred Schmidt indicates that the Marxian concept of modern human praxis is only at first glance characterised by an unshakeable optimism. 'The fact that nature is converted into a "pure object for man" and ceases to "be recognised as a power in itself" is registered but not celebrated by Marx'.[6] While it is true that Marx expresses at various points in his work his fascination with the apparently unlimited power of bourgeois praxis *vis-à-vis* the obstacles previously presented by nature and tradition,[7] on the basis of his fundamental ideas and in an entire series of passages he shows himself to be much more critical;

---

4 In this regard, see the subchapter on Echeverría's Differences *vis-à-vis* the Concept of Praxis in Sánchez Vázquez, pp. 199ff of this book.
5 'Of course, Sánchez Vázquez's affirmation is a reaffirmation of what Marx doubtless poses. But I believe the problem lies precisely in the fact that Marx lacks a definition of what the practical life of the human being consists of' (Bolívar Echeverría: Third interview with the author on 10 July 1996 at the Faculty of Philosophy and Arts of the UNAM, Mexico City. Tape recording, cassette I, side B, pos. 150–3).
6 Schmidt 1973, p. 1119. Here, Schmidt cites the *Grundrisse*: Marx 1983b, p. 323. See, moreover, Schmidt's argument along the lines that Marxian materialism 'is critical, rather than a positive confession of faith': Schmidt 1971, p. 134.
7 Thus, for example, in the *Manifesto*: 'The bourgeoisie cannot exist without constantly revolutionizing the instruments of production, and thereby the relations of production, and with them the whole relations of society.... All that is solid melts into air, all that is holy is profaned, and man is at last compelled to face with sober senses, his real conditions of life, and his relations with his kind' (Marx and Engels 1908, p. 12).

his concept of praxis, especially in reference to the present world, is, instead, a sceptical one.[8]

Sánchez Vázquez, certainly, did not deal explicitly in his work with the Marxian concept of nature, but in his studies on the relationship between praxis and knowledge Marx's sceptical position is present. For example, upon discussion of the problematic of the difference between the concept of pragmatist or empiricist truth and that of Marx, as sketched out in the *Theses on Feuerbach*, among other writings, it becomes clear that Marx does not conceive an immediate relationship with praxis, as the latter is only truly recognisable in theoretical reflection. Or, put differently: not all activity is at the same time praxis, but only that which is undertaken consciously and reflectively. The intimate relationship between theory and praxis is already, for Marx himself, inseparably contained within the concept of praxis. Adolfo Sánchez Vázquez emphasises these facts, as we have seen in our examination of his *Philosophy of Praxis*.

If we interpret Marx's concept of praxis radically in this latter sense, we could even arrive at the conclusion that such praxis in the strict sense scarcely exists under existing social relations. This assertion loses what seems absurd at first glance, if we consider what Marx said on one occasion: that the current form of social reproduction, and with it, the organisation of society as a whole, are to a high degree unreflexive, chaotic, even 'anarchic',[9] and humanity has, therefore, not truly entered the phase of reason, or, in other words, has not left prehistory. But we, the human beings of the present, are not only in a stage of social unconsciousness, as is the case with so-called 'primitives', but rather the polemical Marxian concept of prehistory as nineteenth-century reality (and

---

8 See, for example: 'Capitalist production, therefore, only develops the techniques and the degree of combination of the social process of production by simultaneously undermining the original sources of all wealth – the soil and the worker' (Marx 1976a, p. 638).

   In the prologue to the French edition of his book on the Marxian concept of nature, Alfred Schmidt demonstrates with a wide range of passages in the text that Marx's view of contemporary human praxis – and above all in relation to the destruction of nature – is not simply a euphoric one (see Préface de l'auteur à l'édition française. Pour un matérialisme écologique, in Schmidt 1994). On Marx's non-progressivist reflections, see also our subchapter 'Contribution to the Reconstruction of the Concept of Ideology in the Critique of Political Economy', pp. 313ff.

9 'The capitalist mode of production, while it enforces economy in each individual business, also begets, by its anarchic system of competition, the most outrageous squandering of labour-power and of the social means of production, not to mention the creation of a vast number of functions at present indispensable, but in themselves superfluous' (Marx 1976a, p. 667).

seen from today, twentieth-century reality as well) contains, moreover, something very different.

In their reproductive acts, so-called primitive human beings were closer than we are to the strict Marxian concept of praxis as the unity of activity and understanding. It is true that they had fewer possibilities in terms of the massive technical control over nature, and their instrumental reason was much less dominant than is the case today, but simultaneously, their comprehension of social relations and productive relations themselves was less fetishised than it is the case at present. In the chapter on the fetishism of the commodity, it becomes clear that no previous economic form has been so unfathomable as is the dominant capitalist form. Never before as today, in any historical epoch, was there so little collective and individual consciousness of the process of reproduction and, as a result, of the social structure in all its complexity as well.

In this sense, Marx may be understood in the way that, at first glance, it seems to be that there exists in bourgeois society a highly organised and advanced level of praxis; however, a more rigorous observation offers the opposite image. It is true that the ruling society is untiringly active and has produced a multitude of products that was never before imaginable, but with all this, it remains doubtful as to whether or not this truly constitutes a 'productive praxis'. On the contrary, the critical Marxian conception of praxis is hardly applicable to this myriad of activities, since its level of consciousness is merely technical-immediate and it does not gain a real comprehension of the social relations created with the existing form of production. This lack of consciousness toward activity and its comprehensive meaning results in the fact that we cannot understand it as 'praxis' in the Marxian sense, as interpreted in detail by Adolfo Sánchez Vázquez.

This throws an entirely new light onto the problematic of an overly optimistic concept of praxis in Marx and Sánchez Vázquez, as Bolívar Echeverría observes. When Echeverría spoke of a 'monstrous praxis' in contemporary society, it is clear that he was not referring to praxis in the radically critical sense discussed previously, but rather equated 'praxis' with 'activity', two concepts that – according to Sánchez Vázquez's interpretation of Marx – must be distinguished with precision. This relates to the fact that *consciousness*, which the precise distinction between 'activity' and 'praxis' consists of, is not grasped as critically by Bolívar Echeverría as by Marx himself. In our explanations of Marx's concept of ideology and of Echeverría's concept of *ethos*, which is different from the former, it became clear that Echeverría arrived at his concept of historical *ethos* (one which is critical of Eurocentrism) only at the price of diminishing the critical Marxian impulse of ideology, which was taken up by

Western Marxism. This entailed, moreover, that Echeverría did not look with the most critical eyes upon the current conditions of possibility of a consciousness of social relations, which goes beyond what can be achieved by instrumental reason. In this way, out of a certain necessity he could not arrive at the reflection that a critical interpretation of Marx's concept of praxis cannot grasp this concept in the naïvely optimistic manner typical of dogmatic Marxism.

It is worth recalling that officially approved interpretations of Marx did not only make use of the method of silencing particular texts to arrive at the desired theoretical results. The obsession with a concept of progress limited to new technical discoveries and their industrial applications, which entailed stripping the concept increasingly of its critically polemical components, can be explained largely by the political and economic interest in 'overtaking without catching up to' the capitalist bloc. However, in Marx's own work, there are certain passages which allow one to make this sort of progressivist interpretation without much effort. We should not deny that Marx is contradictory on these questions[10] and that he repeatedly makes claims that could be read as progressivist, as admiring technology, and even as Eurocentric. Their overcoming corresponds, without a doubt, to Marxian theoretical principles; but this cannot occur through simply silencing those vestiges of bourgeois thought that emerge within Marx himself, but rather only through the critical discussion of their theoretical limitations and those of many of his successors in particular. It is to this that Bolívar Echeverría's reflections have contributed, despite their limitations but also because of them. Since these limitations are not the result of chance, but rather the price of his very relevant effort to develop a non-Eurocentic focus *within* Marxist discussions, these are not in and of themselves only an obstacle for the process of knowledge but also simultaneously its preconditions.

But to truly be able to advance in this effort to surpass the Eurocentrism at the heart of Marxism, where it also has a massive presence, without thereby falling into an idealistic reinterpretation of Marx and of human history, we

---

10   Schmidt interprets the fact that Marx's theory is frequently contradictory with regard to the relationship between praxis and nature in the following terms: 'The realm of the forces of nature has something of the "poetic sensuous luster" ascribed to it by the Renaissance and perceived by Marx, in *The Holy Family*, even in Bacon's technologically oriented materialist concept of matter. Nature is not only an immense *material*, present under all human social conditions of existence in all its modes of appearance, but also a *potential*, whose extensive or intensive actualization takes place according to the measure of the existing level of the forces of production' (Schmidt 1971, pp. 161–2. Schmidt here cites Marx 1972, p. 135).

need a persistent critique of the mentioned limitations of Echeverría. For this, we also need again and again new formulations of the Marxian concepts of praxis and ideology, as well as the concept of knowledge, a task that Adolfo Sánchez Vázquez carries out with singular determination. Alfred Schmidt, who we have introduced at various points in the discussion in order to clarify several difficulties, plays – without having known the writings of either author beforehand – a sort of mediating role. Like Sánchez Vázquez, he maintains a critical interpretation of the Marxian concept of praxis and knowledge and, at the same time, has been one of the first to take up the question of nature in Marx, venturing into a problematic, which during the 1960s was still untouched territory in Marxist debates. While his book on the concept of nature in Marx – as he admits in his most recent prologue – does not deal with the question of the destruction of nature on the level that it must unavoidably be studied today, the very fact of having placed the concept of nature, and thereby that of use-value, at the centre of his first book, is sufficient reason to treat him as an author of special relevance with regard to the question of the concept of use-value in Marx, a question that Echeverría would later consider as central.

To summarise, the following could be said regarding the problem posed by Bolívar Echeverría, namely, that Marx's concept of praxis and that of his critical interpreter, Sánchez Vázquez, has been too optimistic: Echeverría's reproach of Marx and Sánchez Vázquez is a pertinent one, and is the basis for some of his primary contributions to the unfolding of a critical Marxist theory and the development of social philosophy more generally; therefore, it is the basis for his theory of the historical *ethos* as a central element of a materialist and non-Eurocentric theory of culture. At the same time, his reproach is misguided and should be understood as a consequence of his major philosophical limitation; namely, the tendency to simplify the problematic of ideology in order to be able to do something correct even on the plane of the existing false. Hence his peculiar oscillation between limiting himself to describing particular social forms of the four *ethe* of capitalist modernity, projected as ideal types, and fixing these in an idealistic fashion, beyond sufficiently broad materialist research.

As regards Sánchez Vázquez and Marx, it is worth noting that, having learned some lessons from Bolívar Echeverría and Alfred Schmidt, we can observe an occasionally excessive optimism toward human praxis and its transformative force, as well as toward their possibility and desirability (under certain specific circumstances).[11] But, at the same time, adopting the perspective of Sánchez

---

11   In this sense, Schmidt criticises Marx's quick rejection of Feuerbach in the *Theses* he dedicates to the latter: 'What the 1845 *Theses* condemn as the merely contemplative character

Vázquez and Alfred Schmidt, we must go more deeply into the Marxian concept of praxis, rediscovering its radicality. Now, this radicalism of the concept of praxis does not encourage a naïve faith in praxis, but, instead, becomes in itself a driving force for grasping its own conceptual as well as real limitations. Praxis is not simply, as Echeverría occasionally suggests, the category that stands opposite nature (or the natural form), but it is, rather, the case that a concept of nature with a qualitative – and not only quantitative – orientation only becomes possible through praxis.[12]

Finally, with regard to Echeverría's critique of a concept of praxis, which is perhaps too non-critical, we must again delve into the historical context. Both the theory of Adolfo Sánchez Vázquez and that of Alfred Schmidt were developed in a historical context completely different from that of the founder of scientific socialism. It is true that both wrote their central texts on the concept of praxis during the early 1960s, that is, in an era of increasing agitation, a prelude to the student movement of almost global reach whose culminating point was 1968, but this is not necessarily the principal historical-political referent of their theories. The fact that the beginning of the elaboration of these theories should be situated, in both cases, even prior to the precursors of the movements of '68 also leads us toward this interpretation. It is clear that in both authors there exists a historical-political reference point that does not allow predominant human praxis to be seen in a positive light. For Sánchez Vázquez and Schmidt, there was nothing comparable to what Marx had with the period prior to the revolution of March 1848; both wrote under the direct influence of the absolutely negative experience of European fascism. Sánchez Vázquez himself fought against Francoism, which rapidly tore to pieces the promising project of a democratic Spanish Left, and Alfred Schmidt came directly from the tradition of the Frankfurt School, whose representatives were forced to flee into exile to escape certain death at the hands of the National Socialist mass movement in Germany. For both authors (as well as for Gramsci, whose *Philosophy of Praxis* was in its majority written, and not by coincidence,

---

of Feuerbachian matérialism, was not only an expression of theoretical-political backwardness, but also contained what Horkheimer and Adorno called "the urge of the living toward peace"' (Schmidt 1974, p. 211. The citation is from the 1971 *postscript*, which is not included in the Spanish, Italian, or English translations of the book). Schmidt is here citing Horkheimer and Adorno 2002, p. 212.

12 'In labour (for Marx in properly organised labour in particular) nature presents to men a more differentiated, as it were "more natural" side ... But in the shape of the material of labour, nature *also* confronts men as something qualitatively determined' (Schmidt 1971, p. 161).

in a fascist prison), the direct experience and memory of the human praxis as radical intervention are in the first instance negative. Here it is worth asking if fascist, Francoist, and National Socialist activity can be simply catalogued as praxis in the strict sense, since such a concept also includes theoretical reflection, but in any case the rise of these forces, which were the most destructive in the society of the late bourgeois period, implied the far-reaching defeat of emancipatory political praxis. Thus, when the works of these authors discuss extensively the problem of the relationship between objectively given conditions and the subjective possibility of influencing these conditions, as well as the problem of the knowledge of these objective conditions, it is possible that this might appear to today's reader – especially one lacking a professional specialised education in philosophy – as a merely scholastic exercise in concepts. But this perception owes more, on the one hand, to political apathy and the resignation which prevails above all at present, and on the other hand, to historical amnesia, than to any internal philosophical exhaustion.

Against all first appearances, the concept of praxis that appears in both authors is not merely a concept of absolute confidence – one emerging from the progressivist bourgeois tradition – in the human capacity to transform the world and knowledge, but is, at the same time and to a greater degree, a concept that springs up from indignation at lived human praxis. The knowledge that accompanies praxis is not knowledge in the sense of Enlightenment thinkers, which inspires the world more and more in the light of truth, but rather knowledge of horror. Perhaps the most brilliant accomplishment of Adolfo Sánchez Vázquez was his ability to develop in Mexican exile, without knowledge of Walter Benjamin's work, a critical concept of history that is included in his concept of praxis.

CHAPTER 19

The Conceptual Determination of Culture and Nature

Adolfo Sánchez Vázquez attempts, with the help of the Marxian concept of praxis, to overcome the disappearance of the subject in different theories, for example in the dogmatic (Stalinist) interpretation of Marx. In so doing, he critiques those formulations which reduce the socially originated to something natural-eternal or, as Marx says with critical distance, to something which is '*naturwüchsig*' [what is believed naïvely to be 'natural'].[13] In their false analysis, the theories he critiques follow ruling social relations, whose own survival becomes the end of history, and the majority of human beings are reduced to guaranteeing the survival of those relations, instead of social relations preparing the organisational social framework for the subjects of history.

But this 'naturalisation' of the social, which perverts relations – insofar as something derived is elevated to the category of being the original substance – does not contain a true approximation to nature. In the words of the Marxian critique of political economy, the 'forgetting' of the social character of production in the prevailing consciousness of bourgeois society, or in other words, the false understanding of value as a magnitude given by nature, is only a negative type of reference to 'nature'; the latter is put forth as a substitute for the omitted real analysis of social relations. Thus, the fixation on the use-value side is something purely instrumental without any real interest in its full comprehension.

Necessarily false consciousness is based on a one-sided understanding of the double character of commodity production as social and private at the same time, which is to say, simultaneously as values and as use-values; as a result, only the private side (productive of use-values) of the process of commodity production is seen. The bourgeois obsession with the private side of production, or in other words, the naturalisation of the historically developed capitalist form of reproduction, *does not* necessarily entail a true interest in grasping the individual, the private, use-value, or the natural form of the commodity. In these instances, what we have is a merely negative reference, since it apparently ignores the need for scientific (which is to say, critical) analysis of the social aspect of production.

---

13   See, for example, Marx 1975a, p. 87.

This represents precisely the difference between bourgeois theories of the 'private side' of production and that formulated by Bolívar Echeverría. The latter attempts to advance in the *material* analysis of the 'private side' in his analysis of use-value, of the natural form of production. For this reason, his theory of the (historical) *ethe* of capitalist modernity demonstrates basic differences *vis-à-vis* Sánchez Vázquez's studies of the concept of praxis, but only at first sight. In both cases, we find an effort to overcome the incapacity of bourgeois society to understand itself. Moreover, both take as their point of departure the fact that their theories should also function critically within Marxist debates. But this is not due to any pedantic sectarianism and nor to the unreflexive adherence to a particular theoretical current that has come into favour, but, rather, to the discovery of the fact that even the theoretical formulations of the Marxist tradition have been affected by the previously mentioned incapacity of bourgeois society to understand itself.

Consequently, while Sánchez Vázquez, with the concept of praxis, attempts to fill with content the programme that Alfred Schmidt would formulate with the words: 'Marxist knowledge has as its end to free again the history paralysed in acknowledged facts';[14] Echeverría, for his part, attempts to contribute to the analysis of what is understood in the Marxian sense as the 'natural form of the commodity'. These are factors that, in a certain sense, precede history, without being totally unconnected to it. They are elements of the natural and human being, situated in strata of human reality, which are deeper than immediate social relations, which, through a revolutionary process, can be modified with *relative* quickness and ease. We are referring to those components of social reality, and, in a certain sense as well, of natural reality, which due to their persistence and inertia occasionally seem immutable and, insofar as these are directly subjected to the laws of nature, may even be so. In any case, it should be observed that the laws of nature are not conceivable beyond their (respective) social reality, thus they exist as non-mediated ones only on their respective historical plane.

The complex relationship between nature and society, between matter and subjectivity, which presents considerable epistemological problems – studied by Alfred Schmidt in detail and in an exemplary fashion for critical Marxist debates – finds, in its own way, a counterpart in the complex relationship between conditions, which are immediately determined by the social relations, on the one hand, and intersubjective structures that are developed and modified during very long lapses of time, on the other: language, traditions, and forms of cultural manifestations in the broadest sense. But Echeverría's

---

14   Schmidt 1973, p. 1120.

focus should not be understood in any way as an attempt to throw Adolfo Sánchez Vázquez's *Philosophy of Praxis* or comparable European formulations overboard entirely, but his theory should instead be understood as an effort to *radicalise* the philosophy of praxis; an attempt, in the etymological sense of the word, conceptually to reach the roots of existing social relations.

So Echeverría is not interested in diluting Marxian theory in bourgeois waters, as he has been accused of occasionally, but rather – on the contrary – to deprive of arguments the superficial naturalising and culturalising interpretations of bourgeois society and capitalist relations of production. Now, it has been the case just as often that natural and cultural aspects – which no doubt exist in every society and frequently slow their direct transformation, which is the reason why such interpretations tend to be applauded by conservative theories – have been studied by such authors with as little seriousness as when they studied the immediate social relations and the human praxis that grounds them. The terminological occupation of the social terrain, and that created directly through praxis, by naturalising and culturalising tendencies has pressed the true analysis of nature-society and culture-society relations out of the conceptual terrain.

Echeverría's purpose in locating these two relations at the centre of his analysis should be understood as another step in what was already Marx's theoretical project: the successive demystification of bourgeois ideas regarding their own existence. While Sánchez Vázquez has as his objective to demystify the distortion of that, which is created by human praxis – or, by conscious human activity – as something 'natural' or 'eternally immutable', Echeverría, by contrast, attempts to overcome another problem that is also contained in this mystification, namely, the sovereign negation of what effectively is 'nature' or 'culture'. This 'nature', 'culture', and such like, which are inserted merely as substitutes for aspects of social relations which are conceptually inaccessible to bourgeois theory, due to its ideological and historical limitations, must now be studied as factors of reality which exist beyond the ideological utilisation of these terms.

Obviously, the descent into *deep* strata cannot be accomplished without the loss of previously developed knowledges, since the prevailing naturalisation and culturalisation of social relations has occupied the terminological terrain with ideological concepts, to such a degree that it is almost impossible to penetrate therein and escape unscathed. Just as Alfred Schmidt rightly emphasises time and again that the philosophy of praxis must necessarily turn for help to the idealist philosophy of knowledge in order to be able to conceptually confront mechanical materialism and dogmatic Marxism, in Echeverría's case, things work very similarly. His effort to overcome the tendency to underestimate the relevance of the natural form of social reproduction, as well as the cultural foundations of all material reproduction and social organisation in the majority of Marxist theories, cannot survive in the face of this conceptual predominance if it does not turn to specific idealist [and Heideggerian] terms and knowledges.

But we must also take into consideration Alfred Schmidt's objection to the excessive emphasis on praxis or the subject. Schmidt – without underestimating the importance of human subjectivity and praxis – indicates that it is not possible to entirely subordinate external objectivity, nature, and matter, to the human capacity to transform the world.[15] Taking up again Marx and Hegel, he underlines the meaning of 'the cunning of man',[16] which must be present in praxis in order to, while respecting the laws of matter, transform it according to human needs and ends.[17] In view of this dialectical relationship between society and world-transforming praxis on the one hand, and external nature and matter on the other, what needs to be sought is the correlate in the relationship between culture, traditions, language, etc. on the one hand, and society and human praxis on the other. In turn, it is clear that this correlation must be developed in a double sense.

On the one hand, the relationship between (cultural) tradition and (revolutionary) praxis is limited insofar as praxis cannot break with these traditions at will; here, too, we must behave 'cunningly'. An example of this is languages, which have no doubt developed within repressive and exploitative relations and, therefore, contain ideological elements, which obstruct knowledge.

---

15 'Nature can neither be dissolved into the moments of a metaphysically conceived "Spirit" nor can it be reduced to the historical modes of its appropriation in practice. Lukács succumbed to this neo-Hegelian "actualist" view in *History and Class Consciousness*, in other respects important for the history of the interpretation of Marx' (Schmidt 1971, p. 69).

16 Schmidt 1971, p. 105.

17 'If the human cognitive apparatus, like the objects toward which it operates, is specifically marked by history, this does not simply imply "historicism". It is true that in the human and material world we cannot really separate what arrives given by nature from what is added on socially. And yet it is not for this that the "priority of external nature" is challenged. The Marxist doctrine of praxis sets out from a structure specific to matter that cannot be dissolved in historical subjectivity; that specific structure acquired, already prior to any "subjective" interpretation (in the relativist sense), a *general form* which results from collective *praxis*' (Schmidt 1973, p. 1121). Schmidt cites the term 'priority of external nature' from *Die Deutsche Ideologie*: Marx and Engels 1969, p. 44. Schmidt also refers to *One Dimensional Man*: Marcuse 1967, pp. 229–31.

For its part, revolutionary praxis has no alternative but to set out from these languages in order to be able to transform social relations as well as these languages themselves.

On the other hand, we must equally bear in mind the inverse direction of the relationship of dependence between the cultural/natural determination of the social and its practical transformation. It is clear that tradition, even more so than matter, never escapes the social praxis of humans unscathed. Recourse to Sánchez Vázquez's concept of praxis and Alfred Schmidt's reflections on the concept of nature could, alongside Bolívar Echeverría's formulations, lead reflections on this relationship of double dependence to the level of precision required to rise to the conceptual level necessary for an examination of existing societies and the possibility of their transformation toward a society which is not self-destructive – meaning, ultimately, a free society.

It would seem as though this transformation were no longer possible today. But it is clear – and the most recent bellicose confrontations show this without a shadow of a doubt – that such a transformation remains a vital necessity if we do not wish to leave human history to the discretion of the self-destructive tendency of the existing social formation (and its blind operators).

CHAPTER 20

The Philosophical Critique of Eurocentrism

To conclude our study, we will return again to the problem of Eurocentrism. As has become evident, the philosophical critique of the latter plays an important role for Bolívar Echeverría, but Sánchez Vázquez also refers to this problem at various points and formulates the concept of praxis in such a way that it cannot coincide with a perspective which is limited to Europe and its traditions. Paradoxically, both authors refer practically only to European or US texts. We will tackle this second element first.

a   On the Problem of Focusing on European Authors

In his study of the relationship between philosophy and praxis in history, the Spanish-Mexican philosopher Sánchez Vázquez remains faithful to his European origins in his exclusive reference to 'Western' intellectual history, and does not dedicate a single word to other philosophical developments. This reflects a certain consistency, since he is primarily interested in the theoretical-historical foundations of the Marxian concept of praxis. Bolívar Echeverría, too, has as his point of reference above all authors from the so-called old continent.

But how can we reconcile this with the stated orientation of Echeverría's theory of the four modern *ethe*, whose intention is to overcome Eurocentrism on at least the terrain of social philosophy? And how does Sánchez Vázquez's critique of Eurocentrism apply to Hegel and, in part, to Marx and a 'certain form of Marxism' as well?

> But it is not sufficient to recognise the historical character of reason if it is understood – as Hegel understands it – teleologically, which is to say, as a reason which is identified with an end that is necessarily and inevitably realised, a realisation which is accomplished by Western peoples and from which those that Hegel calls 'peoples without history' are excluded.
>
> Marxian rationalism is incompatible with this universal and abstract teleological rationalism, which, definitively, conceals and justifies behind the realm of reason the realm of the bourgeoisie and the bourgeois state. But Marx, and above all a certain form of Marxism, have not always

separated themselves from this universal rationality on which Eurocentrism feeds and which leaves non-Western peoples outside of history.[18]

Or is the denomination, taken up again by Hegel, of pre-colonial America as a 'natural culture',[19] nothing more than a 'self-fulfilling prophecy'? The European 'explorers', more than five hundred years ago, began to tyrannise a continent that they described as lacking development – although they took advantage of the history of that continent, and not only with regard to the cultivated plants of which they exported more than thirty varieties just from the current Mexican territory (for example, tomatoes, potatoes, corn, cocoa), but also through their looting of massive quantities of pure gold, which was of enormous importance for the development of European monetary circulation, and with it, of the capitalist mode of production – to thereupon destroy nearly all the documents which would today be able to testify to that history. That destruction, which accompanied that of almost all architectural monuments to that history (the pyramids, which are frequently visited today, are but a stony pedestal, lacking in all adornment, upon which in the past colossal temples were erected and whose beauty has not remained even in the slightest trace, except in a few travel accounts from the participants in the first campaigns of conquest), has led to something like a 'continent without precolonial history', if history is understood as the conscious and documented register of the genesis of our own being. The impressive Museum of Anthropology in Mexico City is a David when compared with the Goliath of the thousands and thousands of bonfires in which the many pre-Hispanic codices burned and to the colossal cathedrals, which were built over the ruins of destroyed pyramids. This David, if we can adopt the emphasis of the metaphor, of course demands respect, but nevertheless one cannot deny how difficult – or perhaps impossible – it would be to revive the philosophical conceptions of the pre-Hispanic era in the Mexico of today.

---

18 From 'La razón amenazada', in Sánchez Vázquez 1987, p. 134. In this text, the critical philosophy that Sánchez Vázquez develops apparently goes further than in his book *Filosofía de la praxis*/*The Philosophy of Praxis*, the primary object of our study.
19 Hegel 1975, p. 163.

b   Critical Concept of Praxis Versus Abstract Universalism, Namely
     Eurocentrism

The critical concept of praxis, whose elaboration is pushed decisively by Adolfo Sánchez Vázquez, can not only be addressed against naïve progressivism and the candid confidence in the apparent human capacity to modify everything at will, but can also make a decisive contribution to the philosophical critique of Eurocentrism, which tends to be accompanied by the previously mentioned faith in progress. In this sense, Sánchez Vazquez's philosophy enjoys, in the final instance, a greater affinity with that of Bolívar Echeverría than might seem to be the case at first sight.

For the former, after all, it is precisely the loss of the concept of praxis that can lead to particular forms of human activity known in Europe to be judged *mechanically* to be the only *redeeming* forms for *all* human beings. In regard to one of his primary fields of analysis – aesthetics – Sánchez Vázquez formulates this critique of Eurocentrism through use of the critical concept of praxis. Theoreticism, which is distinguished precisely by the loss of the concept of praxis, is for this philosopher one of the foundations of Eurocentrism in science:

> Now, the danger for all theory, including true theory, is that it loses consciousness of its own limits. And these limits are none other than those imposed by practice itself. The principles valid for explaining an artistic practice cease to be so when applied to a different one, or when the theorised reality is left behind and another appears which demands new explanatory principles. Such is the limitation of classicist aesthetics in attempting to measure all art according to the classical standard and discredit – as did Winckelmann with the baroque – any art which does not allow itself to be measured by it.[20]

Despite their shared point of departure in a critical and non-dogmatic interpretation of Marx, and despite their shared geographical location (Mexico City) the philosophies of Adolfo Sánchez Vázquez and Bolívar Echeverría developed in very different ways, though converging to a certain degree on this point. While Eurocentrism does not play as much of a role of negative reference in the work of Sánchez Vázquez as is the case in the work of Echeverría,

---

20   Sánchez Vázquez 1992, p. 42.

his theory nevertheless does speak – at the precise moment of the convergence of his two principal objects of study (the concept of praxis and aesthetics) – of this problem which is so serious for the development of a new critical theory adequate to social relations in their totality, which are today seen as globalised. It is no coincidence that both Sánchez Vázquez and Bolívar Echeverría name the baroque as an example of Eurocentric incomprehension of the world. This art form possessed major relevance in Latin America during a long period; it allowed a peculiar mixture of European and indigenous aesthetic elements, something that was produced to a particularly high degree in Mexico, since this art form offered the ability to combine very different traditions and forms, thus avoiding the idea of purity that predominated in other prevailing European artistic styles.

While the transplanted [*transterrado*] philosopher does not justify his reason for entering here into the theme of the baroque and the inability of Johann Joachim Winckelmann – one of the most outstanding German art historians of the eighteenth century – to grasp it, this decision nevertheless expresses with the utmost clarity his critical posture, developed on the basis of the concept of praxis, toward 'aesthetic colonisation'.[21] The closely related critique of 'empty abstractions'[22] also links Sánchez Vázquez with Echeverría. Both, with similar points of departure but nevertheless by different paths, arrive at the critique of 'abstract universalism'[23] and of the distorting elevation of European particularities to the so-called rank of universal human properties.

These reflections, as unusual as they may be among [social] scientists of the so-called First World, including the majority of Marxists, are less remote than is generally assumed from the founder of the scientific critique of currently ruling social relations. Marx had already seen how tightly the ideological affirmation of capitalist relations of productions is linked to Eurocentric theoretical frameworks. While he did not study this aspect of the still persistent false reality in a systematic way, he did nevertheless tackle the question explicitly at

---

21 'Something similar occurs when the prevailing aesthetic principles of Western culture attempt to expand to other cultures, thereby giving rise to a veritable aesthetic colonisation' (ibid.).

22 'If the principles of a theory are extended beyond the reality to which they respond, or if they enter into contradiction with a practice that does not conform to them, they cease to be valid theoretical instruments; that is to say, they lose their explanatory force and become empty abstractions or a simple collection of norms' (ibid.).

23 From 'La identidad evanescente' in Echeverría 1995a, p. 56.

various points, above all in his main work.[24] The fact that these formulations in Marx's work have found no echo whatsoever in later Marxist debates is very revealing with regard to the stubbornness with which the majority of Marxists, as well as communist and socialist activists, felt completely at home in many aspects of bourgeois ideology. They hoped to revolutionise the world without losing their own privileges as Europeans, as whites, and as inhabitants of the First World, socialised in a culture bearing the stamp of Christianity. They sought to square a circle. Their failure does not point toward some falseness of Marxian theory or the communist utopia of a world without oppression and exploitation of human by human, but instead to the falseness of the vestigial tyrants of bourgeois ideology, as well as the attitudes and structures, which still are conveyed in their thoughts and actions. The overcoming of the current situation of deadlock (which, if appearances do not deceive, presses toward a new phase of open self-destruction, which is to say, a proliferation of wars on the global level) cannot be achieved by reintroducing and intermingling bourgeois forms in the project of a new critical theory and emancipatory praxis, but instead by abandoning precisely those false forms of thinking, ways of acting, and structures of the bourgeois world, which are long since antiquated and which flail with an ever-increasing violence for survival.

The adequate response to the failure of the path of self-declared 'actually-existing socialism' lies not in flattening Marx's critique of the capitalist form of socialisation, which is destructive by definition, but in radicalising the critique of the existing, false society, without abandoning any aspect of the Marxian critique. It is precisely where Marx himself shows remnants of that repressive-bourgeois thinking that we have denounced previously that a radicalisation of his own approach must be applied to he himself.[25]

One of the bourgeois remains that is most important to overcome is that of Eurocentrism. Marx also made the initial suggestions in this direction, which were ignored almost systematically by his followers. The discussion of the social philosophies of Bolívar Echeverría and Adolfo Sánchez Vázquez can drive this overcoming of an ancient philosophical taboo in two ways. On the one hand, their very philosophies already constitute a component of this project of non-Eurocentric theoretical elaboration or, at the very least, of a critique of Eurocentrism as the basis for and result of a determinate *praxis* and, therefore, knowing them is greatly helpful, if not indispensable, for this

---

24 Marx 1976, pp. 758f, especially note 51 on Bentham. See also: p. 255, note 189 in this book.
25 This is valid, for example, for the problems of gender relations as socially-constructed relations.

long postponed step. On the other hand, the mere fact of discussing these philosophies in Europe constitutes an act that can only be thought of and realised beyond the Eurocentric logic of the majority of existing philosophies, including those most significant for human emancipation. To study these and other important philosophies of the so-called Third World, to investigate them and discuss with them is to dig the grave for one of the most dubious traditions in the history of European philosophy.

Bibliographical Appendix

A   Bibliography of Adolfo Sánchez Vázquez

a) Books   363
b) Articles   365
c) Existing Translations   387
  To German   387
  To Korean   387
  To Czech   388
  To French   388
  To Galician   388
  To English   388
  To Italian   389
  To Portuguese   390
  To Romanian   390
  To Russian   390
  To Serbo-Croat   390
d) Prologues and Book Reviews   391
  Prologues   391
  Book Reviews   392
e) Interviews and Debates with Sánchez Vázquez, Miscellaneous   395
  Interviews   395
  Debates   396
  Miscellaneous   396
f) Translations of Works by Other Authors   396
  From French   396
  From English   397
  From Italian   397
  From Russian   397
g) Collaboration on Editorial Boards and Editorial Tasks   398
h) Literature about Sánchez Vázquez (selected)   399
  General (selected)   399
  Reviews of and Other Texts about *Philosophy of Praxis*   408
i) Existing Bibliographies about Sánchez Vázquez   409

B   Bibliography of Bolívar Echeverría

a) Books   409
b) Articles   411
c) Existing Translations   419
d) Prologues, Book and Film Reviews   419
   Prologues   419
   Book and Film Reviews   420
e) Interviews   421
f) Translations of Works by Other Authors   421
   From German   421
   From French   422
g) Collaboration on Editorial Boards and Editorial Tasks   422
h) Literature about Bolívar Echeverría   423

C   Selected Bibliography on Marxist Philosophy in Latin America

a) Texts Published in Europe   427
   In Spain   427
   In France   427
   In the Netherlands   428
   In Poland   428
   In the German Democratic Republic   428
   In the German Federal Republic   429
b) Texts Published in Canada and the United States   429
   In Canada   429
   In the United States   429
c) Texts Published in Latin America   430
   In Latin America   430
   In Mexico   431

D   Sources for the Bibliographies

Libraries   432
Catalogues of Books or Journals and Databases   433
Archives   434

N.B. ON BIBLIOGRAPHIES: Universidad Nacional Autónoma de México is mentioned always as 'UNAM'; Bolívar Echeverría Andrade as 'Bolívar Echeverría', as it appears on its books.

A   Bibliography of Adolfo Sánchez Vázquez

a)   *Books*

El pulso ardiendo. Morelia: Voces, 1942. 35 pp. Republished with a preface by Aurora de Albornoz. Madrid: Molinos de Agua, 1980. 53 pp. (Col. España Peregrina, no. 3.) Republication of the entire volume in *El Centavo*, Morelia, October–November 1989, vol. 14, no. 142, pp. 5–18. Republished: Morelia: Universidad Michoacana de San Nicolás de Hidalgo, 2002. Facsimile edition: Malaga: Diputación Provincial de Malaga, 2004. [With an introductory essay by María Dolores Gutiérrez Nava.]

Conciencia y realidad en la obra de arte. San Salvador: Universitaria, 1965. 88 pp. [Presented as a Master's Thesis in 1955 in la Facultad de Filosofía y Letras of the UNAM. 105 pp. Published without the author's permission.]

Las ideas estéticas de Marx. Ensayos de estética marxista. Mexico City: ERA, 1965. 293 pp. [Fourteenth printing, 1989]. Republished: Havana: Instituto Cubano del Libro, 1966 and 1973.

Filosofía de la praxis. Mexico City: Grijalbo, 1967. 383 pp. (Col. Ciencias económicas y sociales.) [Presented as a Doctoral Thesis in Philosophy under the title *Sobre la praxis*, in 1966 at the Universidad Nacional Autónoma de México, mimeograph, 311 pp. Unpublished. Advisor: Eli de Gortari.] Second edition, revised and expanded in 1972: Mexico City: Grijalbo, 1980. 464 pp. (Col. Teoría y Praxis, no. 55.) Published simultaneously in Spain Barcelona: Crítica, 1980. 426 pp. Republished: Mexico City: Siglo XXI, 2003, 528 pp. [With the text according to the second Mexican edition, a prologue by Francisco José Martínez, and an epilogue by the author.]

Ética. Mexico City: Grijalbo, 1969. (Col. Tratados y manuales.) [Fifty-First Edition, 1992]. 240 pp. Republished: Barcelona: Crítica, 1978 (with a prologue for Spanish readers on the history of the work). 285 pp. [Fourth edition, 1984, First edition in the *Biblioteca del bolsillo*: 1999]. The 1978 prologue was incorporated into the Forty-Eighth and subsequent Mexican editions.

Rousseau en México. La filosofía de Rousseau y la ideología de la Independencia. Mexico City: Grijalbo, 1969. 157 pp. Republished: Mexico City: Itaca, 2011.

Estética y marxismo. (Anthology, selection and introduction of texts as well as their translation, and the introduction, 'Los problemas de la estética marxista', by the editor A. Sánchez Vázquez) 2 vols. Vol. 1: *Comunismo y arte*. Vol. 2: *Estética comunista*. Mexico City: Era, 1970. 431 pp. and 525 pp. [5th edition, 1983]. Bibl. pp. 434–7. Name and subject index.

Textos de estética y teoría del arte. Antología. Mexico City: UNAM, Colegio de Ciencias y Humanidades/Dirección General de Publicaciones, 1972. (Col. Lecturas Universitarias no. 14.) [Fifth reprinting, 1996.] 492 pp. (Editor and compiler of the anthology).

La pintura como lenguaje. Monterrey, Universidad Autónoma de Nuevo León, Facultad de Filosofía y Letras, 1974. (Col. Cuadernos de Filosofía, no. 1.) [Second edition, 1976.] 42 pp.

Del socialismo científico al socialismo utópico. Mexico City: Era, 1975. 78 pp. [Second edition, 1981]. (Col. Serie popular Era, no. 32.) [Originally published as an article in 1971.]

Ciencia y revolución. El marxismo de Althusser. Madrid: Alianza Editorial, 1978. 210 pp. New edition, including an interview by Bernardo Lima with A. Sánchez Vázquez and an exchange of letters with Étienne Balibar: Mexico City: Grijalbo, 1983. 220 pp.

Sobre arte y revolución. Mexico City: Grijalbo, 1979. 75 pp. (Col. Textos Vivos, no. 8.)

Filosofía y economía en el joven Marx. Los Manuscritos de 1844. Mexico City: Grijalbo, 1982. 287 pp. Republished with a new title: *El joven Marx. Los manuscritos de 1844*. Mexico City: UNAM, Facultad de Filosofía y Letras/Ed. La Jornada/Itaca. 347 pp.

Ensayos marxistas sobre filosofía e ideología. Barcelona: Océano, 1983. 207 pp.

Sobre filosofía y marxismo. Introduction by Gabriel Vargas Lozano. Puebla: Universidad Autónoma de Puebla, 1983. 111 pp. (Col. Publicaciones de la Escuela de Filosofía y Letras de la UAP, no. 8.)

Ensayos sobre arte y marxismo. Mexico City: Grijalbo, 1984. 218 pp. (Col. Enlace)

Ensayos marxistas sobre historia y política. Mexico City: Océano, 1985. 207 pp.

Escritos de política y filosofía. Madrid: Ayuso/Fundación de Investigaciones Marxistas, 1987. 263 pp.

Del Exilio en México. Recuerdo y reflexiones. Mexico City: Grijalbo, 1991. 105 pp. [Second expanded edition, 1997. 288 pp.]

Invitación a la estética. Mexico City: Grijalbo, 1992. 272 pp. (Col. Tratados y manuales.) [Second edition, 2005. Republished Mexico City: Random House Mondadori, 2007.]

Cuestiones estéticas y artísticas contemporáneas. Mexico City: Fondo de Cultura Económica, 1996. 292 pp. Reprint 2003.

Filosofía y circunstancias. Barcelona: Anthropos/UNAM, Facultad de Filosofía y Letras, 1997. 426 pp.

Recuerdos y reflexiones del exilio. Barcelona: Universitat Autònoma de Barcelona, Grupo de Estudios del Exilio Literario, 1997. 190 pp. [Prologue: Manuel Aznar Soler.]

Filosofía, Praxis y Socialismo. Buenos Aires: Tesis 11, 1998. 136 pp.

Entre la realidad y la utopía. Ensayos sobre política, moral y socialismo. Mexico City: UNAM, Facultad de Filosofía y Letras/Fondo de Cultura Económica, 1999, 329 pp. (Col. Filosofía.) Reprint 2000 and 2007.

De Marx al marxismo en América Latina. Mexico City/Puebla: Itaca/Benemérita Universidad Autónoma de Puebla, Facultad de Filosofía, 1999. 263 pp.

El valor del socialismo. Mexico City: Itaca, 2000. 162 pp.

A tiempo y destiempo. Antología de ensayos. Prologue by Ramón Xirau. Mexico City: Fondo de Cultura Económica, 2003. 616 pp. (Col. Filosofía.)

Poesía. Introduction by María Dolores Gutiérrez Navas. Epílogo Adolfo Castañón. Mexico City/Malaga: Fondo de Cultura Económica/Centro de Estudios de la Generación del 27, 2005. 163 pp.

De la estética de la recepción a una estética de la participación. Mexico City: UNAM, Facultad de Filosofía y Letras, 2005. (Col. Relecciones.) Reprint 2007.

Una trayectoria intelectual comprometida. Mexico City: UNAM, Facultad de Filosofia y Letras, 2006. 123 pp.

Ética y política. Mexico City: UNAM/Fondo de Cultura Económica, 2007. 172 pp. Reprint 2010 and 2013.

Creación, estética y filosofía política. Mi recorrido intelectual. Madrid: Editorial Complutense, 2007. 79 pp.

Incursiones literarias. Sevilla: Renacimiento, 2008. 525 pp. Republished: Mexico City: UNAM, Facultad de Filosofía y Letras, 2009.

b)   *Articles*

When the articles have been later incorporated into books by A.S.V. (published up to 1998), they are referred to with the following acronyms:

AM: *Ensayos sobre arte y marxismo,* 1984.
AR: *Sobre arte y revolución,* 1978.
EX: *Del Exilio en México,* 1991.
IE: *Las ideas estéticas de Marx,* 1965.
FI: *Ensayos marxistas sobre filosofía e ideología,* 1983.
FM: *Sobre filosofía y marxismo,* 1983.
HP: *Ensayos marxistas sobre historia y política,* 1985.
PF: *Escritos de política y filosofía,* 1987.
TO: *En torno a la obra de Adolfo Sánchez Vázquez,* 1995.
FC: *Filosofía y circunstancias,* 1997.

In some select cases, we give details of an oral presentation prior to the printed publication.

'Romance de la ley de fugas'. [Published under the pseudonym 'Darin'.] In *October. Escritores y artistas revolucionarios.* Madrid: August–September 1933, no. 3, p. 26. Facsimile reproduction of the six published issues, with a preface by Enrique Montero ('October: revelación de una revista mítica', pp. IX–XXXVI). [no. 1: June–July 1933, no. 6: April 1934, with which publication ceases], Vaduz/Madrid: Topos/Tumen, 1977.

'Número'. In *Sur. Revista de orientación intelectual.* Malaga: December 1935, no. 1, p. 12. Facsimile edition: Malaga: Centro de Estudios de la Generación del 27, 1994.

'Sentido popular de la poesía española'. In *Mundo obrero*, Madrid: 2 April 1936.
'Hacia un nuevo clima para la poesía'. In *Mundo obrero*, Madrid: 5 May 1936.
'Málaga, ciudad sacrificada'. In *Hora de España*, January–May 1937, no. 1–5, pp. 45–8. Republished in five volumes: Vaduz (Liechtenstein), 1977, Topos. (Col. Biblioteca del 36. Revistas de la Segunda República Española.) Article republished in Various authors, *Crónica de la guerra civil*. Valencia, 1937.
'El Cerco de Teruel'. In *Pasaremos. Órgano de la II División*, Frente de Teruel: 28 December 1937, year 2, no. 67, p. 2.
'José María Tavera, poeta mártir'. In *El Mono Azul. Hoja semanal de la Alianza de Intelectuales Antifascistas para la Defensa de la Cultura*. Madrid: 1 May 1937, year 2, no. 16, p. 111. [Republished: Glashütten im Taunus, 1975.]
'Acero contra acero'. In *Pasaremos. Órgano de la II División*, Frente de Teruel: 6 January 1938, year 3, no. 68, p. 6.
'El 5º Batallón Especial de Ametralladoras'. In *Acero. Órgano del V Cuerpo del Ejército*, Frente del Este: 28 March 1938.
'La ofensiva de Aragón'. In *Acero. Órgano del V Cuerpo del Ejército*, Frente del Este: 28 March 1938.
' "Pasaremos" a Líster y Rodríguez'. In *Pasaremos*, 27 April 1938, year 3, no. 80, p. 1.
'Cómo se resistió en la cota 449'. In *Acero. Órgano del V Cuerpo del Ejército*, Frente del Ebro: 1 September 1938, no. 6.
'La decadencia del héroe'. In *Romance. Revista Popular Hispanoamericana*, Mexico City: 15 March 1940, year 1, no. 4, p. 10. Republished: Glashütten im Taunus: ed. Detlev Auvermann, 1974.
'En torno a la picaresca'. In *Romance. Revista Popular Hispanoamericana*, Mexico City: 15 May 1940, year 1, no. 8, p. 6. Republished: Glashütten im Taunus: ed. Detlev Auvermann, 1974.
'Gil Vicente, poeta lírico'. In *Romance. Revista Popular Hispanoamericana*, Mexico City: 15 May 1940, year 1, no. 8, p. 18. Republished: Glashütten im Taunus: ed. Detlev Auvermann, 1974.
'Mentira de Inglaterra, contra verdad de España'. In *España Peregrina*, Mexico City: Junta de Cultura Española, 15 June 1940, year 1, no. 5. Republished: Mexico City: A. Finisterre, 1977.
'18 de July 1936. Elegía a una tarde de España (Fragmento)'. In *España Peregrina*, Mexico City: Junta de Cultura Española, July 1940, year 1, no. 6, pp. 249 y s.
'Sonetos (I, II, III)'. In *Taller. Poesía y crítica*, Mexico City: January–February 1941, no. 12, pp. 59 y s.
'En el Octavo Aniversario de la muerte de Antonio Machado'. In *Las Españas. Revista Literaria*, Mexico City: 29 March 1947, year 2, no. 4, pp. 8, 10.
'Tiempo de destierro'. In *Revista Mexicana de Cultura*. Supplement to *El Nacional*, Mexico City: 28 May 1948.

'Tierra; Sentencia; Nostalgia; Spring; Guerrillero de la noche; Yo sé esperar' [series of sonnets written in the 1940s] In José Luis Cano (ed.): *Antología de poetas andaluces contemporáneos*. (First ed. Madrid 1952.) Third expanded edition. Madrid: Cultura Hispánica del Centro Americano, 1978. 443 pp. (Col.: La encina y el mar, no. 58.), pp. 372–5.

'Entre la ramas del dolor que anudo…; Si el tiempo se quedara sin medida…; Afirmación de amor; El árbol más entero contra el viento…; En la huesa ya has dado con tu empeño; Un solo pensamiento me detiene…; ¿En qué región del aire, por qué mares….' [series of sonnets written in the 1940s]. In Angel Caffarena Such (ed.): *Antología de la poesía malagueña contemporánea*. Malaga: El Guadalhorce, 1960. (Print run limited by censorship to 238.) pp. 168–72.

'Los libros. Una biografía de "Pedro Calver, el santo de los esclavos". In *México en la Cultura*. Supplement to *Novedades*, Mexico City: 15 October 1950, no. 89, p. 7.

'La poesía de Rafael Alberti'. In *México en la Cultura*. Supplement to *Novedades*, Mexico City: 9 September 1951, no. 136, p. 3.

'Antonio Machado, su poesía y España'. In *Nuestro tiempo. Revista mensual de cultura e información general*, Mexico City: January–February 1952, year 4, no. 5.

'Humanismo y visión de España en Antonio Machado'. In *Filosofía y Letras. Revista de la Facultad de Filosofía y Letras*, UNAM, Mexico City: July–December 1952, vol. 24, no. 47–8, pp. 61–77.

'El tiempo en la poesía española'. In *Universidad Michoacana. Revista de la Universidad Michoacana de San Nicolás de Hidalgo*, Morelia: January–February 1953, no. 29.

'Miseria y esplendor de Gogol'. In *Cuadernos Americanos*, Mexico City: January–February 1953, year 12, vol. 67, no. 1, pp. 247–63.

'Los tratados de Stalin sobre la lingüística y los problemas del materialismo histórico'. In *Nuestro tiempo. Revista mensual de cultura e información general*, Mexico City: 1953, no. 9.

'Trayectoria poética de Antonio Machado'. In *México en la Cultura*. Supplement to *Novedades*, Mexico City: 20 February 1955, no. 309, p. 3.

'Tradición y creación en la obra de arte'. In *Cuadernos Americanos*, Mexico City: November–December 1955, year 14, vol. 84, no. 6, pp. 146–55.

'Sobre el realismo socialista'. In *Nuestras Ideas*, Brussels: 1957, no. 3.

'Vieja y nueva canción de León Felipe'. In *Boletín de Información de la Unión de Intelectuales Españoles*, Mexico City: July–October 1959, no. 10.

'Marxismo y existencialismo'. Supplement to *Seminario de Problemas Científicos y Filosóficos*. UNAM, Mexico City: 1960, Second period, no. 28, pp. 183–98.

'Ideas estéticas en los *Manuscritos económico-filosóficos* de Marx'. In *Diánoia. Anuario de Filosofía*, Mexico City: UNAM, Instituto de Investigaciones Filosóficas, 1961; year 7, no. 7, pp. 236–58. Republished in *Casa de las Américas*, Havana: July October 1962, year 2, no. 13–14, pp. 3–24; and in *Realidad*, Rome: November–December 1963, no. 2, pp. 38–68. Revised version, with the title 'Las ideas de Marx sobre la fuente y naturaleza de lo estético', Included in IE.

'La guerra fría en la cultura'. In *La Cultura en México*. Supplement to *Siempre!*, Mexico City: 3 October 1962.

'Se ponen espoletas a las ideas para que estallen y los dinamiteros de la cultura sólo miden su valor por la fuerza destructiva que encierran'. In *La Cultura en México*. Supplement to *Siempre!*, Mexico City: October 1962, no. 33, pp. 3f.

'La filosofía de Rousseau y su influencia en México'. In Mario de la Cueva *et al.: Presencia de Rousseau. A los 250 años de su nacimiento y a los dos siglos de la aparición del Emilio y el Contrato Social*. Mexico City: UNAM, 1962. 252 pp.

'Vincular las deliberaciones a necesidades vivas'. [On the 13th International Philosophy Congress.] In *La Gaceta*, Mexico City: Fondo de Cultura Económica, October 1963, year 10, no. 110.

'Contribución a una dialéctica de la finalidad y casualidad'. In *Anuario de Filosofía*. Mexico City: Facultad de Filosofía y Letras, UNAM, 1961, year 1, pp. 47–66.

'Mitología y verdad en la crítica de nuestra época'. In *Memorias del XIII Congreso Internacional de Filosofía*. Vol. IV. Mexico City: UNAM, 1963. pp. 301–10. Republished in *Revista mexicana de filosofía*, September 1963, special issue 5/6, pp. 253–62.

'Estética y marxismo'. Speech given 7 February 1964 under the auspices of the Cuban Union of Writers and Artists. In *Unión*. Revista de la Unión de Escritores y Artistas de Cuba, Havana: January–March 1964, year 3, no. 1, pp. 8–23. Republished with some changes in *Cuadernos Americanos*, Mexico City: September–October 1964, year 23, vol. 136, no. 5. Included in IE.

'Un héroe kafkiano: José K'. [Speech given in August 1963 in the conference cycle at the UNAM, Casa del Lago, 'Los grandes personajes de la literatura mundial'.] In *Universidad de México*, Mexico City: UNAM, March 1964, vol. 18, no. 7, pp. 28–32. Republished with the title 'Individuo y comunidad en Kafka' in *Casa de las Américas*, Havana, May–June 1964, year 4, no. 24 and republished in *Realidad*, Rome: 1965, no. 6. Included in IE.

'Sobre arte y sociedad'. In *Calli. Revista analítica de arquitectura contemporánea*, Mexico City: June–July 1964, no. 13. Included in IE.

'La filosofía polaca contemporánea'. In *Homenaje a la Universidad de Cracovia en su sexto centenario*, Mexico City: UNAM, Dirección General de Publicaciones, 1964. 267 pp., pp. 35–95.

'Una fuente de inspiración y de esperanza', in Various, *Asturias*, Paris: Cercle d'art, 1964.

'El marxismo contemporáneo y el arte'. [Republished from the chapter of the same title from *Las ideas estéticas de Marx*, Mexico City: 1965 (IE).] In *Cuadernos de Ruedo Ibérico. Revista bimestral*, Paris, October–November 1965, no. 3, pp. 23–34; in *Arauco. Tribuna del pensamiento socialista*, Santiago de Chile, 1967, no. 288; and in *Casa de las Américas*, Havana: September–October 1965, year 5, no. 32. Republished under the title 'Realismo y creación artística'. In *Universidad de México*, Mexico City: UNAM, August 1965, vol. 19, no. 12, pp. 4–18.

'El arte y las masas'. In *La Cultura en México*. Supplement to *Siempre!*, Mexico City: October 1965, no. 192, pp. 6–8. Included in IE.

'Sobre la praxis'. In *Historia y sociedad. Revista continental de humanismo moderno*, Mexico City: Summer 1966, no. 6.

'La praxis creadora'. In *Cuadernos Americanos*, Mexico City: November–December 1966, year 25, vol. 149, no. 6, pp. 114–25. Included in *Filosofía de la praxis*, as the first section of Chapter III 'Praxis creadora y praxis reiterativa' from the second part: 'Algunos Problemas en torno a la praxis'.

'A Cardoza y Aragón: una crítica constructiva'. In *Revista de la Universidad de México*. Mexico City: UNAM, 1966, no. 7. Included in TO.

'A Ramón Xirau. Hacer real una sociedad ideal'. In *Revista de la Universidad de México*. Mexico City: UNAM, 1966, no. 7. Included in TO.

'Arte y realismo'. In *Plan*, Santiago de Chile: March 1967, no. 11.

'Praxis y violencia'. [Republished from the chapter of the same title in *Filosofía de la praxis*.] In *Casa de las Américas*, Havana: March–April 1967, year 7, no. 41, pp. 5–16.

'Lectura estructuralista de *El Capital*'. In *El Gallo Ilustrado*. Supplement to *El Día*, Mexico City: 19 November 1967.

'La estructura y los hombres'. In *La Cultura en México*. Supplement to *Siempre!*, Mexico City: 6 December 1967, no. 303, pp. VI–VIII.

'El socialismo y el Che'. In *Casa de las Américas*, Havana, January–February 1968, year 8, no. 46, pp. 149–51. Republished as 'Apéndice' in Ernesto Guevara, *Táctica y estrategia de la revolución latinoamericana*, ed. Arturo Garmedia. Mexico City: Nuestro Tiempo, 1977. 188 pp. (Col. La lucha por el poder.), pp. 182–8. Included in HP.

'Vanguardia artística y vanguardia política'. In *La Cultura en México*. Supplement to *Siempre!*, Mexico City: 14 February 1968, no. 313, pp. 7–8. Republished in *Casa de las Américas*, Havana: March–April 1968, year 8, no. 47, pp. 112–15. Included in AM, AR.

'Dos impresiones sobre el Congreso Cultural de La Habana'. In *Cuadernos Americanos*, Mexico City: year 27, May–June 1968, vol. 158, no. 3, pp. 53–67. [With Alonso Aguilar M. These are two separate texts.]

'De la imposibilidad y posibilidad de definir el arte'. In *Deslinde. Revista de la Facultad de Filosofía y Letras*, Mexico City: UNAM, May–August 1968, year 1, no. 1, pp. 12–29. Republished under the title 'La definición del arte', in *Estética y marxismo*, vol. I, Mexico City: Era, 1970, [5th ed.: 1983], pp. 152–69. Included in AM.

'Estructuralismo e historia'. In *Conciencia y autenticidad históricas. Escritos en homenaje a Edmundo O'Gorman*, Mexico City: UNAM, 1968. 434 pp., pp. 317–42. Republished with some changes in Henri Lefebvre, Nils Castro y Adolfo Sánchez Vázquez, *Estructuralismo y marxismo*. Mexico City: Grijalbo, 1970 (Col. Enlace, 88.), pp. 65–79. Included in HP, FC.

'Hacia un concepto abierto del arte'. In *Unión. Revista de la Unión de Escritores y Artistas de Cuba*, Havana, 1968, no. 2.
'Comenzó el año XXVIII de la revista'. In *Cuadernos Americanos*, Mexico City: March–April 1969, year 28, vol. 163, no. 2, pp. 105–10.
'Bertrand Russell, el gran rebelde'. In *Revista Mexicana de Cultura*. Supplement to *El Nacional*, Mexico City: 15 February 1970, no. 55, p. 2.
'Notas sobre Lenin y el arte'. In *Casa de las Américas*, Havana: March–April 1970, year 10, no. 59, pp. 106–15. Included in AM, AR.
'Notas sobre Lenin, el arte y la revolución'. In *Revista de la Universidad de México*, Mexico City: November 1970, vol. 25, no. 3, pp. 8–13. Republished in *Casa de las Américas*, Havana: March–April 1972, year 12, no. 71, pp. 14–19. Included in AR.
'La estética de Brecht'. In *Revista Mexicana de Cultura*. Supplement to *El Nacional*, Mexico City: 1970.
'Del socialismo científico al socialismo utópico'. In Leszek Kołakowski, Edgar Morin, Lucio Colleti, Roger Garaudy and Adolfo Sánchez Vázquez, *Crítica de la utopía*, Mexico City: UNAM, Facultad de Ciencias Políticas y Sociales, 1971. 247 pp. (Col. Estudios, no. 25.), pp. 93–142. [Published as a monograph in 1975.]
'¿Muerte o socialización del arte?'. In *La Cultura en México*. Supplement to *Siempre!*, Mexico City: 17 February 1971, no. 471. [The journal issue is entitled *Crítica de la utopía*. The other authors are: Edgar Morin, Leszek Kołakowski, Roger Garaudy and Alvin Gouldner.] Republished in *Vanguardia Dominical*, Bucaramanga (Colombia): 1972, no. 115; and in *Nuestra Bandera, Revista de debate político y teórico*, Paris: Partido Comunista de España, 1972.
'Vicisitudes del arte bajo el socialismo'. In *Santiago. Revista de la Universidad de Oriente*, Santiago de Cuba, 1971.
'El marxismo de Korsch. Un espíritu crítico que no se postergaba ante ninguna autoridad'. In *La Cultura en México*. Supplement to *Siempre!*, Mexico City: 16 February 1972, no. 523, pp. 4–6.
'Picasso como revolucionario'. In *Oposición*, Mexico City: 1–15 May 1972.
'Temas de la revolución, problemas del arte'. In *La Cultura en México*. Supplement to *Siempre!*, Mexico City: 14 June 1972, no. 540, pp. 7f.
'Socialización de la creación o muerte del arte'. [Presentation to the VII International Congress of Aesthetics in Bucharest, Romania.] In *La Cultura en México*. Supplement to *Siempre!*, Mexico City: 25 October 1972, no. 559. Republished in *Casa de las Américas*, Havana, May–June 1973, year 13, no. 78, pp. 32–43. Included in AM, FM.
'Lo real en el arte y el arte de lo real'. In *Alero*, Universidad de San Carlos, Guatemala: Confederación Universitaria Centroamericana, 1973, no. 1.
'El dinero y la enajenación en las notas de lectura del joven Marx'. In *Zona Abierta*, Madrid: 1974, year 1, no. 1, pp. 3–14. Included in PF.

'La ideología de la 'neutralidad ideológica' en las ciencias sociales'. [Presentation to the First National Philosophy Colloquium, Morelia, August 1975.] In *Historia y Sociedad. Revista latinoamericana de pensamiento marxista*, 2nd series [collective volume], Mexico City: 1975, no. 7, pp. 9–25. Republished in *Zona Abierta*, Madrid: 1976, no. 7 and in *La filosofía y las ciencias sociales*. Mexico City: Grijalbo, 1976. (Col. Teoría y praxis, no. 24.) Included in FI, PF.

'El punto de vista de la práctica en la filosofía'. In *Cathedra. Revista de la Facultad de Filosofía y Letras de la Universidad Autónoma de Nuevo León*, Monterrey: 1975, no. 3. Republished in *Casa de las Américas*, Havana: January–February 1977, year 17, no. 100, pp. 8–17. Included in FI, FC.

'El teoricismo de Althusser. Notas críticas sobre una autocrítica'. In *Cuadernos Políticos*, Mexico City: January–March 1975, no. 3, pp. 82–99.

'Homenaje a Juan Rejano'. In *Cuadernos Americanos*, Mexico City: September–October 1976, year 35, vol. 208, no. 5, pp. 83–5.

'Palabras en la cena homenaje del 4 October de 1976'. In *Argumentos*, Madrid: May 1977, year 1, no. 1. Included, under the title 'Reencuentro en Madrid', in HP; and under the title 'Situación del exilio y situación del intelectual' in PF.

'La filosofía de la praxis como nueva práctica de la filosofía'. In *Cuadernos Políticos*, Mexico City: April–June 1977, no. 12. Republished in *Nuestra Bandera. Revista de debate político y teórico*, Madrid: Partido Comunista de España, 1977, nos. 80–81 and in *La filosofía en América. Trabajos presentados en el IX Congreso Interamericano de Filosofía*, Vol. I. Caracas: Sociedad Venezolana de Filosofía, 1979. 257 pp., pp. 133–6. Included in FI, FM, PF, FC.

'La crítica de la economía política en el joven Marx. El punto de vista del economista y las contradicciones de la economía'. In *Plural. Revista mensual de Excélsior. Crítica y literatura*, Mexico City: June 1977, no. 69, pp. 14–20.

'Ernst Bloch o el marxismo utópico. Utopía y realidad'. In *El Universal*, Mexico City: 15 August 1977, 1st part, pp. 4, 14.

'Cultura y exilio'. In *El Universal*, Mexico City: 22 August 1977, p. 4. Included in HP.

'Los escritores mexicanos y el proceso creador'. In *El Universal*, Mexico City: 29 August 1977, pp. 4, 12.

'Lo nuevo y lo viejo en la 'nueva filosofía''. In *El Universal*, Mexico City: 5 September 1977, pp. 4, 12. Included in HP.

'De nuevo sobre Bloch. Entre el sueño y la realidad'. In *El Universal*, Mexico City: 12 September 1977, 1st part, pp. 4, 10.

'Filosofía y ciencia en el mundo de hoy'. In *El Universal*, Mexico City: 19 September 1977, pp. 4, 17.

'Sartre y la música. La Nota y el Ruido'. In *El Universal*, Mexico City: 26 September 1977, 1st part, pp. 4, 16.

'Sobre la verdad en las artes'. In *Arte, sociedad e ideología*, Mexico City: La Impresora Azteca, August–September 1977, no. 2, pp. 4–9.

'Sobre filosofía y revolución'. [At the Inauguration of the xx National Philosophy Colloquium in Monterrey.] In *El Universal*, Mexico City: 3 October 1977, pp. 4, 20.

'Coloquio de Filosofía. Balance mínimo de una importante reunión'. [On the xx National Philosophy Colloquium in Monterrey.] In *El Universal*, Mexico City: 10 October 1977, pp. 4, 8.

'Aleixandre. Trayectoria de su generación'. In *El Universal*, Mexico City: 17 October 1977, pp. 4, 14.

'Diez años después. La gran lección del Che'. In *El Universal*, Mexico City: 24 October 1977, 1st part, pp. 4, 6. Included in HP.

'De la virginidad filosófica'. In *El Universal*, Mexico City: 31 October 1977, pp. 4, 14.

'Significado actual de la revolución de October'. In *El Universal*, Mexico City: 7 November 1977, pp. 4, 12. Included in HP.

'El mito de la neutralidad filosófica'. In *El Universal*, Mexico City: 21 November 1977, pp. 4, 24.

'La ideología de la que no se liberan los filósofos'. In *El Universal*, Mexico City: 28 November 1977, pp. 4, 10.

'La ciencia une, la filosofía divide'. In *El Universal*, Mexico City: 5 December 1977, pp. 4, 8.

'Diego Rivera: pintura y militancia'. In *El Universal*, Mexico City: 12 December 1977, pp. 4, 9.

'El arma de la crítica'. In *El Universal*, Mexico City: 26 December 1977, p. 4. Included under the title 'De críticas y críticos' in HP.

'Filosofía e ideología'. In *Revista de Filosofía de la Universidad de Costa Rica*, July–December 1977, vol. 15, no. 41, pp. 159–63. Republished in *Argumentos*, Madrid: 1977, no. 5. Included in PF.

'II Coloquio Nacional de Filosofía. Discurso de clausura'. In *Boletín de la Facultad de Filosofía y Letras*, Mexico City: UNAM, November–December 1977, year 1, no. 6, pp. 26f.

'Filosofía y realidad en América Latina'. [Ponencia en el IX Congreso Interamericano de Filosofía, Caracas, June 1977.] In *Diorama de la Cultura*. Supplement to *Excélsior*, Mexico City: 1977. Included in FM, HP.

'Marx en 1844. De la filosofía a la economía'. In *Controversias*, Guadalajara, 1977, no. 3.

'Cuando el exilio permanece y dura'. As epilogue to: *Exilio!* [Preface by Gabriel García Márquez.] Mexico City: Tinta Libre, 1977. 208 pp., pp. 199–203. Republished in *Anthropos. Revista de documentación científica de la cultura*, Barcelona: August 1985, no. 52, pp. 17f. Reproduced, under the title 'Fin del exilio y exilio sin fin', as epilogue to: *Sinaia. Diario de la primera expedición de republicanos españoles a México*. Facsimile edition. Mexico City: UNAM, Coordinación de Difusión Cultural/

Universidad Autónoma Metropolitana/La Oca Editores, 1989. 147 pp., pp. 145–7; and included in HP, EX. Included under the original title in FM, PF.

'La independencia intelectual: ilusión y realidad'. In *El Universal*, Mexico City: 2 January 1978. Included under the title: 'De críticas y críticos, II' in HP.

'El asalto a la razón. Ideología y política'. In *El Universal*, Mexico City: 9 January 1978, 1st part, pp. 4, 14. Included in HP.

'Producción y necesidades en la 'sociedad de consumo''. In *El Universal*, Mexico City: 16 January 1978, p. 4. Included in HP.

'El arte y la cultura en el mundo de hoy'. In *El Universal*, Mexico City: 23 January 1978, pp. 4, 8.

'Las revoluciones filosóficas. De Kant a Marx'. In *Arte, Sociedad e Ideología*, Mexico City: La Impresora Azteca, April–May 1978, no. 6, pp. 13–21. Republished in *Las revoluciones y la filosofía*. Mexico City: Grijalbo, 1979. (Col. Teoría y praxis, no. 47.) Included in FI, FC.

'Marinello en tres tiempos'. [Speech given 29 March 1978 as part of an homage to Juan Marinello, organised by the Instituto Mexicano Cubano de Relaciones Culturales José Martí, Mexico City.] In *Casa de las Américas*, Havana: July–August 1978, year 19, no. 109, pp. 113–16. Included in HP.

'Filosofía, ideología y sociedad'. [Sobre José Ferrater Mora.] In *Cuadernos Americanos*, Mexico City: September–October 1978, year 37, vol. 220, no. 5, pp. 149–69. Included in FI, FM, FC

'Literatura e ideología. Lenin ante Tolstoy'. In *Texto Crítico*, Xalapa: Centro de Investigaciones Lingüístico-Literarias. Instituto de Investigaciones Humanísticas de la Universidad Veracruzana, September–December 1978, year 4, no. 11, pp. 3–14. Republished in *Casa de las Américas*, Havana: July–August 1979, year 20, no. 115, pp. 20–7. Included in FI.

'¿Qué ha significado para ti la Revolución Cubana?'. In *Casa de las Américas*, Havana:November–December 1978, year 18, no. 111, pp. 24–7.

'Por qué y para qué enseñar filosofía'. [Inaugural speech at the First Encounter of Philosophy, Ethics, and Aesthetics Professors of the CCH Sur (Colegio de Ciencias y Humanidades de la UNAM, Plantel Sur), April 1979.] In *Gaceta CCH*, Mexico City: 27 April–4 May 1979, no. 181–2. Republished in *Dialéctica. Revista de la Escuela de Filosofía y Letras de la Universidad Autónoma de Puebla*. Puebla: December 1979, year 4, no. 7, pp. 183–93; and in *Argumentos*, Madrid: November 1980, no. 39. Included in FI, PF, FC.

'Antihumanismo o humanismo en Marx. El marxismo como "antihumanismo teórico"'. In *Nueva Política*. Mexico City: Centro Latinoamericano de Estudios Políticos, July 1979, vol. 2, no. 7, pp. 187–98. Included in *Filosofía y economía en el joven Marx. Los Manuscritos de 1844*. Mexico City: Grijalbo, 1982. pp. 257–71, as subchapter under the title 'El marxismo como "antihumanismo teórico"', of chapter IX 'La querella de los

Manuscritos'. The chapter 'La querella de los *Manuscritos*' was republished in its entirety as an article under the title 'El marxismo como humanismo' (1983).

'Notas sobre la relación entre moral y política'. [Presentation at the III National Philosophy Colloquium, Puebla: December 1979, presented with the title: 'Notas sobre las relaciones entre moral y política'.] In *Thesis. Nueva Revista de Filosofía y Letras*, Mexico City: Facultad de Filosofía y Letras, UNAM, April 1980, year 2, no. 5, pp. 17–19. Included, under the title of the speech, in HP.

'El concepto de praxis en Lenin'. In *Diánoia. Anuario de Filosofía*, Mexico City: UNAM, Instituto de Investigaciones Filosóficas, 1979, year 25, no. 25, pp. 46–61. Included in *Filosofía de la praxis*, Second expanded ed., 1980 (as part of the chapter on Lenin).

'Palabras pronunciadas en el Acto de Clausura por el Dr. Adolfo Sánchez Vázquez en representación por los delegados'. In *La filosofía en América. Trabajos presentados en el IX Congreso Interamericano de Filosofía*. Vol. I. Caracas: Sociedad Venezolana de Filosofía, 1979. 257 pp., pp. 245–7.

'Sobre la teoría althusseriana de la ideología'. In Mario H. Otero (ed.), *Ideología y ciencias sociales*. Mexico City: UNAM, Coordinacion de Humanidades, 1979. 231 pp., pp. 63–76.

'La estética libertaria y comprometida de Sartre'. [Speech in the series: 'Sartre: Filosofía, Literatura y compromiso' in the Facultad de Filosofía y Letras de la UNAM, on the occasion of Sartre's death.] In *Thesis. Nueva revista de Filosofía y Letras*, Mexico City: UNAM, October 1980, year 2, no. 7, pp. 50–7. Included in AM.

'Sobre el partido del nuevo tipo'. In *La Calle*, Madrid: 7–13 July 1981, no. 172. Included in HP.

'Ideal socialista y socialismo real'. [Presentation at the international symposium: 'Del Socialismo existente al nuevo socialismo', Caracas: May 1981.] In *Nexos*, Mexico City: August 1981, year 4, no. 44. Republished in *Teoría*, Madrid: July–September 1981, no. 7. Included in HP.

'Democracia socialista y socialismo real'. In *El Machete*, Mexico City: 1981, no. 11. Included under the title 'Perspectivas de la democracia socialista' in HP.

'Racionalismo tecnológico, ideología y política'. In *Nuestra Bandera. Revista de debate político y teórico*. Madrid: Partido Comunista de España, July 1982. Republished in *Dialéctica. Revista de la Escuela de Filosofía y Letras de la Universidad Autónoma de Puebla*, Puebla: June 1983, year 8, no. 13, pp. 11–26. Included in FI, PF.

'Vuelta al arte simbólico'. In *Revista de Bellas Artes*, Mexico City: October 1982, Third period, no. 7, pp. 33–6. Included in AM.

'Prolegómenos a una teoría de la educación estética'. In *Educación*, Consejo Nacional Técnico de Educación de la SEP [Secretaría de Educación Pública], Mexico City: 1982, no. 41.

'El poder y la obediencia'. In *El Buscón*, Mexico City: January–February 1983, no. 2, pp. 130–50. Included in HP.

'El joven Marx y la filosofía especulativa'. In *Suplemento especial de El País, por el 100 aniversario luctuoso de Karl Marx*, Madrid: 14 March 1983. Republished under the title 'El joven Marx y la filosofía' In *Revista Mexicana de Cultura*. Supplement to *El Nacional*, Mexico City: 10 April 1983, no. 8, p. 2.

'Las ciencias sociales y la enseñanza de la filosofía'. In *Deslinde. Revista de la Facultad de Filosofía y Letras de la Universidad Autónoma de Nuevo León*, Monterrey: January–April 1983, vol. 2, no. 4, pp. 5–8.

'Marx y la democracia'. In *Cuadernos Políticos*, Mexico City: April–June 1983, no. 36, pp. 31–9. Republished in *Sistema. Revista de ciencias sociales*, Madrid: Instituto de Técnicas Sociales de la Fundación Social Universitaria, November 1983, no. 57, pp. 19–30.

'Actualidad de Carlos Marx'. [Presentation on the occasion of the centenary of Karl Marx's death, 14 March 1983, at the Palacio de Bellas Artes, Mexico City] In *Plural. Revista mensual de Excélsior. Crítica y literatura*. Mexico City: May 1983, year 12, no. 140, pp. 7–9. Republished in *Mundo Obrero*, Madrid: 20–26 May 1983, no. 229. Included in PF.

'Marx seguirá vivo'. In *La Cultura en México*. Supplement to *Siempre!*, Mexico City: 6 April 1983, no. 1087, p. 4.

'La estética terrenal de José Revueltas'. In *Sábado*. Supplement to *Unomásuno*, Mexico City: 14 May 1983, no. 288, pp. 1, 3–4. Republished in Emmanuel Carballo *et al.*: *Revueltas en la mira*. Mexico City: Universidad Autónoma Metropolitana, 1984. 164 pp. (Col. Molinos de viento, no. 23.) pp. 129–50; and in *Pie de página*, Mexico City: March–April 1984, no. 10, pp. 2–6. Included in AM.

'Marx y la estética'. In *Ínsula. Revista de Letras y Ciencias Humanas*, Madrid: September 1983, year 38, no. 442, p. 3. Included in AM.

'El marxismo como humanismo. Controversia con el 'antihumanismo teórico''. [Republished version of chapter IX ('La querella de los *Manuscritos*') of *Filosofía y economía en el joven Marx*]. In *Nuestra Bandera. Revista de debate político y teórico*, Madrid: Partido Comunista de España, 1983, no. 118–19.

'Controversia: debate sobre la filosofía del marxismo'. In *Dialéctica. Revista de la Escuela de Filosofía y Letras de la Universidad Autónoma de Puebla*, Puebla: December 1983–March 1984, year 8, no. 14–15, pp. 151–5.

'Racionalidad y emancipación en Marx'. In *Papeles de la FIM* [Fundación de Investigaciones Marxistas]. Madrid: January 1984, no. 9–10. Republished in Ramón Reyes (ed.): *Cien años después de Marx. Ciencia y Marxismo*. Madrid: Akal, 1986. 683 pp. Included in abbreviated form in PF.

'Arquitectura y conceptos básicos'. [On his book *Filosofía de la praxis*. Article written in 1979.] In *El Sol de México en los libros*. Supplement to *El Sol de México*, Mexico City: 29 April 1984, no. 498, p. 7.

'Wilfredo Lam: mundo y lenguaje'. [Presentation at the international colloquium: Wilfredo Lam, Havana, 23/24 March 1983.] In *México en el arte*. New period, Mexico City: Instituto Nacional de Bellas Artes, Summer 1984, no. 5, pp. 72–6.

'La razón amenazada'. [1984 speech at the Universidad Autónoma de Puebla on receiving a Doctor Honoris Causa.] In *Universidad. Órgano de difusión de la Universidad Autónoma de Puebla*, Puebla: 9 August 1984, year 4, no. 20. Republished in *Sábado*. Supplement to *Unomásuno*, Mexico City: 29 September 1984, no. 361, p. 6. Republished, under the title 'Discurso de Adolfo Sánchez Vázquez al recibir la distinción universitaria', in *Dialéctica. Revista de la Escuela de Filosofía y Letras de la Universidad Autónoma de Puebla*, Puebla: December 1984, year 9, no. 16, pp. 13–19. Included in HP, PF, FC.

'Ideología y realismo'. In *Contextos. Revista trimestral de cultura*. Cuenca, Ecuador: Casa de la Cultura, 1985, year 1, no. 1, pp. 6–10.

'El problema de la burocracia en Hegel y Marx'. In *Revista Universidad*, Querétaro: Universidad Autónoma de Querétaro, June 1985, no. 27.

'Mi obra filosófica'. [With the date: 15 November 1978.] In *Anthropos. Revista de documentación científica de la cultura*. Barcelona, August 1985, no. 52 pp. 7–9. Republished in Juliana González, Carlos Pereyra and Gabriel Vargas Lozano (eds.), *Praxis y filosofía. Ensayos en homenaje a Adolfo Sánchez Vázquez*. Mexico City: Grijalbo, 1986. 491 pp., pp. 435–43. Included in FM.

'Vida y filosofía' (political-philosophical postscript to *Mi obra filosófica*, 1985). In *Anthropos. Revista de documentación científica de la cultura*. Barcelona: August 1985, no. 52, pp. 10–16. Republished under the title 'Post scriptum político-filosófico a *Mi obra filosófica*', in Juliana González, Carlos Pereyra and Gabriel Vargas Lozano (eds.), *Praxis y filosofía. Ensayos en homenaje a Adolfo Sánchez Vázquez*. Mexico City: Grijalbo, 1986. 491 pp., pp. 445–69. Republished, in abbreviated form, under the title 'Apuntes a mi obra filosófica', in *La Jornada Libros*. Supplement to *La Jornada*, Mexico City: 2 August 1986, no. 81, pp. 1–3. Included (full version) under the title 'Vida y filosofía. Postscriptum político-filosófico, in EX.

'Reexamen de la idea del socialismo'. [Speech presented at table 85 of the International Colloquium 'Socialism in the world' with the subject 'Socialismo on the threshold of the 21st century', Cavat, Yugoslavia: October 1985.] In *Nexos*, Mexico City: October 1985, year 8, vol. 8, no. 94. Republished in *Leviatán. Revista de hechos e ideas*, Madrid: 1986, pp. 27–39. Included in HP, PF.

'Reconsideración de la explicación histórica teleológica'. In *Teoría. Anuario de Filosofía 1981*, Mexico City: UNAM, Facultad de Filosofía y Letras, Colegio de Filosofía, 1985, vol. 2, no. 2, pp. 161–70. Included, with a response to the commentary by Luis Villoro [see, in the secondary literature on A.S.V.: 'Réplica...'], in HP, FC [under the title 'Las explicaciones teleológicas en la historia'].

'La poética de Lotman. Opacidades y transparencias'. [Presentation to the Interamerican Semiotics Congress, Mexico City: October 1985.] With illustrations by Eduardo Cohen. In *Universidad de México. Revista de la* UNAM, Mexico City: March 1986, vol. 41, no. 422, pp. 11–17.

'Literatura, ideología y realismo'. In *Nuestra Bandera. Revista de debate político y teórico.* Madrid: Partido Comunista de España, December 1986, no. 137, pp. 59–65.

'Claves de la ideología estética de Diego Rivera'. In *Diego Rivera hoy. Simposio sobre el artista en el centenario de su natalicio.* Mexico City: SEP [Secretaría de Educación Pública] and INBA [Instituto Nacional de Bellas Artes], 1986. 256 pp., pp. 205–27.

'Homenaje a Ramón Xirau'. In Juliana González *et al.: Presencia de Ramón Xirau.* Mexico City: UNAM, 1986. 233 pp. (Col. Textos de Humanidades.) pp. 27–30.

'No al dilema de todo o nada'. [Synthesis of A. Sánchez Vázquez's participation in the General Assembly of Professors of the Facultad de Filosofía y Letras de la UNAM sobre el movimiento estudiantil del CEU (Consejo Estudiantil Universitario).] In *La Jornada*, Mexico City: 20 January 1987, p. 4.

'Colegio de filosofía. Sobre la superación académica y los exámenes profesionales. In *Boletín de la Facultad de Filosofía y Letras*, Mexico City: UNAM, January–March 1987, fifth period, year 1, no. 2, pp. 9–10.

'Vicisitudes de la filosofía contemporánea en México'. [Presentation at the 11th Congreso Internacional de Filosofía, Guadalajara, Mexico City: November 1985.] In *Cuadernos Americanos*, Mexico City: new period, July–August 1987, year 1, vol. 4, no. 4, pp. 208–21. Included in FC.

'La situación de la filosofía en el mundo hispánico. El marxismo en América Latina'. In *Arbor. Ciencia, Pensamiento y Cultura.* Madrid: Consejo Superior de Investigaciones Científicas, September 1987, vol. 128, no. 501, pp. 39–58. Republished under the title 'El marxismo en América Latina'. In *Dialéctica. Revista de filosofía, ciencias sociales, literatura y cultura política de la Universidad Autónoma de Puebla*, Puebla: July 1988, year 13, no. 19, pp. 11–28; and in *Casa de las Américas*. Havana: January–February 1990, year 30, no. 178, pp. 3–14. Moreover, in *Temas. Estudios de la cultura.* Havana: Departamento de Ciencia y Técnica del Ministerio de Cultura, 1990, no. 20, pp. 13–26. Republished in abbreviated form in *Mythos und Gesellschaft. Zur Verfassung der cubanischen Gesellschaft zwei Generationen nach der Revolution.* Frankfurt am Main AStA [Allgemeiner Studentenausschuß]/Linke Liste, 1991, pp. 50–3.

'En torno al problema de la burocracia en Hegel y Marx'. In *Investigación humanística. Revista de Filosofía, Historia, Literatura y Lingüística de la* UAM, Mexico City: Universidad Autónoma Metropolitana, autumn 1987, no. 3, pp. 15–26.

'Once Tesis sobre socialismo y democracia'. In *Cuadernos Políticos*, Mexico City: October–December 1987, no. 52, pp. 82–8. Republished in *Sistema. Revista de ciencias sociales*, Instituto de Técnicas Sociales de la Fundación Social Universitaria, Madrid: March 1988, no. 83.

'Significado actual de la Revolución de October. Del October ruso a la "Perestroika" '. In *Boletín del* CEMOS, Mexico City: Centro de Estudios del Movimiento Obrero y Socialista, December 1987, no. 17.

'Marx y el socialismo real. Análisis crítico'. [Speech at the Fundación de Investigaciones Marxistas (FIM), Madrid: 1983.] In *Mundo, problemas y confrontaciones*, Mexico City: Winter 1987, vol. 1, no. 1, pp. 25–35.

'En el homenaje a Leopoldo Zea'. In *Casa de las Américas*, Havana , January–February 1988, year 28, no. 166, pp. 112–14. Republished, with small changes, under the title 'Reflexiones sobre la obra de Leopoldo Zea', In *Anthropos. Revista de documentación científica de la cultura*, Barcelona: October 1988, no. 89, pp. 34–6. Included in FC.

'Filosofía y circunstancias'. [Speech given 15 May 1987 at the Universidad de Cádiz (Spain), on receiving a Doctor Honoris Causa.] In *Boletín Filosofía y Letras*, Mexico City: UNAM, Facultad de Filosofía y Letras, November–December 1997, vol. 3, no. 14, pp. 24–8. Republished in *Cuadernos Americanos*, Mexico City: January–February 1988, new period, vol. 1, no. 7, pp. 170–8. Included in FC.

'Marxismo y socialismo, hoy'. In *Nexos*, Mexico City: June 1988, no. 126, pp. 39–45. Republished in *Leviatán. Revista de hechos e ideas*, Madrid: autumn 1988, second period, no. 33.

'Carlos Pereyra'. [Opening speech at the 'Symposium in memory of Carlos Pereyra', 2 to 4 August 1988, Facultad de Filosofía y Letras, UNAM.] In *Nexos*, Mexico City: November 1988, year 11, vol. 11, no. 131, pp. 55–61. Included in FC.

'El *Ché* y el arte'. In *Casa de las Américas*, Havana: July–August 1988, year 29, no. 169, pp. 123–6. Republished in *Artes. Investigación, educación, crítica*. Mexico City: August 1988, no. 6.

'Universidad, Sociedad y Política – La masificación positiva'. In *Cuadernos de la legislación universitaria*, Mexico City: UNAM, September–December 1988, vol. 3, no. 7, pp. 119–27. Republished, with changes, under the title: 'Universidad, Sociedad y Política', in *Utopías. Revista de la Facultad de Filosofía y Letras de la UNAM*, Mexico City: March–April 1989, no. 1, pp. 22–7. Republished, with changes, under the title 'La Universidad del Futuro', in *Cuadernos Americanos*, Mexico City: March–April 1990, year 4, vol. 2, no. 20, pp. 149–60.

'Neutralidad valorativa, neutralidad ideológica'. In *Terminología científico-social*. Barcelona: Anthropos, 1988.

'Para entrar en materia'. In Alejandro Janet, *En torno al libro universitario*. Mexico City: UNAM, 1988 (Col.: Bibliotéca del editor.) pp. 23–6.

'Pereyra: filosofía, historia y política'. In A.S.V., Ludolfo Paramio *et al.*, *Sobre Carlos Pereyra*. Madrid: Pablo Iglesias, 1988, pp. 13–27 (Special issue of: *Zona Abierta*, Madrid: July–December 1988, no. 48–9). Republished in *En memoria de Carlos Pereyra*. Special issue of: *Jornadas de la Facultad de Filosofía y Letras*, Mexico City: UNAM, 1989, no. 5, 80 pp., pp. 11–24.

'Radiografía del Posmodernismo'. In *Sábado*. Supplement to *Unomásuno*, Mexico City: 18 February 1989, no. 594. Republished In *Nuevo Texto Crítico*, Xalapa: Centro de Investigaciones Lingüístico-Literarias. Instituto de Investigaciones Humanísticas de la Universidad Veracruzana, July–December 1990, vol. 3, no. 6, pp. 5–15. Republished, with the title 'Posmodernidad, posmodernismo y socialismo', in *Casa de las Américas*, Havana: July–August 1989, year 29, no. 175, pp. 137–45; and in *Contrarios*. Madrid: 1989, no. 2; and in *Artes Plásticas. Revista de la Escuela Nacional de Artes Plásticas*, Mexico City: March 1991, vol. 3, no. 12, pp. 57–69. Included with the original title in FC.

'Palabras de reconocimiento a Eduardo Nicol'. In *La Gaceta,* Mexico City: Fondo de Cultura Económica, March 1989, new period, no. 219, pp. 35–7. Included in FC.

'Un espacio más amplio para la democracia'. In *Revista Mexicana de Cultura*. Supplement to *El Nacional*. Mexico City: 30 July 1989, year 10, vol. 2, no. 336, pp. 8f.

'Recordando al 'Sinaia'. Exilio y literatura'. In *Revista Mexicana de Cultura*. Supplement to *El Nacional*, Mexico City: 5 November 1989, no. 350. Republished, as 'Presentación', in *Sinaia. Diario de la primera expedición de republicanos españoles a México*. Facsimile. Mexico City: UNAM, Coordinación de Difusión Cultural/Universidad Autónoma Metropolitana/La Oca Editores, 1989, pp. 7–12. Included in EX.

'Carlos Pereyra: a un año de su muerte'. In *Nexos*, Mexico City: July 1989, year 12, vol. 12, no. 139, pp. 21f.

'La cuestión del poder en Marx'. In *Sistema. Revista de ciencias sociales,* Madrid: Instituto de Técnicas Sociales de la Fundación Social Universitaria, September–October 1989, no. 92, pp. 3–17.

'En homenaje a Wenceslao Roces'. In *Revista Mexicana de Cultura*. Supplement to *El Nacional*, Mexico City: 5 November 1989, 10ª época, vol. 2, no. 350. Republished In Elsa Cecilia Frost, *et al., Cincuenta años de Exilio Español en México*. Tlaxcala: Universidad Autónoma de Tlaxcala y Embajada de España en México, 1991. 215 pp., pp. 207–14. (Col. Materiales para la historia de la filosofía en México, no. 3.)

'Palabras al recibir la Gran Cruz de Alfonso X El Sabio' [at the Spanish Embassy in Mexico City, 25 July 1989.] In *Utopías. Revista de la Facultad de Filosofía y Letras de la UNAM*, Mexico City: October–December 1989, no. 4, pp. 79f. Included in EX.

'La perestroika vista desde México'. [A.S.V. responds, alongside eleven other authors, to four questions from the editorial board.] In *Utopías. Revista de la Facultad de Filosofía y Letras de la UNAM*, Mexico City: October–December 1989, no. 4, pp. 74f.

'Universidad y sociedad. La Universidad del futuro'. In *Cuadernos del Congreso Universitario*, Mexico City: UNAM, 7 January 1990, no. 12, pp. 61–6.

'Democracia, revolución y socialismo'. In *Socialismo. Revista de Teoría y Política*, Mexico City: October–December 1989, no. 3–4. Republished In *Utopías. Revista de la Facultad de Filosofía y Letras de la UNAM*, Mexico City: January–February 1990, no. 5, pp. 15–22; and in *Nuestra Bandera. Revista de debate político y teórico*, Madrid:

Partido Comunista de España, second trimester 1990. Published in five parts in *Revista Mexicana de Cultura.* Supplement to *El Nacional*, Mexico City: new period, vol. 2, first part: 'Una definición mínima de la democracia', 28 January 1990, no. 1, p. 4; second part: 'La veta autoritaria de la izquierda latinoamericana', 4 February 1990, no. 2, p. 4; third part: 'La democracia y la historia', 11 February 1990, no. 3, p. 4; fourth part: 'Las críticas a la democracia', 18 February 1990, no. 4, p. 4; fifth part: 'Revolución y autoritarismo; revolución y democracia', 25 February 1990, no. 5, pp. 4f.

'Modos de hacer y usar la filosofía'. In *Mayéutica*, Mexico City: UNAM, Escuela Nacional Preparatoria no. 5 'José Vasconcelos', February–March 1990, year 3, no. 6, pp. 1–17. Republished in *Topan*, Mexico City: Círculo Mexicano de Profesores de Filosofía, July–December 1993, no. 1, pp. 3–9. Included in FC.

'La democratización como medio'. In *Hacia el Congreso de la UNAM. Un cuestionario*, publicado como: *Cuaderno* no. 23, Supplement to *Nexos*, Mexico City: May 1990, no. 149, p. VIII.

'Fin del socialismo real. El marxismo vive'. Published in three parts in *La Jornada*, Mexico City: 3, 4, and 6 September 1990.

'Libertad, tradición de México'. In *La Cultura en México*. Supplement to *Siempre!*, Mexico City: 12 September 1990, p. 57.

'Humanismo y universidad'. In *Universidad de México. Revista de la Universidad Nacional Autónoma de México*, Mexico City: October 1990, vol. 45, no. 477, pp. 4–9. Republished in *Gaceta UAZ*. Zacatecas: Universidad Autónoma de Zacatecas, February 1991, no. 37, pp. 3–10.

'La utopía de Don Quijote'. In *La Jornada Semanal*, Supplement to *La Jornada*, Mexico City: 25 November 1990, no. 76, pp. 21–7. Republished in Various authors, *Guanajuato en la geografía del Quijote. Cuarto Coloquio Cervantino Internacional*, Guanajuato: Gobierno del Estado de Guanajuato, 1991. 92 pp. (Col. Nuestra Cultura.)

'Los males del capitalismo exigen alternativa socialista'. [Intervention in the closing session of the International Encounter of the journal *Vuelta*.] In *Papeles de la FIM*. Madrid: Fundación de Investigaciones Marxistas, September–December 1990, no. 17, pp. 27–33.

'Novedades bibliográficas'. In *Revista mexicana de política exterior*. Mexico City: Winter 1990, year 7, no. 29, pp. 62–4.

'Modernidad y posmodernidad en América Latina'. In *Nuevo texto crítico*. Stanford, CA: Stanford University, 1990, no. 6.

'¿Capitalismo sin alternativas?' In *Mundo, problemas y confrontaciones*, Mexico City: February 1991, no. 30, pp. 32–4.

'Marx y el poder'. In *Deslinde. Revista de la Facultad de Filosofía y Letras de la Universidad Autónoma de Nuevo León*, Monterrey, October 1990–March 1991, vol. 9–10, no. 30–1, pp. 19–29.

'¿De qué socialismo hablamos?' In *Sistema. Revista de ciencias sociales*, Madrid: Instituto de Técnicas Sociales de la Fundación Social Universitaria, March 1991, no. 101. Republished en *Dialéctica. Revista de filosofía, ciencias sociales, literatura y cultura política de la Universidad Autónoma de Puebla*, Puebla: Winter 1991, year 15, no. 21, pp. 7–27.

'La dimensión estética de lo feo'. In *Artes Plásticas. Revista de la Escuela Nacional de Artes Plásticas*, Mexico City: March 1991, vol. 3, no. 12, pp. 5–12.

'La casa en Minería'. [Attributed to A.S.V.] In *Casa de las Américas*, Havana: April–June 1991, year 31, no. 183, pp. 169–72.

'Homenaje a Eli de Gortari'. In *La Jornada*, Mexico City: 3 August 1991, pp. 1, 12. Included in FC.

'Exilio y filosofía. La aportación de los exiliados españoles al filosofar latinoamericano'. In *Cuadernos Americanos*. Mexico City: November–December 1991, new period, year 5, vol. 6, no. 30, pp. 139–53. Republished, with the title 'Exilio y filosofía', In *Gaceta del Fondo de Cultura Económica*. New period, Mexico City: May 1993, no. 269, pp. 28–34; e Included in FC.

'Socialismo y mercado'. In *El Socialismo del futuro. Revista de debate político*, Fundación Sistema. Madrid: 1991, no. 3, pp. 31–7. Republished In *Socialismo*, Mexico City: February 1992, no. 7.

'Trotsky: el arte y la revolución'. In *Artes. Educación, investigación, crítica.* Mexico City: 1991, no. 19.

'Mitos y realidades de la identidad'. In *Claves de razón práctica.* Madrid: March 1992, year 3, no. 20. Republished, under the title 'Identidad e Historia', in Enrique Hülsz Piccone y Manuel Ulacia (eds.), *Más allá de Litoral*, Mexico City: UNAM, Facultad de Filosofía y Letras, 1994, pp. 341–52. Included, under this latter title, in FC.

'Wenceslao Roces, profesor que supo dar transcendencia al conocimiento'. In *Gaceta UNAM*, Mexico City: 2 April 1992, no. 2642, pp. 12f.

'Filosofía, lenguaje y literatura'. In *La Jornada Semanal*, supplement to *La Jornada*, Mexico City: 25 April 1993, no. 202, pp. 16–19. Republished in *Aproximaciones a Alejandro Rossi*. Mexico City: UNAM, Facultad de Filosofía y Letras e Instituto de Investigaciones Filosóficas/El Equilibrista, 1994, pp. 37–46. Included with the title 'Alejandro Rossi' in FC.

'¿Qué significa filosofar? Discurso de investidura como doctor Honoris Causa por la UNED'. In *Revista Internacional de Filosofía Política*, Madrid/Mexico City: Universidad Nacional de Educación a Distancia/Universidad Autónoma Metropolitana – Iztapalapa, April 1993, no. 1. Included in TO, FC.

'Después del derrumbe: estar o no a la izquierda'. In *Sistema. Revista de ciencias sociales*, Instituto de Técnicas Sociales de la Fundación Social Universitaria. Madrid: May 1992, no. 108, pp. 57–67. Republished in *Dialéctica. Revista de filosofía, ciencias sociales, literatura y cultura política de la Universidad Autónoma de Puebla*, Puebla: Winter 1992–Spring 1993, new period, double issue 23, year 16, pp. 61–76.

'Liberalismo y socialismo'. In *Dialéctica. Revista de filosofía, ciencias sociales, literatura y cultura política de la Universidad Autónoma de Puebla*, Puebla: Spring 1992, new period, year 15, no. 22, pp. 108–14. Republished in *Coloquio de Winter. Los grandes cambios de nuestro tiempo*, Mexico City: UNAM/Consejo Nacional para la Cultura y las Artes/Fondo de Cultura Económica, 1992; and in *El Día*, Mexico City: June 1992 (*Suplemento Especial del XXX Aniversario*, no. 5).

'Wenceslao Roces, maestro en toda extensión de la palabra'. In *Gaceta UNAM*, Mexico City: 13 July 1992, no. 2669, pp. 1, 3.

'Vientos del pueblo: Miguel Hernández. A cincuenta años de su muerte'. In *La Jornada Semanal*. Supplement to *La Jornada*, Mexico City: 27 September 1992, new period, no. 172, pp. 29–31.

'El marxismo latinoamericano de Mariátegui. Grandeza y originalidad de un marxista latinoamericano'. In *América Latina. Historia y destino. Homenaje a Leopoldo Zea*, Volume 2. Mexico City: UNAM, 1992, pp. 331–9. Republished, with the title 'Mariátegui, grandeza y originalidad de un marxista latinoamericano', in *Cuadernos marxistas. Revista del Partido Comunista, de análisis, debates y documentos*, Buenos Aires: 1996, no. 6, pp. 149–58.

'Prólogo a *Obra Estética*'. [Preface, drafted in 1991 for a collective volume contracted by Casa de las Américas (Havana): *Obra Estética*, with essays by A.S.V., which has not appeared as of yet.] In *Casa de las Américas*, Havana: January–March 1993, year 33, no. 190, pp. 136–40. Republished, under the title 'Trayectoria de mi pensamiento estético', in *Memoria*, Mexico City: Centro de Estudios del Movimiento Obrero y Socialista (CEMOS), February 1994, no. 63.

'La pintura como lenguaje'. In *Artes plásticas*, Mexico City: UNAM, Escuela Nacional de Artes Plasticas, spring 1993, year 4, no. 15/16, pp. 5–14.

'La filosofía sin más ni menos'. In *Teoría. Revista de Filosofía*, Mexico City: UNAM, Facultad de Filosofía y Letras, July 1993, year 1, no. 1, pp. 13–24. Included in FC.

'Filosofía, técnica y moral'. In *Claves de razón práctica*. Madrid: October 1993, no. 36. Republished in *Dialéctica. Revista de filosofía, ciencias sociales, literatura y cultura política de la Benemérita Universidad Autónoma de Puebla*, Puebla: Spring 1995, new period, year 18, no. 27, pp. 37–53.

'Estética y modernidad'. In *La modernidad como estética. XII Congreso Internacional de Estética, Instituto de Estética y Teoría de las Artes*. Madrid: 1993. Republished, with the title: 'Modernidad, vanguardia y posmodernismo', In *La Jornada Semanal*. Supplement to *La Jornada. Mexico City:* 28 November 1993, no. 233, pp. 25–30.

'La crítica de la ideología en Luis Villoro'. In Ernesto Garzón Valdés y Fernando Salmerón (eds.), *Epistemología y cultura. En torno a la obra de Luis Villoro*. Mexico City: UNAM, Instituto de Investigaciones Filosóficas, 1993. Included in TO.

'Los maestros del exilio español en la UNAM'. In Various, *Maestros del exilio español*. Mexico City: UNAM, Facultad de Filosofía y Letras, 1993. 33 pp. (Col. Cuadernos de Jornadas.)

La filosofía de la praxis y los manuscritos económico filosóficos de 1844. Balance personal. Mexico City: UNAM, Facultad de Economía, Seminario de El Capital, 1994. 15 pp. Abridged, with the title 'La Filosofía de la praxis (balance personal y general)', included in FC.

'Mi trato con la poesía en el exilio'. In Rose Corral, (ed.) *Los poetas del exilio español en México*. Mexico City: El Colegio de México, 1994. 468 pp., pp. 407–14.

El movimiento del 68. Testimonio y reflexiones. Mexico City: UNAM, Facultad de Economía, Seminario de El Capital, 1994. 12 pp. Republished In *Sociológica*. Mexico City: September–December 1998, year 13, no. 38, pp. 145–52. [Issue on '1968. Significados y efectos sociales'.]

'La utopía del fin de la utopía'. In *Papeles de la FIM*. Madrid: Fundación de Investigaciones Marxistas, second period, no. 5, autumn 1995, pp. 99–110.

'Los *Manuscritos de 1844* de Marx en mi vida y en mi obra'. Mexico City: UNAM, Facultad de Economía, Seminario de El Capital, 1995. Included in TO.

'Apostillas a una crítica'. In Gabriel Vargas Lozano (ed.), *En torno a la obra de Adolfo Sánchez Vázquez*, Mexico City: UNAM, Facultad de Filosofía y Letras, 1995, pp. 247–51.

'Carta a Etienne Balibar'. In Gabriel Vargas Lozano (ed.), *En torno a la obra de Adolfo Sánchez Vázquez*. Mexico City: UNAM. Facultad de Filosofía y Letras, 1995, 640 pp., pp. 509–13.

'Izquierda y derecha en política: ¿y en la moral?' [in four parts] In *La Jornada*. Mexico City: 26 al 29 February 1996. Republished In León Olivé and Luis Villoro (eds.), *Filosofía, moral, educación e historia. Homenaje a Fernando Salmerón*. Mexico City: UNAM, Facultad de Filosofía y Letras e Instituto de Investigaciones Filosóficas, 1996. 776 pp., pp. 37–52; and in *Casa de las Américas*, Havana: October–December 1997, vol. 38, no. 209, pp. 22–31.

'El corto y fecundo exilio de Joaquín Xirau'. In *Theoría. Revistu del Colegio de Filosofía*. Mexico City: UNAM, Facultad de Filosofía y Letras, March 1996, no. 3, pp. 131–5. Included in FC.

'Anverso y reverso de la tolerancia'. In Rafael Cordera Campos and Eugenia Huerta (eds.), *La Universidad y la tolerancia*. Mexico City: UNAM, 1996. 265 pp., pp. 41–52. Republished in *Claves de razón práctica*. Madrid: September 1996, no. 65. Republished, with the title 'Límites de la tolerancia', in Isidro Cisneros, *et al.* (eds.), *Tolerancia e identidades en la ciudad de México*. Mexico City: Gobierno del Distrito Federal, 1999, pp. 9–14.

'Introducción a la ética'. In A. Cervantes *et al., Ética y salud reproductiva*. Mexico City: UNAM and Porrúa, 1997, pp. 29–81. (Col. Las Ciencias Sociales. Estudios de género).

'Reflexiones ¿intempestivas? Sobre la igualdad y la desigualdad'. In *Memoria*. Mexico City: Centro de Estudios del Movimiento Obrero y Socialista [CEMOS], June 1997, no. 100, pp. 23–33.

'Homenaje a Joaquín Xirau'. In *Biblioteca de México*, Mexico City: Consejo Nacional para la Cultura y las Artes, September–October 1997, no. 41, pp. 60–2.

'La filosofía de la praxis'. In Fernando Quesada (ed.), *Filosofía política I. Ideas políticas y movimientos sociales*. Volume 13 of the *Enciclopedia IberoAmericana de Filosofía*. Madrid: Trotta, 1997. 284 pp., pp. 17–35. [Second ed. 2002.]

'Tres referentes de Paz: Marx, el marxismo y el socialismo'. In *Vuelta*, Mexico City: January 1998, year 22, no. 254.

'Sobre la posmodernidad'. In *Memoria*. Mexico City: Centro de Estudios del Movimiento Obrero y Socialista [CEMOS], March 1998, no. 109, pp. 49–52.

'Un movimiento antiautoritario'. In *Etcétera. Semanario de política y cultura*. Mexico City: 1 October 1998.

'El Manifiesto comunista. Actualidad e inactualidad'. In *Democracia y Socialismo. Problemas del cambio*. Mexico City: October 1998, no. 2.

'El antihumanismo ontológico de Heidegger'. In *Islas. Revista de la Universidad Central de Las Villas*, Santa Clara, Cuba, September–December 1998, no. 118, pp. 141–52.

'Proletariado, tradición y vanguardia'. [Presentation in the workshop 'Cultura y Revolución, a cuarenta años de 1959', Havana: 4–5 January 1999.] In *Arena*, 21 February 1999, year 1, vol. 1, no. 3, pp. 1–4.

'Ante la situación creada en la UNAM'. In *La Jornada*, Mexico City: 12 April 1999.

'Una utopía en el siglo XXI'. In *Claves de razón práctica*. Madrid: June 1999, no. 93.

'Ante la grave situación de la UNAM. (Primera parte)'. In *La Jornada*, Mexico City: 6 August 1999.

'Ante la grave situación de la UNAM. (Segunda y última parte)'. In *La Jornada*, Mexico City: 7 August 1999.

'Venturas y desventuras de una propuesta'. In *La Jornada*, Mexico City: 1 October 1999.

[Untitled]. In Eduardo Heras León (ed.), *Cultura y revolución. A cuarenta años de 1959*. Havana: Casa de las Américas, 1999. 188 pp.

Gramsci I. Mexico City: UNAM, Centro de Investigaciones Interdisciplinarias en Ciencias y Humanidades, 1999. 17 pp. (Col. Clásicos.) [Pamphlet.]

'La revolución cubana y el socialismo'. In Roberto Fernández Retamar, *et al.*, *Cultura y revolución. A cuarenta años de 1959*. Havana: Casa de las Américas, 1999. 188 pp. Republished in *Dialéctica. Revista de filosofía, ciencias sociales, literatura y cultura política de la Benemérita Universidad Autónoma de Puebla*, Puebla: spring 1999, new period, vol. 23, no. 32, pp. 146–51.

'Filosofía y vida en el exilio.' [Presentation in the Seminar 'Herencia y recuperación del exilio filosófico'.] In *Gaceta del Fondo de Cultura Económica*, Mexico City: June 1999, no. 342, pp. 22–5.

'El socialismo como utopía'. In *Casa de las Américas*, Havana: July–September 1999, vol. 40, no. 216, pp. 79–84.

'¿A dónde va la universidad?' In *La Jornada*, Mexico City: 15 January 2000.

'La razón de la fuerza y la fuerza de la razón'. In *La Jornada*, Mexico City: 23 February 2000. [Clarification by A.S.V. on two lines omitted from the published dedication: 'Omitieron dedicatoria'. In *La Jornada*, Mexico City: 24 February 2000, p. 2.]
'Respuesta de Adolfo Sánchez Vázquez a Javier Flores'. In *La Jornada*, Mexico City: 29 February 2000. p. 2.
'Los del 96 y la política'. In Leopoldo Zea and María Teresa Miaja (eds.), *98. Derrota pírrica*. Mexico City: Instituto Panamericano de Geografía/Fondo de Cultura Económica, 2000. 246 pp.
'Las humanidades y las artes entre dos siglos y dos milenios'. In Adriana Segovia (ed.), *Memoria del Coloquio Las Humanidades y las Artes ¿Crisis o Revolucion?*, Mexico City: UNAM, Consejo Academico del Area de las Humanidades y de las Artes, 2000. 437 pp., pp. 360-5.
'Del destierro al transtierro'. In *Sólo historia*. Mexico City: 2001, no. 12, pp. 34-47. Republished, with the title 'El exilio del 39. Del destierro al transtierro', In *Claves de razón práctica*. Madrid: April 2002, no. 101.
'El laberinto de la soledad. Cincuenta años después'. [With Roger Bartra.] In *Claves de razón práctica*, Madrid: 2001, no. 112, pp. 47-55.
'Octavio Paz en su "Laberinto"'. In *Anuario de la Fundación Octavio Paz,* Mexico City: 2001, no. 3.
'Miradas sobre -y desde- el exilio'. In Various, *Exilio*. Madrid: Fundación Pablo Iglesias, 2002.
'Juan Rejano en el exilio'. Teresa Hernández (ed.), *Juan Rejano y el exilio de 1936 en México*. [Minutes of the International Congress 'Juan Rejano y el exilio de 1936 en México'.] Córdoba, Spain Diputación de Córdoba, 2002.
'Encuentros y desencuentros entre política y moral'. In *Perfil*. Supplement to *La Jornada*, Mexico City: 3 May 2001, pp. I-IV.
'Emilio Prados entre el olivo y el recuerdo'. In María José Jiménez Tomé (ed.), *Cita sin límites. Homenaje a Emilio Prados en el centenario de su nacimiento*. Malaga: Universidad de Málaga, 2001. Republished, with the title 'Emilio Prados en mis recuerdos', in Manuel Aznar Soler (ed.), *Las Literaturas del exilio republicano de 1939*, Barcelona, Universitat Autònoma de Barcelona, 2002.
'El 'Sueño' metódico de sor Juana'. In *Literatura mexicana*, Mexico City: UNAM, Instituto de Investigaciones Filológicas, 2002, vol. 13, no. 2, pp. 49-63.
'Emilio Prados en los años de la República y la Guerra Civil'. In *Biblioteca de México*, Consejo Nacional para la Cultura y las Artes, Mexico City: January-April 2003, no. 73-74.
'El doble fin del exilio del 39'. In *Claves de razón práctica*. Madrid: July 2003, no. 133.
'Negación y afirmación de la importancia de la filosofía'. [Speech given at the first international day of philosophy, 21 November 2000.] In Gabriel Vargas Lozano (ed.), *Día internacional de filosofía*, Mexico City: Asociación Filosófica de México, 2003. 135 pp, pp. 51-7.

'Vida y filosofía. Páginas de memoria'. In *Gaceta del Fondo de Cultura Económica*, Mexico City: January 2004, no. 397, pp. 11–14.

'Reivindicación de la filosofía en tiempos adversos'. [Speech at the Universidad de Guadalajara upon being named 'Doctor Honoris Causa'.] In *La Jornada*, Mexico City: 12 June 2004.

'Ramón y yo'. In *Revista de la Universidad de México*, Mexico City, August 2004, no. 6, pp. 93–4.

'Por qué ser marxista hoy'. [Speech at the Universidad de la Habana upon being named Doctor Honoris Causa.] In *La Jornada*, Mexico City: 12 September 2004.

'Leopoldo Zea, in memoriam'. In *Cuadernos americanos*, Mexico City: September–October 2004, new period, year 18, vol. 5, no. 107, p. 193.

'Testimonios sobre Leopoldo Zea en la prensa escrita', [by A.S.V. *et al.*]. In *Cuadernos Americanos*, Mexico City: September–October 2004, new period, no. 107, pp. 193–211.

'Reivindicación de la filosofía en tiempos adversos'. In *Casa de las Américas*, Havana, October 2004, year 44, no. 237, pp. 3–6.

'Discurso del doctor Adolfo Sánchez Vázquez en el Acto de Investidura como Doctor Honoris Causa por la Universidad Complutense de Madrid'. In *Dialéctica*, Puebla, Winter 2004, vol. 28, no. 36, pp. 207–10.

'El desafuero de la política y la moral'. In *La Jornada*. Mexico City: 18 March 2005.

'El compromiso político-intelectual de María Zambrano'. In *Casa de las Américas*, Havana, April–June 2005, year. 45, no. 239, pp. 3–11.

'Dos sonetos'. In *La Jornada*. Mexico City: 31 December 2005.

'Don Quijote como utopía'. In *Casa de las Américas*, Havana, April–June 2006, year 46, no. 243, pp. 119–23.

'Por qué ser marxista hoy. Discurso pronunciado al ser investido doctor honoris causa por la Universidad de La Habana'. In *Dialéctica,* Puebla, Winter 2006, vol. 30, no. 38, pp. 213–17.

'Don Quijote como utopía. Discurso pronunciado al ser investido Doctor Honoris Causa por la Universidad Autónoma del Estado de Morelos'. In *Dialéctica*, Puebla, Winter 2006, vol. 30, no. 38, pp. 218–23.

'Ética y marxismo', in Atilio A. Boron, Javier Amadeo, Sabrina González (eds.), *La teoría marxista hoy. Problemas y perspectivas*, Buenos Aires: Consejo Latinoamericano de Ciencias Sociales, 2006, pp. 297–307.

'Socialismo: realidad y utopía', in *Revista de la Universidad de México*, Mexico City: UNAM, May 2007, new period, no. 39, pp. 12–17.

'Crítica y marxismo'. In *Contrahistorias. La otra mirada de Clío*, Mexico City, September 2008–February 2009, no. 11, pp. 19–22.

'Defensa de la filosofía en tiempos adversos'. In *Dialéctica*, Puebla, Winter 2008–Spring 2009, vol. 32, no. 41, pp. 155–8.

'La razón amenazada. Discurso al recibir la distinción universitaria'. In *Dialéctica. Revista de filosofía, ciencias sociales, literatura y cultura política de la Universidad Autónoma de Puebla,* Puebla, Spring–Summer 2011, vol. 34 no. 43 pp. 139–43.
'Actualidad del socialismo'. In Elvira Concheiro, Massimo Modonesi, Horacio Gutiérrez Crespo (eds.) *El comunismo. Otras miradas desde América Latina,* Mexico City: UNAM, 2007 pp. 673–730.

c) *Existing Translations*

The titles of the respective originals in Spanish, if published, appear noted in brackets. If the title of the translation is not listed, this means that it was not possible to determine.

To German

'Hauptmotive der Ästhetik Diego Riveras'. ['Claves de la ideología estética de Diego Rivera'.] In *Diego Rivera 1886–1957. Retrospektive.* [Volume of text and images for the exposition of the same name, 23 July to 16 September, Neue Gesellschaft für Bildende Kunst (GBKB)/Staatliche Kunsthalle Berlin.] Volume conceived by: Olav Münzberg and Michael Nungesser. Berlin (West): Ed. Dietrich Reimer, 1987. 222 pp., pp. 194–208.
'Überprüfung der sozialistischen Idee angesichts ihrer Kritiker'. [Part VI of: 'Reexamen de la idea del socialismo'.] Trans. Wolfgang Gabbert. In Miloš Nikolić (ed.), *Der Sozialismus an der Schwelle zum 21. Jahrhundert.* Volume 2. Berlin (West): Argument, 1985. (Col. Internationale Sozialismus-Diskussion, no. 7, Argument-Sonderband AS 136.) pp. 111–15.
'Demokratie, Revolution und Sozialismus'. ['Democracia, revolución y socialismo'.] Trans. Stefan Gandler. In *Diskus. Frankfurter StudentInnenzeitung,* Frankfurt am Main July 1990, year 39, no. 3, pp. 43–9.
'Wir werden dafür bezahlen müssen. Mexikanische Intellektuelle diskutieren über Sozialismus und Kommunismus'. ['La crisis en Europa del Este'.] Abbreviated translation, by Michael Werz. Discussion with the following participants: Rolando Cordera, Djuka Julys, Eduardo Montes, Luis Salazar C. and Adolfo Sánchez Vázquez. In *Diskus. Frankfurter StudentInnenzeitung,* Frankfurt am Main May 1990, year 39, no. 2, pp. 21–6.
'Die Utopie des Don Quijote'. [Slightly abbreviated translation of: 'La utopía del Don Quijote'.] Trans. Nana Badenberg. In *Das Argument. Zeitschrift für Philosophie und Sozialwissenschaften,* Hamburg: January–February 1994, year 36, no. 203, Vol. 1, pp. 79–84.

To Korean

Yesulgwa sahoe. [*Las ideas estéticas de Marx.*] Trans. Yang Kŏn-yŏl. Seoul: Iron'gwa shilch'ŏn, 1993. 302 pp.

To Czech
'Kafkův hradina Josef K'. ['Un héroe Kafkiano: José K.'] Trans. Zdeněk Kouřím. In *Plamen. Měsíčník pro literaturu, umění a život.* Prague: 1964, year 6, no. 8. pp. 90–5.

To French
'Une source d'inspiration et d'espoir'. ['Una fuente de inspiración y de esperanza'.] In Various, *Asturias*, Paris: Cercle d'art, 1964.

'Socialisation de la création ou mort de l'art'. ['Socialización de la creación o muerte del arte'.] Trans. Simone Degrais. In *L'homme et la société. Revue internationale de recherches et synthèses sociologiques*, Paris: October–December 1972, no. 26, pp. 69–81.

'La philosophie de la praxis comme nouvelle pratique de la philosophie'. ['La Filosofía de la praxis como nueva práctica de la filosofía'.] Trans. K. Nair. In *L'homme et la société. Revue internationale de recherches et synthèses sociologiques*, Paris: January–June 1977, no. 43–4, pp. 141–9.

'Le marxisme et la question nationale en Amérique Latine'. In *Socialism in the World*, Belgrade: 1988, no. 65.

'Socialisme et marché'. ['Socialismo y mercado'.] In *Actuel Marx*, Paris: October 1997, no. 22.

To Galician
'A aportación dos exiliados españois ó filosofar latinoamericano' ['Exilio y filosofía. La aportación de los exiliados españoles al filosofar latinoamericano'], Trans. Alfonso Sola Limia, in Leopoldo Zea et al., *América Latina. Entre a realidade e a utopía*, Vigo: Edicións Xerais de Galicia, 1992, pp. 155–67.

To English
Art and Society. Essays in Marxist Aesthetics. [*Las ideas estéticas de Marx.*] Trans. Maro Riofrancos. New York: Monthly Review Press, 1974; and London: Merlin Press, 1974. 287 pp.

'Vicissitudes of the Aesthetic Ideas of Marx'. ['Vicisitudes de las ideas estéticas de Marx'.] [Chapter I of *Art and Society. Essays in Marxist Aesthetics.*] Trans. Maro Riofrancos. In *Monthly Review. An independent socialist magazine*, New York: February 1974, year 25, no. 9, pp. 37–49.

'Lunacharsky: The Paradoxes of Art and Revolution'. ['Lunacharsky y las aporías del arte y la revolución. (Prefacio, 1975.)'] In *Praxis. A journal of radical perspectives on the arts*, Goleta, CA, 1976, no. 2.

The philosophy of Praxis. [*Filosofía de la praxis.*] [Based on the 1st edition in Spanish.] Trans. Mike González. Atlantic Highlands, N: Humanities Press, 1977; and London: Merlin Press, 1977. 387 pp.

'Are the Theses of Classical Marxism on Just War and Violence Valid Today?' [Trans. of the unpublished speech in Spanish: '¿Son válidas hoy las tesis del marxismo clásico sobre la guerra justa y la violencia?', given in 1973 at the Fifteenth World Philosophy Congress in Varna (Bulgaria).] In John Sommerville (ed.), *Soviet Marxism and Nuclear War. An International Debate.* Westport, CT: Greenwood Press, 1981, pp. 91–5.

'Philosophy, Ideology and Society'. ['Filosofía, ideología y sociedad'.] Trans. Priscilla Cohn. In Priscilla Cohn (ed.), *Transparencies. Philosophical Essays in Honor of J. Ferrater Mora.* Atlantic Highlands, NJ: Humanities Press, 1981, pp. 139–57.

'Marxism as Humanism. Controversy with "Theoretical Antihumanism" '. ['La querella de los *Manuscritos*. 2' (Chapter Nine of *Filosofía y economía en el joven Marx*), also published as: 'El marxismo como humanismo. Controversia con el 'antihumanismo teórico'.'] Trans. Miroslava Janković. In *Socialism in the World. International journal of Marxist and socialist thought*, Belgrade: 1983, year 7, no. 35, pp. 72–82.

'On truth in the arts'. ['Sobre la verdad en las artes'.] Trans. Malicha Delone and Guillermo de la Luna. In *Ufahamu. Journal of the African Activist Association*, Los Angeles: University of California, African Studies Center, 1983, vol. 12, no. 2, pp. 11–19.

'Rationality and Emancipation in Marx'. ['Racionalidad y emancipación en Marx'.] Trans. Mirjana Đukić. In *Socialism in the World. International journal of Marxist and socialist thought*, Belgrade: 1984, year 8, no. 40, pp. 127–38.

'The idea of Socialism re-examined'. ['Reexamen de la idea del socialismo'.] In *Socialism on the threshold of the 21st century.* London: Verso, 1985, pp. 266–82.

'Marxism in Latin America'. ['La situación de la filosofía en el mundo hispánico. El marxismo en América Latina'.] Trans. Jorge J.E. Garcia. In *The Philosophical Forum*, Boston, MA: Autumn-Winter 1988–9, vol. 20, no. 1–2, pp. 114–28.

'The Question of Power in Marx' ['La cuestión del poder en Marx']. In *Synthesis philosophica*, Croatian Philosophical Society and the Union of Philosophical Societies of Yugoslavia. Zagreb: Filozofski Fakultet, 1991, no. 1, pp. 189–204.

To Italian

'Il marxismo in America latina.' ['El marxismo en América Latina']. In Biagio Muscatello (ed.), *Gramsci e il marxismo contemporaneo. Realizioni al convegno organizzato dal Centro Mario Rossi, Siena, 27–30 aprile 1987.* Rome: Riuniti, 1990, pp. 213–31.

Riesame dell'idea di socialismo. Padua: Editore GB, 1988. 199 pp.

'Socialismo e mercato'. ['Socialismo y mercado'.] In *Il socialismo del futuro. Rivista di dibattito politico.* Rome: Edizioni Mondo Operario, 1991, no. 3, pp. 93–8.

To Portuguese

150 anos de manifesto comunista. São Paulo: PT, Secretaria Nacional de Formação Política 1998. 174 pp. [With Jorge Almeida and Vitoria Cancelli.]

As idéias estéticas de Marx. [*Las ideas estéticas de Marx.*] Rio de Janeiro: Paz e Terra, 1968.

Ciência e revolução. O marxismo de Althusser. [*Ciencia y revolución. El marxismo de Althusser.*] Trans. Heloísa Hahn. Rio de Janeiro: Civilização Brasileira, 1980. 177 pp.

Convite à Estética. [*Invitación a la estética.*] Rio de Janeiro: Civilização Brasileira, 1999. 336 pp.

'Do Socialismo Científico ao Socialismo Utópico'. [*Del socialismo científico al socialismo utópico.* Published as a book in Spanish.] Trans. Ana Teresa Jardin Reynaud. In *Encontros com a Civilização Brasileira,* Rio de Janeiro: 1979, no. 14, pp. 95–135.

Entre a realidade e a utopia. Ensaios sobre política, moral e socialismo. [*Entre la realidad y la utopía.*] Trans. Gilson B. Soares. Rio de Janeiro: Civilização Brasileira, 2001. 396 pp.

Ética. [*Ética.*] Trans. João Dell'Anna. Rio de Janeiro: Civilização Brasileira, 1970. 267 pp. (Col.: Perspectivas do homen. Seria filosofia, no. 46.) Twenty-Fourth Edition 2003.

Filosofia da práxis. [*Filosofía de la praxis,* Translation of the First edition.] Trans. Luiz Fernando Cardoso. Rio de Janeiro: Paz e Terra, 1968. Third edition, 1986. 454 pp.

Filosofia da práxis. [*Filosofía de la praxis,* Translation of the Second edition.] Trans. Maria Encarnación Moya, Buenos Aires/São Paulo: Consejo Latinoamericano de Ciencias Sociales/Expressão Popular, Brasil, 2007. 440 pp.

Filosofia e circunstâncias. [*Filosofía y circunstancias.*] Trans. Luiz Cavalcanti de M. Guerra. Rio de Janeiro: Civilização Brasileira, 2002. 555 pp.

To Romanian

'Ideile estetice din 'Manuscrisele economico-filozofice'. Ale lui Marx'. ['Ideas estéticas en los 'Manuscritos económico-filosóficos' de Marx'.] In *Revista de Filosofie,* Bucharest: 1964, no. 2, pp. 201–18.

To Russian

'Naša svjaě' s ěpochoj'. ['Mitología y verdad en la crítica de nuestra época'.] In *Voprosy Filosofii,* Moscow: Akademija Nauk SSSR, Institut Filosofii, 1964, no. 1, pp. 45–54.

['Socialización de la creación o muerte del arte'.] In *Materiali VII Mezhdunarodnogo Esteticheskogo Kongressa v Bujareste v 1972.* Moscow: Znanie, 1973.

To Serbo-Croat

'Definicija umjetnosti'. ['De la imposibilidad y posibilidad de definir el arte'. Also publushed as: 'La definición del arte'.] In *Marksizam, estetika, umjetnost.* (*Anthologie*), Volume 1. Belgrade: Izdavaski Centar Komunist, 1982.

Filozofija praxis. [*Filosofía de la praxis.*] [Trans. of the Spanish second edition.] Trans. Stanko Petković and Gordana Tintor. Zagreb: Naprijed, 1983. 395 pp.
'Od Marxova Socijalizma do Realnog Socijalizma'. ['Ideal socialista y socialismo real'.] Trans. Milivoj Telećan. In *Kulurni radnik*, Zagreb: 1983, no. 5.
'Koncepcija čovjeka u mladog Marxa'. ['La concepción del hombre del joven Marx'.] In Elmar Altvater, Rade Kalanj *et al.: Marx nakon 100 godina.* Zagreb: Globus, 1984. 412 pp.
'Marksizam i socijalizan danas'. ['Marxismo y socialismo, hoy'.] In *Kulturni radnik*, Zagreb: 1988, no. 2.
'Pitanje vlasti u Marxovoj teoriji'. ['La cuestión del poder en Marx'.] Trans. Maya Meixner. In *Filozofska istrazivanja*, Zagreb: 1991, year 11, no. 40, pp. 13–27.

d) **Prologues and Book Reviews**
When the prologues and reviews have a specific title, these appear in brackets at the end of the note.

Prologues

Aznar Soler, Manuel (ed.), *El exilio literario español de 1939*, [Minutes of the Primer Congreso Internacional, Bellaterra: 27 November–1 December 1995.] Barcelona: Universitat Autònoma de Barcelona, 1998.
Kafka, Franz, *El proceso*, Havana: 1967.
Korsch, Karl, *Marxismo y filosofía*, Trans. Elizabeth Beniers. Mexico City: Era, 1971. 137 pp. (Col. El hombre y su tiempo.) [Orig. Marxismus und Philosophie.] ['El marxismo de Korsch', pp. 9–18.]
Kosík, Karel, *Dialéctica de lo concreto. Estudios sobre los problemas del hombre y el mundo*, Trans. A.S.V. Mexico City: Grijalbo, 1967. 269 pp. (Col. Teoría y praxis, no. 18.) [1976 second edition. Orig.: *Dialektika konkretního. Studie o problematice člověka a sveta.*]
Lenin, V.I., Leon Trotsky, Nicolai Bujarin, *Debate sobre la economía soviética y la ley del valor*, Mexico City: Grijalbo, 1975. (Col. Teoría y praxis.) ['La economía como política'.] Prologue included in HP.]
Lunacharsky, Antoly Vasilievich, *El arte y la revolución (1917–1920)*, Trans. Ricardo San Vicente. Selection of texts by A.S.V. Mexico City: Grijalbo, 1975. 372 pp. (Col. teoría y praxis, no. 8.) ['Lunacharsky y las aporías del arte y la revolución'.] Prologue included in AM, AR. Mexico City:
Marx, Karl, *Crítica de la filosofía del Estado de Hegel*, Trans. Antonio Encinares. Mexico City: Grijalbo, 1968. 158 pp. Republished in Spanish: Barcelona: Grijalbo, 1974. 158 pp. ['Marx y su crítica de la filosofía política de Hegel', pp. 5–10.]
Marx, Karl, *Cuadernos de París. Notas de lectura de 1844*, Trans. Bolívar Echeverría. Mexico City: Era, 1974. 192 pp. (Col.: El hombre y su tiempo.) Second edition 1980. ['Economía y humanismo'.]

Mirabeau, Honoré Gabriel Riquetti comte de (Conde de la Borrasca), *Cartas de amor*, Trans. Adolfo Sánchez Vázquez. Mexico City: Centauro, 1944. 290 pp.

Mosquera, Gerardo, *El diseño fue en October*, Havana: 1989.

Pashukanis, E.B., *La teoría general del derecho y el marxismo*, Mexico City: Grijalbo, 1976. 162 pp. (Col. Teoría y praxis, no. 27.) ['Pashukanis, teoría marxista del derecho'.] Prologue reprinted in *Dialéctica. Revista de la Escuela de Filosofía y Letras de la Universidad Autónoma de Puebla*, Puebla: January 1977, year 2, no. 2, pp. 99–119. Included in HP, with the title: 'Entre el derecho y la política'.

Ponce, Aníbal, *Educación y lucha de clases*, Mexico City: Solidaridad, 1969.

Rivadeo, Ana María, *Epistemología y política en Kant. Inmanencias y totalidad en la filosofía moderna*, Mexico City: UNAM, Escuela Nacional de Estudios Profesionales [ENEP] Acatlán, 1987.

Tinoco, Victor Hugo, *Conflicto y Paz. El proceso negociador centroamericano*, Managua: Meztrza/Coordinación Regional de Investigaciones Económicos y Sociales, 1989. 182 pp.

Togliatti, Palmiro, *Escritos políticos*, Trans. Alejandro Rossi. Mexico City: Era, 1971. 440 pp. (Col. El hombre y su tiempo.) [Orig.: *Scritti scelti*.] ['Togliatti o la política como sustancia de la historia'.] Prologue included in HP.

Various, *Sinaia. Diario de la primera expedición de republicanos españoles a México*, Facsimile edition. Mexico City: UNAM, Coordinación de Difusión Cultural/ Universidad Autónoma Metropolitana/La Oca Editores, 1989. 147 pp.

Velasco Gómez, Ambrosio; Elisabetta di Catro; María Julia Bertomeu, *La vigencia del republicanismo*, UNAM, 2006, pp. 7–8.

Book Reviews

Reviews published in the journal *Romance. Revista Popular Hispanoamericana* (published in Mexico City) are referenced in what follows in an abbreviated fashion as *Romance*. Reprint of *Romance*: Glashütten im Taunus: Ed. Detlev Auvermann, 1974.

Ajmanov, A.S., *Loguischeskoe uchenie Aristotelia*, Moscow: Pedagogical Institute, 1954. Reviewed in *Diánoia. Anuario de filosofía*, Mexico City: UNAM, Instituto de Investigaciones Filosóficas, 1956, year 2, no. 2, pp. 373f.

Alonso, Dámaso, *Hijos de la ira. Diario íntimo*, Buenos Aires/Mexico City: Espasa-Calpa Argentina, 1946. 147 pp. (Col. Austral, no. 595.) Reviewed in *Ultramar*, Mexico City: 1947, no. 1.

Álvarez Arregui, Federico, *La respuesta imposible. Eclecticismo, marxismo y transmodernidad*, Mexico City: Siglo XXI, 2002. 311 pp. Reviewed in *Al pie de la letra*. Book supplement to *Universidad de México*, Mexico City: UNAM, June 2003, no. 10, pp. 2–5. ['¿Es salvable el eclecticismo?']

Arguedas, José María, *Pumaccahua. Trabajos de los alumnos del Colegio Nacional de Sicuani, bajo la dirección de José María Arguedas*, Sicuani: 1940. 32 pp. Reviewed in

Romance, Mexico City: 1 June 1940, year 1, no. 9, p. 19. ['En torno a un libro de José Ma. Arguedas. Sobre el arte popular indio y mestizo'.]

Arguedas, José María, *Canto Kechwa. Con un ensayo sobre la capacidad de creación artística del pueblo indio y mestizo*, Lima: Club del Libro Peruano, 1938. 65 pp. Reviewed in *Romance*, Mexico City: 1 June 1940, year 1, no. 9, p. 19. ['En torno a un libro de José Ma. Arguedas. Sobre el arte popular indio y mestizo'.]

Armand, Félix and Maublanc, René, *Fourier*, Mexico City: Fondo de Cultura Económica, 1940. 460 pp. (Col. Serie de los Inmortales.) Reviewed in *Romance*, Mexico City: 15 April 1940, year 1, no. 6, p. 19 ['Fourier o el socialismo utópico'.]

Arriarán, Samuel, *Crítica a la modernidad desde América Latina*, Mexico City: UNAM, Facultad de Filosofía y Letras, 1997. 246 pp. Reviewed in *Iztapalapa. Revista de ciencias sociales y humanidades*. Universidad Autónoma Metropolitana – Iztapalapa, Mexico City: July–December 2000, vol. 20, no. 49, pp. 209–14. ['Sobre la posmodernidad'.]

Bazán, Armando, *Unamuno y el marxismo*, Madrid: Imprenta de Juan Pueyo, 1935. 95 pp. Reviewed in *Sur. Revista de orientación intelectual*, Malaga: 1936, no. 2.

Borbolla, Oscar de la, *Asalto al infierno*, Reviewed in *La Jornada Semanal*, supplement to *La Jornada*, Mexico City: 6 March 1994, no. 247, pp. 41–3.

Camacho Ramírez, Arturo and Eduardo Carranza, et al., *Piedra y cielo*, Reviewed in *Romance*, Mexico City: 15 June 1940, year 1, no. 10, p. 18. ['La nueva generación poética de Colombia'.].

Carneiro, Edison, *Guerras de los Palmares*, Mexico City: Fondo de Cultura Económica, 1946. (Col. Tierra Firme.) Reviewed in *Revista Mexicana de Cultura*. Supplement to *El Nacional*. Mexico City: 11 May 1947 [erroneously published with the date '10 May 1947'], new period, no. 6, p. 12.

Dieterlen, Paulette, *Marxismo analítico. Explicaciones funcionales e intenciones*, Mexico City: UNAM, Facultad de Filosofía y Letras, 1995. 256 pp. Reviewed in *Diánoia*. *Anuario de Filosofía*. Mexico City: UNAM, Instituto de Investigaciones Filosóficas, 1995, year 41, no. 41, pp. 227–33.

Echeverría, Bolívar, *Las ilusiones de la modernidad*, Mexico City: UNAM/El Equilibrista, 1995. 200 pp. Reviewed in *Dialéctica. Revista de filosofía, ciencias sociales, literatura y cultura política de la Universidad Autónoma de Puebla*, Puebla: spring 1997, new period, year 21, no. 29–30, pp. 164–8. ['¿Hacia una nueva modernidad?']

Garaudy, Roger, *La liberté*, Paris: Editions Sociales, 1955. Reviewed in *Diánoia. Anuario de filosofía*, Mexico City: UNAM, Instituto de Investigaciones Filosóficas, 1956, year 2, no. 2, pp. 406–8.

Giner de los Ríos, Francisco, *La rama viva*, Mexico City: Tezontle, 1940. 81 pp. Reviewed in *Romance*, Mexico City: 1 August, 1940, year 1, no. 13, p. 18. ['La rama viva y el amor eterno'.]

Gortari, Eli de, *Introducción a la lógica*, Reviewed in *Diánoia. Anuario de filosofía*, Mexico City: UNAM, Instituto de Investigaciones Filosóficas, 1957, year 3, pp. 363–76. ['La lógica dialéctica de Eli de Gortari'.]

Guzmán, Martín Luis, *Memorias de Pancho Villa*, Third volume: *Panoramas Políticos*. Mexico City: Botas, 1940. [Four volumes in total: 1938–40.] Reviewed in *Romance*, 1 May 1940, year 1, no. 7, p. 18. ['Pancho Villa. El héroe y el hombre'.]

Lefebvre, Henri, *Nietzsche*, Mexico City: Fondo de Cultura Económica, 1940. Reviewed in *Romance*, 15 September 1940, year 1, no. 16, p. 18 ['Nietzsche revivido'.]

Manzor, Antonio R., *Antología del cuento hispanoamericano*, Santiago de Chile: Editorial Zig-Zag, 1940. Reviewed in *Romance*, Mexico City: 15 August, 1940, year 1, no. 14, p. 18. ['Perfil del cuento en América'.]

Marinello, Juan, *Ensayos*, Second edition, Havana: Imprenta La Verónica, 1940. Reviewed in *Romance*, 15 February 1940, year 1, no. 2, p. 19. ['Momento español'.]

Maurois, Andrés, *Eduardo VII en su época*, Buenos Aires: Editorial Claridad, 1940. 306 pp. Reviewed in *Romance*, Mexico City: 1 February, 1940, year 1, no. 1, p. 20. ['Eduardo VII y su época'.]

Omel'Ianovskii, Mijail Erazmovick, *Problemas filosóficos de la mecánica cuántica*, Trans. Adolfo Sánchez Vázquez, Mexico City: UNAM, 1960. Reviewed in *Anuario de filosofía*, Mexico City: 1961, year 1, pp. 229f.

Ortíz Soralegui, Juvenal, *Flor Cerrada. Poemas*, Montevideo: Biblioteca Alfar, 1940. Reviewed in *Romance*, Mexico City: 1 April, 1940, year 1, no. 5, p. 18. ['Una poesía encadenada']

Pereyra, Carlos, *El sujeto de la historia*, Madrid: Alianza Editorial, 1984. Reviewed in *Dialéctica. Revista de la Escuela de Filosofía y Letras de la Universidad Autónoma de Puebla*, Puebla: December 1985, vol. 10, no. 17, pp. 163–70. With the title 'Sobre el sujeto de la historia', included in HP, FC.

Pereyra, Carlos, *Sobre la democracia*, Mexico City: Cal y Arena, 1990. 301 pp. Reviewed in *Revista Mexicana de Política Exterior*, Mexico City: winter 1990, year 7, no. 2, pp. 62–4. Republished in *Utopías. Revista de la Facultad de Filosofía y Letras de la UNAM*, Mexico City: February–March 1991, no. 8, pp. 90f.

Ponce, Manuel, *Ciclo de Vírgenes*, Mexico City: 1940. Reviewed in *Romance*, 15 April, 1940, year 1, no. 6, p. 18. ['Angeles y vírgenes en la poesía'.]

Rebolledo, Francisco, *Rasero de Luces*, Mexico City: Joaquín Mortiz, 1993. Reviewed in *La Jornada Semanal*. Supplement to *La Jornada*, Mexico City: 8 May 1994, no. 256, pp. 5–7. ['Rasero de Luces'.]

Rojo, Vicente, Gral., *Alerta a los pueblos. Estudio político-militar del periodo final de la guerra española*, Buenos Aires: Anicetto López. Reviewed in *España Peregrina, Revista de la Junta de Cultura Española*, Mexico City: 15. March 1940, year 1, no. 2, pp. 85f.

Rosental, M., *Voprosí dialecktiki 'Kapitale' Marxa*, Moscow: 1955. Reviewed in *Diánoia. Anuario de filosofía*, Mexico City: UNAM, Instituto de Investigaciones Filosóficas, 1957, year 3, no. 3, pp. 387–92.

Roxas, Juan Bartolomé, *Tres en uno. Autosacramental a la usanza antigua, en cinco cuadros y tres jornadas*, Havana: Imprenta La Verónica. Reviewed in *Romance*, 5 July, 1940, year 1, no. 12, p. 18.

Vargas Lozano, Gabriel, *Más allá del derrumbe*, Mexico City/Puebla: Siglo XXI/Benemérita Universidad Autónoma de Puebla, 1994. 146 pp. Reviewed in *Dialéctica. Revista de Filosofía, Ciencias Sociales, Literatura y Cultura Política de la Benemérita Universidad Autónoma de Puebla*. Puebla: new period, winter 1995–6, year 19, no. 28, pp. 129–33. [In 'Tres comentarios al libro de Gabriel Vargas Lozano *Más allá del derrumbe*'.]

Vargas Lozano, Gabriel, *¿Qué hacer con la filosofía en América Latina?* Reviewed in *Plural. Revista mensual de Excélsior. Crítica y literatura*, Mexico City: September 1991, new period, vol. 20, no. 240, pp. 129f. ['La filosofía en América Latina'.]

Villoro, Luis, *Creer, saber y conocer*, Mexico City: 1982. Reviewed in *Boletín de la Facultad de Filosofía y Letras*, Mexico City: UNAM, July–August 1982, fourth period, year 1, no. 2, p. 7.

Vicente, Gil, *Poesías de Gil Vicente. Selección y comentario de Dámaso Alonso*, Mexico City: Séneca, 1940. 77 pp. Reviewed in *Romance*, Mexico City: 15 May, 1940, year 1, no. 8, p. 18.

e) *Interviews and Debates with Sánchez Vázquez, Miscellaneous*
    Interviews with Sánchez Vázquez

Abelleyra, Angélica, 'Sin la estética, el mundo caería en lo inhumano: Adolfo Sánchez Vázquez. Honoris Causa de la Universidad de Educación a Distancia, en Madrid. *Invitación a la estética*, nuevo libro del filosofo', in *La Jornada*, Mexico City: 23 January 1993, p. 25 (Sección Cultura).

Aceves, Bertha, 'Sánchez Vázquez y la cuestión estética', Part I: 'La teoría marxista permite replantear los conceptos básicos de la materia artística'; Part II: 'No se justifica la reducción de la estética marxista a una simple sociología del arte', in *Excélsior*, Mexico City: 18 and 19 August 1983. Included in AM.

Bozal, Valeriano, 'De este tiempo, de este país', in *Boletín de Filosofía y Letras*, Mexico City: UNAM, Facultad de Filosofía y Letras, January–February 1977, vol. 3, no. 1, pp. 10–13.

Chávez, Rosa María and Antonio Juárez, 'Sobre el marxismo occidental y la influencia de Marx en América Latina', in *Así Es, Seminario del PSUM* [Partido Socialista Unificado de México]. Mexico City: 1986, no. 167. Included in PF.

Franzé, Javier, 'Entrevista a Adolfo Sánchez Vázquez', in *Cuadernos Hispanoamericanos*, Madrid: Ediciones Cultura Hispánica, May 1999, no. 587, pp. 99–103.

Lima, Bernardo, 'Entrevista con Adolfo Sánchez Vázquez sobre *Ciencia y Revolución*', in *Unomásuno*, Mexico City: 30 April 1979. Republished as a preface in *Ciencia y revolución. El marxismo de Althusser*, new edition, Mexico City: Grijalbo, 1982. 220 pp., pp. iii–viii.

Mikecin, Vjekoslav, 'Cuestiones marxistas disputadas', in *Cuadernos Políticos*, Mexico City: January–March 1985, no. 42, pp. 5–19; and in *Mientras Tanto*, Barcelona: 1985, no. 24. Included in PF.

Molina, Javier 'Sobre Marx y la estética marxista', in *Unomásuno*, Mexico City: 12 and 13 March 1983. Included in AM.

Orgambides, Fernando, ' "El capitalismo es injusto". Adolfo Sánchez Vázquez comenta la evolución del pensamiento socialista y marxista', in *Babelia,* supplement to *El País*, Madrid: 12 September 1992, pp. 2f.

Pereda, Carlos, 'Una conversación con Adolfo Sánchez Vázquez', in *Theoría. Revista del Colegio de Filosofía*. Mexico City: UNAM, Facultad de Filosofía y Letras, February 1997, no. 4, pp. 101–12.

Rocha Urtecho, Luis and July Valle-Castillo, 'Entrevista en Nicaragua', in *Nuevo Amanecer Cultural*. Supplement to *El Nuevo Diario*, Managua: 8 May 1983. Included in AM.

Vargas, Hugo, 'La ronda de las ideologías. Entrevista con Adolfo Sánchez Vázquez', in *La Jornada Semanal*. Supplement to *La Jornada*, Mexico City: 27 August 1989, new period, no. 11, pp. 15–19.

Debates

Cordera, Rolando, Djuka Julys, Eduardo Montes, Luis Salazar C. and Adolfo Sánchez Vázquez: 'La crisis en Europa del Este', [Transcription of a panel discussion transmitted on the television programme *Nexos TV*, Mexico City.] In *Nexos*, Mexico City: March 1990, year 13, vol. 13, no. 147, pp. 27–35.

Miscellaneous

Kismet, destino. Novelización de la película M.G.M. del mismo título, Mexico City: Galatea, 1946. 171 pp. (Col. Grandes novelas cinematográficas.) [Novel based on the movie *Kismet*, 1944, directed by William Dieterle, produced by Metro-Goldwyn-Mayer.]

f) *Translations of Works by Other Authors*

The titles of the respective originals, if they could be determined, appear in brackets at the end of the note.

From French

Mirabeau, Honoré Gabriel Riquetti, Comte de (Conde de la Borrasca), *Cartas de amor*, With a preface by A.S.V. Mexico City: Centauro, 1944. 290 pp. [*Lettres d'amour*.]

Viollet-le-Duc, Eugène Emmanuel, *Historia de la vivienda humana*, Mexico City: Centauro, 1945. 367 pp. [*Histoire de l'habitation humaine depuis les temps préhistoriques jusqu'à nos jours.*]

From English

Hobson, John Atkinson, *Veblen*, Mexico City: Fondo de Cultura Económica, 1941. 160 pp. (Col. Obras de sociología. Grandes sociólogos modernos.) [*Veblen.*]
Irving, Washington, *Vida de Mahoma*, Mexico City: Centauro, 1944. 271 pp. [*Life of Mahomet.*]
Wilde, Oscar, *El retrato de Dorian Gray*, Illustrations by Elvira Gascón. Mexico City: Leyenda, 1946. [*The picture of Dorian Gray.*]

From Italian

Kosík, Karel, *Dialéctica de lo concreto. Estudios sobre los problemas del hombre y el mundo*, with a preface by A.S.V. Mexico City: Grijalbo, 1967. [Second edition: 1976] (Col. Teoría y praxis, no. 18.) [*Dialektika konkretuiko. Studie o problematice cloveka a sveta.*]

From Russian

Alperovich, Moiseï Samoïlovich: *Historia de la independencia de México (1810–1824)*, Mexico City: Grijalbo, 1967. 354 pp.
Arjiptsev, Fedor Timofeevich, *La materia como categoría filosófica*, Mexico City: Grijalbo, 1962. [Second ed. 1966]. 293 pp. (Col. Enciclopedia de filosofía, second series, no. 9.) [*Materiia kak filososkaia kategoriia*, Moscow: Academy of Sciences.]
Cherkasin, P.P., *Raíces y esencia del idealismo filosófico*. Mexico City: Fondo de Cultura Popular, 1967. 295 pp.
Dynnik, M.A. et al. (eds.), *Historia de la filosofía* (in 3 volumes), Mexico City: 1963–9. Volume 1: 'De la antigüedad a comienzos del siglo XIX', 1963. 647 pp. Volume 2: 'Desde finales del siglo XIX hasta la revolución socialista de October de 1917', 1969. 783 pp. Volume 3: 'Segunda mitad del siglo XX', 1968. 552 pp. Republished: Barcelona: Grijalbo, 1985. (Translated in collaboration with José Laín and Augusto Vidal Roget, translation reviewed by A.S.V.) [*Istoriia filosofii*, Moscow: Academy of Sciences].
Frolov, Iurii Petrovich, *Examen de la cibernética*, Mexico City: UNAM, 1958 (Col. Seminario de problemas científicos, Suplementos, second series, no. 13.) pp. 85–126.
Iadov, Vladimir Aleksandrovich, *La ideología como forma de la actividad espiritual de la sociedad*. Mexico City: Fondo de Cultura Popular, 1967. 178 pp.
Konstantinov, F.V. (ed.), *El materialismo histórico*, Seventh edition, Mexico City: Grijalbo, 1980. 446 pp. (Col. Ciencias económicas y sociales.) (Translated with Wenceslao Roces.) [First edition: 1957].
Konstantinov, F.V. (ed.), *Los fundamentos de la filosofía marxista*. Mexico City: Grijalbo, 1959. 651 pp. Second ed., corrected and expanded according to the new Russian edition: 1965. 690 pp. (Col. Enciclopedia de la Filosofía, no. 1.) Republished: Havana:

Editora Política, 1964. 773 pp. (Translated with Wenceslao Roces.) [Orig. published by the USSR Academy of Sciences.]

Lenin, V.I., *Obras completas* (volumes 11 and 21), Buenos Aires: Cartago, 1960.

Omel'Ianovskii, Mijail Erazmovich, *Problemas filosóficas de la mecánica cuántica*, Mexico City: UNAM, Dirección General de Publicaciones, 1960. 302 pp. (Col.: Problemas científicos y filosóficos, no. 24.) [*Filosofskie Voprosi Kvantovoi Mejaniki*, Moscow: Academy of Sciences, 1956.]

Pavlov, Ivan Petrovich, *El reflejo condicionado*, Mexico City: UNAM, 1958 (Col.: Seminario de problemas científicos y filosóficos, Suplementos, 2nd series, no. 8.) pp. 193–213.

Rosental, Mark Moissevich and G.M. Straks, *Categorías del materialismo dialéctico*, Mexico City: Grijalbo, 1958. 372 pp. [Second ed. 1960. Translated with Wenceslao Roces.]

Rozhin Vasillii, Pavlovich, *Introducción a la sociología marxista*, Mexico City: Fondo de Cultura Popular, 1967. 264 pp.

Shishkin, Aleksandr Fedorovich, *Ética marxista*, Mexico City: Grijalbo, 1966. 511 pp. (Col.: Ciencias económicas y sociales.) [*Osnovy marksistskoi etiki*. Translated with Andrés Fierro Merui.]

Shishkin, Aleksandr Fedorovich, *Teoría de la moral*. Mexico City: Grijalbo, 1970. 154 pp.

Moreover, he translated texts by the following authors for his anthology *Estética y marxismo*:

From French: Louis Althusser, Marcel Breazu, Roger Garaudy, Lucien Goldmann, Stefan Morawski, Raymonde Moulin and Yanko Ros.

From Russian: Antoli V. Lunacharsky, Stefan Morawski, G.A. Nedoskivin, V. Pletnev and Y.N. Tynianoy.

From English: Jiri Hayek.

g) Collaboration on Editorial Boards and Editorial Tasks
Collaboration on Editorial Boards

Sur. Revista de orientación intelectual. Malaga: no. 1: December 1935. Ends publication with no. 2, January–February 1936. A.S.V. serves as director alongside Enrique Sanín. Facsimile edition: Malaga: Centro de Estudios de la Generación del 27, 1994.

Ahora. Madrid. [Beginning on 1 January 1937, the journal appears with the subtitle: *Diario de la Juventud.*] Edited by the Juventud Socialista Unificada. Year I: 1930 to year VIII: 1939, ending publication in February 1939.

Pasaremos. Year 1, no. 1: 1º December 1936, ends publication with the end of the Spanish Civil War. It bears different subtitles, beginning with: year 2, no. 48, 30 September 1937, the subtitle is: *Órgano de la II División.*

Acero. Órgano del 5º Cuerpo de Ejército del Centro. [Different places of publication and different subtitles.] 1937 to 1939, publication ends with the end of the Spanish Civil War.

Romance. Revista Popular Hispanoamericana. Mexico City: 1 February 1940 to 31 May 1941. (Year 1, no. 1–year 2, no. 24, with which publication ceases.) Reprint: Glashütten im Taunus, Ed. Detlev Auvermann, 1974.

Boletín de la Unión de Intelectuales Españoles en México. Mexico City: published in the 40s.

España Peregrina. Junta de Cultura Española. Mexico City: year 1, 1941.

Las Españas. Revista Literaria. Mexico City: year 1, no. 1, October 1946; documented until year 6, no. 19–20: 29 May 1950. [A.S.V. is mentioned among the Collaborators for the 29 November 1946 edition, year 1, no. 2, p. 7. Beginning on 29 January 1949, year 4, no. 11 A.S.V. is no longer mentioned (p. 12).]

Ultramar. Mexico City: 1950ies. [Publication ceases after year 1, no. 1.]

Editorial Tasks

Marcuse ante sus críticos. Mexico City: Grijalbo, 1970. 154 pp.

El mundo de la violencia. Mexico City: UNAM, Facultad de Filosofía y Letras/Fondo de Cultura Económica, 1998. 457 pp. ['Presentación' and 'Nota del editor' by A.S.V.]

Moreover, Sánchez Vázquez directed Grijalbo's book collection *Teoría y praxis* from 1973 to 1981, in which approximately sixty books were published.

h) **Literature about Sánchez Vázquez (selected)**
   General (selected)

Anonymous, 'Adolfo Sánchez Vázquez dona a la UNAM el fondo filosófico de su biblioteca', in *Gaceta UNAM,* Mexico City: 31 March 2011. no. 4325, pp. 4–5.

Anonymous, 'Adolfo Sánchez Vázquez. Maestro Distinguido de la Ciudad', in *Boletín Filosofía y Letras,* Mexico City: UNAM, Facultad de Filosofía y Letras, November 2000, new period, vol. 1, no. 2, pp. 25f.

Anonymous, 'Doctorado honoris causa otorgado por la Universidad Autónoma de Nuevo León al doctor Adolfo Sánchez Vázquez', in *Boletín Filosofía y Letras,* Mexico City: UNAM, Facultad de Filosofía y Letras, November–December 1994, no. 2, p. 15.

Anonymous, 'Escritores-profesores, profesores escritores', in *Boletín de la Facultad de Filosofía y Letras,* Mexico City: UNAM, Facultad de Filosofía y Letras, September–December 1978, Second period, vol. 1, no. 4/5, pp. 2–4.

Anonymous, 'Sánchez Vázquez, Adolfo'. In José Ferrater Mora, *Diccionario de filosofía.* Volume 4. Madrid: Alianza Editorial, 1979; pp. 2926f. Republished in *Anthropos. Revista de documentación científica de la cultura.* Barcelona, August 1985, no. 52, pp. 27f.

Anonymous, [review of *Sobre filosofía y marxismo*], in *Dialéctica. Revista de la Escuela de Filosofía y Letras de la Universidad Autónoma de Puebla,* Puebla: June 1983, vol. 8, no. 13, p. 190.

Abellán, José Luis, *Panorama de la filosofía española actual*, Madrid: Espasa-Calpe, 1978, especially pp. 155–60. These pages reprinted in *Anthropos. Revista de documentación científica de la cultura*. Barcelona: August 1985, no. 52, pp. 26f.

Abellán, José Luis, 'Sánchez Vázquez y otros filósofos del exilio', in *Informaciones. Diario independiente*. Madrid: 11 November 1976. Section: Informaciones de las Artes y las Letras, pp. 6f.

Acanda González, Jorge Luis, *Analyse einiger Versuche, die marxistisch-leninistische Philosophie als Praxis-Philosophie zu konzipieren, unter besonderer Berücksichtigung des Werkes von Adolfo Sánchez Vázquez*. Dissertation A, Leipzig: Karl-Marx-Universität. 1988. 120 pp.

Álvarez Arregui, Federico (ed.), *Adolfo Sánchez Vázquez. Los trabajos y los días. Semblanzas y entrevistas*, Mexico City: UNAM, Facultad de Filosofía y Letras, 1995. 411 pp.

Álvarez Arregui, Federico (ed.), 'Homenaje a Adolfo Sánchez Vázquez', in *Boletín Filosofía y Letras*, Mexico City: UNAM, Facultad de Filosofía y Letras, November–December 1995, no. 7, pp. 7–9.

Anthropos, Revista de documentación científica, 'Adolfo Sánchez Vázquez: exilio crítico y marxismo' [editorial note], in *Anthropos. Revista de documentación científica de la cultura*, Barcelona: August 1985, no. 52, pp. 2–6.

Arreola, Gerardo, 'Urge impulsar una opción social al capitalismo: Adolfo Sánchez Vázquez. El marxismo debe desechar las tesis refutadas por la vida y reivindicar las vigentes', in *La Jornada*, Mexico City: 17 September 2004, p. 16.

Arriarán Cuéllar, Samuel, 'La filosofía política en Adolfo Sánchez Vázquez', in Elsa Cecilia Frost, *et al.*, *Cincuenta años de Exilio Español en México*. Tlaxcala: Universidad Autónoma de Tlaxcala y Embajada de España en México, 1991. 215 pp., pp. 139–47. (Col. Materiales para la historia de la filosofía en México, no. 3.)

Balcárcel, José Luis, 'Nueva visión de la estética marxista', in *Diánoia. Anuario de Filosofía*, Mexico City: UNAM, Instituto de Investigaciones Filosóficas, Mexico City: 1971, year 17, no. 17, pp. 250–63.

Barreda, Andrés, 'El maestro Adolfo Sánchez Vázquez', in *La Jornada de enmedio*. Supplement to *La Jornada*, Mexico City: 14 July 2011, p. 5a.

Bautista, M., 'Sánchez Vázquez escribe sobre el arte y lo bello'. [Review of: *Invitacion a la estetica*.] In *Universidad de México*, Mexico City: UNAM, May 1993, vol. 48, no. 508, pp. 53–4.

Berenzon Gorn, Boris, 'Entrevista al Doctor Adolfo Sánchez Vázquez', in *Boletín Filosofía y Letras*, Mexico City: UNAM, Facultad de Filosofía y Letras, November–December 1994, no. 2, pp. 24–7.

Cámara, Pacheco, [Review of Ambrosio Velasco Gómez (ed.) *Vida y obra: Homenaje a Adolfo Sánchez Vázquez*], in *Revista de Hispanismo Filosófico*, Madrid: 2010, year 15, no. 10, pp. 355–8.

Capdeville García, Rubén, *Philosophische Problematik in der 'Philosophie der Praxis' von Sánchez Vázquez*. Dissertation A, Berlin: Humboldt Universität, 1992. 136 pp.

Cardiel, Reyes, *El exilio español en México, 1939–1982*, Mexico City: Fondo de Cultura Económica, 1982, pp. 232f. and p. 856. Republished in *Anthropos. Revista de documentación científica de la cultura*. Barcelona: August 1985, no. 52, p. 32.

Casar, E., 'Lukacs en México', in *Plural. Revista mensual de Excélsior. Crítica y literatura*, Mexico City: August 1981, vol. 10, no. 119, pp. 62–5.

Castañeda Zavala, Jorge, 'Esfuerzos y contribuciones marxistas para la historiografía mexicana', in *Iztapalapa. Revista de ciencias sociales y humanidades*, Mexico City: Universidad Autónoma Metropolitana – Iztapalapa, July–December 2001, vol. 22, no. 51, pp. 239–56.

Castellanos, Laura, 'Mantiene Adolfo Sánchez Vázquez "el pulso ardiendo". Saca a la luz sus poemas', in *Reforma*, Mexico City: 19 January 2005, section 'Cultura', p. 1 C.

Comín, Alfonso, 'Althusser bajo una crítica rigurosa' [Review of *Ciencia y revolución*], in *Plural. Revista mensual de Excélsior. Crítica y literatura*, Mexico City: year 8, August 1979, no. 95, pp. 65–7.

Di Castro Stringer, Elisabetta, 'Adolfo Sánchez Vázquez', in *Humanidades*, Mexico City: 25 March 1998, no. 160, p. 25.

Di Castro Stringer, Elisabetta, 'Adolfo Sánchez Vázquez II', in *Humanidades*, Mexico City: 13 May 1998, no. 163, pp. 3 and 10.

Di Castro Stringer, Elisabetta, 'Doctorado honoris causa a Adolfo Sánchez Vázquez', in *Theoría. Revista del Colegio de Filosofía*. Mexico City: UNAM, Facultad de Filosofía y Letras, July 1993, vol. 1, no. 1, pp. 177–8.

Di Castro Stringer, Elisabetta, 'Premio Nacional de Historia, Ciencias Sociales y Filosofía 2002 a Adolfo Sánchez Vázquez', in *Theoría. Revista del Colegio de Filosofía*. Mexico City: UNAM, Facultad de Filosofía y Letras, June 2003, no. 14–15, pp. 211–12.

Díaz, Elías, *Pensamiento español (1939–1975)*, Second ed., Madrid: Cuadernos para el Diálogo, 1978.

Durán Payán, Silvia, 'Palabras de Silvia Durán en la ceremonia de entrega del doctorado honoris causa', in *Dialéctica. Revista de la Escuela de Filosofía y Letras de la Universidad Autónoma de Puebla*, Puebla: December 1984, year 9, no. 16, pp. 21–5.

Durán Payán, Silvia, 'Sánchez Vázquez: dos raíces, dos tierras, dos esperanzas', in Elsa Cecilia Frost, et al., *Cincuenta años de Exilio Español en México*. Tlaxcala: Universidad Autónoma de Tlaxcala and Embajada de España en México, 1991. 215 pp., pp. 125–37. (Col. Materiales para la historia de la filosofía en México, no. 3.)

Echeverría, Bolívar, 'En torno a la presencia de Adolfo Sánchez Vázquez', in *Boletín de la Facultad de Filosofía y Letras*, Mexico City: UNAM, November/December 1995, no. 7, pp. 10–12.

Echeverría, Bolívar, 'Elogio del marxismo', in Gabriel Vargas Lozano (ed.), *En torno a la obra de Adolfo Sánchez Vázquez*. Mexico City: UNAM, Facultad de Filosofía y Letras, 1995. 640 pp., pp. 77–82.

Enríquez, José Ramón, 'Adolfo Sánchez Vázquez: Entre el rock pesado y el Rey Alfonso X', in *La Jornada Semanal*. Supplement to *La Jornada*. Mexico City: 27 August 1989, new period, no. 11, pp. 20–4.

Escogido Clausen, Ylenia, *Cuatro filósofos ante la Tesis XI. (Bloch, Althusser, Sánchez Vázquez, Echeverría)*, licenciatura dissertation, Mexico City: UNAM, Facultad de Filosofía y Letras, 1998. 44 pp. [Unpublished. Advisor: Margarita Vera Cuspinera.]

Fabelo Corzo, José Ramón and Gilberto Valdes Gutiérrez, 'La empecinada herejía de Adolfo Sánchez Vázquez', in *Casa de las Américas*, Havana: April–June 1996, vol. 36, no. 203, pp. 142–7.

Fernández Retamar, Roberto, 'Sánchez Vázquez: Del pulso ardiendo a la razón apasionada. La obra teórica y la vida militante de uno de los grandes marxistas contemporáneos recibe el reconocimiento de la Revolución Cubana', in *Rebelión*, 28 October 2004. Available at: <http://www.rebelion.org , accessed 12 June 2005>.

Flores, Javier, 'En torno a un artículo de Adolfo Sánchez Vázquez', in *La Jornada*, Mexico City: 29 February 2000, p. 2.

Fuente Escalona, Jorge de la, 'Praxis, ideología y arte en Adolfo Sánchez Vázquez', in *Temas. Cultura, ideología, sociedad*, Havana: 1998, new period, no. 15, pp. 53–65. Republished in *Plural. Revista mensual de Excélsior. Crítica y literatura*, Mexico City: August 1990, Second period, vol. 19, no. 227, pp. 33–40.

Galván Chávez, Ana, 'Adolfo Sánchez Vázquez y el marxismo', in *Configuraciones*, Mexico City: Fundación Carlos Pereyra, July–September 2000, year 1, no. 2, pp. 91–5.

Gandler, Stefan, 'Adolfo Sánchez Vázquez: rebelión, antifascismo y enseñanza', in *La Jornada Semanal*. Supplement of *La Jornada*, Mexico City, 2 October 2011, no. 865, pp. 8–10.

Gandler, Stefan, *'El concepto de ideología. La crítica de Luis Villoro al marxismo crítico de Sánchez Vázquez'*, in *Frontera Interior. Revista de Ciencias Sociales y Humanidades*, Aguascalientes, etcétera: January–April 1999, year 1, no. 1, pp. 109–18. Republished in *Papeles de la FIM. Revista de Investigación Marxista*, Madrid: Fundación de Investigaciones Marxistas, December 2002, no. 18, pp. 19–30.

Gandler, Stefan, *El discreto encanto de la modernidad. Ideologías contemporáneas y su crítica*. Mexico City/Querétaro: Siglo XXI Editores/Universidad Autónoma de Querétaro, 2013, pp. 82–95, 122–9.

Gandler, Stefan, 'Marx in Mexiko', in *Z. Zeitschrift marxistische Erneuerung*, Frankfurt am Main: September 2001, no. 47, pp. 167–80.

Gandler, Stefan, 'Materialismus heute. Alfred Schmidt und Adolfo Sánchez Vázquez', in *Zeitschrift für kritische Theorie*, Lüneburg: 2013, year 19, no. 36/37, pp. 144–59.

Gandler, Stefan, 'Nachruf auf Adolfo Sánchez Vázquez', in *ADLAF-Info, Zeitschrift der Arbeitsgemeinschaft Deutsche Lateinamerikaforschung*, Hamburg: August 2011, no. 2, pp. 12–15.

Gandler, Stefan, 'Sozialphilosophie in Mexiko. Adolfo Sánchez Vázquez und Bolívar Echeverría', in *Concordia. Internationale Zeitschrift für Philosophie*, Aachen: October 2001, no. 40, pp. 27–44.

García Soto, Luis, 'Una idea de moral', in *Agora. Papeles de Filosofía*, Santiago de Compostela: Universidad de Santiago de Compostela, Departaments: 'Filosofía e Antropoloxía social' and 'Lóxica e Filosofía Moral', 2001, vol. 20, no. 1, pp. 221–9. Available at: http://dspace.usc.es/bitstream/10347/1183/1/pg_223-232_agora20-1.pdf

Garrido, Manuel S., 'Contra una caterva de encantadores' [review of *Ciencia y revolución*], in *Plural. Revista mensual de Excélsior. Crítica y literatura*. Mexico City: year 8, August 1979, no. 95, pp. 42–8.

González, Juliana, Carlos Pereyra and Gabriel Vargas Lozano (eds.), *Praxis y filosofía. Ensayos en homenaje a Adolfo Sánchez Vázquez*, Mexico City: Grijalbo, 1985. 491 pp. [Includes contributions by: Guiseppe Prestipino, Gajo Petrović, István Mészáros, Juliana González Valenzuela, Ramón Xirau, Cesáreo Morales, José Ignacio Palencia, Gabriel Vargas Lozano, Luis Villoro, Vjekoslav Mikecin, Gerardo Mosquera, Xavier Rubert de Ventós, Teresa del Conde, Pablo Gonzáles Casanova, Adam Schaff, Manuel Sacristán Luzón, Ludolfo Paramio, Javier Muguerza, Michael Löwy, Wenceslao Roces, Juan Mora Rubio, Carlos Pereyra and Adolfo Sánchez Vázquez.]

González Montiel, A., [review of *Invitacion a la estetica*], in *Revista de filosofía*, Mexico City: September–December 1994, vol. 27, no. 81, pp. 528–30.

Gonzáles Rojo, Enrique, *Epistemología y socialismo. La crítica de Sánchez Vázquez a Louis Althusser*, Mexico City: Diógenes, 1985. 432 pp.

Górski, Eugeniusz, 'Adolfo Sánchez Vázquez i marksizm wspóczesny', [review of G. Vargas Lozano (ed.), *Praxis y filosofía. Ensayos en homenaje a Adolfo Sánchez Vázquez*, Mexico City: Grijalbo, 1985, 491 pp.] in *Studia filozoficzne*. Warsaw: Polska Akademia Nauk, Instytut Filozofii i Socjologii, 1987, vol. 12, no. 265, pp. 184ff.

Güemes, Cesar, 'En juego, la vigencia y validez del marxismo: Sánchez Vázquez', in *La Jornada*, Mexico City: 24 February 2003, p. 2a.

Gutiérrez Navas, María Dolores (ed.), *Homenaje a Adolfo Sánchez Vázquez*, Madrid: Fondo de Cultura Económica/Junta de Andalucía, 2007. 68 pp.

Haug, Wolfgang Fritz, *Orientierungsversuche materialistischer Philosophie. Ein fragmentarischer Literaturbericht*, (particularly point 8: 'Sánchez Vázquez, Holz und Sève über den ideologischen Charakter von Philosophie') In *Das Argument*, Berlin (West): July–August 1981, no. 128, pp. 516–32.

Hermosin, Xavier, *Philosophie et exil. Adolfo Sánchez Vázquez et les penseurs républicains espagnols exilés au Mexique*, Memoria DEA [Diplôme d'études approfondies] [unpublished], Nanterre: Départment d'Etudes Ibériques et Ibéro-américains, Université Paris-X Nanterre, 1998. 81 pp.

Ibargüengoitia Chico, Antonio, 'Filosofía y sociedad en México en el siglo XX', in *Revista de filosofía*, Mexico City: January–April 1996, vol. 29, no. 85, pp. 88–111.

Kohan, Néstor, 'El marxismo crítico de Adolfo Sánchez Vázquez', in *Utopía y praxis latinoamericana. Revista Internacional de Filosofía Iberoamericana y Teoría Social*, Maracaibo: Universidad del Zulia, September 2002, year. 7, no. 18, pp. 101–7.

Labastida, Jaime, 'La capacidad de dudar', in *Excélsior*, Mexico City: 28 December 1982. Republished in *Anthropos. Revista de documentación científica de la cultura*. Barcelona: August 1985, no. 52, p. 32.

Lang, Berel, [Review of: *Art and society. Essays in marxist aesthetics*], in *Leonardo. international Journal of the Contemporary Artist*, Oxford: Pergamon Presss, Winter 1977, vol. 10, no. 1, pp. 73–4.

Leyva Martínez, Gustavo (ed.), *Raíces en otra tierra. El legado de Adolfo Sánchez Vázquez*, Mexico City: Universidad Autónoma Metropolitana/Era, 2013.

Leyva Martínez, Gustavo, 'La teoría crítica en México', in *Theoría. Revista de filosofía*, Mexico City: UNAM, Facultad de Filosofía y Letras, December 2001, no. 11–12, pp. 133–47.

López Cruchet, Julián, [Review of: *Entre la realidad y la utopia: Ensayos sobre politica, moral y socialismo*], in *Revista de Hispanismo Filosófico*, Madrid: 2000, vol. 5, pp. 164–6.

Löwy, Michael, 'Marxismo y utopía', in Juliana González, Carlos Pereyra and Gabriel Vargas Lozano (eds.), *Praxis y filosofía. Ensayos en homenaje a Adolfo Sánchez Vázquez*, Mexico City: Grijalbo, 1985, pp. 387–95.

Magaña, Mariana, 'La pintura como lenguaje de Adolfo Sánchez Vázquez' [review of *La pintura como lenguaje*], in *Zentzontli*, Guadalajara: April–July 1986, no. 2/3, pp. 139–44.

Mance, Euclides André, 'Práxis de Libertação e Subjetividade', in *Revista de Filosofia*, Curitiba: Pontifícia Universidade Católica do Paraná, June 1993, vol. 6, no. 7, pp. 81–109.

Martínez Lorca, Andrés, 'Adolfo Sánchez Vázquez, nuestro filósofo en Méjico', in *Sur*, Malaga: 23 October 1983. Republished in *Anthropos. Revista de documentación científica de la cultura*, Barcelona: August 1985, no. 52, pp. 35f.

Mikecin, Vjekoslav, 'Cuestiones marxistas disputadas' [interview by Vjekoslav Mikecin with Adolfo Sánchez Vázquez], in *Cuadernos Políticos*, Mexico City: January–March 1985, no. 42, pp. 5–19; and in *Mientras Tanto*, Barcelona: 1985, no. 24.

Mitchell S., [review of *Art and society. Essays in marxist aesthetics*] in *The Times Literary Supplement*, London: 1976, no. 3871, pp. 623f.

Monterrubio, Mara I., [review of *El mundo de la violencia*] in *Bien común y gobierno*, Mexico City: Fundacion Rafael Preciado Hernandez, January 1999, vol. 5, no. 50, pp. 125–7.

Montes SaMaya, Cintya Angélica, *La definición abierta de arte en la obra de Adolfo Sánchez Vázquez (1965–1980)*, philosophy licenciatura dissertation, Mexico City: UNAM, Facultad de Filosofía y Letras, 141 pp. [Unpublished. Advisor: Margarita Vera Cuspinera.]

Montiel, Miguel, 'Formalización estética', in *Lotería*, Panama: July 1979, no. 281, pp. 46–61.

Montiel, Oscar González, [review of *Invitación a la Estética*], in *Revista de Filosofía*, Mexico City: September–December 1994, vol. 27, no. 81, pp. 528–30.

Morales, Cesáreo, 'El marxismo inevitable' [review of *Filosofía y economía en el joven Marx*], in *Dialéctica. Revista de la Escuela de Filosofía y Letras de la Universidad Autónoma de Puebla*, Puebla: September 1982, no. 12, pp. 247–51. Republished in *Cuadernos americanos*, Mexico City: November–December 1982, vol. 245, no. 6, pp. 70–3.

Morales, Cesáreo, 'Una reconsideración de Marx: de las condiciones transcendentales de la acción a órdenes colectivos experimentales', in Juliana González, Carlos Pereyra and Gabriel Vargas Lozano (eds.), *Praxis y filosofía. Ensayos en homenaje a Adolfo Sánchez Vázquez*, Mexico City: Grijalbo, 1985, pp. 133–56.

Mosquera, Gerardo, 'Estética y marxismo en Cuba' [drafted as a prologue to the unpublished Cuban edition of *Estética y marxismo*], in *Cuadernos americanos*, Mexico City: UNAM, September–October 1991, pp. 169–86.

Mosquera, Gerardo, 'Sánchez Vázquez. Marxismo y arte abstracto', in *Temas. Estudios de la cultura*, Havana: 1986, no. 9, pp. 23–37.

Muñiz Huberman, Angelina, [review of *Del exilio en México*], in *La Jornada Semanal*. Supplement to *La Jornada*, Mexico City: 1 September 1991, no. 116, pp. 3f.

Nair, K., 'Prefacio a la traducción al francés' [with the title *La philosophie de la praxis comme nouvelle pratique de la philosophie*], in *L'homme et la société*, Paris: 1977, no. 43–4, pp. 141–9.

Olvera, Leticia, 'Homenaje a Sánchez Vázquez en Filosofía', in *Gaceta UNAM*, Mexico City: 20 October 2005, no. 3846, p. 5.

Ortiz Tejada, C., A. Huerta and A. Alatorre, 'La perestroika vista desde México', in *Utopías. Revista de la Facultad de Filosofía y Letras de la UNAM*, Mexico City: October–December 1989, no. 4, pp. 67–76.

Palazón Mayoral, María Rosa, 'Aproximacion dialogica a 'Cuestiones esteticas y artisticas contemporaneas' de Adolfo Sánchez Vázquez', in *Analogía. Revista de filosofía; investigación y difusión*, Mexico City: Centro de Estudios de la Provincia de Santiago de México de la Orden de Predicadores, 1997, vol. 11, no. 2, pp. 183–96.

Palazón Mayoral, María Rosa, 'La filosofía de la praxis según Adolfo Sánchez Vázquez', in Atilio A. Boron, Javier Amadeo, Sabrina González (eds.), *La teoría marxista hoy. Problemas y perspectivas*, Buenos Aires: Consejo Latinoamericano de Ciencias Sociales, 2006, pp. 309–23.

Paramio, Ludolfo, 'Reivindicación de Adolfo Sánchez Vázquez', in *El País*, Madrid: 30 November 1980.
Peikova, E.I., *The Aesthetic Ideas of Sánchez Vázquez* [in Russian], doctoral thesis in philosophical sccciences, Moskow: Universidad Lomnosov, 1986.
Peralta, Alfonso, 'La "etica" de Sánchez Vázquez', in *Hojas de crítica*, supplement to *Revista de la Universidad de México*, Mexico City: 1969, vol. 23, no. 11, pp. 4–6.
Pereda, Carlos, 'Una conversación con Adolfo Sánchez Vázquez', in *Theoría. Revista de filosofía*, Mexico City: UNAM, Facultad de Filosofía y Letras, February 1997, no. 4, pp. 101–12.
Pérez, Federico Augusto, *Alienation in six contemporary Spanish playwrights* [in Spanish], University Park, PA: The Pennsylvania State University, 1980. 265 pp. [doctoral thesis, partly about A.S.V.]
Poniatowska, Elena, 'Adolfo Sánchez Vázquez: los trabajos y los días' [review of Federico Álvarez Arregui (ed.), *Adolfo Sánchez Vázquez. Los trabajos y los días. Semblanzas y entrevistas*, Mexico City: UNAM, Facultad de Filosofía y Letras, 1995. 411 pp.], in *Vuelta*, Mexico City: December 1995, vol. 19, no. 229, pp. 60–4.
Primero Rivas, L.E., 'Filosofía y economía en el joven Marx', in *Plural. Revista mensual de Excélsior. Crítica y literatura*, Mexico City: January 1984, year 13, no. 148, pp. 43–7.
Ribeiro, Gilvan P., 'O marxismo de A. Sánchez Vázquez', in *Encontros com a Civilização Brasileira*, Rio de Janeiro: 1979, no. 8, pp. 69–79.
Sánchez Cuervo, Antolín, [Review of *Creación, estética y filosofía política: Mi recorrido intelectual*], in *Revista de Hispanismo Filosofico*, Madrid: Asociación de Hispanismo Filosófico/Fondo de Cultura Económica de España, 2008, no. 8, pp. 219–22.
Sasso, Javier, 'Sánchez Vázquez y los cuadros de la moral', in *Fragmentos*, Caracas: Centro de Estudios Latinoamericanos 'Romulo Gallegos', 1983, no. 15, pp. 82–117.
Solares, Ignacio, 'Sánchez Vázquez: siempre poeta', in *Revista de la Universidad de México*, Mexico City: UNAM, August 2011, new period, no. 90, pp. 31–4.
Souza, Miliandre Garcia de, [review of the book *Um convite a estetica*, Portuguese trans. of *Invitación a la estética*], in *Historia. Questoes & debates. Publicação semestral da Associação Paranaense de História (APAH) e do Programa de Pós-Graduação em História da UFPR*, Curitiba: Universidade Federal do Paraná, July–December 2002, vol. 19, no. 37, pp. 199–205.
Tomasini Bassols, Alejandro, [review of *Del socialismo científico al socialismo utópico*], in *Crítica*, Mexico City: UNAM, Facultad de Filosofía y Letras, August 1976, year 8, no. 23, pp. 133–6.
Valle-Castillo, 'Sánchez Vázquez, maestro de la estética marxista', in *Nuevo Amanecer Cultural* (Supplement to *El Nuevo Diario*), Managua: vol. 3, 8 May 1983, no. 151. Republished in *Anthropos. Revista de documentación científica de la cultura*, Barcelona: August 1985, no. 52, pp. 33–5.
Vargas, Angel, 'Alerta Sánchez Vázquez sobre una nueva barbarie a manos del capitalismo', *La Jornada*, Mexico City: 4 June 2003, p. 5.

Vargas, Angel, 'La Generación del 98 propició, en España, el pensador comprometido', *La Jornada*, Mexico City: 3 December 1998.

Vargas Lozano, Gabriel, 'Adolfo Sánchez Vázquez, doctorado honoris causa por la UAP', in *Dialéctica. Revista de filosofía, ciencias sociales, literatura y cultura política de la Universidad Autónoma de Puebla*, Puebla: December 1984, year 9, no. 16, pp. 9–12.

Vargas Lozano, Gabriel, 'El humanismo teórico-práctico de Adolfo Sánchez Vásquez', in *Utopía y praxis latinoamericana: revista internacional de filosofía iberoamericana y teoría social*, Maracaibo: Universidad del Zulia, July–September 2006, year. 11, no. 32, pp. 115–24.

Vargas Lozano, Gabriel, [review of *Filosofía y circunstancias*], in *Dialéctica. Revista de filosofía, ciencias sociales, literatura y cultura política de la Universidad Autónoma de Puebla*, Puebla. spring 1998, new period, year 22, no. 31, pp. 173–5.

Vargas Lozano, Gabriel, [review of *Filosofía y economía en el joven Marx*], in *Dialéctica. Revista de la Escuela de Filosofía y Letras de la Universidad Autónoma de Puebla*, Puebla: September 1982, vol. 7, no. 12, pp. 241–6.

Vargas Lozano, Gabriel, 'La obra filosófica de Adolfo Sánchez Vázquez', [as an introduction], in *Sobre filosofía y marxismo*, Puebla: Universidad Autónoma de Puebla, 1983. 111 pp., pp. 11–21, included in FM. Republished in *Anthropos. Revista de documentación científica de la cultura*, Barcelona: August 1985, no. 52, pp. 28–31, included in PF.

Vargas Lozano, Gabriel, 'La relación entre filosofía e ideología. Consideraciones sobre la polémica entre Adolfo Sánchez Vázquez y Luis Villoro', in *Islas. Revista de la Universidad Central de Las Villas*, Santa Clara, Cuba: May–August 1995, no. 111, pp. 164–76.

Vargas Lozano, Gabriel (ed.), *En torno a la obra de Adolfo Sánchez Vázquez. Filosofía, ética, estética, política*, Mexico City: UNAM, Facultad de Filosofía y Letras, 1995. 640 pp.

Various, 'Adolfo Sánchez Vázquez', issue dedicated to A.S.V. in *Anthropos. Revista de documentación científica de la cultura*, Barcelona: August 1985, no. 52, pp. 1–50.

Villoro, Luis, 'Dos comentarios al libro 'Filosofía y circunstancias' de Adolfo Sánchez Vázquez' [review of *Filosofía y circunstancias*], in *Dialéctica. Revista de filosofía, ciencias sociales, literatura y cultura política de la Universidad Autónoma de Puebla*, Puebla: spring 1998, new period, year 22, no. 31, pp. 171–3.

Woldenberg, José, [Review of *Ética y política*], in *Revista de la Universidad de México*, Mexico City: UNAM, December 2007, new period, no. 46, pp. 92–3.

Xirau, Ramón, *Estudios de historia de la filosofía en México*, third edition, Mexico City: UNAM, 1980, pp. 317–18. Reproduction of the pages about Sánchez Vázquez in *Anthropos. Revista de documentación científica de la cultura*, Barcelona: August 1985, no. 52, pp. 31f.

Xirau, Ramón, 'A. Sánchez Vázquez', in *Gaceta del Fondo de Cultura Económica*, Mexico City: January 2004, no. 397, pp. 15–16.

Reviews and Other Texts about the *Philosophy of Praxis*
Including various untitled reviews.
Anonymous, in *El Heraldo Cultural*. Supplement to *El Heraldo*, Mexico City: 4 June 1967, p. 14.
Anonymous, in *Punto Final. Revista de asuntos políticos, informativos y culturales*, Santiago de Chile: October 1967, no. 39.
Anonymous, in *Anthropos. Revista de documentación científica de la cultura*, Barcelona: August 1985, no. 52, pp. 49f.
Albert, Eduardo, 'Reflexiones en torno a la interpretación praxeológica del marxismo de Adolfo Sánchez Vázquez (un espacio abierto al debate con su autor)', in *Islas. Revista de la Universidad Central de las Villas*, Santa Clara, Cuba: January–April 1992, no. 101, pp. 84–100.
Bautista, Miguel, in *El Nacional*, Mexico City: 1 March 1981.
Burguete, Ricardo, in *Filosofskie Nauki*, Moscow, 1969, no. 1, pp. 138–40.
Cantarell Gamboa, Melvin, in *Revista de la Universidad*, Mexico City: vol. XXII, September 1967, no. 1.
Casalla, Mario C., in *Cuadernos de Filosofía*, Buenos Aires: Universidad de Buenos Aires, 1971.
Cogniot, Georges, in *La Pensée*, Paris: March–April 1968, no. 138, pp. 146f.
Flay, J.C., [review of *The Philosophy of Praxis*], in *Human Studies. A journal for philosophy and the social sciences*, Dordrecht: 1980, vol. 3, no. 2, pp. 190–5.
González de Luna, Tomás, 'La categoría de la "praxis" y el problema fundamental del conocimiento', in *Armas y letras. Revista de la Universidad de Nuevo León*, Monterrey: June–August 1970, third period, no. 2, pp. 40–51.
Gutiérrez Castañeda, Griselda, 'El marxismo como filosofía de la praxis', in Elsa Cecilia Frost *et al., Cincuenta años de Exilio Español en México*, Tlaxcala: Universidad Autónoma de Tlaxcala and Embajada de España en México, 1991. 215 pp., pp. 155–64. (Col. Materiales para la historia de la filosofía en México, no. 3.)
Jiménez, José, 'Marxismo y filosofía de la praxis', in Federico Álvarez Arregui (ed.), *Adolfo Sánchez Vázquez. Los trabajos y los días. Semblanzas y entrevistas*, Mexico City: UNAM, Facultad de Filosofía y Letras, 1995. 411 pp., pp. 283–6.
Kohan, Néstor, *Sánchez Vázquez y la Filosofía de la praxis*, Buenos Aires: Universidad de Buenos Aires, Facultad de Filosofía y Letras, c. 1993. 131 pp. [unpublished manuscript].
Labastida, Jaime, in *Política. Quince días de México y el mundo*, Mexico City: 1–14 September 1967, year 8, no. 175, pp. 55f.
Lang, Berel, [review of *The Philosophy of Praxis*], in *The New Republic*, Washington D.C.: 1 April 1978, vol. 178, no. 13, pp. 30f.
Palencia, José Ignacio, 'La práctica de la filosofía de la praxis', in Gabriel Vargas Lozano (ed.), *En torno a la obra de Adolfo Sánchez Vázquez*, Mexico City: UNAM, Facultad de Filosofía y Letras, 1995. 640 pp., pp. 255–65.

Pereyra, Carlos, 'Sobre la práctica teórica', in Juliana González, Carlos Pereyra and Gabriel Vargas Lozano (eds.), *Praxis y filosofía. Ensayos en homenaje a Adolfo Sánchez Vázquez*, Mexico City: Grijalbo, 1986. 491 pp., pp. 425–32.

Prestipino, Guiseppe, 'La filosofía de la praxis y el procedimiento de la ciencia', trans. Roberto Hernández Oramas, in Juliana González, Carlos Pereyra and Gabriel Vargas Lozano (eds.), *Praxis y filosofía. Ensayos en homenaje a Adolfo Sánchez Vázquez*, Mexico City: Grijalbo, 1985, pp. 21–37.

Santos Ribeiro, Maria Luísa, *Eduçacão escolar e práxis*, São Paulo: Iglu, 1991. 72 pp.

Santos Valdés, José, in *El Día*. Mexico City: 3 November 1969.

Swiderski, E.M., [review of *The Philosophy of Praxis*], in *Studies in Soviet Thought*, Freiburg: Universität Freiburg, Osteuropa-Institut, 1982, vol. 23, no. 1, pp. 80–5.

Vlăduiescu, Gh., 'Filozofia praxis-ului', in *Revista de Filosofie*, Bucharest: 1968, no. 5, pp. 645–7.

Xirau, Ramón, in *Diálogos. Artes, letras, ciencias humanas*, Mexico City: El Colegio de México, September–October 1967, no. 5 (17), pp. 36f. Republished in *Anthropos. Revista de documentación científica de la cultura*, Barcelona: August 1985, no. 52, p. 31.

i) **Existing Bibliographies about Sánchez Vázquez**

Anonymous: 'Bibliografía de y sobre Adolfo Sánchez Vázquez', in *Anthropos. Revista de documentación científica de la cultura*, Barcelona: August 1985, no. 52, pp. 19–25.

Anonymous: 'Bibliografía de Adolfo Sánchez Vázquez', in Juliana González, Carlos Pereyra and Gabriel Vargas Lozano (eds.), *Praxis y filosofía. Ensayos en homenaje a Adolfo Sánchez Vázquez*, Mexico City: Grijalbo, 1985, pp. 471–86.

Jiménez Álvarez, Oralia Leticia, *Adolfo Sánchez Vázquez. Bibliografía de un exiliado español* [undergraduate thesis in library science], Mexico City: UNAM, 1992. 273 pp. [Unpublished.] [With short summaries of some texts, as well as selected information about texts available in Mexico City libraries.]

Gandler, Stefan, 'Bibliografía selecta de Adolfo Sánchez Vázquez', in Gabriel Vargas Lozano (ed.), *En torno a la obra de Adolfo Sánchez Vázquez*, Mexico City: UNAM, Facultad de Filosofía y Letras, 1995, pp. 619–29.

B   **Bibliography of Bolívar Echeverría**

a)   *Books*

El discurso crítico de Marx, Mexico City: Era, 1986. 222 pp. (Col. El hombre y su tiempo.)

El problema de la nación desde la crítica de la economía política, Guatemala: Ediciones de la Universidad de San Carlos de Guatemala, 1988.

Sobre el materialismo. Modelo para armar, Mexico City: Facultad de Filosofía y Letras, UNAM, 1990, 12 pp. (Col. Cuadernos de apoyo a la docencia.) [Presented as an undergraduate thesis in philosophy, under the title *Apuntes para un comentario de las Tesis sobre Feuerbach*, in 1974 in the Facultad de Filosofía y Letras de la UNAM, Mexico City. 51 pp.]

La circulación capitalista y la reproducción de la riqueza social. (Apunte crítico sobre los 'Esquemas de reproducción' esbozados por K. Marx en 'El Capital'), Mexico City: UNAM, Facultad de Economía/Seminario de 'El Capital', 1992. 73 pp. [Presented as a master's thesis under the title *Apunte crítico sobre los esquemas de reproducción esbozados por K. Marx en El Capital*, in 1991 in the Facultad de Economía de la UNAM, Mexico City. 73 pp. Advisor: Pedro López Díaz.] Second ed.: *Circulación capitalista y reproducción de la riqueza social. Apunte crítico sobre los esquemas de K. Marx*. Mexico City/Quito: UNAM, Facultad de Economía/Nariz del Diablo, 1994. 103 pp.

Conversaciones sobre lo barroco, [in collaboration with Horst Kurnitzky.] Introduced by Marco Aurelio García Barrios. Mexico City: UNAM, Facultad de Filosofía y Letras, 1993. 87 pp.

Las ilusiones de la modernidad, Mexico City: UNAM/El Equilibrista, 1995. 200 pp. First reprint 1997. Republished: Quito: Tramasocial, 2001.

Valor de uso y utopía, Mexico City: Siglo XXI, 1998. 197 pp.

La modernidad de lo barroco, Mexico City: Era, 1998. 231 pp. [Originally a doctoral thesis in philosophy, Mexico City: UNAM, Facultad de Filosofía y Letras, with the title: *Lo barroco y la historia de la cultura*. 1997. 212 pp. Advisor: Carlos Pereda. Published as a book with some minor changes.]

La contradicción del valor y el valor de uso en 'El Capital' de Karl Marx, Mexico City: Itaca, 1998. 37 pp.

Definición de la cultura. Curso de Filosofía y Economía 1981–1982, Mexico City: Itaca/UNAM, Facultad de Filosofía y Letras, 2001. 275 pp.

Vuelta de siglo, Mexico City: Era, 2006. 272 pp.

Modernidad y blanquitud [posthumous edition, based on manuscript mainly finished by the author], Mexico City: Era, 2010. 243 pp.

Siete aproximaciones a Walter Benjamin [posthumous compilation by Carlos Antonio Aguirre Rojas], Bogotá: Ediciones Desde Abajo, 2010. 133 pp.

El materialismo de Marx. Discurso crítico y revolución. En torno a las tesis sobre Feuerbach de Karl Marx [posthumous compilation by Editorial Itaca], Mexico City: Itaca, 2011. 128 pp.

Crítica de la modernidad capitalista. Antología [posthumous compilation of articles and classroom audio recordings], La Paz: Vicepresidencia del Estado Plurinacional de Bolivia, 2011. 800 pp.

Ensayos políticos [posthumous compilation], introduction and selection by Fernando Tinajero [introduction is a partial reprint of the chapter 'The Life and Work of Bolívar Echeverría' in this book], Quito: Ministerio de Coordinación de la Política y Gobiernos Autónomas Descentralizados, 2011. 260 pp.

Discurso crítico y modernidad. Ensayos escogidos [posthumous compilation by Carlos Antonio Aguirre Rojas], Bogotá: Ediciones Desde Abajo, 2011. 351 pp.

Modelos elementales de la oposición campo-ciudad. Antotaciones a partir de una lectura de Braudel y Marx [posthumous compilation of classroom audio recordings], edited by Jorge Gasca Salas, Mexico City: Itaca, 2013. 107 pp.

b) *Articles*

When articles have later been incorporated into one of B.E.'s books (published up to 1998), this is referred to according to the following acronyms:

DC: *El discurso crítico de Marx*, 1986.
IM: *Las ilusiones de la modernidad*, 1995.
VU: *Valor de uso y utopía*, 1998.
MB: *La modernidad de lo barroco*, 1998.

In some specific cases, we detail the context of an oral presentation prior to the printed publication.

'De la posibilidad de cambio', in *Pucuna*, Quito: April 1965, no. 6, pp. 26–33. Previously published in abbreviated form, without the author's authorisation, in *Pucuna*, Quito: August 1964, no. 5, pp. 3–6.

'La intelectualidad en Latinoamérica. (Trabajos del seminario de la A.E.L.A.)', in *Latinoamérica. Revista bimestral publicada por la Secretaría General de la Asociación de Estudiantes Latinoamericanos en Alemania Occidental*, Göttingen: 1965, no. 2, pp. 8–18.

'Para el planteamiento general de la problemática de los movimientos revolucionarios del Tercer Mundo', in *La Bufanda del Sol. Revista Latinoamericana*. Quito: March–July 1966, no. 3–4, pp. 47–51.

'Rosa Luxemburgo en el cincuentenario de su sacrificio' [published under the pseudonym 'Javier Lieja'], in *Solidaridad*, Mexico City: Sindicato de Trabajadores Electricistas de la República Mexicana, 15 May 1969, no. 4, pp. 32–5. Reprinted [under the author's name], with the title 'Rosa Luxemburgo a los cincuenta años de su muerte', in *Letras del Ecuador*, Quito: Casa de la Cultura Ecuatoriana, August 1969, year 25, no. 143, pp. 34–8.

'Lenin y Rosa Luxemburg', [published under the psudonym 'Javier Lieja'], in *Solidaridad*, Mexico City: Sindicato de Trabajadores Electricistas de la República Mexicana, 15 February 1970, no. 14, pp. 39–41.

'¿Qué significa la palabra *Revolución*?', in *Procontra*, Quito: April 1971, no. 1, pp. 17–20.

'La revolución teórica comunista en las Tesis sobre Feuerbach', in *Historia y sociedad*, Mexico City: Summer 1975, no. 6, pp. 45–63. [Article version of the undergraduate thesis entitled *Apuntes para un comentario de las Tesis sobre Feuerbach*, 51 pp.] Also published, with the title 'Nota para un comentario de las "Tesis sobre Feuerbach"', in *Cuadernos del Seminario de El Capital*, Mexico City: UNAM, Facultad de Economía, January 1975, pp. 1–20. Republished as a book with the title: *Sobre el materialismo. Modelo para armar.* Included, with the title 'El materialismo de Marx', in DC.

'Discurso de la revolución, discurso crítico', in *Cuadernos Políticos*, Mexico City: October–December 1976, no. 10, pp. 44–53. Republished in Agustín Cueva (ed.), *Política y Sociedad*. Quito: 1976, Universidad Central, Escuela de Sociología, pp. 33–48. Included, with the title 'Definición del discurso crítico', in DC.

'Para lectores de *El Capital*', in *Investigación Económica. Revista de la Facultad de Economía*, Mexico City: UNAM, January–March 1977, no. 1, pp. 265–9.

'Para lectores de *El Capital*. Comentario 1', in *Investigación Económica. Revista de la Facultad de Economía*, Mexico City: UNAM, April–June 1977, new period, vol. 36, no. 2, pp. 245–50. Republished in 1979 as the first part of the article 'Comentario sobre el "punto de partida" de *El Capital*'.

'Para lectores de *El Capital*. Comentario dos: Sobre el "punto de partida" en *El Capital*', in *Investigación Económica. Revista de la Facultad de Economía*, Mexico City: UNAM, December 1977, new period, no. 4, pp. 219–37. Republished in 1979 as the second part of the article 'Comentario sobre el "punto de partida" de *El Capital*'.

'Esquemas gráficos para el estudio del capítulo quinto de *El Capital*', in *Investigación Económica. Revista de la Facultad de Economía*, Mexico City: UNAM, December 1977, new period, no. 4, pp. 237–46.

'La atípica Rosa Luxemburgo', in *Sábado*. Supplement to *Unomásuno*, Mexico City: March 1978, no. 77, pp. 2f.

'El concepto de fetichismo en el discurso revolucionario', in *Dialéctica, Revista de la Escuela de Filosofía y Letras de la Universidad Autónoma de Puebla*, Puebla: July 1978, year 3, no. 4, pp. 95–105. Republished in *La filosofía y las revoluciones sociales. Segundo coloquio Nacional de Filosofía*, Mexico City: Grijalbo, 1979. 271 pp., pp. 85–98. (Col. Teoría y praxis, no. 48.) [Speech given at the Segundo Coloquio Nacional de Filosofía, Monterrey, Nuevo León, 3–7 October 1977.]

'Comentario sobre el "punto de partida" de *El Capital*', in Pedro López Díaz et al., *El Capital: teoría, estructura y método*. Mexico City: Ediciones de Cultura Popular, 1979, pp. 29–67. Republished, with the title 'Sobre el "punto de partida" de *El Capital*', in Enrique Leff (ed.), *Teoría del valor*, Mexico City: UNAM, Dirección General de Publicaciones, 1980, pp. 85–112. Republished in *Cuadernos de la DEP* [División de Estudios de Posgrado], Mexico City: UNAM, Facultad de Economía, July 1981, pp. 1–38. Included in DC.

'Cuestionario sobre lo político', in *Palos de la crítica*, Mexico City: July–September 1980, no. 1. Included in DC.

'El problema de la nación (desde de la crítica de la economía política)', in *Cuadernos Políticos*, Mexico City: July–September 1981, no. 29, pp. 25–35. Republished in 1988 as a book. Included in DC.

'Text und Bild in der "Historieta"', in Barbara Beck (ed.), *Das ist Mexiko. México así es* [in the context of the exhibition *Wand Bild Mexiko*, Nationalgalerie Berlin, 5 May to 20 June 1982], Berlin (West): Frölich und Kaufmann, 1982. 47 pp., pp. 36–43.

'En la hora de la barbarie', in *El Buscón*, Mexico City: Metamorfosis, August 1983, no. 5, pp. 114–21. Republished in *Cuadernos de la* DEP, UNAM, Facultad de Economía, Mexico City: January 1985, pp. 1–24.

'En este número' [short commentary on Karl Marx's text: 'Subsunción formal y subsunción real del proceso de trabajo al proceso de valorización', published in this issue of the journal], in *Cuadernos Políticos*, Mexico City: July–September 1983, no. 37, p. 2.

'Aspectos generales del concepto de crisis en Marx', in *Ensayos. Economía, política e historia*, Mexico City: UNAM, Facultad de Economía, March 1984, vol. I, no. 1, pp. 7–14.

'Discurso crítico y desmitificación. El tema del salario', in *Ensayos. Economía, política e historia,* Mexico City: UNAM, Facultad de Economía, June 1984, vol. I, no. 2, pp. 42–8.

'La "forma natural" de la reproducción social', in *Cuadernos Políticos*, Mexico City: July–December 1984, no. 41, pp. 33–46. A revised version was published under the title 'El "valor de uso": ontología y semiótica', included in VU.

'La discusión de los años veinte en torno a la crisis. Grossmann y la teoría del derrumbe', in Pedro López Díaz (ed.), *La crisis del capitalismo. Teoría y práctica*, Mexico City: Siglo XXI, 1984, pp. 173–93.

'Aspectos generales del concepto de crisis en Marx', in *Ensayos. Economía, política e historia,* Mexico City: UNAM, Facultad de Economía, January 1985, pp. 1–24.

'Valor y Plusvalor (I)', in *Ensayos. Economía, política e historia,* Mexico City: UNAM, Facultad de Economía, February 1986, no. 2, pp. 1–25.

'Clasificación del plusvalor', in *Ensayos. Economía, política e historia*, Mexico City: UNAM, Facultad de Economía, July 1986, vol. II, no. 6, pp. 1–54.

'Valor y Plusvalor (II)', in *Ensayos. Economía, política e historia*, Mexico City: UNAM, Facultad de Economía, July 1986, vol. II, no. 8, pp. 56–65.

'Entre la barbarie y la utopía', in *La liebre ilustrada*, supplement to *Hoy*, Quito: November 1986, p. 8.

'Valor y Plusvalor', in *Cuadernos de la* DEP [División de Estudios de Posgrado], Mexico City: UNAM, Facultad de Economía, February 1987, pp. 1–29.

'Discurso crítico y desmitificación. El concepto de ganancia', in *Cuadernos de la* DEP [División de Estudios de Posgrado], Mexico City: UNAM, Facultad de Economía, September 1987, pp. 1–25.

'El concepto de fetichismo en Marx y Lukács', in Gabriela Borja Sarmiento (ed.), *Memoria del Simposio internacional György Lukács y su época*, Mexico City: Universidad Autónoma Metropolitana – Xochimilco, Departamento de Política y Cultura, 1988, pp. 209–22. A revised version, with the title 'Lukács y la revolución como salvación', is included in IM.

'¿La filosofía sólo es posible en Occidente?', in *Palabra Suelta*, Quito: June 1989, year 3, pp. 6–8.

'Heidegger y el ultranazismo'. In *La Jornada Semanal*. Mexico City: 10 de September 1989, new period, pp. 33–6. Expanded version included in IM. Republished in *La nariz del diablo*, Quito: December 1989, 2nd period, no. 14, pp. 66–72.

'Diecinueve tesis sobre modernidad y capitalismo', in *Cuadernos de la* DEP [División de Estudios de Posgrado], Mexico City: UNAM, Facultad de EconomíaMarch 1987, pp. 1–23, [new versions of this text, with important modifications, are published beginning in 1989 with the title 'Quince tesis sobre modernidad y capitalismo'].

'Discurso crítico y desmitificación. El concepto de ganancia', in *Cuadernos de la* DEP [División de Estudios de Posgrado], Mexico City: UNAM, Facultad de Economía, September 1987, pp. 1–25.

'Quince tesis sobre modernidad y capitalismo', in *Cuadernos Políticos*, Mexico City: September–December 1989, no. 58, pp. 41–62, republished, revised and with the title 'Modernidad y capitalismo. Quince tesis', [in Spanish] in *Review. A Journal of the Fernand Braudel Center for the Study of Economies, Historical Systems, and Civilisations*, Binghamton, NY: Autumn 1991, vol. 14, no. 4, pp. 471–515. Republished, further revised and with the title 'Modernidad y capitalismo (15 Tesis)', in Norbert Lechner *et al.*, *Debates sobre modernidad y postmodernidad*, Quito: Editores Unidos Nariz del Diablo, 1991. 187 pp. Included, with the latter title, in IM. [A first preliminary version was published in 1987 with the title 'Diecinueve tesis sobre modernidad y capitalismo'.]

'La Izquierda: reforma y revolución', in *Utopías. Revista de la Facultad de Filosofía y Letras*, Mexico City: UNAM, January–March 1990, no. 6, pp. 10–14. [Speech presented in the series 'Cuestiones políticas', organised by the Facultad de Filosofía y Letras of the UNAM, January 1990.] Included, with the title 'A la izquierda', in IM.

'Presentación' [in the monographical issue of the journal on the subject '1989: Doce meses que cambiaron a Europa del Este'], in *Cuadernos Políticos*, Mexico City: autumn 1990, no. 59. Included, with the title '1989', in IM.

'Europa del Este y América Latina', in C. Maya, F. Burgueño, Bolívar Echeverría *et al.*, *El sentido histórico del año 1989. Debate político*, Culiacán: Dirección de Investigación and Fomento de Cultura Regional, 1990. 118 pp., pp. 52–64.

'El dinero y el objeto del deseo', in *Debate feminista*, Mexico City: 1991, year 2, no. 4, pp. 155–60. Included in IM.

'Malintzin, la lengua', in *La Jornada Semanal*, Mexico City: 28 February 1993, new period, pp. 16–20. Republished in Margo Glantz (ed.), *La malinche, sus padres y sus hijos*, Mexico City: UNAM, Facultad de Filosofía y Letras, 1994, pp. 129–38. Included in MB.

'Ceremonia festiva y drama escénico', in *Cuicuilco. Arte, Estética y Antropología*, Mexico City: January–June 1993, no. 33/4, pp. 7–10.

'La actitud barroca en el discurso filosófico moderno', in *Teoría. Revista de Filosofía*, Mexico City: UNAM, Facultad de Filosofía y Letras July 1993, year 1, no. 1, pp. 53–66. Included in MB.

'El concepto de capitalismo en Braudel y Marx', in Carlos Antonio Aguirre Rojas *et al.*, *Primeras Jornadas Braudelianas*, Mexico City: Instituto de Investigaciones Dr. José María Luis Mora, 1993, pp. 54–70. Included, with some changes and under the title 'La comprensión y la crítica. (Braudel y Marx sobre el capitalismo)', in IM.

'Estilo barroco y *ethos* barroco', in B.E. and Horst Kurnitzky, *Conversaciones sobre lo barroco*. Mexico City: UNAM, Facultad de Filosofía y Letras, 1993, pp. 67–74.

'La fragmentación de Alberto Castro Leñero', in *La fragmentación*. Mexico City: ICON/Centro Cultural San Angel, 1993, pp. 3–6.

'Sobre el barroco romano y la Roma de Bernini', in B.E. and Horst Kurnitzky, *Conversaciones sobre lo barroco*, Mexico City: Universidad Nacional Autónoma de México, 1993, pp. 75–85.

'Postmodernismo y cinismo'. In *Viento del Sur. Revista de ideas, historia y política*, Mexico City: April 1994, year 1, no. 1, pp. 55–61. Republished, with the title 'Posmodernismo y cinismo', in Mariflor Aguilar Rivero (ed.), *Diálogos sobre filosofía contemporánea, modernidad, sujeto y hermenéutica*, Mexico City: UNAM, Coordinación de Humanidades/Asociación Filosófica de México, 1995, pp. 15–30. Included in IM with the title 'Postmodernidad y cinismo'.

'La identidad evanescente', in Enrique Hülsz Piccone and Manuel Ulacia (eds.), *Más allá del litoral*, Mexico City: UNAM, Facultad de Filosofía y Letras, 1994. 485 pp., pp. 389–403.

'El *ethos* barroco', in B.E. (ed.), *Modernidad, mestizaje cultural, 'ethos' barroco*, Mexico City: UNAM/El Equilibrista, 1994, pp. 13–36. Republished in *La nariz del diablo*, Quito: May 1994, second period, no. 20, pp. 27–45; and in *Debate feminista*, Mexico City: April 1996, year 7, vol. 13, pp. 67–87. [Theme of this issue: *Otredad*.] With some changes, included in MB.

'El mestizaje y las formas', in *Epitafios*, Mexico City: June 1994, no. 9, pp. 17–21.

'Las aventuras de la abstracción', in *Estructura Esencial. Francisco Castro Leñero* [Catalogue of the exhibition of the same name at the Museo de Arte Moderno, Mexico City: 27 October 1994 to 5 February 1995. The other author of the catalogue was Teresa del Conde.], Mexico City: La Sociedad Mexicana de Arte Moderno/Museo de Arte Moderno, 1994, pp. 27–38.

'La muerte de Dios y la modernidad como decadencia', in *Theoría. Revista del Colegio de Filosofía*, Mexico City: UNAM, Facultad de Filosofía y Letras, November 1995, no. 2, pp. 11–26. Republished in Herbert Frey (ed.), *La muerte de Dios y el fin de la metafísica (simposio sobre Nietzche)*, Mexico City: UNAM, Facultad de Filosofía y Letras, 1997. 161 pp., pp. 39–56. With the title 'La modernidad como "decadencia"', included in VU.

'En torno a la presencia de Adolfo Sánchez Vázquez', in *Boletín de la Facultad de Filosofía y Letras*, Mexico City: UNAM, November/December 1995, no. 7, pp. 10–12.

'Elogio del marxismo', in Gabriel Vargas Lozano (ed.), *En torno a la obra de Adolfo Sánchez Vázquez*, Mexico City: UNAM, Facultad de Filosofía y Letras, 1995, pp. 77–82.

'En torno a la presencia de Adolfo Sánchez Vázquez', in *Boletín Filosofía y Letras*, Mexico City: UNAM, Facultad de Filosofía y Letras, November–December 1995, no. 7, pp. 10–12.

'La Era de *Cuadernos Políticos*', in *Ediciones ERA 35años. Neus Espresate*, Guadalajara: Universidad de Guadalajara, 1995, pp. 35–40. (Col. Homenaje a un editor.)

'La transición histórica', in Carlos Barros (ed.), *A Historia a debate*. Volume: *América Latina*. Santiago de Compostela (Coruña): Historia a Debate, 1995, pp. 39–43.

'El ethos barroco y la estetización de la vida cotidiana', in *Escritos. Revista del Centro de Ciencias del Lenguaje*, Puebla: Universidad Autónoma de Puebla, January–December 1996, no. 13/14, pp. 161–88.

'Por una modernidad alternativa', in *Viento del Sur. Revista de ideas, historia y política*, Mexico City: Summer 1996, no. 7, pp. 57–61.

'En busca de una modernidad', in *Intercambio académico*, October–November 1996, no. 79/80, pp. 1–10.

'La compañía de Jesús y la primera modernidad de América Latina', in *Procesos. Revista ecuatoriana de historia*, Quito: 1996, no. 9, pp. 21–37. Republished in Petra Schumm (ed.), *Barrocos y modernos. Nuevos caminos en la investigación del Barroco iberoamericano*, Frankfurt am Main/Madrid: Vervuert/Iberoamericana, 1998. (Col. Berliner Lateinamerika-Forschungen, no. 8), pp. 49–65. Included in MB.

'Lo político en la política', in *Chiapas*, Mexico City: Era/UNAM, Instituto de Investigaciones Económicas, 1996, no. 3, pp. 7–17. Republished in *Theoría. Revista del Colegio de Filosofía*, Mexico City: UNAM, Facultad de Filosofía y Letras, February 1997, no. 4, pp. 11–21. Included in VU. Republished as *Lo político en la política. Exposición del autor en el Centro de Estudos Sociais de la Universidade de Coimbra, July 1996*, Coimbra, Portugal: 1996. 16 pp. [Pamphlet.]

'Modernidad y revolución', in Ruy Mauro Marini and Márgara Millán (eds.), *La teoría social latinoamericana*, volume IV, Mexico City: El Caballito, 1996.

'Deambular (Walter Benjamin y la cotidianidad moderna)', in *Dialéctica. Revista de filosofía, ciencias sociales, literatura y cultura política de la Universidad Autónoma de Puebla*, Puebla: spring 1997, new period, year 21, no. 29–30, pp. 72–9. Republished in *Debate Feminista*, Mexico City: April 1998, year 9, vol. 17, pp. 237–44.

'*Queer*, manierista, *bizarre*, barroco', in *Debate feminista*, Mexico City: October 1997, year 8, vol. 16, pp. 3–10. [Theme of this issue of the journal: *Raras rarezas*.]

'Benjamin mesianismo y utopía', in Patricia Nettel and Sergio Arroyo (eds.), *Aproximaciones a la Modernidad. París, Berlín, siglos XIX y XX*, Mexico City: Universidad Autónoma Metropolitana – Xochimilco, 1997, pp. 39–67. Republished in Laura Baca Olamendi and Isidro Cisneros H. (eds.), *Los intelectuales y los dilemas políticos en el siglo XX*, Mexico City: Facultad Latinoamericana de Ciencias Sociales [FLACSO]/Triana, 1997. Included in VU.

'Nietzsche. La decadencia y la "muerte de Dios" ', in Herbert Frey (ed.), *Nietzsche y la 'muerte de Dios'*, Mexico City: UNAM, Facultad de Filosofía y Letras, 1997.

'Carlos Pereyra y los tiempos del "desencanto". De la revolución a la modernización: un recentramiento', in *Universidad de México*, Mexico City: UNAM, October–November 1998, no. 573/4, pp. 47–9.

'Violencia y modernidad', in A. Sánchez Vázquez (ed.), *El mundo de la violencia*, Mexico City: UNAM, Facultad de Filosofía y Letras/Fondo de Cultura Económica, 1998, pp. 365–82. Included in VU.

'Lejanía y cercanía del manifiesto comunista. A ciento cincuenta años de su publicación', in *Viento del Sur. Revista de ideas, historia y política*, Mexico City: March 1999, year 5, no. 14, pp. 41–8.

'América como sujeto', in *Correo del maestro*, Mexico City: 2000, no. 53.

'Las distintas modernidades en América Latina', in *Presencia*, Universidad de San Carlos, Guatemala: 2001.

'Octavio Paz, muralista mexicano', in *Anuario de la Fundación Octavio Paz. Memoria del coloquio internacional 'Por el laberinto de la soledad a 50 años de su publicación'*, Mexico City: Fondo de Cultura Económica, 2001. 245 pp.

'El olmo y las peras', in *Universidad de México*, Mexico City: UNAM, April 2002, no. 610, pp. 52–5.

'Apuntes para salir de cierta Antropología de la miseria', in *Universidad de México*, Mexico City: UNAM, 2002.

'La injusticia de la Historia'. In *Los Universitarios*, Mexico City: UNAM, 2002.

'El discurso filosófico en América Latina', in *Universidad de México*, Mexico City: UNAM, 2002.

La dimensión cultural de la vida social, Quito: Casa de la Cultura Ecuatoriana Benjamín Carrión, 2002. 32 pp. [Booklet.]

'El sentido del siglo XX', in *ESECONOMÍA. Revista de la Escuela Superior de Economía*, Instituto Politécnico Nacional, Mexico City: winter 2002–3, no. 2.

'Desalojo', in *Universidad de México*, Mexico City: UNAM, April 2003, no. 622, pp. 62f.

'Como en un espejo', in *Universidad de México*, Mexico City: UNAM, June 2003, new period, no. 624, pp. 6of.

'Homo legens', in *Universidad de México*, Mexico City: UNAM, July–August 2003, no. 11, pp. 12–15.

'La religión de los modernos', in *Fractal*, Mexico City: autumn 2002, year 7, no. 26, pp. 101–12. Republished in Hermann Herlinghaus (ed.), *Fronteras de la Modernidad en América Latina*, Pittsburgh: University of Pittsburgh, Instituto Internacional de Literatura Iberoamericana, 2003, 309 pp.

'La historia como desencubrimiento', in *Contrahistorias*, Mexico City: September 2003–February 2004, no. 1, pp. 29–34.

'El juego, la fiesta y el arte', in Patricia Ducoing (ed.), *Lo otro, el teatro y los otros*, Mexico City: UNAM, Centro de Investigaciones Interdisciplinarias en Ciencias y Humanidades, 2003. 246 pp.

'Teratológica', in *Universidad de México*, Mexico City: UNAM, December 2003–January 2004, new period, no. 630–1, p. 79.

'¿Un socialismo barroco?', in *Diánoia. Anuario de Filosofía*, UNAM, Instituto de Investigaciones Filosóficas, Mexico City: November 2004, year 49, no. 53, pp. 125–7.

'La historia como desencubrimiento', in *Contrahistorias. La otra miradad de Clío*. Mexico City: September 2004–February 2005, vol. 1, no. 1, pp. 29–34.

'El breve siglo veinte mexicano', in *Contrahistorias. La otra miradad de Clío*. Mexico City: March–August 2005, no. 4, pp. 39–54 [together with Carlos Monsivais].

'La múltiple modernidad de América Latina', in *Contrahistorias. La otra miradad de Clío*. Mexico City: March–August 2005, no. 4, pp. 57–70.

' "Renta Tecnológica" y Capitalismo Histórico', in *Mundo siglo XXI*, Mexico City: Summer 2005, no. 2, pp. 18–20.

'Lefebvre y la crítica de la modernidad', in *Veredas. Revista del Pensamiento Sociológico*, Mexico City: January–June 2006, vol. 7, no. 12, pp. 33–7.

'Alonso Quijano y los indios', in *Revista de la Universidad de México*, Mexico City: May 2006, new period, no. 27, pp. 21–6.

'El humanismo del existencialismo', in *Diánoia*, Mexico City: November 2006, vol. 51, no. 57, pp. 189–99.

'Acepciones de la ilustración', in *Mundo siglo XXI*, Mexico City: Fall 2007, no. 10, pp. 5–10. Republished in *Contrahistorias. La otra mirada de Clío*, Mexico City: September 2007–February 2008, no. 9, pp. 39–46.

'Un concepto de modernidad', in *Contrahistorias. La otra mirada de Clío*, Mexico City: September 2008–February 2009, no. 11, pp. 7–18.

'De la academia a la bohemia y más allá', in *Theoría. Revista del Colegio de Filosofía*. Mexico City: UNAM, Facultad de Filosofía y Letras, June 2209, no. 19, pp. 49–62.

'Independientes, ¿quiénes?', in *Casa de las Américas*, Havana: October–December 2009, year. 49, no. 257, pp. 124–5.

'Crítica a "La posibilidad de una Teoría Crítica" de György Márkus', in *Mundo siglo XXI*, Mexico City: June 2012, no. 21, pp. 9–12.

'Una introducción a la Escuela de Frankfurt', in *Contrahistorias. La otra mirada de Clío*, Mexico City: September 2010–February 2011, vol. 8, no. 15, pp. 19–50.

'Una Lección sobre Walter Benjamin', in *Contrahistorias. La otra mirada de Clío*, Mexico City: September 2010–February 2011, vol. 8, no. 15, pp. 51–62.

'El aporte político de Rosa Luxemburgo', in *Contrahistorias. La otra mirada de Clío*, Mexico City: September 2010–February 2011, vol. 8, no. 15, pp. 63–78.

'América Latina: 200 años de fatalidad', in *Contrahistorias. La otra mirada de Clío*, Mexico City: September 2010–February 2011, vol. 8, no. 15, pp. 79–85.

c) *Existing Translations*
The title of the Spanish original is noted in brackets.

To German
'Postmoderne und Zynismus. Revolution, Nation und Demokratie – die drei Mythen der Moderne' ['Postmodernidad y cinismo', slightly summarised], trans. Stefan Gandler, in *Die Beute. Politik und Verbrechen*, Berlin, Autumn 1996, year 3, no. 11, pp. 80–94.

d) *Prologues, Book and Film Reviews*
When the prologues and reviews have a particular title, these appear in brackets at the end of the note.

Prologues
Benjamin, Walter, *El autor como productor*, trans. Bolívar Echeverría, Mexico City: Itaca, 2004. 60 pp.
Benjamin, Walter, *La obra de arte en la época de su reproductibilidad técnica*, trans. Andrés Echeverría Weikert. Mexico City: Itaca, 2003. 127 pp. ['Arte y utopía'.] Republished: Quito: Rayuela/Diagonal, 2010.
Benjamin, Walter, *Tesis sobre el concepto de la historia y otros fragmentos*, trans. Bolívar Echeverría, Mexico City: Contrahistorias, 2005. 67 pp. ['Benjamin, la condición judía y la política'.]
Echeverría, Bolívar and Carlos Castro (eds.), *Sartre, los intelectuales y la política*, Mexico City: Siglo XXI, 1969. [Sixth ed: 1980, Prologue by Carlos Castro Valverde.]
Frank, André Gunder, Ernesto [*Ché*] Guevara et al., *Kritik des bürgerlichen Antiimperialismus. Entwicklung der Unterentwicklung. Acht Analysen zur neuen Revolutionstheorie in Lateinamerika*, [preface by Horst Kurnitzky], Berlin (West): Wagenbach, 1969 (Col. Rotbuch, no. 15.), pp. 7–13. [Second edition, 1975, with the title *Lateinamerika. Entwicklung der Unterentwicklung*, 142 pp. (Col. Politik, no. 15.)]
Guevara, Ernesto Che, *¡Hasta la victoria, siempre! Eine Biographie mit einer Einführung von Bolívar Echeverría*, comp. Horst Kurnitzky, trans. Alex Schubert. Berlin (West): Peter von Maikowski, 1968. 208 pp., pp. 7–18.
Horkheimer, Max, *Estado Autoritario*, trans. Bolívar Echeverría, Mexico City: Itaca, 2006.
López Díaz, Pedro (ed.), *Marx y la crisis del capitalismo*, Mexico City: Quinto Sol, 1986, pp. 7–10.

Luxemburgo, Rosa, *Obras escogidas. Escritos políticos*, two volumes, Mexico City: Era, 1978 and 1981, pp. 9–26 (vol. I) and pp. 9–23 (vol. II). Included, with the title: 'Rosa Luxemburgo. Espontaneidad revolucionaria e internacionalismo', in DC.

Mercado, Pedro de, *Destrucción del ídolo: ¿qué dirán?*, Mexico City: UNAM/Porrúa, 2004. 163 pp. ['Un enemigo hecho de voces. El padre Pedro de Mercado S.J. y el nuevo catolicismo en el nuevo mundo.']

Book and Film Reviews

Aguirre Rojas, Carlos Antonio, *Antimanual del mal historiador. O ¿Cómo hacer hoy una buena historia crítica?* Mexico City: Ed. Contrahistorias, 2005. Reviewed in *Contrahistorias. La otra mirada de Clío*, Mexico City: September 2010–February 2011, vol. 8, no. 15, pp. 89–91.

Álvarez Arregui, Federico, *La respuesta imposible*, Mexico City: Siglo XXI, 2002. Reviewed in *Theoría. Revista del Colegio de Filosofía*, Mexico City: UNAM, June 2003, no. 14–15, pp. 193–7. ['Federico Alvarez y el elogio del eclecticismo'.]

Burnier, Michel-Antoine, *Les existentialistes et la politique*. Paris: Gallimard, 1966. 109 pp. Reviewed in *Revista de la Universidad de México*, Mexico City: UNAM, August 1967, vol. XXI, no. 12, pp. 32–4.

Castañón, Adolfo, *Cercanía de Montaigne*. Mexico City: Ensayo, 1995. (Col. Cuadernos de Montaigne.) Reviewed in *Theoría. Revista del Colegio de Filosofía*, Mexico City: UNAM, Facultad de Filosofía y Letras, March 1996, no. 3, pp. 155–60. ['Cercanía de Montaigne'.]

Díaz Polanco, Héctor *et al.*, *La nación contra las culturas nacionales*. Reviewed in *Cuadernos Políticos*. Mexico City: December 1987, pp. 4f.

Martiarena, Oscar, *Culpabilidad y resistencia. Ensayo sobre la confesión en los indios de la Nueva España*. Mexico City: Universidad Iberoamericana, Departamento de Historia, 1999. 228 pp. Reviewed in *Theoría. Revista del Colegio de Filosofía*. Mexico City: UNAM, Facultad de Filosofía y Letras, December 2001, no. 11–12, pp. 151–6. ['Una ambigüedad histórica'.]

Ruy Guerra: *Os Fuzis*, 1964. Film, reviewed in *Pucuna*, Quito: April 1965, no. 6, pp. 7–10. [' "Los fusiles", Brazilian film by Ruy Guerra (1963)'.]

Tablada, José Juan, *En el país del sol*. Mexico City: UNAM, 2006. Reviewed in *Literatura mexicana*, Mexico City, 2007, vol. 18, no. 2, pp. 221–8. ['Tulipanes en suelo de nopales. El "modernismo" literario y el primer "japonismo" de José Juan Tablada'.]

Various, *Los escritores contra Sartre*, Buenos Aires: Proteo, 1966. Reviewed in *Revista de la Universidad de México*, Mexico City: UNAM, March 1967, vol. XXI, no. 7, pp. 27–30.

Villoro, Luis, *El poder y el valor, fundamentos de una ética política*, Mexico City: Fondo de Cultura Económica, 1997. Reviewed in *Theoría. Revista del Colegio de Filosofía*, Mexico City: UNAM, June 2000, no. 10, pp. 145–8. ['Hacia una ética disruptiva'.]

e) *Interviews*

Cue, Alberto, 'Por una modernidad alternativa. Entrevista con Bolívar Echeverría', in *La Jornada Semanal*. Supplement to *La Jornada*. Mexico City: 2 June 1996, pp. 10f.

Aguirre Rojas, Carlos Antonio, 'Chiapas y la conquista inconclusa. Entrevista con Bolívar Echeverría', in *Chiapas*, Era/UNAM, Instituto de Investigaciones Económicas, Mexico City: 2001, no. 11, pp. 45–59. Republished in Carlos Antonio Aguirre Rojas (ed.), *Chiapas en perspectiva histórica*, Barcelona: Viejo Topo, 2001. 178 pp.

Fernando Rojas, 'Entrevista a Bolívar Echevería' [video recordings], Havana: Videoteca Contracorriente del ICAIC [Instituto Cubano del Arte e Industria Cinematográficos]. available at: http://www.youtube.com/watch?v=lTnGZSz5Qrs.

f) *Translations of Works by Other Authors*

The titles of the respective originals, if these could be determined, are noted in brackets at the end of the note.

From German

Benjamin, Walter, 'El autor como productor', in *La Cultura en México*, supplement to *Siempre!*, Mexico City: 1971. Republished as a book: *El autor como productor*, Mexico City: Itaca, 2004. 60 pp. ['Der Autor als Produzent'.]

Benjamin, Walter, *Tesis sobre el concepto de la historia y otros fragmentos*, with an introduction by Bolívar Echeverría, Mexico City: Contrahistorias, 2005, 67 pp. Republished: Mexico City: Itaca/Universidad Autónoma de la Ciudad de México, 2008.

Brecht, Bertolt, 'La efectividad de las antiguas obras de arte', in A. Sánchez Vázquez (ed.), *Estética y Marxismo* [two volumes], *Volume 1: Comunismo y arte*, Mexico City: Era, 1970, p. 330.

Brecht, Bertolt, 'El formalismo y las formas', in A. Sánchez Vázquez (ed.), *Estética y Marxismo* [two volumes], *Volume 1: Comunismo y arte*, Mexico City: Era, 1970, pp. 230–3.

Brecht, Bertolt, 'El Goce Artístico', in A. Sánchez Vázquez (ed.), *Estética y Marxismo* [two volumes], *Volume 1: Comunismo y arte*, Mexico City: Era, 1970, p. 210.

Brecht, Bertolt, 'Juanita, la pirata', in *Pucuna*, Quito: April 1965, no. 6, p. 11. ['Die Seeräuber-Jenny'.]

Brecht, Bertolt, 'Meti. El libro de las variaciones', in *Casa de las Américas*, Havana: September–October 1967, no. 44, pp. 62–82. ['Meti. Buch der Wendungen'.]

Brecht, Bertolt, 'Novedades formales y refuncionalización artística', in A. Sánchez Vázquez (ed.), *Estética y Marxismo*, vol. 2, *Estética comunista*, Mexico City: Era, 1970, pp. 161f.

Brecht, Bertolt, 'Del realismo burgués al realismo socialista', in A. Sánchez Vázquez (ed.), *Estética y Marxismo*, vol. 2, *Estética comunista*, Mexico City: Era, 1970, pp. 250–5.

Brecht, Bertolt, 'Sobre el modo realista de escribir', in A. Sánchez Vázquez (ed.), *Estética y Marxismo*, vol. 2, *Estética comunista*. Mexico City: Era, 1970, pp. 59–73.

Habermas, Jürgen, 'La soberanía popular como procedimiento', in *Cuadernos Políticos*, Mexico City: May–August 1989, no. 57, pp. 53–69.

Horkheimer, Max, 'El Estado Autoritario', in *Palos de la crítica*, Mexico City, July–September 1980, no. 1, pp. 113–35. ['Autoritärer Staat']. Republished as book: *Estado Autoritario*, prologue Bolívar Echeverría, Mexico City: Itaca, 2006.

Kozlik, Adolf, *El capitalismo del desperdicio. El milagro económico norteamericano*, Mexico City: Siglo XXI, 1968. 364 pp. (Col. El mundo del hombre. Economía y demografía.) [*Der Vergeudungskapitalismus. Das amerikanische Wirtschaftswunder.* Vienna: Ed. Europa, 1966. (Col.: Europäische Perspektiven.)]

Marx, Karl, *Cuadernos de París. Notas de lectura de 1844*, with an introductory study by Adolfo Sánchez Vázquez, Mexico City: Era, 1974. [Second edition: 1980.] 192 pp. (Col. El hombre y su tiempo.)

Marx, Karl, 'Subsunción formal y subsunción real del proceso de trabajo al proceso de valorización' [extracts from the 1861–3 *Manuscripts*, comp. B.E.], in *Cuadernos Políticos*, Mexico City: July–September 1983, no. 37, pp. 5–14.

Marx, Karl, 'La tecnología del capital. Subsunción formal y subsunción real del proceso de trabajo al proceso de valorización (extractos del manuscrito 1861–1863)' [comp. B.E.] Mexico City: Itaca, 2005. 61 pp.

Marx, Karl, 'La mercancía', in *Anales. Revista de la Universidad Central el Ecuador.* Quito: 1976, no. 354, pp. 7–58.

Musil, Robert, 'La casa encantada', in *Palos*, Mexico City: 1981, no. 2 [translated with Ingrid Weikert].

From French

Echeverría, Bolívar and Carlos Castro Valverde (eds.), *Sartre, los intelectuales y la política*, Mexico City: Siglo XXI, 1969. 106 pp. [Sixth edition: 1980. Trans. with Carlos Castro Valverde.]

Sartre, Jean-Paul, 'La larga noche del socialismo', in *La Cultura en México*, supplement to *Siempre!*, Mexico City: 1970.

Sartre, Jean-Paul, 'El socialismo que llegó del frío', in *La Cultura en México*, Mexico City: 1978.

g)   *Collaboration on Editorial Boards and Editorial Tasks*
   Collaboration on Journal Editorial Boards

Latinoamérica. Revista bimestral publicada por la Secretaría General de la Asociación de Estudiantes Latinoamericanos en Alemania Occidental (A.E.L.A.). Göttingen: 1965–8.

Cuadernos Políticos, [every four months], Mexico City: Era, 1974–1990. [Echeverría was a founding member of this journal and worked on it until its final issue.]

Editorial Tasks

Echeverría, Bolívar (ed.), *Modernidad, mestizaje cultural, ethos barroco*. Mexico City: UNAM/El Equilibrista, 1994. 393 pp. [With contributions by Bolívar Echeverría, Carlos Pereda, Xavier Rubert de Ventós, Horst Kurnitzky, Solange Alberro, Antonio García de León, Raquel Serur, Carlos Espinosa Fernández de Córdoba, María Alba Pastor, Teresa del Conde, Margo Glantz, Jorge Alberto Manrique, Javier G. Vilaltella, Petra Schumm, Carlos Monsiváis, Boaventura de Sousa Santos, Gonzalo Celorio and Carlos Rincón.]

Echeverría, Bolívar (ed.), *La Mirada del ángel. En torno a las 'Tesis sobre la historia' de Walter Benjamin*, Mexico City: UNAM/Era. 2005. 252 pp.

Echeverría, Bolívar (ed.), *La americanización de la modernidad*, Mexico City: UNAM/Era. 2008. 307 pp.

Echeverría, Bolívar and Carlos Castro Valverde (eds.), *Sartre, los intelectuales y la política*, (with Carlos Castro Valverde). Mexico City: Siglo XXI, 1969. [Sixth edition, 1980].

Frank, André Gunder, Ernesto Ché Guevara, et al., *Kritik des bürgerlichen Antiimperialismus. Entwicklung der Unterentwicklung. Acht Analysen zur neuen Revolutionstheorie in Lateinamerika*, Berlin (West): Wagenbach, 1969. 188 pp. (Col. Rotbuch, no. 15) [Second edition, 1975, with the title: *Lateinamerika. Entwicklung der Unterentwicklung*. 142 pp. (Col. Politik, no. 15.) Prologue with Horst Kurnitzky.]

Luxemburgo, Rosa, *Obras escogidas. Escritos Políticos I*, Mexico City: Era, 1978.

Luxemburgo, Rosa, *Obras escogidas. Escritos Políticos II*, Mexico City: Era, 1981.

h) *Literature about Bolívar Echeverría*

Aguilar Piña, René, *Historia, modernidad y discurso crítico en América Latina. Un estudio sobre el concepto de Ethos histórico de Bolívar Echeverría*, master's thesis in Latin American Studies, Mexico City: UNAM, Facultad de Filosofía y Letras, 2003. 108 pp. [Unpublished. Advisor: José Antonio Matesanz Ibañez.]

Arriarán Cuéllar, Samuel, 'Una alternativa socialista al ethos barroco de Bolívar Echeverría', in *Diánoia. Anuario de Filosofía*, UNAM, Instituto de Investigaciones Filosóficas, Mexico City: November 2004, vol. 49, no. 53, pp. 111–24.

Bartra, Roger, 'Definición de la cultura. A propósito de un libro de Bolívar Echeverría' [review of *Definición de la cultura*], in *Universidad de México*, Mexico City: UNAM, February 2002, no. 608, pp. 74–6.

Beuchot, Mauricio, [review of *Definicion de la cultura*], in *Analogía. Revista de filosofía; investigación y difusión*, Mexico City: Centro de Estudios de la Provincia de Santiago de México de la Orden de Predicadores, 2002, vol. 16, no. 2, pp. 183–6.

Bosteels, Bruno, 'El materialismo de Marx según Bolívar Echeverría', [paper presented at the XXXI International Congress of the Latin American Studies Association, Washington, DC, 29 May–1 June 2013]. Available at http://www.academia.edu/3631790/El_materialismo_de_Marx_segun_Bolivar_Echeverria.

Castañón, Adolfo, 'El barroco: una forma de ser' [review of: Echeverría, Bolívar (ed.), *Modernidad, mestizaje cultural*, ethos barroco. Mexico City: UNAM/El Equilibrista, 1994. 393 pp.], in *Theoría. Revista del Colegio de Filosofía*, Mexico City: UNAM, Facultad de Filosofía y Letras, November 1995, no. 2, pp. 171–6.

Cuéllar, Samuel Arriarán, 'Una alternativa socialista al ethos barroco de Bolívar Echeverría', in *Diánoia*, Mexico City: November 2004, vol. 49, no. 53, pp. 111–24.

Escogido Clausen, Ylenia, *Cuatro filósofos ante la Tesis XI. (Bloch, Althusser, Sánchez Vázquez, Echeverría)*, undergraduate thesis, Mexico City: UNAM, Facultad de Filosofía y Letras, 1998. 44 pp. [Unpublished. Advisor: Margarita Vera Cuspinera.]

Fuentes, Diana; Isaac García Venegas and Carlos Oliva Mendoza (eds.), *Bolívar Echeverría. Crítica e interpretación*, Mexico City: UNAM/Itaca, 2012. 465 pp.

Gandler, Stefan, 'Alltag in der kapitalistischen Moderne aus peripherer Sicht. Nichteurozentrische Theoriebeiträge aus Mexiko', in *Review. A Journal of the Fernand Braudel Center*, Binghamton, NY: Fall 2003, year XXVI, no. 3, pp. 407–22.

Gandler, Stefan, 'Bolívar Echeverría (1941–2010)', in *Das Argument. Zeitschrift für Philosophie und Sozialwissenschaften*, Berlin: October 2010, year 52, vol. 288, no. 4–5, p. 10.

Gandler, Stefan, 'Bolívar Echeverría para "dummies"', in *El Comercio*, Quito: 10 November 2013.

Gandler, Stefan, 'Der barocke Charme der Moderne. Echeverrías Philosophie einer (nicht–) kapitalistischen Gesellschaft', in *iz3w. Blätter des Informationszentrums Dritte Welt*, Freiburg: February/March 2001, no. 251, pp. 14–16.

Gandler, Stefan, *El discreto encanto de la modernidad. Ideologías contemporáneas y su crítica*. Mexico City/Querétaro: Siglo XXI Editores/Universidad Autónoma de Querétaro, 2013, pp. 96–121.

Gandler, Stefan, 'El intelectual de la emancipación', in *Masiosare. Política y sociedad*, Supplement of *La Jornada*, Mexico City: 23 October 2005, no. 409, pp. 7–8.

Gandler, Stefan, 'In Memoriam Bolívar Echeverría', in *International Sociology*, London: March 2011, vol. 26, no. 2, pp. 266–7.

Gandler, Stefan, [introduction to] Bolívar Echeverría, 'Postmoderne und Zynismus. Revolution, Nation und Demokratie – die drei Mythen der Moderne', in *Die Beute. Politik und Verbrechen*, Berlin: Fall 1996, year 3, no. 11, pp. 80f.

Gandler, Stefan, 'Kulturtheorie in Mexiko. Das viergesichtige Ethos der kapitalistischen Moderne', in *Jura Soyfer. Internationale Zeitschrift für Kulturwissenschaften*, Vienna: Spring 2001, year 10, no. 1, pp. 11–16.

Gandler, Stefan, 'Meksika'da Elestirel Teori', in *Felsefelogos*, Istanbul: Buluy Yayinlari, September 2002, year 6, no. 19, pp. 73–8.

Gandler, Stefan, 'Mestizaje cultural y ethos barroco. Una reflexión intercultural a partir de Bolívar Echeverría', in *Signos filosóficos*, Mexico City: Universidad Autónoma

Metropolitana – Iztapalapa, January–June 2000, vol. 1, no. 3, pp. 53–73. Republished in *Itinerarios,* Warsaw: University of Warsaw, Institute of Iberian and Iberian-American Studies, 2001, no. 4, pp. 77–98.

Gandler, Stefan, 'Primeras aportaciones para una teoría crítica no eurocéntrica. Marxismo occidental bajo el volcán', in *Argumentos. Estudios críticos de la sociedad,* Mexico City: Universidad Autónoma Metropolitana – Xochimilco, August 2001, no. 39, pp. 117–35.

Gandler, Stefan, 'Producir y significar', [review of *Definición de la cultura. Curso de Filosofía y Economía 1981–1982.*], in *Polylog. Forum für interkulturelles Philosophieren,* Vienna: Winter 2003, no. 4. Available online at: <http://lit.polylog.org/4/rgs-es.htm > (consulted 12 June 2005).

Gandler, Stefan, '¿Quién es Bolívar Echeverría?', in *La Jornada Semanal,* Supplement of *La Jornada,* Mexico City: 8 August 2010, no. 805, pp. 5–7.

Gandler, Stefan, ' "Reconocimiento del otro" vs "mestizaje cultural". La convivencia de culturas diferentes bajo el ethos realista o bajo el ethos barroco', in *Memorias del Tercer Congreso Europeo de Latinoamericanistas,* Amsterdam: July 2002 (CD-Rom).

Gandler, Stefan, 'Reification versus ethos moderne. Conscience quotidienne en Georg Lukács et Bolívar Echeverría', in *Actuel Marx en Ligne,* Paris: 3 de November 2003, no. 26, available at: <http://netx.u-paris10.fr/actuelmarx/mainnfm.htm> (consulted 12 June 2005).

Gandler, Stefan, 'Sozialphilosophie in Mexiko. Adolfo Sánchez Vázquez und Bolívar Echeverría'. In *Concordia. Internationale Zeitschrift für Philosophie,* Aachen: October 2001, no. 40, pp. 27–44.

Gandler, Stefan, ' "Verdinglichung" versus "Ethos der kapitalistischen Moderne". Zur Lukács-Rezeption in Lateinamerika', in Frank Benseler y Werner Jung (eds.), *Jahrbuch der Internationalen Georg-Lukács-Gesellschaft,* Berlin: Aisthesis, September 2000, vol. 4, pp. 95–114.

Gandler, Stefan, 'Zum Ethos-Begriff in der heutigen lateinamerikanischen Philosophie', in *Deutsche Zeitschrift für Philosophie,* Berlin: November 2006, year 54, no. 5, pp. 767–83.

García Barrios, Marco Aurelio, 'Bolívar Echeverría', in *Educación UACM,* Mexico City: La Jornada/Universidad Autónoma de la Ciudad de México, 3 July 2010, no. 12, p. 15.

García Barrios, Marco Aurelio, *Economía y cultura política barroca en América Latina,* economics licenciatura dissertation, Mexico City: UNAM, Facultad de Economía, 1993. 89 pp. [Unpublished.]

García Barrios, Marco Aurelio, *Lo político y el ethos histórico en el México del siglo XX,* master's thesis in political analysis, Querétaro: Universidad Autónoma de Querétaro, Facultad de Ciencias Políticas y Sociales, 2002. 131 pp. [Unpublished. Advisor: Stefan Gandler.]

Gilly, Adolfo, 'Lo que el ángel miraba: Bolívar Echeverría. Violencia y utopía', in *Revista de la Universidad de México*, Mexico City: UNAM, February 2011, new period, no. 84, pp. 42–6.

Gilly, Adolfo, 'Polifonía para un maestro', in *La Jornada*, Mexico City: 16 November 2012. p. 16.

Grave, Crescenciano, 'Esencia y crítica de la modernidad' [review of: Bolívar Echeverría, *Las ilusiones de la modernidad*], in *Theoría. Revista del Colegio de Filosofía*, Mexico City: UNAM, Facultad de Filosofía y Letras, March 1996, no. 3, pp. 173–8.

Labastida, Jaime, 'Bolivar Echeverría. Pensador que permanecerá', in *Revista de la Universidad de México*, Mexico City: UNAM, July 2010, new period, no. 77, pp. 50–1.

Leal Fernández, Gustavo, *La crítica de la economía política en los tres libros de El Capital*, doctoral thesis, Mexico City: UNAM, Facultad de Economía, 1981. [Unpublished.]

Leyva, Gustavo, 'La teoría crítica en México', in *Theoría. Revista de filosofía*, Mexico City: UNAM, Facultad de Filosofía y Letras, December 2001, no. 11–12, pp. 133–47.

Habermann, Friederike, 'Zapatistischer Nationalismus? Einige Gedanken zum Thema Nation', in *Friedolin. Zeitschrift für Kriegsdienstverweigerung und Gewaltfreiheit*. Graz: Arbeitsgemeinschaft für Kriegsdienstverweigerung und Gewaltfreiheit, 1997, no. 1.

Manrique, Jorge Alberto, 'Conversando acerca de unas conversaciones (sobre lo barroco)', in B.E. (ed.), *Modernidad, mestizaje cultural, 'ethos' barroco*, Mexico City: UNAM/El Equilibrista, 1994.

Moreano, Alejandro; Rosa Echeverría and Fernando Tinajero, *Homenaje póstumo a Bolívar Echeverría Andrade. Filósofo, Intelectual, Académico e Investigador Ecuatoriano*. Quito: Universidad Central del Ecuador, 2010. 35 pp.

Ortega Esquivel, Aureliano, 'Contra lo que ya es. A propósito de "Posmodernismo y cinismo" de Bolívar Echeverría', in Mariflor Aguilar Rivero (ed.), *Diálogos sobre filosofía contemporánea, modernidad, sujeto y hermenéutica*, Mexico City: UNAM, Coordinación de Humanidades/Asociación Filosófica de México, 1995, pp. 31–46.

Sánchez Vázquez, Adolfo, '¿Hacia una nueva modernidad?' [review of *Las ilusiones de la modernidad*], in *Dialéctica. Revista de filosofía, ciencias sociales, literatura y cultura política de la Universidad Autónoma de Puebla*, Puebla: Spring 1997, new period, year 21, no. 29–30, pp. 164–8.

Tonda Mazón, María de la Concepción, *El proceso de trabajo en la crítica de la economía política. El capital, libro I, capítulo V. Glosa crítica a la interpretación de Bolívar Echeverría*, Mexico City: Itaca, 1997. 46 pp.

C Selected Bibliography on Marxist Philosophy in Latin America

a) *Texts Published in Europe*

In Spain

Fernández Díaz, Osvaldo, 'Sobre los orígenes del marxismo en América Latina. En el centenario de Carlos Marx', in *Araucaria de Chile*, Madrid: 1983, no. 23, pp. 49–63.

Fernández Díaz, Osvaldo, 'Teoría y práctica en América Latina', in *Araucaria de Chile*, Madrid: 1984, no. 27, pp. 57–68.

Gomáriz, Enrique, Carlos Franco, José Aricó y André Gunder Frank, 'La crisis del marxismo en América Latina' [debate organised in Trier during the Commemorative Congress for Marx's Centenary], in *Leviatán. Revista de hechos e ideas*, Madrid: spring 1983, second period, no. 11, pp. 73–82.

Posada, Francisco, *Los orígenes del pensamiento marxista en Latinoamérica. Política y cultura en José Carlos Mariátegui*, Madrid: 1968. 89 pp. (Col. Ciencia Nueva.)

In France

Ayoub Karaa, Habiba, *La philosophie politique en Amérique Latine. Étude de cas l'Argentine*, specialised doctoral thesis, Toulouse: Université de Toulouse 2, 1983.

Gachie-Pineda, Maryse, 'La diffusion du marxisme au Mexique à travers la revue "Futuro" (1933–1939)', in *América. Cahiers du CRICCAL*, Paris: Centre de Recherches interuniversitaires sur les champs culturels en Amérique Latine, 1990, no. 4–5, pp. 151–64. Bibliography.

Gachie-Pineda, Maryse, *Les intellectuels mexicains face au cardenisme. Réel, idéologie et pensée politique dans le Mexique cardéniste (1933–1940): Vicente Lombardo Toledano, José Vasconcelos*, Paris: 1984, doctoral thesis, Université de Paris III, Études ibériques, 1027 pp., 132 pp. Bibliography.

Gachie-Pineda, Maryse, *Recherche sur le courant marxiste dans le Mexique cardéniste*, doctoral thesis, Université de Haute Bretagne, Rennes: 1980. 377 pp. 29 pp. Bibliography.

Gall, O., *Trotsky et la vie politique dans le Mexique de Cardenas (1937–1940)*, Grenoble: 1986, political sciences doctoral thesis at the Université des Sciences Sociales de Grenoble, Institut d'Études Politiques. 668 pp.

Groupe de recherches sur l'Amérique Latine (G.R.A.L.) – Toulouse, *Intellectuels et État au Mexique au XXe siècle*, Paris: Centre National de recherches Scientifiques, 1979. 149 pp.

Lempérière, Annick, *Les intellectuels mexicains entre l'État et la société civile (1920–1968)*, Paris: Université de Paris I, 1988. 477 pp. Bibliography: pp. vii–xxii.

Löwy, Michael, *Le Marxisme en Amérique latine de 1909 à nos jours. Anthologie*, Paris: Maspero, 1980. 455 pp.

Löwy, Michael, 'Marxisme et christianisme en Amérique Latine', in *Tiers Monde*, Paris: Université de Paris, Institut d'Etude du Développement Economique et Social/ Presses Universitaires de France, July-September 1990, year. 31, no. 123, pp. 667-82.

Pares, Carmen, *Théorie marxiste et pratique politique en Amérique Latine (1870-1948)*, doctoral thesis, Grenoble: Université Grenoble 2, 1980.

Paris, Robert, 'Mariátegui et Gramsci. Quelques prolégomènes à une étude contrastive de la diffusion du marxisme', in *Économies et Sociétés. Cahiers de l'I.S.M.E.A.; Marx au lendemain d'un centenaire*, Paris: July-August 1984, no. 23-24 series S.

Paris, Robert, 'Diffusion et appropriation du marxisme en Amérique latine', in *Amérique Latine*, Paris: Centre de recherche sur l'Amérique Latine et le tiers monde, 1985, no. 21, pp. 28-34.

Sidicaro, Ricardo, Robert Paris, Hugo Moreno, Hernán Gutiérrez, Cary Hector, Marcos Wincour, Jorge Rhenan Segura and Hugo Neira, 'Les gauches d'Amérique Latine. Histoires et horizons', in *Amérique Latine*, Paris: Centre de recherche sur l'Amérique Latine et le tiers monde, 1985, no. 21, pp. 27 et sqq.

In the Netherlands

Paris, Robert, 'Difusión y apropiación del marxismo en América Latina', trans. Ricardo Falcón, in *Boletín de estudios latinoamericanos y del Caribe*, Amsterdam: 1984, no. 36, pp. 3-12.

In Poland

Czyżowicz, Wiesław Eugeniusz, 'La teoría marxista-leninista y la teoría de la dependencia', *Coloquio Internacional 'Alternativas del Desarrollo Social en América Latina. Pasado y actualidad'*, Rostock, 2-28 de May 1989, Warsaw: Acad. Nauki Sosialski, 1989.

In the German Democratic Republic

Caregorodčeo, V., 'Die Linksradikalen in Lateinamerika', in *Lateinamerika*, Rostock: spring 1977, pp. 25-33.

Kaeselitz, Rudi, 'Linksradikalismus in Lateinamerika. Entwicklung und Aktivitäten', in *Asien, Afrika, Lateinamerika*, Berlin: 1980, vol. 8, no. 4, pp. 726-34.

Pallinger, Karl, 'Marxismus in Lateinamerika', in *Die Zukunft. Sozialistische Zeitschrift für Politik, Wirtschaft und Kultur*, Vienna: Dr.-Karl-Renner-Institut, January 1976, no. 1/2, pp. 10-16.

Reuter, Walter, 'Einige Tendenzen in der Entwicklung der revolutionär-demokratischen Ideologie und der Annäherung nichtproletarischer Kräfte an den Marxismus-Leninismus seit der kubanischen Revolution', in *Lateinamerika*, Rostock: Spring 1983, pp. 76-96.

Vargas Lozano, Gabriel, 'La filosofía latinoamericana en el siglo XX', in *Lateinamerika*, Rostock: 1990, year 25, no. 2, pp. 9-17.

Vetter, Ullrich B., 'Aktuelle Tendenzen der philosophischen Diskussion in Lateinamerika und ihr historischer Hintergrund', in *Asien. Afrika, Lateinamerika*, Berlin: 1990, volume 18, no. 2, pp. 320-31.

In the German Federal Republic

Barreda, Andrés, 'Entwicklung der Diskussion und Erforschung der Werke von Marx und Engels in Mexiko während der letzten drei Jahrzehnte', in *Marxistische Studien. Jahrbuch des IMSF*, Frankfurt am Main: Institut für Marxistische Studien und Forschungen [IMSF], 1987, no. 12, p. 277.

Fornet-Betancourt, Raúl, *Kommentierte Bibliographie zur Philosophie in Lateinamerika*, Frankfurt am Main: Lang, 1985. 156 pp. (Col. Europäische Hochschulschriften, Col. 20, Philosophie no. 158.)

Fornet-Betancourt, Raúl and Alfredo Gomez-Muller (eds.), *Positionen Lateinamerikas*, prologue by Walter Biemel, trans. Astrid Peters and Raúl Fornet-Betancourt, Frankfurt am Main: Materialis, 1989. 146 pp. (Col. Lateinamerika-Solidarität, no. 1.)

Hoellhuber, Ivo, *Geschichte der Philosophie im spanischen Kulturbereich*. Munich/Basel: Reinhardt, 1967. 267 pp.

Krumpel, Heinz, *Philosophie in Lateinamerika. Grundzüge ihrer Entwicklung*, Berlin: Ed. Akademie, 1992. 390 pp.

Löwy, Michael, *Marxismus in Lateinamerika 1909-1987*, trans. Willy Boepple, Frankfurt am Main: Isp, 1988. 108 pp.

Mires, Fernando, 'Die Unterentwicklung des Marxismus in Lateinamerika', in Veronika Bennholdt-Thomsen, T. Evers, K. Meschat, C. Müller, V. Müller, W. Olle and W. Schoeller (eds.), *Lateinamerika. Analysen und Berichte*, vol. 1: *Kapitalistische Entwicklung und politische Repression*, Berlin: Olle & Wolter, 1977, pp. 12-52.

In Switzerland

Guy, Alain, *Panorama de la philosophie ibero-américaine de XVIe siècle à nos jours. XVI*, Geneva: Paitno: 1989. 285 pp. Bibliography: pp. 245-60.

b) *Texts Published in Canada and the United States*

In Canada

Mires, F., *El subdesarrollo del marxismo en América Latina y otros ensayos*, Montreal: Alai, 1985. 126 pp. (Col. Documentación política, vol. III, no. 1.)

In the United States

Aguilar, Luis E., *Marxism in Latin America*. New York: Alfred A. Knopf, 1968; and Philadelphia: Temple University Press, 1978. 412 pp.

Carefoot, David Rollins, *Che Guevara: Existentialist*, PhD thesis, Tallahassee, FL: Florida State University, 1990. 113 pp.

Carr, Barry, 'The development of communism and Marxism in Mexico. A historiographical essay', in Roderic A. Camp, Charles A. Hale and Josefina Zoraida Vázquez (eds.), *Los intelectuales y el poder en México*, Los Angeles/Mexico City: University of California at Los Angeles, Latin American Center Publications/El Colegio de México, 1991, pp. 377–94.

Chang-Rodriguez, Eugenio, *La literatura política de González Prada, Mariátegui y Haya de la Torre*, PhD thesis, Seattle, WA: University of Washington, 1955. 564 pp.

Chilcote, Rh., 'Post-marxism. The retreat from class in Latin-America', in *Latin American Perspectives. A journal on capitalism and socialism*, Riverside, CA: Spring 1990, vol. 17, no. 2, pp. 3–24.

García, Jorge J.E. (ed.), 'Latin American Philosophy Today', in *The Philosophical Forum*, Boston, MA: Boston University, Department of Philosophy, 1988–9, vol. 20, no. 1–2, special edition, pp. 1–158.

Liss, Sheldon B., 'Marxist thinkers in Mexico. Each to his own revolution', in Roderic A. Camp, Charles A. Hale and Josefina Zoraida Vázquez (eds.), *Los intelectuales y el poder en México*, Los Angeles/Mexico City: University of California at Los Angeles, Latin American Center Publications/El Colegio de México, 1991, pp. 359–76.

Liss, Sheldon B., *Marxist Thought in Latin America*, Berkeley, CA: University of California, 1984. 344 pp.

Löwy, Michael, 'Marxism and Romanticism in the Work of José Carlos Mariátegui', trans. Penelope Duggan, in *Latin American Perspectives. A journal on capitalism and socialism*, Riverside, CA: July 1998, year 25, no. 4, pp. 76–88.

Romero Cantarero, Ramón Antonio, *The New Marxism of José Carlos Mariátegui (Peru)*, PhD thesis, Tallahassee, FL: Florida State University, 1990. 197 pp.

Sánchez Vázquez, Adolfo, 'Marxism in Latin America', trans. Jorge J.E. Garcia, in *The Philosophical Forum*, Boston, MA: Autumn-Winter 1988–9, vol. 20, no. 1–2, pp. 114–28.

Stoltz Chinchilla, Norma, 'Marxism, Feminism and the Struggle for Democracy in Latin America', in *Gender & Society*, Thousand Oaks, CA: 1 September 1991, vol. 5, no. 3, pp. 291ff.

Vandern, Harry E., *National Marxism in Latin America. José Carlos Mariátegui's thought and politics*, Boulder, CA: L. Riemer, 1986. 198 pp.

c)   *Texts Published in Latin America*
     In Latin America

Aguirre, Manuel Agustín, *Marx ante América Latina. Homenaje a Carlos Marx por el centenario de su muerte*, Quito: Universidad Central, Instituto de Investigaciones Económicas, 1985. 200 pp.

Cueva Dávila, Agustín, 'El marxismo latinoamericano. Historia y problemas actuales', in *Homines. Publicación del Departamento de Ciencias Sociales*, San Juan, Puerto

Rico: Universidad Interamericana de Puerto Rico, January–July 1986, vol. 10, no. 1, pp. 197–210. Republished in Aline Frambes-Bruxeda, *Nuestra América Latina*, San Juan, Puerto Rico: Universidad Interamericana de Puerto Rico, 1989, pp. 428–41. (Col. Libros Homines, no. 6.) [Annotation: vol. 13, no. 1, February–July 1989.]

Franco, Carlos, *Del marxismo eurocéntrico al marxismo latinoamericano*, Lima: Centro de Estudios para el Desarrollo y la Participación, 1981. 112 pp. (Col. Textos de contrapunto, no. 1.)

Gaete Avaria, Jorge, 'Historia de una experiencia infortunada. La difícil sobrevivencia del marxismo mariateguiano', in *Fragmentos*, Caracas: 1983, no. 16, pp. 18–60.

Guevara, Ernesto *Ché*, José Carlos Mariátegui, July Antonio Mella, Carlos Romero *et al. El marxismo en América Latina. (Antología)*, Buenos Aires: Centro Editor de América Latina, 1972. 140 pp. (Col. Biblioteca fundamental del hombre moderno, no. 58.)

Löwy, Michael, 'Los intelectuales latinoamericanos y la crítica social de la modernidad', in *Casa de las Américas*, Havana: April–June 1993, no. 191, pp. 100–5.

Mayz Vallenilla, Ernesto (ed.), *La filosofía en América. Trabajos presentados en el IX Congreso Interamericano de Filosofía*, Caracas: Sociedad Venezolana de Filosofía, 1979, two volumes, 257 pp. and 258 pp.

Mella, July Antonio, *et al.*, *Marxistas de América*, Managua: 1985. 465 pp. (Col. Biblioteca popular de la cultura universal.)

Mires, Fernando, 'El subdesarrollo del marxismo en América Latina', in *Revista de filosofía de la Universidad de Costa Rica*, San José, Costa Rica: 1980, vol. 18, no. 47, pp. 87–108.

Posada, Francisco, *Los orígenes del pensamiento marxista en Latinoamérica*, Havana: 1968. 65 pp. [Also: *Los orígenes del pensamiento marxista en Latinoamérica. Política y cultura en José Carlos Mariátegui*, Madrid: 1968. 89 pp. Col. Ciencia Nueva. A further edition was published in Bogotá: Nuevas Ediciones, 1977.]

Ramos Serpa, Gerardo, 'Política y concepción del mundo. Antinomias del marxismo latinoamericano', in *Revista cubana de ciencias sociales*, Havana: 1988, year 6, no. 17, pp. 35–51.

Vargas Lozano, Gabriel, 'La función actual de la filosofía en México. La década de los setenta', in *1. Congreso Internacional de Filosofía Latinoamericana. Ponencias*, Bogotá: 1981, pp. 83–107.

Vasconi, Tomás Amadeo, 'El pensamiento marxista a partir de la revolución cubana', in *Tareas*, Panama: no. 58, 1984, pp. 69–85.

In Mexico

Aricó, José (ed.), *Mariátegui y los orígenes del marxismo latinoamericano*, Mexico City: Pasado y Presente/Siglo XXI, 1978. 321 pp.

Bernstein, Harry, 'Marxismo en México, 1917–1925', in *Historia Mexicana*, Mexico City: El Colegio de México, 1958, vol. 7, no. 4 (28), pp. 497–516.

Davis, Harold Eugene, *La historia de las ideas en Latinoamérica*, Mexico City: UNAM, Facultad de Filosofía y Letras, Coordinación de Humanidades, Centro de Estudios Latinoamericanos, 1979. 23 pp. (Col. Cuadernos de cultura latinoamericana, no. 47.)

Gándara Vázquez, Manuel, Fernando López e Ignacio Rodríguez García, 'Arqueología y marxismo en México', in *Boletín de antropología americana*, Mexico City: 1985, no. 11, pp. 5–17.

Gilly, Adolfo, 'Mariátegui y la Revolución Mexicana', in *Viento del Sur. Revista de ideas, historia y política*, Mexico City: April 1994, year 1, no. 1, pp. 29–45.

Löwy, Michael (ed.), *El Marxismo en América Latina (de 1909 a nuestros días)*, Mexico City: Era, 1982. 430 pp.

Medina Hernández, Andrés, 'El pensamiento marxista en la antropología mexicana', in *Boletín de la Escuela de Ciencias Antropológicas de la Universidad de Yucatán*, Mérida: 1979, year 7, no. 37, pp. 2–20.

Miranda, José Porfirio, *Marx en México. Plusvalía y política*, Mexico City: Siglo XXI, 1972. 136 pp.

Montalvo, Enrique, 'La lucha por el socialismo y la super-estructura ideológica en México', in *Arte, sociedad, ideología*, Mexico City: La Impresora Azteca, 1979, no. 7, pp. 93–114.

Osornio Urbina, Jaime, 'El marxismo latinoamericano y la dependencia', in *Cuadernos Políticos*, Mexico City: 1984, no. 39, pp. 40–59.

Roig, Arturo Andrés, *Teoría y crítica del pensamiento latinoamericano*, Mexico City: Fondo de Cultura Económica, 1981. 313 pp. (Col. Tierra Firme.)

Various, *Karl Marx y América Latina*, Mexico City: UNAM, Centro Coordinador y Difusor de Estudios Latinoamericanos, 1983. 140 pp. [Monographic issue of the journal: *Nuestra América*, 1983, vol. 3, no. 9.]

D Sources for the Bibliographies

For the elaboration of the bibliographies included in this book we referred, aside from the existing provisional bibliographies for Sánchez Vázquez, to other general bibliographies and the bibliographical notes in books by Adolfo Sánchez Vázquez and Bolívar Echeverría, as well as the following resources.

Libraries
Biblioteca Central de la UNAM, Mexico City.
Biblioteca Daniel Cosío Villegas, El Colegio de México, Mexico City.
Biblioteca de la Facultad de Filosofía y Letras de la Universidad Complutense, Madrid.
Biblioteca de la Fundación de Investigaciones Marxistas (FIM), Madrid.

SOURCES FOR THE BIBLIOGRAPHIES 433

Biblioteca Nacional, Madrid.
Biblioteca Nacional, Mexico City.
Biblioteca Samuel Ramos, Facultad de Filosofía y Letras, UNAM, Mexico City.
Bibliothèque de documentation internationale contemporaine, Nanterre, France.
Bibliothèque Nationale, Paris.
Bibliothèque Universitaire de Paris X, Nanterre, France.
Deutsche Bibliothek, Frankfurt am Main.
Hemeroteca Municipal, Madrid.
Hemeroteca Nacional, Madrid.
Hemeroteca Nacional, Mexico City.
Iberoamerikanisches Institut, Berlin.
Stadt- und Universitätsbibliothek Frankfurt am Main.
Universitätsbibliothek Innsbruck, Austria.

Catalogues of Books or Journals and Databases

General catalog of the UNAM libraries [Librunam]. Available at: <http://www.dgbiblio.unam.mx/>.
Catálogo Hemerográfico Nacional, México [Seriunam]. Available at: <http://www.dgbiblio.unam.mx/>.
Catálogo de Tesis, UNAM [Tesiunam]. Available at: <http://www.dgbiblio.unam.mx/>.
CLASE. Citas Latinoamericanas en Ciencias Sociales y Humanidades. Available at: <http://clase.unam.mx/>
Directorio de publicaciones seriadas de América Latina. Global Books in Print Plus.
Karlsruher Virtueller Katalog, Universität Karlsruhe, Alemania Available at: <http://www.ubka.uni-karlsruhe.de/kvk.html>.
Library of Congress Online Catalog. Available at: <http://catalog.loc.gov/>.
Melvyl. The Catalog of the University of California Libraries. Available at: <http://melvyl.worldcat.org/>.
Österreichischer Verbundkatalog, Austria. Available at: <http://opac.bibvb.ac.at/acc01/>.
Philosopher's Index. Available at: <http://philindex.org/>.
REDALYC. Red de Revistas Científicas de América Latina y el Caribe, España y Portugal. Available at: <http://www.redalyc.org/>.
Verbundkatalog des Deutsches Bibliotheksinstitut Berlin.
World Cat. Available at: <http://www.worldcat.org/>.
Zeitschriften Datenbank [ZDB]. Editado por el Deutsches Bibliotheksinstitut. Staatsbibliothek zu Berlin. Preußischer Kulturbesitz. Available at: <http://dispatch.opac.dnb.de/>.

Archives

Acero. Organo del 5° Cuerpo de Ejército del Centro. [Different places of publication and subtitles.] 1937 to 1939, publication ceases with the end of the Spanish Civil War. In Hemeroteca Municipal de Madrid. (Existing originals up to Madrid: 15 June 1937, year 1, no. 8.)

Ahora, Madrid. [With the following subtitle after 1 January 1937: *Diario de la Juventud.*] Edited by the Juventud Socialista Unificada. Year 1: 1930 to year 8: 1939, publication ceases in February 1939. In Hemeroteca Municipal de Madrid. (Exists on microfilm up to 16 February 1939.)

La Hora, Diario de la juventud. Valencia. (National edition of *Ahora.*) Edited by the Juventud Socialista Unificada. Year 1, no. 1: 8 June 1937 to year 3: 1939, publication ceases in February 1939. In Hemeroteca Municipal de Madrid. (Originals exist up to 19 February 1939, no. 526.)

Pasaremos, Year 1, no. 1, 1 December 1936, publication ceases with the end of the Spanish Civil War. Subtitles: Beginning with year 1, no. 2, 13 December 1936: *Órgano de la 1st Brigada Mixta;* from year 2, no. 5, 24 January 1937: *Órgano de la primera Brigada Mixta de Líster;* from year 2, no. 6, 13 February 1937: *'Órgano de la 11st División – Líster';* from year 2, no. 13, 27 March 1937: *'Órgano de la 11st División'* (in no. 13 *'Líster'* is bolded); from year 2, no. 48, 30 eptember 1937: *'Órgano de la 11 División'.* Editorial location: from year 1, no. 1, 1 December 1936: Madrid; from year 2, no. 37, August 1937: Caspe; from year 2, no. 61, November 1937: 'on the front'. In Hemeroteca Municipal de Madrid (Originals exist up to 10 December 1938, year 3, no. 100).

Romance. Revista Popular Hispanoamericana, Mexico City: 1 February 1940–31 May 1941. (Year 1, no. 1 to year 2, no. 24, with which publication ceases.) In Stadt- und Universitätsbibliothek Frankfurt am Main (original and reprint).

References

Acanda González, Jorge Luis 1988, *Analyse einiger Versuche, die marxistisch-leninistische Philosophie als Praxis-Philosophie zu konzipieren, unter besonderer Berücksichtigung des Werkes von Adolfo Sánchez Vázquez*, Dissertation A, Karl Marx University of Leipzig.

Aguilar Rivero, Mariflor (ed.) 1995, *Diálogos sobre filosofía contemporánea, modernidad, sujeto y hermenéutica*, Mexico City: UNAM.

Althusser, Louis 1965a, *Pour Marx*, Paris: Maspero.

―― 1965b, *Lire le Capital*, Paris: Maspero.

―― 1965c, 'Teoría, práctica teórica y formación teórica. Ideología y lucha ideological', trans E. Román, *Casa de las Américas*, 34: 5–31.

―― 1976, *Posiciones (1964–75)*, Mexico City: Grijalbo.

Álvarez, Santiago 1986, *Memorias II. La Guerra civil de 1936–1939*, La Coruña: Edicios do Castro.

―― 1989, *Los comisarios politicos en el Ejército Popular de la República*, La Coruña: Edicios do Castro.

Anders, Günther 1947 'Nihilismus und Existenz', *Die neue Rundschau*, 48: 48–76.

Anonymous 1984, 'Diez años de *Cuadernos Políticos*', *Cuadernos Políticos*, 41.

―― 1985: 'Bibliografía de y sobre Adolfo Sánchez Vázquez', *Anthropos. Revista de documentación científica de la cultura*, 52: 19–25

―― 1987, 'Riobamba' in *El Pequeño Espasa*, Madrid: Espasa-Calpe.

Ardao, Arturo et al., (ed.) 1976, *La filosofía actual en América Latina*, Vol. 3, 'Primer Coloquio Nacional de Filosofía', Mexico City: Grijalbo.

Aricó, José 1990, 'Introducción', in *Mariátegui y los orígenes del marxismo latinoamericano*, Mexico City: Siglo XXI.

Aristotle 1948, *Politik*, trans. E. Rolfes, Leipzig: Felix Meiner.

―― 2000, *Nicomachean Ethics*, trans. R. Crisp, Cambridge: Cambridge University Press.

Axelos, Kostas 1961, *Marx, penseur de la technique*, Paris: Minuit.

Baudrillard, Jean 1972, *Pour une critique de l'économie politique du signe*, Paris: Gallimard.

Beck, Barbara and Horst Kurnitzky 1975, *Zapata: Bilder aus der Mexikanischen Revolution*, Berlin: Wagenbach.

―― 1982, *Wand Bild Mexico*, Berlin: Frölich & Kaufmann.

Benítez, Fernando 1960, *La batalla de Cuba*, with an essay by Enrique González Pedrero, Mexico City: Era.

―― 1995, *Ediciones Era. 35 años. Neus Espresate*, Guadalajara: Universidad de Guadalajara.

Benjamin, Walter 1966, 'Über Sprache überhaupt und über die Sprache des Menschen', in *Angelus Novus. Ausgewählte Schriften 2*, Frankfurt am Main: Suhrkamp.

—— 1968, 'Theses on the Philosophy of History', in *Illuminations*, ed. and introd. H. Arendt, New York: Harcourt, Brace & World.

—— 1978, 'Über den Begriff der Geschichte', in *Gesammelte Schriften*, Vol 1/II, Second edition, Frankfurt am Main: Suhrkamp.

—— 1982, 'Das Passagen-Werk', in *Gesammelte Schriften*, Vol. 5/II, Frankfurt am Main: Suhrkamp.

—— 1999, *The Arcades Project*, trans. H. Eiland and K. McLaughlin, Cambridge, MA: Harvard University Press.

—— 2003, *La obra de arte en la época de su reproductibilidad técnica*, trans. Andrés Echeverría Weikert, prologue Bolívar Echeverría, Mexico City: Itaca. 127 pp., [Republished: Quito: Rayuela/Diagonal, 2010.]

Biese, F. 1842, *Die Philosophie des Aristoteles*, Vol. 2, Berlin.

Bowers, Claude G. 1955, *Misión en España 1933–1939*, Mexico City: Grijalbo.

Braudel, Fernand 1992, *Civilisation and Capitalism, 15th–18th Century*, trans. S. Reynold, Berkeley, CA: University of California Press.

Brecht, Bertolt 1949, *The Threepenny Opera*, New York: Grove.

—— 1961, *Flüchtlingsgespräche*, Frankfurt am Main: Reclam.

—— 1986, 'Conversations in Exile', adapted by Howard Brenton from a translation by David Dollenmayer, *Theater*, 17, 2.

—— 2003, 'Legend of the Origin of the Book Tao-Te-Ching on Lao-Tsu's Road into Exile', in *Poetry and Prose*, edited by R. Grimm, London: Continuum.

Brentel, Helmut 1989, *Soziale Form und ökonomisches Objekt. Studien zum Gegenstands- und Methodenverständnis der Kritik der politischen Ökonomie*, Opladen: Westdeutscher.

Bundschuh, Stephan 1998, *'Und weil der Mensch ein Mensch ist...' Anthropologische Aspekte der Sozialphilosophie Herbert Marcuses*. Lüneburg: Zu Klampen, 1998.

Cabrera, H. 1965 'A la Redacción de *Latinoamérica*. Comentarios sobre el primer número', *Latinoamérica*, 2.

Caffarena Such, Angela 1960, *Antología de la poesía malagueña contemporánea*, Malaga: El Guadalhorce.

Camp, Roderic A., Hale, Charles A., and Zoraida Vázquez, Josefina 1991, *Los intelectuales y el poder en México*, Los Angeles: UCLA.

Cantarell Gamboa, Melvin 1967, review of *Filosofía de la praxis, Revista de la Universidad*, XXII, 1.

Capdeville García, 1992, *Philosophische Problematik in der 'Philosophie der Praxis' von Sánchez Vázquez*, Dissertation A, Humboldt University of Berlin.

Carr, Barry 1991, 'The Development of Communism and Marxism in Mexico: A Historiographical Essay', in Camp, Hale and Zoraida Vázquez 1991.

Carrillo, Santiago 1974, *Demain l'Espagne. Entretiens avec Régis Debray et Max Gallo*, Paris: Seuil.
Casterás, Ramón 1977, *Las JSUC: ante la guerra y la revolución (1936–1939)*, Barcelona: Nova Terra.
Cogniot, G. 1968, 'Filosofía de la praxis" (review), *La Pensée*, 138.
Cortada, James W. (ed.) 1982, *Historical Dictionary of the Spanish Civil War, 1936–1939*, Westport, CT: Greenwood.
Cueva Dávila, Agustín 1974, *El proceso de dominación política en Ecuador*, Mexico City: Diógenes.
────── 1986, 'El marxismo latinoamericano. Historia y problemas actuales', *Homines. Publicación del Departamento de Ciencias Sociales, Universidad Interamericana de Puerto Rico*, 10, 1: 197–210.
────── 1987, *Entre la ira y la esperanza*, Quito: Planeta.
────── 1988, *Ideología y Sociedad en América Latina*, Montevideo: Banda Oriental.
────── 1990, 'La hora de las elecciones en Ecuador', *Secuencia*, 18: 105–12.
Cuyas, Arturo 1956, *Appleton's revised Cuyas dictionary*. New York/Toronto: Grolier.
Della Volpe, Galvano 1978 [1956], *Rousseau and Marx and Other Writings*, London: Lawrence and Wishart.
Deutscher, Isaac 1970, *Lenin's childhood*, Oxford: Oxford University Press.
Diccionario ideológico de la lengua española 1990, Second edition, Barcelona: Gustavo Gili.
Dittmar, Frieder 1995, 'Wale und Atome. Greenpeace als Institution der globalen Öffentlichkeit', *Die Beute. Politik und Verbrechen*, 7: 9–17.
Dussel, Enrique 1993, *Las metáforas teológicas de Marx*, Estella: Verbo Divino.
Dutschke, Gretschen 1996, *Rudi Dutschke. Eine Biographie*, Cologne: Kiepenheuer & Witsch.
Dutschke, Rudi 1981, *Aufrecht gehen. Eine fragmentarische Autobiographie*, Berlin: Olle & Wolter.
Echeverría, Bolívar 1965a, 'La intelectualidad el Latinoamérica. Trabajos del seminario de la AELA', *Latinoamérica*, 2.
────── 1965b 'De la posibilidad de cambio', *Pucuna*, 6: 26–33.
────── 1965c ' "Los fusiles," filme brasileño de Ruy Guerra (1963)', *Pucuna*, 6: 7–10.
────── 1967a, review of *Los escritores contra Sartre*, *Revista de la Universidad de México*, XXI, 7: 27–30.
────── 1967b, review of Michel-Antoine Burnier, *Les existentialistes et la politique*, *Revista de la Universidad de México*, XXI, 12: 32–4.
────── 1968, 'Einführung', in Guevara 1968–1977a, 'Para lectores de *El Capital*', *Investigación Económica. Revista de la Facultad de Economía*, 1: 265–9.
────── 1977b, 'Para lectores de *El Capital*. Comentario 1', *Investigación Económica. Revista de la Facultad de Economía*, 2: 245–50.

―― 1977c, 'Para lectores de *El Capital*. Comentario 2. Sobre el "punto de partida" en *El Capital*', *Investigación Económica. Revista de la Facultad de Economía*, 4: 21–37.

―― 1977d, 'El concepto del fetichismo en el discurso revolucionario', *Dialéctica. Revista de la Escuela de Filosofía y Letras de la Universidad Autónoma de Puebla*, 4.

―― 1977e, 'Esquemas gráficos para el estudio del capítulo quinto de *El Capital*', *Investigación Económica. Revista de la Facultad de Economía*, 4: 237–46.

―― 1984, 'La "forma natural" de la reproducción social', *Cuadernos Políticos*, 41: 33–46.

―― 1986, *El discurso crítico de Marx*, Mexico City: Era.

―― 1987, 'Diecinueve tesis sobre modernidad y capitalismo', *Cuadernos de la* DEP, March: 1–23.

―― 1989, 'Quince tesis sobre modernidad y capitalismo', *Cuadernos Políticos*, 58: 41–62.

―― 1990a, *Sobre el materialismo. Modelo para armar*, Mexico City: UNAM.

―― 1990b, 'Presentación', *Cuadernos Políticos*, 59.

―― 1991, 'Quince tesis sobre modernidad y capitalismo', *Review*, 14, 4: 471–515.

―― 1992, *La circulación capitalista y la reproducción de la riqueza social. (Apunte crítico sobre los 'Esquemas de Reproducción esbozados por K. Marx en 'El Capital'*, Mexico City: UNAM.

―― 1994a, *Circulación capitalista y reproducción de la riqueza social. Apunte crítico sobre los Esquemas de K. Marx*, Mexico City: UNAM.

―― 1994b (ed.), *Modernidad, mestizaje cultural, ethos barroco*, Mexico City: UNAM.

―― 1994c, 'Postmodernidad y cinismo', *Viento del sur*, 1: 55–61.

―― 1995a, *Las ilusiones de la modernidad*, Mexico: UNAM/El Equilibrista.

―― 1995b, 'Elogio del marxismo', in *En torno a la obra de Adolfo Sánchez Vázquez*, edited by Gabriel Vargas Lozano, Mexico City: UNAM.

―― 1995c, 'En torno a la presencia de Adolfo Sánchez Vázquez', *Boletín de la Facultad de Filosofía y Letras*, 7: 10–12.

―― 1995d, 'La Era de *Cuadernos Políticos*', in Benítez 1995.

―― 1996a, 'Curriculum Vitae', unpublished.

―― 1996b: 'Postmoderne und Zynismus', trans. S. Gandler, in *Die Beute. Politik und Verbrechen*, 11: 80–94.

―― 1998a, La *modernidad de lo barroco*, Mexico City: Era.

―― 1998b, 'El "valor de uso" ontología y semiótica', in *Valor de uso y utopía*, Mexico City: Siglo XXI.

Echeverría, Bolívar and Horst Kurnitzky 1993, *Conversaciones sobre lo barroco*, edited by M.A. García Barrios, Mexico City: UNAM.

Echeverría, Bolívar, Horst Kurnitzky, and Raquel Serur 1993, 'Segunda conversación', in Echeverría and Kurnitzky 1993.

REFERENCES

El pequeño Espasa 1987, Madrid: Espasa-Calpe.

Engels, Friedrich 1907, *Socialism, Utopian and Scientific*, Chicago: Charles H. Kerr.

―――― 1955, *Dialektik der Natur*, Berlin: Dietz.

―――― 1961, 'Brief an Joseph Bloch', 21–2 September 1890 in *Werke*, Vol. 37, Berlin: Dietz.

Etymologisches Wörterbuch des Deutschen 1989, Vol. 2, edited by the Autorenkollektiv des Zentralinstituts für Sprachwissenschaft [collective of authors of the Central Institute for Linguistics] coordinated by Wolfgang Pfeiffer, Berlin: Akademie.

Farías, Víctor 1987, *Heidegger und der Nazionalsozialismus*, Frankfurt: Fischer.

Foucault, Michel 1970, *The Order of Things*, New York: Vintage.

―――― 1988, *Les mots et les choses*, Paris: Gallimard.

Frank, André Gunder et al. 1969, *Kritik des bürgerlichen Antiimperialismus. Entwicklung der Unterentwicklung. Acht Analysen zur neuen Revolutionstheorie in Lateinamerika*, edited by Bolívar Echeverría and Horst Kurnitzky, Berlin: Wagenbach.

Fremdwörterbuch 1974, Third edition, Mannheim: Dudenverlag.

Galeano, Eduardo 1973, *Open veins of Latin America. Five centuries of the pillage of a continent*, trans. Cedric Belfrage, New York: Monthly Review Press.

Gandler, Stefan 1990, 'Was passiert in Alemania?', *Diskus. Frankfurter Student-Innenzeitung*, 39, 2, 8–13. Republished in *Gemeinsam sind wir unausstehlich. Die Wiedervereinigung und ihre Folgen*, edited by K. Bittermann, Berlin: Tiamat. Abbreviated version in Spanish in *Perspektiven. Die Internationale Student-Innenzeitung*, 4.

―――― 2009, 'Modernidad e identidad', in *Fragmentos de Frankfurt. Ensayos sobre la Teoría Crítica*, Mexico City: Siglo XXI.

―――― 2010, '¿Quién es Bolívar Echeverría?', in *La Jornada Semanal*, 805, 8 August, 5–7. Also available at: <http://www.jornada.unam.mx/2010/08/08/sem-stefan.html>. Also included in Gandler 2013a.

―――― 2011 'Adolfo Sánchez Vázquez: rebelión, antifascismo y enseñanza', in *La Jornada Semanal*, 865, 2 October, 8–10. Also available at: <http://www.jornada.unam.mx/2011/10/02/sem-stefan.html>. Also included in Gandler 2013a.

―――― 2013a, *El discreto encanto de la modernidad. Ideologías contemporáneas y su crítica*. Mexico City: Siglo XXI.

―――― 2013b, 'Moderne und Identität', in *Frankfurter Fragmente. Essays zur kritischen Theorie*, Frankurt: Peter Lang.

Gemoll, Wilhelm (ed.) 1965, *Griechisch-Deutsches Schul- und Handwörterbuch*, revised and expanded by Karl Vretska, Vienna: Freytag.

Germani, Gino 1970, 'Political Socialization of Youth in Fascist Regimes: Italy and Spain', in *Authoritarian Politics in Modern Society*, edited by Samuel P. Huntington and Clement H. Moore, London: Basic Books.

Goldhagen, Daniel 1996, *Hitler's Willing Executioners: Ordinary Germans and the Holocaust*, New York: Alfred A. Knopf.

González Rojo, Enrique 1985, *Epistemología y socialismo. La crítica de Sánchez Vázquez a Louis Althusser*, Mexico City: Diógenes.

González, Juliana, Carlos Pereyra and Gabriel Vargas Lozano (eds.) 1985, *Praxis y filosofía. Ensayos en homenaje a Adolfo Sánchez Vázquez*, Mexico City: Grijalbo.

GRAL [Groupe de recherches sur l'Amérique latine] 1979, *Intellectuels et État au Mexique au XXeme siècle*, Paris: Editions du CNRS.

Guevara, Ernesto 1968 *¡Hasta la victoria siempre! Eine Biographie mit einer Einführung von Bolívar Echeverría. Zusammengestellt von Horst Kurnitzky*, trans. A. Schubert, Berlin: Peter von Maikowski.

Haug, Wolfgang Fritz 1981, *Orientierungsversuche materialistischer Philosophie. Ein fragmentarischer Literaturbericht*, (particularly point 8: 'Sánchez Vázquez, Holz und Sève über den ideologischen Charakter von Philosophie'), *Das Argument*, 128, 516–32.

Hegel, Georg Wilhelm Friedrich 1932, *Jenenser Realphilosophie*, Leipzig.

―――― 1970, *Grundlinien der Philosophie des Rechts oder Naturrecht und Staatswissenschaft im Grundrisse*, Vol. 7 of *Werke*, Frankfurt am Main: Suhrkamp.

―――― 1975, *Lectures on the Philosophy of World History*, trans. H.B. Nisbet, Cambridge: Cambridge University Press.

―――― 1986, *Enzyklopädie der philosophischen Wissenschaften. Erster Teil. Die Wissenschaft der Logik*, Vol. 8 of *Werke*, in 20 volumes, compiled on the basis of his works from 1832 to 1845. Edited by E. Moldenhauer and K.M. Michel, Frankfurt am Main: Suhrkamp.

―――― 1991, *Elements of the Philosophy of Right*, trans. H.B. Nisbet, Cambridge: Cambridge University Press.

―――― 2002, *Science of Logic*, London: Routledge.

Heidegger 1990 [1933], 'The Self-Assertation of the German University', in *Martin Heidegger and National Socialism*, edited by Gunther Neske and Emil Kettering: New York: Paragon House.

Hirsch, Joachim 1990, *Kapitalismus ohne Alternative? Materialistische Gesellschaftstheorie und Möglichkeiten sozialistischer Politik heute*, Hamburg: VSA.

Hjelmslev, Louis 1971 [1954], *La stratification du langage*, in *Essais linguistiques*, Paris: Minuit.

Horkheimer, Max 1982, 'The Authoritarian State', in *The Essential Frankfurt School Reader*, edited by A. Arato and E. Gephardt, New York: Continuum.

Horkheimer, Max and Theodor W. Adorno 2002, *Dialectic of Enlightenment: Philosophical Fragments*, ed. G. Schmid Noerr, trans. E. Jephcott, Stanford, CA: Stanford University Press.

Jakobson, Roman 1960, *Closing Statement: Linguistics and Poetics*, in *Style and Language*, New York: Wiley.

—— 1971, 'Two Aspects of Languages and Two Types of Aphasic Disturbances' in *Selected Writings, II: World and Language*, The Hague: Mouton.
Jato, David 1953, *La rebellion de los estudiantes*, Madrid: CIES.
Korsch, Karl 1965, '10 Thesen über Marxismus heute', in *Alternative. Zeitschrift für Literatur und Diskussion*, 8, 41.
—— 1971, *Marxismo y filosofía*, trans. E. Beniers, Mexico City: Era.
Kosik, Karel 1967, *Dialéctica de lo concreto*, prologue by Adolfo Sánchez Vázquez, Mexico City: Grijalbo.
—— 1976, *Dialectics of the Concrete: A Study on Problems of Man and World*, Dordrecht: D. Reidel.
Kozlik, Adolf 1968, *El capitalismo del desperdicio. El milagro económico norteamericano*, trans. Bolívar Echeverría, Mexico City: Siglo XXI.
Kurnitzky, Horst 1970, *Versuch über den Gebrauchswert*, Berlin: Wagenbach.
—— 1974, *Triebstruktur des Geldes. Ein Beitrag zur Theorie der Weiblichkeit*, Berlin: Wagenbach.
—— 1978a, *Museum des Geldes. Über die seltsame Natur des Geldes in Kunst, Wissenschaft und Leben. Eine Ausstellung*, Düsseldorf: Städtische Kunsthalle.
—— 1978b, *Ödipus. Ein Held der westlichen Welt. Über die zerstörerischen Grundlagen unserer Zivilisation*, Berlin: Wagenbach.
—— 1994, *Der heilige Markt. Kulturhistorische Anmerkungen*, Frankfurt: Suhrkamp.
Labastida, Jaime 1967, 'Reseña de *Filosofía de la praxis*', *Política. Quince días de Mexico y el Mundo*, 8, 175.
Lang, Berel 1978, review of the English translation of *The Philosophy of Praxis*, *New Republic*, 178, 13, 1 April.
Langenscheidts Taschenwörterbuch der spanischen und deutschen Sprache. I: 'Spanisch-Deutsch' 1985, Berlin: Langenscheidt.
Langenscheidts Taschenwörterbuch der spanischen und deutschen Sprache. II: 'Deutsch-Spanisch' 1985, Berlin: Langenscheidt.
Largend, Etienne 1995, 'Was gibt die Bestie im Tausch für das, was sie nimmt? Zum Kräfteverhältnis zwischen EZLN und dem mexikanischen Regime', *Die Beute. Politik und Verbrechen*, 6: 7–18.
Leroi-Gourham, André 1964, *Le geste et la parole, I: Technique et langage*, Paris: A. Michel.
Lexicon der alten Welt 1965, Zürich: Artemis.
Lieber, Hans-Joachim (ed.) 1988, *Marx Lexikon. Zentrale Begriffe der politischen Philosophie von Karl Marx*, Darmstadt: Wissenschaftliche Buchgesellschaft.
Liss, Sheldon B. 1991, 'Marxist Thinkers in Mexico: Each to His Own Revolution' in Camp, Hale and Zoraida Vázquez 1991.
Líster, Enrique 1966, *Nuestra Guerra*, Paris: Ebro.
Löwy, Michael 1985, 'Marxismo y utopia', in González, Pereyra and Vargas Lozano (eds.) 1985.

Lucas, Ana 1987, 'Adolfo Sánchez Vázquez: vida y obra', in Sánchez Vázquez 1987.
Lukács, György 1971, *History and Class Consciousness: Studies in Marxist Dialectics*, trans. R. Livingstone, London: Merlin Press.
Macdonald, Dwight 1941, 'The End of Capitalism in Germany', *Partisan Review*, May–June: 198–220.
Magalhaes-Vilhena, V. 1962, 'Progrès technique et blocage social dans la cité Antique"', *La Pensée*, 102: 103–20.
Manrique, Jorge Alberto 1994, 'Conversando acerca de unas conversaciones (sobre lo barroco)', in Echeverría 1994b.
Marcuse, Herbert 1955, *Reason and Revolution: Hegel and the Rise of Social Theory*, Second edition with supplementary chapter, London: Routledge & Kegan Paul.
———— 1958, *Soviet Marxism*, New York: Columbia University Press.
———— 1967, *Der eindimensionale Mensch*, trans. A. Schmidt, Berlin.
Marx, Karl 1904, *Contribution to the Critique of Political Economy*, trans. Nahum Issac Stone, Chicago: Charles Kerr.
———— 1954, *Capital. A Critique of Political Economy*, Vol. I, trans. S. Moore and E. Aveling, Moscow: Progress Publishers.
———— 1959a 'Tesis sobre Feuerbach', in *La ideología alemana*, trans. W. Roces, Montevideo: Pueblos Unidos.
———— 1959b, *Economic and Philosophic Manuscripts of 1844*, trans. M. Milligan, Moscow: Progress Publishers.
———— 1962a, 'Manuscritos económico-filosóficos de 1844,' in Karl Marx and Friedrich Engels, *Escritos económicos varios*, trans. W. Roces. Mexico City: Grijalbo.
———— 1962b, 'Thesen über Feuerbach', in Marx and Engels, *Werke*, Vol. 3, Berlin: Dietz.
———— 1964, *El capital*, Vol. I, trans. W. Roces, Mexico City: FCE.
———— 1970, 'Critique of the Gotha Programme', in *Marx and Engels Selected Works*, Vol. III, Moscow: Progress Publishers.
———— 1972, *Die heilige Familie oder Kritik der kritischen Kritik gegen Bruno Bauer und Konsorten*, in Marx and Engels, *Werke*, Vol. 2, Berlin: Dietz.
———— 1974, *Cuadernos de París. Notas de lectura de 1844*, ed. and introd. A. Sánchez Vázquez, trans. B. Echeverría, Mexico City: Era.
———— 1975a, *Das Kapital*, Vol. I, in Marx and Engels, *Werke*, Vol. 23, Berlin: Dietz.
———— 1975b *El capital. Crítica de la economía política. Libro primero. El proceso de producción de capital*, trans. Pedro Scaron, Mexico City: Siglo XXI.
———— 1976a, *Capital: A Critique of Political Economy*, Vol. I, trans. B. Fowkes, London: Penguin.
———— 1976b, 'Preface to A Contribution to the Critique of Political Economy', in *Preface and Introduction to A Contribution to the Critique of Political Economy*, Peking: Foreign Languages Press.
———— 1978a, 'Economic and Philosophical Manuscripts of 1844', in Marx and Engels 1978b.

―― 1978b, 'Theses on Feuerbach', in Marx and Engels 1978b.
―― 1981, *Capital*, Vol. III, London: Penguin.
―― 1983a, 'Marx to Ferdinand Lassalle in Düsseldorf. London, 22 February 1858', in *Marx-Engels Collected Works*, Vol. 40, London: Lawrence & Wishart.
―― 1983b, *Grundrisse*, in Marx and Engels, *Werke*, Vol. 42, Berlin: Dietz.
―― 1985a, *Ökonomisch-philosophische Manuskripte aus dem Jahre 1844*, in Marx and Engels, *Werke*, Vol. 40, Berlin: Dietz.
―― 1985b, *Zur Kritik der Politischen Ökonomie*, in Marx and Engels, *Werke*, Vol. 13, Berlin: Dietz.
―― 1987, 'Tesis sobre Feuerbach' in *La ideología alemana*, trans. W. Roces, Mexico City: Grijalbo.
―― 1993, *Grundrisse: Foundations of the Critique of Political Economy (Rough Draft)*, trans. M. Nicolaus, London: Penguin.
―― 1996, 'Notes on Adolph Wagner', in *Marx: Later Political Writings*, trans. and ed. T. Carver, Cambridge: Cambridge University Press.
Marx, Karl and Friedrich Engels 1908, *Manifesto of the Communist Party*, New York: New York Labor News.
―― 1969, *Die Deutsche Ideologie*, in *Werke*, Vol. 3, Berlin: Dietz.
―― 1978a, 'The German Ideology', in Marx and Engels 1978b.
―― 1978b, *The Marx-Engels Reader*, ed. R.C. Tucker, Second edition, New York: W.W. Norton.
Merleau-Ponty, Maurice 1968, *Die Abenteuer der Dialektik*, trans. A. Schmidt and H. Schmitt, Frankfurt: Suhrkamp.
Meyers Kleines Konversationslexicon in sechs Bänden 1908, Vienna: Bibliographisches Institut.
Morales, Cesáreo 1985, 'Una reconsideración de Marx: de las condiciones transcendentales de la acción a órdenes colectivos experimentales', in González, Pereyra and Vargas Lozano (eds.) 1985.
Müller, Jost 1990, 'Rassismus und die Fallstricke des gewöhnlichen Antirassismus', *Diskus. Frankfurter StudentInnenzeitung*, 39, 2, 38–45.
Musil, Robert 1981, 'La casa encantada', *Palos*, Mexico City, 2 [translated with Ingrid Weikert].
Neumann, Franz 2009, *Behemoth: The Structure and Practice of National Socialism, 1933–1944*, Chicago: Ivan R. Dee.
Orozco, Teresa 1995, *Platonische Gewalt. Gadamers politische Hermeneutik in der NS-Zeit*, Hamburg: Argument.
Ortega Esquivel, Aureliano 1995, 'Contra lo que ya es. A propósito de *Posmodernidad y cinismo* de Bolívar Echeverría', in *Diálogos sobre filosofía contemporánea, modernidad, sujeto y hermenéutica*, edited by Mariflor Aguilar Rivero, Mexico City: UNAM.

Petrović, Gajo (ed.) 1969, *Revolutionäre Praxis. Jugoslawischer Marxismus der Gegenwart*, trans. K. Held, Freiburg: Rombach.
Poniatowska, Elena 1989, *La noche de Tlatelolco. Testimonios de historia oral*, Mexico City: Era.
—— 1995, 'Neus, Nieves, Neus Espresate, el ojo infallible', in Benítez 1995.
Sánchez Barbudo, Antonio 1975, 'Introducción', in *Romance*, reprint, Glashütten im Taunus: Detlev Auvermann.
Sánchez Vázquez, Adolfo 1933, 'Romance de la ley de fugas', *Octubre. Escritores y Artistas Revolucionarios*, 3, August–September. [published under the pseudonym 'Daris'].
—— 1942, *El Pulso Ardiendo*, Morelia: Voces.
—— 1960, 'Marxismo y existencialismo', *Suplemento del Seminario de Problemas Científicos y Filosóficos*, 2, 28.
—— 1961, 'Ideas estéticas en los *Manuscritos económico-filosóficos* de Marx', in *Diánoia. Anuario de Filosofía*. México, UNAM, Centro de Estudios Filosóficos.
—— 1963, 'Un héroe kafkiano: José K', *Revista de la Universidad*, September.
—— 1965a, *Conciencia y realidad en la obra de arte*, San Salvador: Universitaria.
—— 1965b, *Las ideas estéticas de Marx. Ensayos de estética marxista*, Mexico City: Era.
—— 1967a, 'Prólogo', in Franz Kafka, *El proceso*, Havana: Instituto del Libro.
—— 1967b, *Filosofía de la praxis*, Mexico City: Grijalbo.
—— 1967c, 'Praxis y violencia', *Casa de las Américas*, 7, 41: 5–16.
—— 1970 (ed.), *Estética y marxismo*, 2 vols., Vol. I: *Comunismo y arte*. Vol. II: *Estética comunista*, Mexico City: Era.
—— 1974, *Art and Society. Essays in Marxist Aesthetics*, trans. Maro Riofrancos, New York: Monthly Review Press.
—— 1975a, *Del socialismo científico al socialismo utópico*, Mexico City: Era.
—— 1975b, 'El teoricismo de Althusser. Notas críticas sobre una autocrítica', *Cuadernos Políticos*, 3.
—— 1977a, *The Philosophy of Praxis*, trans. M. Gonzalez, New Jersey: Humanities Press.
—— 1977b, 'La philosophie de la praxis comme nouvelle pratique de la philosophie', trans. K. Nair, *L'homme et la societé. Revue internationale de recherches et synthèses sociologiques*, 43–4: 141–9.
—— 1977c, 'La filosofía de la praxis como nueva práctica de la filosofía', *Cuadernos Políticos*, 12.
—— 1978a, 'Marinello en tres tiempos', *Casa de las Américas*, 19, 109: 113–16.
—— 1978b, *Ciencia y revolución. El marxismo de Althusser*, Madrid: Alianza Editorial.
—— 1978c, '¿Qué ha significado para ti la Revolución Cubana?', *Casa de las Américas*, 18, 111: 24–7.

——— 1979, 'El concepto de la praxis en Lenin', *Diánoia, Anuario de Filosofía*, 25, 25.
——— 1980a, 'La estética libertaria y comprometida de Sartre', *Thesis*, 7: 50–7.
——— 1980b, *Filosofía de la praxis*, Second corrected and expanded edition, Mexico City: Grijalbo.
——— 1982, *Filosofía y economía en el joven Marx. Los Manuscritos de 1844*, Mexico City: Grijalbo.
——— 1983a, 'Actualidad de Carlos Marx', *Plural*, 12, 140: 7–9.
——— 1983b, 'La filosofía de la praxis como nueva práctica de la filosofía', in *Ensayos marxistas sobre filosofía e ideología*, Mexico City: Océano.
——— 1984, *Ensayos de arte y marxismo*, Mexico City: Grijalbo.
——— 1985a, 'Vida y filosofía', *Anthropos*, 52: 10–16.
——— 1985b, 'La estética de Sartre', *Antropos*, 52: 19–25.
——— 1985c, 'Actividad académica', *Anthropos*, 52: 18.
——— 1987, *Escritos de política y filosofía*, Madrid: Ayuso.
——— 1989, 'Democracia, revolución y socialismo', *Socialismo. Revista de Teoría y Política*, 3–4.
——— 1992, *Invitación a la estética*, Mexico City: Grijalbo.
——— 1997, 'La filosofía de la praxis', in *Filosofía política I. Ideas políticas y movimientos sociales*, edited by Fernando Quesada, Vol. 13 of the *Enciclopedia iberoamericana de filosofía*, Madrid: Trotta.
——— 1998, 'Sobre la posmodernidad', *Memoria*, 109.
Saussure, Ferdinand de 1966, *Course in General Linguistics*, trans. W. Baskin, New York: McGraw-Hill.
——— 1979 [1915] *Cours de linguistique générale*, Paris: Payot, 1979.
Saussure, Horace Bénédict de 1979, *Premières ascensions au Mont Blanc: 1774–1787*, Paris: Maspero.
Schmidt, Alfred (ed.) 1969a, *Beiträge zur marxistischen Erkenntnistheorie*, Frankfurt: Suhrkamp.
——— 1969b, 'Der strukturalistische Angriff auf die Geschichte', in Schmidt 1969a: 194–267.
——— 1969c, 'Einleitung', in Schmidt 1969a: 7–17
——— 1971 [1962], *The Concept of Nature in Marx*, trans. B. Fowkes, London: NLB.
——— 1972, 'Zum Erkenntnisbegriff der Kritik der politischen Ökonomie', in *Kritik der politischen Ökonomie heute. 100 Jahre 'Kapital'. Referate und Diskussionen vom Frankfurter Colloquium 1967*, edited by Walter Euchner and Alfred Schmidt, Frankfurt: Europäische Verlagsanstalt.
——— 1973, 'Praxis', in *Handbuch Philosophischer Grundbegriffe. Studienausgabe*, Vol. 4, edited by Hermann Krings, Hans Michael Baumgartner, and Christoph Wild, Munich: Kösel.

―――― 1974, *Der Begriff der Natur in der Lehre von Marx*, republished in revised and expanded form, Frankfurt am Main: Europäische Verlagsanstalt.

―――― 1977 'Herrschaft des Subjekts. Über Heideggers Marx-Interpretation', in *Martin Heidegger: Fragen an sein Werk. Ein* Symposium, Stuttgart: Reclam.

―――― 1993, *Der Begriff der Natur in der Lehre von Marx*, Fourth edition, Hamburg: Europäische Verlagsanstalt.

―――― 1994, *Le concept de nature chez Marx*, trans. Jacqueline Bois. Paris: Presses Universitaires de France.

Shelly, Percy Bysshe 1989, 'Mont Blanc, Lines Written in the Vale of Chamouni', in Mary Wollstonecraft Shelley, History of a Six Weeks' Tour (London: Hookham, 1817, facsimile reprint: Oxford, Woodstock).

Thomas, Hugh 1961, *The Spanish Civil War*, New York: Harper and Brothers.

Tinajero Villamar, Fernando 1983, *El desencuentro*, Quito: El Conejo.

―――― 1987, *De la evasión al desencanto*, Quito: El Conejo.

Togliatti, Palmiro 1971, *Escritos politicos*, trans. A. Rossi, Mexico: City: Era.

Troubetzkoy, Nicolas S. 1970, *Principes de Phonologie*, trans. J. Cantineau, Paris: Klincksieck.

Tuñón de Lara, Mañuel 1966, 'Resumen de un optimista. El último año de la República', in *Crónica de la guerra española*, Vol. 5, Buenos Aires: Codex.

Vargas Lozano, Gabriel (ed.), *En torno a la obra de Adolfo Sánchez Vázquez*, Mexico City: UNAM.

Vázquez Montalbán, Manuel 1998, *Y Dios entró en La Habana*, Madrid: Santillana.

Villegas, Paloma and Marcelo Uribe 1995, 'Entrevista con Neus Espresate y Vicente Rojo', in Benítez 1995.

Villoro, Luis 1995, 'El concepto de ideología en Sánchez Vázquez', in *En torno a la obra de Adolfo Sánchez Vázquez*, Mexico City: UNAM.

Viñas, Ricard 1978, *La formación de las Juventudes Socialistas Unificadas, 1934–1936*, Madrid: Siglo XXI.

Wörterbuch der spanischen und deutschen Sprache 1975, Vol. I: *Spanisch-Deutsch*, edited by Rudolf J. Slabý and Rudolf Grossmann, Third edition, revised and expanded by J.M. Banzo Sáenz de Miera, Wiesbaden: Brandstetter.

Wörterbuch der Sprachswierigkeiten 1989, edited by Joachim Dückert and Günther Kempcke, Leipzig: Bibliographisches Institut.

Zapata Galindo, Martha 1995, *Triumph des Willens zur Macht. Zur Nietzsche-Rezeption im NS-Staat*, Hamburg: Argument.

Index of Titles

10 Thesen über Marxismus heute   236n135
1989   74n261, 193, 331, 333
1989: Twelve Months that hanged Eastern Europe   74
20 months of a youth daily   21n25

Aesthetics and Marxism   66
Aesthetic Ideas in Marx's Economical-Philosophical Manuscripts   15, 34
Ahora. Diario de la Juventud   19n22, 21, 33n96
Amauta   59n191
Angelus Novus   212n76
Anthropos   17n7
Antología del Cuento Hispanoamericano   29n75
Apuntes para un Comentario de las Tesis sobre Feuerbach   66n223
Art and society. Essays in Marxist Aesthetics   15, 35, 178, 179, 180
Artistic Enjoyment   66n220
Anschlag, Der   52

Barroque and the History of Culture, The   81n282
Barroque ethos, The   190n3, 198n22, 268n208, 308
Battle of Cuba, The   68
Being and Time   48
Brecht and Lukács' conceptions of realism   39n125
Bufanda del Sol, La   78n269

Capital: Critique of Political Economy   55, 55n175, 66, 66n226, 67, 77n268, 107, 121, **122n137**, 123, 127, 134n186, 146, 146n234, 155, 176, 177, 178, 180, 181n353, 182, 188n1, 202, 206n50, **207, 210**, 211, 216, 219, 220, 222n96, 230n121, 238n138, 241n145, 258, 286, 290, 291n285, 292, 297, 314, 315, 317n358, 318, 323, 325, 326n387, 326n388, 327n388, 328
Casa de las Américas   15, 72
Ciclo de Vírgenes   29n75
Circulación Capitalista y Reproducción de la Riqueza Social, La   78n273

Ciudad sin Ángel   46n145
Comprensión y la crítica de Braudel y Marx sobre el capitalismo   190n5
Concept of cultural mestizaje and the history..., The   78
Concept of Nature in Marx, The   168n319, 215n80
Concept of political culture and political life..., The   79
Consciousness and Reality in Artwork   32
Contribution to the Critique of Political Economy   129, 191, 217, 313, 324
Conversations in Exile   174n333
Conversation on the baroque   268n208
Critical note on the outlines of reproduction sketched..., A   78
Critique of Bourgeois Anti-Imperialism, The   54
Critique of Pure Reason   167n317
Critique of the Gotha Programme   123n140, 254n188, 336
Cuadernos Políticos   56n180, 67, 68n233, 69, 70, 71, 72, 73n255, 74n258, 74n259, 75, 76, 77, 78n269
Cuestiones Marxistas Disputadas   68n233

De la Evasión al Desencanto   47n153
Decadencia del Héroe, La   29, 30
Del Sentimiento Trágico de esta Vida   46n148
Del Socialismo Científico al Socialismo Utópico   68n233
Desencuentro, El   47n153
Dialectic of Enlightenment   237n136, 279n242, 306n326
Dialectics of the Concrete: A Study on Problems of Man and World   116n103, 117n103
Diccionario ideológico de la lengua española   270n215, 311n339
Discourse on Revolution, Critical Discourse   78n269

Economic and Philosophic Manuscripts of 1844   66, 128, 326n387

Eduardo VII y su época 29n75
Effectiveness of antique artworks, The 66n220
Ensayos 29n75
Entorno a la Picaresca 29
Entre Marx y una Mujer Desnuda 46n145
Escrito Políticos 68n233
Escritos de política y filosofía 103n42
España Peregrina 30
Estética y Marxismo 68n233

Filosofía Actual en América Latina, La 37
Filosofía de Praxis como una Nueva Práctica de la Filosofía, La 68n233
Flor Cerrada. Poemas 29n75
Formalism and Forms 66n220
Fourier 29n75
From Bourgeois realism to socialist realism 66n220

General Introduction to the Critique of Political Economy 163, 164
Generelle Morphologie 215
German Ideology, The: Critique of Modern German... 127, 128, 129, 130, 136, 138, 170, 353n17
Gonzalo Sánchez Vázquez, our beloved director 21n25
Graphic diagrams for the study of the fifth chapter of Capital 230n121
Grundisse der Kritik der politischen Ökonomie (Rohentwurf) 176, 177, 178, 180, 198, 202, 216, 343n6
Guardian, The 36

Heidegger 49n158
Heidegger y el ultranazismo 50n159
Heilige Markt, Der. Kulturhistorische Anmerkungen 78n270
Hitler's Willing Executioners. Ordinary Germans and the Holocaust 50n159
Historia y Sociedad 66n223
Historical Materialism: A System of Sociology 154n265
History and Class Consciousness 61, 272, 277, 312, 313, 317n360, 328, 329, 329n394, 353n15

Holy Family or Critique of Critical Criticism, The. Against... 128, 129, 346n10
Hora de España 27
Hora, La. Diario Juvenil 21n25, 33n96

Ideas Estéticas de Marx, Las. Ensayos de estética marxista 68n233
Ideas of Marx on the Source and Nature of the Aesthetic, The 15n5
Ideología y sociedad en América Latina 47n153
Illusions of Modernity, The 80, 226n109, 278, 309, 310
Intellectuality in Latin America 60
Introduction. From ordinary consciousness to the philosophical... 95
Introduction to the Critique of Hegel's Philosophy of Right 127, 129

Jornada, La 81

Langenscheidts Taschenwörterbuch der spanischen und... 94n4
Latinoamérica 60
Legend of the Origin of the Book Tao-Te-Ching on Lao-Tsu's Road... 200
Letras del Ecuador 78n269
Línea 18
Lire le Capital 155n270, 165n312

Manifesto of the Communist Party 128, 130, 131, 132, 181n353, 343n7
Marcha 70, 70n239, 70n243
Marx, Engels y la Revolución de 1848 33n96
Marx Lexikon. Zentrale Begriffe del politischen Philosophie von Karl Marx 62n204
Marx y la Democracia 68n233
Marxism-Leninism, Lenin and Trotskyism... 21n27
Marxismo latinoamericano, El. Historia y Problemas actuales 47n153
Marxismo y Filosofía 68n233
Marx's Critical Discourse 78, 206n50, 209n64
Materialismo de Marx, El 66n223
Materialismo storico e la filosofia di Benedetto Crocce, Il 154n265

INDEX OF TITLES

Meaning of Truth, The   153
Memorias de Pancho Villa. Tercera Parte: panoramas políticos   29n75
Metáforas teológicas de Marx, Las   291n284
Meyers Kleines Konversationslexikon   49n158, 270n217
Modernidad de lo Barroco, La   81n282
Modernity and Capitalism   81, 226, 226n109, 227n109, 268n208, 307, 335
Modernity, Cultural Mestizaje, Baroque Ethos   80, 198n22, 281, 309, 311n339
Modernity Outside Europe: the Case of Latin America   42, 280n249
Monde, Le   36
Mont Blanc, Line Written in the Vale of Chamouni   170
Mots et les choses, Les   227
Mundo Obrero   18, 27
Museum des Geldes. Über die seltsame Natur des Geldes...   78n270

Nariz del Diablo   78
"Natural form" of social reproduction, The   197n21, 201, 201n39, 206n50, 215, 216, 225n104, 230, 251, 261n198,
New Left Review   72
Nexos   74, 74n258
Nicomachean Ethics   123n140
Nietzsche   29n75
Novelties of form and artistic refunctionalism   66n220

Octubre   17
Odyssey, The   298
On Praxis   35
On the concept of history   190
On the Realist Way of Writing   66n220
Once Tesis sobre Socialismo y Democracia   68n233
One Dimensional Man   353n15
Ödipus. Ein Held der westlichen Welt...   78n270

Palabra Suelta   78n269
Paris Manuscripts of 1844   127, 128n158, 130, 131, 138, 177
Pasado y Presente   70, 70n239

Pasaremos. Órgano de la 11a División   23, 23n36, 23n38
Pensamiento Crítico   70n239, 71
Pequeño Espasa, El   270n215
Philosophical conceptions and practical results   153
Philosophy of Nature   261n198
Philosophy of Praxis, The   15, 33n96, 35, 35n106, 35n108, 85, 87n304, 89, 90, 93, 93n1, 95, **96**, 97, 97n16, **97n17, 97n18**, 98, 99n24, 101n29, 101n31, 104n45, 110, 112n78, **113**, 115, 117n109, 122, 122n137, 124n142, 125, 133, 134, 142n222, 145, 148, 149n243, 149n245, 150, 151, 154, 177, 179, 181, **183**, 183n355, 184, 184n359, 185, 199, 344, 348, 352, 356n18
Philosophy of praxis as a new philosophical practice   96, 99
Philosophy of Right, The   150
Piedra y cielo   30n75
Poesía de Gil Vicente   29n75
Politeia   117n110
Politics   119
Postmodernity y Cynism   82n286, 195,196n8, 263, 331n398
POUM youth continue their politics of blackmail, The   21n27
Pour Marx   130, 155n270, 165n312
Pragmatism: a new name for some old ways of thinking   153
Procontra   78n269
Pucuna   59, 78n269
Pumaccahua   29n75
Pulso Ardiendo, El   18
Punto Crítico   74n259
Punto Final   70, 70n239, 70n241

Rama Viva, La   29n75
Razón Amenazada, La   103n42
Reading Capital   155, 156
Reason and Revolution   150, 217
Refugee Dialogues   174
Reification and the consciousness of the proletariat   275, 328
Review   227n109
Revista Latinoamericana   78n269
Revolución Teórica Comunista en las Tesis sobre Feuerbach, La   66n223

Revolutionäre Praxis. Jugoslawischer Marxismus der Gegenwart   117n103
Revolutions in Philosophy, The   38
Rhetoric and the baroque   281
Rifles, The   60
Rivoluzione contro il capitale, La   154n265
Romance de la Ley de Fugas   17n9
Romance, Revista Popular Hispanoamericana   26, 27, 29, 29n72, 29n75
Rousseau and Marx   129

Schriften, Briefe in 7 Bänden (8 Teilbände)   61n204
Self-Assertation of the German University, The   49n158
Sense of Time in the Poetry of Antonio Machado, The   31
Seven Interpretive Essays on Peruvian Reality   58n190
Sobre el barroco romano y la Roma de Bernini   282n258
Sobre el Materialismo. Modelo para Armar   66n223
Socialism, Utopian and Scientific   151
Solidarity   72n249
Sprachphilosophie   254
Sur   18

Taller   27
Texto con personajes   46n145

Teoría, práctica teórica y formación teórica. Ideología y luhca...   165n312
Teoricismo de Althusser, El: notas críticas sobre una autocrítica   68n233, 161n291
Theory and practice   37
Theses on Feuerbach   66, **99**, 99n24, 100, 106n54, 117, 126, **127**, 128, 131, **132**, 133, 134, 135, 138, 139, 139n209, 140, 140n214, 141, 142, 143, 144n226, 146, 147, 147n240, 148, 148n242, 149n243, 151, 151n260, 152, 153, 158n284, 163, 168, 175, 178, 181, 199, 199n28, 202, 255n188, 330n395, 344, 347n11
Tres en Uno. Auto sacramental a la usanza antigua...   29n75
Triebstruktur des Geldes. Ein Beitrag zur Theorie der Weiblichkeit   78n270

Versuch über den Gebrauchswert   78n270
Vida de Don Quijote y Sancho   46n148
Viento del Sur   81n283, 195n8

Wasteful Capitalism. The North American Economical Miracle   64
Wesen des Christentums, Das   134
Works and Days   124
Wörterbuch der spanischen und deutschen Sprache   94n4, 270n215
Wretched of the Earth, The   52n165, 60

Index of Concepts

Abstract   164n306
Accumulation
    Primitive accumulation   292, 292n287
Activity   see Praxis
Aesthetics   110n72, 113, 135, 158n283, 176, 277, 314
    Aesthetic attitude   179
    Aesthetic criteria   179
    Aesthetic sensibility   179
Alienation   263, 312
Althusserianism   161, 177
Anarchism   17, 18, 20, 20n24, 23, 118n113
Anthropologism   85, 108n62, 130
Anthropology   177
Antiquity   117, 121, 122, 243n156, 278, 298
    Ancient Greece   117, 117n110, 118, 118n112, 118n113, 119n117, 121, 123, 123n140, 124, 125
Anti-semitism   134n186, 237n136, 255, 256
Aristotelianism   106
Art   119, 121, 145n231, 179, 229, 281, 281n253, 282n258
    Architecture   281
    Art criticism   255n189
    Art history   262n201, 280, 281, 282, 295, 311
    Artistic creation   145n231
    Artistic development   180
    Audience   179
    Baroque   213, 268, 280, 281, 282, 282n258, 306, 311n339
    Classicism   295
    Literature   179, 280
    Mannerism   282, 282n258
    Mechanical art   125
    Post-renaissance   303n318
    Western art   303n318
Asceticism   291n284
Aufheben   100, 301
Authoritarianism   160, 173
    Anti-authoritarianism   302

Barbarism   272, 283
Base   314
    Economic base   314, 315n352

Behavior   163, 293, 296, 303, 306n326
    Scientific behavior   237n136
Bios Theoretikós   119, *from now on see* Theoretical life
Bourgeoisie   167, 233n130, 234n130, 254n188, 255, 255n189, 276, 284, 285n266, 286, 297n301
    Bourgeois ideology   255
    Bourgeois philosophy   107n55, 177, 256
    Bourgeois state   150
    Bourgeois stupidity   255, 255n189
    Bourgeois thinkers   167
    Revolutionary bourgeoisie   146

Capital   188, 259, 296, 298, 306, 309n337
    Commercial capital   121
Capitalism
    Anti-capitalism   285, 301
    Capitalist economy   305
    Liberal capitalism   258
    Pro-capitalism   174n335
    Puritan capitalism   289
    Spirit of capitalism   289, 290
    State capitalism   258, 258n193, 260, 283
Category
    Cognitive category   143
    Sociological category   143
Censorship   264n204
Chauvinism   237
Christianity   118n113, 255n189, 290, 291, 291n284, 292, 292n287, 293, 305n325
    Catholicism   49, 287, 289, 291n285, 304, 311, 311n339
    Christian antisemitism   300n309
    Franciscans   311, 311n339
    Jesuits   304, 305, 305n325, 306, 311, 311n339
    Paradoxical christianity   300n309
Circulation   285
    Mercantil ciruclation   301
Citizenship   119, 243n156
Civilisation   286, 288n272
Class   108, 129, 182, 233n130, 255n188, 276, 284, 285

Clas ideology   179
Class relations   *see* Relations *and subentries*
   Dominant class   124, 124n142, 284, 298, 315
   Dominated class   284
   Middle class   250
   Ruling class   *see* Dominant Class
   Urban middle class   250
   Working class   174n333, 235 *see also* Proletariat
Codification   254
Collectivity   229
   Bureaucratic collectivity   258n193
   Collective subject   303
Colony   292n287
Commerce   138n206
Commodity   107, 121, 122n137, 123n140, 146, 160, 274, 275, 291, 291n285, 292, 305, 306n326, 315, 316, 317
   Commodity exchange   278, 279
   Commodity fetishism   *see* Fetishism *and subentries*
   Commodity production   122, 158, 182, 274, 291, 312, 315, 315n352, 316, 317
   Spirit of commodity   291n285
Common sense   101n30, 102, 255n189
Commonplace   233n130
Communication   229, 231, 233, 234, 238, 239n141, 245, 246
   Communicative act   233, 239
   Means of communication   239
   Process of communication   230, 231
Communism   17, 20, 20n24, 55, 56, 56n179, 58n190, 61, 128n158, 158, 159, 164, 174n333, 233n130, 255, 276
   Anti-communism   61, 62n204, 167
   Pseudo-communism   57
Concentration camps   24
Concrete   164n306
   Real concrete   164
   Concrete thought   164
Conformism
   Non-conformism   301, 302
Conscious objective activity   *see* Praxis
Consciousness   85, 99, 101, 102n39, 103n41, 105, **106**, 109, 111, 114, 126, 132, 137, 144, 145n231, 147, 149, 160, 169, 169n322, 171, **179**, **181**, **182**, 183, 259, 275, 291n285, 312, **314**, 316n356

Class consciousness   33, 179, 183
Consciousness manipulation   179, 180
Consciousness of praxis   101, 103, 118n112
Critical consciousness   106
Emancipatory consciousness   181
Enlightened consciousness   181
Everyday consciousness   101n30, 102, 103, 104, 104n44, 105, 106, 107, 107, 107n55, 108, 109, 109n65, 110, 111, 112, 113, 115, 117, 234n132
Everyday consciousness of praxis   102, 110, 111, 113
False consciousness   107, 314, 318
Free consciousness   181
Ideological consciousness   107
Ordinary consciousness   *see* Everyday consciousness
Ordinary proletarian consciousness   103
Philosophical consciousness   109, 109n65, 114, 115, 315n352
Philosophical consciousness of praxis   103, 104, 114, 115
Philosophy of consciousness   171
Political consciousness   113
Proletarian consciousness   103
Reified consciousness   145, 275, 299
Socialist consciousness   183
Unconsciousness   175, 297n302
Conservatism   285n266, 301, 302
   Enlightened conservatives   174
Consumption   188, 229, 231, 232, 233, 234, **235**, 236, 239n141, 240, 241, 249, 251, 252, 255n188, 266, 271, **277**, 284, 285, 293, **294**, 295, 297, 298, 307
   Productive consumption   241n144, 248
Crisis
   Revolutionary crisis   288
Criticism   137
Culture   229, 250, 252, 254, 282, 301, 303
   Cultural determinations   229, 285
   Cultural process   259
   Culturalism   282
   Cultures   253n184, 259, 278, 303n317, 304
   High culture   281
   History of culture   282
Cynism   124, 125n148

Democracy   263
   Bourgeois Democrats   167

INDEX OF CONCEPTS 453

Social-democracy 174, 174n335, 255n188, 299
Depoliticisation 112
Development 236, 237, 250, 255, 296, 316
    Capitalist development 293
    Industrial development 170
    Underdevelopment 236, 250
Dialectics 32, 103, 150, 154, 171, 175, 178n344, 248, 262, 317n358
Dictatorship 258n193
Discourse 234n130, 245, 249
Discrimination 264n204

Economism 180, 182
Economics 230n121, 293, 305
    Capitalist economy 258n193
    Economic circulation 258n193
    Economic structure 307, 314
Education 106, 143, 144, 146
Effectivity 150, 153
Emancipation 179, 181
Emigration 178n344
Empiricism 140, 141,142, 143n224, 153, 156, 160, 164, 316n356
End of time 113
Ends 169, 247n171
Enlightenment 76, 106n52, 123n140, 144, 237n136, 279
    German Enlightenment 144
Epistemology 168, 175
Equality 123n140, 254n188, 255, 255n188, 261n199
    Inequality 254, 255n188
Eros 279
Eroticism 303
Ethics 150, 277, 289n278
    Protestan ethic 289
Ethnicity 182
Ethnology 229
Ethnocentrism 237n136, 255n189, 265
    Non-ethnocentrism 290
    Structural ethnology 114n87
Ethos 42, 188, 265, 266, **268n208, 269, 270,** **270n217, 270n219, 271, 271n219, 271n220, 271n221,** 274, 276, 277, 280, 281n253, 282, 284, 285, 288, 289, 289n278, 290, 293, 295, 297, 298, 299, 300, 301, 303, 304, 304n320, 306, 307, 308, 309, 312, 313

Baroque ethos 266, 267, 268n208, **280, 281n253, 285,** 288, 288n272, **289,** 294, 295, 300, 300n309, 301, 301n309, **302, 303,** 303n318, **304,** 304n320, 306, 307, 308, 311, 312
Classic ethos 280, 295, 299, 299n304, 300
Custom 269
Ethos of capitalist modernity 284
Everyday life ethos 266
Habit 269
Historical ethos 268, 268n208, 269, 271, 273, 277, 277n235, 281, 306, 307, 311
Modern ethos 42, 264, 265, 281n253, 311
Personality 269
Professional ethos 271n220
Realist ethos 280, 288, 289, 293, 294, 295, 296, 297, 299, 300, 301, 306, 307, 308, 309
Romantic ethos 280, 295, 297, 297n302, 298, 299, 300, 301
Use 269
τὸ ἦθος 269, *from now on see* Ethos
Eurocentrism 84, 236, 236n134, 237, 237n136, 251, 254, 255, 257, 258, 265, 265n206, 267, 275, 276, 285n266, 312
    Anti-eurocentrism 58n190
    Tsarist eurocentrism 236n134
Everyday *see* Everydayness
Everydayness 101n30, 104, 107n55, 113, 250, 272, 273, 281, 291n285, 304n320, 305n325, 309n337
    Capitalist everydaynes 251
    Everyday man 101n30
    Everyday consciousness *see* Consciousness *and subentries*
    Everyday forms of reproduction *see* Reproduction
    Everyday knowledge *see* Knowledge *and subentries*
    Everyday political praxis *see* Praxis *and subentries*
    Everyday understanding of praxis 101n30
    Ordinary man *see* Everyday man
Exchange 316, 317
Exile 178, 179, 182, 185
Existencialism 32
Experience 152
Exploitation 118n113

Fact
  Capitalist fact   299n304
  Practical fact   142
Faith   291n285, 304
Falseness   141, 276, 301, 312
  Falsification   178
  Social falseness   284
Fascism   19, 20n24, 106, 145n231, 275
  Anti-fascism   15, 75, 275n231
Feminism   118n113
Fetishism   107, 160, 247n168, 291, 292, 313, 315, 316
  Commodity fetishism   158, 182, 312, 315, 316, 317n360
Feuerbachianism   114n87, 130
Folklore   307
Folklorisation   307
Form   167n317
Form of production   see Mode of production
Francoism   16, 19, 19n23, 20, 24, 25, 26, 26n54, 47n149, 68
  Anti-Fracoism   20n24
Frankfurt School   105, 170, 237n136, 300n309
Freedom   229, 238, 240n142, 261n199, 266, 315
Friendship   123n140
  Political Friendship   123n140

Gegenstand   134, 135
Gegenständliche   see Objectivity
  Gegenständlicher Schein   108n58, from now on see Objective appearance
Gender   118n113
Genocide   283, 283n262
Geometry   119
  Non-Euclidean geometry   157
Gnoseology   114n88
Government   314n351
Grand narratives   257

Happiness   301
Hegelianism   100, 102, 129, 150, 248, 260, 262, 262n201
  Left Hegelianism   128
  Hegelianising   130, 261, 262, 317n360
Heideggerianism   61, 62, 286
Hitoricism   133n184

History   157, 230, 238, 244, 263, 272, 278, 287n272, 288n272, 297, 301, 301n309, 302, 316
  Historical act   238n138
  History of ideas   115, 125, 157
  History of praxis   157
  History of theory   see History of ideas
  Real history   115
Holy Inquisition   257
Humanism   133n184, 309n337

Ideal process   172
Idealism   32, 100, 101, 102, 112, 120, 132, 134, 135, 137, 139,142, 143n224, 149, 152, 153, 164, 165, 167, 168, 172, 175, 249, 314n352
  Dialectical idealism   248
  German idealism   101n31, 103, 151
  Hegelian idealism   129
  Idealist epistemology   132
Identity   160, 167n317, 242n147
Ideology   106, 107, **129**, 177, 180, 181, **182**, 188, 232n127, 233n130, 237, 243n156, 251, 253n184, 272, 274, 275, 276, **277**, 279, 290, 293, 293n292, 299, 302, **313, 314**, 314n351, 315, 315n352, 317, **324**, 331, 352
Imaginary   306
Immanentism   133n184
Imperialism   56, 66n226, 103n41, 234n130
  Anti-imperialism   56n181
Indigenous   292n287, 304n320, 305
Individualism   114
Individuality   229
Industry   138n206
Industrialisation   250, 251
Irony   264n204
  Self-irony   263n204

Judaism   49
Justice   305, 305n325
  Bourgeois justice   306n326

Knowledge   15, 101n29, 105, 107, 114n87, 115, 117, 127, **132, 133**, 134, 135, 136, 137, 138, 139n209, 140, 140n214, 141, 141n216, 142, 143, 143n224, 151n260, **153**, 153n263, 154, 156, 157, 159, 160, 161, 161n291, 162, 164, 165, 167, 167n317, 168, 172, 175, 176, 176n338, 178, 232, 234, 259, 264, 312, 313, 315, **317n356, 349**
  Anticipatory knowledge   172

INDEX OF CONCEPTS 455

Basis of knowledge   159, 160
Contemplative knowledge   124n142
Cognoscitive relationship   135, 137, 170
Criterion of truth   132, 133, 138, 142, 142n220, 143, 153, 154, 157, 159, 160, 164, 165
Economic knowledge   182
End of knowledge   132, 133, 157, 160, 161, 164, 165
Everyday knowledge   108
Experimental knowledge   114n87
Experimentation   114n87
Knowledge act   300
Process of knowledge   133, 246n164
Theoretical knowledge   101, 142, 174

Labour   **118, 123n140**, 230n121, 236, 240n143, 241, 241n144, 241n145, 243, 243n155, 244, 244n157, 245, 253n186, 254n188, 255n188, 291, 304, 306n326, 315, 316, 317, **322**
  Alienated labour   130
  Division of labour   118n113
  Human labour   107, 122n137, 123, 123n140, 124, 124n143
  Instruments of labour   241, 241n144, 241n145, **242**, 242n148, 243, 243n155, 244, 244n157, 244n158, 244n159, 245n159, 246, 247n170, 248n176
  Labour force   159, 261n199
  Labour of education   144, 147
  Labour-power   123n140, 124n143, 159, 254, 306n326
  Labour process   171, 242n148, 244n157, 245, 246n164, 248, 248n176, 274
  Labourer   245, 246, 293, 316
  Manual labour   124n142
  Means of labour   243n153, 245n159, 247n170
  Object of labour   241, 241n144, 242, 242n148, 243, 243n153, 244, 245, 245n161, 246
  Servile labour   124
  Slave labour   121, 123n140
  Social labour   169
  Subject of labour   245n161
  Tool   241, 241n146, 242, 243, 243n155, 244, 244n157, 244n158, 244n159, 245, 246, 246n167, 247, 247n168, 247n171, 248, 249, 292

Workshop   244n157
Langage   *see* Speech
Faculté de langage   *see* Speech
Language   232, 232n126, 233n130, 234n130, 238, **239**, 240, **240n141, 240n142**, 241, 242, 246, 251, 252, 252n183, 266
  Everyday language   297
  Nature of language   232
  Propaganda language   297
  Spoken language   233n130, 234n130
Law   161, 240n143, 305
Lenguaje   *see* Speech
Leninism   57n186, 74n259, 86, 183, 184
Liberalism   56n181
Libertarianism   *see* Anarchism
Linguistics   169, 229n120, 232, 232n125, 233, 239, 249, 252, 287n272
Logic
  Attribute   141
  Formal logic   141
  Indicator   141

Machinery   293
Market   235, 305, 305n323
  Free law of the market   305
Marxism   15, 18, 25, 31, 32, 33, 34, 35, 37, 38, 40, 55, 56n181, 58, 61, 61n204, 62, 62n206, 63, 65, 68n233, 71, 81, 84, 85, 86, 87, 87n304, 88, 88n305, 89, 89n311, 90, 101, 102, 118n113, 123n140, 126n153, 128, 131, 151, 153, 154, 156, 164, 245, 254, 296
  Academic Marxism
  Anti-Marxism   62n204, 123n140
  Classical Marxism   103n42
  Critical Marxism   58n191, 84, 85, 86, 88, 88n307, 104n45, 167, 168, 185, 188, 245, 260, 299
  Dogmatic Marxism   *see* Orthodox Marxism
  French Marxism   161
  Hegelian Marxism   102, 150
  Marxian concept of praxis   131
  Marxian theory   126
  Marxism-Leninism   *see* Orthodox Marxism
  Marxist activist   167
  Marxist authors   103, 106, 134n186, 139, 152, 156, 164, 167

Marxist criticism 135
Marxist epistemology 109, 156
Non-dogmatic Marxism *see* Critical Marxism
Orthodox Marxism 58, 84, 85, 86, 87, 88, 89, 89n311, 104, 167, 168, 173, 179, 179n350, 180, 181, 182, 235, 245, 259, 272, 286, 296
Petrifications of Marxism *see* Orthodox Marxism
Scientific character of Marxism 156
Western Marxism 127, 167, 182, 237n136, 272, 274, 275, 276, 279
Mass 173
Mass media 182
Material process 172
Materialism 34, 85, 100, 102, 132, 134, 144, 167, 167n317, 168, 169, 169n322, 171, 229, 248, 264
  Anthropological materialism 99
  Diamat 33, 34
  Dialectical materialism 102, 114n87, 167n317, 169n322, 171
  Existing materialism 134, 135, 137
  Historical materialism 172, 233n130, 246, 246n164
  Marxist materialism 171
  Materialist appearance 282
  Materialist doctrine 143
  Materialist history of culture 281, 282
  Materialist metaphysics 154
  Mechanical materialism 175
  Pre-Marxist materialism 136, 167
  Old materialism 154
  Traditional materialism 132, 135, 137, 139, 149, 152, 247
  Vulgar materialism 102
Materiality 176, 231
Mathematics 230n121
Matter 167n317, 169
  Law of matter 169, 171
Means 246n164, 247
  Means of production *see* Production *and subentries*
  Means of reproduction *see* Reproduction *and subentries*
  Means of transformation 162
Meanings 234, 234n132, 239n141
  Meaningful 234

Mechanicism 102
Mediation 105, 172
Medium 161
Messianism 272, 313
Mestizaje 77n268, 79, 80, 303, 303n317
  Cultural mestizaje 79, 80, 303n317, 304
  Mestiza food 80
Metaphysics 237
Method 164n306, 233, 264, 266
  Baroque method 306
  Dialectical method 261
  Semiotic method 266
Mode of Production 74, 121, 124, 282, 286, 291n285
  Capitalist mode of production 74, 76, 83, 111, 170, 173, 174, 188, **235**, 236, 237, 253, 253n186, 254, 272, 273, 277, 280, 283n262, 284, 285, 286, 289, 290, 291, 291n285, 293, 295, 296, 297, 297n302, 298, 299, 300, 301, 302, 304, 309, **335**, 356
  Commodity mode of production 273
  Feudal mode of production 276
  Pre-capitalist mode of production 286
  Slave-holding mode of production 125
Modernity 237n136, 253, 257, 258, 259, 260, 261, 262, 265n206, 266, 267, 268n208, 278, 279, 280, 283n262, 284, 284n265, 285, 286, 287, 289, 295, 303n318, 305, 307, 309, 310, 312
  Actually-existing modernity 257, 258, 259, 260, 261, 262, 263, 264, 265
  Baroque modernity 308, 309
  Capitalist modernity 188, 259n195, **264**, 266, 268n208, 273, 276, **278**, 284, 285, 286, 287, 288, 289, 290, 295, 298, 299, 300, 301, 303, 304, 304n320, 306, 307, 308, 311, 312
  Classic modernity 308, 309
  Concrete modernity 262, 264
  Cruelty of modernity 283n262
  Dominant modernity 286
  Jesuit modernity 304, 305
  Modernisation 302, 305n325
  Modernities *see* Modernity
  Non-capitalist modernity 264, 266, 280, 287, 305
  Post-capitalist modernity 285, 287, 288, 302, 312

INDEX OF CONCEPTS 457

Pre-modernity   308, 309
Real modernity   262, 262n201, 263, 312
Realist modernity   309, 310
Religious modernity   304
Romantic modernity   308, 309
Monarchy   287n272
Money   316
Monopoly   305
Moral   172, 270, 271n219, 271n220, 305n325
   Moral action   95, 166n316
Mysticism   142, 306
Myth   279
   Modern myth   279, 309
   Myth of democracy   309, 310
   Myth of nation   309, 310
   Myth of revolution   309, 310
   Mythical complex   309n337

Nation   242n147
Nationalism   20, 49, 49n158, 251n181
National Socialism   19, 49, 49n158, 50n163, 73n255, 75, 106, 106n52, 131n176, 252n183, 253n184, 258n193, 275
Natural form   229n120, 230n121, 266, 271, 298
Nature   176n338, 177, 231, **234**, 234n132, 240n143, 242, 243, 243n156, 245, 245n160, 247, 254, 255n188, 279, **321**, **347**, 350
   External nature   146, 171n326, 172, 172n330, 245, 247n171, 283, 283n262
   Human nature   243n156
   Humanised nature   138
   Internal nature   146
   Laws of nature   171, 238
   Naturalisation   284, 298
   Virgin nature   138
Nazism   *see* National Socialism
Neoliberalism   83
Neurology   188
Nihilism   49

Object   105, 109, **132**, 133, **135**, 136, 137, 138, 146, 149n245, 150, 161, 162, 164, 166, 167n317, 169, 170, 173, 184, 231, 233, 234, 235, 238, 243, 246, 246n167, 248, 277n235, 316n356, 317n356
   Object of labour   *see* Labour *and subentries*

Objekt   134, 135
Practical object   111
Social object   241n145

Objectification   123, 135
Objective appearance   **261**, 261n199, 272, 275, **317**, 317n358
Objectivism   *see* Objectivity
   Simple objectivism   175
Objectivity   85, 99, 99n24, 100, 103, 107, 110, 111, 126, 132, 134, 135, 146, 147, 153, 154, 162, 163, 166, 169, 173, 175, 182, 234n132, 270n219, 274, 277, 306
   Material objectivity   169
Objektiv   99n24, *from now on see* Objectivity
Obscurantism   144
Ontology   169, 176
Oppression   118n113

Pacifism   118n113
Paradox   300, 300n309, 301n309, 302, 303
Party   106, 276n233
   Revolutionary party   184
   Workers' party   184n361
Peace
   Internal peace   288
Perceptions   161
Pessimism   110, 111, 283
Philosophy   *see* Theory
   Philosopher king   120, 121
Pinochetism   70n240
Platonism   120n128, 292, 293
Plurality   258, 288n272
Poiesis (ποίησις)   95, 118n112
Point of view   *see* Standpoint
   Economic point of view   258n193
Polis   118
Political economy   130, 176, 188, 290, 305, 305n325, 313
   Classical political economy   111
   Critical political economy*   177, 180, 181, 182, 188, 232, 313
Politicism   112n78
   Practical politicism   112
   Practical apoliticism   112
Politics   145n231, 312, 313
   Emancipatory politics   152
   Modern political culture   309n337

Political culture   309, 309n337
Political currents   251
Political groups   251
Realist political culture   309n337
Popularisation   306
Positivism   154, 182, 238n138, 265, 265n206, 309n337
  Neopositivismo   102
Postmodernity   253n184, 254, 257, 258, 261, 261n199, 279, 288
  Actually-existing postmodern spirit   257, 259n195
  Actually-existing postmodern thought   257
Power   112, 139, 139n209, 141, 176n338, 237, 243, 246, 285n266, 288n272
  Empowerment   296
  Labour-power   see Labour *and subentries*
Practical   *see* Utilitarianism
Practice   94, 94n7, 95, 96, 96n13, 97, 98, 98n20, 105n49, 107, 109, 119, 120n128, 121, 125, 134, 135, 137, 142, 142n220, 154, 158, 158n281, 166, 166n316, 172
  Historical practice   *see* Historical praxis
  Mediating practice   171
  Práctica   93, 94n4, *from now on see* Practice
  Practical life   121
  Practical reason   121
  Practices   94n7
  Practicism   *see* Utilitarianism
  Práctico   94n7
  Praktik   94, 94n7, 95, 98
  Praktiken   94
  Pratica   93
  Pratique   94
  пра́ктика (russian)   94
  Theoretical practice   97n17
Pragmatism   140, 141, 141n216, 153, 153n263, 156
Praxis   15, 34, 35n108, 37, 57, 63, 71, 75, 76, 81, 86, 87n304, 89, 188, 229, 234, 238n138, 260, 261n199, 277
  Anti-francoist praxis   132
  Artistic praxis   108, 113, 176, 177
  Consumptive praxis   229
  Continuos praxis   146
  Cosmic praxis   157
  Creative praxis   108
  Dirty judaical praxis   134n186
  Economic praxis   233n130
  Emancipatory praxis   93, 152
  Everyday political praxis   103
  Future praxis   156
  Historical praxis   105, 105n49, 169, 174
  Imposed praxis   140
  Objective praxis   114n87, 165
  Political praxis   15, 93, 95n8, 120, 121, 126n153, 130, 131, 172, 176, 177, 178, 233n130, 299
  Prassi   93
  Praxis of social emancipation   *see* Emancipatory praxis
  Productive material praxis   119
  Productive praxis   118, 119, 119n116, 120, 121, 123, 124, 124n146, 131, 171, 229
  Progressive praxis   160
  Proletarian praxis   130
  Reproductive praxis   178
  Revolutionary praxis   103, 104n44, 104n45, 106n54, 108, 110, 113, 143, 144, 144n226, 146, 147, 149, 151, 154, 156, 160, 164, 177, 233n130
  Social praxis   15, 37, 93, 156, 158, 283
  Still non-existent praxis   157
  Theoretical praxis   158n280, 161, 162, 163, 164, 165, 166
  Total praxis   158n281
  Transformative praxis   93, 143, 144n226, 156, 157, 162
  πρᾶξις (greek)   93
Pre-hispanic Civilization   58n191, 64, 79, 80, 303
Production   111, 188, 229, 231, 232, 233, 234, 235, 236, 239, 239n141, 240, 240n143, 241, 245, 246, 249, 250, 251, 252, 266, 271, 272, 275, 277, 284, 285, 293, 294, 295, 297, 298, 307, 314, 316
  Capitalist relations of production   167, 182, 188, 272, 273, 276, 277, 289, 296, 301
  Ends of production   247
  Intellectual production   159
  Material production   159
  Means of production   26, 159, 254, 258n193
  Production of knowledge   163

INDEX OF CONCEPTS   459

Production of value   see Production
Productive force   250, 278, 279, 289, 292,
    296, 309n337, 316
Relations of production   233n130, 291,
    296, 313, 314, 314n347, 315
Productivism   236
    Capitalist productivism   302
    Economic productivism   236
    Western productivism   236
Progress   125, 144, 309n337
    Socio-historic progress   109
    Technical progress   125
Progressivism   236
Proletariat   25, 32, 57n182, 72, 103, 103n41,
    103n42, 151n260, 174n333, 179, 180, 181, 182,
    184, 233n130, 234n130, 235, 275, 276
    Proletarian revolution   see Revolution
        and subentries
    Revolutionary proletariat   179
Pronounceability   169
Propaganda   178, 233n130, 311n339
Property   313, 316
    Private property   128n158
Protestantism   289, 290, 291, 291n284,
    291n285, 305, 308
    Calvinism   289
    Puritanism   291n285, 293, 294
Psychoanalysis   297n302
Psychology   162, 188, 232, 232n127, 301
    Social Psychology   232, 232n127

Racism   145n231, 236n134, 237n136, 253n184,
    303, 304, 304n320
Radicalism   312
Raw material   241, 241n144, 242, 243,
    243n153, 248, 248n176
Realism   104n44, 110n72, 262n201, 293, 295
    Ingenuous realism   110, 110n72, 111,
        132
    Political realism   299
    Socialist realism   33, 135, 135n194,
        158n283, 179
Reality   126, 133, 139, 139n209, 140n214, 150,
    152, 154, 162, 163, 164n306, 180, 230,
    253n184, 257, 260, 261, 261n198, 261n199,
    262n201, 274, 312, 316n356
    Capitalist reality   296, 300
    External reality   169, 169n322,

Magic realism   307
Material reality   154
Monolithic reality   284n265
Sensuous reality   137
Reason   121, 141, 144, 172, 245, 246, 246n167
Rationalism   144, 266, 278, 299, 309n337
Reflection   158n283
Reflejo   158n283, *from now on see*
    Reflection
Reflexión   158n283, *from now on see*
    Reflection
Reformism   173, 174, 175, 263, 299
Refugee   178n344
Reification   263, 313, 317, 317n360
Religion   146, 166n316, 182, 277, 287n272, 291,
    311n339, 314
    Church   305n325
    Deism   291
    Monotheism   287n272
    Polytheism   287n272
    Salvation   294
Reproduction   229, 233, 238, 245, 249, 259,
    266, 271
    Capitalist reproduction   264
    Everyday form of reproduction   229
    Material reproduction   229, 233
    Means of reproduction   316
    Process of reproduction   230, 231, 233,
        248, 296
    Spiritual reproduction   164
Revolution   236n135, 261, 263, 278, 286, 314,
    314n347
    Bourgeois revolution   276
    Counter-revolution   275, 278
    Myth of the revolution   234n130
    Proletarian revolution   159
    Revolutionary pulse   302
    Revolutionary subjectivity   275
Richtigkeit   139n209
Romanticism   112

Sandinism   38, 131, 185
Saussureanism   252
Scarcity   253n186
Skepticism   147
Science   125, 143, 158, 160, 229, 232n127, 250
    Natural science   114n87, 138n206, 140,
        232n127

Positive science 160
Scientifiscism 102, 103, 154
Social sciencie 232n127, 266
Technology 125
Scholasticism 126n153, 139
Secularisation 306
Semiology 229n120, 232, 232n125, 232n126, 232n127
Semiotics 229, 230, 232, 232n127, 233, 238, 239n141, 240, 241, 248, 249, 251, 252, 256, 264, 267, 303n317
  Semiotic exchange 188
  Semiotic process 303n317
Senses 137n199, 138n206, 152, 161
Sign 230, 231, 232, 232n127, 233, 234, 239, 240, 241, 252, 266, 277, 283
  Codigo-phagia 303, 303n317
  Sign system 239, 249, 266, 277, 301, 303, 307, 309
Signified 238, 240, 240n142, 241, 242, 248, 249
Signifier 238, 240, 240n142, 241, 242, 248, 249
Slavery 118n114, 121, 124, 124n142, 249, 258n193, 292, 293
Social movement 118n113
Social relations 316
  Class relations 176
Socialisation 279, 305, 309
  Capitalist mode of socialisation 283
Socialism 20, 20n24, 22, 39, 40, 58, 58n190, 74, 75, 83, 86, 87n304, 88, 89, 104n44, 118n113, 145n231, 173, 174, 179, 245, 259, 260, 272
  Actually-existing socialism 167, 260
  Real socialism 260
  Revolutionary socialism 260
  Scientific socialism 129, 151n260
  Socialist revolution 174
  Utopian socialism 144
Society 108n62, 115, 118n113, 119, 122, 123n140, 126, 136, 137n199, 143, 144, 159, 160, 176n338, 179, 181, 182, 185, 232n127, 242, 242n147, 243n156, 255, 263, 271n219, 278, 279, 281, 281n253, 284, 289, 291, 292, 314, 316
  Bourgeois society 182, 188, 261n199, 296, 297, 302, 317
  Capitalist society 179

Competitive society 303
Modern society 312
Post-capitalist society 304
Social creation 145n231
Socialist society 260
Sociology 172
Socratic 125n148
Sophism 124
Sovereignty 236n134, 263
Speaking 240, 241, 242n147
Speech 231, 231n123, 238, 239n141, 240n141, 240n142, 251, 252, 253, 266
  Faculty of speech see Speech
Spirit 126, 137, 145n231, 176, 245, 298
  Militant spirit 184n361
  Spirit of seriousness 264n204
Spontaneism 151
Stalinism 25, 58, 58n190, 70n240, 104, 173, 185, 236, 236n134
Standpoint 175
  Capitalist standpoint 111
  Socio-historical standpoint 154
  Standpoint of the proletariat 316n356
State 150, 305
  Religious state 305
  Satellite state 283
  State institutions 287n272
Structuralism 249
Subject 105, 110, 135, 137, 146, 167n317, 169, 170, 172, 173, 179, 182, 184, 238, 241, 277n235
  Active subject 110
  Autonomous subject 229
  Cognizant subject 110
  Mental subject 175
  Passive subject 135
  Revolutionary subject 235
Subjectivism see Subjectivity
  Simple subjectivism 175
Subjectivity 85, 99, 100, 111, 135, 137, 147, 153, 154, 162, 175, 229, 270n219, 299, 306
Subsumption
  Real subsumption to value 188
Success see Effectivity
Superstructure 314, 315n352
  Juridical 314
  Political 314
Symbolisation 254

INDEX OF CONCEPTS 461

Tatsächlichkeit see Effectivity
Technology   278, 280
Teleology   150
Terrenalidad see This-sidedness
Theory   114, 120, 120n128, 125, 130, 131n176,
    140, 142, 142n222, 143, 147, 149n245, 153, 156,
    157, 158, 158n281, 159, 160, 161, 162, 163, 164,
    165, 168, 171, 175, 178, 178n344, 234
  Critical theory   104n44, 243n156, 278n242
  Dogmatic theory   104n44
  Emancipatory theory   164
  Hypotheses   161, 162
  Political theory   140
  Theoretical life   119, 120, 121
  Theoretical revolution   151
  Theoreticism   173, 174n333
  Theory of knowledge see Epistemology
  Social theory   140
Theory of relativity   157
Thing see Gegenstand
  Capitalist thing   296, 298, 312
This-sidedness   139, 139n209, 141
Tolerance   304
Tradition   229
Trotskyism   21n27
Truth   139, 139n209, 140, 141, 142, 143n224,
    153, 165, 178, 301
  Criterion of truth see Knowledge *and
    subentries*
  Objective truth   139n209, 140
  Law of truth   154
Tsarism   236n134, 276n233

Universalism   49, 249, 254, 257, 261, 261n199
  Abstract universalism   254n188, 257, 258,
    261, 261n199
  Concrete universalism   253, 254, 257, 261
  Eurocentric universalism   253
  False universalism   252, 254
Utilitarianism   95, 97, 98, 104, 105, 110, 111, 113,
    114, 118, 153, 173
Utopia   112, 292, 305n323, 309n337

Value   107, 111, 121, 122, 122n137, 123, 123n140,
    124, 124n143, 179, 235, 245, 250, 251,
    253n184, 272, 274, 275, 277, 295, 297,
    299, 306n326, 315, 315n352, 316, 317,
    317n360
  Abstract value   274
  Creation of value   188, 235, 251
  Commodity value   123n140
  Exchange-value   121, 122, 122n137
  Law of value   111, 301
  Money value   291n285
  Surplus value   111, 235, 272, 306n326
  Use-value   78n270, 107, 121, 188, 230, 233,
    234, 235, 236, 237, 238, 239, 240, 241,
    241n144, 245, 247n168, 248, 248n176,
    249, 250, 251, 252, 253, 266, 267, 271, 2
    72, 273, 274, 275, 277, 284, 293, 295,
    297, 298, 299, 300, 301, 302, 303, 307,
    308, 315
  Valorisation process   230n121, 295, 296,
    297, 298
  Value of labour   122, 124n143
  Value consumption   230
  Value production   230, 235, 271, 295, 297,
    315
Verdad see Truth
Violence   145n231, 233n130, 246n167, 257,
    263, 303
  Counter-violence   145n231
  Revolutionary violence   234n130

Wahrheit   139n209
Wealth   274, 285, 309n337, 317n360
Will   171, 240n143, 313
Wirklichkeit   139n209, 150

Xenophobia   303

Zapatist rebellion   263, 302, 304n320
Zoon politikon   118

Index of Names

Note: Adolfo Sánchez Vázquez has not been indexed in chapter 1 'The Life and Work of Adolfo Sánchez Vázquez' and in part 2 'Adolfo Sánchez Vázquez: Praxis and Knowledge'. Bolívar Echeverría Andrade has not been indexed in chapter 2 'The Life and Work of Bolívar Echeverría' and in part 3 'Bolívar Echeverría: Use-Value and *Ethos*'.

Acanda González, Jorge Luis   85, 86, 86n298, 87, 88, 88n305, 88n307, 90, 168
Adorno, Theodor W.   42, 56n180, 189, 205, 278n242, 300n309, 306n326, 348n11
Adoum, Jorge Enrique   46n145
Aguilar Rivero, Mariflor   195n8
Aguirre, Carlos   80n276, 80n277
Alberti, Leon Battista   116
Alberti, Rafael   17, 22n29, 22n30
Alighieri, Dante   219
Allende Gossens, Salvador   59n192, 70, 70n240
Alonso, José Ramón   24n40
Althusser, Louis   37, 97n17, 117, 117n105, 129, 130, 155, 155n270, 156, 158n280, 161, 161n291, 165, 165n312, 177, 178, 183, 202
Altoaguirre, Manuel   18, 22n30
Álvarez, Santiago   20n23, 22n29, 23, 23n33, 24n40, 25
Anaya, José Vicente   185n362
Anders, Günther   49n156, 50n159
Andrade Velasco, Rosa (madre)   43
Antipater   293
Antiphon   124, 124n146
Antisthenes   124, 124n148
Aragon, Louis   22
Arguedas, José María   29n75
Aricó, José   58n191
Aristotle   95, 95n10, 116, 119, 120, 121, 122, 123, 123n140, 124, 125, 209, 209n66, 210, 210n68, 211, 212, 230n120, 243n156, 292, 293
Armond   29n75
Arouet, François-Marie   *see* Voltaire
Axelos, Kostas   158, 158n284, 159, 159n285
Azaña, Manuel   19
Azorín, José   68

Bacon, Francis   116, 346n10
Bahro, Rudolf   87
Balibar, Etienne   155, 161n291
Balmat, Jacques   171n326
Barga, Corpus   22n29
Barros Sierra, Javier   36
Barthes, Roland   230n120
Bastiat, Frédéric   209n66, 290
Bataille, Georges   230n120, 303
Batista, Fulgencio   48
Baudrillard, Jean   215n79, 227, 228, 228n118, 292
Benjamin, Walter   56n180, 189, 190, 190n3, 190n5, 212n76, 230n120, 239, 239n140, 239n141, 265, 349
Benítez, Fernando   68
Bentham, Jeremy   255n189
Benveniste, Émile   230n120
Bergamín, José   22n29
Bloch, Ernst   89, 136
Borbón y Borbón-Dos Sicilias, Juan Carlos de   39
Borges, Jorge Luis   77n267
Braudel, Fernand   190n5, 335n407
Braus, J.   22n29
Brecht, Bertolt   16, 37, 39, 41, 66, 66n220, 174n333, 178n344, 200, 221n94, 265n206
Brentel, Helmut   326
Brenton, Howard   174n333
Briones   24n40
Bronshtein, Lev Davidovich   *see* Leon Trotsky
Bruno, Giordano   116
Bukharin, Nikolai   116, 154

Cabrera Sevilla, Luis   64
Callois, Roger   230n120
Camacho, Manuel   205, 205n48
Camus, Albert   47
Cano, José Luis   18
Cantarell Gamboa, Melvin   122n137, 145n231
Capdeville García, Rubén   88, 89, 90
Carbajal, Iván   47, 47n153

INDEX OF NAMES 463

Cárdenas del Río, Lázaro   25, 25n49, 31
Carrero Blanco, Luis   38
Carpentier, Alejo   22n29
Carrillo Solares, Santiago   20n24, 21
Castañeda, Fernando   185n362
Castells, Manuel   185n362
Casterás, Ramón   20n24, 21n25
Castro, Fidel   48, 88
Castro Jijón, Ramón   64
Celine, Louis-Ferdinand   30, 30n77
Chabás, Juan   22n30
Che Guevara, Ernesto   34, 48, 54, 55, 56, 56n179, 57, 58, 63
Cicero   293
Claudín, Fernando   33n96
Cogniot, Georges   145n231, 184n361
Compostela   24n41
Cordera, Ronaldo   67, 73, 74n258
Córdoba Iturburo, Cayetano   22n29
Córdova, Arnaldo   67, 73
Corral, Luis   47, 47n152, 50, 51, 52n163, 59n193
Cortada, James W.   20n24
Crusoe, Robinson   321, 322
Cueva Dávila, Agustín   47, 47n153, 78n269

Da Vinci, Leonardo   116
Daedalus   292
David   356
Davydova, G. A.   116
De Gortari, Eli Eduardo   31, 35, 36
De la Cruz, Juan   18
De Loyola, Ignacio   305n325
De Saussure, Ferdinand   189, 192, 229, 230, 231n123, 232, 232n127, 233, 239, 240, 240n142, 241, 242n147, 249, 251, 252, 252n183, 266
De Saussure, Horace Bénédict   171n326
De Unamuno, Miguel   46, 46n148, 46n149, 47, 47
Del Conde, Teresa   80n277
Della Volpe, Galvano   129
Descartes, René   116
Deutscher, Isaac   57n186
Díaz Canedo, Enríque   27n61
Díaz, Porfirio   204n47
Diogenes Laertius   124n148
Diogenes of Sinope   125n148
Dollenmayer, David   174n333

Domenchina, Juan José   28
Dühring, Eugen   145n231
Dussel, Enrique   37, 291n284
Dutschke, Gretchen   53n165, 54n168
Dutschke, Rudi   52n165, 53n165, 59, 60, 61, 62
Duverger, Maurice   185n362

Echeverría Andrade, Bolívar   90, 90n317, 340, 341, 342, 343, 345, 346, 347, 348, 351, 352, 354, 355, 357, 358, 359
Echeverría Andrade, Eduardo (brother)   44
Echeverría Andrade, Elena (sister)   44
Echeverría Andrade, Julio (brother)   44, 78
Echeverría Andrade, Marco (brother)   44
Echeverría Andrade, Rosa (sister)   44
Echeverría Paredes, Bolívar (father)   43
Echeverría Serur, Albert (son)   77
Echeverría Serur, Carlos (son)   77
Echeverría Weikert, Andrés (son)   77
Ehrenberg, Ilya   22
Einstein, Albert   157
Eles, F.   116
Engels, Friedrich   33n96, 114n87, 116, 128, 131, 144n226, 148n242, 151n260, 165n310, 167n317, 198n24, 215, 255, 314, 315n352, 321n373
Escarpit, Fracoise   82n284
Escudero, Roberto   36, 65
Esperate, Fracisco   68
Esperate, Jordi   68
Esperate, Neus   67, 68, 70, 72, 74n259, 75, 75n262
Esperate, Tomás   68
Esperet   24n40
Establet, Roget   155
Estrella, Ulises   47, 47n153

Fanon, Frantz   52, 60
Fernández Montesinos, José   18
Feuerbach, Ludwig   96n13, 98n20, 99, 99n24, 100, 116, 117, 127, 130, 134, 135, 136, 137n199, 138, 144, 151, 158n284, 163, 172n330, 255n188, 347n11
Fichte, Johann Gottlieb   102, 116, 172
Flores Olea, Victor   185n362
Forno, Estela   68
Foucault, Michel   215n79, 227, 227n112, 227n113

Fowkes, Ben   123n140, 146n234, 244n157, 245n161, 247n170
Franco, Francisco   17, 19, 19n23, 32, 38, 68
Franklin, Benjamin   243, 243n156
Freile Posso, Guillermo   64
Fromm, Erich   185n362

Gaidukov, D.A.   116
Gallego, Rómulo S.   27n61
Gándara Enrique, Marcos   64
Gandler, Stefan   82n286
Ganivet, Paco   24n40
Gaos, José   18, 31, 32, 35
García Barrios, Marco Aurelio   80n277
García de León, Antonio   80n277
Garfias Zurita, Pedro   22n30, 27
Gilly, Adolfo   81n283
Giménez Siles, Rafael   28, 28n70
Giner, Francisco   29n75
Giono, Jean   30
Goldhagen, Daniel Jonah   50n159, 75n262
Goliath   356
González Martínez, Enrique   27n61
González, Mike   141n216, 162n300
González, Ramón   24n40
Gramsci, Antonio   86, 87, 88n307, 107n55, 117, 117n105, 133, 133n184, 154, 154n265, 155, 155n269, 155n270, 156, 159n285, 348
Grlić, Danko   116n103
Guerra, Ricardo   35
Guerra, Ruy   60
Guillén, Nicolás   22n29
Gumplowicz, Ludwig   145n231
Guzmán, Martín Luis   27n61, 28, 28n70, 29, 29n75

Haeckel, Ernst   215
Hegel, Georg Wilhelm Friedrich   102, 105, 109n64, 116, **117**, 127, **150**, 151, 164n306, 167n317, 169, 171, 174n333, 175n337, 176, 216, 217, 218, 218n87, 245, **246**, 246n164, 246n167, **247**, 247n168, 247n170, **248**, 249, **261**, 261n198, **262**, 265, 265n206, 313, 353, 355, 356
Heidegger, Martin   42, 47, 48, 48n154, 49, 49n156, 49n158, 49n159, 50, 50n159, 51n161, 56n180, 59, 62, 62n206, 73n255, 107n55, **226, 228**, 230n120, 237, 286, 328

Heine, Heinrich   255
Heller, Agnes   107n55
Hemingway, Ernest   22n29
Henríquez Ureña, Pedro   27n61
Hernández, Miguel   22n30, 24n40
Hephaestus   292
Herrera Petere, José   18, 22n30, 24n40, 27, 29n72, 30
Hesiodo   124
Hilferding, Rudolf   258
Hjelmslev, Louis   229, 229n120
Hirsch, Joachim   336, 337
Hobsbawm, Eric   185n362
Horkheimer, Max   56n180, 168n316, 189, 205, 278n242, 300n309, 306n326, 348n11
Huidobro, Vicente   22n29
Husserl, Edmund   50n159, 107n55

Izcaray, Jesús   22n30

Jakobson, Roman   229, 229n120
James, William   153n263, 159n285
Jara, Victor   70n240
Jaspers, Karl   107n55

Kafka, Franz   30, 30n77
Kangrga, Milan   116n103
Kant, Immanuel   102, 137, 167n317, 175n337, 218n87, 221n94
Karol, K.S.   185n362
Kay Ogden, Charles   230n120
King Juan Carlos I   see Borbón y Borbón-Dos Sicilias, Juan Carlos de
Kisch, Egon Erwin   22n29
Klee, Paul   212n76
Korsch, Karl   68n233, 116, 189, 236n135
Kosík, Karel   37, 107n55, 116, 116n103, 133, 168, 185n362
Kozlik, Adolf   64
Krauze, Rosa   37
Kurnitzky, Horst   54, 54n171, 56n180, 78, 78n270, 79, 80n276, 268n208

Labastida, Jaime   96n12, 145n231
Lang, Berel   124n142
Lao-Tsu   200
Lasalle, Ferdinand   326
Lazaruz   109n65

INDEX OF NAMES

Lefèbvre, Henri   29, 29n75, 37, 107n55
Lemper, Ute   265n206
Lenin   34, 57n186, 87n304, 89, 117, 117n109, 131,183, 184, 184n361, 236n134, 246n164
Leroi-Gourhan, André   230n120
Lévi-Strauss, Claude   114n87, 230n120
Lieber, Hans-Joachim   61, 61n204, 62n204
Lieja, Javier (pseudonym for B.E.)   72n249
Lima, Bernardo   161n291
Líster Forján, Enrique   22, 23, 24, 24n41
Lobachevsky, Nikolai   157
López, Juan   19n22
López Díaz, Pedro   78n273
Lukács, György   39, 88n307, 107n55, 114n87, 116, 172, 189, 198n22, 230n120, **259**, 259n194, **272**, 274, **275**, 275n231, 276, 276n234, 277, 299, 312, 313, 316, **317n356**, 317n360, 325n385, **328, 329**, 329n394, 329n395, 353n15
Luxemburg, Rosa   183, 213, 263, 272
Lyotard, Jean-François   257

MacCulloch   290
Machado, Antonio   31, 46n149
Macherey, Pierre   155
Machiavelli, Niccolò   116
Malraux, André   22
Manjarrez, Héctor   68
Manrique, Jorge Alberto   280, 281, 282, 282n258, 311, 311n340
Manzar, Antonio R.   29n75
Mao Tse-tung   176n338
Marcos, Subcomandante   73n255, 82n284
Marcović, Mihailo   116n103
Marcuse, Herbert   42, 48n154, 60, 88n307, 89, 90, 150, 184, 184n361, 185n362, 217, 218, 243n156
Mariátegui, José Carlos   58, 58n190, 58n191, 59n191, 63, 84, 84n289
Marinello, Juan   22, 27, 29, 29n75
Marini, Ruy Mauro   67
Marx, Karl   15, 15n5, 18, 33n96, **34**, 35, 39, 39n127, 42, 48, 49n156, **55**, 55n175, 60, 61, 61n204, 62, 66, 67, 98n20, 99, 99n24, 100, 101, 102, 104, 105, 107, 107n55, 108, 108n58, 114n87, 116, 117, **121, 122, 122n137**, 123, 123n140, 124, 124n146, 126, **127**, 128, 128n158, 129, **130**, 132, 133, 134, **134n186**, 135, 136, 137,

138, 139n209, 140, 141, 143, 143n224, 144, 144n226, 145, 146, 147, 147n240, 148n242,149, 151, 152, 155, 156, 158, 159, 160, 163, **164**, 165, 167n317, 168, 169, 171, 172, 172n330, 173, 175, 175n337, 176, **177**, 178, 180,181,181n353, 182, 184, 184n361, 185, 188, 188n1, 190n5, 191, 192, 193, 195, 196, 198, 189n22, 198n24, 199, 200, 202, 203n45, **206**, 206n50, 207, 207n53, 208, 208n60, **209**, 209n64, 209n66, 210, 210n68, 211, 212, 214, 215, 216, 216n82, 217, 218, 218n88, 219, 219n92, 220, 221, 221n94, 222, 222n96, **223**, 224, 225, 225n103, 226, 227, 228, 232, 232n127, 233, 235, 237, 238, 240n143, 242, **243**, 243n156, 244, 244n157, 244n158, 244n159, 245, 245n160, 246, 247, 247n170, 248, 249, 253, 254, 254n188, 255, 256, 256n188, 258, 259n194, 261, 261n198, 264, 266, 267, 272, 276, 286, 290, **291, 291n284, 291n285, 292, 293**, 293n292, 296, 302, 305n326, 306n326, 313, 314, 314n351, 315n352, 315n355, 317, 317n358, 317n360, 318, 319, 320, 322, 323, 324,325, 325n385, 326, 326n387, 327, 327n288, 327n289, 327n390, 330n395, 334n405, 335n407, 336, 343, 343n5, **344**, 344n8, 345, 346, 346n10, 347, 347n11, 348n12, 350, 352, 353, 353n15, 355, 357, **358**, 359
Massa, María   80n277
Maubliac   29n75
Maurois, André   29n75
Mayo, Faustino   24n40
Medusa   220n93
Mena, Tania   80n277
Merleau-Ponty, Maurice   114n87, 230n120
Mery   287n272
Mészáros, István   185n362
Meyer, Joseph   49n156
Miliband, Ralph   185n362
Mikecin, Vjekoslav   68n233
Mills, Wright   185n362
Monsiváis, Carlos   80n277
More, Thomas   116
Muñoz Ledo, Porfirio   205, 205n48

Neruda, Pablo   18, 22n29, 27
Nettel, Patricia   80n277
Neummann, Franz   258n193

Odysseus 298
Orfila, Arnaldo 64
Ortega Esquivel, Arueliano 90n317, 331n398
Ortega y Gasset, José 18, 35, 107n55
Ortiz Soralegui, Juvenal 29n75

Paccard, Michel 171n326
Palazón, María Rosa 37
Paredes, Juan 24n40
Pastor, María Alba 80n276, 80n277
Paz, Octavio 22, 27, 36, 203n46
Peñaloza, Eduardo 80n277
Pereda, Carlos 81n282
Pereyra, Carlos 65, 67
Perseus 220n93
Petrović, Gajo 116n103, 117n103
Pinochet, Augusto 59n192, 70, 70n240
Pita Rodríguez, Félix 22n29
Plato 116, 117n110, 119, 120, 121, 124n147, 125, 125n148, 212, 212n75, 292, 293
Plutarch 119
Ponce, Manuel 29, 29n75
Prados, Emilio 17, 22n30
Prieto, Miguel 27
Prodicus of Ceo 124, 124n147

Queneau, Raymond 30

Rabehl, Bernd 60, 62
Rancière, Jacques 155
Rebolledo, Aurora (wife A.S.V.) 31
Rebolledo, Enrique 18
Rejano, Juan 22n30, 25, 27
Remedios Vázquez Rodríguez, María (mother) 16
Renn, Ludwig 31
Reyes, Alfonso 31
Reyes, Pedro Joel 80n277
Ricardo, David 116
Richards, Ivor Armstrong 230n120
Roces, Wenceslao 18, 22n29, 32, 35, 98n20, 99n24, 128n158, 134, 148
Rojas Paz, Pablo 22n29
Rojo, Vicente 68
Rossanda, Rossana 37, 185n362
Rousseau, Jen-Jacques 116
Roxas, Juan Bartolomé 29, 29n75
Rubel, Maximilen 184n361

Rutkevisch, Mikhail N. 116

Saint-Simon, Claude Henri 116
Salinas de Gortari, Carlos 74n257, 191n7, 205, 205n48
Sánchez Barbudo, Antonio 26, 27, 28n70, 29, 29n72
Sánchez Calderón, Benedicto (father) 16
Sánchez Rebolledo, Adolfo (son) 31, 67, 67n230, 73, 74n259
Sánchez Rebolledo, Juan Enrique (son) 31n82, 36,
Sánchez Rebolledo, María Aurora (daughter) 31n82
Sánchez Vázquez, Adolfo 46n149, 47n149, 62, 63, 64, 65, 65n216, 66, 67n230, 68n233, 69, 85, 86, 87, 87n304, 88, 89, 89n311, 90, 90n315, 188, 193, 195, 199, 200, 201, 202, 202n43, 204, 205, 206, 224, 234, 234n132, 275n231, 276, 276n234, 330n395, 340, 341, 342, 343, 343n5, 344, 345, 347, 348, 349, 350, 351, 352, 354, 355, 357, 358, 359
Sánchez Vázquez, Ángela (sister) 17
Sánchez Vázquez, Gonzalo (brother) 17, 21n25
Sartre, Jean-Paul 30, 30n77, 47, 47n151, 48n154, 64, 230n120
Schaff, Adam 37, 88n307, 116
Schmidt, Alfred 42, **105, 105n49**, 114n87, 139n209, 168, 168n319, 169, 170, 170n325, 171, 171n327, 172, 173, 174, **175**, 176, 176n338, 177, 179, 180, 215, **216**, 217, 218, 218n88, 219, 219n92, 221, 223, 224, 224n100, 225, 244n158, 245, 245n160, 246, 246n164, 247, 280n249, 324, 343, 343n6, 344n8, 347, 347n11, **348**, 351, 352, 353, 353n17, 354
Schopenhauer, Arthur 108, 109n65
Seghers, Anna 22
Sender, Ramón José 22n29
Serrano Plaja, Arturo 22n29, 22n30
Serrano Poncela, Segundo 33n96
Serur, Raquel (second wife B.E.) 44n134, 77, 77n267, 80, 80n277
Shelley, Percy Bysshe 170n324
Singer, Peter 106n52
Smith, Adam 116, 212
Snoth 30
Somoza Debayle, Anastasio 39

INDEX OF NAMES

Spender, Stephen   22n29
Stalin, Joseph   59n191, 183
Supek, Rudi   116n103

Taylor, Sedley   321, 321n373
Tell, Wilhelm   252n183
Tinajero Villamar, Fernando   47, 47n153
Togliatti, Palmiro   68n233
Tolstoi, Alexei   22n29
Tornú, Sara   22n29
Trotsky, Leon   183
Tuñón de Lara, Manuel   22n30
Tupper, Martin   255
Tzara, Tristan   22n29

Ulyanov, Vladimir Ilyich   *see* Lenin

Vallejo, César   22n29
Varela, Lorenzo   27
Vázquez, Alfredo (uncle)   17
Vázquez Días, Fracisco   *see* Compostela
Vázquez Montalbán, Manuel   86, 87, 88
Velasco Ibarra, José María   44, 64
Vicente, Gil   29, 29n75
Villa, Francisco   82n287

Villaurutia, Xavier   31
Villoro, Luis   35, 179n350, 180n350
Villoro, Juan   198n22, 289, 293, 293n292
Voltaire   144
Von Humboldt, Wilhelm   253, 254
Vranicki, Predrag   116n103

Wallerstein, Immanuel   81, 81n282
Weber, Max   198, 288, 289, 290, 293
Weikert, Ingrid (first wife B.E.)   52, 64, 65, 77
Whal Jean   185n362
Winckelmann, Johann Joachim   357
Wirth, Max   321n373
Wittfogel, Karl August   230n120

Xenophon   212n75
Xirau, Joaquín   31

Yerobi Indaburu, Clemente   64

Zapata, Emiliano   82n287
Zea, Leopoldo   37
Zelený, Jindrich   37
Zurián, Karla   80n277

www.ingramcontent.com/pod-product-compliance
Lightning Source LLC
Chambersburg PA
CBHW071144070526
44584CB00019B/2650